the Unofficial Guide® to Bed & Breakfasts in California

1st Edition

D0048601

Also available from IDG Books Worldwide:

the Unofficial Guide® to

Bed & Breakfasts in California

1st Edition

Mary Anne Moore
and Maurice Read

Every effort has been made to ensure the accuracy of information throughout this book. Bear in mind, however, that prices, schedules, etc., are constantly changing. Readers should always verify information before making final plans.

IDG Books Worldwide, Inc.
An International Data Group Company
919 E. Hillsdale Blvd., Suite 400
Foster City, California 94404

Produced by Menasha Ridge Press

MACMILLAN is a registered trademark of Macmillan General Reference USA, Inc., a wholly owned subsidiary of IDG Books Worldwide, Inc.
UNOFFICIAL GUIDE is a registered trademark of Macmillan General Reference USA, Inc., a wholly owned subsidiary of IDG Books Worldwide, Inc.

ISBN   0-02-863267-2

ISSN   1527-1676

Manufactured in the United States of America

10 9 8 7 6 5 4 3 2 1

Contents

List of Maps

About the Authors
and Illustrator

Mary Anne Moore and **Maurice Read** are freelance writers and editors who have contributed to a number of travel books, including *Northern California Best Places* (two editions), *Northern California Cheap Sleeps,* and *Northern California Budget Traveler.* They have written articles on a variety of subjects for magazines and newspapers such as *California Magazine, Parenting,* the *Sacramento Bee,* and the *San Francisco Chronicle.* They are now branching out into cyberspace, writing reviews of products and places for various dot-coms. In her non-writing life, Mary Anne is a legislative consultant in the California State Capitol, spending her off-hours traveling the globe in search of great getaways, first-class restaurants, idyllic jogging trails, and the world's best bookstores. Maurice is a Sacramento-based lobbyist and a gourmet cook. He tours California with his Australian shepherd looking for dog-friendly lodgings, great fly-fishing streams, and memorable meals.

Born and raised in New York City, illustrator **Giselle Simons** received her Bachelor of Fine Arts degree from Cornell University. She currently lives on Manhattan's Upper West Side, where she works as an illustrator, architectural design drafter, and graphic designer. She is caretaker to a dog, two cats, an increasing number of fish, and her husband, Jeff.

Acknowledgments

For us, touring California's beautiful inns was great fun and hugely time-consuming, given the sheer size of the state—nearly 160,000 square miles. Suffice it to say, we could not have completed this book without some help. Most notably, we'd like to thank our persistent and patient co-worker, fact-checker extraordinaire, and good friend Norma Clevenger, and also our Southern California expert, writer Bobbi Zane. In traveling around the state we found the various visitors and convention bureaus to be very accommodating. We would particularly like to thank Maggie Schaeffer of the Napa Valley Conference and Visitors Bureau; Koleen Hamblin, public relations consultant for the Santa Barbara Convention and Visitors Bureau; and Amy Herzog, marketing communications director for the Monterey Peninsula Visitors and Convention Bureau. Two industry groups went out of their way to offer help and advice. Thank you, Michael Richardson, president, California Association of Bed and Breakfast Inns, and Jim Abrams, executive vice president, California Hotel and Motel Association.

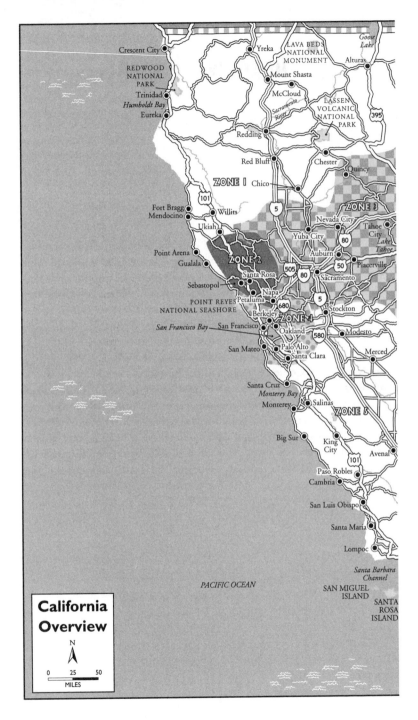

California Overview

N

0   25   50
MILES

PACIFIC OCEAN

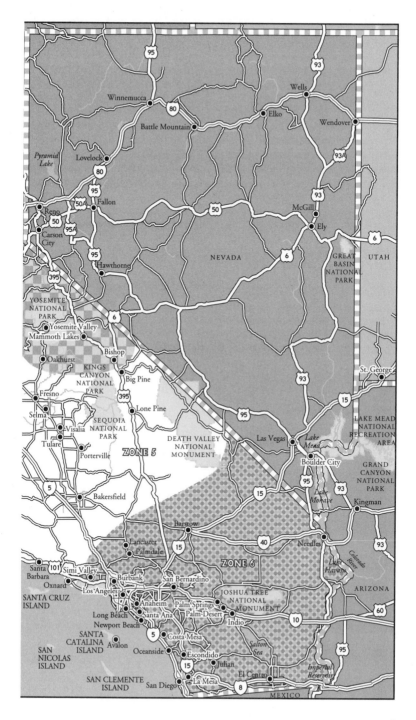

Introduction

For those who frequent B&Bs and are true aficionados of these quirky and interesting places, there may not be any surprises at the range, nature, and caliber of inns you will find described in this book. On the other hand, if your preconceived idea of a B&B is a place where you sleep in rooms filled with ruffles and teddy bears and stagger down to breakfast at a specified time, forced to converse with strangers before you've even had a cup of coffee, be prepared to broaden your horizons. While there are still plenty of traditional B&Bs around because lots of people love them, they are a dwindling group, in California at least. They are gradually being replaced, not only by corporations with the bucks to build or renovate beautiful mansions and fill them with every creature comfort imaginable, but also by fashionable folk abandoning large cities in droves to create a dream of a place that represents their unique sensibilities. The result is a choice of inns that are hugely varied in style, location, and price, and many of them are just splendid.

After touring hundreds of B&Bs, it became clear to us that the creation and maintenance of these inns is truly a form of art-in-progress: many of them are as lovely and personal as any other work of fine art. Forget the notion of a spare bedroom in somebody's rumpled home or in a seedy old mansion stuffed full of dusty furniture, because you won't find any of those in this guide. Instead, think of unique combinations of lodging and locale that can meet all your expectations of a totally great place to be.

B&Bs have evolved from humble origins into highly creative means of bedding and feeding travelers of all sorts—vacationers, businesspeople, couples seeking romance, folks traveling solo who want to avoid lonely hotel rooms, and, increasingly, people who understand that a few days in a perfect location is a mini-vacation you can have numerous times during the year.

Exploring B&Bs is a way to indulge in a variety of travel experiences. California has hundreds of miles of beaches, the mountains, the desert, exciting cities, and acres of vineyards, and there are small inns at all of them. You can spend a few days in a sunny Italian villa or in a castle or in a lighthouse on an island. You can stay in a pretty room or spacious suite filled with every amenity you can think of, or you can stay in a restored historic gold rush hotel with plank floors, shared baths, and the echo of spurs ringing down the halls. In these pages, you will find an inn in a coast guard station, a Russian dacha, a house shaped like an ink bottle, French châteaux, and elegant Victorian mansions that will make you feel like a character in a Henry James novel.

Wherever you want to go, whatever you intend to do, there's a great place waiting for you, and it isn't some cookie-cutter hotel room with a strip of paper across the toilet seat. After all, this is California, the garden of earthly delights. Indulge.

About *Unofficial Guides*

HOW COME "UNOFFICIAL"?

The book in your hands is part of a unique travel and lifestyle guidebook series begun in 1985 with *The Unofficial Guide to Walt Disney World.* That guide, a comprehensive, behind-the-scenes, hands-on prescription for getting the most out of a complex amusement park facility, spawned a series of like titles: *The Unofficial Guide to Chicago*, *The Unofficial Guide to New Orleans*, and so on. Today, dozens of *Unofficial Guides* help millions of savvy readers navigate some of the world's more complex destinations and situations.

The *Unofficial Guides to Bed-and-Breakfasts* continue the tradition of insightful, incisive, cut-to-the-chase information, presented in an accessible, easy-to-use format. Unlike with some popular books, no property can pay to be included—those reviewed are solely our choice. We visit the good, the bad, and the quirky. We finger the linens, chat with the guests, and sample the scones. We screen hundreds of lodgings, affirming or debunking the acclaimed, discovering or rejecting the new and the obscure. In the end, we present detailed profiles of the lodgings we feel are the best among a selection of inns representing a broad range of prices, styles, and geographical areas.

We have arbitrarily, but reasonably we hope, divided the state into six geographical zones, and we provide introductions for each zone to give you an idea of the nearby general attractions. These introductions also feature helpful phone numbers for further information. Within each zone, bed-and-breakfasts and small inns are listed alphabetically by city or town (or the closest one). Area maps with the properties marked help you pinpoint your general destination. (And detailed mini-indexes help you look up properties by categories and lead you to places that best fit your needs.) The difference, by the way, between the terms "bed-and-breakfast" and "small inn" is a rapidly blurring one. Bed-and-breakfast used to refer exclusively to lodgings in private homes, while inns were commercial operations in larger facilities that commonly served dinner. In California, the largest official association for the industry, the California Association of Bed and Breakfast Inns, simplifies the matter by referring to all its member lodgings as "bed-and-breakfast inns."

With *The Unofficial Guides to Bed-and-Breakfasts,* we strive to help you find the perfect lodging for every trip. This guide is unofficial because we answer to no one but the reader.

LETTERS, COMMENTS, AND QUESTIONS FROM READERS

We expect to learn from our mistakes, as well as from the input of our readers, and to improve with each book and edition. Many of those who use the *Unofficial Guides* write to us to ask questions, make comments, or share their own discoveries and lessons learned in California. We appreciate all such input, both positive and critical, and encourage our readers to write. Readers' comments and observations will contribute immeasurably to the improvement of revised editions of the *Unofficial Guides.*

How to Write the Authors

Maurice Read and Mary Anne Moore
The Unofficial Guide to Bed-and-Breakfasts in California
P. O. Box 43673
Birmingham, AL 35205

When you write, be sure to put your return address on your letter as well as on the envelope—sometimes envelopes and letters get separated. And remember, our work takes us out of the office for long periods of time, so forgive us if our response is delayed.

What Makes It a Bed-and-Breakfast?

A bed-and-breakfast or small inn, for the purposes of this book, is a small property—from about 3 to 25 guest rooms (with a few exceptions), with hosts, a distinct personality, individually decorated rooms, and breakfast included in the price. Many of these smaller properties have hosts living right there; in others, the hosts are nearby, in an adjoining house or a phone call away.

Recently, the bed-and-breakfast and small inn trade in California has taken off—with mixed results. This growth, for the most part, has taken place on two fronts: the low end and the high end. As bed-and-breakfasts gain popularity, anyone with a spare bedroom leaps into the fray, popping an ad in the Yellow Pages for "Billy's Bedroom B&B." These enterprises often lack professionalism; they may not keep regular hours or days of operation, are sometimes unlicensed, and were avoided in this guide. However, many smaller B&Bs, particularly in less traveled areas, are great bargains and can be marvelous places to stay. A number of these are included in the directory section of the book to give you a broader choice when traveling. On the other end of the spectrum is the new breed of high-end bed-and-breakfasts—luxury premises with more amenities than the finest hotels. Often, these are lodgings built to be bed-and-breakfasts or inns, with exteriors resembling a Victorian or Craftsman, perhaps, but interiors that are spacious and posh, sporting designer decor. All baths are private and en suite; breakfasts are often gourmet affairs. In-room whirlpool tubs and fireplaces are de rigueur, and extras range from in-room refrigerators (perhaps stocked with champagne) to complimentary high tea to free use of state-of-the-art recreational equipment to . . . the list goes on! (One longtime innkeeper, whose historic home was tidily and humbly maintained by hours of elbow grease and common sense, dubbed this new state of affairs "the amenities war.")

The result is a changing industry that's hard to describe in a nutshell. A simple homestay bed-and-breakfast with a shared bath and common rooms can be a budget experience, while a new, upscale bed-and-breakfast can be the luxury venue of a lifetime.

Who Stays at Bed-and-Breakfasts?

American travelers are finally catching on to what Europeans have known for a long time. Maybe it's a backlash against a cookie-cutter, strip-mall landscape, or longing for a past that perhaps never was, or for an idealized, short-term interaction with others. Maybe it's a need for simple pleasures in a world over the top with theme parks and high-tech wonders. Who can say for sure?

The bed-and-breakfast trade has grown so large that it includes niches catering to virtually every need. Some bed-and-breakfasts and small inns are equipped to help travelers conduct business, others provide turn-down service and fresh flowers by the honeymooners' canopied bed, and still others are just the right size for reunions or conferences. Whatever your needs, there is a bed-and-breakfast or small inn tailored to your expectations. The challenge, and one this guide was designed to help you meet, is sifting through the choices until you find the perfect place.

Romantics

More and more properties are establishing at least one room or suite with a fireplace, a whirlpool tub for two, a king-size canopy bed, breakfast in bed, and all the rest of the trappings of romance. Theme rooms can also be especially fun for fantasizing. Always check out the privacy factor. Sometimes a property has a carriage house in the back, or a top-floor room away from the others. Some inns have more substantial walls between guest rooms than others and go out of their way to say so. Many inns have a room designated as the Honeymoon Suite or indicate that a particular room is especially popular with honeymooners. If an inn welcomes kids, and you and your honey are trying to have a romantic getaway from yours, you may want to find one that discourages child guests.

Families

Face it, moms and dads: a casual setting where children are welcome with open arms will sometimes have to be your goal. You may have to give up pristine decor and breakfast tea served in bone china for a more relaxed atmosphere, but on the upside, you won't have to worry as much about Caitlin or Michael knocking over the Wedgwood collection on the sideboard. While California law forbids innkeepers from refusing any guests without just cause, a new statute permits innkeepers to require adults, in writing, not to leave children age 12 or younger unattended at any time, and to preserve the peace and quiet for other guests.

When an establishment says kids are "OK," that usually means it's a safe, kid-friendly place. Check the age recommendations. If your children are under the recommended age but well behaved, let the host know. Generally, bed-and-breakfasts are not ideal for high-action kids. Aside from noise considerations, some inns are perched beside cliffs or bodies of water or busy streets, or they have accessible swimming pools or upper floors with balconies. Safety is a legitimate concern. But if your children enjoy games, puzzles, books, and other quiet pleasures, and the site is appropriate for them, you and your kids can have a wonderful experience together—and so can the rest of the guests. The inn profiles identify which ones welcome children without qualification, and which ones consider their premises suitable for older or younger children, or not suitable for children at all.

Business Travelers

For individual business travelers, bed-and-breakfasts and small inns are becoming much more savvy at anticipating your needs, but they still do so to differing degrees. While phone lines and data ports are fairly common, they vary from one bed-and-breakfast to another. Some say they offer data ports when in fact they have two phone jacks in every room but only one phone line servicing the entire property. This can be fine for a three-room inn in the off-season, but if you're trying to conduct business, look for the properties with private lines and/or dedicated data ports. If in doubt, ask. Some rooms have desks, but these also vary, particularly in surface area and quality of lighting. If this is an important feature, ask for specifics and make sure you secure a room with a desk at the time of your reservation.

Some establishments even make services such as couriers, secretarial support, fax, e-mail, and laundry/dry cleaning available. And for business travelers who don't have time to take advantage of a leisurely and sumptuous breakfast, hosts often provide an early morning alternative, sometimes continental, sometimes full.

Finally, there are intangibles to consider. After the sterile atmosphere of the trade show, meeting hall, or boardroom, a small inn with a host and a plate of cookies and a personal dinner recommendation can be nice to come home to.

The atmosphere is also a plus for business meetings or seminars: the relaxed surroundings are quite conducive to easy-going give-and-take. During the week, when guest rooms are often available, bed-and-breakfasts and small inns are usually eager to host business groups. Discounts are often included, and special services such as catering and equipment are offered if you rent the entire property. But forget weekends; these properties are still tourist-oriented.

Singles

If you are on your own, small lodgings are ideal. Look for a place with single rates, and even if a special rate isn't listed, you can often negotiate a small discount. If you're feeling sociable, you can sit in the parlor, lounge, or common rooms and chat with other guests. If you're looking for peace and quiet, most guest rooms have a comfortable chair, often by a fireplace or a window with a view. Many inns have small libraries or stashes of videos to catch up on. Single female travelers might find a measure of security in coming "home" to a facility like this rather than an impersonal, 150-room hotel.

Groups

Whether you are part of a wedding, reunion, or just a group of people who want to travel together, an inn or bed-and-breakfast is a delightful place to stay. The atmosphere is special, your needs are taken care of in a personal way, the grounds are most often spacious and lovely, and in the evening you can all retire in close proximity. It's especially fun when you take over the whole place, so you may want to choose a small property if that's your goal.

Special Needs

Look in our entries for mention of special needs facilities or access. Then call for details to determine just how extensive the accessibility is. Remember that many of these houses are quite old, and owners of a small bed-and-breakfast will not have a team of accessibility experts on hand, so be specific with your questions. If doorways must be a certain width to accommodate a wheelchair or walker, know how many inches before you call; if stairs are difficult for Great Aunt Agnes, don't neglect to find out how many are present outside as well as inside. Older properties that have been extensively remodeled may very well have a room or rooms (and bathrooms) that are disabled accessible. And if a property that seems otherwise special doesn't have the facilities you need, perhaps you can patch things together, such as a room on the first floor. Although many older buildings contain lots of stairs and steps and may be situated on hilltops or in rural terrain, California has strict building codes that require new structures to be accessible, so the situation is improving.

If you suffer from allergies or aversions, talk it over when you book; a good innkeeper will make every attempt to accommodate you. As for food, if you request a special meal and give enough notice, you can often get what you like. That's one of the joys of a small, personalized property.

You and Your Hosts

Hosts are the heart of your small inn or bed-and-breakfast experience and color all aspects of the stay. They can make or break a property, and sometimes an unassuming place will be the most memorable of all because of the care and warmth of the hosts. Typically, they are well versed in navigating the area and can be a wealth of "insider information" on restaurants, sight-seeing, and the like.

While many hosts live on the premises, they often have designed or remodeled their building so that their living quarters are separate from the guest rooms. Guests often have their own living room, den, parlor, and sitting room; you may be sharing with other guests, but not so much with your hosts. The degree of interaction between hosts and guests varies greatly. In most cases, hosts are accessible but not intrusive; they will swing through the common areas and chat a bit but are sensitive to guests' need for privacy.

SOME CONSIDERATIONS

No two bed-and-breakfasts are alike. Some are housed in historic homes or other buildings (train stations, hospitals, barns, castles, stagecoach stops!). Some are humble and unpretentious, some are grand and opulent. Some are all in one building, while others are scattered among individual, free-standing units. Some offer a breakfast over which you'll want to linger for hours; others—well, others make a darn good muffin. Bed-and-breakfasts are less predictable than hotels and motels but can be much more interesting. A few bed-and-breakfast aficionados have discovered that "interesting" sometimes comes at a price. This guide takes the "scary" out of "interesting" and presents only places that meet a certain standard of cleanliness, predictability, and amenities. However, there are certain questions and issues common to bed-and-breakfasts and small inns that first-time visitors should consider:

Check-In/Check-Out

As small operators, most bed-and-breakfast hosts need to know approximately when you'll be arriving. Many have check-in periods (specified in the profiles) during which the hosts or staff will be available to greet you. Most can accommodate arrival outside their stated check-in period but need to be advised so they can arrange to be home or get a key to you. Think about it—they have to buy groceries and go to the kids' soccer games and get to doctors' appointments just like you. And they have to sleep sometime. Don't show up at 11:30 at night and expect a smiling bellhop—the same person who lets you in is probably going to be up at 5 or 6 a.m. slicing mushrooms for your omelet!

Check-in times are often flexible, but, as with any commercial lodging, check-out times can be critical, as the innkeeper must clean and prepare your room for incoming guests. If you need to stay longer, ask. If the room hasn't been rented, a late check-out will sometimes be possible, and a host will generally let you leave your bags and enjoy the common areas after check-out, as long as you vacate your room.

Please take cancellation policies seriously. A "no-show" is not a cancellation! If an establishment has a cancellation policy of seven days, or 72 hours, or whatever, you are expected to call and cancel your reservation prior to that time, or you could be liable for up to the full amount of your reserved stay. After all, a four-unit bed-and-breakfast has lost 25% of its revenue if you arbitrarily decide not to show up.

Choosing Your Room

Check out your room before lugging your luggage (an absence of elevators is usually part of the charm). This is standard procedure at small properties and saves time and trouble should you prefer another room. When a guest room has an open door, it usually means the proud innkeeper wants you to peek. You may just find a room that you like better than the one you are assigned, and it may be available, so ask.

Four-legged Family Members

In general, we haven't mentioned inn-house pets in the profiles, as these may change (more or fewer or different) over a short period of time. Don't assume that because an establishment does not allow guests to bring pets that pets aren't around. Dogs and cats and birds (and monkeys, pigs, goats, llamas, etc.) are often very around. If you foresee a problem with this, be sure to clarify "how around" before booking. And in case you can't bear to leave your own beloved Barkly or Miss Kitty for long periods, we have indicated which facilities allow pets, although it's best to check beforehand. One bad experience can change a pet policy overnight. Good innkeepers often know of reputable boarding facilities nearby.

Bathrooms

Americans are picky about their potties. The traditional (sometimes referred to as "European-style") bed-and-breakfast setup involved several bedrooms sharing a bath, but this is becoming less common. Even venerable old Victorians are being remodeled to include private baths. In fact, many bed-and-breakfasts offer very luxurious bath facilities, including jetted tubs, dual vanities, and so forth. Our advice is not to reject shared bath facilities out of hand. Sometimes these can be excellent values. Many inns with shared baths are that way to preserve an architectural gem. Do check the bedroom-to-bath ratio, however. Two rooms sharing a bath is excellent, but three or more can be problematic with a full house.

Meals

For starters, bed-and-breakfasts by definition offer breakfast—sometimes a continental or expanded continental, but more often a full breakfast. The former usually includes cold items such as cereal, fruit, and yogurt (and hot beverages), the latter a hot entrée with accompaniments. (To make matters more confusing, however, some B&Bs that describe their breakfasts as "expanded continental" offer eggs or some other hot dish!) Of course, many hotels and even motels now provide breakfasts. In most cases, a bed-and-breakfast breakfast—even a continental—tends to include more homemade items, greater selection, and greater care in presentation.

Some inns' breakfasts are quite elaborate, even gourmet, experiences, and refreshments upon arrival or in the evening are becoming commonplace as well. Many inns have self-serve beverages and/or snacks, or such items are available upon request. Usually food and beverages are complimentary. Innkeepers are sensitive to dietary needs and preferences but need to be warned of them in advance. When you make your reservation, be sure to explain if you are diabetic, wheat- or dairy-intolerant, vegetarian or vegan, or otherwise restricted. Many proprietors pride themselves on accommodating difficult diets, and a few of our inns don't serve meat at all. You'll find this information in the inn profiles.

Smoking

Californians are notoriously on the cutting edge of health and environmental concerns, and smoking is more frowned upon here, in general, than in other states. Virtually all the bed-and-breakfasts profiled in this book prohibit smoking anywhere indoors. A few don't even allow smoking outside on their premises; most do, however. Smoking in restaurants and bars is now prohibited in California, too, in order to prevent employee exposure to secondhand smoke.

Security

Many bed-and-breakfasts have property locks and room locks as sophisticated as those at hotels and motels. Others do not. Beyond locks, however, most bed-and-breakfasts provide an additional measure of security in that they are small properties, generally in a residential district, and typically with live-in hosts on the premises.

Privacy

At a hotel, you can take your key and hole up in solitude for the duration of your stay. It's a little harder at a bed-and-breakfast, especially if you take part in a family-style breakfast (although many inns offer the option of an early continental breakfast if you're pressed for time or feeling antisocial, and some offer en suite breakfast service, and others will let you make up a tray and take it to your room yourself—these options are noted in the inn profiles). Most bed-and-breakfast hosts we've met are very sensitive to guests' needs for privacy and seem to have a knack for being as helpful or as unobtrusive as you wish.

Autonomy

Most bed-and-breakfasts provide a key to the front door and/or an unlocked front door certain hours of the day. While you might be staying in a family-style atmosphere, you are seldom subject to rules such as a curfew.

Planning Your Visit

If you're not sure where you want to travel, browse through our listings. Maybe from an introduction or from a description of a property, you'll find something to spark your interest. If you know you are going to a certain location, note the properties in that zone, then read the entries. You can also call for brochures or take a further look at Web sites, especially to see rooms or to book directly.

Most of the inns in this book have Web sites, and most of the rest are in the process of getting one. Four other addresses that may be helpful are the California Division of Tourism at www.gocalif.ca.gov, the California Association of Bed and Breakfast Inns at www.cabbi.com, the California Hotel and Motel Association at www.chma.com, or the Independent Innkeepers Association at www.innbook.com.

WHEN YOU BOOK

With small properties you usually have to book on your own. Some travel agents will help you out with these reservations but may charge a fee, because many small properties don't give travel agent commissions. The fastest, easiest way to book is through the Internet. Many inns report that up to 50% or 60% of their reservations are now made over the Web, and the Web sites will often have detailed pictures and descriptions of the rooms. You can also use a reservation service, but if you have special needs or questions, we suggest contacting properties directly to get exactly what you want, when you want it.

Ask about any special needs or requirements, and make sure your requests are clear. Also specify what amenities are important to you—privacy, king-size bed, fireplace, tub versus shower, view, first-floor access. Note the room you want by name, if you know it, or ask for the "best" room (in your price range) if you're not sure. Remember to ask about parking conditions—does the property have off-street parking or will you have to find a place on the street? And if air-conditioning is a must for you, always inquire—some bed-and-breakfasts do not have it, and many inns in mild summer climates like San Francisco and the Sierras don't need it.

Verify prices and conditions and any factors or amenities that are important to you. The best time to call is in the early afternoon, before new guests arrive for the day and when hosts have the most free time. Book as soon as possible—for weekends and holidays, preferred properties could be filled a year or more in advance.

A WORD ABOUT NEGOTIATING RATES

Negotiating a good rate is more straightforward at a bed-and-breakfast than at a hotel. For starters, the person on the other end of the line at the bed-and-breakfast may be the owner and thus may have the authority to offer you a discount if she's so inclined. Second, the bed-and-breakfast owner has a smaller number of rooms and guests to keep track of than a hotel manager and won't have to do a lot of checking to know whether something is available. Also, because the number of rooms is small, each room is more important. In a bed-and-breakfast with four rooms, the rental of each room increases the occupancy rate by 25%. To get the best rate, just ask. If the owner expects a full house, you'll get a direct and honest "no deal." On the other hand, if she has rooms and knows that you are sensitive about price, chances are she'll work with you.

What the Ratings Mean

We have organized this book so that you can get a quick idea of each property by checking out the ratings, reading the information at the beginning of each entry, and then, if you're interested, reading the more detailed overview of each property. Obviously ratings are subjective, and people of good faith (and good taste) can and do differ. But you'll get a good, relative idea, and you'll be able to quickly compare properties.

Overall Rating   The overall ratings are represented by stars, which range in number from one to five and represent our opinion of the quality of the property as a whole. The ratings are defined as follows:

★★★★★	The Best
★★★★½	Excellent
★★★★	Very Good
★★★½	Good
★★★	Good Enough
★★½	Fair
★★	Not So Good
★½	Barely Acceptable
★	Unacceptable

The overall rating for the bed-and-breakfast or small inn experience incorporates all factors of the property, including guest rooms and also public rooms, food, facilities, grounds, maintenance, hosts, ambience, the surroundings, the view, and something we'll call "specialness," for lack of a better phrase.

Some properties have fairly equal star levels for all of these things, but most have some qualities that are better than others. Also, large, ambitious properties that serve dinner would tend to have a slightly higher star rating for the same level of qualities than a smaller property (the difference, say, between a great novel and a great short story; the larger it is, the harder it is to pull off, hence the greater the appreciation). Yet a small property can earn five stars with a huge dose of "specialness."

Overall ratings and room quality ratings do not always correspond. While guest rooms may be spectacular, the rest of the inn may be average, or vice versa. Generally, though, we've found through the years that a property is usually consistently good, or bad, throughout. You will note that none of the properties that are profiled in this book have less than three stars. That is because there are so many fine inns in California that it was difficult to decide what to include, but no problem at all to know what to exclude.

Room Quality Rating The quality ratings, stated in the form of letter grades, represent our opinion of the quality of the guest rooms and bathrooms only. For the room quality ratings we factored in view, size, closet space, bedding, seating, desks, lighting, soundproofing, comfort, bathrooms (or lack), style, privacy, decor, "taste," and other intangibles. A really great private bathroom with a claw-foot tub and antique table might bring up the rating of an otherwise average room. Conversely, poor maintenance or lack of good lighting will lower the rating of a spacious, well-decorated room. The ratings are defined as follows:

> A = Excellent
>
> B = Very Good
>
> C = Good
>
> D = Acceptable

Value Rating The value ratings—A to D—are a combination of the overall and room quality ratings divided by the cost of an average guest room. If getting a good deal means the most to you, choose a property by looking at the value rating. Otherwise, the room quality and overall stars are better indicators of a satisfying experience. A five-star inn or bed-and-breakfast with an A value and quality would be ideal, but most often you'll find a mix. If a wonderful property is fairly priced, it may only get a B or C value rating, but you still might prefer it to an average property that gets an A value rating. In general, there are a lot more bargains in more remote and less-traveled locales.

Price Our price range is the lowest-priced room in low season to the highest-priced room in high season. The range does not usually include specially priced times such as holidays and special events. (This is especially important to remember in major tourist areas, where some inns' rates not only double but even triple for certain events and times of year!) The room rate is based on double occupancy and assumes that breakfast is included. Unless specifically noted, prices quoted in the formats do not include gratuities or state taxes, which can be fairly steep. Gratuities are optional; use your own discretion. Prices change constantly, so check before booking.

The Inn Profiles Clarified

The bulk of information about properties is straightforward, but much of it is in abbreviated style, so the following clarifications may help. They are arranged in the order they appear in the profile format.

Location

First, check the map for location. Our directions are designed to give you a general idea of the property's location. For more complete directions, call the property when you are in town. Web sites almost always have a map and directions to the inn.

Building

This category denotes the design and architecture of the building. Many of the properties in the *Unofficial Guides* are historically and architecturally interesting. You may want to brush up on your nineteenth- and early-twentieth-century architecture. Styles you will see here include Queen Anne Victorian, Italianate Victorian, Tudor Revival, Stick-style Victorian, Arts and Crafts, and Spanish Mission Revival. You'll notice numerous references to wallpapers made by Bradbury & Bradbury. This California firm meticulously handmakes nineteenth- and early-twentieth-century silk-screened wallpapers using as many as 1,000 individual impressions for an average Victorian room. You may see their work at www.bradbury.com. If it weren't for bed-and-breakfast inns, a great many of our country's unique and irreplaceable architectural masterpieces would have long ago been demolished. To become more informed on American architecture, you might pick up a copy of Marilyn Klein and David Fogle's inexpensive ($7.95) handbook *Clues to American Architecture,* ISBN 0–913515–18–3.

Food and Drink

Most properties go all out to fill you up at breakfast, so that you could easily skip lunch (factor that into the value). If a full-scale morning meal, including a hot entrée or two, is a major part of the B&B experience for you, note in the profiles whether we specify "full breakfast." Extended continental breakfasts are often quite elaborate as well, with fresh fruit, juices, a variety of cereals and granola, yogurt, pastries and bagels, and hot beverages. Many inns and bed-and-breakfasts also offer some or all of the following: afternoon tea (sometimes a "high tea"), predinner hors d'oeuvres, postdinner desserts, sherry, or wine, and "bottomless" cookie jars. Quite honestly, in some inns you will never be hungry enough to go out and dine unless you exercise great restraint or remove yourself from temptation by fleeing the premises.

Recreation

We try to indicate whether the activities noted in the format are on-site. With a very few exceptions, assume that golf, tennis, fishing, canoeing, downhill skiing, and the like are not on-site (since these are small properties, not resorts). Assume that games and smaller recreational activities are on the property. But there are exceptions, so ask. There are good places to walk, jog, or hike around virtually every property, so walking, jogging, and hiking are not usually listed as recreational activities.

Amenities and Services

These blend a bit. Generally, amenities include extras such as swimming pools and games, or services such as business support and turning down beds in the evening, plus special services that you will have to pay for. Business travelers should note whether any services are mentioned and whether there are public rooms, group discounts, and so forth to back them up. Almost all bed-and-breakfasts and inns can provide advice regarding touring, restaurants, and local activities; many keep maps and brochures on hand.

Deposit

Most inns require a credit card, check, or cash for the deposit, which may range from one night's lodging to the entire amount. Few inns will charge your credit card before you arrive. If you cancel in advance of their stated deadline, some will give a full refund, and others will charge a nominal fee for the extra paperwork you have put them through. If you cancel after the deadline, you may be responsible for part or all of the time you had reserved. Quite a few inns, however, will refund most or all of your money if the room is re-rented. Cancellations can be really costly, so pay close attention to the deadline if it appears you may have to cancel.

Discounts

Discounts may extend to singles, long-stay guests, kids, seniors, packages, and groups, even if there are none listed in the text. It doesn't hurt to ask, as these sorts of things are especially flexible in small establishments, or midweek, or off-season, or at the last minute, when innkeepers may want to fill their rooms. We've also used this category to tell you how much an extra guest will cost at some establishments.

Credit Cards

For those properties that do accept credit cards (we note those that do not), we've listed accepted credit cards with the following codes:

V	VISA	MC	MasterCard
AE	American Express	D	Discover
DC	Diner's Club International	CB	Carte Blanche

Check-In/Out

A late check-out is often OK if you request it. Sometimes it's possible to store luggage at the property before or after check-out to extend your recreational time in the area. If you plan to check in very late, call the hosts and let them know.

Open

Properties often claim that they are open all year, but they can close at any time, at the last minute, for personal reasons, or if business is slow. Similarly, properties that close during parts of the year may open specially for groups. If you can get a bunch of family or friends together, it's a great way to stay at popular inns and bed-and-breakfasts that would be otherwise hard to book. And remember that in low season, things slow down, dinners may not be served, and even when some properties are "open," they may be half-closed. Also remember that the low-/high-season distinction varies a lot depending on geography. Inns in the desert invariably close in the summer; their high season is in the winter. Sierra inns may close in the winter if they are not near an all-weather highway. If they are near a ski resort, however, their high season will be when the slopes are open.

Changing Times

Nothing stays the same for long in the small-lodging business. Innkeepers get divorced, prices go up, chefs quit in the middle of a quiche, and rooms get redecorated, upgraded, and incorporated. So use this format as a means to get a good overall idea of the property, and then when you book inquire about the specific details that matter most to you. Changes will definitely occur, so check to be sure.

Making the Most of Your Stay

Once you're settled in, it's a good idea to scope out the entire place, or you may not realize until too late that your favorite book was on the shelf, or that an old-fashioned swing would have swung you into the moonlight on a warm evening. If you are alone in the inn, it can feel like the property is yours (and that, in fact, is a good reason to go midweek, off-season).

Do take advantage of the unique charms of these lodgings: the fireplace, the piano, other guests, the gardens. What makes an inn or bed-and-breakfast experience so integral a part of a trip are small moments that can become special memories.

Did you love it? You can perhaps duplicate in your daily life some of the touches that made the experience special, whether it was warm towels, an early weekend breakfast by candlelight, or a special recipe for stuffed French toast. Hosts usually enjoy sharing ideas and recipes.

A small inn or bed-and-breakfast, perhaps set in a village or town where at least a few blocks retain a look of history and often grace, encourages you to relax, lie back, unwind, open up, read, talk, get romantic, dream, slow down, look up at the stars and down at the grass, and smell the coffee—and, of course, the roses, climbing on the pergola or lining the walkway. These small lodgings are stress-busters, far away from sitcoms and fast food and the media mania du jour. They are intimate places to settle into and curl up with a book, or a honey, or a dream, or, if you must, a laptop and a cell phone.

Authors' Selection of Interesting and Unusual Inns

St. Orres   An inn on the Sonoma coast with striking pseudo-Russian architecture, a famous restaurant and rooms from budget to posh

Brigadoon Castle   A fairyland castle in the little-visited Trinity Alps

Coast Guard House   Arts and Crafts in a former living quarters for lighthouse keepers on the Sonoma Coast

Sonoma Chalet   An inexpensive and secluded getaway with 1920s and 1930s decor, just blocks from downtown Sonoma

Ink House   Napa's imposing Victorian mansion shaped like an ink bottle

Columbia City Hotel and Fallon Hotel   Authentic gold rush hotels in a restored gold rush town

Heirloom Bed-and-Breakfast Inn   A small Greek Revival Victorian with a sod roof annex in the Gold Country

Piety Hill Inn Bed-and-Breakfast Cottages   A restored 1920s auto court in Nevada City

Indian Creek Bed-and-Breakfast   A historic gold rush building-cum-1930s Hollywood getaway in a rural gold rush locale

Cottage Inn at Lake Tahoe   1930s log cabins with funky theme rooms on the shore of California's most spectacular lake

Blackthorne Inn   A soaring four-story tree house in a quiet redwood forested canyon on Point Reyes

East Brother Light Station   A working lighthouse on an island in San Francisco Bay

Château Tivoli   A sterling example of an exotic Châteauesque-style Victorian mansion in San Francisco's Victorian-studded Alamo Park district

Panama Hotel and Restaurant   Tropical wackiness and down-home charm in Marin County

Casa Del Mar   Light and airy rooms decorated with folk art and bright prints in a former botanical garden on Marin County's most popular beach

Union Hotel and Victorian Mansion   A restored stage-stop hotel and a surreal Victorian with Disneyland-like theme rooms, just north of Santa Barbara

Bed-and-Breakfast Inn at La Jolla   A rare example of early 1900s Cubist-style architecture and tropical landscaping in La Jolla

Bracken Fern Manor   A prohibition-era brothel and mob hangout in Lake Arrowhead

Inn at 657   The only B&B in California's largest city is both good and affordable

Korakia Pensione   A continuing work by an architect/artist that is an exotic mixture of Moroccan and Greek styles

Venice Beach House   Lodgings with character close to L.A.'s most colorful beach

Mini Indexes

Top 30 Overall

Five Stars
The Archbishop's Mansion
Carter House Victorians
Château du Sureau
Gaige House Inn
Glendeven
The Inn at Depot Hill
The Inn on Mount Ada
Kenwood Inn
Orchard Hill Country Inn
The Sherman House
Simpson House Inn
Victorian Gardens
The Willows Historic Palm
    Springs Inn

Four-and-a-Half Stars
Abigail's Elegant Victorian
    Mansion
Agate Cove Inn Bed and Breakfast
Albion River Inn
Amber House Bed and Breakfast
Applewood Inn and Restaurant
Arbor Inn Bed and Breakfast
Artists' Inn
Avila Valley Inn

Babbling Brook Bed and
 Breakfast Inn
The Ballard Inn
The Bed and Breakfast Inn at
 La Jolla
Belle de Jour Inn
The Bissell House Bed and
 Breakfast
Blue Whale Inn
Brigadoon Castle
Campbell Ranch Inn
Captain Walsh House

Top 30 by Room Quality

1. Château du Sureau
2. Simpson House Inn
3. The Willows Historic Palm
 Springs Inn
4. The Archbishop's Mansion
5. The Inn on Mount Ada
6. The Sherman House
7. Victorian Gardens
8. Gaige House Inn
9. Glendeven
10. Kenwood Inn
11. The Inn at Depot Hill
12. Carter House Victorians
13. Inn at Playa del Rey
14. Old Monterey Inn
15. Seal Cove Inn
16. Seven Gables Inn
17. The Just Inn
18. Windy Point Inn
19. Albion River Inn
20. Applewood Inn and Restaurant
21. Belle de Jour Inn
22. Grand View Inn
23. Inn at Occidental
24. Mangels House
25. Oak Knoll Inn
26. Orchard Hill Country Inn

27. Rachel's Inn
28. The Honor Mansion
29. The Martine Inn
30. Two Angels Inn

Top Values

American River Inn
Avalon House
Baywood Bed-and-Breakfast Inn
Blue Spruce Inn
Cain House: A Country Inn
Camino Hotel—Seven Mile House
Carriage House Bed-and-Breakfast
Cavanagh Inn
Chalfant House
Chichester-McKee House: A Bed-
 and-Breakfast Inn
Columbia City Hotel and Fallon
 Hotel
Cleone Gardens Inn
Cornelius Daly Inn
Cowper Inn
DeHaven Valley Farm and
 Restaurant
Dorrington Hotel and Restaurant
Dorris House
Faulkner House
Feather Bed
Fitzpatrick Winery and Lodge
Forbestown Inn
Garratt Mansion
Hanford House B&B Inn
Harper House Bed-and-Breakfast
Heirloom Bed-and-Breakfast Inn
High Country Inn
Hollyhock Farm Bed-and-
 Breakfast
Hotel Mac
Imperial Hotel
Inn 1890
Inn at 657

Inn at Shallow Creek Farm
Jamestown Hotel
Jamestown National Hotel:
    A Country Inn
Johnson's Country Inn
Julian Gold Rush Hotel
Lodge at Noyo River
Lord Bradley's Inn
Madison Street Inn
McCloud Bed-and-Breakfast Hotel
Mendocino Farmhouse
Moon's Nest Inn
Mount Shasta Ranch Bed-and-
    Breakfast
New Davenport Bed-and-
    Breakfast Inn
Nob Hill Inn
Old Lewiston Inn
Panama Hotel and Restaurant
Piety Hill Inn Bed-and-Breakfast
    Cottages
Rainbow Tarns Bed-and-Breakfast
    at Crowley Lake
Roughley Manor
St. George Hotel
Sanford House
Snow Goose Inn
Strawberry Creek Inn
Tahoma Meadows Bed-and-
    Breakfast
Theodore Woolsey House
Tiffany House Bed-and-Breakfast
    Inn
Victorian Gardens
Wild Goose Country Victorian
    Bed-and-Breakfast
The Willows

Work on Your Winter Tan
Casa Cody B&B Country Inn
Homestead Inn
Korakia Pensione
L'Horizon

Roughley Manor
Tres Palmas Bed-and-Breakfast
Two Angels Inn
Willows Historic Palm Springs Inn

Close to the Ski Slopes
Apples Bed-and-Breakfast
Bracken Fern Manor
Carriage House Bed-and-Breakfast
Chalfant House
Chaney House
Château du Lac
Christiania Inn
Cottage Inn at Lake Tahoe
Dorrington Hotel and Restaurant
Eagle's Landing
Grandmere's Inn—Aaron Sargent
    House
Hollyhock Farms Bed-and-
    Breakfast
Inn at Fawnskin
Lodge at Manuel Mill
McCaffrey House Bed-and-
    Breakfast Inn
McCloud Bed-and-Breakfast Hotel
Mount Shasta Ranch Bed-and-
    Breakfast
Rainbow Tarns Bed-and-Breakfast
    at Crowley Lake
Richardson House
Rockwood Lodge
Snow Goose Inn
Sunnyside Restaurant and Lodge
Tahoma Meadows Bed-and-
    Breakfast
Truffles Bed-and-Breakfast
Windy Point Inn

Great Views
Agate Cove Inn Bed-and-Breakfast
Beltane Ranch
Campbell Ranch Inn
Casa Del Mar
Darling House

East Brother Light Station
Evergreen
Green Gables Inn
Hollyhock Farm Bed-and-Breakfast
Ink House
Inn at Playa del Rey
Inn on Mount Ada
La Mer
Lake Oroville Bed-and-Breakfast
Martine Inn
Mount Shasta Ranch Bed-and-Breakfast
Mountain Home Inn
New Davenport Bed-and-Breakfast Inn
Roundstone Farm
Sea Rock Bed-and-Breakfast Inn
Seven Gables Inn/Grand View Inn
Vine Hill Inn Bed-and-Breakfast
Wine Country Inn

For Lovers

Albion River Inn
Amber House
Avila Valley Inn
Babbling Brook Bed-and-Breakfast Inn
Ballard Inn
Bed-and-Breakfast Inn at La Jolla
Château de Vie
Château du Lac
Château du Sureau
Cheshire Cat Inn
Cottage Grove Inn
Deer Run
Doryman's Oceanfront Inn
Gingerbread Mansion
The Homestead
Inn at Playa del Rey
Johnson's Country Inn
Just Inn
L'Horizon

Lost Whale Bed-and-Breakfast Inn
Moon's Nest Inn
Old Monterey Inn
Pelican Inn
Sandy Cove Inn
Seal Beach Inn and Gardens
Seal Cove Inn
Spencer House
St. Orres
Whale Watch Inn by the Sea
Windy Point Inn
Zosa Gardens Bed-and-Breakfast

On the Water

Albion River Inn
Baywood Bed-and-Breakfast Inn
Chaney House
Cypress Inn on Miramar Beach
DeHaven Valley Farm and Restaurant
Doryman's Oceanfront Inn
Eagle's Landing
East Brother Light Station
Elk Cove Inn
Greenwood Pier Inn
Griffin House at Greenwood Cove
Harbor House Inn
High Country Inn
Inn at Fawnskin
Jenner Inn and Cottages
Lodge at Manuel Mill
Lost Whale Bed-and-Breakfast Inn
New Davenport Bed-and-Breakfast Inn
Old Lewiston Inn
Old Milano Hotel
Pillar Point Inn
Portofino Beach Hotel
Sandpiper House Inn
Sandy Cove Inn
Scripps Inn
Sunnyside Restaurant and Lodge
Two Angels Inn

Vichy Hot Springs Resort
Whale Watch Inn by the Sea
The Willows
Windy Point Inn

Kid-Friendly (children OK with no qualifications)

Albion River Inn
Amber House Bed-and-Breakfast
Anderson Creek Inn
Archbishop's Mansion
Bath Street Inn
Ballard Inn
Baywood Bed-and-Breakfast Inn
Cain House: A Country Inn
Camino Hotel—Seven Mile House
Carriage House
Carter House Victorians
Casa Cody B&B Country Inn
Casa Laguna Inn
Channel Road Inn
Château Tivoli
Christmas House Bed-and-
  Breakfast Inn
Coast Guard House
Coloma Country Inn
Columbia City Hotel and Fallon
  Hotel
Cornelius Daly Inn
Cowper Inn
Cypress Inn on Miramar Beach
Darling House
Doryman's Oceanfront Inn
Fetzer Vineyards Bed-and-
  Breakfast
Foxes in Sutter Creek
Garratt Mansion
Gingerbread Mansion
Green Gables Inn
Green Lantern Inn
Grey Whale Inn

Groveland Hotel
Heritage Park Bed-and-Breakfast
  Inn
Hollyhock Farm Bed-and-
  Breakfast
Homestead Inn
Inn at 657
Inn at Playa del Rey
Inn on Summer Hill
Jamestown Hotel
La Residence Country Inn
Lake Oroville Bed-and-Breakfast
Lodge at Noyo River
Lost Whale Bed-and-Breakfast Inn
Madison Street Inn
Martine Inn
Mount Shasta Ranch Bed-and-
  Breakfast
Mountain Home Inn
Nob Hill Inn
Old Lewiston Inn
Panama Hotel and Restaurant
Pelican Inn
Piety Hill Inn Bed-and-Breakfast
  Cottages
Point Reyes Seashore Lodge
Scotia Inn
Sherman House
Snow Goose Inn
Strawberry Creek Inn
Sunnyside Restaurant and Lodge
Theodore Woolsey House
Twenty Mile House
Union Street Inn
Venice Beach House
Vichy Hot Springs Resort
Victorian Inn on the Park
Vintage Towers Bed-and-Breakfast
Vizcaya
Washington Square Inn
Wine and Roses Country Inn

Rural or Farm Setting

Apple Lane Inn
Ballard Inn
Beltane Ranch
Bidwell House
Campbell Ranch
Coloma Country Inn
DeHaven Valley Farm
    and Restaurant
Hollyhock Farm Bed-and-
    Breakfast
The Homestead
Howard Creek Ranch
Inn at Shallow Creek Farm
Johnson's Country Inn
Just Inn
LeeLin Wikiup Bed-and-Breakfast
Mendocino Farmhouse
Pelican Inn
Roundstone Farm
Vine Hill Inn Bed-and-Breakfast
Wine and Roses Country Inn
Zosa Gardens Bed-and-Breakfast

Pet-Friendly Inns (special conditions may apply)

American River Inn
Anderson Creek Inn
Apple Lane Inn
Boonville Hotel and Restaurant
Carriage House
Casa Cody B&B Country Inn
Casa Laguna Inn
Château de Vie
Château Tivoli
Cleone Gardens Inn
Greenwood Pier Inn
Groveland Hotel
Hollyhock Farm Bed-and-
    Breakfast
Howard Creek Ranch

Inn 1890
Inn at Schoolhouse Creek
Jamestown National Hotel:
    A Country Inn
Jenner Inn and Cottages
Lake Oroville Bed-and-Breakfast
Moon's Nest Inn
Mount Shasta Ranch Bed-and-
    Breakfast
Old Lewiston Inn
Panama Hotel and Restaurant
Rachel's Inn
San Antonio House
Spencer House
St. George Hotel
Tahoma Meadows Bed-and-
    Breakfast
Twenty Mile House
Vagabond's House
Wine and Roses Country Inn

Inns by a Vineyard

Arbor Inn Bed-and-Breakfast
Belle de Jour Inn
Beltane Ranch
Campbell Ranch
Château de Vie
Fetzer Vineyards Bed-and-
    Breakfast
Fitzpatrick Winery and Lodge
Hope-Merrill House and Hope
    Bosworth House
Ink House
Just Inn
Kenwood Inn
Loma Vista Bed-and-Breakfast Oak
    Knoll Inn
Oleander House
Shady Oaks Country Inn
Wine Country Inn
Zinfandel Inn

Zone I
Northern California

North Coast

Starting 50 miles north of San Francisco at Bodega Bay, following Highway 1 north along the coast to the Oregon border.

Cities and Towns Bodega, Jenner, Gualala, Point Arena, Manchester, Elk, Albion, Little River, Mendocino, Fort Bragg, Westport, Ukiah, Scotia, Ferndale, Eureka, Arcata, Trinidad.

Attractions Miles and miles of uncrowded **beaches and state parks** with tide pools and more than 300 species of birds, seals, whales, and otters; **Fort Ross State Historic Park**, a nineteenth-century Russian fur-trapping settlement; **Point Arena Lighthouse**; the picture-postcard town of **Mendocino**, with shops, restaurants, and numerous parks and beaches; **redwoods**, 50,000 acres of them just in the Avenue of the Giants along Highway 101, south of **Scotia**; **Ferndale**, a historic landmark full of well-preserved Victorians; **Eureka**, beaches, bay cruises, a national wildlife preserve, and well-preserved Victorians; **Trinidad**, a tiny fishing village with still more beaches and redwoods.

Contact Information Bodega Bay Visitors Center, (707) 875-3422; Fort Ross State Historic Park, (707) 847-3221; Fort Bragg/Mendocino Coast Chamber of Commerce, (800) 726-2780; Russian Gulch State Park, (707) 937-5804; Skunk Train, (800) 77-SKUNK; Mackerricher State Park, (707) 937-2434; Humboldt Redwood State Park, (707) 946-2263; Eureka/Humboldt County Convention and Visitors Bureau, (800) 346-3482 (www.redwoodvisitor.org); Patrick's Point State Park, (707) 677-3570; Redwood National Park Information Center, (707) 464-6101.

Shasta Cascade Mountains

An off-the-tourist-track paradise at the northern end of the Central Valley, stretching from the Trinity Alps east to Mount Shasta and Mount Lassen, then north to the Oregon, California, and Nevada borders.

Cities and Towns Lewiston, Weaverville, Fort Jones, Dunsmuir, Mount Shasta City, Gazelle, McCloud, Chester, Alturas.

Attractions   The unspoiled **Trinity Alps**, with the historic mining towns of **Lewiston** and **Weaverville**, the latter containing the country's oldest Chinese temple; **Fort Jones**, an isolated, unspoiled ranching town; mystical **Mount Shasta** and the three lovely towns on its flanks—**Dunsmuir**, a railroad buff's heaven; **Mount Shasta City**, a sophisticated mix of New Agers and yuppies; and **McCloud**, a newly revived company lumber town with a restored railroad; **Mount Lassen** blew its stack in '15 and is still fuming and steaming, and **Lassen Volcanic National Park** has sights like **Boiling Springs Lake**, the **Sulphur Works**, and **Bumpass Hell** to prove it; **Lava Beds National Monument**, an unlikely but hypnotically fascinating area of lava, sagebrush, and cinder cones; **Lake Almanor**, like a tiny Tahoe, with great fishing, waterskiing, and perfect summer weather.

Contact Information   Trinity County Chamber of Commerce, (800) 487-4648; Joss House State Historic Park in Weaverville, (530) 623-5284; Dunsmuir Chamber of Commerce, (800) DUNSMUIR (www.dunsmuir. com); Mount Shasta Visitors Bureau, (800) 926-4865 (www.mtshasta. com/chamber); Shasta Sunset Dinner Train, (800) 733-2141; Lassen Volcanic National Park Headquarters, (530) 595-4444; Chester–Lake Almanor Chamber of Commerce, (530) 258-2426; Alturas Chamber of Commerce, (530) 233-4434; Modoc National Wildlife Refuge, (530) 233-3572.

North Central Valley

Starting at Redding, south to Red Bluff on I-5, then south on Highway 99 to Chico and Oroville.

Cities and Towns   Redding, Igo, Red Bluff, Orland, Chico, Oroville, Berry Creek.

Attractions   Sacramento River, a mountain stream at its source near Mount Shasta, becomes a major river in the Central Valley, watering thousands of acres of rice, olives, almonds, walnuts, and prunes; **Redding**, the north valley's largest city, and nearby 3,640-foot-long **Shasta Dam**, second largest in the country; **Red Bluff**, quiet farming and ranching town, with many Victorian homes; **Chico**, a classic college town and farm center with much charm and sophistication; **Oroville**, historic mining town on the Feather River; and the 770-foot-high **Oroville Dam**, tallest in the United States.

Contact Information   Redding Convention and Visitors Bureau, (800) 874-7562 (www.shastacascade.org); Red Bluff–Tehama County Chamber of Commerce, 800-655-6225 (www.redblufftehamacntyinfo.com/chamber/ cvb); Chico Chamber of Commerce and Visitors Bureau, (800) 852-8570 (www.chicochamber.com/ visitor.htm); Oroville Chamber of Commerce, (800) 655-GOLD.

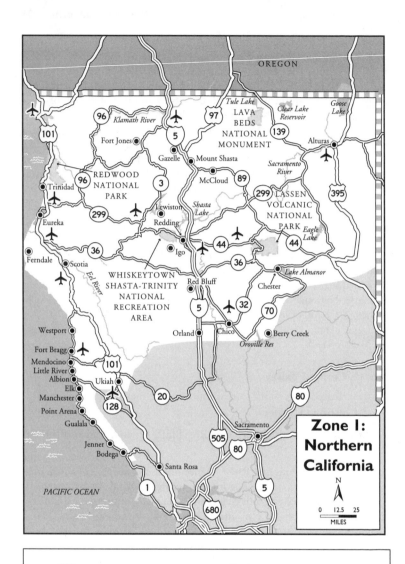

Zone 1:
Northern
California

N

0   12.5   25
MILES

PACIFIC OCEAN

ALBION RIVER INN, Albion

| Overall: ★★★★½ | Room Quality: A | Value: B | Price: $170–$260 |

If your idea of bliss is a spectacular ocean view, this is your spot. Built right on the cliffs, all 20 of these luxury cottages follow the curve of Albion Cove. A nearby Coast Guard harbor horn sounds its haunting call day and night—so if you're a light sleeper, you may want to stay farther inland or use the earplugs provided in each room. You will find yourself immersed in sea air and sunsets, and, in season, you'll enjoy the passage of migrating whales. Many of the cottages contain spas or tubs for two with the same dramatic ocean view. The Albion River Inn Restaurant, located on the premises, features fresh seafood, locally grown produce, and an award-winning selection of 450 wines and 100 single-malt Scotch whiskeys. A full, chef-prepared, complimentary breakfast is served in the restaurant, and the menu changes daily.

SETTING & FACILITIES

Location: 6 mi. south of Mendocino at the Albion River, 3.5 hours north of San Francisco on Hwy. 1

Near: State parks, beaches, redwood forests, art galleries, restaurants, theater and musical events, scuba diving, fishing

Building: Contemporary, New England-style cottages

Grounds: 10 acres of ocean bluffs above Albion Cove and the Pacific Ocean, landscaped w/ flowers, wild headland grasses, native shrubs and pines

Public Space: Restaurant, bar, gift shop, grounds

Food & Drink: Chef-cooked breakfast in the restaurant DR 8–9:45 a.m.

Recreation: Tennis, horseback riding, canoeing, bicycling, golf

Amenities & Services: Hot tub, binoculars for whale- and wildlife-viewing, fresh-roasted coffee and teas, wine, fires laid each day, and a morning newspaper delivered to your room; private parking, disabled access, fax avail. during office hours

ACCOMMODATIONS

Units: 20 guest rooms
All Rooms: Ocean view, fireplace, fridge, phone, private bath
Some Rooms: Private deck, four-poster, sleeper sofa
Bed & Bath: Queens and kings, some spas or 2-person tubs, robes
Favorites: The 3 larger, newer rooms

with spas—17, 19, and 20
Comfort & Decor: Rooms medium to large, individually decorated w/ mix of contemporary/country/antique furniture, handpainted sponge detailing on walls, wingback chairs in front of fireplace, Adirondack chairs on decks

RATES, RESERVATIONS, & RESTRICTIONS

Deposit: 1st night's lodging; must cancel 7 days in advance
Discounts: None
Credit Cards: All
Check-in/Out: After 3/noon
Smoking: No
Pets: No
Kids: OK
No-Nos: TVs
Minimum Stay: 2 nights on weekends, 3 on holiday weekends

Open: All year
Hosts: Flurry Healy and Peter Wells
P.O. Box 100
3790 Hwy. 1
Albion, CA 95410
(707) 937-1919
(800) 479-7944
Fax: (707) 937-2604
www.albionriverinn.com
innkeepers@albionriverinn.com

FENSALDEN INN, Albion

| Overall: ★★★½ | Room Quality: B | Value: B | Price: $120–$175 |

In Norwegian, Fensalden means "home of the mist and sea." The name seems entirely apt for this cedar-shingled, two-story inn sitting in lonely splendor on a rise overlooking 20 acres of wildflower-dotted pasturelands that sweep down to the ocean. Once an 1860s stagecoach stop and tavern, the inn now offers an attractive array of five pleasing guest rooms in the main house, two more in the antique water tower, and a rustic, very private bungalow with large wooden beams and a full kitchen. A large breakfast of things like homemade applesauce, pear-stuffed French toast, and homemade banana bread is served in the handsome Tavern Room, and there's a champagne brunch on Sundays. It's so quiet here, you will swear you can hear the creaking and jingling of the last stagecoach to leave the inn, echoing down the road.

SETTING & FACILITIES

Location: Off Hwy. 1, 7 mi. south of Mendocino, .25 mi. down Navarro Ridge Rd.
Near: Airport, state parks, beaches, redwoods, restaurants, shopping, art

galleries, theater and musical events
Building: Gabled farmhouse, separate bungalow, and water tower w/ guest rooms

Grounds: 20 acres of rolling meadows, lined w/ cypress trees

Public Space: The Tavern Room, the parlor, and an office for guests

Food & Drink: 3-course breakfast in the Tavern Room 8:30–10 a.m., champagne on Sun.

Recreation: Croquet, horseshoes, badminton, volleyball on the premises; tennis, horseback riding, canoeing, biking, golf nearby

Amenities & Services: Wine, hors d'oeuvres, office for guests w/ fax, copier, telephone, computer hookup; private parking, disabled access

ACCOMMODATIONS

Units: 8 guest rooms, including 2 suites, and a bungalow w/ kitchen, 2 BRs, and 2 single-bed lofts

All Rooms: Fireplace, fridge, private bath

Some Rooms: Private porch or balcony overlooking garden, ocean view (6)

Bed & Bath: All queens, plus twins in bungalow and Hide-a-Bed in the Tower Suite, some shower/tubs

Favorites: Hawthorne Suite, w/ canopy bed, sitting room, and ocean view; Tower Suite, w/ cathedral ceiling and tall windows

Comfort & Decor: Rooms individually decorated w/ antiques, art, carpets and oriental rugs; bungalow has wood-burning stove, redwood kitchen counters

RATES, RESERVATIONS, & RESTRICTIONS

Deposit: No deposit; must cancel 7 days in advance, 14 days on holiday weekends

Discounts: Long stays, weekday business, groups

Credit Cards: MC, V

Check-In/Out: 3/11, late check-out by arrangement

Smoking: No

Pets: No

Kids: 16 or over

Minimum Stay: 2 nights on weekends

Open: All year

Host: Evelyn Hamby

P.O. Box 99

33810 Navarro Ridge Rd.

Albion, CA 95410

(707) 937-4042

(800) 959-3850

Fax: (707) 937-2416

www.fensalden.com

ehamby@mcn.org

DORRIS HOUSE, Alturas

Overall: ★★★	Room Quality: B	Value: A	Price: $49

Dorris House is far, far from everything except birds, cattle, mountains, water, and sky. On the shores of Dorris Lake in Modoc County, the 1912 farmhouse is on 35 acres that encompass part of a federal wildlife refuge. This is bird-watcher heaven, the absolute quiet disturbed only by raucous flights of Canada geese. Guest rooms are homey and comfortable, decorated with great-grandma's quilts and the owners' collection of Indian beadwork. Host Karol Woodward has lived in this off-the-beaten-track area for 75 years and can answer any questions you might think of.

SETTING & FACILITIES

Location: 3 mi. east of Alturas, on shores of Dorris Lake; call for precise directions

Near: Ski area, Warner Mountains Wilderness Area, Lava Beds Nat'l Monument, Fort Bidwell, Modoc County museum, small airport

Building: 2-story farmhouse, circa 1912

Grounds: 35 acres situated on Dorris Lake, part of the wildlife refuge

Public Space: Parlor w/ pump organ and piano, deck, front screened porch, kitchen

Food & Drink: Expanded cont'l breakfast served at guests' convenience on deck in summer, in ranch kitchen in winter

Recreation: Biking, bird-watching, golf, X-C skiing, ice-skating, sailing, fishing

Amenities & Services: Evening wine, owners' TV and phones avail. to guests; private parking; pasture for horses w/ prior notification; assistance w/ dining, fishing and hiking areas; can arrange pickup at airport

ACCOMMODATIONS

Units: 4 guest rooms, 3 larger than average

Some Rooms: View of Warner Mountains, lake, bird refuge, extra twin beds (3)

Bed & Bath: Doubles, 2 shared baths

Favorites: 3 upstairs rooms w/ family heirlooms, views

Comfort & Decor: Rooms individually decorated w/ heirloom antiques, Indian beadwork, quilts, area rugs on pine floors, new double-glazed windows

RATES, RESERVATIONS, & RESTRICTIONS

Deposit: $10 deposit; must cancel 10 days in advance

Discounts: Long stays, singles

Credit Cards: None

Check-In/Out: After 4/before 11 a.m.

Smoking: No

Pets: No

Kids: 12 or over

Minimum Stay: None

Open: All year

Hosts: Karol and Mary Woodward
P.O. Box 1575
County Rd. 57, 3 mi. east of Hwy. 395
Alturas, CA 96101
(530) 233-3786

LAKE OROVILLE BED-AND-BREAKFAST, Berry Creek

Overall: ★★★½	Room Quality: B	Value: B	Price: $105–$145

This buttercup yellow B&B sits high on a hill overlooking Lake Oroville on 40 acres of pine woods. Although it was built in 1991 specifically to be an inn, the rooms and decor—wallpaper and lace curtains, overstuffed chairs, and crocheted antimacassars—will remind you a bit of a visit to grandmom's house. The wraparound covered porch is a treat, with views in every direction. If you sit quietly, you may see a deer stroll by. The friendly owners like children and pets and encourage family reunions. They feed you well, too, with fresh-squeezed orange juice, asparagus quiche, sausage, and stuffed French toast or eggs Benedict.

Setting & Facilities

Location: On the north side of Lake Oroville, 15 mi. east of Oroville (call for directions), 1.5 hours north of Sacramento

Near: Shopping, golf courses, marinas; Lake Oroville, the 2nd largest lake in California; Feather Falls, the 6th highest waterfall in the United States

Building: Recently built Country French house w/ wraparound porch on all 4 sides

Grounds: 40 acres on top of a hill w/ views of Lake Oroville and the coastal range, gardens

Public Space: Parlor w/ fireplace, library w/ puzzles and videos, over-stuffed chairs and footstools, billiard room

Food & Drink: Full breakfast served at 9 a.m. in the parlor, at other times by arrangement; cater to vegetarian, vegan, and other dietary needs

Recreation: Billiards and pool on premises; fishing, golf, horseback riding, mountain biking, snowmobiling

Amenities & Services: Afternoon snacks, sodas, avail. 24 hours; private parking, disabled access

Accommodations

Units: 6

All Rooms: Private entrance and bath, phone; TV/VCR furnished on request

Some Rooms: Whirlpool tubs (5)

Bed & Bath: Queens and kings

Favorites: Rose Petal, w/ rose-colored Victorian wallpaper, white Battenberg

covering on a king bed, full bath w/ whirlpool tub, exceptional view over lake and valley

Comfort & Decor: Individually themed rooms w/ antiques to match, wallpaper, lace curtains, floral draperies and matching fabrics, carpets

Rates, Reservations, & Restrictions

Deposit: Payment in advance; must cancel 5 days in advance; $25 cancellation fee

Discounts: Weekday business, AAA

Credit Cards: AE, D, MC, V

Check-In/Out: 3-6/11:30, late check-out OK

Smoking: No

Pets: OK

Kids: OK

Minimum Stay: 2 nights on holiday

weekends

Open: All year

Hosts: Ronald and Cheryl Damberger

240 Sunday Dr.

Berry Creek, CA 95916

(916) 589-0700

(800) 455-5253

Fax: (530) 589-4761

www.lakeoroville.com/lakeoroville

lakeinn@now2000.com

SONOMA COAST VILLA, Bodega

Overall: ★★★★½	Room Quality: B	Value: B	Price: $185–$295

If you can't find time to visit Italy this year, you can check into this villa near Bodega Harbor and pretend. Pink stucco buildings with arched doors and windows, red-tiled roofs, and rooms with Italian slate floors, beamed ceilings, and wood-burning fireplaces will lull you into a Mediterranean frame of mind. Fine wines, spa amenities, and continental cuisine will round out the illusion. A full breakfast of seasonal fresh fruit, baked goods, and a hot entrée is served in the inn's dining room. Of course, if the European odyssey grows tiresome, California beaches, golf courses, shopping, and wineries are right at hand.

SETTING & FACILITIES

Location: 5 mi. south of Bodega Bay on Hwy. I, set back 100 yards from road, I hour north of San Francisco
Near: Bodega Harbor, beaches, shopping, restaurants, galleries, wineries, redwoods
Building: Mediterranean, w/ red-tiled roofs, terra-cotta stucco walls, arched doors and windows, carriage house
Grounds: 60 acres including extensive gardens, giant cacti, organic garden, pond
Public Space: Reception area w/ oriental rugs, art objects; tower library w/ books, magazines, videos, telescope; carriage house has pool table, Ping-Pong table, putting green

Food & Drink: Full country breakfast served 9–10 a.m. in the main DR; 3-course prix fixe dinner avail. on weekends
Recreation: Billiards, Ping-Pong, putting green on premises, nearby horseback riding on beach, tide pooling, bird-watching, boating, ocean and stream fishing, surfing, rafting, golf
Amenities & Services: Swimming pool, evening wine and complimentary beverages in Tower Room, fresh flowers, robes and toiletries, in-room VCRs; private parking, massage and spa services avail., concierge services for reservations and touring

ACCOMMODATIONS

Units: 12 guest rooms, 5 larger than average, including I suite
All Rooms: Fireplace, private bath, fridge, TV, reading lamp, sitting area, freshly ground coffee, herb teas, and fully stocked complimentary minifridge w/ bottle of local wine, fruit basket, fresh flowers
Some Rooms: Spanish-style blond wood furniture, large armoire, wrought-iron table and lamp, private terrace, extra twin bed (2)

Bed & Bath: Kings and queens, jetted tubs, Jacuzzis, or marble walk-in showers
Favorites: No. 4, the honeymoon suite, w/ walnut furniture, a plush sofa, deep pile carpet, private deck (John Travolta stayed here 30 days during filming of *Phenomenon,* followed by Robert Duvall)
Comfort & Decor: Rooms individually decorated in Mediterranean style: drapes and wooden shutters, exposed wooden beams, Italian green slate floors, carpets, natural materials

RATES, RESERVATIONS, & RESTRICTIONS

Deposit: Credit card or I night's lodging; must cancel 3 days in advance; cancellation fee I night's lodging
Discounts: No; extra person $50
Credit Cards: AE, MC, V

Check-In/Out: 3/11, late check-out when using spa facilities
Smoking: No
Pets: No
Kids: Not suitable

Minimum Stay: None
Open: All year
Hosts: Cyrus and Susan Griffin
P.O. Box 236
16702 Coast Hwy. 1

Bodega, CA 94922-0236
(707) 876-9818
(888) 404-2255
www.scvilla.com
reservations@scvilla.com

BIDWELL HOUSE, Chester

Overall: ★★★★	Room Quality: B	Value: B	Price: $60–$160

Where the heck is Chester? Well, it's at the north end of Lake Almanor, and down the road a piece from Lassen Volcanic Park. (Lassen is 108,000 acres of uncrowded, strange, and beautiful wilderness complete with 10,457-foot Lassen Peak, the largest plug dome volcano in the world.) Bidwell House is a great place to stay while you're exploring this lively area. Bird-watchers love it here, and there's a 10-mile paved trail on the west side of Lake Almanor that's fun to bicycle or hike in the summer and cross-country ski in the winter. The lake is also well-known for its large trout. Cohost Ian James prepares excellent breakfasts and is also chef for the popular restaurant on the premises. Chester may be a tad remote, but it is a robust and friendly place with a good mix of shops and restaurants.

SETTING & FACILITIES

Location: At the east end of Chester on the main street, 1 hour 15 min. from Chico, 3 hours from Sacramento, 2 hours from Reno
Near: Shopping, restaurants, Lake Almanor, airport, Lassen Volcanic Nat'l Park, Feather River, Caribou Wilderness Area
Building: Turn-of-the-century Victorian summer home for the founder of Chico, General John Bidwell
Grounds: 2 acres of lawns, aspen grove, herb garden, 2 vegetable gardens, gazebo, many flower gardens, view of meadow and Lake Almanor
Public Space: Parlor, DR, sunroom/game room
Food & Drink: Full breakfast in DR 8:30–10 a.m.
Recreation: Biking, golf, fishing, all water sports, bird-watching, X-C/downhill skiing, snowmobiling
Amenities & Services: Dinner by reservation Thurs., Fri., Sat.; disabled access

ACCOMMODATIONS

Units: 14 guest rooms, including 1 cottage, 3 suites
Some Rooms: Wood-burning stove, four-poster, fridge, private entrance, TV, cable, phone, extra twin bed, private baths (12), shared baths (2)
Bed & Bath: Queens and doubles, Jacuzzis (7)
Favorites: Robin's Roost, a large, private corner room w/ double Jacuzzi and shower, queen bed, and excellent view of meadow and lake

Comfort & Decor: Individually decorated rooms w/ walnut and mahogany antiques, lace curtains, original pine floors w/ oriental rugs, high ceilings

RATES, RESERVATIONS, & RESTRICTIONS

Deposit: 50% of bill or credit card number; must cancel 4 days in advance
Discounts: Long stays, weekday business, groups, AAA
Credit Cards: MC, V
Check-In/Out: 3/1, late check-out OK if room not rented
Smoking: No
Pets: No
Kids: OK with supervision

Minimum Stay: 2 nights on July and Aug. weekends
Open: All year
Hosts: Kim and Ian James
P.O. Box 1790
1 Main St.
Chester, CA 96020
(530) 258-3338
Fax: (530) 258-3187
www.bidwellhouse.com

JOHNSON'S COUNTRY INN, Chico

Overall: ★★★★   Room Quality: A   Value: A   Price: $72–$125

In the midst of a peaceful almond orchard and minutes from a pedestrian-friendly college town, this comfortable "farmhouse" with its inviting wraparound, covered porch was actually designed to be a B&B from its inception. As a result, the four handsome guest rooms are particularly quiet and private. Farm-hearty breakfasts may include a vegetable-cheese frittata, locally made apple sausage, and sour cream coffeecake with almonds grown right on the premises.

SETTING & FACILITIES

Location: 5 min. from downtown on the western edge of Chico, 1.5 hours north of Sacramento
Near: Feather River Scenic Byway, Chico State University, airport, downtown shopping, Bidwell Mansion and park (3rd largest city park in United States)
Building: Neo-Victorian farmhouse built in 1992; the looks of a former time w/ modern conveniences
Grounds: 10-acre almond orchard, 1-acre landscaped garden area rolling to orchard
Public Space: Garden Room w/

puzzles, checkers, cards, and piano; parlor w/ fireplace, TV, reading/conversation area
Food & Drink: Breakfast hours flexible until 9:30 a.m.
Recreation: Croquet, horseshoes, badminton on premises, bicycle rentals near park area, 4 golf courses and 2 tennis courts within 4 mi.
Amenities & Services: Coffee, tea, and juice served to rooms before breakfast, locally made juices, soft drinks during the day, evening wines and sherry; private parking, phone in rooms, disabled access on lower floor

ACCOMMODATIONS

Units: 3 guest rooms, I suite
All Rooms: Individually controlled AC, private bath, double shower, phone
Some Rooms: Fireplace, Jacuzzi for 2
Bed & Bath: Queens and extended double
Favorites: Harrison Suite, romantic and intimate, w/ cutwork duvet piled high on an 1860s Victorian double bed
Comfort & Decor: Spacious individual "theme" guest rooms furnished w/ antiques: Art Deco (1920), Art Nouveau (1900), Eastlake (1860), Arts and Crafts movement (1895)

RATES, RESERVATIONS, & RESTRICTIONS

Deposit: Hold w/ credit card; must cancel 48 hours in advance; cancellation fee $15
Discounts: Sun.–Thurs., $65 w/out breakfast
Credit Cards: AE, MC, V
Check-In/Out: 4–6 p.m. or by special arrangement/11
Smoking: No
Pets: No
Kids: 10 or over
Minimum Stay: None except for a few weekends w/ special Chico State College activities
Open: Closed Dec. 30–Jan. 1
Hosts: Joan and David Johnson
3935 Morehead Ave.
Chico, CA 95928
(530) 345-7829
Fax: (530) 345-7829
www.chico.com/johnsoninn
j.c.inn@pobox.com

ELK COVE INN, Elk

Overall: ★★★½	Room Quality: B	Value: B	Price: $98–$278

Informal and comfortable, this inn is a friendly, homey kind of place—if your home just happens to be on a gorgeous oceanfront lot, that is. All rooms have down comforters, robes, good chairs, reading lights, and fresh flowers. The inn is famous for its large breakfast buffet, so you can stuff yourself with juices, fruit, yogurt, and up to a dozen hot dishes such as Belgian waffles, polenta, frittatas, and assorted meats. Later in the day, the inn's full bar serves local wines, beer, and a special martini menu. The inn is open for dinner on Tuesday and Wednesday nights.

SETTING & FACILITIES

Location: On the ocean side of Hwy. 1, just south of the village of Elk, 2.5 hours north of San Francisco
Near: Beaches, shopping, restaurants, state parks, jogging path, golf, wineries
Building: 1872 Victorian mansion, cottages, new Arts and Crafts–style building w/ suites
Grounds: 1.5 acres of gardens on a bluff over the ocean, surrounded by parkland and beach, gazebo, creek
Public Space: Oceanfront DR and restaurant, common room w/ VCR/TV, microwave, fridge, phone, full cocktail bar w/ 25 different kinds of martinis, Anderson Valley wines, several local microbrews

Food & Drink: Large buffet breakfast served 8:30–9:30 a.m. in DR; special dietary needs accommodated

Recreation: Horseback riding, numerous hiking trails, kayaking, golf, tennis, biking; commercial guided kayak tours nearby

Amenities & Services: Gift basket w/ wine and cookies, evening port and chocolates; spa/massage services avail., private parking

ACCOMMODATIONS

Units: 14 guest rooms, including 4 suites, 12 rooms larger than average

All Rooms: Private bath, down comforter, reading light, chair, in-room tea- and coffeemaker, antique linens, fresh flowers

Some Rooms: Four-poster, sleeper sofa, fridge, skylight, stereo, microwave, fireplaces (13), extra twins (5), queen sofa beds (3)

Bed & Bath: Kings and queens, robes, Jacuzzis (4)

Favorites: Seascape in main building, w/ king bed, fireplace, fine view of ocean; Surf Song suite, w/ queen bed, remote-controlled fireplace, oceanfront window seat, bath w/ ocean view

Comfort & Decor: Rooms individually decorated w/ pottery collection, antiques, carpet; oceanfront suites have redwood ceilings, handcrafted lights, stonework, and oak furniture

RATES, RESERVATIONS, & RESTRICTIONS

Deposit: Credit card, 100% of bill; must cancel 14 days in advance; cancellation fee $10/night

Discounts: Long stays, groups, AAA, weekdays Nov.-April; extra person $30

Credit Cards: AE, MC, V

Check-In/Out: 2–6/11, late check-out by arrangement

Smoking: No

Pets: No

Kids: 11 or over

Minimum Stay: 2 nights on weekends, 3 on holiday weekends

Open: All year

Host: Elaine Bryant
P.O. Box 367
6300 S. Hwy. 1
Elk, CA 95432
(707) 877-3321
(800) 275-2967
www.elkcoveinn.com
elkcove@mcn.org

GREENWOOD PIER INN, Elk

Overall: ★★★½	Room Quality: B	Value: B	Price: $120–$235

This probably isn't the place for folks on a quest for the perfect little Victorian B&B. Quirky and eclectic, with a certain laid-back charm, the Greenwood Pier Inn is a collection of Victorian, Craftsman, and hybrid buildings practically hanging off the ocean cliff on one side and buried under a massive flower garden on the other. There's a redwood cabin right on the bluff, cliffside "castles," and an assortment of guest rooms in the main house, most only 100 feet from the edge of the cliff overlooking the surf. On the premises is a country store and garden shop and the Greenwood Pier Café.

SETTING & FACILITIES

Location: On Hwy. 1 in downtown Elk, 3 hours north of San Francisco
Near: Next to state park w/ large beach, shopping
Building: 9 Victorian/Craftsman/eclectic buildings, all remodeled, several over 100 years old
Grounds: Ocean bluff w/ views, year-round colorful gardens
Public Space: Country store and garden shop featuring local arts, boutique, books, jewelry, plants, and a café (dinner can be delivered to room)
Food & Drink: Extended cont'l breakfast 8 a.m. in room (outside door if you're asleep), other times by special arrangement
Recreation: Whale-watching, biking, tennis, golf, kayaking, horseback riding
Amenities & Services: Hot tub on cliff; private parking, massage avail.

ACCOMMODATIONS

Units: 12 guest rooms, 6 larger than average, including 4 suites
All Rooms: Private bath, handpainted tiles, homemade quilt, CD player, coffeemaker, fridge
Some Rooms: Fireplaces/woodstoves (11), gas fireplace, four-poster, sleeper sofa
Bed & Bath: Mostly kings and queens, Jacuzzis (3)
Favorites: Lighthouse suite, w/ ocean views from 2 levels, cupola viewing area, Jacuzzi upstairs overlooking ocean, double bed and double futon
Comfort & Decor: Rooms individually decorated w/ antiques, original art, stained glass, skylights, imported hardwood and some painted furniture, wrought iron, pink marble surround on fireplace

RATES, RESERVATIONS, & RESTRICTIONS

Deposit: 1st night's lodging; must cancel 7 days in advance
Discounts: Long stays; 2 or more weeknights in winter; extra person $15
Credit Cards: AE, MC, V
Check-In/Out: After 2/noon, late check-out by arrangement
Smoking: No
Pets: In 5 rooms, $15 extra
Kids: In 7 rooms
Minimum Stay: 2 nights on weekends, 3 on holiday weekends (4 rooms)
Open: All year
Host: Kendrick Perry
P.O. Box 336
5926 Hwy. 1
Elk, CA 95432
(707) 877-9997
www.greenwoodpierinn.com
gwpier@mcn.org

GRIFFIN HOUSE AT GREENWOOD COVE, Elk

Overall: ★★★	Room Quality: C	Value: B	Price: $75–$225

No cable and no telephone—no, not even a signal for your cell phone—so kick back, build a fire in the potbellied stove, and enjoy stunning ocean views or a colorful garden replete with hummingbirds, plus good food delivered to the door of your quaint cottage. While the garden cottages are a good value, the real attraction here is the cottages overlooking the ocean. The tiny village of Elk was a turn-of-century lumber town and shipping port, but nowadays it's a refuge for folks who yearn to return to the coast of the past. Elk is quieter, folksier, and decidedly less trendy than Mendocino, and everybody seems to like it just fine that way.

SETTING & FACILITIES

Location: In the middle of the village of Elk, 2.5 hours north of San Francisco on Hwy. I

Near: Anderson Valley wineries, redwoods, beaches, whale-watching

Building: Main House built in 1890, 7 cottages built in 1925, Carriage House built circa 1900

Grounds: Half-acre oceanfront property, picket fences, informal gardens with native plants, lots of flowers and hummingbirds

Public Space: Pub is a local meeting place open 3–10 daily, beer and wine, full dinners Thurs.-Mon.

Food & Drink: Full, hot breakfast served to rooms, attention given to dietary restrictions

Recreation: Fishing, tennis, ocean and river kayaking, canoeing, whale-watching

Amenities & Services: Wine on arrival, snacks in pub; private parking; some disabled access; VCRs avail.; room service for dinner; fax, copier

ACCOMMODATIONS

Units: 8 guest rooms, all cottages, 4 w/ private ocean-view decks; I is a separate house with a kitchen, right on the bluff; some of the cottages sleep up to 4

All Rooms: Wood-burning stove, private bath

Some Rooms: Parlor, sleeper sofa, fridge, sofa bed/daybed

Bed & Bath: Queens and doubles, most baths have tub/showers or tubs w/ handheld showers

Favorites: Carriage House, a bluff-top

cottage renovated in 1973 by local craftsmen to preserve its original character; LR w/ stone fireplace, den w/ queen bed and trundle, bath with whirlpool tub for 2, and private wraparound deck w/ unobstructed view of Greenwood Cove

Comfort & Decor: Clean and simply furnished cottages with a Cape Cod feel, claw-foot tubs, a mahogany bed, stained glass, and French doors; ocean-view cottages have windows and decks

RATES, RESERVATIONS, & RESTRICTIONS

Deposit: Ist night's lodging; must cancel 72 hours in advance

Discounts: Long stays, weekday business travelers

Credit Cards: AE, MC, V

Check-In/Out: 2/noon

Smoking: No

Pets: No

Kids: In 4 cottages

Minimum Stay: 2 nights on weekends

Open: All year

Host: Leslie Griffin Lawson
P.O. Box 172
5910 S. Hwy. I
Elk, CA 95432
(707) 877-3422
Fax: (707) 877-1853
www.griffinn.com
griffinn@mcn.org

THE HARBOR HOUSE INN, Elk

| Overall: ★★★★½ | Room Quality: B | Value: B | Price: $195–$315 |

There's a darkly dramatic, brooding quality to this beautiful old inn sitting on a bluff overlooking a wonderfully craggy stretch of private beach. You can easily imagine Heathcliff and Catherine murmuring before the huge fireplace in the high-beamed living room built of redwood from the nearby Albion forest. Choose one of the guest rooms with an ocean view and a fireplace and you, too, will have a setting for high drama. The inn operates on a modified American plan, including breakfast and dinner. And what a dinner it is: the inn's restaurant, considered the best in the area, nightly prepares a leisurely four-course dinner with one seating for 24 people.

SETTING & FACILITIES

Location: On ocean side of Hwy. 1 at the north end of Elk, 3 hours north of San Francisco
Near: Private beach, state parks, restaurants, galleries, shopping
Building: 1916 Craftsman-style building, built by a lumber company as executive residence; 4 cottages built in 1940s
Grounds: 3.5 acres, seaside gardens, paths to private beach, secluded sitting areas, ocean views
Public Space: Virgin redwood parlor/ LR w/ fireplace, DR
Food & Drink: Full breakfast served in DR 8:30–9:30 a.m., 4-course dinner included in fee
Recreation: Whale-watching, kayaking, bird-watching
Amenities & Services: Robes, down comforters and pillows; private parking

ACCOMMODATIONS

Units: 10 guest rooms, including 5 large rooms in the main house, 4 cottages
All Rooms: Private bath, CD player, individually controlled heat
Some Rooms: Fireplaces (9), private decks (5), four-poster
Bed & Bath: Kings and queens
Favorites: Harbor Room, large, w/ stunning view, mahogany four-poster, fireplace, sitting area
Comfort & Decor: Rooms newly refurbished and redecorated throughout w/ antiques, custom window treatments, carpets

RATES, RESERVATIONS, & RESTRICTIONS

Deposit: Credit card or 1 night's lodging; must cancel 14 days in advance; cancellation fee $20
Discounts: Winter weekdays; extra person $100
Credit Cards: MC, V
Check-In/Out: 2/noon
Smoking: No
Pets: No
Kids: 12 or over
Minimum Stay: 2 nights on weekends, 3 on holiday weekends

Open: Closed Dec. 1–15
Hosts: Sam and Elle Haynes
P.O. Box 369
5600 Hwy. 1
Elk, CA 95432

(707) 877-3203
(800) 720-7474
Fax: (707) 877-3452
www.theharborhouseinn.com
innkeepers@theharborhouseinn.com

SANDPIPER HOUSE, Elk

Overall: ★★★★	Room Quality: B	Value: B	Price: $130–$220

This pristinely pretty, gray-shingled home with a white picket fence and perennial flower garden in front shows no trace of its secret. As you continue inside, the interior of the classic country house with coffered ceilings, raised-panel walls, and decorously formal furnishings is serenely appealing. It isn't until you look out the windows toward the ocean that you realize that behind the quiet facade lies a wild, gorgeous ocean setting—kind of like scarlet undies under a gray wool suit. Four of the five guest rooms have this great view. The fifth, and least expensive, faces a pastoral view of the meadow and hills of Greenwood Ridge. Breakfast in the gracious, wood-paneled dining room is served on fine china and may feature poached pears, gingerbread pancakes, and chicken-basil sausage.

SETTING & FACILITIES

Location: On ocean side of Hwy. 1, 3 hours south of San Francisco
Near: Wineries, art galleries, shopping, restaurants
Building: Gray-shingled 83-year-old California Craftsman
Grounds: Half-acre oceanfront, rural countryside, perennial gardens, lawns w/ garden chairs, rose arbor, picket fence, private beach

Public Space: LR w/ fireplace, DR
Food & Drink: Full breakfast served 8:30–9:30 a.m. in DR
Recreation: Ocean kayaking, diving, river canoeing
Amenities & Services: Fresh baked goods, hot tea, chocolate, cider avail. in afternoon, evening sherry 4–6 p.m. in LR, massage services avail.; private parking

ACCOMMODATIONS

Units: 5 guest rooms, 3 larger than average, including 1 suite
All Rooms: Private bath, down comforter, fine linens, fresh flowers, fridge
Some Rooms: Fireplace, four-poster, sleeper sofa, extra bed (1)
Bed & Bath: Queens
Favorites: Weston, w/ fireplace, panoramic view of Greenwood Cove,

wing chairs at window, large bath w/ antique vanity
Comfort & Decor: Rooms individually decorated w/ mix of traditional and antique furniture, including wing chairs, wicker accents, a lace-covered canopy bed, bookshelves, wallpaper, drapes and lace curtains, oriental rugs and carpet

RATES, RESERVATIONS, & RESTRICTIONS

Deposit: 1st night's lodging, 50% for 3 or more nights; must cancel 7 days in advance; $10 cancellation fee
Discounts: None
Credit Cards: AE, D, MC, V, cash, traveler's checks, or personal checks
Check-In/Out: 2/11, 2-hour-late check-out $20
Smoking: No
Pets: No
Kids: 12 or over

Minimum Stay: 2 nights on weekends, 3 on holiday weekends
Open: All year
Host: Claire Melrose
P.O. Box 149
5520 S. Hwy. 1
Elk, CA 95432
(707) 877-3587
(800) 894-9016
www.sandpiperhouse.com

ABIGAIL'S ELEGANT VICTORIAN MANSION, Eureka

| Overall: ★★★★ | Room Quality: A | Value: B | Price: $85–$185 |

Abigail's is about as Victorian as you can get on this side of the ocean. It is used as an interactive living history house museum, and the period furnishings are impressive in their scope and quality. And the owners? Well, they pull out all the stops to make your visit memorable. They get into costume to drive guests around town in their antique cars. Doug dons an English butler's uniform to greet guests at the door. Lily, who was born in Belgium and studied cooking with a four-star French chef, puts her talent to work at breakfast using fresh produce from the inn's organic gardens and orchard. Her breakfast specialties are eggs *en croute*—creamed and scrambled eggs with smoked salmon or ham in a puffed pastry crust. She is also available for Swedish massages. Doug is an actor, writer, and world traveler as well as a gracious host.

SETTING & FACILITIES

Location: Half-mile east of Hwy. 101 at C and 14th Sts., 5 hours north of San Francisco

Near: Redwood state parks, beaches, airport, shopping, restaurants

Building: An 1888 Queen Anne Victorian home w/ Eastlake influences, on the Nat'l Register of Historic Places, carriage house w/ 3 antique automobiles

Grounds: Half-acre of Victorian gardens including a formal rose garden w/ over 100 roses, croquet field, organic orchard and garden, statuary, fountain, lawn and garden furniture

Public Space: 2 large parlors, sitting room, library w/ 10,000 books, DR, all w/ fireplaces

Food & Drink: Full French breakfast w/ fresh-squeezed orange juice served in DR at 9 a.m., special dietary needs accommodated w/ advance notice

Recreation: Croquet, darts, bicycles on premises, tennis, golf, deep-sea fishing, sailing on bay

Amenities & Services: Full Finnish sauna, half-hour horseless carriage ride round town, pump organ, afternoon ice cream sodas on request, evening classic movies in sitting room, robes, VCR avail., fridge for guests, barbecue; German, Dutch, and French spoken; resident ghost, Abigail; private parking, covered parking, Swedish massage, conference room

ACCOMMODATIONS

Units: 4 guest rooms, 2 larger than average, and 1 suite

All Rooms: Desk, sitting area, phone, AC, ceiling fan, radio

Some Rooms: Four-poster, views of Eureka, Humboldt Bay, ocean, and Samoa Peninsula; extra twin (1), private bath (2)

Bed & Bath: Queens; 2 rooms share 3 baths

Favorites: Lily Langtry Room, named after the 19th-century actress who was a guest here, dark oak four-poster queen bed, view of the bay from a Palladian window, choice of 3 baths down the hall

Comfort & Decor: Rooms and public spaces decorated w/ authentic High Victorian furnishings; original wood trim, gas and electric light fixtures; custom-made historic wallpapers; European rugs and curtains, original art

RATES, RESERVATIONS, & RESTRICTIONS

Deposit: Entire amount charged to credit card at time of reservation; must cancel 14 days in advance; cancellation fee $25

Discounts: AAA, NRA, weekday business, singles, other (inquire); extra person in suite $50

Credit Cards: MC, V

Check-In/Out: 3–6/11

Smoking: No

Pets: No

Kids: 12 or over

Minimum Stay: 2 nights on Humboldt State University graduation in May

Open: All year

Hosts: Doug and Lily Vieyra
1406 C St.
Eureka, CA 95501
(707) 444-3144
Fax: (707) 442-5594
www.bbchannel.com/bbc/p214341.asp

CARTER HOUSE VICTORIANS, Eureka

| Overall: ★★★★★ | Room Quality: A | Value: B | Price: $152–$495 |

The Carter House Victorians in Eureka currently include four properties: the original Carter House, the Hotel Carter, Bell Cottage, and Carter Cottage. All of them are splendid. Filled with handsome furniture, tasteful original art, graceful fireplaces, gleaming floors and lush carpets, they combine the elegance of the past with contemporary good taste and comfort. It's hard to choose a favorite. Carter House is a four-story mansion built in the early 1980s using the house plan of a San Francisco Victorian destroyed in the 1906 earthquake. Across the street, the larger, more contemporary Hotel Carter is modeled after a nineteenth-century Eureka hotel. Bell Cottage is a renovated nineteenth-century Victorian with three lovely guest rooms, two parlors, and a kitchen that guests can use. The newest jewel in the Carter crown is Carter Cottage, a Colonial-era Victorian that contains a master suite and a parlor with a fireplace and features a large outdoor deck and panoramic view of Humboldt Bay. Breakfast for all guests is provided in the Hotel and is justifiably famous, reputed to be the best in California. All meals here employ herbs and produce from the hotel's organic garden and the region's seasonal offerings.

SETTING & FACILITIES

Location: At the north end of Eureka, 1 block from the bay, 2 blocks north of Hwy. 101

Near: Beaches, redwood forests, harbor cruises, historic old town/Victorian homes, airport, shopping

Building: Carter House, authentic re-creation of 4-story San Francisco Victorian mansion; Carter Hotel, re-creation of a 3-story 19th-century Eureka hotel; Bell Cottage, restored 1880s 1-story stick-style Victorian residence; Carter Cottage, a newly restored 1-story Victorian cottage

Grounds: Urban landscaped lots including organic gardens furnishing more than 300 varieties of fruits and vegetables for the hotel's restaurant

Public Space: Carter House, 3 parlors w/ marble fireplaces; Carter Hotel, lobby w/ fireplace; Bell Cottage, 2 parlors w/ fireplace, contemporary kitchen for guest use; Carter Cottage, parlor area w/ fireplace, large deck, contemporary demonstration kitchen
Food & Drink: Full breakfast served 7:30–10 a.m. in Restaurant 301 at Carter Hotel for all 4 properties; Carter Hotel guests may also be served in their rooms

Recreation: Boating, biking, surfing, whale-watching, day use of nearby health club, antiquing, fishing, kayaking, river rafting
Amenities & Services: Evening wine and hors d'oeuvres, homemade cookies and herbal teas, fresh flowers, fine contemporary paintings and ceramics; private parking, disabled access, full-service restaurant, concierge and valet services, baby-sitting, turn-down, VCR tape library

ACCOMMODATIONS

Units: Carter House, 7 guest rooms, including 4 suites; Carter Hotel, 23 guest rooms, including 6 suites; Bell Cottage, 3 guest rooms; Carter Cottage, 1 suite
All Rooms: Cable TV, phone, down comforter
Some Rooms: Fireplace, four-poster, fridge, entertainment center w/ VCR/CD/TV/stereo, featherbed, halogen lights, kitchen, sitting area, dressing area, views of marina
Bed & Bath: Carter House, beds vary, all private baths, spa tub for 2 (1); Hotel Carter, mostly queens and doubles, all private baths, Jacuzzis for 2 (6), whirlpool tubs (6); Bell Cottage, mostly queens, all private baths, Jacuzzis for 2; Carter Cottage, king, Jacuzzi for 2

Favorites: Carter House, Library Suite w/ 2 large BRs, Jacuzzi spa tub for 2, fireplace, dressing area; Hotel Carter, Rooms 301 and 302, w/ queen bed, sitting room w/ tiled fireplace and couch, French doors, oversized shower for 2 and deep spa tub for 2 w/ views of local landmark Carson Mansion and marina; Bell Cottage, Rooms 1 and 3, w/ fireplaces, hardwood and marble trim, halogen lights, queen beds, modern art, marble-faced spa tubs for 2
Comfort & Decor: Rooms individually decorated w/ local art, Victorian antiques, shutters, hardwood floors w/ oriental rugs, bay windows, carved headboards, canopy beds, marble facings, window seats

RATES, RESERVATIONS, & RESTRICTIONS

Deposit: 1st night's lodging; must cancel 72 hours in advance
Discounts: Long stays, groups, AAA, seniors, singles, corporate; extra person $25
Credit Cards: All
Check-In/Out: 3–6/11, late check-out by arrangement
Smoking: No
Pets: No
Kids: OK

Minimum Stay: None
Open: All year
Hosts: Mark and Christi Carter
301 L St.
Eureka, CA 95501
(707) 445-1390
(800) 404-1390
Fax: (707) 444-8067
www.carterhouse.com
carter52@carterhouse.com

CORNELIUS DALY INN, Eureka

Overall: ★★★★	Room Quality: B	Value: A	Price: $75–$150

Those Daly brothers knew how to live! Cornelius and John Daly were Irish immigrants who founded the Daly Brothers Department Stores in the late 1800s. They were so successful that they built mansions next door to each other. This stately inn, all 6,000 sq. ft. of it handsomely restored, has a library, a ballroom, four wood-burning fireplaces, and a Victorian garden complete with gazebo. The five guest rooms have individual touches such as a hand-carved bedroom set from Belgium, a French oak bedroom set ornamented with gold ormolu, and authentic reproductions of Victorian wall coverings. A full breakfast of fresh juice, fruit, eggs, and coffeecake is served in the formal dining room. The inn is within walking distance of Eureka's Old Town and a few blocks from the bay.

SETTING & FACILITIES

Location: On the north side of downtown Eureka (from Hwy. 101 take H St. south to 11th St.), 5 hours north of San Francisco
Near: Humboldt Bay, Eureka's historic Old Town, Redwood Nat'l Park, zoo, restaurants, shopping, airport
Building: A 3-story, 6,000-sq.-ft. Colonial Revival building built in 1905
Grounds: Half-block, Victorian gardens, gazebo

Public Space: 2 parlors w/ fireplaces, library w/ fireplace, 3rd-floor "ballroom," formal DR, breakfast room
Food & Drink: Full breakfast served at 9 a.m. in DR, earlier by request
Recreation: Croquet, badminton on premises; nearby golf, tennis, boating
Amenities & Services: Evening wine and hors d'oeuvres, barbecue, guests' fridge; private parking, concierge services for reservations

ACCOMMODATIONS

Units: 5 guest rooms, including 2 suites, 1 smaller BR
Some Rooms: Private sunporch, sitting room, fireplace, private bath (3), shared bath (2)
Bed & Bath: Mostly queens
Favorites: Annie Murphy's Room, w/ fireplace, French oak BR suite, gentle-

man's armoire, lady's dressing table, view of garden
Comfort & Decor: Rooms individually decorated w/ antique furniture and lighting fixtures, white wicker, Victorian wall coverings, hardwood floors, oriental or hooked rugs, custom bedspreads

RATES, RESERVATIONS, & RESTRICTIONS

Deposit: Credit card; must cancel 7 days in advance; cancellation fee first night's lodging
Discounts: Long stays, AAA, singles, winter, corporate, family; extra person $20

Credit Cards: AE, D, MC, V
Check-In/Out: 4–7/11, late check-out by arrangement
Smoking: No
Pets: No
Kids: OK

Minimum Stay: 2 nights on holiday weekends
Open: Feb. 2–Dec. 24
Hosts: Sue and Gene Clinesmith
1125 H St.
Eureka, CA 95501

(707) 445-3638
(800) 321-9656
Fax: (707) 444-3636
www.humboldt1.com/~dalyinn
dalyinn@humboldt1.com

GINGERBREAD MANSION, Ferndale

Overall: ★★★★½	Room Quality: A	Value: B	Price: $140–$350

If you hard-core B&B explorers think you've exhausted the genre, but you haven't been to the Gingerbread Mansion, pack your little carpetbag. Over-the-top-but-with-taste might be a description of this ultimate Victorian house in the ultimate Victorian town. The entire town of Ferndale is a National Historic Landmark because it has changed so little since the late 1800s, but even so, this peach and yellow Queen Anne stands out. Its architect wanted to make a statement and succeeded for 100 years—it is the most photographed Victorian in the state and perhaps the country. Dripping, well, gingerbread outside, the inn has guest rooms that range from the merely pretty to seriously awesome. How many beds have you slept in that were anchored by Ionic columns? Innkeeper Torbert is particularly good at interesting ways to immerse you in water—from matching his-and-hers claw-foot tubs to a sit-down shower with pulsating jets everywhere. A full breakfast and English high tea are equally opulent.

SETTING & FACILITIES

Location: In the village of Ferndale, 5 mi. west of Hwy. 101 and 17 mi. south of Eureka
Near: Victorian Village shops, galleries, restaurants, historic walking tours, wilderness trails, old-growth redwood forests, beaches
Building: 1899 Queen Anne/Eastlake Victorian with spindlework, turrets and gables, icicle eaves, bay windows
Grounds: 1.5 acres, formal English gardens, brick pathways, sculptured boxwood, topiary, fountains

Public Space: 4 parlors, library, DR, 2nd-floor veranda
Food & Drink: Full breakfast in DR and breakfast nook upstairs, choice of seatings at 8, 8:30, 9, or 9:30 a.m., prepared by professional chef
Recreation: Biking
Amenities & Services: Afternoon English tea, evening turn-down service w/ hand-dipped chocolates, robes, umbrellas, hairdryers; private parking, concierge service for reservations

ACCOMMODATIONS

Units: 11 guest rooms, 9 larger than average, including 5 suites
All Rooms: Egyptian cottons, fine

linens, private bath
Some Rooms: Fireplace or 2, four-poster, extra twin (2)

Bed & Bath: Queens and kings, some claw-foot tub(s), bidets
Favorites: Empire Suite, w/ king bed surrounded by Ionic columns, large bathing area w/ marble and glass sit-in shower w/ multiple showerheads and massage sprays, a claw-foot tub in front of a fireplace, sitting area w/ 2nd fireplace, breakfast area
Comfort & Decor: Rooms individually decorated w/ Victorian antiques, wallpapers, carpets, fabrics, side-by-side tubs in bathroom w/ tiled fireplace, toe-to-toe matching claw-foot tubs on a raised platform, canopy beds, French windows

RATES, RESERVATIONS, & RESTRICTIONS

Deposit: Credit card, full prepayment; must cancel 7 days in advance, $10/night cancellation fee, no refund unless room is rebooked
Discounts: Weekday business travelers, winter specials; extra person $40
Credit Cards: AE, MC, V
Check-In/Out: 3–6/11, late check-in/out by arrangement
Smoking: No
Pets: No
Kids: OK

Minimum Stay: None
Open: All year
Host: Ken Torbert
P.O. Box AA40
400 Berding St.
Ferndale, CA 95536
(707) 786-4000
(800) 952-4136
Fax: (707) 786-4381
www.gingerbread-mansion.com
innkeeper@gingerbread-mansion.com

AVALON HOUSE, Fort Bragg

Overall: ★★★★	Room Quality: B	Value: A	Price: $80–$140

Nicely located on a quiet residential street, the three-story Avalon House is within walking distance of the beach and close to shops, galleries, and restaurants in Fort Bragg. Built at the turn of the century, the former home has been carefully restored to preserve its California Craftsman style. It blends the best of the past and the present with a judicious use of antiques and period detailing enhanced by all the modern conveniences, such as good mattresses, reading lights, whirlpool tubs, thick towels, and soundproofed walls. You'll also like the omelets, scones, and muffins that come out of the commercial kitchen the owner installed.

SETTING & FACILITIES

Location: On the northwest edge of downtown Fort Bragg (going north turn left on Fir St. and go 1 block to Stewart), 4 hours north of San Francisco
Near: Beaches, whale-watching, shopping, restaurants, galleries, steam locomotive excursion train, deep-sea/surf fishing
Building: 1905 Craftsman home restored to original style
Grounds: Large garden in quiet residential neighborhood w/ secluded seating

Public Space: Parlor, library
Food & Drink: Full breakfast served
8:30–10:30 a.m. in dining area
Recreation: Horseback riding,

biking, tennis
Amenities & Services: Evening
sherry; private parking

ACCOMMODATIONS

Units: 6 guest rooms, 3 larger than
average
All Rooms: Private bath, 2 reading
lamps per bed, new Posturepedic mattress, down pillows, comforter
Some Rooms: Private deck, fireplace,
fridge
Bed & Bath: Mostly queens, whirlpool
tubs (4)
Favorites: Quilt Room, w/ private
deck, ocean view, gas fireplace, patch-

work quilt wall hangings, whirlpool tub,
fridge; Yellow Room, w/ large private
deck, ocean view, willow four-poster
canopy bed, gas fireplace, skylights,
whirlpool tub/shower
Comfort & Decor: Rooms individually decorated in Craftsman style w/
antiques, handcrafted willow furniture,
comfortable chairs, tasteful art, stained-
glass windows

RATES, RESERVATIONS, & RESTRICTIONS

Deposit: Credit card; must cancel 3
days in advance, or 5 days in advance for
holidays
Discounts: Weekday business travelers
Credit Cards: All
Check-In/Out: 3–7/noon, late check-in
by prior arrangement
Smoking: No
Pets: No
Kids: Only 1 room suitable for 3
persons
Minimum Stay: 2 nights on weekends,

2 June–Nov., 3 on holiday weekends
Open: All year, closed daily noon–
3 p.m.
Host: Anne Sorrells
561 Stewart St.
Fort Bragg, CA 95437
(707) 964-5555
(800) 964-5556
Fax: (707) 964-5555
www.theavalonhouse.com
anne@theavalonhouse.com

CLEONE GARDENS INN, Fort Bragg

Overall: ★★★½	Room Quality: C	Value: A	Price: $76–$140

The community of Cleone is the gateway to MacKerricher State Park, with
its miles and miles of beaches, a knockout bike and jogging path right
along the water, and even a nearby fen (a primordial bog, the only one in
the western United States). The aptly named "garden" inn offers a variety
of accommodations and options—large guest rooms, suites, a cottage, and
an outlying beach house. Although the main building is motel-like in
structure, the current owner has done such good things to the lovely
grounds that only the snootiest B&B-o-phile will care. If you stay in one
of the rooms in the main building on the bed-and-breakfast plan, a substantial breakfast of melon, scrambled eggs, bacon, and muffins will be

delivered to your room. And guess what? The nice owner not only likes kids, he also likes dogs—a rarity in the B&B world.

SETTING & FACILITIES

Location: 2 mi. north of Fort Bragg in the village of Cleone, 4 hours north of San Francisco

Near: 5 blocks from 10 mi. of sandy ocean beaches and dunes that are being restored to their original state, bringing back native grasses, wildflowers, and birds (all part of popular MacKerricher State Park), country market, restaurants, riding stable, Mendocino

Building: Ranch-style inn w/ separate cottage and beach house

Grounds: 5 acres w/ beautifully kept gardens, trails, and a meadow with a redwood grove, fir trees, and flowers

Public Space: Library

Food & Drink: Full breakfast for 2 served 8–9 a.m. in 5 guest rooms in the main building; rooms are also avail. without breakfast at a reduced rate

Recreation: Fishing, reduced rates for guests at nearby health club

Amenities & Services: Barbecue, spa (which can be reserved for a fee for private use), gazebo, large decks and sitting areas, classical music piped to back deck, picnic areas; private parking, 1 room w/ disabled access

ACCOMMODATIONS

Units: 8 guest rooms, including 5 suites, plus 1 cottage and 1 beach house

All Rooms: Cable TV, private bath

Some Rooms: Fireplace, sleeper sofa, phone, extra bed (6), private entrance off private deck, garden court, forest or meadow view

Bed & Bath: Queens and kings, shower/tubs (5)

Favorites: MacKerricher Room, a romantic room with king bed, fireplace, shower, garden entry, large private deck, view of the meadow and gardens

Comfort & Decor: Lots of redwood in large rooms individually decorated, mixed periods, comfortably and simply furnished, carpet and vinyl floor coverings

RATES, RESERVATIONS, & RESTRICTIONS

Deposit: 1st night's lodging; must cancel 72 hours in advance; $12 cancellation fee

Discounts: None; extra bed/ person $10

Credit Cards: AE, D, MC, V

Check-In/Out: 1:30/11; $12/hr. late check-out, if approved

Smoking: No

Pets: Dogs allowed in 3 units with prior arrangement

Kids: OK; beach house limited to children 10 or over

Minimum Stay: 2 nights on weekends, 3 on holiday weekends

Open: All year

Host: Lar Krug
24600 N. Hwy. 1
Fort Bragg, CA 95437
(707) 964-2788
(800) 400-2189
www.cleonegardensinn.com
lar@cleonegardens.inn

GREY WHALE INN, Fort Bragg

Overall: ★★★★	Room Quality: A	Value: B	Price: $100–$180

It is safe to say you will never encounter another B&B quite like this one. Constructed in 1915, the four-story structure was originally the town hospital, as you will quickly see from the ramps between floors, the wide doors, and the unusually spacious rooms, which were formerly wards, operating rooms, and the dispensary. Because it was built by a lumber company, the entire building is constructed from clear heart redwood. Each of the 14 beautiful guest rooms has a special amenity: view, fireplace, interior patio, private deck, or whirlpool tub. Besides beautiful rooms, the inn has a ground-floor recreation area, a fireside lounge, and a conference room. The ramp substitutes for a staircase, so getting to the fourth floor is a mite like climbing a hill. Breakfast is a full buffet with a hot entrée, all sorts of bagels, muffins, and coffeecake, plus cereals, fresh fruit, and yogurt.

SETTING & FACILITIES

Location: On Main St. (Hwy. 1) just north of downtown Fort Bragg and 5 blocks from the ocean, 4 hours north of San Francisco
Near: Shopping, galleries, beaches, state parks, the Mendocino Botanical Gardens, theater, Skunk Train (excursion train through the redwoods from Fort Bragg to Willits), microbrewery
Building: 4-story redwood building in Classical Revival style, built in 1915 by the lumber company as a town hospital
Grounds: Landscaped urban lot with flower beds, native shrubs, lawns, and a 10-foot sculpture of a gray whale by a local artist

Public Space: Parlor w/ fireplace, couches, tea, restaurant menus and reviews, TV/VCR room, game room w/ billiard table, wide-ranging collection of books, magazines, puzzles, and board games
Food & Drink: Full buffet breakfast including hot entrée, breads, bagels, muffins, prizewinning coffeecake
Recreation: Billiards on premises; nearby biking, tennis, golf, whale-watching, surf and deep-sea fishing
Amenities & Services: Fresh fruit, tea, and sodas always avail.; off-street parking, disabled access

ACCOMMODATIONS

Units: 14 guest rooms, including 1 suite
All Rooms: TV, cable, phone, coffeemaker, private bath
Some Rooms: Fireplaces (4), small kitchenettes (4), VCRs, modem access (1), private enclosed terrace (1), private sundeck/patio (2), room for more than 2 people (3)

Bed & Bath: Mostly queens and kings, some shower/tubs, 1 disabled-accessible shower
Favorites: 2 penthouse rooms—Sunrise, w/ wicker furniture, a double whirlpool bath, and a view of town in the distance, and Sunset, w/ ocean view, private deck

Comfort & Decor: Large rooms w/ custom fabrics, antiques, wallpaper, wicker, local art, and a remarkable collection of patchwork quilts used as wall hangings

RATES, RESERVATIONS, & RESTRICTIONS

Deposit: 1st night's lodging; must cancel 7 days in advance
Discounts: AAA, corporate rates, winter weekdays
Credit Cards: AE, D, MC, V
Check-In/Out: Noon/noon, late check-out possible depending on occupancy
Smoking: No
Pets: No
Kids: OK
No-Nos: More than 2 guests only in specified rooms
Minimum Stay: 2 nights on weekends, 3 on holiday weekends
Open: All year
Hosts: John and Colette Bailey
615 N. Main St.
Fort Bragg, CA 95437
(707) 964-0640
(800) 382-7244
Fax: (707) 964-4408
www.greywhaleinn.com
stay@greywhaleinn.com

LODGE AT NOYO RIVER, Fort Bragg

Overall: ★★★½	Room Quality: B	Value: A	Price: $75–$155

In a wooded glade, perched high on a hill overlooking Fort Bragg's colorful working harbor, the Lodge at Noyo River is a study in contrasts. The main house, which displays the craftsmanship of the Scandinavian shipbuilders who constructed it, is right out of a European film about times gone by. The dark redwood and heartwood fir paneling, large fireplace, and genteel Victorian decor are an emphatic contrast to the very modern suites in the adjacent annex. A substantial "lumberjack" breakfast is served in the sunny dining room or on a deck overlooking the picturesque harbor. This is a very popular inn.

SETTING & FACILITIES

Location: On the south end of Fort Bragg, just east of Hwy. 1 at the entrance to Noyo Harbor, 3.5 hours north of San Francisco on Hwy. 1
Near: One block to Noyo Harbor, 10-minute walk to the ocean, garden paths along the Noyo River, Mendocino Botanical Gardens, shopping
Building: Craftsman-style residence and later a lodge for fishermen built on the Noyo River in 1868; modern annex and cottages built in 1990
Grounds: 2.5 acres of gardens and cypress trees
Public Space: Parlor and DR
Food & Drink: Full breakfast served 8:30–10 a.m. in the dining area in the main house or, weather permitting, on the deck
Recreation: Whale-watching, deep-sea fishing, Skunk Train, scuba diving for abalone and sports fish, bike rentals

Amenities & Services: Afternoon local wines, snacks, and hors d'oeuvres, outdoor deck overlooking the harbor and fishing vessels; private parking, disabled access

ACCOMMODATIONS

Units: 16 guest rooms, including 9 suites
All Rooms: View, teddy bear, feather comforter and pillows, coffeemaker, private bath
Some Rooms: TV, fireplace, extra beds (3)
Bed & Bath: Queens and kings, some double soaking tubs
Favorites: Upstairs BRs in the main lodge, old-fashioned, w/ walls of burnished heart of redwood, antiques, views of the harbor, ghosts; spacious modern suites in the annex, w/ private balconies overlooking the harbor, plus all the modern conveniences
Comfort & Decor: Rooms in the historic inn are simple but pleasantly furnished w/ antiques and floral prints. Annex suites have private decks, sunken LRs, fireplaces, and contemporary, upscale motel decor

RATES, RESERVATIONS, & RESTRICTIONS

Deposit: 1 night's lodging during high season (May–Oct.) and holidays; must cancel 3 days in advance
Discounts: AAA, AARP
Credit Cards: AE, MC, V
Check-In/Out: 3/11
Smoking: No
Pets: No
Kids: OK

Minimum Stay: 2 nights on weekends
Open: All year
Host: Charles Reinhart
500 Casa del Noyo Dr.
Fort Bragg, CA 95437
(707) 964-8045
(800) 628-1126
www.noyolodge.com
innkeeper@noyolodge.com

WELLER HOUSE INN, Fort Bragg

Overall: ★★★★	Room Quality: B	Value: B	Price: $95–$175

Built in 1886, this inn opened its handsomely restored doors to the public in 1998. The seven guest rooms are decorated in High Victorian style with English wallpaper, wainscoting, stained-glass windows, and bath tiles hand-painted by co-owner Eva Kidwell. Breakfast is served in a splendid 900-square-foot ballroom on Dresden china with gold flatware. The hosts have succeeded in creating a period Victorian experience, albeit with modern plumbing. The reconstructed water tower on the property is the tallest point in Fort Bragg, and you can climb it for a bird's-eye view of the formal gardens, the blue Pacific, and perhaps even a passing whale or two. The town's lumber mill is nearby, but it is a quiet neighbor.

SETTING & FACILITIES

Location: On the northwest edge of downtown Fort Bragg (going north, turn left on Pine and right on Stewart), 4 hours north of San Francisco
Near: Shopping, galleries, beaches, state parks, Mendocino Botanical Gardens, theater, live music, local history museum, historic excursion railroad
Building: 120-year-old Italianate house listed on Nat'l Registry of Historic Places
Grounds: Formal English gardens on 3 sides of house, statuary, fountain, pond
Public Space: 900-sq.-ft. ballroom

paneled in California redwood, 53-ft.-tall water tower for views
Food & Drink: Full breakfast served at 8 or 9:30 a.m. in the ballroom; vegetarian or low-cal breakfast may be ordered when making reservations
Recreation: Canoeing, surfing, diving, tennis, golf, biking, deep-sea and surf fishing, horseback riding on the beach
Amenities & Services: Hot tub, evening wine and hors d'oeuvres, hot tea and coffee around the clock; private parking

ACCOMMODATIONS

Units: 7 guest rooms, 4 larger than average
All Rooms: Plug-in for cable TV, phone, VCR (by request); private bath, down comforter
Some Rooms: Fireplace, extra bed (4)
Bed & Bath: Mostly queens, king (1), Jacuzzi (1), claw-foot tubs (3)
Favorites: Aqua Room, w/ handpainted murals on all 4 walls and large

bath w/ Jacuzzi for 2, view of formal gardens and limited ocean view
Comfort & Decor: Rooms individually decorated w/ oil paintings, watercolors and prints, antiques, Victorian period wallpapers, original hardwood floors, area rugs, handpainted tiles, wall murals by local artists, stained glass, faux-grained doors

RATES, RESERVATIONS, & RESTRICTIONS

Deposit: 1st night's lodging or 50% of room fee; must cancel 10 days in advance (21 days in advance for holidays); full refund if room subsequently rented
Discounts: Long stays, weekday business travelers, AAA; low-/high-season rates, $20 discount Sun.–Thurs., 3rd night free Sun.–Thurs., extra bed $25
Credit Cards: All
Check-In/Out: 3/11
Smoking: No
Pets: No
Kids: In 1 room

Minimum Stay: 2 nights on weekends in summer, Nov.-May no minimum; check for major holidays
Open: All year
Hosts: Ted and Eva Kidwell
P.O. Box 248
524 Stewart St.
Fort Bragg, CA 95437
(707) 964-4415
(877) 893-5537
Fax: (707) 964-4198
www.wellerhouse.com
innkeeper@wellerhouse

WILD GOOSE COUNTRY VICTORIAN B&B, Fort Jones

Overall: ★★★½	Room Quality: B	Value: A	Price: $67

The Wild Goose is a small and lovely B&B in a small and lovely town. Because it's small, you get a lot of care and feeding here. The two (soon to be three) guest rooms are Victorian in style, and breakfast is country hearty—pumpkin-oat waffles, sautéed pears, and homemade muffins. Most Californians have never heard of Fort Jones, much less gone there, and, though they've missed a treat, perhaps it's for the best. Lying in a verdant little valley surrounded by some of California's most beautiful (and least visited) mountains, Fort Jones is just far enough off the beaten path to keep from getting spoiled. It's a thriving community that many visitors cherish and seek out in order to enjoy the small-town feeling and step back into a simpler, rich time. Those seeking action and a scene will prefer the road more traveled.

SETTING & FACILITIES

Location: 18 min. west of Hwy. I-5 on Hwy. 3, 17 mi. southwest of Yreka, 2 hours from Redding, and 1 hour from Medford, Oregon
Near: Shopping, antiques, restaurants, historic church, airport, 2 local history museums, Marble Mountain Wilderness, Scott River, Trinity Alps
Building: 2-story Country Victorian built in 1890, restored in 1990 with original doors, parlor windows, gingerbread
Grounds: 2/3 acre w/ garden, court-yard, and seasonal garden plantings
Public Space: Parlor, DR, upstairs covered veranda with views of the town, mountains, and sunsets
Food & Drink: Full breakfast served in DR 9–10 a.m., freshly ground coffee outside each door by 7:30 a.m.
Recreation: Biking and mountain biking, fishing, horseback riding, llama pack trips, rafting, airplane tours, X-C/downhill skiing, dog sledding, rodeos
Amenities & Services: Private parking, disabled access

ACCOMMODATIONS

Units: 2 guest rooms; additional room and a cottage to be added 1999/2000
All Rooms: Cable TV, ceiling and window fans, individual room heat, vanity/dressing area, private bath
Bed & Bath: High old-fashioned double beds
Favorites: Father Goose Room, w/ plaids, checks, and ruffled skirts on a big brass bed, white walls adorned w/ rambling vines and country florals; Gander's Garden Room, w/ rose prints, soft pastel-striped bedskirts, carved mahogany furnishings
Comfort & Decor: Individually decorated w/ antiques, family heirlooms, local arts and crafts (some handcrafted by the owners)

RATES, RESERVATIONS, & RESTRICTIONS

Deposit: 100% of bill; must cancel 7 days in advance (30 days for holidays); $15 cancellation fee
Discounts: For stays over 4 days
Credit Cards: None
Check-In/Out: 3–6/11, other by prior arrangement
Smoking: No
Pets: No
Kids: Not suitable

Minimum Stay: 2 nights on weekends and all holidays
Open: Closed Dec. 20–28
Hosts: Terry and Cindy Hayes
P.O. Box 546
11624 Main St.
Fort Jones, CA 96032
(530) 468-2735
wildgoose@sisqtel.net

HOLLYHOCK FARM B&B, Gazelle

Overall: ★★★½	Room Quality: B	Value: A	Price: $80

Hollyhock Farm is on old Hwy. 99, almost forgotten since I-5 was built several miles to the east. That makes it a convenient place to stay for the passing traveler or visitor to the area. This handsome old farmhouse is in a country setting where you can still hear the birds and see the stars, but it's not too far from Weed (10 miles) or the many shops and restaurants in Mt. Shasta (16 miles). The best feature of this nice B&B is the mountain, which appears to be just across the street—the view of Mt. Shasta is amazing. While Hollyhock Farm is small and a mite off the beaten path, it is definitely worth a visit. Guest rooms are tastefully decorated in a country farmhouse style, and the country theme extends to breakfasts of eggs, hot links, and casseroles. If you happen to be traveling with your dog and horse, you're in luck: your hostess has accommodations for them, too.

SETTING & FACILITIES

Location: 30 mi. south of the Oregon border, 20 min. north of the town of Mt. Shasta off Hwy. I-5
Near: Shopping, Lake Siskiyou, Mt. Shasta, restaurants
Building: 1902 Normandy-style stone farmhouse, recently constructed guest house
Grounds: 50-acre alfalfa farm, a private country setting with spectacular view

of Mt. Shasta, large front lawn, gardens
Public Space: Parlor w/ fireplace, 2 couches, TV, VCR, DR w/ 2 large tables
Food & Drink: Full breakfast served in DR to meet guests' schedules
Recreation: Fishing, hunting, golf, downhill/X-C skiing
Amenities & Services: Dog kennel and horse pens avail., unheated swimming pool; private parking

ACCOMMODATIONS

Units: 3 guest rooms, 1 suite upstairs, separate guest house

All Rooms: AC

Some Rooms: Private baths (3); guest house has vaulted redwood ceiling, woodstove, extra twin, full kitchenette with refrigerator, stove, microwave, TV; suite has extra daybed
Bed & Bath: Queens, full roll-away

beds avail.
Favorites: Upstairs suite has sunroom and a view of Scott Mountains
Comfort & Decor: An eclectic mix of antiques, period reproductions, lace curtains

RATES, RESERVATIONS, & RESTRICTIONS

Deposit: Deposit charged to credit card; must cancel 48 hours in advance; cancellation fee 1 night's lodging
Discounts: None; extra person $10
Credit Cards: MC, V
Check-In/Out: 2/11, late check-out with prior agreement
Smoking: No
Pets: OK in kennels on premises
Kids: OK

Minimum Stay: 2 nights Fourth of July weekend
Open: All year
Host: Beth Pokorny
P.O. Box 152
18705 Old Hwy. 99
Gazelle, CA 96034
(530) 435-2627
Fax: (530) 435-0158

NORTH COAST COUNTRY INN, Gualala

Overall: ★★★★	Room Quality: B	Value: B	Price: $150–$195

Once part of a coastal sheep ranch, this carefully tended inn is a cluster of rustic redwood buildings in a redwood and pine forest on a hillside across Hwy. 1 from the ocean. With their beamed ceilings, large fireplaces, and beautifully coordinated fabrics, the guest rooms are very appealing. If you can tear yourself away from the comfortable chair in front of the fireplace, there's a peaceful gazebo and sitting deck in a secluded glen and a hot tub set in a two-level deck. A full buffet breakfast is served in the wood-paneled common room at tables for two with pretty floor-length tablecloths. The menu may include a ham and potato quiche, sliced melon, croissants and scones.

SETTING & FACILITIES

Location: On Hwy. 1 at Fish Rock Rd., across highway from ocean, 4 mi. north of Gualala and .25 mile north of Anchor Bay, 2 hours north of San Francisco
Near: Shopping, beaches, galleries, wineries, redwoods
Building: Redwood board-and-batten multilevel buildings with shake roofs built between 1984 and 1997
Grounds: 1 acre of forested hillside with many separate gardens, an upper garden with gazebo, cobblestone

garden courtyard, ocean views
Public Space: Wood-paneled common room, library w/ fireplace, TV/VCR, and CD player
Food & Drink: Full breakfast served 8:30–10 a.m. on individual tables for 2, or on patio umbrella table in courtyard
Recreation: Biking, tennis, golf, kayaking, fishing, diving, horseback riding, bird-watching
Amenities & Services: Hot tub, evening sherry; private parking

ACCOMMODATIONS

Units: 6 large guest rooms
All Rooms: Fireplace, private bath, private deck w/ deck chairs, fridge, coffeepot, coffee, tea, and juice
Some Rooms: Four-poster, minikitchen, wet bar
Bed & Bath: Queens, kings (2), new penthouse guest rooms have whirlpool tubs
Favorites: Sea Urchin, w/ covered wraparound deck, fireplace, filtered ocean view, and minikitchen; South-wind, w/ view of South Coast, private deck, hillside garden
Comfort & Decor: Rooms individually decorated using carefully coordinated antiques, wallpaper, wood paneling, wainscoting, and rugs. Open-beamed ceilings, large fireplaces with matching comfortable chairs

RATES, RESERVATIONS, & RESTRICTIONS

Deposit: Hold room w/ credit card; must cancel 5 days in advance; no cancellation fee
Discounts: Long stays
Credit Cards: AE, MC, V
Check-In/Out: 2/11
Smoking: No
Pets: No
Kids: No

Minimum Stay: 2 nights on weekends, 3 on holiday weekends
Open: All year
Hosts: Loren and Nancy Flanagan
34591 S. Hwy. 1
Gualala, CA 95445
(707) 884-4537
(800) 959-4537

OLD MILANO HOTEL, Gualala

Overall: ★★★★½	Room Quality: B	Value: B	Price: $115–$210

This may just be the pick of the litter when it comes to the combination of good rooms, good food, and a fabulous ocean view. The six guest rooms upstairs in the inn share two large baths but are otherwise so delightfully wallpapered and furnished that you don't care. Among the six cottages with a variety of amenities to choose from is a genuine railroad caboose, cute and private. The inn's best attribute, however, is a gift from nature—a view of the ocean and beach that is amazing even for jaded beachophiles. Sitting in the late afternoon on the sloping back lawn in an Adirondack chair with the old hotel twinkling in the background, a glass of Sonoma cabernet in hand, waiting for a spectacular sunset over the Pacific, is a memory no one will forget.

SETTING & FACILITIES

Location: 1 mile north of Gualala on the west side of Hwy. 1, 2 hours north of San Francisco on the south Mendocino coast
Near: Beaches, picturesque coast towns, state parks, shopping, art galleries
Building: Victorian inn built in 1905 on bluffs overlooking the ocean, listed in Nat'l Registry of Historic Places

Grounds: 3-acre estate w/ gardens, fountain, rolling lawn right on cliffs overlooking the Pacific

Public Space: Parlor w/ fireplace, seating on front porch and bluffs

Food & Drink: Full breakfast served 8:15–10 a.m. in DR in front of fireplace or outside on patio; room service

breakfast avail. in main inn

Recreation: Fishing, diving, kayaking, golf, biking, horseback riding, wine tasting, movie theater

Amenities & Services: Cliffside hot tub, which can be reserved for privacy; full-service restaurant; private parking, 1 cottage disabled-accessible

ACCOMMODATIONS

Units: 13 guest rooms, 5 larger than average, including master suite in main inn w/ private sitting room; 6 freestanding cottages, including 1 railroad caboose

All Rooms: No TV, radio, or phone

Some Rooms: Fireplace, wood-burning stove, canopy and brass beds, goose down comforter and pillows, stained-glass window, skylight, reading loft; private baths (7), 2 shared baths w/ double showers (6); Caboose has private deck and 2 upstairs brakemen's seats for ocean viewing

Bed & Bath: Queens and doubles; spa tubs w/ handheld showers (2), double showers (2)

Favorites: Iris Cottage, where you can hear the ocean and feel the sea breeze, w/ stained glass window above the sunken spa tub, fireplace, wrought-iron bed w/ down comforter

Comfort & Decor: Rooms are individually decorated w/ antiques, Victorian furniture and wallpaper, some have lace curtains, all are carpeted, fresh flowers in each room

RATES, RESERVATIONS, & RESTRICTIONS

Deposit: 1st night's lodging; must cancel 72 hours in advance; $10 cancellation fee

Discounts: 25% discount Mon.–Thurs./Nov.–March, excluding holidays

Credit Cards: MC, V; credit cards are not accepted in restaurant

Check-In/Out: 2/noon

Smoking: No

Pets: No

Kids: OK in Caboose and Garden Vine cottages

Minimum Stay: 2 nights on weekends

Open: All year

Host: Leslie Linscheid
38300 S. Hwy. 1
Gualala, CA 95445
(707) 884-3256
Fax: (707) 884-4249
www.oldmilanohotel.com
coast@oldmilanohotel.com

ST. ORRES, Gualala

Overall: ★★★★½	Room Quality: B	Value: B	Price: $60–$225

The exotically beautiful St. Orres with its famous onion-shaped, copper-plated domes was inspired by early-eighteenth-century Russian fur-trading settlements in the area. It was originally intended to be a toy factory, but a change of plans by the owners led to the opening of the hotel in 1976. The restaurant on the premises is perhaps more famous than the hotel, known for its inventive and sometimes fanciful (wild raspberries with cut-out stars of jicama, local greens, and sprinkles of red hots) North Coast cuisine that features choices like steelhead, salmon, wild boar, venison, wild mushrooms, huckleberries—anything that's native to the area. The eight rooms in the main lodge are pleasant and a good value, though very small, and they share baths. The cottages tucked discreetly here and there on the extensive grounds are imaginative, varied in size and amenities, and altogether delightful. Most have fireplaces, redwood decks, sitting areas, wet bars, and ocean or forest views. If you're staying in one of the cottages, breakfast is delivered to your door. The hotel's glassed-in, plant-filled breakfast area is pretty, too.

SETTING & FACILITIES

Location: North of Sea Ranch and Gualala, and south of Anchor Bay, 1.5 hours north of San Francisco on Hwy. 1
Near: Shopping, beaches, galleries, wineries, redwoods
Building: Russian style with copper domes, constructed in the 1970s with timbers from a 100-year-old sawmill and surplus copper circuit boards
Grounds: 50 acres of colorful landscaping edged by redwood forest
Public Space: An attractive bar, a restaurant under a dramatic 3-story Russian dome with open beams and leaded glass windows, w/ a plant-filled solarium
Food & Drink: Full breakfast served 9–10 a.m. in the hotel or, if you're staying in one of the cottages, delivered to your door at 9 a.m.
Recreation: Tennis, golf
Amenities & Services: The Creekside cottages share a hot tub, sauna, and sundeck spa; disabled access

ACCOMMODATIONS

Units: 20 guest rooms, 8 small Euro-style rooms in hotel, 12 cottages spread out over 50 acres
All Rooms: Ocean, meadow, or creekside view; hotel rooms, double bed, 3 shared baths; cottages, private baths w/ tub/shower
Some Rooms: Fireplace, sleeper sofa, fridge, Jacuzzi, wet bar, coffeemaker, extra bed (5)
Bed & Bath: Beds vary
Favorites: Wildflower has a very private outside shower w/ forest view; Sequoia has an elevated BR w/ skylight and ocean view plus a soaking tub; Treehouse has a sitting area w/ Franklin fireplace, French doors to a deck w/ ocean view and soaking tub
Comfort & Decor: Hotel rooms and cottages artistically decorated in wealthy California hippie style—lots of wood, handmade quilts, tiled floors, stained glass windows by local artisans, skylights, French doors, views

RATES, RESERVATIONS, & RESTRICTIONS

Deposit: 100% of bill; must cancel 72 hours in advance; cancellation fee $10 per night per accommodation
Discounts: None
Credit Cards: MC, V, checks
Check-In/Out: 3–7/noon
Smoking: No
Pets: No
Kids: OK in cabins
Minimum Stay: 2 nights on weekends

Open: All year
Hosts: Rosemary Campiformio, Eric
Black, and Ted Black
P.O. Box 523
36601 S. Hwy. 1
Gualala, CA 95445

(707) 884-3303
Fax: (707) 884-1840
www.saintorres.com
rosemary@mcn.org

WHALE WATCH INN BY THE SEA, Gualala

Overall: ★★★★½	Room Quality: A	Value: B	Price: $170–$270

The Whale Watch carves out a unique niche among small California coastal inns, offering unabashed luxury, privacy, and personal service for clients who seek a high degree of comfort in a contemporary setting. Perched on what is arguably the best real estate in the area for ocean views, the inn takes every advantage to dazzle you with the scenery. It is possible in some rooms to move from deck to bed to bath without ever losing sight of water. Add to that carefully coordinated color schemes, fireplaces, deluxe furnishings, and fine linens, and you have a cool elegance that appeals to those who are most comfortable in first-class hotels. Some more laid-back souls may be turned off by the formal perfection of the inn. Breakfast is delivered to guests' rooms and features a daily entrée, fresh fruit, and baked goods.

SETTING & FACILITIES

Location: On coastal side of Hwy. 1, just north of the village of Anchor Bay, 2 hours from San Francisco
Near: Small airport, shopping, beach, restaurants
Building: 5 contemporary buildings, 2 completed in the mid-1970s, 3 in the mid-1980s, sit 90 feet above the ocean. Wraparound deck on Whale Watch building allows prime viewing of whales
Grounds: 2 cliff-side acres overlooking Anchor Bay, private stairway to half-mile-long beach with tidal pools
Public Space: Large reception area in

Pacific Edge building, Whale Watch building has large common room with a circular fireplace and sweeping ocean view from floor to ceiling windows
Food & Drink: Full, hot breakfast delivered to rooms at prearranged time
Recreation: Biking, tennis, golf, tide pooling
Amenities & Services: Afternoon snacks avail. on request, wine and hors d'oeuvres served on Saturday evening, quiet music piped into rooms; private parking, disabled access

ACCOMMODATIONS

Units: 18 guest rooms, 14 larger than average, including 8 suites
All Rooms: Very private, w/ private deck, view, fireplace, and phone if requested; fine linens and down

comforter, private bath
Some Rooms: Four-poster, full kitchen, small fridge, icemaker, skylight over the bed for stargazing, private hot tubs on decks (3), sauna (1), sofa beds (2)

Bed & Bath: Queens, robes, some 1- and 2-person whirlpool baths, some tub/showers
Favorites: Bath Suite, w/ a 2nd-floor 2-person whirlpool w/ ocean view; Golden Voyage Suite, w/ full kitchen, window seats, skylights; Crystal Sea, w/ amazing view
Comfort & Decor: All rooms individually decorated in styles varying from Queen Anne to Neo-Classic, w/ custom furniture, subtle colors, high ceilings, skylights, carpet, fine linens

RATES, RESERVATIONS, & RESTRICTIONS

Deposit: 1st night's lodging; must cancel 5 days in advance; no cancellation fee
Discounts: None
Credit Cards: AE, MC, V
Check-In/Out: 3–7/11 late check-out possible depending on occupancy
Smoking: No
Pets: No
Kids: In 2 rooms
Minimum Stay: 2 nights on weekends, 3 on holiday weekends
Open: All year
Hosts: Dr. James Popplewell and Mrs. Kazuo Popplewell
35100 Hwy. 1
Gualala, CA 95445
(707) 884-3667
(800) 942-5342
www.whale-watch.com
whale@mcn.org

BRIGADOON CASTLE, Igo

Overall: ★★★★½	Room Quality: B	Value: B	Price: $150–$285

Just when you think you've seen everything, you hear about this fabulous castle in Igo. Igo? Well, it turns out Igo is a farming and retirement community in the Trinity mountains. It's reached by a narrow, winding, forested road that leads you through the mists to a castle aptly named Brigadoon. Built by a previous owner in 1983, the design of the Gothic "Elizabethan" castle was inspired by buildings at the University of Washington. There's a 30-foot-high Great Hall with a scissor-beamed ceiling and floor-to-ceiling windows, and a library mezzanine with a hand-carved mahogany railing, oak paneling, and an antique brick fireplace. Velvet-draped Gothic arches lead the way to a formal dining room. Guest rooms vary in decor, from the two-level room in the turret, with a featherbed surrounded by ivy-covered, arrow port windows, to rose-colored Feona's Suite, with taffeta wall coverings, a fireplace, a four-poster bed, and a steam spa. Breakfasts often feature egg casseroles and seasonal fruit from the inn's orchard. The forested creekside setting is the perfect backdrop for a castle.

SETTING & FACILITIES

Location: 15 mi. southwest of Redding in Igo, call inn for precise directions
Near: Airport, Lake Shasta, Trinity Alps, Shasta Caverns, Whiskeytown Reservoir

Location: 15 mi. southwest of Redding in Igo, call inn for precise directions
Near: Airport, Lake Shasta, Trinity Alps, Shasta Caverns, Whiskeytown Reservoir
Building: 5,000-sq.-ft. Elizabethan castle built in 1983
Grounds: 86 acres bounded by natural forest
Public Space: Great Hall w/ fireplace, loft library, game room w/ fireplace, DR, brick terrace
Food & Drink: Full breakfast served at 9:30 in DR; dinner avail. on Fri., Sat., Sun.
Recreation: Fishing, swimming, mountain biking
Amenities & Services: Hot tub, barbecue, evening wine and hors d'oeuvres, down comforters, robes; private parking, 61-in. TV in TV room, kitchen avail. to guests

ACCOMMODATIONS

Units: 5 guest rooms, 2 larger than average, including 1 suite; separate cottage w/ private hot tub
All Rooms: AC, forest and mountain view, private bath
Some Rooms: Fireplace, four-poster, fridge, extra queen Hide-a-Bed (1)
Bed & Bath: Queens, king (1); suite has steam bath
Favorites: The Cottage, beside stream w/ trout pond in front, w/ full kitchen, sitting area, sleeping loft, skylights, deck w/ hot tub, fireplace, bay windows, walk-in shower, extra queen sofa bed; Feona's Suite, w/ watermarked taffeta wall coverings, fireplace, sitting area, windows overlooking forest and South Fork mountains, Italian slab marble bath w/ steam spa
Comfort & Decor: Rooms individually decorated in eclectic/contemporary style w/ painted murals, stained glass windows, antiques, upholstered chairs and couches, marble baths w/ Gothic arches, brass fixtures, Axminister wool carpet, carved oak window frames w/ cornices

RATES, RESERVATIONS, & RESTRICTIONS

Deposit: 1st night's lodging; must cancel 7 days in advance
Discounts: None; extra person $25
Credit Cards: All
Check-In/Out: 3:30/noon, late check-in/out by arrangement
Smoking: No
Pets: No
Kids: Not suitable
Minimum Stay: None
Open: All year
Host: Geri MacCallum
P.O. Box 324
9036 Zogg Mine Rd.
Igo, CA 96047
(530) 396-2785
(888) 343-2836
Fax: (530) 396-2784
www.brigadooncastle.com
inquiry@brigadooncastle.com

JENNER INN, Jenner

| Overall: ★★★ | Room Quality: C | Value: B | Price: $95–$235 |

The 70-mile Sonoma Coast has more than 20 easy-to-get-to sandy beaches, several bird and wildlife preserves, and Fort Ross, a historic Russian fort and trading post. The village of Jenner is located on an estuary where the Russian River enters the sea, creating a sanctuary for a colony of more than 300 harbor seals, river otters, and a wide variety of native and migratory birds. It is a gentle, peaceful place to kayak or canoe and be a part of it all. Not only that, but it also has the mildest weather on the Northern California coast. The Jenner Inn is a collection of guest rooms, cottages, and suites scattered about this small village that can meet just about any need you might have. The accommodations range from modest rooms across the highway from the estuary to glamorous units with fireplaces, hot tubs, and private decks so close to the water you could drop a line in and catch your dinner while you watch the sunset. An expanded continental buffet breakfast is served in the lodge parlor on weekdays, and there is a full breakfast on weekends.

SETTING & FACILITIES

Location: On the Sonoma Coast at the end of the Russian River, junction of California's Scenic Hwys. 1 and 116, 1.5 hours north of San Francisco
Near: Beaches, redwoods, fishing port, shopping, galleries, historic Fort Ross, Kruse Rhododendron State Reserve, seal- and whale-watching
Building: A collection of 8 California- and New England-style cottages, 4 on the estuary and 4 on the landward side, plus a separate building containing the parlor and DR
Grounds: 2.5-acre meadow with year-round creek, and bocce ball court
Public Space: Wood-paneled parlor with woodstove and antiques
Food & Drink: Expanded continental buffet served in the parlor 8:30–10 a.m., full breakfast on weekends
Recreation: Tide pooling, ballooning, kayaking, canoeing, fishing, horseback riding, swimming, golf, tennis, biking, wine tasting
Amenities & Services: Tea and aperitifs in afternoon and evening in parlor; private parking

ACCOMMODATIONS

Units: 20 guest rooms, including 7 suites and 2 minisuites
All Rooms: Private bath
Some Rooms: Fireplaces, four-posters, fridges, private spas (2), shared spas (5), saunas (3), kitchens (4), kitchenettes (4), extra beds (6)
Bed & Bath: Queens, kings (3), double (1)
Favorites: Heron, sitting above the river, w/ sunporch and French windows, done in blue w/ white wicker furniture; Rosewater, a spacious cottage w/ stone fireplace, large sitting area w/ daybed, separate BR w/ four-poster, deck above the river, garden, outdoor spa overlooking the water
Comfort & Decor: Rooms individually decorated w/ antiques, wicker furniture, hardwood floors with carpets, tiles, each room unique in shape, size, location

RATES, RESERVATIONS, & RESTRICTIONS

Deposit: 1st night's lodging; must cancel 7 days in advance; $10 cancellation fee, 1 night's charge with less than 7 days notice
Discounts: Long stays, weekday business travelers Nov.–Mar, groups, AAA, AARP; extra person $15

Credit Cards: AE, MC, V
Check-In/Out: 3/11:30
Smoking: No
Pets: Allowed in certain rooms only, $25 fee
Kids: OK except for waterfront rooms
Minimum Stay: 2 nights on weekends, 3 on holiday weekends
Open: All year

Hosts: Richard and Sheldon Murphy, owners
P.O. Box 69
10400 Hwy. 1
Jenner, CA 95450
(707) 865-2377
(800) 732-2377
Fax: (707) 865-0829
www.jennerinn.com
inkeeper@jennerinn.com

OLD LEWISTON INN, Lewiston

Overall: ★★★★	Room Quality: B	Value: A	Price: $75–$95

Lewiston is a jewel of a town. It has a feeling of real California history that is fast disappearing in many gold rush towns "discovered" and made over for tourists. And the Old Lewiston Inn is just the place to stay and sample the myriad local delights. Fly fishers, mountain bikers, history buffs, and seasoned backpackers have long been hip to this place. The innkeepers are of that increasingly rare breed that like children and dogs and say this policy has never drawn any problems or complaints from their guests. The inn itself is clean and comfortable, and the antique decor in the guest rooms is done nicely but sparingly. This is not a fussy place. Breakfasts are simple and hearty, too, running to fresh fruit, French toast, eggs, sausages, and cereal.

SETTING & FACILITIES

Location: In the Trinity Alps, 30 mi. west of Redding on Hwy. 299, 3 mi. north in the historic eastern section of Lewiston
Near: The fly-fishing-only section of the Trinity River, antique shops, restaurant next door
Building: 2 buildings—a historic home that has been restored to 1870s gold rush standards and a more recent addition built in an 1870s style. The main building is on the Nat'l Register of Historic Places.
Grounds: Flower gardens in both front and back yards, back lawn slopes down to the Trinity River, hot tub is in separate building that opens

onto the river
Public Space: Parlor and game room, DR
Food & Drink: Full country-style breakfasts cooked by Mr. Nixon served 7–9:30 a.m. on back decks overlooking the river in warm weather or in DR other times
Recreation: Mountain and regular biking, bird-watching, fly fishing for steelhead or trout on the grounds, golf, picnicking (box lunches avail. from inn)
Amenities & Services: Hot tub; 1 room w/ handicapped access and bath, concierge services for picnic and excursion planning, fly-fishing guides, whitewater rafting

ACCOMMODATIONS

Units: 7 guest rooms, 4 of which are larger than average
All Rooms: TV/VCR, phone, AC, gold era antiques, fridge, private bath
Some Rooms: Four-poster, private entrance, river-view deck, adjoining room w/ 2 twins for kids (1),

extra twins (3)
Bed & Bath: Queens, king (1)
Favorites: None
Comfort & Decor: Comfortably furnished with antiques and historic photos of Lewiston's glory days during the 1880s gold rush

RATES, RESERVATIONS, & RESTRICTIONS

Deposit: Credit card number to hold room
Discounts: Long stays, groups
Credit Cards: MC, V
Check-In/Out: 11/10, late check-out avail. by request
Smoking: No
Pets: OK
Kids: OK
Minimum Stay: 2 nights on weekends spring–fall

Open: All year
Hosts: Connor and Mary Nixon
P.O. Box 688
On Deadwood Rd., half-block from the Lewiston Bridge
Lewiston, CA 96052
(530) 241-9705
(800) 286-4441
Fax: (530) 778-0309
www.oldlewistoninn.com
nixons@snowcrest.com

GLENDEVEN, Little River

Overall: ★★★★★	Room Quality: A	Value: B	Price: $98–$240

Recognized as one of the best inns in the United States, Glendeven is simply the epitome of good taste. Its focal point is a handsome New England Federalist farmhouse, built in 1867, on two and a half acres of meticulously kept grounds and gardens. Although the inn recently changed ownership, its previous owner had an architectural background who applied his knowhow to perfection in the Stevenscroft addition, a separate building that contains four spacious, private suites with a simple but elegant mix of antiques and contemporary art, custom woodwork, tile, fireplaces, and outdoor balconies or porches. Be forewarned: the guest rooms here are so attractive that you will go home and stare balefully at your own furniture. The hosts jump-start the day with a breakfast of fresh fruit or baked apples, eggs, muffins, and coffeecake served in your room or the farmhouse dining room.

SETTING & FACILITIES

Location: On east side of Hwy. 1, 2 mi. south of Mendocino, 3.5 hours north of San Francisco
Near: Shopping, beaches, state parks, restaurants, galleries, art center, theater
Building: 19th-century New England-style farmhouse and country inn, restored barn and water tower w/ large suite, and the recent Stevenscroft annex
Grounds: 2.5-acre rural setting on headland meadows with views of Little River Bay, flower gardens; renovated barn is a gallery featuring fine arts, crafts, jewelry, and handcrafted furniture

Public Space: Sitting room in the farmhouse, w/ fireplace, baby grand piano, and patio
Food & Drink: Full breakfast served 8:30–9 a.m. in room or at the farmhouse table
Recreation: Biking, golf, tennis, art galleries
Amenities & Services: Afternoon snacks, evening sherry, wine and cheese, home-baked cookies, coffee and tea all day; 1 disabled-accessible room (not shower)

ACCOMMODATIONS

Units: 10 guest rooms, including 3 suites. The Barn House suite is a 2-story house w/ full kitchen, DR, LR, 2 BRs, 1.5 baths.
All Rooms: Private bath; no TV, hot tub, or phone
Some Rooms: Fireplaces (8), four-poster (1), balconies (4), private porch (3), deck (3), extra bed (3)
Bed & Bath: Queens, tubs (2), showers (8)

Favorites: The Pinewood or Bayloft Suites in the Stevenscroft annex; the modestly priced Garret in the farmhouse, w/ dormer windows and views of the bay
Comfort & Decor: All rooms are individually decorated w/ house plants and blooming orchids, antiques, handcrafted furniture, contemporary arts and crafts, some quilts mounted on walls

RATES, RESERVATIONS, & RESTRICTIONS

Deposit: 1st night's lodging for short stays, 50% for longer stays; must cancel 7 days in advance; no cancellation fee
Discounts: Weekday business travelers, winter specials
Credit Cards: AE, MC, V
Check-In/Out: 2/11
Smoking: No
Pets: No
Kids: In 2 rooms
Minimum Stay: 2 nights on weekends, 3 on holiday weekends
Open: All year
Hosts: Sharon and Higgins
8221 Hwy. 1
Little River, CA 95456
(707) 937-0083
(800) 822-4536
Fax: (707) 937-6108
www.glendeven.com
inkeeper@glendeven.com

INN AT SCHOOLHOUSE CREEK, Little River

| Overall: ★★★★ | Room Quality: B | Value: B | Price: $95–$175 |

From its humble origins as a collection of turn-of-the-century logging and mill worker cottages, a 1930s motor court, and a 1960s motel, this inn has evolved into a destination of great charm and distinction. Situated on eight and a half acres of flower-filled gardens, rolling meadows, and an old-growth redwood forest overlooking the ocean, there are accommodations of varying sizes, some with kitchens, all beautifully renovated, restored, and decorated in a comfortable country cottage style. The recent completion of a hot tub with a panoramic view of the adjoining meadow is an added enticement. A sample breakfast menu includes lemon-cranberry popovers, fresh fruit compote, banana and carrot breads, coffeecake, granola with yogurt, and hot and cold cereals.

SETTING & FACILITIES

Location: On the east side of Hwy. 1, 3 mi. south of Mendocino, 3.5 hours north of San Francisco
Near: Private airport, shopping, beaches, state parks, Mendocino, Anderson Valley Wine region, historical excursion railroad, whale-watching excursions
Building: Main building, the historic Ledford House, serves as a guest lounge and is a renovated country ranch house, circa 1862; cottages— recently renovated—are turn-of-the-century; 1932 motor court, remodeled, was the first in the area
Grounds: 8.5 acres of gardens, meadow, and redwood forest on a hillside overlooking the ocean; includes a fern glen, creek, and outdoor picnic area
Public Space: Parlor, library, dining porch, game room/guest reception area, hot tub, outdoor sitting area
Food & Drink: Expanded cont'l breakfast w/ home-baked goods served in the Ledford House 8:30–10 a.m.
Recreation: Croquet, horseshoes, and volleyball on premises, beach access 4 min. away, fishing, sea and river kayaking, golf
Amenities & Services: Hot tub, wine and hors d'oeuvres, games, puzzles, videos, picnic lunches avail., "swap" library, concierge service for reservations, telescope, fenced area for dogs; private parking, fax, e-mail, copying, computer access

ACCOMMODATIONS

Units: 13 guest rooms, 11 larger than average, including 4 cottages w/ separate BRs and full kitchens, 1 cottage w/ minikitchen
All Rooms: Private bath, TV, cable, fireplace, ocean view, private entrance
Some Rooms: Phone/modem connection (9), fridge (7)
Bed & Bath: Mostly queens; 2 rooms sleep 4, 1 cottage sleeps 5, 4 rooms sleep 3; whirlpool tub (1)

Favorites: Fuchsia Cottage has separate BR, LR w/ Franklin fireplace and sofa bed, kitchen, large claw-foot soaking tub, deck, and excellent ocean view; Cypress Cottage has potbellied stove, ocean view, and sitting area

Comfort & Decor: Rooms individually decorated w/ local art, attic treasures, down comforters, some featherbeds, redwood and cypress paneling, country curtains, original redwood floors, and some carpet

RATES, RESERVATIONS, & RESTRICTIONS

Deposit: 1 night's lodging; must cancel 7 days in advance, 14 days in advance for holidays; $15 cancellation fee
Discounts: Occasional specials, off-season rates
Credit Cards: AE, D, MC, V
Check-In/Out: 2/11, late check-out by arrangement
Smoking: No
Pets: Limited, $15 fee
Kids: OK w/ supervision
Minimum Stay: 2 nights on week-

ends, 3 on holiday weekends
Open: All year
Hosts: Al and Penny Greenwood
P.O. Box 1637
7051 N. Hwy. 1
Little River, CA 95456
(707) 937-5525
(800) 731-5525
Fax: (707) 937-2012
www.schoolhousecreek.com
innkeeper@schoolhousecreek.com

RACHEL'S INN, Little River

Overall: ★★★★½	Room Quality: A	Value: B	Price: $96–$220

Little River, a few miles south of Mendocino, is home to the dazzling Van Damme State Park, with its 2,337-acre fern and redwood forest and beach, and to some of the best B&Bs in California. This inn is one of them. There's no substitute for taste, and owner Rachel Binah has it. The Main House, an 1860s Victorian farmhouse, was renovated in the 1980s. The simple, clean lines of the interior of the inn and the adjoining new structure, the Barn, are complemented by an uncluttered mix of contemporary and antique furniture. Nature is the star performer here, however—you'll revel in the gorgeous gardens, old cypress trees, and trails to meadows, the park, and the beach. All that, and the food is exceptional, too, ranging from the traditional to the exotic. One menu includes a fresh fruit compote, herbed cheese omelet with southwestern-style black beans, buttermilk corn muffins, and cinnamon-walnut sour cream coffeecake.

SETTING & FACILITIES

Location: 2 mi. south of Mendocino at Little River, on ocean side of Hwy. 1, 3.5 hours north of San Francisco

Near: Beach access and park trails (a 320-acre section of Van Damme State Park is adjacent to property), shopping, restaurants, galleries, historic excursion railroad, art center, theater, airport

Building: The main house, built in 1860s and renovated in 1980s, has DR and 5 guest rooms; the Barn, w/ a more contemporary feeling, was built in 1990 and has central sitting room and 4 guest rooms

Grounds: Surrounded by informal gardens and 100-year-old cypress trees, as well as by state park w/ trails to cliffs overlooking the ocean and beach

Public Space: DR in main house w/ fireplace, upstairs sitting room overlooking state park, sitting room w/ fireplace in the Barn

Food & Drink: Breakfast served in DR 8:30–10 a.m., coffee avail. at 7 a.m., will accommodate special dietary needs

Recreation: Whale- and bird-watching, deep-sea fishing, canoeing, kayaking, wind surfing, scuba diving, biking, tennis, golf

Amenities & Services: Sherry; private parking, disabled access

ACCOMMODATIONS

Units: 9 guest rooms, including 3 suites

All Rooms: Private bath, art by local artists

Some Rooms: Fireplace, fridge, extra bed (4)

Bed & Bath: Queens, claw-foot tub (1), tub/showers (3), disabled-accessible shower w/ seat (1)

Favorites: Parlor Suite, w/ sitting room, fireplace, piano, ocean view, separate BR; South Room in the Barn, w/ garden view, fireplace, disabled-accessible outside ramp, and bathroom w/ disabled-accessible seat; Upper Suite in the Barn, w/ spacious sitting room, private balcony, fireplace, wet bar and fridge, and additional queen bed

Comfort & Decor: Guest rooms individually decorated—the Main House has more traditional comfortable furniture, carpets, fresh flowers, fine linens, and the Barn has a more contemporary look, w/ wicker and white furniture, down comforters, balconies or private decks

RATES, RESERVATIONS, & RESTRICTIONS

Deposit: 1 night's lodging; must cancel 7 days in advance, 14 days for holidays or for 2 or more rooms; $12 cancellation fee

Discounts: None; extra person $18

Credit Cards: MC, V

Check-In/Out: 2/11

Smoking: No

Pets: No

Kids: OK w/ supervision

Minimum Stay: 2 nights on weekends, 3 on holiday weekends, 4 on Thanksgiving weekend

Open: All year

Host: Rachel Binah
P.O. Box 134
8200 N. Hwy. 1
Little River, CA 95456
(707) 937-0088
(800) 347-9252
Fax: (707) 937-3620
www.rachelsinn.com

VICTORIAN GARDENS, Manchester

Overall: ★★★★★	Room Quality: A	Value: B	Price: $135–$185

Once in awhile you find an inn so perfect, you'd like to keep it a secret. This is one. The innkeepers, one a gifted designer and the other a divine Italian chef disguised as a physician, have brought together the talents and passions of two lifetimes and focused them on this splendid inn. Each room is a treasure-house of original art (contemporary, antique, folk), hand-stenciled wallpaper, 120-year-old Italian lace curtains, and elegant bathrooms, including one with a breathtaking original Victorian glass etching as a window. A woodworker lived on the premises for three years matching and restoring banisters, baseboards, and ceiling trim with native woods. If you arrange to have dinner at the inn, prepare yourself for the same attention to detail. At least once a week, Luciano Zamboni drives a 12-hour circuit from Fort Bragg to Healdsburg to the Bay Area for the freshest and best sources of fish, poultry, olives, bread, wine, and produce. He hand-writes the menus (in a beautiful script) and keeps a log of what each guest has been served to avoid repeating it in the future. Bravo! Bravissimo!

SETTING & FACILITIES

Location: On the Mendocino County coast, 9 mi. north of Point Arena and 8 mi. south of Elk, 3 hours north of San Francisco

Near: State parks, state beaches, wineries, Point Arena lighthouse, boutiques and galleries in Mendocino

Building: 1904 classic Victorian farmhouse

Grounds: 92 acres of rolling hills, forests and meadows w/ free-roaming farm animals, such as Barbados sheep, donkeys; miles of paths and trails, flower and vegetable gardens, Malo Paso Creek

Public Space: LR, library, parlor, kitchen, veranda, picnic tables and chairs

Food & Drink: Full breakfast served at 9 a.m. in the garden room or kitchen next to the fire, at other times by arrangement, 5-course regional Italian dinners avail. by reservation w/ I seating, served on embroidered damask or linen cloths, Italian china, sterling silver and crystal

Recreation: Biking, horseback riding, boat trips, kayaking

Amenities & Services: Aperitifs and hors d'oeuvres served in the evening, robes and slippers, artesian well water, luncheons and picnic baskets avail. by request, homemade jams and preserves, tea service in room by arrangement; private parking, massage by arrangement, concierge services for reservations

ACCOMMODATIONS

Units: 4 guest rooms, 2 larger than average

All Rooms: Down quilt, fine linens, seating and reading area

Some Rooms: Balcony w/ French doors, private bath (2 or 3), shared bath (1 or 2)

Bed & Bath: Queens

Favorites: Master BR, w/ sitting and reading area w/ coffee table and armchairs, deck, private bath w/ shower, claw-foot tub, pedestal sink, bidet; Northwest, w/ four-poster, rocking chair, reading area, private bath w/ tub for 2, tiled shower, pedestal sink, and bidet

Comfort & Decor: Rooms individually decorated w/ original, signed artwork by Picasso, Warhol, Burri, Afro, et al., eclectic combination of contemporary and original antique furniture, authentic Victorian light fixtures, signed rugs from Sardinia, Morocco

RATES, RESERVATIONS, & RESTRICTIONS

Deposit: Checks or credit card

Discounts: Single occupancy

Credit Cards: AE, MC, V

Check-In/Out: No rules

Smoking: No

Pets: No

Kids: Very small or well-behaved

Minimum Stay: 2 nights on holiday weekends

Open: All year

Hosts: Luciano and Pauline Zamboni
14409 S. Hwy. 1
Manchester, CA 95459
(707) 882-3606

MCCLOUD BED AND BREAKFAST HOTEL, McCloud

Overall: ★★★★	Room Quality: B	Value: A	Price: $74–$163

McCloud sprang up as a picturesque company-built lumber-mill town on the south slope of Mt. Shasta. The 90-room McCloud Hotel, on the main street of town, was home to mill workers, teachers, and occasional visitors until it was closed in 1985. Lee and Marilyn Ogden have totally renovated the hotel in exquisite detail and turned the 90 workers' rooms into 17 spacious guest rooms. The Ogdens send you off to play in the morning with a full stomach—apricot ravioli, cheese blintzes, ham, and custard, for example. In the summer you can hike, swim (the town swimming hole on the McCloud River is a must), or fish in this wonderful area; in the winter, you can ski and play in the snow.

SETTING & FACILITIES

Location: 9 mi. east of I-5 at Mt. Shasta on Hwy. 89 in the historic district of McCloud, 4 hours north of Sacramento
Near: Shopping, restaurants, Shasta Sunset Dinner Train
Building: Modified Craftsman built by the lumber mill in 1915, on Nat'l Register of Historic Places, completely restored in 1995
Grounds: Half-acre w/ perennial gardens, garden room, and lawn
Public Space: Spacious, comfortable lobby and parlor with overstuffed sofas, wingback chairs, fireplace, garden room, 6 porches, conference room, TV rooms upstairs and downstairs
Food & Drink: Full breakfast served at individual tables in lobby, suites, or garden room in summer, at 8–9 a.m., coffee bar at 7 a.m.; full service at tables for 2, 4, or 6; restaurant planned for 1999/2000
Recreation: Biking, golf, skiing, fly fishing, square dancing, swimming, snowmobiling
Amenities & Services: Wine service, Saturday tea, barbecue, books, puzzles and games avail. in lobby, picnic lunch tours of area in hotel's van, hairdryers; concierge service will book guides, rent snowmobiles, make restaurant reservations, provide maps; private parking, fax, copier; 1st floor and 1 room meet ADA requirements

ACCOMMODATIONS

Units: 17 guest rooms, 10 larger than average, 4 suites
All Rooms: AC, private bath w/ tub/shower
Some Rooms: Four-poster, sleeper sofa, balcony, extra bed (2)
Bed & Bath: Queens, twins (2); suites have whirlpool tubs for 2 and oversized showers
Favorites: The 2 upstairs suites, 211 and 217, are L-shaped and spacious, w/ whirlpool tubs for 2, separate showers, queen canopy beds, and a view of the old town from private balconies
Comfort & Decor: Rooms are individually decorated w/ artwork of local scenes, coordinated decorator fabrics, original wood floors w/ oriental rugs, original (and now quite rare) clear honey pine trims and doors. Furniture rescued and restored from the original hotel includes antique vanities, trunks used as tables or benches, and four-posters

RATES, RESERVATIONS, & RESTRICTIONS

Deposit: Credit card, 1 nights' deposit for holidays; must cancel 10 days in advance; cancellation fee $10

Discounts: Long stays, off-season rates, AAA, AARP, 20% discount if traveler arrives in a pre–World War II car

Credit Cards: AE, D, MC, V

Check-In/Out: 3–7, late arrival by arrangement/11

Smoking: No

Pets: No

Kids: OK w/ advance arrangement

Minimum Stay: 2 nights on holiday weekends

Open: All year

Hosts: Lee and Marilyn Ogden

P.O. Box 730

408 Main St.

McCloud, CA 96057

(530) 964-2822

(800) 964-2823

Fax: (530) 964-2844

www.mchotel.com

mchotel@snowcrest.net

AGATE COVE INN B&B, Mendocino

Overall: ★★★★	Room Quality: B	Value: B	Price: $109–$250

The owners here clearly know what they're doing. Every advantage is taken to display the splendid views of this rugged section of the Mendocino Coast, and the lavish flower beds on parklike grounds will melt a gardener's heart. Rooms in the 1860s clapboard farmhouse and the cottages are purposefully "casual country" (not "cute country"), with light pine or white furniture and floral wallpaper with complementary fabrics. Other nice touches are a morning San Francisco newspaper on your doorstep, award-winning bread served at a big country breakfast, and a crystal decanter of sherry in your room.

SETTING & FACILITIES

Location: At the north end of the village on Lansing Street, the main north-south street; 3.5 hours north of San Francisco

Near: Beaches, headlands, botanical gardens, state parks, restaurants, galleries, art center, shopping, theater, airport

Building: 1860s farmhouse, 4 single cottages, 2 duplex cottages

Grounds: 1.5 acres, landscaped lawn w/ gardens and sitting areas facing the ocean, original candlestick fence

Public Space: Reception area, breakfast room w/ view of cove, LR furnished w/ antiques and family treasures

Food & Drink: Country breakfast in breakfast room at 8:45, 9, 9:15, and 9:30 a.m.

Recreation: Whale- and bird-watching, chartered fishing trips, canoeing, kayaking, wind surfing, scuba diving, biking, tennis, golf

Amenities & Services: Candies and cookies set out in main house; each room has live orchids or fresh flowers; library of CDs/VCR tapes, sherry in rooms, coffee or tea all day; private parking, concierge service for reservations, fax machine, in-room massage, gift shop; gift baskets may be ordered ahead

ACCOMMODATIONS

Units: 10 guest rooms, 2 in farmhouse w/ separate entrances, 4 single cottages, 4 in duplex cottages
All Rooms: TV/VCR, CD player, Scandia down comforter, private bath
Some Rooms: View of ocean (8), gardens (2), Franklin or gas fireplaces (8), four-posters, private deck (8), sofa bed (2)
Bed & Bath: Queens and kings, spa tub (1), soaking tubs (2)
Favorites: Emerald or Obsidian, each w/ king four-poster, whitewater ocean views, gas fireplace, armchairs, down comforter, sofa bed in sitting area, tub for 2
Comfort & Decor: Rooms individually decorated w/ comfortable furniture, floral print wallpaper, custom fabrics and bedding

RATES, RESERVATIONS, & RESTRICTIONS

Deposit: Credit card or full payment; must cancel 7 days in advance; $25 cancellation fee
Discounts: Nov.–March Sun.–Thurs.; extra person $25
Credit Cards: AE, MC, V
Check-In/Out: 3–7/11, late check-in by arrangement
Smoking: No
Pets: No
Kids: Over 12
Minimum Stay: 2 nights on weekends, 3 on holiday weekends, 4 on Thanksgiving and Christmas weekends
Open: All year
Hosts: Scott and Betsy Buckwald
P.O. Box 1150
11201 N. Lansing St.
Mendocino, CA 95460
(707) 937-0551
(800) 527-3111
Fax: (707) 937-0550
www.agatecove.com
info@agatecove.com

JOHN DOUGHERTY HOUSE, Mendocino

Overall: ★★★★	Room Quality: B	Value: B	Price: $95–$205

The original settlers of Mendocino were loggers from Maine, and they built the kind of houses they had back home. That's how the New England saltbox now called the John Dougherty House was designed in 1867. It's one of the oldest houses in the village. Located at the end of the road in the small village of Mendocino, it looks out over the wildly beautiful Mendocino Headlands State Park, and if the sun didn't set over the ocean, you might swear you were in New England. At John Dougherty's you can sit a spell, watch the whales migrating or the ospreys fishing, and listen to the gulls. Breakfast is served in the New England "keeping room," and it's always a hot entrée such as quiche, frittata, or sausage rolls, plus the Wells' famous homemade scones.

SETTING & FACILITIES

Location: From Hwy. 1, use Main St. exit to Kasten, turn right onto Ukiah (2 streets up), and turn left to inn; 3.5 hours north of San Francisco
Near: Beaches, headlands, botanical gardens, state parks, restaurants, galleries, art center, shopping, theater, airport
Building: 1867 blue saltbox w/ historic water tower and separate building containing 2 cottages, several large verandas on back of main house

Grounds: 3/4 acre w/ view of ocean
Public Space: New England-style keeping room w/ fireplace
Food & Drink: Full breakfast served in the keeping room at 9 a.m., breakfast basket delivered to some cottages
Recreation: Whale- and bird-watching, chartered fishing trips, canoeing, kayaking, wind surfing, scuba diving, biking, tennis, golf
Amenities & Services: Antiques, country quilts; private parking

ACCOMMODATIONS

Units: 11 guest rooms, 6 larger than average, including 4 suites, also guest house and cottage off premises
All Rooms: Private bath, fridge
Some Rooms: Four-poster, sleeper sofa, cable TV (10), fireplace or wood-burning stove (10), extra bed (3)
Bed & Bath: Queens, kings (2); guest house has 2 queens and 2 twins; deep tub (1), Jacuzzis (2), tub/shower (1)
Favorites: Captain's Room, w/ view of

ocean, bay, and town, wood-burning stove, hand-stenciled walls, soaking tub; Starboard Cottage, a 2-room suite at the bottom of the garden w/ wood-burning stove, sitting room, and veranda, all with ocean view
Comfort & Decor: Rooms individually decorated with English and American antiques, redwood beam ceilings, carpet, country pine furnishings

RATES, RESERVATIONS, & RESTRICTIONS

Deposit: Credit card or 1st night's lodging; must cancel 7 days in advance, 14 for holidays and for 2 or more rooms; you will be charged for any nights they are unable to rebook; $15 cancellation fee
Discounts: Long stays; extra person $20
Credit Cards: MC, V
Check-In/Out: 3–6/11
Smoking: No
Pets: No
Kids: Over 12

Minimum Stay: 2 nights on weekends, 3 on holiday weekends, 4 on Thanksgiving weekend
Open: All year
Hosts: Marion and David Wells
P.O. Box 817
571 Ukiah St.
Mendocino, CA 95460
(707) 937-0421
(800) 486-2104
Fax: (707) 937-4139
www.jdhouse.com

JOSHUA GRINDLE INN, Mendocino

Overall: ★★★★½   Room Quality: A   Value: B   Price: $109–$195

The first bed-and-breakfast in Mendocino, this popular New England-inspired inn opened in 1978, setting a high standard for the many inns that were to follow. Built in 1879 as a wedding present to town banker Joshua Grindle, the inn retains its original beauty and style and has been thoughtfully expanded to include lovely rooms in a historic water tower and a saltbox cottage. It's renowned for its breakfasts: guests waddle away from the antique pine harvest table in the dining room to explore rugged coastal headlands or the proliferating smart shops and art galleries in wonderful Mendocino, or perhaps only as far as the Adirondack chairs on the lawn to relax and mimic banker Grindle taking his ease.

SETTING & FACILITIES

Location: In Mendocino proper at the northeast corner of the village, 3.5 hours north of San Francisco
Near: Shopping and restaurants, ocean headlands, beaches, galleries, state parks, theater
Building: 1879 New England-style farmhouse w/ 5 rooms and a wrap-around porch, 1890 redwood saltbox cottage w/ 2 rooms, and 1895 water tower w/ 3 rooms
Grounds: 2 landscaped acres overlooking village and ocean

Public Space: Parlor w/ pump organ and fireplace, DR
Food & Drink: Full breakfast served 8:15–9:30 a.m. in DR or outdoors on veranda, weather permitting
Recreation: Croquet on premises, nearby biking, tennis, golf, whale-watching, horseback riding, canoeing/kayaking, scuba diving, fishing
Amenities & Services: Fruit, sherry, tea, and treats in the parlor, Adirondack chairs and picnic tables outside; private parking

ACCOMMODATIONS

Units: 10 guest rooms, 8 larger than average

All Rooms: Private bath, sitting area, view of ocean or garden

Some Rooms: Fireplace, four-poster, bookshelves (with real books!), extra bed (3)

Bed & Bath: Mostly queens, some deep soaking tubs, whirlpool bath (1)

Favorites: Master Room in the main house, w/ sitting area, wood-manteled fireplace, whirlpool bath; Room 1 in the historic water tower, w/ redwood-beam ceiling and lots of windows

Comfort & Decor: Rooms individually decorated w/ local and historical art, hand-decorated tiles, an eclectic mix of early American, New England, and Shaker antiques, including a collection of rare old clocks and an antique pump organ

RATES, RESERVATIONS, & RESTRICTIONS

Deposit: 1st night in advance; must cancel 7 days in advance; cancellation fee $10

Discounts: AAA

Credit Cards: MC, V

Check-In/Out: 1/11

Smoking: No

Pets: No

Kids: OK at a self-governing age

Minimum Stay: 2 nights on week-ends, 3 on holiday weekends

Open: Closed Dec. 24–25

Hosts: Jim and Arlene Moorhead
P.O. Box 647
44800 Little Lake Rd.
Mendocino, CA 95460
(707) 937-4143
(800) 474-6353
www.joshgrin.com
stay@joshgrin.com

MENDOCINO FARMHOUSE, Mendocino

Overall: ★★★½	Room Quality: B	Value: A	Price: $85–$135

When you seriously want to get away from it all, try this cheery farmhouse tucked deep in a quiet redwood forest. Surrounded by beautiful English-cottage-style flower gardens and a white picket fence, the main house has the appearance of a turn-of-the-century property but was actually built in 1975 to match the owner's fond memories of old houses. The separate Barn Cottage rooms have sitting areas, stone fireplaces, and gardens. Fresh flowers fill the house, and the country breakfasts benefit from the fresh herbs, the homemade jams, and the chickens in residence.

SETTING & FACILITIES

Location: From Hwy. 1 just south of Mendocino, turn east on Comptche-Ukiah Rd., drive 1.5 mi. to Olson Lane, turn left, and go to the end of the road, on the right; 3.5 hours north of San Francisco
Near: Ocean, state parks, Mendocino shopping and restaurants
Building: 2-story high-ceiling farmhouse w/ paned windows built in 1975.
Grounds: 5 acres of forest, meadows, gardens among the most beautiful in the area, duck pond, stream
Public Space: Parlor, library w/ an extensive collection of books
Food & Drink: Full country breakfast served 8:45–10 a.m. in DR at tables for 2, or outside on the deck in the summer
Recreation: Canoeing, scuba diving, Mendocino shopping and restaurants
Amenities & Services: Picnic baskets and mats for beach; private parking, concierge services for reservations, etc.

ACCOMMODATIONS

Units: 5 guest rooms, 3 in main house, 2 w/ private entrances in separate building
All Rooms: Private bath, views of forest, meadow, and pond
Some Rooms: Fireplaces (4), fridges (2), extra bed (1)
Bed & Bath: Queens, king (1)
Favorites: The secluded Barn Cottage: its Pine and Cedar Rooms have stone fireplaces, their own gardens, and private entrances
Comfort & Decor: Casual, cheerful wallpapered rooms eclectically decorated w/ antiques, down comforters, corner window seats, stone and Franklin fireplaces

RATES, RESERVATIONS, & RESTRICTIONS

Deposit: 50% of bill; must cancel 7 days in advance (weekends) or 10 days in advance (holidays), refunds if able to rent room; $15 credit card cancellation fee
Discounts: Long stays, weekday business travelers
Credit Cards: MC, V
Check-In/Out: 2/11:30, late check-out with notice
Smoking: No
Pets: No
Kids: OK in 1 room, but no highchairs or cribs avail.
Minimum Stay: 2 nights on weekends, 3 on holiday weekends
Open: All year
Host: Margie Kamb
P.O. Box 247
43410 Comptche-Ukiah Rd.
Mendocino, CA 95460
(707) 937-0241
(800) 475-1536
Fax: (707) 937-2932
www.mendocinofarmhouse.com
mkamb@mcn.org

PACKARD HOUSE B&B, Mendocino

Overall: ★★★★½	Room Quality: B	Value: B	Price: $85–$210

The exciting new inn in Mendocino, this 1878 Victorian is not only beautiful, it's also perfectly located so that guests are only steps away from everything the village has to offer—shops, restaurants, and the headlands, with its famous views. The restored mansion is a work of art in itself, and inside the owners have used their own museum-quality art collection as part of the decor. Breakfast is equally artistic—typical fare includes a pear in pastry, artichoke soufflé, and fresh cornmeal muffins. If you want to work off some of those calories, hosts Daniel and Maria will lead you on a guided mountain bike tour.

SETTING & FACILITIES

Location: Centrally located in Mendocino; from Hwy. 101 turn left on Little Lake St., left on Lansing, immediate right back onto Little Lake to corner of Little Lake and Kasten Sts.
Near: Beaches, botanical gardens, state parks, historical excursion railroad, airport, restaurants, galleries, art center, shopping, theater
Building: An 1878 "Carpenter's Gothic" Victorian
Grounds: 2/3 acre, private cottage looks out on courtyard, private sitting areas, gardens, old water tower

Public Space: Parlor w/ fireplace and old (1700) French armoire used to display antiquities
Food & Drink: Full breakfast served at 9 a.m. in DR, delivered to cottage
Recreation: Whale- and bird-watching, chartered fishing trips, canoeing, kayaking, wind surfing, scuba diving, biking, tennis, golf
Amenities & Services: Evening sherry, wine, hors d'oeuvres in parlor; robes, slippers, and Spanish sherry in rooms; private parking, guided mountain bike tours

ACCOMMODATIONS

Units: 4 guest rooms, 1 larger than average; private cottage can accommodate 4
All Rooms: Fireplace, cable TV, VCR

and videos, phone, private bath
Some Rooms: Four-poster, sleeper sofa, fridge, ocean or garden view, sophisticated ventilation system

Bed & Bath: Queens (2), kings (2), cottage w/ queen and 2 twins, jet massage tubs and separate showers, marble surrounds, limestone floors
Favorites: Pacific View, w/ ocean and village views, king carved bed, French antique furniture, decorative wall finishes; Garden Cottage, rustic, sleeps 4,
allows children, and features queen featherbed and pull-out twin sofa bed, full kitchen, and fireplace
Comfort & Decor: Rooms professionally decorated w/ museum-quality artifacts, antiques, custom draperies, hardwood floors w/ rugs, fine linens

RATES, RESERVATIONS, & RESTRICTIONS

Deposit: 1st night's lodging; must cancel 7 days in advance
Discounts: Long stays, weekday business travelers; extra person $15
Credit Cards: D, MC, V
Check-In/Out: 2–6/11
Smoking: No
Pets: No
Kids: In cottage
Minimum Stay: 2 nights on weekends, 3 on holiday weekends

Open: All year
Hosts: Maria, Dan, and Bette Levin
P.O. Box 1065
45170 Little Lake St.
Mendocino, CA 95460
(707) 937-2677
(888) 453-2677
Fax: (707) 937-1323
www.packardhouse.com
info@packardhouse.com

SEA ROCK B&B INN, Mendocino

Overall: ★★★★	Room Quality: B	Value: B	Price: $105–$250

This comfortable, well-run inn is the kind of place you could come to year after year just for the fun of it. Wonderfully located on a grassy hillside overlooking rocky cliffs and crashing breakers, the inn offers a wide variety of accommodations, all tasteful, immaculate, and unfussy, and almost all with views that will knock your sou'wester off. All rooms have queen beds and private baths, and most have wood-burning Franklin fireplaces. The two guest rooms with kitchens are perfect for an extended stay, and you will want to stay! It's just a great spot to hang out. An expanded continental breakfast is set out every morning in the pretty breakfast room, which has lots of windows overlooking the sea.

SETTING & FACILITIES

Location: Half-mile north of Mendocino on Hwy. 1 (turn left on Little Lake Rd., drive one block to Lansing), 3.5 hours north of San Francisco
Near: Beaches, headlands, botanical gardens, state parks, historical excursion railroad, restaurants, galleries, art center, shopping, theaters, airport

Building: Individual cottages with private decks, newly constructed 2-story building w/ suites, views of ocean and coastline
Grounds: 2 acres on a hillside overlooking the ocean; cottages are surrounded by century-old cypress trees, landscaped gardens, spacious lawns

Public Space: DR overlooking the ocean just off main lobby, picnic tables and benches in the garden areas
Food & Drink: Expanded cont'l breakfast served 8–10 a.m. in DR
Recreation: Whale- and bird-watching, deep-sea fishing, canoeing, kayaking, golf, state parks, biking
Amenities & Services: Firewood, ice, fresh flowers in season, wineglasses; private parking; disabled access in 1 room

ACCOMMODATIONS

Units: 14 guest rooms, including a 2-BR cottage w/ full kitchen, and 4 large suites, 1 w/ kitchen
All Rooms: Private bath, deck, cable TV, VCR, phone, wired for Internet access
Some Rooms: Wood-burning fireplace, kitchen, four-poster, featherbed, extra bed (9)
Bed & Bath: Mostly queens; whirlpool baths (2), 2-person soaker tubs (2), tubs (2)

Favorites: Cottage 1 has 2 BRs w/ full kitchen and fireplace (plan ahead—it's popular)
Comfort & Decor: Rooms individually decorated w/ original art, specially designed bird's-eye pine furniture, valances and blinds, carpet and tile; new units are 600 sq. ft., 2 w/ vaulted ceilings, 2 w/ oversized tubs w/ window view of ocean; suites have telephones wired for Internet access and desks

RATES, RESERVATIONS, & RESTRICTIONS

Deposit: 50% of bill; must cancel 2 weeks in advance; $20 cancellation fee
Discounts: None
Credit Cards: All
Check-In/Out: 2–7/11
Smoking: No
Pets: No
Kids: In 5 units
Minimum Stay: 2 nights on weekends, 3 on holiday weekends

Open: All year
Hosts: Susie and Andy Plocher
P.O. Box 906
11101 Lansing St.
Mendocino, CA 95460
(707) 937-0926
(800) 906-0926
www.searock.com
searock@mcn.org

WHITEGATE INN, Mendocino

Overall: ★★★★½	Room Quality: A	Value: B	Price: $139–$229

Described aptly by a guest as "the ultimate B&B," Whitegate Inn has been the setting for several movies and the subject of various magazine articles. It is an over-the-top confection of riotous flower gardens, French, Italian, and Victorian antiques, crystal chandeliers, featherbeds, fireplaces, bone china and sterling silver, and decadent breakfasts. In the hands of someone less skilled, the onslaught of colors, patterns, and accents could have gotten entirely out of hand, but the owners, an interior decorator and a contractor, achieve a certain kind of milieu that approaches B&B heaven for many. Others may feel like a bit like bulls in the proverbial china shop. Don't plan to stay on your diet here, because breakfast entrées include dishes like caramel-apple French toast or pecan-and-date pancakes.

SETTING & FACILITIES

Location: Just off Hwy. 1 in the village of Mendocino (turn west at Little Lake Rd., then left on Howard St. for 2 blocks), 3.5 hours north of San Francisco
Near: Shopping, restaurants, beaches, headlands, state parks, historical excursion railroad, galleries, art center, theater, airport
Building: A restored 1883 Victorian on the Nat'l Register of Historic Places
Grounds: Ancient cypress trees and Victorian gardens enclosed by a white picket fence, w/ many sitting areas

Public Space: Parlor w/ fireplace, gazebo
Food & Drink: 2-course breakfast 8:30–9:30 a.m. in DR
Recreation: Whale- and bird-watching, deep-sea fishing, canoeing, kayaking, wind surfing, scuba diving, biking, tennis, golf
Amenities & Services: Welcome basket and chocolates in all rooms, evening wine and hors d'oeuvres, high tea served for an additional charge, homemade cookies; private parking, concierge service for reservations

ACCOMMODATIONS

Units: 7 guest rooms, 2 larger than average
All Rooms: Private bath, fireplace, European featherbed, down comforter, blooming orchids, cable TV, phone
Some Rooms: Four-poster, sleeper sofa, fridge, ocean view, extra bed (1)
Bed & Bath: Queens, king (1), rollaway may be added to 2 rooms; claw-foot tubs or showers or both

Favorites: Enchanted Cottage, w/ private entrance in secluded garden, antique French BR w/ king bed, sleeper sofa, claw-foot tub and shower, fireplace, French doors to private deck
Comfort & Decor: Rooms individually decorated w/ original artwork, antiques, wallpaper, custom window treatments, carpet, fresh flowers

RATES, RESERVATIONS, & RESTRICTIONS

Deposit: 50% of bill; must cancel w/in 14 days, 30 days on holidays or w/ 2 or more rooms
Discounts: Long stays, midweek in winter
Credit Cards: All
Check-In/Out: 3–6/11, no extra charge for noon check-out
Smoking: No
Pets: No
Kids: 10 or over in main house, under 10 in cottage
Minimum Stay: 2 nights on week-

ends, 3 to 4 on holiday weekends
Open: All year
Hosts: George and Carol Bechtloff, owners; Vince and Gigi, innkeepers
P.O. Box 150
499 Howard St.
Mendocino, CA 95460
(707) 937-1131
(800) 531-7282
Fax: (707) 937-1131
www.whitegateinn.com
staff@whitegateinn.com

MOUNT SHASTA RANCH B&B, Mount Shasta

Overall: ★★★½	Room Quality: B	Value: A	Price: $50–$95

The Mount Shasta area is Northern California's best-kept secret. Beautiful, clean, uncrowded, and with every form of recreation you can think of, it remains unspoiled, unselfconscious, and untouristy. This B&B shares all those qualities. The hosts will knock themselves out to ensure that your stay is a fun one, and they welcome children. Spacious, comfortable, and attractive, the inn is conveniently located for exploring the area's charms. In fact, golf, tennis, fishing, and boating are available within a short walk. A full country breakfast is served in the home's dining room, and popular items include blackberry crepes and a ranch stratta.

SETTING & FACILITIES

Location: At the western edge of the town of Mt. Shasta, west of I-5 and south of the fish hatchery (call for directions)
Near: Shopping, airport, Amtrak, Lake Siskiyou, fish hatchery, local history museum, Mt. Shasta
Building: 2-story ranch house w/ gambrel roof and 3 dormer windows, 60-ft. covered porch, carriage house, cottage, built in 1923
Grounds: 2.5 acres w/ tiered lawn and view of Mt. Shasta, flower garden

Public Space: LR w/ massive rock fireplace, game room, DR, gazebo
Food & Drink: Full country breakfast in DR 8:30–9 a.m., other times by request
Recreation: Horseshoes, volleyball, Ping-Pong, pool table on premises, biking, tennis, golf, water sports, downhill/X-C skiing
Amenities & Services: Hot tub, barbecue, afternoon snacks and wine, VCR, piano; private parking

ACCOMMODATIONS

Units: 10 guest rooms, including 4 suites, cottage w/ 2 BRs
All Rooms: TV, cable, AC
Some Rooms: Sleeper sofa, kitchen, private bath (5)
Bed & Bath: Queens; cottage has private bath, 2 queen sleeper sofas and 2 twins; 5 rooms in carriage

house share 2 baths
Favorites: Northwest room, w/ view of Mt. Shasta, private bath, original oak floors
Comfort & Decor: Early American and Art Deco antiques, collectibles, and china, oriental rugs, matching curtains and bedcovers

RATES, RESERVATIONS, & RESTRICTIONS

Deposit: Credit card or 50% of bill; must cancel 3 days in advance
Discounts: Weekdays in winter and spring, ski packages
Credit Cards: AE, D, MC, V
Check-In/Out: 3/11, late check-out by

arrangement
Smoking: No
Pets: OK, $10 extra
Kids: OK
Minimum Stay: 2 nights on summer and holiday weekends

Open: All year
Hosts: Bill and Mary Larsen
1008 W. A. Bar Rd.
Mt. Shasta, CA 96067

(530) 926-3870
www.travelassist.com/reg/ca121s.html
alpinere@snowcrest.net

INN AT SHALLOW CREEK FARM, Orland

Overall: ★★★½	Room Quality: B	Value: A	Price: $60–$85

This is a real old-fashioned farm in farm country. Just beyond the traffic sounds of I-5, the chickens and ducks are the first thing you see as you approach the quiet, ivy-covered gray-and-white farmhouse surrounded by mandarin orange, black walnut, and almond trees. Since the inn is on the Pacific Flyway, it's an excellent place to see snow geese and a wide variety of ducks and wading birds. It's also a good place to get away from the urban grind, yet Chico, a surprisingly cosmopolitan town, is just 20 miles away if you get desperate for a cappuccino and a *Wall Street Journal*. Breakfast features fresh fruit from the farm in season, custard made with farm eggs, and wild elderberry muffins.

SETTING & FACILITIES

Location: Off I-5 at Chico/Orland exit, 2.2 mi. west to County Rd. DD, and go .5 mile; 1.5 hours north of Sacramento
Near: Nat'l wildlife refuge, Black Butte Lake, golf, biking
Building: Renovated turn-of-the-century farmhouse, cottage, red barn
Grounds: 3-acre working farm, flower garden, citrus orchard, variety of fruit and shade trees, free-roaming ducks, chickens, and geese, Shallow Creek

Public Space: Parlor w/ fireplace, leather sofas, library, piano, TV
Food & Drink: Extended cont'l breakfast featuring fresh fruit from the farm in season, home-baked pastries, served in DR at 8:30 a.m., other times by arrangement
Recreation: Fishing and water sports at lake, golf, bird-watching
Amenities & Services: Guest fridge on sunporch; private parking

ACCOMMODATIONS

Units: 4 guest rooms, 2 larger than average, 1 4-room cottage w/ fully stocked kitchen
All Rooms: Phone, AC, books
Some Rooms: Fireplace, sleeper sofa, kitchen, private bath (2), shared bath (2)
Bed & Bath: Queens, 1 room w/ 2

twins, sofa beds in cottage
Favorites: Penfield Suite in main house, w/ sitting area, private bath, collection of Americana
Comfort & Decor: Rooms individually decorated w/ antiques, comfortable chairs, carpet

RATES, RESERVATIONS, & RESTRICTIONS

Deposit: Credit card or 1st night's lodging; must cancel 6 days in advance; no cancellation fee
Discounts: Long stays; extra person $15
Credit Cards: MC,V
Check-In/Out: 4–7/noon, late check-out by arrangement
Smoking: No
Pets: No

Kids: Not suitable
Minimum Stay: None
Open: All year
Hosts: Mary and Kurt Glaeseman
4712 County Rd. DD
Orland, CA 95963
(530) 865-4093
(800) 865-4093
Fax: (530) 865-4093

COAST GUARD HOUSE, Point Arena

Overall: ★★★★   Room Quality: B   Value: B   Price: $115–$175

Standing high on a hill overlooking the rocky shore of the North Coast, this two-story Cape Cod harbors the history of the "Surfmen," Coast Guard crewmen who performed many daring sea rescues over a 50-year span. Built in 1901 by the U.S. Life-Saving Service, the inn still retains its nautical spirit. In addition to maritime memorabilia throughout, one guest room has the air of a shipmaster's quarters, with a captain's bed built into a many-windowed alcove, and the cottage is a replica of the original boathouse from which the lifeboats were launched. Thankfully, the breakfasts aren't hardtack served on mess trays, but more likely homemade granola, Gruyère potato pie, and fresh melon.

SETTING & FACILITIES

Location: From Hwy. 1 at the town of Point Arena, go west 1 mile on Iversen Ave.; 3 hours north of San Francisco
Near: Beaches, public fishing pier, fishing harbor, sea lions, birds, restaurants, shopping, galleries
Building: 1901 Cape Cod house, restored cottage
Grounds: 2 acres, between headlands, among cypress trees and gardens

Public Space: Parlor, DR
Food & Drink: Full breakfast served at 9:30 a.m. in DR, other times by arrangement
Recreation: Tide pooling, whale-watching, surfing, fishing, horseback riding, kayaking, biking, tennis, golf
Amenities & Services: Hot tub; concierge service for reservations, massages

ACCOMMODATIONS

Units: 6 guest rooms, including 1 suite and a small cottage
All Rooms: Private bath, Arts and Crafts furniture, nautical memorabilia
Some Rooms: Fireplace, sitting area, private patio, extra bed (1)
Bed & Bath: Queens, 2-person whirlpool spa (1), deep Japanese soaking tub/shower (1)

Favorites: Surfmen Cove, spacious, w/ Arts and Crafts furnishings, wood-burning stove, sitting area, view of ocean and cove, Japanese-style deep tile soaking tub/shower

Comfort & Decor: Handcrafted furniture, uncluttered rooms w/ nautical pictures of the inn's maritime history, brass and flags, local artwork, patchwork quilts, wood floors, and rugs

RATES, RESERVATIONS, & RESTRICTIONS

Deposit: 1 night's lodging; must cancel 7 days in advance; no cancellation fee
Discounts: Long stays, AAA
Credit Cards: MC, V
Check-In/Out: 3–6/11:30, late checkout by arrangement
Smoking: No
Pets: No
Kids: OK
Minimum Stay: 2 nights on weekends

Open: All year
Hosts: Mia and Kevin Gallagher
P.O. Box 117
695 Arena Cove
Point Arena, CA 95468
(707) 882-2442
(800) 524-9320
Fax: (707) 882-3233
www.coastguardhouse.com
coast@mcn.org

FAULKNER HOUSE, Red Bluff

Overall: ★★★½	Room Quality: B	Value: A	Price: $65–$90

Red Bluff is a medium-sized town along the upper Sacramento River that most tourists barely glance at as they make their way along I-5. A quiet residential community with an economy centered around cattle and farming, it has its charms—great fishing for sturgeon, trout, bass, and salmon on the Sacramento River, and Mount Lassen, both an hour away. Faulkner House is a traditional B&B and the best in the area, as well as one of the reigning monarchs in a town that has more than its share of immaculately kept Victorians and some fine antique stores. The inn serves fresh orange juice, fresh fruit, and often an entrée such as French toast and bacon in the formal dining room.

SETTING & FACILITIES

Location: 2 blocks west of Main St. in a quiet residential neighborhood w/ many Victorians, 2 hours north of Sacramento
Near: Riverfront park, antique shopping, restaurants, Victorian museum, the Ide adobe (home of California's first and only president), Victorian home walking tour, airport, Lassen Nat'l Park
Building: 1890 Queen Anne Victorian
Grounds: City lot w/ large side yard,
rose garden, small backyard w/ tree swing and brick terrace
Public Space: Parlor/LR w/ fireplace, couches, TV, library, DR, screened porch
Food & Drink: Full breakfast served 8–9 a.m. in DR, earlier by arrangement
Recreation: Fishing, biking, golf
Amenities & Services: Sherry, M&Ms in rooms, beverages on arrival; on-street parking

ACCOMMODATIONS

Units: 4 guest rooms, 2 larger than average

All Rooms: Private bath

Some Rooms: Brocade fainting couch

Bed & Bath: Queens, double (1)

Favorites: Arbor Room, w/ carved European BR set w/ floral wallpaper;

Wicker Room, w/ iron bed and wicker furniture

Comfort & Decor: Rooms individually decorated w/ iron beds, European carved antique furniture, wicker chairs, burgundy velvet curtains, area carpets over hardwood floors, stained glass

RATES, RESERVATIONS, & RESTRICTIONS

Deposit: Credit card, 3 days

Discounts: Long stays

Credit Cards: AE, MC, V

Check-In/Out: 4–7/11, other by special arrangement

Smoking: No

Pets: No

Kids: 10 or over

Minimum Stay: None

Open: All year

Hosts: Harvey and Mary Klinger
1029 Jefferson St.
Red Bluff, CA 96080
(530) 529-0520
(800) 549-6171
Fax: (530) 527-4970
www.snowcrest.net/faulknerbb
faulknerbb@snowcrest.net

TIFFANY HOUSE B&B INN, Redding

Overall: ★★★½	Room Quality: B	Value: A	Price: $85–$135

On a hilltop in a quiet neighborhood setting, this Victorian-style inn built in the 1930s is pretty inside and out. Its many windows frame panoramic views of the Mt. Lassen range, or you can commune with nature firsthand in the landscaped garden or the swimming pool. The bedrooms in the main house have sitting areas, hand-crocheted bedspreads, and embroidered pillowcases, plus individual features such as a claw-foot tub in a cupola window setting. The cottage has knotty pine walls, a high, romantic bed, and a seven-foot spa tub. A sample breakfast menu features baked pears, homemade bread, artichoke-mushroom stratta, and homegrown tomatoes in season, served in the dining room. If you feel energetic, you can jog the seven miles of paved path along the Sacramento River or enjoy its renowned trout, salmon, and steelhead fishing.

SETTING & FACILITIES

Location: Just north of downtown Redding (call for directions)

Near: Restaurants, museums, little theater, antique stores, outlet shopping mall, Shasta Lake

Building: 60-year-old, 2-story Victorian; cottage

Grounds: Landscaped gardens, white picket fence, double-sized city lot

Public Space: Parlor, music room w/ piano and sheet music, game room w/ games and books, large shaded deck, gazebo
Food & Drink: Full breakfast served in DR at 9 a.m., special consideration for dietary restrictions, special arrangements for early departure
Recreation: Fishing, swimming, boating, tennis, golf, biking, river rafting, canoeing
Amenities & Services: Swimming pool, refreshments on arrival, beverages avail. all day, evening wine and hors d'oeuvres, robes; private parking, concierge service for reservations, free transportation to and from airport, golfing at one of the area's premier private golf courses

ACCOMMODATIONS

Units: 4 guest rooms, 1 larger than average
All Rooms: Private bath, AC, crocheted bedspread, embroidered pillow covers, down and synthetic pillows
Some Rooms: Four-poster, sofa bed (1)
Bed & Bath: Queens, whirlpool spa (1)

Favorites: Lavinia's Cottage, secluded, w/ laurel wreath iron bed, sitting area, chairs and desk, private entrance
Comfort & Decor: Rooms individually decorated w/ painted and needlepoint artwork, wallpaper, carpet and area rugs, window treatments that enhance views

RATES, RESERVATIONS, & RESTRICTIONS

Deposit: Credit card or 1st night's lodging; must cancel 7 days in advance; cancellation fee $10
Discounts: None; extra person $25
Credit Cards: AE, D, MC, V
Check-In/Out: After 4/11:30, late check-out by arrangement
Smoking: No
Pets: No
Kids: Not suitable

Minimum Stay: 2 nights on holiday weekends
Open: All year
Hosts: Susan and Brady Stewart
1510 Barbara Rd.
Redding, CA 96003
(916) 244-3225
www.sylvia.com/tiffany.htm
tiffanyhse@aol.com

SCOTIA INN, Scotia

Overall: ★★★½	Room Quality: C	Value: B	Price: $85–$195

Scotia is the town that lumber built—literally and figuratively. Owned by the world's largest lumber company, Pacific Lumber Company, it is home to the world's largest redwood mill and the Scotia Museum (not the world's largest), which features the history of the timber industry, the company, and the Scotia area. The handsome three-story Scotia Inn is built entirely of redwood, of course, and has 21 attractive rooms. It's noted for its restaurant, with a pretty redwood dining room (notice the trend here). The restaurant has an extensive menu featuring fresh fish from the North

Coast and locally grown fruits and vegetables. There's also a Steak and Potato Pub for more casual dining.

SETTING & FACILITIES

Location: In the town of Scotia: from Hwy. 101 take Scotia exit, turn left on Main St.
Near: Airport, shopping, restaurants, tour of mill, Eel River, Avenue of the Giants Scenic Drive, Humboldt Bay Wildlife Refuge, state parks
Building: Historic Mission-style residential hotel for lumber mill, built in 1923
Grounds: .3-acre groomed grounds

w/ seasonal flowers, a wedding garden
Public Space: Library, gazebo
Food & Drink: Extended cont'l breakfast served 7–9:30 a.m. in the main lobby
Recreation: Biking, tennis, golf, fishing, bird-watching
Amenities & Services: Hot tub, irons, private parking, disabled access to DR, copier, fax, wine and gift shop

ACCOMMODATIONS

Units: 21 guest rooms, 7 larger than average, including 5 suites
All Rooms: Private bath, cable TV, phone
Some Rooms: Views of town and forest, four-poster, hand-carved headboard, extra bed (6)
Bed & Bath: Queens and kings, double (1), Jacuzzi for 2 (1), Jacuzzi (1)

Favorites: Large Bridal Suite decorated in white, w/ king bed draped w/ half-canopy, antiques, Jacuzzi for 2 in separate room
Comfort & Decor: Rooms individually decorated w/ old posters, historic photographs, and modern art, furniture from the 1920s, 1930s, and 1940s, lace curtains, carpet

RATES, RESERVATIONS, & RESTRICTIONS

Deposit: Credit card guarantee; must cancel 10 days in advance; cancellation fee $10
Discounts: Weekday business, groups, AAA; extra person $20
Credit Cards: D, MC, V
Check-In/Out: 3/11, late check-out by arrangement
Smoking: No
Pets: No
Kids: OK
Minimum Stay: 2 nights on holiday weekends, 1 weekend in May and 1 in

Oct. for special events
Open: All year
Hosts: Charles Oppitz and Jonathon Schleef
P.O. Box 248
Mill St. (directly across from the mill)
Scotia, CA 95565
(707) 764-5683
(888) 764-2248
Fax: (707) 764-1707
www.scotiainn.com
scotiain@scotiainn.com

LOST WHALE B&B INN, Trinidad

Overall: ★★★★	Room Quality: B	Value: B	Price: $118–$178

Located on one of the most beautiful sections of the Pacific coastline, the Lost Whale is not just a place to stay on your way from A to B, but a true journey's end. And for children, it's heaven. They're welcomed here with open arms to enjoy the enclosed play area, the menagerie of horses, pygmy goats, and other farm animals down the road, and the miles and miles of private beaches, tide pools, and sea lion homesteads. The hearty, five-course meals each morning draw rave reviews.

SETTING & FACILITIES

Location: A 25-minute drive north of Eureka, 4.5 mi. north of Trinidad, off Hwy. 101: either take Patrick's Point Drive, then go 1 mile south, or take the Seawood Drive exit and go north 1.8 mi.
Near: Redwood Nat'l Park, Patrick's Point State Park, restaurants, airport
Building: 1989 Cape Cod-style inn
Grounds: 4 acres of lawn and gardens, woods w/ ferns, pines, and alders, private beaches, 2-mile cove w/ sea lions
Public Space: LR w/ woodstove, floor-to-ceiling windows, DR with view windows, library, decks
Food & Drink: Full buffet breakfast served at 8:30 a.m. in DR
Recreation: Fishing, horseback riding, whale-watching, biking, tennis, golf, river rafting
Amenities & Services: Hot tub, barbecue, afternoon tea, evening sherry and wine w/ hors d'oeuvres, complimentary sodas, chocolates, private parking, concierge service for reservations, fax

ACCOMMODATIONS

Units: 8 guest rooms, 4 larger than average, also a 2-BR farmhouse w/ kitchen that sleeps 6
All Rooms: Private bath, lots of windows, soundproofing
Some Rooms: Ocean views (5), sleeping loft for extra guests (2), private balcony, sitting alcove, skylight, daybed (1)
Bed & Bath: Queens, plus futon or twins in lofts
Favorites: Beluga Whale, spacious, w/ sliding door to private balcony, ocean view
Comfort & Decor: Rooms individually decorated w/ large windows, dormer windows, hardwood floors and area rugs, oak beds, art by local artists

RATES, RESERVATIONS, & RESTRICTIONS

Deposit: Credit card, 50% of bill; must cancel 7 days in advance; $15 cancellation fee; no refund unless room is subsequently rented
Discounts: AARP, cash, singles; extra adults $25, children 3–16 $20
Credit Cards: AE, D, MC, V
Check-In/Out: 3/11, late check-in by arrangement
Smoking: No
Pets: No
Kids: OK
Minimum Stay: 2 nights on weekends and June 15–Sept. 15, 3 on holiday weekends
Open: All year
Hosts: Lee Miller and Susanne Lakin
3452 Patrick's Point Dr.
Trinidad, CA 95570
(707) 677-3425
(800) 677-7859
Fax: (707) 677-0284
www.lost-whale-inn.com
lmiller@lost-whale-inn.com

SANFORD HOUSE, Ukiah

Overall: ★★★½   Room Quality: C   Value: A   Price: $100

The Manogue family aims to provide your home-away-from-home when you visit the pretty little town of Ukiah. Their Queen Anne Victorian is located in a quiet neighborhood within walking distance of restaurants, theaters, the public golf course, and the Ukiah Conference Center. The five guest rooms are pleasantly unfussy. There's wicker furniture on the large front porch, and a koi pond in the flower-filled garden. You can have breakfast at the time you choose, use the family fridge, and even walk the family dogs.

SETTING & FACILITIES

Location: From Hwy. 101 in Ukiah, take Perkins St. exit, go west to Pine, and turn left; 2 hours north of San Francisco
Near: Ukiah Conference Center, theaters, restaurants, public golf course, courthouse, Lake Mendocino 10 min. away
Building: 1904 Queen Anne Victorian, remodeled
Grounds: 2/3 acre in quiet neighborhood setting w/ old trees, gardens w/ koi pond, cherry trees
Public Space: Parlor w/ original bird's-eye maple fireplace, turret sitting area, DR, library, front porch w/ wicker furniture
Food & Drink: Full breakfast of seasonal fresh food served in DR, anytime 6:30–10 a.m.
Recreation: Fishing, free passes to health club for swimming, exercise, spa, etc.
Amenities & Services: Home-baked cookies, nuts, lemonade, coffee, tea, evening wine, fax, computer hookups, TV/VCR and large movie selection, house fridge avail. to guests, private parking

ACCOMMODATIONS

Units: 5 guest rooms, 2 larger than usual
All Rooms: Private bath, individual heat and AC
Some Rooms: Four-poster
Bed & Bath: Queens, roll-away avail., claw-foot tubs (3)
Favorites: The Wilson Room, upstairs in the turret
Comfort & Decor: Rooms individually decorated with original art and family memorabilia, floral overstuffed couches, lace and balloon curtains, hunter green carpet

RATES, RESERVATIONS, & RESTRICTIONS

Deposit: Credit card; must cancel 7 days in advance; cancellation fee full price if room can't be rented
Discounts: Long stays, singles; extra person $25
Credit Cards: AE, MC, V
Check-In/Out: Anytime/noon, late check-out by arrangement
Smoking: No
Pets: No
Kids: Over 10

Minimum Stay: None
Open: All year
Hosts: Dorsey and Bob Manogue
306 S. Pine St.
Ukiah, CA 95482

(707) 462-1653
Fax: (707) 462-8987
www.sanfordhouse.com
sanhouse@bullhead.net

VICHY HOT SPRINGS RESORT, Ukiah

Overall: ★★★½   Room Quality: C   Value: B   Price: $99–$225

It's rare to be able to use the word "unique" and really mean it, but that's what the 700-acre Vichy Springs Ranch is. The springs are the only carbonated hot springs in the United States, and the spritzy "Champagne Baths" will literally tickle you. The resort has been a big deal since 1854. Mark Twain, Robert Louis Stevenson, Jack London, three presidents, and prize-fighters Gentleman Jim Corbett and John L. Sullivan all came to soak in the therapeutic and restorative waters. In the 1950s and 1960s it fell on hard times and was almost torn down. Today the resort's popularity is again on the rise, and in the summer you definitely need a reservation. The old buildings have been renovated, and new ones are being added. There are both rooms and one- and two-bedroom cottages with kitchens and porches. Futons are available for extra guests, and a full breakfast is served in the lodge dining room. The future here is definitely, may we say, sparkling?

SETTING & FACILITIES

Location: From Hwy. 101 in Ukiah, take Vichy Springs turnoff and follow the state historical landmark signs; 2 hours north of San Francisco
Near: Redwoods, wineries, brandy distilleries, shopping, restaurants, airport, 2 local history museums, steam locomotive excursion train, boating
Building: 1870 1-story, 12-room redwood lodge, 1870 creekside lodge w/ 5 rooms, 3 redwood cottages built in 1854, the oldest buildings in Ukiah, a California Historical Landmark; 2 newer cottages, DR, office
Grounds: 700-acre ranch, 100-gallon naturally carbonated warm (90°) springs and hot soaking pool (104°) in a travertine and onyx grotto lined
w/ ferns, waterfall, meadows, and forest of oak, madrone, and California nutmeg
Public Space: Olympic swimming pool, indoor and outdoor bathing tubs, hot soaking pool, DR
Food & Drink: Full buffet breakfast served 7:30–10 a.m. in DR, special dietary needs accommodated
Recreation: Nature trails, swimming, picnicking on premises, hang gliding, mountain biking, tennis, golf, fishing, sailing, Jet Skiing
Amenities & Services: Mineral baths, hot soaking pool, barbecues, picnic tables, basketball, horseshoes; massage and facials, private parking, disabled access, RV parking $20/night

ACCOMMODATIONS

Units: 22 guest rooms, 12 rooms in main lodge, 5 rooms in creekside lodge, 3 1-BR cottages, 2 2-BR cottages
All Rooms: Private bath, individual heat and AC, phone, hardwood floors, porch
Some Rooms: Kitchen, sleeper sofa, fridge, fireplace
Bed & Bath: Mostly queens; beds vary, esp. in cottages; futons/sleeper sofas

avail. for extra occupancy; tubs (3)
Favorites: 1854 1-BR cottage w/ LR and kitchen, fireplace, lots of windows, panoramic views of grounds, private porch
Comfort & Decor: Rooms individually decorated using Waverly chintz fabric (used extensively in the White House), overstuffed chairs and sofas, throw rugs on original fir floors

RATES, RESERVATIONS, & RESTRICTIONS

Deposit: Credit card or 100%; must cancel 7 days in advance, 14 days on holidays; cancellation fee $10
Discounts: None; extra person $35
Credit Cards: All
Check-In/Out: 3–9/noon, other by arrangement
Smoking: No
Pets: No
Kids: OK
Minimum Stay: 2 nights cottages and

creekside rooms, main lodge July–Sept., weekends April–Nov., holiday weekends
Open: All year
Hosts: Gilbert and Marjorie Ashoff
2605 Vichy Springs Rd.
Ukiah, CA 95482
(707) 462-9515
Fax: (707) 462-9516
www.vichysprings.com
info@vichysprings.com

DEHAVEN VALLEY FARM & RESTAURANT, Westport

Overall: ★★★★	Room Quality: C	Value: A	Price: $85–$140

On Dehaven Valley's beautiful 20 acres, a one-minute walk from the ocean, owner Christa Stapp takes in "retired" farm animals—horses, donkeys, goats, sheep, geese—and she'll take you in, too. She'll put you up in comfortable, pretty rooms in this old-fashioned farmhouse and feed you great food. You can hike, beachcomb, and explore the odd history of Westport, once home to 3,000 but now inhabited by only 200 hardy souls.

SETTING & FACILITIES

Location: Off Hwy. 1, 1.7 mi. north of Westport, just past Branscomb Rd.; 4.5 hours north of San Francisco
Near: Beach, state park, shopping, Westport, airport, Fort Bragg
Building: White clapboard manor house built in 1875, broad front veranda; 2 adjacent cottages
Grounds: 20 acres of meadows, rolling

hills, trees, and pastures; hiking trails
Public Space: Large LR with fireplace, couches, books, games, VCR, DR (part of the restaurant), gazebo
Food & Drink: Full breakfast served in DR 8:30–9:30 a.m.
Recreation: Tide pooling horseback riding on the beach, biking, golf

Amenities & Services: Hot tub, barbecue, afternoon snacks, evening sherry; parking on private road w/ no through traffic

ACCOMMODATIONS

Units: 8 guest rooms, 2 larger than average, 5 rooms in main house, 2 cottages, one with 2 units
All Rooms: Phones
Some Rooms: Fireplace (6), firewood, fridge (2), sleeper sofa, private bath (6), shared bath (for 2-unit cottage)
Bed & Bath: Queens, kings (2, can be rearranged as twins)
Favorites: Acacia is a family cottage w/ LR and Franklin stove, wet bar, coffeemaker and refrigerator, can accommodate 4; Eagle's Nest has huge picture window overlooking meadows and rolling hills, sitting area, Franklin stove
Comfort & Decor: Rooms individually decorated with, antiques, lace curtains, wallpaper, wool carpet, large windows facing mountains, large balconies facing ocean

RATES, RESERVATIONS, & RESTRICTIONS

Deposit: Credit card or 50% of bill; must cancel 72 hours in advance
Discounts: Long stays, groups, AAA, former guests, some off-season discounts subject to availability; extra person $25
Credit Cards: MC, V
Check-In/Out: 3/11
Smoking: No
Pets: No
Kids: In cottage

Minimum Stay: 2 nights on weekends, none in off-season
Open: All year
Host: Christa Stapp
39247 Hwy. 1
Westport, CA 95488
(707) 961-1660
Fax: (707) 961-1677
www.dehaven-valley-farm.com
dehaven@dehaven-valley-farm.com

HOWARD CREEK RANCH, Westport

Overall: ★★★★	Room Quality: C	Value: A	Price: $75–$160

This 40-acre oceanfront farm has accommodations ranging from pretty rooms in the 1871 farmhouse and the 1880 carriage house to a separate redwood beach house, a cabin built around a beached boat, and a rustic meadow cabin from which you walk to the commode. The ranch is populated by horses, cows, sheep, and llamas, plus lots of wildlife—deer, porcupines, bears, bobcats, and birds. The Griggs serve a farm breakfast that varies but often includes bacon, sausage, hotcakes, fried potatoes, grits, and baked apples with granola and whipped cream.

SETTING & FACILITIES

Location: 28 mi. north of Mendocino and 3 mi. north of Westport on Hwy. 1 (turn right after milepost 80.4), 4 hours north of San Francisco
Near: Beach, old-growth redwoods, Sinkyome Wilderness State Park

Building: Victorian farmhouse built in 1871, 7 other buildings

Grounds: 40 acres w/ lawn, award-winning flower gardens

Public Space: Parlor, library, game room, DR

Food & Drink: Full ranch breakfast served 9 a.m. in DR

Recreation: Swimming on premises, whale- and bird-watching, tide pooling, horseback riding on beach, biking, deep-sea/surf fishing

Amenities & Services: Large hot tub, pool table, barbecue, piano and organ, domestic livestock, wildlife, ocean and mountain views, private parking, massage

ACCOMMODATIONS

Units: 11 guest rooms, including 3 suites

All Rooms: Homemade quilts

Some Rooms: Fireplace, woodstove, four-poster, microwave, fridge, outdoor (covered) Jacuzzi, skylight, private deck, balcony, original 6-ft.-long claw-foot tub, extra bed (1), private bath (8)

Bed & Bath: Kings, queens, doubles

Favorites: Redwood Suite, w/ 2 floors, BR w/ king bed upstairs, large skylights, downstairs LR, freestanding fireplace, microwave, fridge, ocean view, Jacuzzi

Comfort & Decor: Rooms individually decorated w/ antiques, handcrafted redwood interiors, Victorian wallpaper, old-growth redwood finished floors, antique rugs, plush carpet

RATES, RESERVATIONS, & RESTRICTIONS

Deposit: Half of bill; must cancel 7 days in advance; cancellation fee 3% of credit card deposit

Discounts: Winter (inquire); extra person $15

Credit Cards: AE, MC, V

Check-In/Out: 2/11, late check-out by arrangement

Smoking: No

Pets: Dogs, by prior arrangement

Kids: Not suitable

Minimum Stay: 2 nights on holiday weekends

Open: All year

Hosts: Charles and Sally Grigg
P.O. Box 121
40501 Hwy. 1
Westport, CA 95488
(707) 964-6725
Fax: (707) 964-1603
www.howardcreekranch.com

Zone 2
Wine Country

Starting at the north end of San Francisco Bay, including Napa County, west and north to Sonoma and Lake Counties, then north and west to the inland portions of Mendocino County.

Cities and Towns Napa County, including towns of Yountville, St. Helena, and Calistoga; Sonoma County, including Sonoma, Glen Ellen, Kenwood, Santa Rosa, Petaluma, Sebastopol, Occidental, Guerneville, Healdsburg, Geyserville, and Cloverdale; Lake County, including Lakeport; inland Mendocino County, including Hopland and Boonville.

Attractions Wines, vines, redwoods, beaches, and world-class restaurants and shops; **Napa Valley**, chic and touristy, comfortably seen from the **Wine Train**; the **Sonoma Mission** and the pre–gold rush Mexican adobes around its **plaza**; Jack London's tragically beautiful **Beauty Ranch** near Glen Ellen; river rafting and canoeing down the **Russian River; Calistoga**, with hot springs, mud baths, gliders, and hot air balloons; Robert Louis Stevenson's home and state park north of Calistoga; **Santa Rosa**, home of Luther Burbank; **Healdsburg**, small, smart, and hip; **Petaluma's** restored waterfront; rural **Boonville**, center of the **Anderson Valley** wine region.

Contact Information Napa Valley Wine Train, (800) 253-2111; Napa Valley Conference and Visitors Bureau, (707) 226-7459 (www.napavalley.com/nvcvb.html); Sonoma Valley Visitors Bureau, (707) 996-1090 (www.visitsonoma.com); Petaluma Visitors Program (www.petaluma.org/visitor); Russian River Region Visitors Bureau (www.russianriver.org); Greater Santa Rosa Conference and Visitors Bureau (www.visitsantarosa.com); Lake County Information and Visitor Center, (800) LAKESIDE (www.lakecounty.com); Anderson Valley Chamber of Commerce, (707) 895-2379.

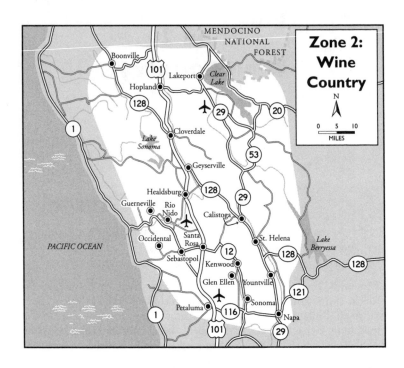

ANDERSON CREEK INN, Boonville

Overall: ★★★½	Room Quality: B	Value: B	Price: $110–$170

Those who eschew Victoriana, couldn't care less about trendy, and love big, wide-open landscapes in a country setting should try the Anderson Creek Inn. Essentially a sprawling ranch house on 16 acres in the lovely Anderson Valley, the inn has five rooms that are very, very large and have fireplaces. All five have king-size beds and private baths. The swimming pool and patio are attractive, and the friendly innkeepers provide bikes and helmets so you can toodle around the countryside when you're not busy petting llamas or hanging out in the tree house. Breakfast is served in the dining room or in the two guest rooms that have dining facilities. A typical menu includes bacon-broccoli frittata, apple cream cake, and a medley of fresh fruit.

SETTING & FACILITIES

Location: Just past Boonville and south of Hwy. 128: after crossing small concrete bridge, take first left and go 1.75 mi. to inn sign and follow signs to parking lot
Near: Wineries and wine tasting, Hendy Woods State Park, Boonville shops, 30 min. to Mendocino coast
Building: Contemporary California ranch house
Grounds: 16 acres of ranchland at the junction of 2 creeks, gardens, fishpond, friendly farm animals—horses, pigs, sheep, goats, pigs, and llamas
Public Space: Large LR and DR with oversized fireplace; courtyards and patios
Food & Drink: Full breakfast served at 9 a.m. in DR or in 2 guest rooms w/dining areas
Recreation: Biking (bicycles and helmets provided), swimming, horseshoes
Amenities & Services: Evening sherry, wine, and hors d'oeuvres beside swimming pool, in room, or in adult-sized tree house in a big oak tree overlooking the creek, private parking, disabled access, concierge service for reservations

ACCOMMODATIONS

Units: 5 guest rooms, 3 larger than average
All Rooms: Private bath, views, privacy
Some Rooms: Fireplace (3), VCR (1)
Bed & Bath: Kings, robes, claw-foot tub (1)
Favorites: Meadow Room Suite, w/ fireplace, windows on 3 sides, easy access to pool and cabana, antique dining set for in-room breakfast service
Comfort & Decor: Rooms individually decorated w/ mix of antique and contemporary furniture, including a wrought-iron four-poster bed w/ canopy, love seat, wicker accents, a claw-foot tub in Courtyard Room

RATES, RESERVATIONS, & RESTRICTIONS

Deposit: Credit card guarantee; must cancel 72 hours in advance
Discounts: Long stays, off-season specials; extra person $25
Credit Cards: MC, V
Check-In/Out: 4–6/11, late check-out by arrangement
Smoking: No

Pets: By arrangement, $20
Kids: OK
Minimum Stay: 2 nights on weekends
May 1–Oct. 31, 3 on holiday weekends
Open: All year
Hosts: Rod and Nancy Graham
P.O. Box 217

12050 Anderson Valley Way
Boonville, CA 95415
(707) 895-3091
(800) 552-6202
Fax: (707) 895-9466
www.andersoncreekinn.com
innkeeper@andersoncreekinn.com

BOONVILLE HOTEL & RESTAURANT, Boonville

Overall: ★★★½	Room Quality: B	Value: B	Price: $75–$200

The Boonville Hotel isn't for everyone—not a teddy bear in sight—but if you love simple, clean lines, white walls, bright abstract paintings, and sublime food, this is your place. The building is a historic roadhouse and hotel in the heart of Mendocino County's beautiful Anderson Valley, famous for some of California's best wineries, apples, and sheep. The hotel interior was recently remodeled from designs by the hotel's executive chef in a Shaker style using local artisans and artists. Nearby Hendy Woods offers visitors an opportunity to appreciate California's famous redwoods. A light continental breakfast of juice, fresh fruit, cereal, toast and bagels, and coffee is served in the bar area, and espresso is available.

SETTING & FACILITIES

Location: On Main St. (Hwy. 128) in downtown Boonville at Lambert Lane, 2.5 hours north of San Francisco
Near: Small airport, redwoods, wineries, Mendocino coast
Building: Historic 2-story wooden roadhouse/hotel and restaurant, built in 1862 and recently remodeled, a new creekside annex w/ 2 suites behind the main building
Grounds: 2 acres of rolling hills, vegetable and herb gardens, gazebo
Public Space: Parlor w/ fireplace, games, magazines, restaurant, noted wood-crafted bar

Food & Drink: Cont'l breakfast served in the bar area 8:30–9:30 a.m., adjoining restaurant open for lunch and dinner using fresh ingredients from house vegetable garden and local organic farms
Recreation: Biking, tennis, wine tasting, Saturday farmers' market with local produce, cheeses, and crafts held in hotel parking lot May–Oct.
Amenities & Services: Fresh flowers displayed in local pottery, handmade furniture by local craftspeople; on-premises salon for haircuts, massages, and manicures; private parking, disabled access

ACCOMMODATIONS

Units: 10 guest rooms—6 rooms and 2 suites upstairs in main building, 2 suites w/ sitting areas in detached annex
All Rooms: Private bath, wooden shutters, colorful duvet cover, no TV

or phone
Some Rooms: Private balcony, sleeper sofa, skylight, garden views, private screened porch, extra twin (1)

Bed & Bath: Queens and doubles, Italian plumbing fixtures, some tub/showers
Favorites: The 2 Creekside Suites, w/ private entrance and yard, disabled-accessible and child- and pet-friendly; No. 2 in the hotel, a large and spacious suite w/ sitting room, bar, private balcony, and geometric blond wood and ebony bed and matching armoire made by a local artisan
Comfort & Decor: "Shaker-inspired" furnishings, austere white walls, pale oak floors, and splashes of vibrant color, many handcrafted details such as a steel shower curtain rod, a marble star set into the bathroom tile, all-natural materials in linens and towels, and natural wood venetian blinds

RATES, RESERVATIONS, & RESTRICTIONS

Deposit: Credit card number; must cancel 7 days in advance
Discounts: Long stays, groups on weekdays, room upgrades in off-season
Credit Cards: MC, V
Check-In/Out: 3/noon, late check-out by arrangement
Smoking: No
Pets: OK by arrangement in detached suites
Kids: In detached suites

Minimum Stay: 2 nights on holiday weekends
Open: Closed Jan. 3–Feb. 5
Hosts: John Schmitt and Jeanne Eliades
P.O. Box 326
Hwy. 128 at Lambert Lane
Boonville, CA 95415
(707) 895-2210
Fax: (707) 895-2243
www.boonvillehotel.com

BRANNON COTTAGE INN, Calistoga

Overall: ★★★½	Room Quality: B	Value: B	Price: $90–$200

This is one of the last remaining cottages built by Calistoga's founder, gold rush legend Sam Brannon. His dream was to establish a spa to rival those of the East Coast (like Saratoga, New York, which provided the last half of Calistoga's name). Sam went bankrupt before his dream succeeded, but this delightful cottage is here in its original location, with its white picket fence, its five graceful roof arches crowned by a striking gingerbread gable board, and its inviting wraparound front porch. The Brannon Cottage Inn is unusual for a small Victorian B&B in that each of the light, airy guest rooms has its own entrance and bath. A full buffet breakfast is served in the game room or, weather permitting, outside, and may include a breakfast casserole, plus eggs and ham.

SETTING & FACILITIES

Location: At the northwest edge of downtown Calistoga, half-block west of the main street, 1.5 hours north of San Francisco
Near: Shopping, restaurants, spas, wineries, local history museum
Building: Victorian, gabled single-story house built in 1862, on Nat'l Register of Historic Places

Grounds: Quarter-acre of well-groomed grounds, including rose garden, lemon trees
Public Space: Parlor, game room
Food & Drink: Full buffet breakfast served in parlor 8:30–9:30 a.m., out-doors in the garden in warm weather
Recreation: Biking, tennis, golf, horseback riding, glider rides, wine tasting
Amenities & Services: Sherry, port, fresh flowers, concierge service for reservations, private parking

ACCOMMODATIONS

Units: 6 guest rooms, including 2 suites
All Rooms: Private bath and entrance, clock radio, fridge, AC and ceiling fan, down comforter
Some Rooms: Sleeper sofa (1)
Bed & Bath: Queens
Favorites: All
Comfort & Decor: Rooms individually decorated w/ a mix of antique pine furniture and contemporary white wicker, lace curtains, individually stenciled walls, hardwood floors, and 11-ft. ceilings

RATES, RESERVATIONS, & RESTRICTIONS

Deposit: 1st and last nights' lodging; must cancel 7 days in advance, cancellation fee $20
Discounts: None
Credit Cards: MC, V
Check-In/Out: After 2/11, for late check-out add half of daily rate
Smoking: No
Pets: No
Kids: Over 12
Minimum Stay: 2 nights on weekends
Open: All year
Hosts: Dieter and Ruth Back
P.O. Box 81
109 Wapoo Ave.
Calistoga, CA 94515
(707) 942-4200
www.napalinks.com/website/017/
    brannon2.htm

CHATEAU DE VIE, Calistoga

Overall: ★★★★	Room Quality: B	Value: B	Price: $145–$195

Screened from Highway 128 by dense vegetation and vineyards, this graceful French Country estate on the outskirts of Calistoga is one of the area's newest B&Bs. The furnishings are trés chic in a Ralph Lauren kind of way. Though it's just a few minutes from downtown Calistoga, the site is quiet and rural and, with all the vines, reminiscent of the French countryside. The two and a half acres of formal gardens surrounding the property contain 100 different roses, fruit and nut trees, exotic flowers, areas for sunbathing, and offer views of Mount Saint Helena and the Palisades. A lavish breakfast of fresh-baked scones, breads and muffins, country sausage, and vegetable quiche or eggs Benedict is served in the formal dining room or on the sunny deck.

SETTING & FACILITIES

Location: Just north of Calistoga on Hwy. 128, .25 mile past Tubs Lane
Near: Wineries, antique shopping, restaurants, mud baths and spas
Building: French Country estate built in 1981
Grounds: 2.5 acres of formal gardens surrounded by vineyards with a mix of 5 different bordeaux grapes
Public Space: Parlor w/ fireplace, library

Food & Drink: Morning coffee and tea outside door, full breakfast served at 9 a.m. in DR or on the deck
Recreation: Biking, tennis, golf, horseback riding, hot air ballooning
Amenities & Services: Hot tub, complimentary refreshments from guest fridge, oversized robes, private parking, assistance w/ reservations for winery tours, restaurants, massages

ACCOMMODATIONS

Units: 3 guest rooms
All Rooms: AC, garden and vineyard views
Some Rooms: Four-poster, private bath (2), hall-access bath (1)
Bed & Bath: Queens
Favorites: Mustard Room, w/ four-poster, very large bath w/ views of vineyards and gardens
Comfort & Decor: Rooms individually decorated w/ earth- and jewel-tone colors, hardwood floors w/ rugs, fine linens

RATES, RESERVATIONS, & RESTRICTIONS

Deposit: Credit card to hold reservation; must cancel 7 days in advance
Discounts: Long stays
Credit Cards: AE, MC, V
Check-In/Out: 3/noon, ask at time of reservation for late check-out
Smoking: No
Pets: Well-behaved pets, if in company of owner
Kids: Not suitable
No-Nos: No more than 2 guests per room
Minimum Stay: None
Open: All year
Hosts: Phillip Barragan and Peter Weatherman
3250 State Hwy. 128
Calistoga, CA 94515
(707) 942-6446
Fax: (707) 942-6456
www.chateaudv.com
chateaudv@aol.com

COTTAGE GROVE INN, Calistoga

Overall: ★★★★½	Room Quality: A	Value: B	Price: $195–$245

You'll no doubt want to move right into one of these adorable cottages and stay forever. Lined up side by side in a long parklike setting, they may just look like nice, cute cottages with white wicker rockers on the porches, but step inside and you're in a self-contained world of color and comfort and sybaritic pleasure. The overstuffed chairs are pulled up next to a wood-burning fireplace, the beds are luxurious, and the Jacuzzis are seriously deep, with little bottles of scents to appeal to every sense. Breakfast is a lavish spread of fruit, cereal, pastries, and yogurt that you can eat in the pretty breakfast room or take to your room on a tray.

Setting & Facilities

Location: At the north edge of downtown Calistoga, 1.5 hours north of San Francisco
Near: Hot springs, spas, shopping, restaurants, wineries, local history museum, state parks, petrified forest, balloon rides
Building: 16 recently constructed cottages
Grounds: Landscaped grounds w/ flowers, vines, shrubs and gazebos in a grove of Siberian elms
Public Space: Common room for breakfast and afternoon wine and cheese

Food & Drink: Expanded cont'l breakfast w/ fresh fruit, cereals, freshly baked pastries, yogurt, etc., served in common room 8:30–10 a.m.
Recreation: Biking (2 bikes on premises), golf, glider rides, tennis, horseback riding, 12 hot spring spas
Amenities & Services: Large selection of local wines and cheeses; parking space at each cottage, 1 disabled-accessible cottage, concierge service for restaurants, spas, horseback riding, winery tours

Accommodations

Units: 16 guest rooms in freestanding cottages
All Rooms: Private bath w/ 2-person deep Jacuzzi soaking tubs, front porch w/ 2 wicker rockers, wood-burning fireplace, CD/stereo system, VCR, cable TV, phone, modem line, individual AC and heat, vaulted ceiling, skylight, fridge and wet bar, coffeemaker w/ locally roasted coffee, ironing board and iron
Some Rooms: Extra twin sofa bed (8)
Bed & Bath: Kings and queens, hairdryers, separate showers
Favorites: Each cottage is the same except for art and variations in color schemes
Comfort & Decor: All cottages have antique fir floors, white louvered closets and armoires, custom furniture and fabrics, down comforters and pillows, all-cotton sheets and towels, and guest robes. Each cottage has a "theme" reflected in the selection of fabrics and artwork: for instance, the Architectural Cottage has Beaux Arts architectural drawings and a bed headboard inspired by the pediment from a San Francisco Victorian

Rates, Reservations, & Restrictions

Deposit: 1st night's lodging; must cancel 7 days in advance; $15 cancellation fee
Discounts: None; extra person $50
Credit Cards: AE, D, MC, V
Check-In/Out: 3/11, late check-out if arranged in advance
Smoking: No
Pets: No
Kids: Over 12
Minimum Stay: 2 nights on weekends or holidays
Open: All year
Hosts: Bob and Valerie Beck, Larry and Monica Williams, Tom and Georgie Stimpert
1711 Lincoln Ave.
Calistoga, CA 94515
(707) 942-8400
(800) 799-2284
www.cottagegrove.com
innkeeper@cottagegrove.com

THE ELMS, Calistoga

Overall: ★★★½	Room Quality: B	Value: B	Price: $125–$200

On a quiet, tree-lined, neighborhood street, this perfectly restored French Victorian mansion built in 1871 is the last of the "Great Eight" homes that graced historical Calistoga. There are four guest rooms in the main house and three in the adjacent carriage house, small to medium-large in size. All have different, interesting features such as a lace-covered Versailles canopy bed, French doors and windows leading to a private patio, a skylight and dormer window seat, and Victorian tin ceilings. Four have spa tubs. Katherine Hepburn slept in the Palisades Garden room during a movie filmed at the Elms. Perhaps she also dined on the baked pears, sour cream coffeecake, and elaborate entrées the inn is noted for.

SETTING & FACILITIES

Location: Residential neighborhood just west of downtown Calistoga, 1.5 hours north of San Francisco
Near: Hot springs, wineries, restaurants, galleries, local history museum, Old Faithful geyser, state parks
Building: French Victorian mansion built in 1871, listed in Nat'l Register of Historic Places
Grounds: Spacious grounds located on the Napa River next to a city park, lawns, white picket fence, brick patios, lawn chairs, and hammock

Public Space: Parlor w/ fireplace, sitting room, gazebo, patio
Food & Drink: Multicourse breakfast served 8:30–9:30 a.m. in DR
Recreation: Biking, ballooning, glider rides, golf, horseback riding, swimming, tennis
Amenities & Services: Afternoon wine, cheese, and hors d'oeuvres served in parlor, coffee or tea in rooms, decanter of port in room, chocolates at bedtime, robes, private parking, concierge service for reservations

ACCOMMODATIONS

Units: 7 guest rooms, 2 larger than average, 1 minisuite
All Rooms: Private bath, cable TV, AC, down comforter
Some Rooms: Fireplace, four-poster canopy bed, fridge, VCR
Bed & Bath: Kings and queens, spa tubs (4)
Favorites: Le Chambre, w/ private balcony, wicker love seat under the elms, marble gas fireplace, queen lace-topped

canopy bed; Carriage House, large room w/ king brass bed, fireplace, leather sofa, recliner chair, kitchenette, French doors and windows w/ view of Napa River, private patio, double shower
Comfort & Decor: Rooms individually decorated w/ antiques and some contemporary touches, lots of pillows, reading lamps, carpets

RATES, RESERVATIONS, & RESTRICTIONS

Deposit: Credit card; must cancel 7 days in advance; cancellation fee $20
Discounts: Weekday business

travelers
Credit Cards: MC, V
Check-In/Out: 3–6/11

Smoking: No
Pets: No
Kids: Not suitable
Minimum Stay: 2 nights on weekends, 3 on major holidays, 4 on holiday weekends
Open: Jan. 22–Jan. 4
Hosts: Stephen and Karla Wyle

1300 Cedar St.
Calistoga, CA 94515
(707) 942-9476
(800) 235-4316
Fax: (707) 942-9479
www.theelms.com
103702.1043@compuserve.com

FOOTHILL HOUSE, Calistoga

Overall: ★★★★½	Room Quality: B	Value: B	Price: $165–$300

Small but darn near perfect, this B&B has three spacious, beautifully appointed suites in the main house, and the area's most romantic cottage just up the hill. In fact, romance is the theme here. Fireplaces that can be viewed from four-poster beds, love seats, Jacuzzis with a view—this is a likely spot to fan those embers. On the other hand, if you prefer to feed your embers, co-owner Doris Beckert is a fabulous cook who will ply you with her breakfast specialties, wonderful appetizers in the afternoon, and fresh cookies at night.

SETTING & FACILITIES

Location: Just past Calistoga on Hwy. 128 (Foothill Blvd.), 1.5 hours north of San Francisco
Near: Hot springs, spas, shopping, restaurants, galleries, wineries, local history museum, state parks, petrified forest
Building: Turn-of-the-century farmhouse, remodeled w/ separate cottage, private entrances, decks
Grounds: Country setting in the foothills of Calistoga, surrounded by 1.5 acres of landscaped gardens, gazebo, oaks, redwoods and Douglas firs, waterfalls and fishponds
Public Space: Sunroom, spa
Food & Drink: Full breakfast, 8:30–9:30 a.m., served in room, on private deck, in gazebo, in sunroom, or on patio
Recreation: Biking, horseback riding, glider rides, tennis, golf
Amenities & Services: Hot tub, sherry, wine, hors d'oeuvres, coffeepot, robes, private parking, concierge service to make reservations and plan itineraries

ACCOMMODATIONS

Units: 4 guest rooms, all larger than average, including 3 suites and 1 cottage
All Rooms: Private bath, sitting area, fireplace, TV/VCR, cable, phone, AC, ceiling fan, four-poster
Some Rooms: Extra bed (3); Cottage has kitchen and wet bar, washer/dryer; Evergreen Suite has a bay window, private patio w/ tiled waterfall
Bed & Bath: Kings, queen (1), Jacuzzi/shower (3), tub/shower (1)

Favorites: Quail's Roost Cottage is 1,000 square feet; private, w/ open-beamed ceilings, skylights; Jacuzzi and shower look out a glass wall to a waterfall coming down the hillside; fully equipped kitchen, washer/dryer, private patio

Comfort & Decor: Antique oak and pine furniture, Laura Ashley linens, carpet, color schemes for each room centered around handmade quilts on four-poster beds

RATES, RESERVATIONS, & RESTRICTIONS

Deposit: 1 night's lodging; must cancel 8 days in advance; $10 cancellation fee
Discounts: None
Credit Cards: AE, D, MC, V
Check-In/Out: 3/11, late check-out noon
Smoking: No
Pets: No
Kids: In 1 room, 12 and over
Minimum Stay: 2 nights on weekends

Open: Closed Thanksgiving and Christmas Days
Hosts: Doris and Gus Beckert
3037 Foothill Blvd.
Calistoga, CA 94515
(707) 942-5692
(800) 942-6933
Fax: (707) 942-4592
www.foothillhouse.com

LA CHAUMIERE, Calistoga

Overall: ★★★	Room Quality: C	Value: B	Price: $150–$225

In a charming older neighborhood, La Chaumiere is a quiet hideaway that is popular with other innkeepers from outside the area. Innkeeper Gary Venturi's love of gardening, cooking, and design stand him in good stead for this intimate, but not cramped, getaway place. The sounds of birds and water and the bliss of the unique tree house in a redwood will keep bringing you back, whether you come for the local mud baths or to write the Great American Novel.

SETTING & FACILITIES

Location: Half a block west of downtown Calistoga in a quiet residential neighborhood, 1.5 hours north of San Francisco
Near: Hot springs, spas, restaurants, shopping, galleries, wineries, a local history museum, state parks, petrified forest
Building: A 1930s Cotswold cottage w/ peaked roof and arched windows, an adjoining cottage suite

Grounds: Well-tended grounds w/ gardens, a courtyard, and towering incense cedars
Public Space: DR, LR, courtyard w/ brick patio, redwood deck, groupings of tables and chairs, a 2nd-story deck/tree house in a redwood tree
Food & Drink: Full gourmet breakfast served in DR or courtyard at 9 a.m.
Recreation: Biking, tennis, golf, glider rides, spas, wine tasting

Amenities & Services: Hot tub, barbecue, wine and hors d'oeuvres in evening, port in rooms for a nightcap; concierge services for spa and restaurant reservations, wine tours, on-premises massages, facials, and bodyworks avail. in summer

ACCOMMODATIONS

Units: 3 guest rooms—1 cottage w/ LR, BR, and kitchen, 1 single room, 1 minisuite w/ sitting room
All Rooms: Private bath, AC
Some Rooms: TV/VCR, wood-burning stove, fridge, sleeper sofa, kitchen w/ modern range, French doors
Bed & Bath: Queens, king (1), tub/shower (1), shower only (2)
Favorites: The Cottage, very romantic and private, w/ king bed, wood-burning stove in fireplace, TV and VCR, and view of the mountains across an open field of valley oaks
Comfort & Decor: An eclectic mix, including wicker, a French walnut antique bed, marble-topped tables, a large mirror framed by an antique pool cue rack, and a pull-chain w.c.

RATES, RESERVATIONS, & RESTRICTIONS

Deposit: Total amount; must cancel 7 days in advance; $20 cancellation fee
Discounts: None; extra person $30
Credit Cards: MC, V, personal checks
Check-In/Out: 4–6/11, late check-in/out by prior arrangement
Smoking: No
Pets: No
Kids: No
Minimum Stay: 2 nights on weekends, 3 on holiday weekends
Open: All year
Host: Gary Venturi
1301 Cedar St.
Calistoga, CA 94515
(707) 942-5139
(800) 474-6800
www.lachaumiere.com
calist9578@aol.com

SCOTT COURTYARD, Calistoga

Overall: ★★★½	Room Quality: B	Value: B	Price: $125–$175

This is a place for those who love the 1930s and 1940s, eschew Victorian bibelots and lace curtains, but kind of miss chenille bedspreads and pink flamingos. The Scotts obviously had great fun scouring antique shops and flea markets to find the array of memorabilia they have artfully sprinkled around for their guests' delight. However, it is the privacy and spaciousness of the accommodations, in combination with the large pool and poolside social room, that have made this inn so popular. The six suites in 1920s and 1940s California bungalow style, peach-and-white with black-and-white awnings, are built around the pool and gardens. The complex has the aura of a private villa. The breakfast menu changes daily but might include ham with soft-boiled eggs and bread pudding.

SETTING & FACILITIES

Location: At the northwest edge of downtown Calistoga, 2 blocks from the main street, 1.5 hours from San Francisco
Near: Hot springs, spas, wineries, restaurants, galleries, petrified forest, local history museum, state parks, glider rides, jogging path
Building: 1920s–1940s California bungalows, peach-and-white wood and stucco w/ black-and-white awnings
Grounds: Secluded gardens w/ fruit and walnut trees, many roses, Confederate jasmine and grapevines, walkways,

lawns, secluded sitting areas, gazebo
Public Space: Poolside social room w/ vaulted ceiling and fireplace, aviary, art studio w/ TV, music and art projects, library
Food & Drink: Full breakfast menu served in bistro-style kitchen 9–10 a.m.
Recreation: Biking, tennis, golf, wine tasting
Amenities & Services: Swimming pool, wine and snacks served afternoons in social room; cold drinks, soda, and coffee always avail.; private parking

ACCOMMODATIONS

Units: 6 guest rooms, including 3 suites in 1 building, 3 bungalows w/ kitchens
All Rooms: LR, BR, private bath and entrance, AC, irons, coffeemakers, cable TV
Some Rooms: Fireplace, four-poster, extra bed (4), sleeper sofa, fridge
Bed & Bath: Queens, robes, hairdryers, claw-foot tub (1), tub (4), oversized tile shower (1)
Favorites: Tropical Bungalow is close to the pool, w/ a Balinese feeling—rattan chairs, large round glass-topped

coffee table held up by carved Balinese figures, leather sofa, kitchen w/ black-and-green palm-leaf wallpaper, black-and-white floor, and a mini Wedgwood stove
Comfort & Decor: All rooms w/ different decor emphasizing 1930s and 1940s styles: a tropical, Southern California kind of aesthetic, w/ original art, oriental rugs, Mexican tile floor, antiques, vintage rattan furniture, hardwood floors, French doors, 1940s tilework

RATES, RESERVATIONS, & RESTRICTIONS

Deposit: 1st night's lodging; must cancel 7 days in advance; cancellation fee $12.50
Discounts: Dec.–March $99 special weekday walk-in rate, April/May/Nov. $110 special weekday walk-in rate
Credit Cards: AE, D, MC, V
Check-In/Out: 3/11:30
Smoking: No
Pets: No
Kids: Over 7

Minimum Stay: 2 nights on weekends
Open: All year
Hosts: Derek and Robin Werrett, owners and innkeepers
1443 2nd St.
Calistoga, CA 94515
(707) 942-0948
(800) 942-1515
Fax: (707) 942-5102
www.scottcourtyard.com

VINTAGE TOWERS B&B, Cloverdale

Overall: ★★★   Room Quality: B   Value: B   Price: $75–$160

The quiet, small town of Cloverdale is the junction for roads leading to the coast, the redwoods, and the wine country. This interesting Queen Anne Victorian is located on one of the town's neighborhood streets. It has three unusual towers: a round one, a square one, and a hexagonal one. Each tower contains a suite with a sitting area, and there are five other guest rooms as well. The inn's hosts plan special events year-round, such as murder mystery weekends, wine-maker dinners, and barrel-tasting weekends. After you've captured your murderer and drunk your barrel, you can rest on the nice 40-foot veranda and make the porch swing squeak.

SETTING & FACILITIES

Location: In Cloverdale, from Hwy. 101 take Citrus Fair Dr. exit, turn left at the light, then right on Cloverdale Blvd., then right on 3rd St.; inn is at corner of 3rd and Main Sts.
Near: Wineries, redwoods, coast
Building: 1901 Queen Anne Victorian on Nat'l Register of Historic Places
Grounds: Neighborhood oversized corner lot w/ landscaping
Public Space: Parlor, library w/ fireplace and TV, upstairs sitting room,
40-ft. wraparound veranda, gazebo
Food & Drink: Full breakfast served in DR at 9 a.m.
Recreation: Biking, tennis, golf, boating
Amenities & Services: Afternoon tea and lemonade, evening milk and cookies, TV/VCR in library; concierge service for reservations, special house events—murder mystery weekends, wine-maker dinners, barrel-tasting of upcoming wine releases

ACCOMMODATIONS

Units: 8 guest rooms, including 3 suites
All Rooms: AC, heat
Some Rooms: Private balcony, private bath (6), shared bath (2)
Bed & Bath: Queens, king (1), double (1)
Favorites: Vintage Tower Suite, w/ Eastlake Victorian furnishings, claw-foot
tub/shower, sitting room, private porch with telescope
Comfort & Decor: Rooms individually decorated w/ antiques, collectibles, brass, oak, maple, and white iron beds, matching armoires, marble-topped nightstands, wicker furniture

RATES, RESERVATIONS, & RESTRICTIONS

Deposit: Credit card or personal check within 1 week of making reservation; must cancel 5 days in advance
Discounts: Winter weekdays, Internet specials; extra person $35
Credit Cards: AE, D, MC, V
Check-In/Out: 4–8/11, early or late check-in by arrangement, late check-out by arrangement
Smoking: No
Pets: No
Kids: OK

Minimum Stay: 2 nights on weekends
May–Nov.
Open: All year
Hosts: Cindy and Gus Wolter
302 N. Main St.
Cloverdale, CA 95425

(707) 894-4543
(888) 886-9377
www.vintagetowers.com
gus@vintagetowers.com

CAMPBELL RANCH INN, Geyserville

Overall: ★★★★	Room Quality: B	Value: B	Price: $125–$225

On top of a hill surrounded by 1,000 acres of vineyards, this inn is a combination resort and B&B. There's swimming and rafting on the Russian River and water sports and fishing on Lake Sonoma, just a few miles down the road. The bright lights of Healdsburg with its good restaurants and shops are not much farther. Campbell Ranch Inn is a modern, nicely furnished property with many amenities. Its five spacious guestrooms all have special features—one has a piano, for instance, and the cottage in a separate building has a fireplace, stereo, tub for two, and a hot tub on the deck overlooking the vineyards. You actually have a choice of juices, entrées, and breads for breakfast, which you select from a menu, and each evening there's a homemade pie or cake for dessert.

SETTING & FACILITIES

Location: From Hwy. 101, take Canyon Rd. exit in Geyserville and go west 1.6 mi., 1.5 hours north of San Francisco
Near: Dry Creek wineries, Lake Sonoma, Russian River, airport, shopping, restaurants, Armstrong Redwoods State Reserve
Building: Split-level traditional home, cottage, built in 1968
Grounds: 35 acres on a hilltop in the Dry Creek wine region, gardens, greenhouse
Public Space: Family room w/ games and puzzles, TV, VCR, and satellite dish,
LR w/ vaulted ceiling and fireplace, dining area off kitchen, terrace
Food & Drink: Full breakfast from menu 8–10 a.m. in dining area
Recreation: Bicycles, swimming, horseshoes, Ping-Pong, tennis, and model trains on premises; nearby ballooning, horseback riding, fishing, water sports, golf
Amenities & Services: 20-by-40-ft. swimming pool, large hot tub, professional tennis courts, lemonade and iced tea always avail., evening dessert of homemade pie or cake, fruit, fresh flowers, robes, private parking, massage

ACCOMMODATIONS

Units: 5 guest rooms, all larger than average, including 1 suite, cottage w/ 2 BRs
All Rooms: Private bath, sitting area
Some Rooms: Dressing area, fire-
place, hot tub on deck, balcony, fridge, piano, stereo
Bed & Bath: Kings; cottage has king and double

Favorites: The Cottage, w/ fireplace, fridge, deck w/ hot tub for 2, soaking tub for 2 in front of window overlooking vineyards and sunset
Comfort & Decor: Rooms individually decorated w/ photos of world travel, curtains w/ blackout drapes at sliding doors to balconies, rugs, tiled fireplace, overstuffed chairs, wicker and hardwood furniture, reading lamps

RATES, RESERVATIONS, & RESTRICTIONS

Deposit: Credit card; must cancel 3 days in advance; no cancellation fee
Discounts: None; extra person $25
Credit Cards: AE, MC, V
Check-In/Out: After 1/noon, late check-out by arrangement
Smoking: No
Pets: No
Kids: Over 8
Minimum Stay: 2 nights on week-

ends, 3 on holiday weekends
Open: All year
Hosts: Jerry and Mary Jane Campbell
1475 Canyon Rd.
Geyserville, CA 95441
(707) 857-3476
(800) 959-3878
Fax: (707) 857-3239
www.campbellranchinn.com

HOPE–MERRILL HOUSE AND HOPE BOSWORTH HOUSE, Geyserville

Overall: ★★★★½   Room Quality: A   Value: B   Price: $111–$174

You might think of these two homes facing each other across the street as the gorgeous sister and the merely pretty one. Hope-Merrill, a meticulously restored two-story Eastlake and Stick Victorian design, gets star billing and, in fact, won a beauty contest of sorts—first place as an outstanding B&B in a National Trust for Historic Preservation competition. The house, built entirely of redwood, has the original quarter-sawn oak graining on all doors and woodwork, the original Lincrusta-Walton wainscoting, and Bradbury silk-screened wallpapers. The Hope-Bosworth House, a pretty Queen Anne Craftsman style, is more informal, but charming and cheerful—you know, the sister who had to develop personality. Guests here share access to the lovely pool and garden area at Hope-Merrill. For wine-making wannabes, the inn offers a unique four-day wine event where the guests spend two days in the fall picking and crushing grapes, then two more days in the spring blending and bottling them. At the end, participants get a case each of red and white wine to take home.

SETTING & FACILITIES

Location: In Alexander Valley, take Hwy. 101 to Exit 128, East Geyserville; at end of ramp, turn right onto Geyserville Ave. and drive just over 1 mi.
Near: Vineyards, wineries, Russian River, Lake Sonoma, shopping, restaurants

Building: Hope-Merrill is 1870 Eastlake Stick Victorian, Hope-Bosworth is 1904 Queen Anne Craftsman
Grounds: 2 acres w/ pool, vineyard, gardens
Public Space: Parlors, DRs, library, gazebo
Food & Drink: Full country breakfast

served at 9 a.m. in both DRs, coffee and tea served at 8 a.m.
Recreation: Biking, tennis, golf
Amenities & Services: Swimming pool, private parking, disabled access, concierge service for reservations, wine, beer, and beverages

ACCOMMODATIONS

Units: Hope-Merrill has 8 guest rooms, including 1 suite; Hope-Bosworth has 4 guest rooms
All Rooms: Private bath
Some Rooms: Fireplace, four-poster, chaise lounge, sitting room, private entrance, skylight, ceiling fan, French doors
Bed & Bath: Hope-Merrill, queens; Hope-Bosworth, queens, claw-foot tub/showers, Jacuzzis for 2, double showers, whirlpool tub/shower
Favorites: Hope-Merrill has the Sterling Suite, w/ four-poster cherry-wood

bed, alcove w/ 2 chairs, large sitting area w/ couch and 2 chairs, fireplace, Bradbury & Bradbury wallpaper, lace curtains, private entrance from pool, and private entrance from parking lot; Hope-Bosworth has the Oak Room, w/ ceiling fan, wicker chairs, view of Geyser Peak and Saint Helena
Comfort & Decor: Rooms individually decorated w/ antiques, wall coverings hand-screened by Bruce Bradbury, hardwood floor and area rugs, antique light fixtures, original wainscoting

RATES, RESERVATIONS, & RESTRICTIONS

Deposit: 1st night's lodging in advance; 50% of bill for multiple nights; must cancel 7 days in advance; $10 cancellation charge/night
Discounts: Seasonal specials; extra person $30
Credit Cards: AE, D, MC, V
Check-In/Out: After 3:30/11
Smoking: No
Pets: No
Kids: Not suitable
Minimum Stay: 2 nights on week-

ends, no minimum Dec. 1–March 31 except holiday weekends
Open: All year
Hosts: Cosette and Ron Scheiber
P.O. Box 42
21253 and 21238 Geyserville Ave.
Geyserville, CA 95441
(707) 857-3356
(800) 825-4233
Fax: (707) 857-4673
www.hope-inns.com
info@hope-inns.com

BELTANE RANCH, Glen Ellen

Overall: ★★★★	Room Quality: B	Value: B	Price: $130–$210

As you drive up the long, winding road to the pretty yellow ranch house, you'll feel like you're about to step into the setting for some Western like *Shane*. But the cattle and sheep are long gone, supplanted by olives and the chardonnay grapes that produce the prizewinning Kenwood Beltane

Ranch Chardonnay. With the Mayacamas Mountains in the background and the house itself surrounded by extensive flower and vegetable gardens, the views from each room are extensive and admirable. Guests come here because they enjoy the quiet and the feeling of being at a real working ranch. And nothing beats sitting on the porch swing on the veranda after a hard day's leisure, sippin' some of the local vintage, watching the sun go down beyond the Valley of the Moon.

SETTING & FACILITIES

Location: 8 mi. north of Sonoma on the east side of Hwy. 12, 1.25 hours north of San Francisco
Near: Wineries, Jack London State Historic Park, Sonoma Valley Regional Park, shopping, restaurants
Building: 2-story Southern Louisiana ranch-style house built in 1892 w/ wraparound veranda, cottage
Grounds: 1,600-acre working ranch with vineyards, olive trees, large lawn, gardens, vegetable garden

Public Space: DR/LR w/ fireplace
Food & Drink: Full breakfast served 8–10 a.m. in DR, outside in nice weather
Recreation: Tennis and volleyball courts, miles of hiking trails on premises; bird- and wildlife-watching, golf, warm springs
Amenities & Services: Cookies, fridge for guests' use; concierge service for reservations

ACCOMMODATIONS

Units: 6 guest rooms, including 3 suites
All Rooms: Private bath and entrance
Some Rooms: Sitting room w/ daybed, wood-burning stove, hammock
Bed & Bath: Queens
Favorites: No. 2 upstairs, large roman-

tic room w/ view, couch, oak armoire, vanity
Comfort & Decor: Spacious rooms individually decorated w/ local art, antiques, wooden shutters, hardwood floors, carpet

RATES, RESERVATIONS, & RESTRICTIONS

Deposit: 1 night's lodging; must cancel 5 days in advance; no cancellation fee
Discounts: None
Credit Cards: None
Check-In/Out: 2/11, late check-out by arrangement
Smoking: No
Pets: No
Kids: 5 and over

Minimum Stay: None
Open: All year
Hosts: Rosemary Wood, owner; Anne Marie Soulier, mgr.
P.O. Box 395
11775 Sonoma Hwy.
Glen Ellen, CA 95442
(707) 996-6501

GAIGE HOUSE, Glen Ellen

Overall: ★★★★★	Room Quality: A	Value: B	Price: $195–$355

This is an inn other innkeepers speak of reverently. The turn-of-the-century Victorian in a creekside setting has been stripped to its handsome bones, artfully restored, and then furnished in a subtly beautiful and cosmopolitan mixture of West African, Indonesian, and Southeast Asian Plantation styles. The owners have collected art from around the world, commissioned hand-carved teak furniture from Indonesia, and here and there tucked in small delights such as a Japanese fountain gurgling gently in a courtyard. Not a teddy bear in sight: it's a place for people who don't usually like B&Bs. The pool and grounds are remarkably pretty, and breakfasts are prepared by a professional chef.

SETTING & FACILITIES

Location: Off Hwy. 12 north from Sonoma (turn left on Arnold Drive; inn is on right just before the town of Glen Ellen), 1.25 hours north of San Francisco

Near: Restaurants, wineries, state parks, balloon rides, shopping

Building: 1890 Queen Anne Italianate, pool house and garden annex recently built

Grounds: 1.5 acres on Calabasas Creek w/ landscaped gardens, herb garden

Public Space: LR, parlor, DR w/ large deck, deck overhanging creek

Food & Drink: Full 2-course breakfast served 8:30–10 a.m. at private tables in DR, professional chef

Recreation: Biking, horseback riding, golf

Amenities & Services: Passes to local health club, hot tub, swimming pool, creekside hammock, complimentary premium Sonoma wines, hors d'oeuvres, cold drinks, hot tea, and fresh cookies always avail., private parking, full-service concierge, massage treatments arranged in room or at the pool

ACCOMMODATIONS

Units: 13 guest rooms, 10 larger than average, including 2 suites; 6 rooms are in the original house, 7 in pool house and the garden annex

All Rooms: Private bath, cable TV, CD player, phone, AC, iron, down pillows and comforter

Some Rooms: Fireplace, four-poster, fridge, daybed (1)

Bed & Bath: Kings and queens, whirlpool baths (3), robes, hairdryers

Favorites: Room 10, w/ teak bed, French bronze reading lamps, Indonesian lazy chair, fireplace, large 2-person shower, whirlpool bath, view of rose gardens and pool, private deck

Comfort & Decor: Rooms individually decorated w/ mix of antiques and museum-quality art, carpet and hardwood floors, designer linens and down comforters

RATES, RESERVATIONS, & RESTRICTIONS

Deposit: 1st night's lodging; must cancel 7 days in advance; no cancellation fee

Discounts: None; extra person $25

Credit Cards: AE, D, MC, V

Check-In/Out: 3–7/11, late check-out

by arrangement

Smoking: No

Pets: No

Kids: Over 12

Minimum Stay: 2 nights on weekends

Open: All year
Hosts: Ken Burnet and Greg Nemrow,
owners; Sue Burnet, mgr.
13540 Arnold Dr.
Glen Ellen, CA 95442

(707) 935-0237
(800) 935-0237
Fax: (707) 935-6411
www.gaige.com
gaige@sprynet.com

GLENELLY INN, Glen Ellen

Overall: ★★★½	Room Quality: B	Value: B	Price: $125–$150

Jack London loved this area for good cause. It has a wild, remote feeling
that you don't get in Napa or Sonoma, and the Glenelly Inn—built in the
1920s for railroad travelers—has that same feel, with its country furnishings, ancient oaks, and a view of the Valley of the Moon from the veranda
outside each room. Kids love it here, and so do honeymooners. The inn is
laid-back and comfortable, without a lot of frou-frou. The innkeeper, who
studied cooking at a Norwegian culinary academy, whips up a mean breakfast, including fresh-squeezed OJ—surely one of the more reliable indicators of a good B&B.

SETTING & FACILITIES

Location: In the village of Glen Ellen in
the Valley of the Moon, just off Arnold
Dr., which connects Hwy. 116 to Hwy.
12; 1.25 hours north of San Francisco
Near: Wineries, restaurants, shopping,
galleries, Jack London State Park, mineral warm springs, hiking trails
Building: 1916 French Colonial-style
inn, w/ wraparound verandas, Stick-
style cottage
Grounds: 1-acre hillside setting w/
deer, oaks, madrones, and wildflowers,
flagstone patio w/ tables, chairs, hammock, swing, gardens
Public Space: Common room w/
cobblestone fireplace and leaded-glass

windows overlooking the Sonoma
Mountains
Food & Drink: Full buffet breakfast
served in common room of the main
building, on the patio, or delivered to
room at 9 a.m., special requests accommodated for earlier or later breakfasts
Recreation: Swimming in warm
springs, hot air ballooning, biking,
tennis, golf
Amenities & Services: Outdoor
Jacuzzi in rose garden, robes, hairdryers, cookies, hot and cold drinks, "I forgot" basket for forgetful travelers,
private parking, massage, aromatherapy,
spa treatments

ACCOMMODATIONS

Units: 8 guest rooms—6 in inn building, 2 in cottage
All Rooms: Private bath, private
entrance onto veranda or deck, ceiling
fan, firm custom mattress, individual
reading lights, 6+ pillows per bed, down

comforter
Some Rooms: Fireplace, claw-foot
tub, four-poster bed, sitting area, couch
Bed & Bath: Queens, double and twin,
roll-away beds and cribs avail.

Favorites: Valley of the Moon, w/ queen brass bed, couch, wood-burning stove, old hotel dresser and armoire, view of sunset from veranda; St. Jean, w/ pine four-poster, light pine furniture, decorated in peach-and-white Laura Ashley

Comfort & Decor: Rooms individually decorated w/ country and antique furnishings, 1 room w/ a hat collection, queen wooden sleigh bed, marble-topped nightstands

RATES, RESERVATIONS, & RESTRICTIONS

Deposit: Credit card; must cancel 7 days in advance; no cancellation fee
Discounts: None; extra person $25
Credit Cards: MC, V
Check-In/Out: 3/11, late check-out by arrangement
Smoking: No
Pets: No
Kids: OK if well-behaved
Minimum Stay: 2 nights on weekends, 3 on holiday weekends

Open: All year
Host: Kristi Hallamore Jeppeson
5131 Warm Springs Rd.
Glen Ellen, CA 95442
(707) 996-6720
www.glenelly.com
glenelly@vom.com

APPLEWOOD INN AND RESTAURANT, Guerneville

Overall: ★★★★½	Room Quality: A	Value: B	Price: $135–$275

Fancy a trip to the Mediterranean, but can't find the time? Indulge yourself with a visit to this small luxury inn complete with villa-style architecture, sunny colors, private patios with well-tended gardens and splashing fountains, and, of course, a pool to recline and dine by. The small restaurant on the premises, specializing in fresh, regional fare, became so popular that a new restaurant was built in 1999. Although there are lots of ways to amuse yourself in the Russian River area, you may decide you're already in the best imaginable spot and never budge.

SETTING & FACILITIES

Location: Just across the Russian River from downtown Guerneville on Hwy. 116, 1.5 hours north of San Francisco
Near: Wineries, Russian River beaches, redwoods
Building: California Mission Revival villas
Grounds: 6-acre hillside setting w/ redwood groves, apple orchards, terraced herb, vegetable, and flower gardens
Public Space: Solarium, sitting room, library, formal DR, game room

Food & Drink: Full breakfast served in DR or by the pool 9–10 a.m., champagne brunch on Sun., gourmet dining in restaurant on premises Tues.–Sat.
Recreation: Swimming, biking, canoeing, massage, wine tasting
Amenities & Services: Swimming pool and hot tub, sunset wine hour, evening turn-down service, fresh flowers, private parking, disabled access, concierge service for reservations, fax, computer hookups, meeting areas

ACCOMMODATIONS

Units: 16 guest rooms, including 7 suites
All Rooms: Private bath, TV, cable, phone
Some Rooms: Patio, balcony, fireplace, four-poster, courtyard w/ fountain
Bed & Bath: Queens, double showers (5), Jacuzzis for 2 (5)
Favorites: Honeymoon Penthouse, w/

private rooftop deck, lofted ceiling w/ tropical fan, wicker chaise lounge, and an iron bed created by a local artisan
Comfort & Decor: Rooms individually decorated w/ warm colors, custom fabrics, original art and antique prints, down comforters and pillows, Egyptian cotton towels and fine hand-pressed linens, carpet

RATES, RESERVATIONS, & RESTRICTIONS

Deposit: 1st night's lodging or, for reservations for 5 or more nights, 1st and last nights' lodging; must cancel 14 days in advance; cancellation fee $20
Discounts: Weekday groups
Credit Cards: AE, D, MC, V
Check-In/Out: 3–10/noon, late checkout by arrangement
Smoking: No
Pets: No
Kids: Not suitable

Minimum Stay: 2 nights on weekends, 3 on holiday weekends
Open: All year
Hosts: Darryl Notter and Jim Caron
13555 Hwy. 116
Guerneville, CA 95446
(707) 869-9093
(800) 555-8509
Fax: (707) 869-9170
www.applewoodinn.com
norton@applewoodinn.com

THE WILLOWS, Guerneville

Overall: ★★★	Room Quality: C	Value: A	Price: $59–$139

On five grassy acres bordering the Russian River, The Willows guest house and campground is a playground for grown-ups. It has a private dock and canoes for guests' use, an outdoor hot tub and sauna, and an open-air kitchen and outdoor barbecue. The guest rooms range from attractive to very basic, but they are clean and comfortable, and some have nice views of the grounds and river . . . and the river is what this whole town seems to live for from spring to fall. If you're looking for a laid-back resort to soak up some rays and hang loose, this may be your kind of place.

SETTING & FACILITIES

Location: Near Hwy. 116 on River Rd. in downtown Guerneville on the Russian River, 1.5 hours north of San Francisco

Near: Russian River, Armstrong Redwoods State Reserve, restaurants, shopping, wineries

Building: Redwood country lodge built in 1940s

Grounds: 5 acres on banks of Russian River, parklike grounds w/ redwoods, willows, maples, dock

Public Space: Common room and library w/ stone fireplace and grand piano, sundecks over the river

Food & Drink: Expanded continental buffet served 8–10:30 a.m. in the common room

Recreation: Swimming, sunbathing, fishing, kayaking, canoeing, golf, tennis, biking

Amenities & Services: Hot tub, barbecue, open-air community kitchen, sauna, private dock w/ canoes and kayaks, community Jacuzzi and sauna, phones, private parking, VCRs in rooms, large video library, masseur seasonally avail.

ACCOMMODATIONS

Units: 13, 1 larger than average

All Rooms: Ceiling fan

Some Rooms: Fireplace, private balcony, private bath (9)

Bed & Bath: Queens, 4 rooms share 2 baths

Favorites: No. 5, w/ small balcony; No. 8, w/ fireplace

Comfort & Decor: Rooms individually decorated w/ antiques and antique photos, country curtains, carpet, old-fashioned country motif

RATES, RESERVATIONS, & RESTRICTIONS

Deposit: Credit card or 1st night's lodging; must cancel 3 days in advance; cancellation fee 1st night's lodging unless room can be rented

Discounts: 7th night free, weekday, off-season rates; extra person $18

Credit Cards: AE, D, MC, V

Check-In/Out: After 2/noon, late check-out by arrangement

Smoking: No

Pets: No

Kids: Not suitable

Minimum Stay: 2 nights on weekends May–Sept.

Open: All year

Host: Rick Reese
P.O. Box 465
15905 River Rd.
Guerneville, CA 95446
(707) 869-2824
(800) 953-2828
Fax: (707) 869-2764
willowsrussianriver.com

BELLE DE JOUR INN, Healdsburg

Overall: ★★★★½   Room Quality: A   Value: B   Price: $165–$275

"Wow" is the spontaneous reaction when you walk into any one of this inn's five cottages. They're that pretty. Each one is spacious, high-ceilinged, and light-filled, with gleaming wood floors, beautiful colors, and a judicious use of showcase antiques. Instead of ponderous Victoriana, the owners have selected simple, clean-lined furniture such as a tall, light pine four-poster bed with a delicate lace canopy, and wicker accents. The Hearns maintain lovely, private grounds with views of woods and rolling hills, offer excellent breakfasts with things like spinach-feta cheese tarts and raspberry kuchen, and even sun-dry the sheets. If you're in the mood, and if he's in the mood, resident cat Ivan the Terrible will let you pet him. By the way, this Belle de Jour is named for a flower, not the movie of the same name.

SETTING & FACILITIES

Location: At the northern edge of Healdsburg, take Hwy. 101 to Dry Creek Rd. exit, turn east, turn left at light onto Healdsburg Ave., go 1 mile, note the Simi winery on left, turn right up tree-lined drive to top of hill
Near: Wineries, redwood groves, restaurants, shopping, Russian River, Lake Sonoma, airport
Building: Innkeepers' residence is 1873 Italianate farmhouse; 4 cottages are gabled 1-story wood-framed structures of various ages; carriage house is 2-story gabled wood-framed structure
Grounds: 6 acres on a hilltop w/ mixed trees, flower and vegetable gardens, expanses of lawn, hammocks and picnic tables
Public Space: Breakfast Room in main house
Food & Drink: Full breakfast served in the breakfast room at 9 a.m., early tea and coffees starting at 7:30 a.m., includes espresso, latte, cappuccino, mocha
Recreation: Biking, tennis, golf, canoeing, kayaking, fishing, bird-watching
Amenities & Services: Wine at check-in, robes, hairdryers, private parking, concierge service for reservations

ACCOMMODATIONS

Units: 5 guest rooms, 3 larger than average, including 4 accommodations in cottages with private entrances, 1 suite entire second floor of carriage house

All Rooms: Private bath, phone, ceiling fan, AC, AM/FM/CD tape player, down comforter

Some Rooms: Fireplace, four-poster, fridge

Bed & Bath: Kings and queens, Jacuzzi tubs for 2 (3), hairdryers

Favorites: Caretaker's Suite, w/ king canopy bed, sitting area w/ fireplace, whirlpool tub for 2 and shower, trellised entry deck w/ view

Comfort & Decor: Rooms individually decorated w/ framed prints, etchings, antiques, pine, rattan and oak furniture, overstuffed love seats, lace curtains, plantation shutters, hardwood floors w/ area rugs

RATES, RESERVATIONS, & RESTRICTIONS

Deposit: 1 night's lodging in advance paid by check, credit card OK for final bill; must cancel 14 days in advance for refund less cancellation fee; cancellation fee $20

Discounts: None

Credit Cards: AE, MC, V

Check-In/Out: 4/11, late check-in/out by arrangement

Smoking: No

Pets: No

Kids: Not suitable

No-Nos: No more than 2 guests per room

Minimum Stay: 2 nights on weekends, 3 on major holidays

Open: All year

Hosts: Tom and Brenda Hearn
16276 Healdsburg Ave.
Healdsburg, CA 95448
(707) 431-9777
Fax: (707) 431-7412
www.belledejourinn.com

CALDERWOOD, Healdsburg

Overall: ★★★★	Room Quality: B	Value: B	Price: $135–$200

The original owners of Calderwood were friends of legendary horticulturist Luther Burbank (a local boy). The fountain, koi ponds, and old rose garden all vie for your attention and invite your contemplation. And what better place to contemplate from than the porch swing on the room-sized front porch? Though the house is a Victorian, it doesn't have the familiar gingerbread, and the result is quietly elegant, a feeling the current owners have carried through in the interior. The handcrafted wall and ceiling papers by Bay Area artisans Bradbury & Bradbury are so eye-catching that you almost have to force yourself to look down to avoid stumbling. Breakfast is served in the formal dining room and sometimes includes eggs Benedict, potatoes, and a special fresh fruit dish. Port and dessert are served in the evening.

SETTING & FACILITIES

Location: 3 blocks north of downtown Healdsburg: from Hwy. 101, take Central Healdsburg exit, go 1 mi. to Grant St., turn left and drive 1 block
Near: Wineries, restaurants, antique shops, theaters, shopping, Armstrong Redwoods State Reserve, Lake Sonoma, Russian River, airport
Building: 1902 Queen Anne Victorian
Grounds: 1-acre estate w/ 100+-year-old cypress, redwood, and cedar trees, heritage rose gardens, 2 fountains, 3 koi ponds; original landscape designed and planted by Luther Burbank

Public Space: LR w/ player grand piano, DR, 2 large porches w/ antique wicker furniture and porch swing
Food & Drink: Full breakfast served at 9 a.m. in DR
Recreation: Biking, tennis, golf, water sports, ballooning, fishing
Amenities & Services: Barbecue, afternoon snacks, early evening wine tasting and appetizers, late evening port and dessert, private parking, concierge service for reservations, copier, fax, TV avail. on request

ACCOMMODATIONS

Units: 6 guest rooms, 1 larger than average
All Rooms: Private bath, AC, down comforter, stereo alarm clock/cassette player
Some Rooms: Fireplace, four-poster, fridge, cable TV/VCR, window seat, overstuffed chair
Bed & Bath: Queens, claw-foot tub/showers, whirlpool tubs, or tiled showers

Favorites: Cotswold, a dormer room w/ sunny window seat, floral "English cottage" wallpapers and antique furnishings, claw-foot tub
Comfort & Decor: Rooms individually decorated w/ oil paintings, custom handcrafted Victorian wallpapers, hardwood floors w/ Persian and Indian area rugs, custom-made furniture, leaded-glass windows, writing desks

RATES, RESERVATIONS, & RESTRICTIONS

Deposit: 1st night's lodging; must cancel 7 days in advance for 1 room, 14 days in advance for more than 1 room; cancellation fee $20
Discounts: Long stays
Credit Cards: None
Check-In/Out: 3–6/11, late check-out by arrangement
Smoking: No
Pets: No
Kids: Not suitable

No-Nos: No more than 2 persons per room
Minimum Stay: 2 nights on weekends, 3 on holiday weekends
Open: All year
Hosts: Jennifer and Paul Zawodny
25 W. Grant St.
Healdsburg, CA 95448
(707) 431-1110
www.calderwoodinn.com

CAMELLIA INN, Healdsburg

| Overall: ★★★★ | Room Quality: B | Value: B | Price: $80–$185 |

The camellias this pretty inn is named for are in great profusion: there are over 80 bushes in the garden, and some were gifts from Luther Burbank. The remarkably well-preserved building, with its clean Italian styling, looks just like it did in steel engravings done in 1900. Rooms have been simply wallpapered and painted so that the original inlaid hardwood floors, chandeliers, and decorated friezes that initially graced the house could prevail. Breakfast is a full buffet in the dining room with fresh fruit, cereals, a hearty main dish such as artichoke-cheese baked omelets, and homemade preserves. The inn is just two blocks from Healdsburg's plaza, which features interesting shops and restaurants.

SETTING & FACILITIES

Location: From Hwy. 101, take the Central Healdsburg exit, take Healdsburg Ave. to North St., right on North St. to inn
Near: Wineries, restaurants, shopping, Armstrong Redwoods State Reserve, Lake Sonoma
Building: 1869 Italianate Victorian
Grounds: Half-acre of landscaped grounds w/ over 50 varieties of camellias, 1920s tiled fishpond, 65-ft. cedar of Lebanon planted in 1870 in front, brick walkways

Public Space: Double parlors w/ twin marble fireplaces, DR w/ fireplace, swimming pool
Food & Drink: Full buffet breakfast served 8:30–10 a.m. in DR
Recreation: Canoeing, kayaking, ballooning, biking, golf
Amenities & Services: Afternoon snacks and evening hors d'oeuvres served in the parlor or poolside, robes, hairdryers, irons, cassette players, off-street private parking, concierge service for reservations

ACCOMMODATIONS

Units: 9 guest rooms, 2 larger than average, and a family suite
All Rooms: Private bath, AC
Some Rooms: Fireplace, four-poster
Bed & Bath: Queens, family suite has extra BR w/ twin trundle, Jacuzzis for 2 (4), soaking tubs (2)
Favorites: Memento Room, w/ mementos from 1890s, queen brass

bed, spacious bath w/ claw-foot tub and shower, door can be opened from dressing area to another room to form suite
Comfort & Decor: Rooms individually decorated w/ antiques, Bradbury & Bradbury handcrafted wallpapers, inlaid hardwood floors and carpet, canopy beds, oriental rugs, chandeliers

RATES, RESERVATIONS, & RESTRICTIONS

Deposit: Credit card or check for 1st night; must cancel 7 days in advance
Discounts: None
Credit Cards: AE, MC, V
Check-In/Out: 3:30–6/11, late check-

out by arrangement
Smoking: No
Pets: No
Kids: In family suite

Minimum Stay: 2 nights on weekends, 3 on holiday weekends or special-event weekends
Open: All year
Hosts: Ray, Del, and Lucy Lewand
211 N. St.

Healdsburg, CA 95448
(707) 433-8182
(800) 727-8182
Fax: (707) 433-8130
www.camelliainn.com
info@camelliainn.com

HEALDSBURG INN ON THE PLAZA, Healdsburg

Overall: ★★★★	Room Quality: B	Value: C	Price: $205–$265

The lovely, shady plaza in downtown Healdsburg is fringed on all sides by good restaurants, interesting little shops, and the Healdsburg Inn on the Plaza. It's a good place for lovers of traditional B&B's: gracious innkeeper Ginny Jenkins does her utmost to assure that her guests are comfortable and that they gain at least five pounds during their stay. Hearty breakfasts, bottomless cookie jars, wine tasting and appetizers, a champagne brunch on weekends and holidays, and, finally, dessert wines and chocolates on weekend evenings—that should round you out nicely.

SETTING & FACILITIES

Location: In downtown Healdsburg on the south side of the plaza
Near: Wineries, Russian River, Lake Sonoma, redwoods, shopping, museum, restaurants, airport
Building: Victorian commercial hotel built in 1900 as a professional office building, used as a Wells Fargo Stage Coach stop, architectural details still preserved
Grounds: On the Plaza, shops on first level
Public Space: Upstairs lounge w/ fireplace, books, and puzzles, large solarium overlooking the town, gift shop in lobby
Food & Drink: Extended cont'l breakfast at 7:30 a.m., full breakfast at 9 a.m. served buffet-style in the solarium, champagne brunch 9–10 a.m. Sat. and Sun.
Recreation: Bike rental next door, massage therapy spa, tennis, golf nearby
Amenities & Services: All day, cookies w/ tea, coffee, and juice; 5:30 wine tasting and appetizers; evening dessert wine and chocolates on weekends; fridge stocked w/ beverages; VCR library, fax, copy machine

ACCOMMODATIONS

Units: 10 guest rooms, 9 larger than average
All Rooms: Private bath, claw-foot tub, cable TV/VCR, phone, AC
Some Rooms: Fireplace (9), extra twin bed (2)
Bed & Bath: Queens and kings, whirlpool tub for 2 (1)
Favorites: Garden Suite, w/ king bed, corner fireplace, whirlpool tub for 2, stall shower, balcony
Comfort & Decor: Rooms individually decorated w/ original local art, antiques, white iron and brass beds, formal drapes in front bay windows, carpets, 13-ft. ceilings, skylights, balconies, Egyptian cotton towels, rubber duckies

RATES, RESERVATIONS, & RESTRICTIONS

Deposit: Must cancel 3 days in advance to avoid room charge; $15 cancellation fee per night per room

Discounts: Long stays, weekday, winter; extra person $35

Credit Cards: MC, V

Check-In/Out: 3/11, will try to accommodate early check-ins or late check-outs

Smoking: No

Pets: No

Kids: By special arrangement

Minimum Stay: 2 out of 3 nights on holiday weekends

Open: All year

Hosts: Genny Jenkins and Leroy Steck
P.O. Box 1196
110 Matheson St.
Healdsburg, CA 95448
(707) 433-6991
(800) 431-8663
Fax: (707) 433-9513
www.healdsburginn.com

HONOR MANSION, Healdsburg

Overall: ★★★★½	Room Quality: A	Value: B	Price: $130–$350

In 1994 Steve and Kathy Fowler set about restoring the 111-year-old home of a prominent old Healdsburg family. They did it right—with respect and modern plumbing. Their aim was to create a luxury B&B. How well did they succeed? Well, they didn't stop with a picture-perfect house and grounds. They chose fine furnishings and antiques and added details such as a hand-painted mural of Renaissance angels behind a bed with crisp white linens topped with heirloom quilts and comforters. The resulting rooms are lavish, but not kitschy. The Fowlers also go all out for the holidays—on a recent Christmas they individually decorated 18 Christmas trees with themes like an heirloom Raggedy Ann and Andy tree, a cow tree, and, in the kitchen, a pasta tree. Breakfast, served on antique china, sometimes features particularly notable Honor Mansion versions of eggs Benedict, baked pears with poached dried fruits, fresh pumpkin muffins, and cappuccino.

SETTING & FACILITIES

Location: On the northwest side of Healdsburg; from Hwy. 101, take Dry Creek Rd. exit east

Near: Wineries, Lake Sonoma, restaurants, shopping, antique shops

Building: 1883 Italianate Victorian, cottage, award of merit for historic home preservation by Healdsburg Museum and Historic Society

Grounds: 1+ acre landscaped grounds, gardens, fountains, koi pond, waterfall, 100-year-old magnolia tree and redwoods

Public Space: Parlor w/ fireplace, parlor games, swimming pool, gazebo, 4,000 sq. ft. of decks, porches w/ rocking chairs

Food & Drink: Full breakfast served at 9 a.m. in DR

Recreation: Biking, tennis, golf, canoeing, ballooning

Amenities & Services: Afternoon snacks, evening sherry, 24-hour cappuccino machine, tea and homemade cookies, down comforters, robes, hairdryers, garment steamers, lap desks, turn-down service w/ mints, seasonal fresh flowers, private parking, phone, fax, and modem hookup, concierge services for reservations

ACCOMMODATIONS

Units: 8 guest rooms, 4 larger than average, including 3 suites

All Rooms: Private bath, AC, armoire, featherbed

Some Rooms: Fireplace, four-poster, fridge, cable TV/VCR, in-room coffee service, hand-painted mural, extra daybed (1)

Bed & Bath: Queens and kings, Jacuzzi tubs (2), claw-foot tubs (4), tiled shower (2)

Favorites: Rose Room, in warm shades of rose and green w/ hand-carved antique bed and matching armoire, TV/VCR and video library, sitting area w/ fireplace, secluded porch w/ wicker furniture, very large bathroom w/ claw-foot soaking tub/shower

Comfort & Decor: Rooms individually decorated w/ antiques and carpet, fine linens, Egyptian cotton towels, ceiling fans, English oak antiques, softly lighted sitting areas, a four-poster so high you need a stool to get in bed

RATES, RESERVATIONS, & RESTRICTIONS

Deposit: 1st night's lodging; must cancel 15 days in advance; cancellation fee $25

Discounts: Long stays, weekday business

Credit Cards: D, MC, V

Check-In/Out: 4–8/11, late check-out by arrangement

Smoking: No

Pets: No

Kids: 12 and over

No-Nos: No more than 2 guests per room

Minimum Stay: 2 nights on weekends, 3 on some holiday weekends

Open: All year

Hosts: Steve and Cathi Fowler
14891 Grove St.
Healdsburg, CA 95448
(707) 433-4277
(800) 554-4667
Fax: (707) 431-7173
www.honormansion.com
cathi@honormansion.com

MADRONA MANOR, Healdsburg

Overall: ★★★★	Room Quality: B	Value: B	Price: $155–$250

When you stay in one of the rooms in this imposing three-story mansion, or even in its carriage house, you get a real sense of what life must have been like for the very wealthy in the nineteenth century. Or perhaps it's just the resident ghost whispering her story in your ear that makes you feel so involved in the house's history. Built in 1881 as the home and weekend retreat of a San Francisco businessman, the wooded estate now occupies 8 of the original 240 acres. Many of the furnishings in the spacious, high-ceilinged rooms are wonderful examples of American Victorian craftsmanship from the original home.

SETTING & FACILITIES

Location: Just west of Healdsburg; from Hwy. 101, take Central Healdsburg exit, go north on Healdsburg Ave. to Mill Rd., which becomes Westside Rd., and go to the end
Near: Wineries, farmers' market, antique stores, Armstrong Redwoods State Reserve
Building: 3-story Victorian built in 1881, carriage house also built in 1881, Meadow Wood complex, garden cottage
Grounds: 8 acres of landscaped grounds w/ fountain, vegetable garden, fruit trees, roses, abundant flowers
Public Space: Parlor, lounge, music room w/ grand piano and fireplace, swimming pool, palm terrace, veranda
Food & Drink: Full buffet breakfast in DR 8–9:45 a.m.
Recreation: Biking, tennis, golf
Amenities & Services: Robes, swimming pool, makeup mirrors, hairdryers, private parking, disabled access, fax, e-mail, restaurant serves candlelight dinners in 3 DRs

ACCOMMODATIONS

Units: 22 guest rooms, 8 larger than average, including 5 suites
All Rooms: Private bath, phone, AC
Some Rooms: Fireplace (20), four-poster, extra twin (2)
Bed & Bath: Queens, kings, doubles, Jacuzzis (3), sunken tub (1), claw-foot tubs/showers (2)
Units: 22 guest rooms, 8 larger than average, including 5 suites
Favorites: Rooms on the mansion's 2nd floor are the most requested; No. 204 often used as honeymoon suite, w/ bay window, balcony, original furniture from 1881, view of Dry Creek Valley
Comfort & Decor: Spacious rooms individually decorated w/ Victorian, contemporary, and hand-carved redwood furniture from Nepal, velvet curtains; carriage house has hand-carved rosewood detailing, French doors, and balconies

RATES, RESERVATIONS, & RESTRICTIONS

Deposit: 1 night's lodging; must cancel 5 days in advance; $10 cancellation fee
Discounts: Winter specials; extra person $30
Credit Cards: All
Check-In/Out: 3/11, late check-out on request
Smoking: No
Pets: No
Kids: 18 and over in main house, 14 and over in carriage house
Minimum Stay: 2 nights on week-ends, mansion only
Open: All year
Hosts: John and Carol Muir
P.O. Box 818
1001 Westside Rd.
Healdsburg, CA 95448
(707) 433-4231
(800) 258-4003
Fax: (707) 433-0703
www.madronamanor.com
info@madronamanor.com

FETZER VINEYARDS B&B, Hopland

| Overall: ★★★★ | Room Quality: B | Value: B | Price: $120–$175 |

Traveling with someone who doesn't like cutesy B&Bs? Try this one. Part of the Fetzer Vineyard complex, this delightful ten-room inn is nestled right in the vineyards and is handsomely furnished in an uncluttered contemporary decor. There's lots to see and do without leaving the premises. Besides sampling wine in the tasting room (without having to worry about driving), you can tour the winery and visit the five-acre Bonterra Garden, with its showcase organic fruits, vegetables, flowers, and herbs. There's also a wine library where you can taste, for a nominal charge, and purchase reserve wines and rarities available nowhere else.

SETTING & FACILITIES

Location: Just east of Hopland; from Hwy. 101, take Hwy. 175 approx. 1 mi. east to junction w/ East Side Rd.
Near: Rural location surrounded by vineyards, nearby lakes, hot air ballooning, Skunk Train (narrow-gauge excursion train), winery tours
Building: Historic turn-of-the-century ranch buildings—Bed & Breakfast Building; the carriage house, w/ 4 rooms and 2 suites; Haas House, the mansion w/ 3 suites; cottage, 2-room suite w/ kitchen
Grounds: Located on Valley Oaks Ranch, 5-acre Bonterra Organic Garden, landscaped, picnic sites, vineyards surround buildings
Public Space: Hospitality Room in Information Center
Food & Drink: Expanded continental served 8–9 a.m. in the Hospitality Room
Recreation: Biking, water sports, all nearby
Amenities & Services: Bottle of Fetzer wine, summer barbecues, swimming pool, private parking, disabled access, Bonterra Garden tours, deli, gift shop, tasting room

ACCOMMODATIONS

Units: 10 guest rooms, all larger than average, including 6 suites
All Rooms: Private bath, AC, phone, coffeemaker
Some Rooms: Private patio, fireplace, TV, CD player, fridge, library, kitchenette, kitchen, sleeper sofa (3), extra twin (1)
Bed & Bath: Queens, Jacuzzis (2)

Favorites: Rooms 5 and 6 are the largest suites, w/ kitchenettes and Jacuzzis
Comfort & Decor: Rooms individually decorated w/ comfortable, contemporary furniture, white louvers, rugs, hardwood floors, art, fresh flowers; views of surrounding vineyards

RATES, RESERVATIONS, & RESTRICTIONS

Deposit: Credit card number; must cancel 72 hours in advance
Discounts: AAA, AARP; extra adult $25, no extra charge for children
Credit Cards: AE, D, MC, V
Check-In/Out: 3/11
Smoking: No
Pets: No
Kids: OK
Minimum Stay: None

Open: All year
Hosts: Jo Gennuso and Joel Clark
P.O. Box 611
13601 Eastside Rd.
Hopland, CA 95449
(800) 846-8637
Fax: (707) 744-7488
www.fetzer.com/tasting
inez_guevarra@b-f.com

KENWOOD INN AND SPA, Kenwood

Overall: ★★★★★	Room Quality: A	Value: B	Price: $225–$395

On secluded hillside amid 1,000 acres of estate vineyards, the Kenwood Inn and Spa looks like an elegant old Tuscan villa magically transported to the Valley of the Moon. Luxury is the word here—from the use of fine decorator fabrics in rich colors of burgundy, gold, mango, and ochre, to spa offerings such as body wraps and scrubs and a two-hour East Indian Ayurvedic healing treatment. You may want to spend all your time at the lovely patio and pool area, however, where it is quite possible to believe you are lounging in a sun-soaked Mediterranean villa. *La dolce vita*, indeed.

SETTING & FACILITIES

Location: On Hwy. 12 between Sonoma and Santa Rosa in Kenwood, 1.5 hours north of San Francisco
Near: Wineries, shopping, restaurants
Building: Mediterranean-style, ivy-covered main building and DR is joined with 3 smaller Italianate buildings, each containing 2 to 4 suites

Grounds: A flagstone terraced courtyard w/ fountain, gardens, grapevines, swimming pool, Jacuzzi, arbor w/ persimmon, fig, and olive trees
Public Space: DR, LR
Food & Drink: 3-course breakfast served at 9:30 in DR at tables for 2 or outside in the courtyard

Recreation: Biking, tennis, golf
Amenities & Services: Swimming pool, hot tub, afternoon snacks w/ sherry, wine, fruit and cheese, compli-

mentary bottle of wine in room, private parking, disabled access, VCRs in room on request, spa w/ massages, facials, body wraps

ACCOMMODATIONS

Units: 12 guest rooms, all suites
All Rooms: Private bath, stereo/CD player, featherbed, down comforter, fireplace, AC
Some Rooms: Upstairs suites have balconies, downstairs suites have private terraces
Bed & Bath: Queens, Jacuzzis
Favorites: Tuscan suite, w/ private LR,

balcony, whirlpool bath for 2, walls in BR hand-painted w/ Arts and Crafts–style trompe l'oeil
Comfort & Decor: Antiques, coordinated armoire and bed sets, fine fabrics including silk drapes and Egyptian cotton sheets, marble-topped washstands, brass fixtures in baths

RATES, RESERVATIONS, & RESTRICTIONS

Deposit: Credit card or 1 night's lodging; must cancel 7 days in advance
Discounts: None
Credit Cards: AE, MC, V
Check-In/Out: 3/11
Smoking: No
Pets: No
Kids: 16 and over
Minimum Stay: 2 nights on weekends

Open: All year
Hosts: Terry and Roseann Grimm
10400 Sonoma Hwy.
Kenwood, CA 95452
(707) 833-1293
(800) 353-6966
Fax: (707) 833-1247
www.kenwoodinn.com

FORBESTOWN INN, Lakeport

Overall: ★★★½	Room Quality: C	Value: A	Price: $85–$115

Clear Lake is California's largest freshwater lake, attracting lots of summer campers, fishers, waterskiers, and Jet Skiers. The Forbestown Inn is also old-fashioned and quiet. Covered with wisteria, the Victorian inn has four pretty guest rooms in the main house and a carriage house with a private suite, including a living room. The backyard is a big attraction, with a beautiful black-bottomed swimming pool under a giant redwood tree and a hot tub nearby. The innkeepers like to cook and will feed you handsomely.

SETTING & FACILITIES

Location: In a residential neighborhood in downtown Lakeport between 8th and 9th Sts., 1 block west of Main St., 2 blocks from Clear Lake

Near: Clear Lake, orchards, vineyards, wildflowers, fall colors
Building: Victorian farmhouse built in 1863

Grounds: Half city block w/ street-front lawns, old wisteria, roses, mature walnut trees, rear garden w/ swimming pool, redwood and fig trees, roses
Public Space: LR w/ woodstove, DR, large front porch
Food & Drink: Full breakfast served in DR or garden 8–10 a.m., earlier by request

Recreation: Water sports, boating, and fishing on Clear Lake, biking, antiquing, golf
Amenities & Services: Swimming pool, hot tub, evening wine, snacks and hors d'oeuvres, hammock for 2 in hidden corner of garden; street parking, VCRs in public rooms

ACCOMMODATIONS

Units: 4 guest rooms, 2 larger than average, separate carriage house sometimes avail.
All Rooms: AC
Some Rooms: Private bath (2), shared bath (1)
Bed & Bath: Queens, king (1), roll-away avail., extra-long claw-foot tub (1)
Favorites: Bartlett Suite, in ivory and

floral prints, sunny, w/ antique fainting couch and armoire, velvet side chairs
Comfort & Decor: Rooms individually decorated w/ American antique oak furniture, extra-tall windows, color-coordinated fabrics, hand-stitched pillows, carpet, hardwood floors and area rugs, stained-glass window in bath

RATES, RESERVATIONS, & RESTRICTIONS

Deposit: Credit card guarantee; must cancel 5 days in advance
Discounts: Long stays, weekday business, winter singles; extra person $20
Credit Cards: AE, DC, D, MC, V
Check-In/Out: 3/11, noon check-out by arrangement
Smoking: No
Pets: No
Kids: Not suitable for small children

Minimum Stay: 2 nights on holiday weekends
Open: All year
Hosts: Wally and Pat Kelley
825 Forbes St.
Lakeport, CA 95453
(707) 263-7858
Fax: (707) 263-7878
www.innaccess.com/fti
forbestowninn@zapcom.net

BEAZLEY HOUSE, Napa

Overall: ★★★½	Room Quality: B	Value: B	Price: $115–$250

Roomy and comfortable, the Beazley House sits on a half acre on a neighborhood street in Old Napa, convenient to shops and restaurants in the area. The first B&B in Napa, the big, brown, Edwardian mansion contains six spacious guest rooms, most with views of the flower-filled garden. A reproduction of the mansion's original carriage house contains five more "country" decor guestrooms, all with fireplaces and two-person spas. The two loft guestrooms have 15-foot ceilings and arched windows. Breakfast is a buffet in the dining room with fresh fruit, muffins, quiche, and just-ground coffee.

SETTING & FACILITIES

Location: In the historic section of downtown Napa, at the corner of 1st St. and Warren

Near: Wine touring, restaurants, mud baths and spas, shopping

Building: 1902 Edwardian mansion, carriage house

Grounds: Half acre of lawns and gardens

Public Space: Large sitting room w/ fireplace, library, music room w/ French doors to the gardens, formal DR

Food & Drink: Full breakfast served 8:30–10 a.m. in DR

Recreation: Bicycles avail. for rent, hot air ballooning, wine train, horseback riding, historic Napa walking tour

Amenities & Services: Bathrobes, hairdryers in rooms, coffeemakers in carriage house, fresh chocolate chip cookies daily, unlimited soft drinks, lemonade, and iced tea in summer, afternoon cheese and crackers, cream sherry, and hot mulled wine; assistance w/ reservations; off-street parking

ACCOMMODATIONS

Units: 11 guest rooms, 6 in the mansion, 5 in the carriage house

All Rooms: Private bath; phone avail. on request

Some Rooms: Carriage house rooms have fireplaces (5)

Bed & Bath: Queens and kings, double (1); private 2-person spas in carriage house rooms (5)

Favorites: The Sun Room in the mansion, w/ 6-ft. soaking tub, private garden-view balcony; Enchanted Rose in the carriage house, w/ fireplace, Victorian bed, 2-person spa, beamed ceiling, cedar-lined bathroom

Comfort & Decor: Rooms individually decorated w/ antiques, wicker, comforters and country quilts, carpets, some wallpapered

RATES, RESERVATIONS, & RESTRICTIONS

Deposit: 50% of stay; must cancel 7 days in advance; $10 cancellation fee

Discounts: AAA, winter specials

Credit Cards: AE, MC, V

Check-In/Out: 3–6/noon, by special arrangement

Smoking: No

Pets: No

Kids: OK in all rooms except Sunroom (w/ balcony) and Master BR (w/ fireplace)

Minimum Stay: 2 nights on weekends, 3 on weekends May–Oct.

Open: All year

Hosts: Jim and Carol Beazley
1910 1st St.
Napa, CA 94559
(707) 257-1649
(800) 559-1649
Fax: (707) 257-1518
www.beazleyhouse.com
innkeeper@beazleyhouse.com

CEDAR GABLES INN, Napa

Overall: ★★★★	Room Quality: B	Value: B	Price: $139–$199

This inn is the size of a small country. Designed by an English architect in the 1890s, the handsome, dark-brown shingle-covered mansion could easily have sheltered the king's entire guard. Winding staircases take you to six guest rooms filled with interesting antiques, chandeliers, and private baths; most have gas-fired coal-burning fireplaces. If you can find your way back, you're invited to the Lower Parlor in the evening to sip wine in front of another fireplace, this one large enough to roast a whole haunch of beef. Breakfast includes seasonal fruits, homemade muffins and breads, and specialties such as French pancakes, almond French toast, or cheese blintzes.

SETTING & FACILITIES

Location: On a residential street in a Nat'l Register historic district, 4 blocks south of downtown
Near: Wineries, restaurants, shopping
Building: "Olde English," built in 1892, designed by English architect Ernest Coxhead, styled after English country manors in Shakespeare's time, dark-brown shingled, 10,000 sq. ft.
Grounds: Oversized urban lot in residential neighborhood, shady, landscaped w/ tall cedars in front
Public Space: Parlor w/ paneled walls

and fireplace, formal DR, breakfast area
Food & Drink: Full breakfast served 9–9:30 a.m. in the downstairs sunroom, cont'l breakfast for earlier departures, can accommodate most dietary restrictions
Recreation: Golf, hot air ballooning, biking, antiquing
Amenities & Services: Evening wine and hors d'oeuvres, VCR and big-screen TV, decanter of port in room, private parking, discount packages for golf, hot air ballooning, honeymoon special

ACCOMMODATIONS

Units: 6 guest rooms, 4 larger than average, including 1 suite
All Rooms: Private bath, AC, iron and ironing board
Some Rooms: Fireplace, double sofa bed (1), twin roll-away (1)
Bed & Bath: Queens; some claw-foot tubs, Jacuzzi tubs for 2, or oversized showers; hairdryers
Favorites: Count Bonzi's Room, queen

featherbed w/ 8-ft. headboard, sunny window seat, gas-fired coal-burning fireplace, 2-person whirlpool tub and shower
Comfort & Decor: Rooms individually decorated w/ antique beds—walnut, oak, wrought iron, or brass, comfortable seating, coordinated fabrics, carpet, 4 antique motorcycles in Lower Parlor

RATES, RESERVATIONS, & RESTRICTIONS

Deposit: Credit card guarantee or 1 night's lodging sent by check; must cancel 7 days in advance for full refund, or forfeit unless room rebooked
Discounts: Long stays; extra person $50 **Credit Cards:** AE, D, MC, V
Check-In/Out: 3–6/11, late check-out by arrangement
Smoking: No
Pets: No
Kids: 14 and over

Minimum Stay: 2 nights on weekends
Open: Closed Dec. 23–26
Hosts: Craig and Margaret Snasdell
486 Coombs St.
Napa, CA 94559
(707) 224-7969
(800) 309-7969
Fax: (707) 224-4836
www.cedargablesinn.com
info@cedargablesinn.com

CHURCHILL MANOR, Napa

| Overall: ★★★★½ | Room Quality: A | Value: B | Price: $95–$205 |

Step under a rose-covered archway into the Churchill Manor estate and leave the real world behind. The stately 10,000-sq.-ft., three-story mansion on an acre of manicured grounds will knock your socks off even if Queen Victoria wasn't your type. Rose gardens, hundred-year-old cedars and redwoods, and a formal fountain are the setting, but the manor is the star. Regal white columns surround a wraparound veranda on the exterior, and original redwood moldings, beveled leaded glass, and four original fireplaces on just the first floor alone grace the interior. The guest rooms are spacious, are furnished in an un-busy way with fine antiques, and retain interesting features such as gold leaf or blue Delft tiles around the original bedroom fireplaces and bathtubs. A full breakfast buffet is served in the solarium or on the veranda; fresh fruit and baked goods are provided, plus made-to-order omelets and French toast.

SETTING & FACILITIES

Location: On a residential street in a Nat'l Register historic district, 4 blocks south of downtown

Near: Wineries, restaurants, antiques, shopping, mud baths and spas, galleries

Building: 3-story 1889 Italianate mansion w/ extensive Greek Revival veranda surrounding 3 sides, listed on Nat'l Register of Historic Places

Grounds: 1 acre w/ 100-year-old cedars, redwoods, expansive lawns, rose and perennial gardens, formal fountain

Public Space: Parlor w/ TV/VCR, movies, game room, library, music room w/ grand piano, original solarium w/ mosaic marble tiled floor, covered veranda supported by 20 white columns

Food & Drink: Full breakfast served 8:30–10 a.m. in the solarium or on the veranda

Recreation: Tandem bicycles and croquet avail. at the manor; balloon rides, tennis, golf nearby

Amenities & Services: Afternoon snacks of freshly baked cookies and refreshments, evening wine and hors d'oeuvres, private parking, disabled access, full concierge services 8:30 a.m.–9 p.m. daily

ACCOMMODATIONS

Units: 10 guest rooms, 5 larger than usual

All Rooms: Private bath, phone, AC, down comforter and pillows

Some Rooms: Fireplace, four-poster, sleeper sofa, original gold-leaf tiles surrounding original fireplaces, sofa bed or roll-away (3)

Bed & Bath: Queens and kings, some 2-person showers or showers w/ leaded glass, brass fixtures, giant antique claw-footed tubs for 2, basket of toiletries

Favorites: Victoria's Room, w/ hand-painted blue Delft tiles framing original fireplace, king bed, leaded glass shower, large claw-foot tub in corner next to fireplace; Edward Churchill Room, w/ matching antique BR set, 2-person tiled shower, fireplace, large soaking tub sitting on mahogany pedestal

Comfort & Decor: Rooms individually decorated w/ historic photos of Napa, European antiques, lace curtains, custom wallpaper, carpet, bay windows

RATES, RESERVATIONS, & RESTRICTIONS

Deposit: Credit card guarantee; must cancel 5 days in advance

Discounts: None; extra person $25

Credit Cards: D, MC, V

Check-In/Out: After 3–9/11, late check-out by arrangement

Smoking: No

Pets: No

Kids: 12 and over

No-Nos: Only 3 rooms accommodate

more than 2 persons

Minimum Stay: 2 nights on weekends

Open: Closed Dec. 24–25

Hosts: Brian Jenson and Joanna Guidotti

485 Brown St.

Napa, CA 94559

(707) 253-7733

Fax: (707) 253-8836

www.churchillmanor.com

HENNESSEY HOUSE B&B, Napa

Overall: ★★★★	Room Quality: B	Value: B	Price: $85–$210

Hennessey House, with its Eastlake/Queen Anne features and cast-iron fence, was clearly designed to be the home of someone of stature. Napa's mayor, circa 1900, lived here, and the current owners have lovingly restored it to a state the mayor would approve of. In a semiurban but quiet neighborhood six blocks from downtown, it is a fine headquarters from which to explore Napa and environs, particularly the increasingly popular Carneros wine-growing region just west of town. The rooms are affordable and elegant, and the four rooms in the carriage house are downright luxurious. The meals are elaborate, including the inn's famous homemade granola, and something to sip or munch never seems far from hand—or mouth. The four-course breakfast is served in a formal dining room with a hand-stamped tin ceiling. Entrées vary but can include blueberry-stuffed French toast or oatmeal-buttermilk pancakes and bacon or sausage.

Setting & Facilities

Location: In a semiurban area near historic downtown Napa; take Hwy. 29 to Lincoln Ave. exit, east on Lincoln to 3rd stop light, and turn right on Main St.

Near: Wineries, Napa Valley Wine Train, restaurants, shopping

Building: 1889 Queen Anne Victorian, carriage house, on Nat'l Register of Historic Places

Grounds: Double-sized lot w/ landscaped gardens, fountain

Public Space: Parlor w/ woodburning fireplace, DR w/ hand-painted stamped tin ceiling, deck overlooking garden and fountain

Food & Drink: Full 4-course breakfast served 9–10 a.m. in DR, will accommodate special diets, cont'l breakfast for early departures

Recreation: Biking, tennis, golf, hot air ballooning, horseback riding

Amenities & Services: 24-hour sauna, afternoon snacks, evening wine and hors d'oeuvres, in-room sherry and chocolates, robes, discount packages for Napa Valley Wine Train, guest discounts for Chardonnay golf course, in-room massages avail., fax, phone, off-street parking on premises; concierge services for reservations

Accommodations

Units: 10 guest rooms (6 in main house, 4 in carriage house), 5 larger than average

All Rooms: Private bath, AC, armoire

Some Rooms: Fireplace (5), extra twin (1)

Bed & Bath: Queens, king (1), Jacuzzis (4), claw-foot tubs w/ shower (3), glass-enclosed showers (3)

Favorites: The Fox's Den in carriage

house, large and private w/ private patio and garden, king bed, gas fireplace, 2-person whirlpool bath, dual antique sinks in vanity

Comfort & Decor: Rooms individually decorated w/ English and Belgian antiques, marble floors in bathrooms, carpet, stained-glass windows, canopy, brass, or feather beds

Rates, Reservations, & Restrictions

Deposit: Credit card or 1 night's lodging by check; must cancel 7 days in advance; deposit forfeited if less than 7 days and room not re-rented; cancellation fee $15

Discounts: Long stays, weekday business, groups, AAA, seniors; extra person $25

Credit Cards: AE, D, MC, V

Check-In/Out: 3:30–6:30/11, late check-out by arrangement

Smoking: No

Pets: No

Kids: In 1 room

Minimum Stay: 2 nights on weekends

Open: All year

Hosts: Gilda and Alex Feit

1727 Main St.

Napa, CA 94559

(707) 226-3774

Fax: (707) 226-2975

www.hennesseyhouse.com

inn@hennesseyhouse.com

LA BELLE EPOQUE, Napa

| Overall: ★★★★ | Room Quality: A | Value: B | Price: $159–$220 |

A painstakingly restored Queen Anne Victorian, this inn has beautiful stained-glass windows and a lavish collection of antiques, oriental carpets, and period wallpapers and drapes. Breakfast is a major event here. Served by candlelight in the formal dining room with fireplace blazing, the meal includes house specialties such as Grand Marnier French toast, pork or beef tenderloin, and lemon scones. The inn has a wine cellar with a fireplace where guests gather in the evening for vintage local wines and hors d'oeuvres.

SETTING & FACILITIES

Location: In historic Old Town Napa; from Hwy. 29, take 1st St. exit to 2nd St. (one way), go 4 blocks to Jefferson and turn left, go 4 blocks to Calistoga, turn right on Calistoga and go 1 block
Near: Wineries, restaurants, shopping, Napa Valley Wine Train
Building: 1893 Queen Anne Victorian, 12 colors, stained glass
Grounds: Double lot in a quiet residential neighborhood, landscaping w/ flowers, rose garden, pocket fuchsia garden, fountains
Public Space: Parlor, gazebo, wine cellar w/ fireplace, wet bar, and entertainment center
Food & Drink: Full 4-course breakfast served at 9 a.m. in parlor in front of fireplace, or on porch
Recreation: Biking, tennis, golf, hot air ballooning, horseback riding
Amenities & Services: Evening wine w/ Napa Valley wines and hors d'oeuvres in the wine cellar, hot and cold beverages avail. 24 hours, private parking, copier, fax and modem avail., in-room massages can be arranged, 1 disabled-accessible room

ACCOMMODATIONS

Units: 7 guest rooms, 4 larger than average, including 2 suites
All Rooms: Private bath, cable TV/VCR, phone, AC, secretarial desk, reading lamps
Some Rooms: Fireplace, four-poster, sleeper sofas (2)
Bed & Bath: Queens and kings, whirlpool tub (1), showers for 2 (3), hairdryers
Favorites: Gamay Room, w/ large fleur-de-lis stained-glass bay window surrounding small sitting area, walnut Victorian queen BR set, Belgian armoire, and ornate ceiling treatment; Cabernet Room, w/ elevated king canopy bed, sitting area, fireplace, oriental carpet, French oak armoire
Comfort & Decor: Rooms individually decorated w/ original paintings, period antiques, period drapes and wallpaper, oriental carpet and hardwood floors or wall-to-wall carpet, original ceiling treatments, Victorian light fixtures

RATES, RESERVATIONS, & RESTRICTIONS

Deposit: $25 nonrefundable deposit credited to account; must cancel 72 hours in advance; $25 cancellation fee
Discounts: Weekday business, AAA; extra person $30

Credit Cards: AE, D, MC, V
Check-In/Out: 3–6/11, late check-out
by arrangement
Smoking: No
Pets: No
Kids: 12 and over
Minimum Stay: 2 nights on week-
ends, 3 on holiday weekends
Open: All year

Host: Georgia Jump
1386 Calistoga Ave.
Napa, CA 94559
(707) 257-2161
(800) 238-8070
Fax: (707) 226-6314
www.labelleepoque
innkeeper@labelleepoque.com

LA RESIDENCE COUNTRY INN, Napa

Overall: ★★★★½   Room Quality: B   Value: B   Price: $175–$295

One of the nicest inns in the Napa area, La Residence offers 20 lovely rooms in 2 buildings, one a Gothic Revival mansion and the other a graceful contemporary structure, reputedly in the style of a French barn. Oh, those French. Guest rooms in the barn are furnished in a delicate French Provincial fashion, and all have sitting areas, fireplaces, and, guess what, French doors leading to balconies. The mansion features American walnut and oak antiques, plantation shutters, and coordinated fabrics and wall coverings. The spa and heated swimming pool are in an inviting parklike setting surrounded by brick patios, a gazebo, and shady gardens. The inn is noted for great breakfasts in its large, sunny dining area.

SETTING & FACILITIES

Location: On Napa's northern outskirts between Napa and Yountville,
where the vineyards begin, on the east
side of Hwy. 29 frontage road, between
Salvador and Oak Knoll
Near: Napa Valley wineries, redwoods,
shopping, restaurants, wine train, balloon rides
Building: 2 buildings, an 1870 Gothic
Revival mansion and a contemporary
structure
Grounds: 2 acres of formal gardens
with pool, spa, ponds, paths, 200-year-
old oaks and French plane trees

Public Space: DR w/ French doors to
patios, gazebo, wooden terraces and
brick patios overlooking vineyards, 2nd-
floor salon in French barn
Food & Drink: Full breakfast served
9–10 a.m. in DR or on terrace
Recreation: Biking, tennis, golf, mud
baths in Calistoga
Amenities & Services: Hot tub,
swimming pool, evening wine and hors
d'oeuvres, private parking, disabled
access, concierge services for
reservations

ACCOMMODATIONS

Units: 20 guest rooms, most larger than average, including 5 suites, 1 room totally disabled-accessible
All Rooms: Private bath, AC, phone, CD player
Some Rooms: Fireplace, balcony, four-poster, extra twin (1); Junior Suite and Deluxe Suite each have fridge, TV
Bed & Bath: Queens, soaking tubs for

2 (7), shower for 2 (2)
Favorites: No. 22, w/ French doors to redwood balcony, "pineapple" four-poster; No. 31, w/ four-poster, fireplace, chandelier, sitting area
Comfort & Decor: Rooms individually decorated w/ designer fabrics, carpet; French barn has European pine antiques, patios or balconies

RATES, RESERVATIONS, & RESTRICTIONS

Deposit: Credit card, 1st night's lodging; must cancel 10 days in advance; $20 cancellation fee; 3-day cancellation forfeits full amount unless room is re-rented
Discounts: None; extra person $20
Credit Cards: AE, DC, MC, V
Check-In/Out: 2/11, late check-out by arrangement, hourly charge
Smoking: No
Pets: No
Kids: OK

No-Nos: No more than 3 guests per room
Minimum Stay: 2 nights on weekends, 3 on holiday weekends
Open: All year
Hosts: David Jackson and Craig Claussen
4006 St. Helena Hwy.
Napa, CA 94558
(707) 253-0337
Fax: (707) 253-0382
www.laresidence.com

OAK KNOLL INN, Napa

Overall: ★★★★½   Room Quality: A   Value: C   Price: $250–$395

As you sit on the deck outside your elegant room gazing across thousands of grapevines to the mountains beyond, it seems impossible that downtown Napa is just four miles behind you. The inn is so private and sequestered by the cedars in front, and by its orientation toward the vineyards to the north, that it's easy to overlook. But once you've found it, you'll want to come back, and many if not most of the guests are repeats. The guest room decor is an austere but tasteful mix of contemporary and antique furnishings. Each of the rooms is over 500 square feet, with distinctive features such as great stone walls, a canopy bed with curtains that close, and beautiful fireplaces. Special private tours of wineries are arranged, and local vintners visit to pour and discuss their offerings. This is a place owned and designed by wine lovers for wine lovers, as well as plain old lovers. Breakfast, served in your room, the dining room, or, weather permitting, outside overlooking the vineyards is first-rate. A recent entrée was Anaheim chile quiche, fresh avocado salsa, chorizo, black beans, and corn muffettes.

SETTING & FACILITIES

Location: On the northeastern outskirts of Napa, on Oak Knoll Ave., 2 mi. east of Hwy. 29, almost to Silverado Trail (Hwy. 221)

Near: Surrounded by 600 acres of vineyards, within 20 min. of 250 wineries, art galleries, restaurants, shopping, airport

Building: French Country building w/ thick fieldstone walls, guest rooms remodeled in 1993 and recently redecorated

Grounds: 3+ acres, flower and organic vegetable gardens, views across 600 acres of vineyards to Stags Leap Mountain

Public Space: Country French reception and dining areas, library w/ current and local-interest books, swimming pool, gazebo

Food & Drink: Full breakfast served in DR at communal table or tables for 2, outside overlooking vineyards, or in room

Recreation: Biking, tennis, golf, hot air ballooning, bird-watching

Amenities & Services: Outdoor Jacuzzi spa, swimming pool, evening cheese and local wines (often poured by wine maker), fresh flowers, down pillows and duvets, featherbeds, hypoallergenic bedding avail.; phones, satellite TV, and VCR by request; private parking, full-time concierge, special individualized itineraries: e.g., red wine drinkers, first-time visitors who want to see everything, private tours of wineries

ACCOMMODATIONS

Units: 4 guest rooms, all considerably larger than average

All Rooms: Private bath, AC, fireplace, fridge, vaulted ceiling w/ exposed beams, iron and ironing board, current periodicals, umbrella, double-thick soundproofed walls, deck, binoculars

Bed & Bath: Kings, roll-aways w/ featherbeds avail.

Favorites: No. 1, an end room, very private and romantic, w/ tall cathedral windows, view of vineyard, 2 overstuffed chairs in sitting area in front of fireplace, sofa, king brass bed, and a small outdoor patio; No. 6, a mirror image of No. 1

Comfort & Decor: Rooms individually decorated w/ local art, overstuffed chairs and love seat, brass or canopy beds, stone on some walls, grass cloth on others, upholstery-weight designer curtains w/ blackout lining, carpet in guest rooms, marble in baths; all rooms have private entrances through French doors

RATES, RESERVATIONS, & RESTRICTIONS

Deposit: Hold w/ credit card; must cancel 7 days in advance

Discounts: Return guests get preferred rates and availability; extra person $50

Credit Cards: MC, V

Check-In/Out: 4/noon, late or early check-in and late check-out avail.

Smoking: No

Pets: No

Kids: 14 and over

Minimum Stay: 3 nights on weekends, 4 on holiday weekends

Open: All year
Hosts: Barbara Passino and John
Kuhlmann
2200 E. Oak Knoll Ave.
Napa, CA 94558

(707) 255-2200
Fax: (707) 255-2296
www.virtualcities.com/ons/ca/
   w/caw9602.htm

OLD WORLD INN, Napa

Overall: ★★★½	Room Quality: B	Value: B	Price: $125–$205

In the historic Old Town section of Napa on a busy street, the Old World
Inn is a handsome Victorian in an eclectic combination of architectural
styles, detailed with wood shingles, wide shady porches, clinker brick, and
leaded and beveled glass. Each room has been decorated with coordinated
linens and fabrics, and the bedrooms feature decor in pastel blue, rose,
peach, and mint. Bright fresh colors also dominate the parlor, with its
hand-painted wall decorations, tiled fireplace, and soft classical background music. In addition to a full breakfast, the inn provides homemade
cookies and a predinner assortment of herbed cheeses, smoked salmon,
and a Moroccan eggplant spread. After dinner, guests return to a chocolate
splurge of homemade truffles, fudge, and chocolate-amaretto torte.

SETTING & FACILITIES

Location: In historic Old Town Napa;
from Hwy. 29, take Lincoln East exit, go
to Jefferson light, turn right
Near: Wineries, Napa Valley Wine
Train, shopping, museums, restaurants
Building: Queen Anne Victorian built
in 1906, 2-BR cottage in back
Grounds: Large city lot, pine and wal-
nut trees, large patio w/ outdoor spa
Public Space: Parlor w/ tiled and
wood-manteled fireplace, DR
Food & Drink: Full breakfast served

8:30–9:30 a.m. in DR
Recreation: Biking, tennis, golf, horseback riding, hot air ballooning
Amenities & Services: Outdoor
custom Jacuzzi, carafe of wine in room,
afternoon snacks, tea and an assortment of cookies, early evening wine and
an assortment of cheeses and spreads,
evening chocolate desserts, fresh flowers, private parking, concierge service
for reservations, fax, computer
hookups

ACCOMMODATIONS

Units: 10 guest rooms, 2 larger than
average, including 2 suites, 2-BR cottage
All Rooms: Private bath, AC
Some Rooms: Fireplace, four-poster,
refrigerator, extra bed (3)
Bed & Bath: Queens and kings, some
Jacuzzi tubs
Favorites: Birch Room, w/ white eyelet

spread, sitting area, small balcony; the
cottage, w/ French Country decor,
Jacuzzi in front of fireplace, private
patio, sleeps 4
Comfort & Decor: Rooms individually decorated w/ painted antique
furniture, including canopied beds, wallpapers, hardwood floors and carpet

RATES, RESERVATIONS, & RESTRICTIONS

Deposit: Credit card for 1st night's
lodging; must cancel 7 days in advance;
$10 cancellation fee
Discounts: Long stays, AAA, Internet
specials
Credit Cards: AE, D, MC, V
Check-In/Out: 3–6/11:30
Smoking: No
Pets: No
Kids: 2 larger rooms suitable for
children

No-Nos: Only 2 persons per room
Minimum Stay: 2 nights on weekends
April–Dec.
Open: All year
Host: Sam Van Hoeve
1301 Jefferson St.
Napa, CA 94559
(707) 257-0112
(800) 966-6624
Fax: (707) 257-0118
www.oldworldinn.com

INN AT OCCIDENTAL, Occidental

| Overall: ★★★★½ | Room Quality: A | Value: B | Price: $175–$270 |

California has more than its share of amazingly attractive, well-run inns, and this is one of them. Occidental, a charming little village handily located between the coast and the vineyards, was once a railroad stop between San Francisco and the Northwest. Innkeeper Jack Bullard and family transformed an original homestead from that era into this fine country inn and filled it with beautiful, comfortable furnishings, oriental carpets on gleaming fir floors, and a lifetime of antique and art collections. The staff is friendly and helpful, the food is delicious, and all the delights of the area are nearby. What more can you ask?

SETTING & FACILITIES

Location: 15 mi. west of Santa Rosa
via Hwy. 12 and the Bohemian Hwy., in
downtown Occidental, 1 block east of
the main street; 1 hour north of San
Francisco

Near: Wineries, Sonoma Coast
beaches, Armstrong Redwoods State
Reserve, antiquing in Sebastopol, Western Hills Rare Plant Nursery and Vintage Gardens

Building: 1877 Victorian homestead restored in 1988, oldest homestead in Occidental
Grounds: Half-acre English courtyard w/ fountain and cottage garden, lawn and flagstone sitting areas
Public Space: Covered veranda w/ wicker furniture, LR w/ fireplace, oriental carpets, antiques, wine cellar w/ huge stone fireplace
Food & Drink: Full breakfast served 8–10 a.m. in the wine cellar, outdoors when weather permits
Recreation: Croquet on premises; river canoeing, whale-watching, swimming, fishing, biking, golf, horseback riding, hot air ballooning nearby
Amenities & Services: Refreshments served in the afternoon, Sonoma County wine in the evening in LR w/ hors d'oeuvres, private parking, fax and e-mail service avail., Sugar Room equipped for physically challenged, concierge service for reservations

ACCOMMODATIONS

Units: 8 guest rooms, including 3 suites
All Rooms: Private bath, phone, cable TV avail., featherbed, down comforter, sitting area
Some Rooms: Fireplace, spa tub, hot tub, private entrance, private patio, garden view, private deck
Bed & Bath: Queens and kings (4 each), kings can be converted to twins; hairdryers, spa tubs (3), double shower (1)
Favorites: Cut Glass Room, w/ own garden, private patio and hot tub, king bed, collection of contemporary photographs, innkeeper's collection of antique English and Irish cut glass pickle jars; Tiffany Room, w/ canopy mahogany four-poster, original 1877 wood-burning fireplace, private balcony w/ table and chairs and chaise lounges, collection of Tiffany silver
Comfort & Decor: Rooms individually decorated w/ antiques, collections of silver, netsuke, quilts, Sandwich glass, cut glass, and shooting marbles, original art, comfortable sitting areas or rooms, coordinating fabrics, unique lamps, oriental rugs, carpet

RATES, RESERVATIONS, & RESTRICTIONS

Deposit: 1st night's lodging; must cancel 10 days in advance; $10 cancellation fee
Discounts: AAA, midweek/off-season
Credit Cards: All
Check-In/Out: 3/noon, late check-out by arrangement
Smoking: No
Pets: No
Kids: 10 and over
No-Nos: No more than 2 guests per room
Minimum Stay: 2 nights on weekends
Open: All year
Hosts: Jack, Bill, and Jean Bullard
P.O. Box 857
3657 Church St.
Occidental, CA 95465
(707) 874-1047
(800) 522-6324
Fax: (707) 874-1078
www.innatoccidental.com
innkeeper@innatoccidental.com

CAVANAGH INN, Petaluma

Overall: ★★★½	Room Quality: C	Value: A	Price: $85–$130

Petaluma is often overlooked by tourists in their quest to experience the wine country. An agricultural center that became a haven for high-tech companies, Petaluma has just about everything the towns in Napa Valley have except high prices and hordes of people with cameras. The historic restored downtown hugging the Petaluma River, with its boat harbor and 300-passenger paddlewheeler, has loads of Victorians and Iron Fronts and more than 24 antique shops. It also has a fine B&B. In 1902, Mr. Cavanagh, who owned the local lumber mill, built the mansion using clear heart redwood that would today cost a fortune, and 12 years later he built an Arts and Crafts cottage next door. Ray and Jeanne Farris have transformed the two into a well-run B&B. Mrs. Farris's meals are famous, and many return just for more of her overnight French toast and apple sausage.

SETTING & FACILITIES

Location: Just west of Hwy. 101, on a quiet residential street within walking distance of historic downtown Petaluma, 45 min. north of San Francisco
Near: Antique shops, local history museum, restaurants, wineries, redwoods
Building: 1902 3-story Georgian Revival mansion, 1912 California Craftsman cottage
Grounds: Half-acre of gardens with persimmon and other large trees
Public Space: Mansion has parlor, library, and DR; cottage has parlor and sitting area
Food & Drink: Full breakfast served at 8:30 a.m. weekdays, 9 a.m. weekends in the main DR, early morning coffee
Recreation: Golf, biking
Amenities & Services: Afternoon wine, evening turn-down w/ sweets, extensive library, fax, copy machine, "I forgot" basket, soundproofing; some private parking, TV in parlor and library, Spanish spoken, concierge services for reservations

ACCOMMODATIONS

Units: 7 guest rooms, 4 larger than average
Some Rooms: Featherbeds, extra twin (1), private bath (5), shared bath (2)
Bed & Bath: Queens, king (1), 2 twins (1), Jacuzzi (1)
Favorites: Magnolia Room in mansion, w/ massive wooden headboard, private bath and shower walled by old etched glass windows; in the cottage, the Victorian Rose Room, w/ twin beds
Comfort & Decor: Mansion decorated w/ more formal Victorian decor and original artwork, including trompe l'oeil mural in library and an unusual octagonal redwood landing in the stairwell; cottage has wicker and more casual garden cottage furnishings

RATES, RESERVATIONS, & RESTRICTIONS

Deposit: Credit card or 1st night's lodging, full payment 30 days prior to arrival; must cancel 10 days in advance
Discounts: Long stays, weekday business, winter specials; extra person $28
Credit Cards: AE, MC, V
Check-In/Out: 4–7/11
Smoking: No
Pets: No
Kids: 12 and over
Minimum Stay: 2 nights on holiday

weekends
Open: Feb. 1–Jan. 13
Hosts: Ray and Jeanne Farris
10 Keller St.
Petaluma, CA 94952
(707) 765-4657
(888) 765-4658
Fax: (707) 769-0466
www.cavanaghinn.com
info@cavanaghinn.com

THE GABLES, Santa Rosa

Overall: ★★★★	Room Quality: B	Value: B	Price: $135–$225

This perfectly kept inn looks like something out of a Gothic fantasy—you can easily imagine someone sweeping down the dramatic, spiraling mahogany staircase and vanishing into the night. It has 15 gables over unusual keyhole-shaped windows, 12-foot ceilings, and 3 Italian marble fireplaces that were brought around Cape Horn. The guest rooms are fresh and pretty, and the innkeepers pride themselves on their excellent, varied breakfasts; they go for long stretches without repeating a menu.

SETTING & FACILITIES

Location: On east side of Santa Rosa; from Hwy. 101, take Rohnert Park Expressway exit, go 2.5 mi. east to Petaluma Hill Rd., left 4 mi. to inn
Near: Wineries, redwoods, Luther Burbank home and gardens, Sonoma Mission, Sonoma Fort, antiquing, shopping, restaurants
Building: 1877 Victorian Gothic Revival on Nat'l Register of Historic Places, recently constructed cottage next to the creek
Grounds: 3.5 acres in country setting, 150-year-old barn with resident owl,

rose and kitchen gardens, footbridge over creek
Public Space: Parlor and DRs w/ 12-ft. ceilings, large deck
Food & Drink: Full breakfast served at 9 a.m. in DR, tray breakfast for early departures or late sleepers, special diets accommodated
Recreation: Biking, horseback riding, spas, tennis, golf, river rafting
Amenities & Services: Afternoon snacks, hospitality center w/ fridge, beverages, private parking, disabled access, concierge service for reservations

ACCOMMODATIONS

Units: 8 guest rooms, including 4 suites, 2-room cottage w/ kitchenette
All Rooms: Private bath, AC, iron, ironing board, down comforter, books,

fresh flowers
Some Rooms: Fireplace, four-poster, fridge, daybed (1)

Bed & Bath: Queens and kings, hairdryers, main house has claw-foot tubs w/ showers, cottage has whirlpool tub w/ handheld shower
Favorites: Parlor Suite, w/ king four-poster, marble fireplace, hunter green and burgundy decor; William and Mary's Cottage, w/ woodstove, kitchenette, double whirlpool tub, queen bed in upstairs loft BR, luxurious bathrobes, TV/VCR, video library
Comfort & Decor: Rooms individually decorated w/ antiques, fabrics from white eyelet to burgundy velvet, wallpaper, handcrafted furniture by owner, Franklin gas fireplaces, carpet, every room uniquely shaped due to gabled architecture

RATES, RESERVATIONS, & RESTRICTIONS

Deposit: 100% of bill; must cancel 14 days in advance; $10 cancellation fee per night
Discounts: Long stays; extra person $25
Credit Cards: All
Check-In/Out: 3–8/11, will extend to noon if requested
Smoking: No
Pets: No
Kids: By arrangement
No-Nos: No more than 2 guests per room

Minimum Stay: 2 nights on weekends, 3 on holiday weekends and during harvest in Sept., Oct.
Open: All year
Hosts: Mike and Judy Ogne
4257 Petaluma Hill Rd.
Santa Rosa, CA 95404
(707) 585-7777
(800) 422-5376
Fax: (707) 584-5634
www.thegablesinn.com
innkeeper@thegablesinn.com

GRAVENSTEIN INN, Sebastopol

Overall: ★★★½	Room Quality: B	Value: B	Price: $100–$135

The Gravenstein Inn and its neighbor, the Vine Hill Inn, are B&B rarities. They're country and proud of it. And the country around here is some of the prettiest in the state—rolling hills, with orchards and vineyards, valley oaks and redwoods, and a mild climate to boot. The site couldn't be better, the food is excellent (particularly the oatmeal-corn pancakes), and the furnishings are comfortable and not at all cutesy. Also, the local Farmtrails program offers a variety of self-guided tours of nearby farms that grow/raise things like pumpkins, bees, lambs, bunnies, Christmas trees, apples, llamas, and wine grapes.

SETTING & FACILITIES

Location: Northwest of Sebastopol; take Hwy. 116 north, go 2.5 mi., turn left on Graton Rd., go .4 mile to corner of Graton and Hicks, turn right, then left at first driveway
Near: Redwoods, wineries, Sonoma Coast, galleries, Farmtrails for produce and local crafts, osmosis Japanese enzyme baths, native plant nurseries, restaurants, antiquing

Building: 1872 3-story Greek Revival farmhouse, elegantly restored, on Nat'l Register of Historic Places, carriage house, chicken house and resident chickens

Grounds: 6 acres, orchards w/ 18 varieties of apples plus other fruit trees, rose garden, redwood grove, patio, fishpond, 1 acre of gardens, organic vegetables, berries, and fruits

Public Space: Parlor w/ oak-manteled fireplace, square grand piano, pump organ, front porch w/ hammock, gazebo

Food & Drink: Full breakfast served 8:30–9:30 a.m. in DR, or outside under the wisteria arbor

Recreation: Horseshoes on premises; biking, horseback riding, golf nearby

Amenities & Services: Solar-heated swimming pool, barbecue, robes, books, custom mattresses, private parking, concierge services for reservations

ACCOMMODATIONS

Units: 4 guest rooms in the main house; 5th room (in carriage house) is 2-room studio w/ full kitchen

Some Rooms: Fireplace, balcony (2), private deck (1), private bath (3), shared bath (2), twin trundle bed (1)

Bed & Bath: Queens, claw-foot tubs (3)

Favorites: Victorian, romantic, w/ high oak bed, marble-topped tables, needlepoint rugs, private balcony w/ views

of redwoods, claw-foot tub/shower, old-fashioned water closet; the 2-room suite in the Carriage House, w/ kitchen, private sundeck overlooking the gardens

Comfort & Decor: Rooms individually decorated w/ antiques, family photos and art, books and plants, lace curtains, wood floors and area rugs, Pennsylvania Dutch quilt

RATES, RESERVATIONS, & RESTRICTIONS

Deposit: 1st night's lodging or credit card; must cancel 7 days in advance

Discounts: Long stays

Credit Cards: AE, MC, V

Check-In/Out: 3–7, later by arrangement/11, late check-out by arrangement

Smoking: No

Pets: No

Kids: In carriage house

No-Nos: No more than 2 guests

per room

Minimum Stay: 2 nights on weekends and holidays for rooms w/ private baths

Open: Closed Dec. 15–Feb. 1

Hosts: Frank and Kathleen Mayhew
3160 Hicks Rd.
Sebastopol, CA 95472
(707) 829-0493
Fax: (707) 824-9382
www.metro.net/gravensteininn
gravensteininn@metro.net

VINE HILL INN B&B, Sebastopol

Overall: ★★★★	Room Quality: B	Value: B	Price: $125–$150

Smack-dab in the middle of rolling foothills of vineyards and apple orchards is Vine Hill Inn, a new arrival in the B&B firmament. With a view in every direction, the inn is definitely away from it all. Even so, both Sebastopol and Santa Rosa are close (3 and 10 miles) and offer a variety of urban things to do if you get bored. But there's a lot to be said for this kind of boredom—lounging around the pool, taking long walks along country lanes with apple trees on both sides, watching the sun rise over hundreds of acres of chardonnay grapes. The four gabled bedrooms on the second floor of the Victorian farmhouse are nicely appointed and nicely priced.

SETTING & FACILITIES

Location: 3 mi. north of Sebastopol off Hwy. 116; turn right on Vine Hill Rd.
Near: Country setting w/ vineyard and mountain ridge views, wineries, Russian River, ocean beaches, restaurants, antiquing, hot air ballooning
Building: 1897 2-story remodeled Victorian farmhouse
Grounds: 2 acres of trees, garden, orchards, fountain

Public Space: Parlor, DR, deck, front porch and screened side porch
Food & Drink: Full breakfast served 8:30–9:30 a.m. in DR, will accommodate dietary needs
Recreation: Ping-Pong table on premises; tennis, golf, biking nearby
Amenities & Services: Swimming pool, robes, private parking, concierge service for reservations

ACCOMMODATIONS

Units: 4 guest rooms
All Rooms: Private bath, AC, balcony
Some Rooms: Skylight, French doors, lace curtains, private deck (2), shared deck (2)
Bed & Bath: Queens, double (1), clawfoot tub/shower or whirlpool tubs
Favorites: Laguna Room, w/ Bedouin-

style canopy bed, skylights, private deck
Comfort & Decor: Rooms individually decorated in a casual country farmhouse style w/ antiques, oriental rugs, a bed w/ an antique shutter for a headboard, a white iron bed, a white iron and brass bed

RATES, RESERVATIONS, & RESTRICTIONS

Deposit: Must cancel 7 days in advance or forfeit full reservation unless room is subsequently rented
Discounts: Winter specials, long stays, weekdays
Credit Cards: AE, MC, V
Check-In/Out: 3–7/11, late check-out by arrangement
Smoking: No
Pets: No
Kids: Over 6

Minimum Stay: None
Open: All year
Host: Ann K. Deickmann
3949 Vine Hill Rd.
Sebastopol, CA 953472
(707) 823-8832
Fax: (707) 824-1045
www.vine-hill-inn.com
innkeeper@vine-hill-inn.com

CEDAR MANSION B&B, Sonoma

Overall: ★★★★½	Room Quality: A	Value: B	Price: $160–$210

Pack your tiara, mama, because yes indeedy, this is a genuine mansion. Standing just a hop and a skip away from the Sonoma Plaza on 1.6 park-like acres, this Italianate mansion is beautiful outside and in. All the rooms have 12-foot ceilings, the bathrooms are tiled with Italian marble, and the common area contains three of the original marble fireplaces. Guest room furnishings are a mix of antique and contemporary, with iron beds and sitting areas. And, naturally, there's daily maid service and a nightly turndown. A recent breakfast included Belgian waffles with strawberries and whipped cream, plus fruit, muffins, and cereals.

Setting & Facilities

Location: 1 block southeast of historic Sonoma Plaza, 1 hour north of San Francisco
Near: Wineries, restaurants, General Vallejo's home, Jack London State Park, shopping, galleries
Building: Italianate mansion built in 1876, 2 cottages added
Grounds: 1.6 acres landscaped in parklike setting w/ large sun patios and rose-covered arbor

Public Space: Parlor, formal DR, gazebo, decks and patios
Food & Drink: Expanded cont'l breakfast served 8:30–10 a.m. in the formal DR, outside, or in room
Recreation: Badminton, croquet on premises; biking, golf nearby
Amenities & Services: Gated parking, concierge service for reservations, picnic baskets by request, refrigerator for guests' use

Accommodations

Units: 5 guest rooms, all larger than average, including 2 minisuites in a cottage near the main residence
All Rooms: Private bath, sitting area, high ceiling, AC, cable TV, down comforter during winter
Some Rooms: Fireplace, love seat

Bed & Bath: Queens, king (1), Jacuzzis (2)
Favorites: Veranda Room downstairs in the mansion, w/ marble fireplace, French doors to private wisteria-covered veranda

Comfort & Decor: Rooms individually decorated w/ mixture of antique and conventional furniture, antique iron beds, shutters, miniblinds, Persian/oriental rugs on hardwood floors, Italian tiled bathrooms

RATES, RESERVATIONS, & RESTRICTIONS

Deposit: 1st night's lodging; must cancel 7 days in advance in high season; must cancel 72 hours in advance in low season
Discounts: None
Credit Cards: D, MC, V
Check-In/Out: 3:30/11:30, late checkout by request
Smoking: No
Pets: No
Kids: Not suitable
No-Nos: No more than 2 guests per room

Minimum Stay: 2 nights on high-season weekends, holiday weekends
Open: Closed Dec. 23–27
Hosts: Horst Kubler, owner; Dagmara Castro and Maria Castro-Asbell, innkeepers
531 2nd St. East
Sonoma, CA 95476
(707) 938-3206
(800) 409-5496
Fax: (707) 935-7721
www.cedarmansion.com
info@cedarmansion.com

COTTAGE INN AND SPA, Sonoma

Overall: ★★★½	Room Quality: B	Value: B	Price: $125–$235

Conveniently located on a quiet urban street a short walk from the Sonoma Mission and Plaza, this inn is a cool Mediterranean/Southwestern-style oasis surrounded by a high, white stucco wall. The courtyard inside the wall has a splashing fountain, a spa, and an interesting original sculpture by one of the owners. The two largest rooms have Mexican tile floors, arched fireplaces, cathedral ceilings, and skylights. All rooms have a completely equipped dining area with fresh fruits, cereals, and beverages; freshly baked goods are delivered in the morning. Plans are under way to add three additional rooms in the summer of 2000.

SETTING & FACILITIES

Location: 1 block north of Sonoma Plaza and historic Mission
Near: 3 wineries and 6 tasting rooms within walking distance, shops, galleries, museums, restaurants
Building: Mediterranean/Southwestern-style structure built in 1947, remodeled 1990s, won Sonoma League of Historic Preservation award of excellence for remodel
Grounds: City lot, courtyard w/ fountain and seating
Public Space: LR/lobby w/ fireplace, courtyard
Food & Drink: Expanded continental served on table in guest rooms
Recreation: Biking, golf, complimentary membership in health club
Amenities & Services: Outdoor spa for 6 in courtyard, private parking, disabled access, in-room massages avail., facials avail. at next-door clinic

ACCOMMODATIONS

Units: 4 guest rooms, 3 larger than average, including 2 suites

All Rooms: Private bath and garden entrance, cable TV, phone, fresh flowers, fridge

Some Rooms: Fireplace, kitchen, sofa bed (2)

Bed & Bath: Queens, Jacuzzi (1)

Favorites: The cottage, w/ private patio, raised arched fireplace, cathedral ceiling, skylight, double French doors in dining area, kitchen, French doors to private garden w/ redwood deck, can accommodate up to 5 guests

Comfort & Decor: Rooms individually decorated in southwestern style, w/ original art, Mexican tile floors, ceiling fans, carpet, cathedral ceilings in cottage and studio

RATES, RESERVATIONS, & RESTRICTIONS

Deposit: 50% of bill; must cancel 72 hours in advance; $10 cancellation fee, rest of deposit returned

Discounts: Long stays, winter weekdays; extra person $20

Credit Cards: All

Check-In/Out: 4/11, late check-out by arrangement

Smoking: No

Pets: No

Kids: Not suitable

Minimum Stay: 2 nights on weekends

Open: All year

Hosts: Robert Behrens and Marga Friberg
302 1st St. East
Sonoma, CA 95476
(707) 996-0719
(800) 944-1490
Fax: (707) 939-7913
www.cottageinnandspa.com
cottageinn@aol.com

SONOMA CHALET, Sonoma

Overall: ★★★½	Room Quality: B	Value: A	Price: $85–$170

Words fail to describe the whimsical charm of this rustic Swiss-style farmhouse and its three cottages, right out of a fairy tale. Although you're only three-quarters of a mile from downtown Sonoma, you're on three acres of eucalyptus trees and lawns and at the edge of an adjoining 200-acre ranch. You may not be remote, but you feel remote. Surrounded by flowering things—trees, vines, shrubs—you're kept company by deer from the nearby hills. The rooms, particularly the cottages, are a composite of interesting furniture, art, quilts, oriental carpets, and collectibles, assembled with great style, taste, and occasionally humor. In Sara's Cottage there's a 1920s four-burner Magic Chef stove that works just fine and looks like new. In Laura's Cottage, the baseboards were hand-painted by a local artist to match the stained-glass window. All the rooms are nice in the main house, even the ones that share a bath, although the cottages offer the most privacy. If you're on a budget, you'll be intensely happy to know about this appealing, affordable place.

SETTING & FACILITIES

Location: .75 mi. northwest of downtown Sonoma; from Hwy. 12, take 5th St. West to the north to the end
Near: Wineries, shopping, Sonoma Mission, Jack London State Park, General Vallejo home, Armstrong Redwoods State Reserve, airport
Building: Swiss chalet–style country house w/ hand-painted murals, separate cottages
Grounds: 3 acres of 100-year-old eucalyptus trees, lawns and flower gardens next to 200-acre farm at the edge of Sonoma
Public Space: Lawns, decks
Food & Drink: Extended cont'l breakfast served 8:30–9:30 a.m. in kitchen, on deck, or on trays to cottages
Recreation: Biking, tennis, golf, hot air ballooning, horseback riding
Amenities & Services: Hot tub, sherry in rooms, private parking

ACCOMMODATIONS

Units: 4 guest rooms in farmhouse, including 2 small rooms that share a bath, and a suite w/ sitting area and private bath, 3 separate cottages w/ private baths, fridges, coffee service
All Rooms: AC, balcony or deck
Some Rooms: Fireplace, fridge, private bath (5), shared bath (2)
Bed & Bath: Queens and doubles
Favorites: Honeymoon Cottage, separate, w/ woodstove, books, spacious bath w/ claw-foot tub, sleeping area and loft, fridge, coffee service
Comfort & Decor: Rooms individually decorated w/ country antiques, quilts and collectibles, sitting areas, deck or balconies w/ views

RATES, RESERVATIONS, & RESTRICTIONS

Deposit: 1st 2 nights in advance; must cancel 7 days in advance; $10 cancellation fee, refunded only if room is rebooked
Discounts: Winter; extra person $25
Credit Cards: AE, MC, V
Check-In/Out: 3–6/noon, late checkout by arrangement
Smoking: No
Pets: No
Kids: In cottages
Minimum Stay: 2 nights on weekends
Open: All year
Host: Joe Leese
18935 5th St. West
Sonoma, CA 95476
(707) 938-3129
(800) 938-3129
Fax: (707) 996-0190
www.sonomachalet.com
sonomachalet@cs.com

SONOMA HOTEL, Sonoma

| Overall: ★★★½ | Room Quality: B | Value: B | Price: $110–$220 |

When you rent a room in this small, pleasant hotel right on the plaza, you're renting a bit of history. The hotel has been providing shelter to the area's visitors for almost 120 years (though they've done away with the chamber pots and spittoons, of course). While Sonoma is not as trendy as some other wine country burgs, it's also not as expensive or crowded, but it's just as interesting and a lot less self-conscious. Everything you need is within a short walk. The rooms in the historic hotel are all newly redecorated and refurbished. They are comfortable in an old-fashioned hotel sort of way, and the proprietors are friendly and helpful. Leave your spurs at the door.

SETTING & FACILITIES

Location: Across from the northwest corner of Sonoma Plaza
Near: Wineries, restaurants, art galleries, historic sites
Building: Historic Victorian building circa 1879, newly renovated and decorated
Grounds: Urban lot across from plaza
Public Space: Parlor w/ stone fireplace, comfortable chairs for plaza-watching
Food & Drink: Extended cont'l breakfast served 8–10 a.m. in the adjoining Heirloom Restaurant, awarded 4 stars by the local newspaper
Recreation: Biking, tennis, golf
Amenities & Services: Complimentary evening selection of local wines, disabled access, concierge service for reservations

ACCOMMODATIONS

Units: 16 guest rooms, 5 larger than average, including 4 suites w/ adjoining sitting rooms
All Rooms: Private bath, cable TV, phones, AC
Some Rooms: Sleeper sofas (4)
Bed & Bath: Queens, 2 twins (2), doubles (4)
Favorites: Large suite on 3rd floor, corner room, large sitting room, and large bathroom
Comfort & Decor: Light and airy, w/ fine linens and bedding, mixture of new and antique Country French and American Country furnishings, rusted iron beds, twin nightstands, pine cabinetry

RATES, RESERVATIONS, & RESTRICTIONS

Deposit: 1 night's stay; must cancel 72 hours in advance
Discounts: None; extra person $30 (5 years and over)
Credit Cards: All
Check-In/Out: After 2/noon
Smoking: No
Pets: No
Kids: By arrangement
Minimum Stay: 2 nights on weekends
April 1–Oct. 31
Open: All year
Hosts: Craig Miller and Tim Farfan
110 W. Spain St.
Sonoma, CA 95476
(707) 996-2996
(800) 468-6016
Fax: (707) 996-7014
www.sonomahotel.com
sonomahotel@aol.com

THISTLE DEW INN, Sonoma

Overall: ★★★½	Room Quality: B	Value: B	Price: $115–$210

The Thistle Dew's owners have built their interests right into their inn, and the result is a really interesting place. First, there's the assemblage of collector-quality, quarter-sawn Arts and Crafts furniture designed in the early twentieth century by such craftsmen as Gustave Stickley. Their design is based on simplicity, and they were handmade by artisans with the best workmanship and materials possible. Guests eat a hearty breakfast on a Stickley table and chairs, or, for a small charge, in their rooms. Owner Larry Barnett's garden contains 450 varieties of cacti and other succulents, including some rare eight-foot tree aloes, and many subtropical ferns. Guests have described the grounds as a botanical garden. You'll find the guest rooms attractive and comfortable, and the Barnetts go all the way to make your stay pleasant.

SETTING & FACILITIES

Location: Half-block from the northwest corner of Sonoma Plaza

Near: Wineries, 2 state parks, hot air ballooning, restaurants, shopping

Building: 2 houses built in 1869 and 1905, w/ 2 guest rooms in the front house and 4 in the back

Grounds: City lot, 450 varieties of cactus and succulents, perennial gardens, wisteria-covered arbor, subtropical fern garden, benches and fountain, decks

Public Space: Common room w/ wood-burning fireplace, DR

Food & Drink: Full breakfast served 8–9 a.m. in DR, or in room w/ prior arrangement and additional charge

Recreation: Bicycles on premises; golf, water sports, fishing nearby

Amenities & Services: Hot tub, afternoon snacks served inside near fireplace or outside at umbrella table, passes to local health club, private parking, disabled access

ACCOMMODATIONS

Units: 6 guest rooms, 3 larger than average, including 1 suite

All Rooms: Private bath, AC, phone w/ voice mail, jack for modems and laptops, ceiling fan

Some Rooms: Fireplace, private entrance, deck, extra bed (2)

Bed & Bath: Queens, whirlpool baths for 2 (3), some rooms have grab bars for disabled

Favorites: Mimosa, w/ sitting area and

couch, gas fireplace w/ brick mantel, French doors to private deck w/ porch swing, "log cabin" quilt, whirlpool bath for 2 in large, terra-cotta-tiled bath, private entrance

Comfort & Decor: Rooms individually decorated w/ original Stickley and Limbert Arts and Crafts furniture, antiques, wicker, sponge-painted walls, handmade quilts, oriental rugs, carpet

RATES, RESERVATIONS, & RESTRICTIONS

Deposit: 1st night's lodging; must cancel 48 hours in advance; $10 cancellation fee

Discounts: Internet specials; extra person $30

Credit Cards: AE, MC, V

Check-In/Out: 3–7/noon

Smoking: No

Pets: No

Kids: 12 and over

Minimum Stay: None

Open: All year

Hosts: Larry and Norma Barnett
171 W. Spain St.
Sonoma, CA 95476
(707) 938-2909
(800) 382-7895
Fax: (707) 996-8413
www.thistledew.com
tdibandb@aol.com

VICTORIAN GARDEN INN, Sonoma

Overall: ★★★½	Room Quality: B	Value: B	Price: $99–$185

On an urban street in the picturesque town of Sonoma, this 1870s farm-house is hard to see from the sidewalk because of the lush English gardens burying it in greenery. Once inside the picket fence, you can stroll through parklike grounds with gnarled trees, moss-covered walkways, and a creek meandering through the property. If you tire of the natural play-ground, around back there's a great pool and spa. There are four guest rooms, each quite different, all sweetly appealing and comfortable; three have private entrances.

SETTING & FACILITIES

Location: 1.5 blocks east of Sonoma Plaza in a residential neighborhood
Near: Historic Town Square, wineries, restaurants, General Vallejo's home and barracks, St. Francis Mission, shopping
Building: 1870 Greek Revival farm-house, wraparound veranda, water tower building
Grounds: 1 acre of authentic Victorian gardens, fruit trees, stream, secret gardens, creekside patios

Public Space: Parlor w/ fireplace, DR
Food & Drink: Full breakfast served 9–10 a.m. in DR or guest's room, or on the garden patios
Recreation: Biking, tennis, golf
Amenities & Services: Swimming pool, hot tub, afternoon snacks, tea cart with sweets, evening sherry, robes, fridge for guests, private parking, concierge service for reservations

ACCOMMODATIONS

Units: 4 guest rooms, including 1 suite
All Rooms: AC, down comforter
Some Rooms: Fireplace, private entrance, 2 extra twins (1), private bath (4)
Bed & Bath: Queens, double (1), suite also avail. as 2 rooms w/ shared bath
Favorites: Woodcutter's Cottage, w/ fireplace and sitting area, large claw-foot

tub and shower, stained glass window in bath, country-style antiques, queen brass bed, steps away from swimming pool and spa
Comfort & Decor: Rooms individu-ally decorated w/ antiques, down com-forters, carpet, Laura Ashley or Marrimekko prints, wicker furniture

RATES, RESERVATIONS, & RESTRICTIONS

Deposit: 100% in advance; for 2 or more rooms for 2 or more nights, must pay by check, cash, or money order; must cancel 7 days in advance or 14 days for 2 or more and holidays; $10 cancellation fee per room per night
Discounts: None
Credit Cards: AE, DC, MC, V
Check-In/Out: 2–4:30/noon

Smoking: No
Pets: No
Kids: By arrangement in suite
No-Nos: No more than 2 guests per room
Minimum Stay: 2 nights on week-ends, 3 on holiday weekends and week-ends April–Oct.

Open: All year
Host: Donna Lewis
316 E. Napa St.
Sonoma, CA 95476
(707) 996-5339

(800) 543-5339
Fax: (707) 996-1689
www.victoriangardeninn.com
vgardeninn@aol.com

DEER RUN INN, St. Helena

Overall: ★★★½	Room Quality: B	Value: B	Price: $140–$195

Up a winding, 4.5-mile road on Spring Mountain, Deer Run is a cedar bungalow set deep in the woods with a rustic exterior, stone chimney, and rugged beamed ceilings but with all the amenities you could want, including rooms decorated with the eminently civilizing influences of Ralph Lauren and Laura Ashley. There's a grand wraparound deck, a heated swimming pool, a hiking trail, horseshoes, Ping-Pong, and homegrown berries. Cody, the chocolate lab, will show you his favorite haunts, too. Homegrown berries grace the breakfast table in season, followed by the Deer Run version of entrées such as crepes; Belgian waffles; cheese, egg, and asparagus casserole; frittatas; and muffins.

SETTING & FACILITIES

Location: Northwest of St. Helena; in town, turn on Madrona Ave., go 3 blocks, and turn right on Spring Mountain Rd.
Near: Wineries, shops, restaurants, airport
Building: 1929 remodeled cedar-shingled ranch
Grounds: 4 forested acres in Spring Mountain above the Napa Valley
Public Space: Library, LR, DR,
outdoor picnic areas
Food & Drink: Full breakfast served 8:30–9:30 a.m.
Recreation: Biking, horseshoes, Ping-Pong, swimming on premises; tennis, wineries, golf nearby
Amenities & Services: Swimming pool, brandy and mints in room, robes, hairdryers, coffee and tea service, private parking

ACCOMMODATIONS

Units: 4 guest rooms, all larger than average, including 1 suite
All Rooms: Private bath and entrance, cards and games, stereo, TV, fridge, AC, down comforter, featherbed
Some Rooms: Fireplace, Italian hideaway twin bed (1)
Bed & Bath: Queens, king (1)
Favorites: Studio Bungalow, w/ cherrywood queen bed, carpeted sitting area w/ gas fireplace and stone hearth, out-
door stone patio; or the cottage, w/ private deck, Cape Cod furnishings, separate carpeted BR, oak and brass and glass bathroom, personal breakfast delivery
Comfort & Decor: Rooms individually decorated w/ local art, antique dressers and beds, miniblinds and wood blinds, carpet; bathrooms have Spanish tile or pine floors

RATES, RESERVATIONS, & RESTRICTIONS

Deposit: 1st night's lodging; must cancel 7 days in advance, 30 days for holidays and multiple room bookings; $20 cancellation fee
Discounts: None; extra person $25
Credit Cards: AE, MC, V
Check-In/Out: 3–6/11, late check-out by arrangement
Smoking: No
Pets: No
Kids: 1 year or younger
No-Nos: No more than 2 guests per room except in suite

Minimum Stay: 2 nights on weekends and holidays
Open: Closed Dec. 17–24
Hosts: Tom and Carol Wilson
P.O. Box 311
3995 Spring Mountain Rd.
St. Helena, CA 94574
(707) 963-3794
(800) 843-3408
Fax: (707) 963-9026
www.virtualcities.com/~virtual/ons/ca/w/caw3602.htm

THE INK HOUSE, St. Helena

Overall: ★★★★½	Room Quality: B	Value: B	Price: $99–$195

This is true: the Ink House was built in the shape of an ink bottle by a St. Helena pioneer named Ink. And he did a bang-up job of it. It's not kitschy or funky, but a stately mansion with grand rooms and grand views. The cap of the ink bottle, on the fourth floor, is an observatory with 360° views of the vineyards of Napa Valley. With their 14-foot-high ceilings and quality antique furnishings, the rooms don't have the glossy, newly restored feel of so many Victorian inns; instead, they have the smooth, burnished patina of cherished heirlooms. The food is varied and good, and in late afternoons wine and appetizers are served, often by local wine makers sharing their secrets and insights with the guests. While Ink House is in a rural setting on large estatelike grounds, it faces Hwy. 29, which can be awfully busy. Not to worry, though: the innkeepers have installed double- and triple-paned windows to shut out any traffic noise.

SETTING & FACILITIES

Location: Between Rutherford and St. Helena, on the west side of Hwy. 29 at Whitehall Lane
Near: Wineries, restaurants, glider port, spas, shopping, airport
Building: Italianate Victorian estate built in 1884, on Nat'l Register of Historic Places
Grounds: 2 acres of Victorian gardens, 250-year-old redwoods and pines, garden swing, original historic barn
Public Space: 2 parlors w/ grand piano, pump organ, crystal chandeliers, original stained glass, game room, 4th-

floor glass-enclosed observatory, antique pool table, wraparound veranda w/ white wicker furniture
Food & Drink: Full 3-course breakfast served 8:30–10 a.m. in DR and parlor
Recreation: 18-speed bicycles and pool table on premises; croquet, bocce ball, darts, hot air ballooning, horseback riding, golf nearby
Amenities & Services: Evening wine, champagne, and hors d'oeuvres, TV/VCR in observatory, sherry, brandy, and port all the time, private parking, concierge services for reservations

ACCOMMODATIONS

Units: 7 guest rooms, 3 larger than average
All Rooms: AC, views
Some Rooms: Private bath (5), shared bath (2)
Bed & Bath: Queens, roll-away avail.
Favorites: French Room, w/ carved French oak quarter-canopied bed, glass-

fronted French armoire
Comfort & Decor: Rooms individually decorated w/ original art and family heirloom photos; English, French, Italian, Eastlake, Georgian, Eastern European, and American antiques, period window treatments and wall coverings, oriental rugs on oak floors, 14-ft. ceilings

RATES, RESERVATIONS, & RESTRICTIONS

Deposit: 100% of bill; must cancel 7 days in advance; $10 cancellation fee
Discounts: Midweek in winter; extra person $25
Credit Cards: MC, V
Check-In/Out: 3/11
Smoking: No
Pets: No
Kids: Not suitable
Minimum Stay: 2 nights on weekends

for some rooms
Open: Closed Dec. 24–25
Host: Diane De Filipi
1575 St. Helena Hwy.
St. Helena, CA 94574
(707) 963-3890
Fax: (707) 968-0739
www.inkhouse.com
Inkhousebb@aol.com

INN AT SOUTHBRIDGE, St. Helena

Overall: ★★★★½	Room Quality: B	Value: D	Price: $235–$490

St. Helena is busily carving out a reputation as the trendiest area of the California wine country, with its upscale luxury accommodations and world-class restaurants. The Inn at Southbridge is one of its stars. Designed by noted architect William Turnbull Jr., its rooms follow the less-is-more design philosophy, with clean-lined furnishings, simple but elegant fabrics and linens, and fine detailing such as vaulted ceilings, fireplaces, and French doors onto private balconies.

SETTING & FACILITIES

Location: In the heart of St. Helena on the east side of Main St. (Hwy. 29), 1 hour north of San Francisco
Near: Restaurants, shopping, ballooning, golf, tennis, wine tasting
Building: Contemporary, architect-designed building built around a courtyard
Grounds: 1 acre of landscaped grounds, courtyard and patio
Public Space: Reception and LRs
Food & Drink: Expanded cont'l breakfast served 7–10:30 a.m. in parlor at tables for 2, or in room

Recreation: Health spa (operated by inn) next door; nearby biking, golf, billiards, tennis, fishing, horseback riding; guests can use nearby Meadowood Resort's golf course, tennis courts, and swimming pools for a small fee
Amenities & Services: Adjacent Mediterranean restaurant, VCRs avail. at front desk, 2 dual-line phones w/ voice mail and fax/modem ports, robes, private parking, concierge services for reservations, disabled access, use of resort amenities at Meadowood (5 min. away)

ACCOMMODATIONS

Units: 21, 20 larger than average, and 1 suite, all rooms on 2nd floor
All Rooms: Private bath w/ tub/shower, private balcony, smoke detector, fridge, skylight, safe, coffeemaking facility, AC, clock radio, down comforter, soundproofing
Some Rooms: Suite has a LR, sitting area, and sleeper sofa
Bed & Bath: Kings

Favorites: All rooms are similarly decorated; King Suite has separate sitting/meeting room
Comfort & Decor: Butter yellow walls, vaulted ceilings w/ skylights, Shaker-like cherry furniture, French doors open to minibalconies w/ view, black-and-white photographs of local vineyards, wrought-iron floor and table lamps, Pottery Barn decor

RATES, RESERVATIONS, & RESTRICTIONS

Deposit: Credit card; must cancel 7 days in advance; cancellation fee 1 night's lodging
Discounts: None
Credit Cards: AE, DC, MC, V

Check-In/Out: 4/noon, late check-out by arrangement
Smoking: No
Pets: No
Kids: In suite

Deposit: Credit card; must cancel 7 days in advance; cancellation fee 1 night's lodging
Discounts: None
Credit Cards: AE, DC, MC, V
Check-In/Out: 4/noon, late check-out by arrangement
Smoking: No
Pets: No
Kids: In suite

Minimum Stay: 2 nights on weekends
Open: All year
Host: Jeff Niezgoda
1020 Main St.
St. Helena, CA 94574
(707) 967-9400
(800) 520-6800
Fax: (707) 967-9486
www.placestostay.com/napa-south bridge/

SHADY OAKS COUNTRY INN, St. Helena

Overall: ★★★	Room Quality: B	Value: B	Price: $159–$195

Shady Oaks Country Inn is on a quiet country lane surrounded by hundreds of acres of vineyards that produce some of the world's finest wines—Raymond, Heitz, Mumm, and Grgich Hills are all close by. The inn consists of an old stone winery and a 1920s Craftsman farmhouse with a wisteria-covered arbor nestled between the two. The rooms are fine. Those in the farmhouse are sunny and bright, with the requisite antiques, love seats, and brass beds; however, it is the two rooms in the winery, with its two-feet-thick walls, that make this a country inn. The innkeepers serve a champagne breakfast with eggs Benedict, Belgian waffles, fresh fruit, and home-baked breads.

SETTING & FACILITIES

Location: 2 mi. south of St. Helena, .5 mile east of Hwy. 29
Near: Wineries, restaurants, shopping
Building: 1920s Craftsman-style house and 1880s stone winery building
Grounds: 2 acres of 300-year-old oak and walnut trees among vineyards, lawn and gardens
Public Space: Parlor w/ fireplace, games, magazines, books, refrigerator, patio and arbor built in 1800s w/ Roman pillars and covered w/ 100-year-old wisteria

Food & Drink: Full breakfast w/ champagne served on patio, in DR, or in your room
Recreation: Croquet and horseshoes on premises; biking, tennis, golf, hot air ballooning, glider rides, mud baths, spas nearby
Amenities & Services: Premium wine and cheeses in parlor or on patio, private off-street parking, concierge services for reservations, disabled access

ACCOMMODATIONS

Units: 5 guest rooms, 3 larger than average, including 1 suite
All Rooms: Private bath, AC, radio, views

Some Rooms: Fireplace, private entrance, private balcony/deck
Bed & Bath: Queens, king (1), roll-away avail., antique claw-foot tub (1)

Favorites: Sunny Hideaway, w/ private deck entrance, white iron and brass bed, white rattan love seat and chairs, fireplace, claw-foot tub/shower, balcony w/ views of vineyards

Comfort & Decor: Rooms individu-ally decorated w/ antiques, carpet, fine linens, triple-mirrored armoire; beds of hand-carved oak, white iron, and brass; heirloom furniture, love seats, sitting areas

RATES, RESERVATIONS, & RESTRICTIONS

Deposit: 100% of bill in advance; must cancel 10 days in advance

Discounts: Off-season/midweek; extra person $29

Credit Cards: MC, V

Check-In/Out: After 2/11, late check-out by arrangement

Smoking: No

Pets: No

Kids: Accepted, not encouraged

Minimum Stay: 2 nights on week-ends, usually

Open: All year

Hosts: John and Lisa Wild-Runnells
399 Zinfandel Lane
St. Helena, CA 94574
(707) 963-1190
Fax: (707) 963-9367
www.napavalley.com/shadyoaks
shdyoaks@napanet.net

WINE COUNTRY INN, St. Helena

Overall: ★★★★½	Room Quality: B	Value: B	Price: $96–$268

If you added a few centuries, this wood and stone inn, with its mansard roof, would look like a chateau in the French countryside, complete with dazzling views of the vineyards in the valley below. Inside, it's pure Califor-nia hedonism. Although the rooms are furnished with country antiques, they are contemporary in feeling. Most have fireplaces and balconies, and some have private hot tubs on your own patio. If you're feeling social, there's a large heated pool and spa and an evening wine social with local wineries sharing their wares along with the inn's homemade appetizers. A full buffet at breakfast wards off hunger by plying you with fresh fruit, homemade breads and granola, and varying egg dishes.

SETTING & FACILITIES

Location: Approx. 1.5 mi. north of St. Helena off Hwy. 29 at Lodi Lane
Near: Wineries, restaurants, shopping, mineral baths, Robert Louis Stevenson Park
Building: New England–style inn, built in the 1970s, on a hillside overlooking vineyards; 3 buildings—main, Brandy Barn, and Hastings House
Grounds: 12 acres, extensive annual and perennial gardens, patios, 3 acres of olives

Public Space: Common room
Food & Drink: Full buffet breakfast served 7:30–9:30 a.m. weekdays, 10 a.m. weekends, in the common room
Recreation: Biking, tennis, golf, hot air ballooning, mud baths
Amenities & Services: 48-ft. swimming pool, hot tub, afternoon wine social w/ hors d'oeuvres, private parking, 3 disabled-accessible rooms

ACCOMMODATIONS

Units: 24 guest rooms, all larger than average, including 3 suites
All Rooms: Private bath, phones, AC
Some Rooms: Fireplace, four-poster, fridge, wet bar, balcony, views of vineyards and mountains, private entrance, private patio, extra daybed (8)
Bed & Bath: Mostly queens, some kings, Jacuzzis for 2 (4)

Favorites: Hastings House rooms, 3 w/ private hot tubs on deck or patio, 1 w/ Jacuzzi for 2, 2 rooms w/ views of vineyards
Comfort & Decor: Rooms individually decorated w/ country antique furnishings, quilts, wallpaper, carpets, wicker accents, iron or brass beds

RATES, RESERVATIONS, & RESTRICTIONS

Deposit: 1st night's lodging; must cancel 22 hours in advance; $10 cancellation fee
Discounts: Return guests; extra person $20
Credit Cards: MC, V
Check-In/Out: 3/noon
Smoking: No
Pets: No
Kids: Not suitable
Minimum Stay: 1, 2, and 3 nights on various rooms
Open: Closed Christmas week, first 2 weeks in Jan.
Host: Jim Smith
1152 Lodi Lane
St. Helena, CA 94574
(707) 963-7077
Fax: (707) 963-9018
www.winecountryinn.com
romance@winecountryinn.com

ZINFANDEL INN, St. Helena

Overall: ★★★½	Room Quality: B	Value: B	Price: $165–$330

This turreted stone castle appears at first glance to be somebody's feudal manor mysteriously teleported to the Napa vineyards. On closer inspection, you'll find a contemporary home behind that brooding facade, with two very large guest rooms and one of average size, all decorated with a lavish hand. The backyard, with its hot tub, free-form swimming pool, velvety lawn, and gazebo, is a major attraction. Though quite close to town, the inn is on a quiet country road almost surrounded by some of America's most prestigious vineyards, a great location for sampling the wine country's many pleasures.

SETTING & FACILITIES

Location: 2 mi. south of St. Helena, .25 mile east of Hwy. 29 on Zinfandel Lane
Near: Wine tasting, spas, restaurants, shopping
Building: English Tudor–style 2-story building built in 1984
Grounds: 2 acres of landscaped grounds w/ gardens, gazebo, fountains, aviary w/ cockatiels, lagoon-like pool

Public Space: Common area, DR
Food & Drink: Full breakfast served at 8:45 a.m. in DR
Recreation: Tennis, golf, swimming, horseback riding, canoeing
Amenities & Services: Champagne and truffles on arrival, evening sherry, private parking

ACCOMMODATIONS

Units: 3 guest rooms, including 2 suites
All Rooms: Private bath, AC, phones, cable TV
Some Rooms: Fireplace, four-poster, VCR, sleeper sofa, panoramic vineyard view, private entrance, balcony
Bed & Bath: Kings, queen (1), Jacuzzis (2)

Favorites: Chardonnay, w/ 14-ft. corner stone fireplace, beamed ceiling, bay window, king brass bed, oval Jacuzzi, private entrance to garden
Comfort & Decor: Rooms individually decorated w/ balloon-type curtains, carpet, sitting areas

RATES, RESERVATIONS, & RESTRICTIONS

Deposit: Credit card to hold, 1st night's lodging; must cancel 10 days in advance; cancellation fee $15
Discounts: Midweek winter; extra person $50
Credit Cards: MC, V
Check-In/Out: 3–5/11, late check-in/out by arrangement
Smoking: No
Pets: No

Kids: Not suitable
Minimum Stay: 2 nights on weekends, 3 on holiday weekends
Open: All year
Hosts: Jerry and Diane Payton
800 Zinfandel Lane
St. Helena, CA 94574
(707) 963-3512
Fax: (707) 963-5310
www.zinfandelinn.com

BURGUNDY HOUSE, Yountville

| Overall: ★★★★ | Room Quality: B | Value: B | Price: $100–$160 |

Originally a distillery, this century-old building has been used, abused, neglected, and finally, in the 1960s, rescued and rehabilitated as an inn. But as with good brandy, its age has only given it more character. The 22-inch-thick river rock and fieldstone walls and the hand-hewn beams and lintels all contribute to the inn's rustic charm. Its ideal location, in the middle of popular Yountville yet on a quiet street (even if it is the main street in town), makes it an ultrapopular place to stay. People enjoy the peaceful surroundings, colorful and copious plantings of flowers, and the homey feeling of harmony in its small but sturdy rooms.

SETTING & FACILITIES

Location: In Yountville; from Hwy. 29, take Yountville exit to Washington St. and turn left, .5 mile to Burgundy House
Near: Wineries, mud baths and spa treatments, shopping, restaurants
Building: 1891 2-story Country French stone structure, on Nat'l Register of Historic Places
Grounds: Double-sized lot, garden setting w/ trees, hedges, roses

Public Space: Parlor and common area, patio
Food & Drink: Full breakfast served 8:30–9:30 a.m. in the common area or outdoors
Recreation: Biking, golf, hot air ballooning, glider rides
Amenities & Services: Afternoon tea w/ port and sherry, fresh flowers, private parking, concierge service for reservations

ACCOMMODATIONS

Units: 6 guest rooms
All Rooms: Private bath, AC
Some Rooms: Fireplace, extra twin (2)
Bed & Bath: Queens, doubles (2)
Favorites: Pommard, w/ separate entrance off garden, fireplace,

white iron bed
Comfort & Decor: Rooms individually decorated w/ antique country furniture, quilted bedspreads, carpet, fresh flowers, beamed ceilings w/ hand-hewn posts and lintels

RATES, RESERVATIONS, & RESTRICTIONS

Deposit: 1st and last night's lodging by check; must cancel 7 days in advance; $20 cancellation fee
Discounts: Off-season, midweek; extra person $25
Credit Cards: MC, V
Check-In/Out: 3–6/11, late check-out by arrangement
Smoking: No
Pets: No

Kids: 10 and over
Minimum Stay: 2 nights on weekends, 3 on holiday weekends
Open: All year
Host: Deanna Roque
P.O. Box 3156
6711 Washington St.
Yountville, CA 94599
(707) 944-0889
www.bbinternet.com/burgundy

MAISON FLEURIE, Yountville

Overall: ★★★★	Room Quality: B	Value: B	Price: $115–$245

There's something about a building with ivy-covered stone walls and flowers out front that sends out a siren song to travelers and travel writers alike. Maybe that's why Maison Fleurie is in virtually every travel book and is generally full. Now restored as a "French" country inn, it oozes charm (though the charm in some of the rooms is a bit worn), making it an ideal place to stay if you are serious about such French passions as good wine and good food. The inn provides bikes for guests, so why not bike to nearby Domaine Chandon for a tasting, or down the street for dinner at one of the country's finest restaurants, the French Laundry? Maison Fleurie is one of the Four Sisters inns, all of which are sources of excellent breakfasts, afternoon hors d'oeuvres, and "bottomless" cookie jars, using recipes from a family-based cookbook.

SETTING & FACILITIES

Location: Just east of Hwy. 29, in Yountville on Yount St., which runs north/south
Near: Wineries, restaurants, shopping
Building: 3 vine-covered stone and brick buildings, the main house built in 1873 w/ 7 guest rooms, carriage house w/ 2 rooms, and bakery building w/ 4 rooms
Grounds: 1 acre of landscaped gardens w/ brick pathways, potted flowers
Public Space: Main building lobby area w/ large stone fireplace, DR w/ fireplace, 2nd-floor sundeck
Food & Drink: Full breakfast served 8–10 a.m. in DR
Recreation: Bicycles avail. at inn; golf, tennis, nearby
Amenities & Services: Swimming pool and spa, teakwood lawn furniture; evening sherry, wine, and hors d'oeuvres; ever-full cookie jar, evening turndown, morning paper, robes, oversized pool towels, hot and cold beverages all day, private parking, disabled access

ACCOMMODATIONS

Units: 13 guest rooms, 5 larger than average
All Rooms: Private bath, phones, AC
Some Rooms: Fireplace, sleeper sofa, cable TV, sofa bed (1), daybed (1)
Bed & Bath: Kings and queens, double (1), Jacuzzis (5)
Favorites: Deluxe room in carriage house, w/ king bed, fireplace, next to pool, private entrance, quiet
Comfort & Decor: Rooms individually decorated w/ antiques, carpet, fine fabrics, whimsical hand-painted wall designs in each room, Country French handcrafted furniture, terra-cotta tile floors

RATES, RESERVATIONS, & RESTRICTIONS

Deposit: Credit card guarantee; must cancel 2 days in advance
Discounts: Repeat guests; extra person $15
Credit Cards: AE, DC, MC, V
Check-In/Out: 3/noon

Smoking: No
Pets: No
Kids: In 6 rooms
No-Nos: No more than 1 bed per room
Minimum Stay: None
Open: All year
Hosts: Roger and Sally Post, owners;

Virginia Marzen, mgr.
6529 Yount St.
Yountville, CA 94599
(707) 944-2056
(800) 788-0369
Fax: (707) 944-9342
www.foursisters.com

OLEANDER HOUSE, Yountville

Overall: ★★★★	Room Quality: B	Value: B	Price: $145–$180

Guests at Oleander House have several car-free entertainment options. It's a very short walk to nearby wineries as well as to Mustard's, among the wine country's best restaurants. Oleander House, a handsome two-story French-style country home, sits back from busy Highway 29, and though the highway noise is not generally bothersome, the most serene rooms are at the back. Oenophiles will like Room 4, which faces one of Napa Valley's most famous vineyards, source of the fabled (and expensive) Joseph Heitz's Martha's Vineyard Cabernet Sauvignon. Guest rooms are very pretty, with high ceilings, Laura Ashley wallcoverings and fabrics, and light, graceful furnishings. Most have fireplaces and French doors leading to balconies. Breakfast, served in the dining room, is pretty special, with entrées like cinnamon-apple flan or soufflé accompanied by apple-cranberry-pecan bread pudding with custard sauce or plum tart.

SETTING & FACILITIES

Location: 3 mi. north of Yountville on the west side of Hwy. 29, just north of Mustard's Grill
Near: Wineries, vineyards, restaurants, spas, shopping, airport
Building: French country–style home
Grounds: 3/4 acre, set back from road by an English rose garden, surrounded by vineyards
Public Space: 2nd-floor guest lounge, formal DR
Food & Drink: Full breakfast served at 9 a.m. in DR
Recreation: Ballooning, golf, biking
Amenities & Services: Outdoor hot tub, evening brandy, complimentary wet bar and fridge, books, Napa Valley guides, private parking, concierge service for reservations, fax, copier, computer hookups

ACCOMMODATIONS

Units: 5 guest rooms, all larger than average
All Rooms: Private bath, AC, vaulted ceiling, ceiling fan
Some Rooms: Fireplaces (4), French doors (4), balcony (4), roll-away avail. (3)
Bed & Bath: Queens

Favorites: No. 1, w/ fireplace, Laura Ashley fabrics, private balcony
Comfort & Decor: Rooms individually decorated w/ four-poster and brass beds, country quilts, antiques, Laura Ashley wallpapers, fine linens, wood blinds, carpet, knotty pine

RATES, RESERVATIONS, & RESTRICTIONS

Deposit: Credit card guarantee; must cancel 7 days in advance or forfeit 1 night's charge if unable to rent
Discounts: AAA, airline employees; extra person $30
Credit Cards: AE, MC, V
Check-In/Out: 3/11, late check-out noon by arrangement
Smoking: No
Pets: No
Kids: 12 and over
Minimum Stay: None

Open: All year
Hosts: Jack and Barbara Kasten, owners; Kathleen Matthews, innkeeper
P.O. Box 2937
7433 St. Helena Hwy.
Yountville, CA 94599
(707) 944-8315
(800) 788-0357
Fax: (707) 944-0980
www.oleander.com
innkeeper@oleander.com

Zone 3
Sacramento, Gold Rush
Country, Lake Tahoe,
and the Sierras

Starting at Sacramento, northeast to the Sierra Nevadas at Quincy, south to Lake Tahoe, then southwest to Yosemite, and across the Sierras to Bridgeport and Mammoth Lakes.

Cities and Towns Sacramento, Lodi, Loomis, Auburn, Nevada City, Grass Valley, Quincy, Cromberg, Sierra City, Truckee, Tahoe City, Homewood, Tahoma, South Lake Tahoe, Coloma, Placerville, Camino, Plymouth, Fair Play, Amador City, Ione, Sutter Creek, Jackson, Volcano, Angels Camp, Murphys, Dorrington, Arnold, Columbia, Twain Harte, Sonora, Jamestown, Groveland, Ahwahnee, Oakhurst, Bridgeport, Bishop, Mammoth Lakes, Georgetown.

Attractions Sacramento, the **California State Capitol**; **Sutter's Fort**; paddlewheel steamboats on the **Sacramento River**; the **California State Railroad Museum**, the finest in the United States, set amid the restored gold rush and Pony Express buildings in **Old Sacramento**; Highway 49, running from **Sierra City** in the north, ending at **Oakhurst** in the south, with mines, mining towns, gold panning, and echoes of the gold rush in between; the **Empire Mine State Park** in Grass Valley, with 360 miles of underground shafts; **Malakoff Diggins** Historic State Park, a hydraulic mining site; **Coloma**, where gold was first discovered; **Columbia**, restored gem of the southern mines, with no cars and lots of family fun; **Angels Camp**, once home to Mark Twain's Jumping Frog; **Lake Tahoe's** resorts, with skiing, fishing, casinos, nightlife, shops, and restaurants and the nearby **Donner Party Memorial** in Truckee; **Calaveras Big Trees**, the largest and oldest living things on Earth; the one and only **Yosemite Valley**, possibly the most beautiful place on Earth; hauntingly beautiful **Mono Lake** and **Bodie**, the most authentic ghost town in California; **Mammoth Lakes** resort area, with skiing, mountain biking, restaurants, resorts, shops, and nearby **Devils Postpile National Monument**.

Contact Information   Sacramento International Airport, (916) 929-5411; California State Railroad Museum, (916) 552-5252, category 7245; Old Sacramento Visitors Center, (916) 442-7644; Sutter's Fort and State Indian Museum, (916) 445-4422; Grass Valley and Nevada County Chamber of Commerce, (800) 655-4667; Nevada City Chamber of Commerce, (800) 655-6569; Plumas County Museum (530) 283-6320; North Lake Tahoe Resort Association, (530) 581-6900 (www.tahoefun. org); Truckee-Donner Chamber of Commerce, (530) 587-2757; Gold Discovery Museum, (530) 622-3470; Hangtown Goldbug Park and Mine, (530) 642-5232; Sutter Creek Visitor Information, (800) 400-0305; Calaveras County Visitors Association, (800) 225-3764; Gold Country Visitors Association, (800) 225-3764 (www.calgold.org); Tuolumne County Visitors Association, (800) 446-1333 (www.tcvb.com); Columbia State Historic Park, (209) 532-0150; Mariposa County Visitors Bureau, (209) 966-6168 (mariposa.yosemite.net/visitor); Yosemite National Park Information, (209) 372-0265; Yosemite Sierra Visitors Association (www.yosemite-sierra.org); Mammoth Lakes Visitor Information, (800) GO-MAMMOTH (www.visitmammoth.com)

Ahwahnee
The Homestead, p. 174

Amador City
Imperial Hotel, p. 175

Arnold
Lodge at Manuel Mill, p. 176

Auburn
Power's Mansion Inn, p. 177

Bishop
Chalfant House, p. 178

Bridgeport
Cain House, p. 179

Camino
Camino Hotel—Seven Mile House,
   p. 181

Coloma
Coloma Country Inn, p. 182

Columbia
Columbia City Hotel & Fallon
   Hotel, p. 183

Cromberg
Twenty Mile House, p. 185

Crowley Lake
Rainbow Tarns B&B at Crowley
   Lake, p. 186

Dorrington
Dorrington Hotel and Restaurant,
   p. 187

Fair Play
Fitzpatrick Winery and Lodge,
   p. 188

Georgetown
American River Inn, p. 189

Grass Valley
Murphy's Inn, p. 191

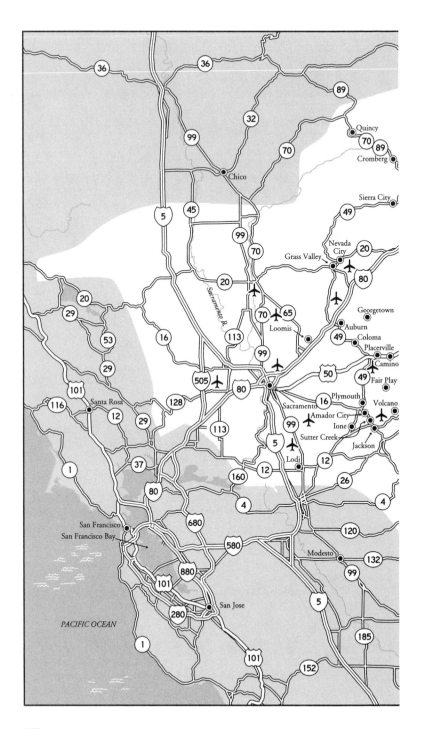

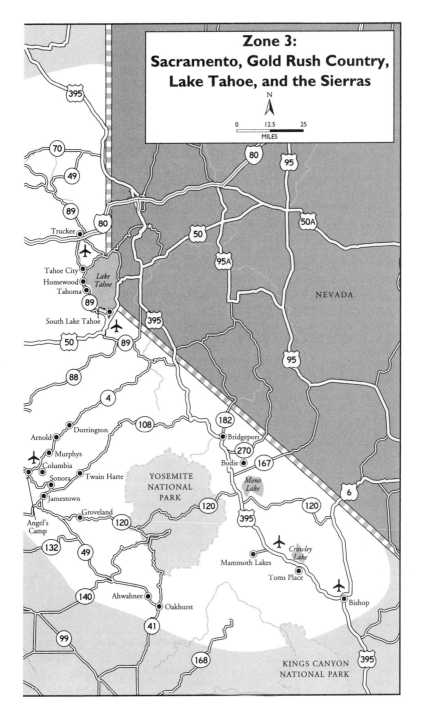

Zone 3:
Sacramento, Gold Rush Country,
Lake Tahoe, and the Sierras

N

0   12.5   25
MILES

395

70

49

89

80

Truckee

Tahoe City

Homewood

Lake
Tahoe

Tahoma

89

South Lake Tahoe

50

89

88

4

108

Arnold

Dorrington

Murphys

Columbia

Sonora

Twain Harte

Jamestown

Groveland

120

Angel's
Camp

132

49

140

Ahwahnee

Oakhurst

41

99

168

80

95

50

50A

95A

NEVADA

395

95

182

Bridgeport

270

Bodie

167

Mono
Lake

YOSEMITE
NATIONAL
PARK

120

120

395

6

Crowley
Lake

Mammoth Lakes

Toms Place

Bishop

KINGS CANYON
NATIONAL PARK

395

THE HOMESTEAD, Ahwahnee

Overall: ★★★★½	Room Quality: A	Value: B	Price: $125–$225

These beautifully constructed and handsomely furnished cottages are a perfect place to stay when you visit the Yosemite area. Individually situated among ancient oaks, each of the four cottages has a living room and fireplace, a fully equipped kitchen, and a separate, comfortable bedroom and bath, plus an outdoor sitting area and barbecue. Details such as leather couches, oak tables, and nice sets of dishes and cookware take this place way out of the "roughing it" category, even though you're definitely in the country. There's a smaller, less expensive "stargazing loft," too. All are very private, and there are 160 wooded acres to explore. Beverages are stocked in your kitchen, and a basket of goodies is delivered to your doorstep in the morning.

SETTING & FACILITIES

Location: 4.5 mi. from Oakhurst on Hwy. 49; go to Rd. 600, then 2.5 mi. to entrance
Near: Yosemite Nat'l Park, shopping, restaurants
Building: Stone and adobe cottages built in 1992
Grounds: 160 acres featuring meandering rock walls and gardens
Food & Drink: Extended cont'l breakfast served in the cottage
Recreation: Golf, mountain biking, fishing, horseback riding
Amenities & Services: Barbecue, robes, private parking, disabled access, satellite television, in-cottage massages, concierge services, telephone and fax machine in office, equine layover possible

ACCOMMODATIONS

Units: 4 guest cottages w/ sitting area, BRs, and kitchens, and stargazing loft w/ smaller kitchen
All Rooms: Fully equipped kitchen, private bath, cable TV, AC, private entrance
Some Rooms: Fireplaces (4), four-poster, sofa bed (2), view of trees and mountains
Bed & Bath: Queens
Favorites: Country, w/ antique Morris chair, dark green leather couch, oak inlay dining table, log bed, fireplace; kitchen equipped w/ wineglasses, dishes, and pans; barbecue, outdoor sitting area
Comfort & Decor: Cottages individually decorated w/ artwork, Levelors and valances, hand-trowelled plaster, Saltillo tile floors and rugs, pine and stone fireplaces, pine ceilings and framings, woven baskets

RATES, RESERVATIONS, & RESTRICTIONS

Deposit: 50% of bill on booking; must cancel 7 days in advance
Discounts: Long stays; extra person $50
Credit Cards: AE, D, MC, V
Check-In/Out: 3/11, late check-out possible
Smoking: No
Pets: No
Kids: Limited availability

Minimum Stay: 2 nights on week-
ends, 3 on holidays
Open: Open all year
Hosts: Larry Ends and Cindy Brooks
41110 Rd. 600
Ahwahnee, CA 93601

(209) 693-0495
Fax: (559) 683-8165
www.homesteadcottages.com
homesteadcottages@sierratel.com

IMPERIAL HOTEL, Amador City

Overall: ★★★½	Room Quality: C	Value: A	Price: $75–$105

This picturesque two-story brick building is the real deal, historically
speaking. It opened as a hotel in 1879, stayed in business almost a half-
century, and was resurrected in all its whimsical glory in 1988 by the current owners. Acclaimed for its innovative restaurant and lively bar, the
hotel has six guest rooms upstairs that are a combination of antiques, modern plumbing, and decor that ranges from very pretty to pretty amusing.
A lovely, secluded patio made of native stone, awash in greenery and lulled
by the trickle of fountains, is a splendid place to chill out. A recent breakfast included French toast and all the trimmings. Amador City is the smallest incorporated city in California, and it won't take you long to see the
sights. There's lots to do in the surrounding countryside, however, including 16 up-and-coming California wineries.

SETTING & FACILITIES

Location: Amador City, on Hwy. 49 in
the foothills of the Sierra Nevada, 35
mi. from Sacraemnto
Near: 16 nearby wineries, antique and
specialty shops, galleries, state parks,
local airport
Building: 1879 2-story Gothic
Victorian
Grounds: Stone paved patio w/ 3 fountains, flower beds, upper lawn area w/
hammocks, herb garden

Public Space: Library, DR
Food & Drink: Full breakfast served
8–10 a.m. in room, DR, or patio
Recreation: Golf, tennis, river rafting,
fishing
Amenities & Services: Hairdryers,
heated towel racks, public DR and
Oasis Bar open nightly 5–9 p.m., picnic
baskets avail. w/ 1 day's notice, private
parking, local airport pickup

ACCOMMODATIONS

Units: 6 guest rooms, 1 larger than
average, 2 suites avail. by combining
rooms
All Rooms: Private bath, AC
Some Rooms: Four-poster, sleeper
sofa (1)
Bed & Bath: Queens, king (can also be
2 twins)

Favorites: No. 1, w/ queen canopy bed,
sitting area, sunny high-ceilinged room,
balcony w/ French doors, large windows overlooking Main St., tub/shower
Comfort & Decor: Rooms individually decorated w/ antiques, wicker, Art
Deco accents

RATES, RESERVATIONS, & RESTRICTIONS

Deposit: 1st night's lodging; must cancel 7 nights in advance
Discounts: Weekday business, AAA, singles; extra person $15
Credit Cards: AE, D, MC, V
Check-In/Out: 3/noon
Smoking: No, except in adjoining bar
Pets: No
Kids: Not suitable for young children
Minimum Stay: 2 nights on weekends

Open: All year
Hosts: Bruce Sherrill and Dale Martin
P.O. Box 195
14202 Hwy. 49
Amador City, CA 95601
(209) 267-9172
(800) 242-5594
Fax: (209) 267-9249
www.imperialamador.com
Host@Imperialamador.com

LODGE AT MANUEL MILL, Arnold

Overall: ★★★½	Room Quality: C	Value: B	Price: $95–$130

This is a place you're never going to stumble over by accident. Nestled in the Stanislaus National Forest near Calaveras Big Trees State Park, the lodge is located at the end of an unpaved road in 43 acres of woods and right next to a 4.3-acre millpond. Although the guest rooms are comfortable, the best features here are the expansive deck overhanging the pond; the charming Great Room, with cushy red couches, a stone fireplace, and windows overlooking the water; and, of course, the wonderful forest location. In spring, wildflowers abound. Breakfast is served in the dining room or on the deck, if you can eat your fruit, French toast, and ham with all of those trout hungrily staring up at you.

SETTING & FACILITIES

Location: Just east of the town of Arnold on Hwy. 4, 21 mi. east of Angels Camp, 2.5 hours from Sacramento, 3 hours from San Francisco; call for directions
Near: Surrounded by Stanislaus Nat'l Forest, near Calaveras Big Trees State Park, w/ giant sequoias, caverns, wineries
Building: Main lodge is log construction circa 1950, located on the millpond of a 19th-century lumber mill
Grounds: 43 acres in Stanislaus Forest
Public Space: Main lodge room w/ massive stone fireplace, DR, gazebo, deck
Food & Drink: Full breakfast served at 9 a.m. in DR or on the deck overlooking the pond
Recreation: Rowing on millpond, swimming, fishing, bird-watching; X-C/downhill skiing, golf, river rafting, and mountain biking nearby
Amenities & Services: Barbecue, evening wine and hors d'oeuvres, hot soup during winter weekends, complimentary bottle of wine on arrival, private parking

ACCOMMODATIONS

Units: 5 guest rooms, 2 larger than average
All Rooms: Private bath and entrance, wood-burning stove
Some Rooms: Four-poster
Bed & Bath: Mostly queens
Favorites: Mr. Manuel Room, w/ oak canopy bed, Victorian decor, black-and-beige-striped chintz; Lillie Coit Room, w/ white enamel and brass bed, pink and blue color scheme
Comfort & Decor: Rooms individually decorated w/ antiques, lace curtains, wood floors w/ area rugs

RATES, RESERVATIONS, & RESTRICTIONS

Deposit: 50% of bill; must cancel 72 hours in advance; $10 processing fee
Discounts: Sun.–Thurs. business
Credit Cards: MC, V
Check-In/Out: 3/11, late check-out by arrangement
Smoking: No
Pets: No
Kids: Not suitable
No-Nos: No more than 2 guests per room
Minimum Stay: 2 nights on weekends and holidays
Open: All year
Hosts: Linda and Ray Johnson, owners; Dee and Stan Bouchard, innkeepers
P.O. Box 998
1573 White Pine Rd.
Arnold, CA 95223
(209) 795-2622

POWER'S MANSION INN, Auburn

Overall: ★★★½   Room Quality: B   Value: B   Price: $89–$169

Auburn is the Gold Country's largest town, with a busy Old Town area and several very good restaurants. It also has Power's Mansion Inn, built in 1898 by a family with a gold-mining fortune. Although the inn is distinctively pink and almost fills a city block, the town has grown up around it, and it's nearly invisible from the street. There's a choice of 13 attractive guest rooms, some with skylights, fireplaces, four-poster beds, and Jacuzzis. Breakfast is a hearty affair in the pretty dining room that still has the original heavy wood beams and curved glass bay windows.

SETTING & FACILITIES

Location: In Auburn; from Hwy. 80, going east, take Elm St. exit, then turn left on Elm St., right on High St., and left on Cleveland
Near: Restaurants, shopping, antiques, Mother Lode Trail
Building: 1898 Victorian built w/ Power family's gold-mining fortune
Grounds: Landscaped urban lot w/ 100-year-old trees, terraced garden w/ patio and sitting areas
Public Space: Parlor, DR w/ original curved glass bay windows, beamed ceilings and fireplace, entry w/ fireplace, 2nd parlor w/ fireplace, wraparound porch and deck
Food & Drink: Full breakfast served 8–9 a.m. on weekdays, 8–10 a.m. on weekends, in DR
Recreation: Gold panning, fishing, horseback riding, water sports, golf, mountain biking, river rafting
Amenities & Services: Morning newspaper, robes, private parking

ACCOMMODATIONS

Units: 13 guest rooms, all larger than average, including 4 suites
All Rooms: Private bath, TV, phone, AC
Some Rooms: Fireplace, four-poster, fridge, skylight, private entrance, city view, extra bed (1)
Bed & Bath: Queens, heart-shaped Jacuzzi (1), Jacuzzi and claw-foot tub (1)
Favorites: Power Family Master BR, w/ original bay windows, four-poster, sitting area; Honeymoon Suite, w/ fireplace, mirrored and inlaid armoire, brick window seat, heart-shaped Jacuzzi for 2
Comfort & Decor: Rooms individually decorated w/ antiques, Bradbury & Bradbury wallpaper, carpet, Persian rugs, original hardwood floors; historic photos of Power family, mansion, and mine

RATES, RESERVATIONS, & RESTRICTIONS

Deposit: Credit card; must cancel 3 days in advance
Discounts: Long stays, weekday business; extra person $10
Credit Cards: AE, MC, V
Check-In/Out: 2–10/11, late checkout by arrangement
Smoking: No
Pets: No
Kids: By arrangement

Minimum Stay: None
Open: All year
Hosts: Arno and Jean Lejnieks
164 Cleveland Ave.
Auburn, CA 95603
(530) 885-1166
Fax: (530) 885-1386
www.vfr.net/~powerinn
powerinn@westsierra.net

CHALFANT HOUSE, Bishop

Overall: ★★★½	Room Quality: B	Value: A	Price: $60–$100

This innocently pretty house has a checkered past. Built in 1898 by the publisher of the first newspaper in the area, it later became a lodging house catering to miners and, gasp, foreigners. But that wasn't the end of its slide into decadence: for almost 20 years it was a brothel. Bishop is in the eastern Sierra Nevada Mountains, and there are lot of lakes, mountain trails, and the Mammoth Mountain Ski Area to try in this uncrowded, unspoiled part of California. A recent breakfast menu at the inn included peaches and cream, French toast, and juice made from grapes grown on the property.

SETTING & FACILITIES

Location: Centrally located in Bishop, 1 block west of Hwy. 395
Near: Shopping, theater, restaurants, park, airport, petroglyphs
Building: 1898 Victorian house
Grounds: Landscaped triple urban lot w/ gardens
Public Space: Parlor, library, gazebo
Food & Drink: Full breakfast served in DR at 7:30 or 8:30 a.m.
Recreation: Golf, fishing, 45 min. to Mammoth ski area and bristlecone pines, hot springs, rock climbing
Amenities & Services: Afternoon beverages, hot apple cider, iced tea, evening ice cream sundaes, private parking

ACCOMMODATIONS

Units: 8 guest rooms, 3 larger than average, including 3 suites
All Rooms: Private bath, AC, ceiling fan
Some Rooms: Fireplace (1), four-poster (1), sleeper sofa (1), extra bed (2); 1 suite has full kitchen, TVs and VCRs
Bed & Bath: Mostly queens
Favorites: Flora, w/ fireplace and four-poster, sitting room, TV/VCR, in mauves and greens; Pleasant Room, in rose and blue, w/ antique white iron bed, stone wall and oak wainscoting in bathroom, oak armoire and dresser, private side entrance and patio w/ table and chairs under a grape arbor
Comfort & Decor: Rooms individually decorated w/ antiques and country furnishings, handmade quilts and comforters, ceiling fans

RATES, RESERVATIONS, & RESTRICTIONS

Deposit: Credit card to hold; must cancel 24 hours in advance; $15 cancellation fee
Discounts: Long stays
Credit Cards: AE, D, MC, V
Check-In/Out: 3/11, late check-in by arrangement
Smoking: No
Pets: No
Kids: Over 8

Minimum Stay: None
Open: All year
Hosts: Fred and Sally Manecke
213 Academy St.
Bishop, CA 93514
(760) 872-1790
www.chalfanthousebb.com
chalfantbb@qnet.com

CAIN HOUSE: A COUNTRY INN, Bridgeport

Overall: ★★★★   Room Quality: B   Value: A   Price: $80–$135

Bridgeport is a pretty little town situated in a lush High Sierra valley. It's surrounded by mountains with a picture-postcard backdrop provided by the sawtooth peaks of the nearby Hoover Wilderness—and that's the view you get out the front door of Cain House. This 1920s ranch house with a white picket fence and Arts and Crafts furnishings has the greenest lawn you ever saw, as green as any in Switzerland—ideal for a game of croquet or badminton. The inn is a superior place from which to investigate the many charms of the eastern Sierras. Some of the West's largest trout are caught in lakes and reservoirs within casting distance (well, darn near) of the inn. Bodie, that legendary and most authentic of western ghost towns, is only 21 miles away. The friendly hosts knock themselves out to get you fed in the morning—they'll fix you something light if you're in a hurry, or "to go" if you're in a serious hurry. Otherwise you get the full treatment of French toast stuffed with raspberries, potatoes roasted in olive oil and thyme, and fresh fruit. Now that's roughing it!

SETTING & FACILITIES

Location: On the north side of Main
St. at the west end of Bridgeport, next
to the courthouse; 4 hours west of
Sacramento, 2.5 hours south of Reno
Near: Shopping, Bodie ghost town,
Mono Lake, Bridgeport Reservoir, hot
springs, airport
Building: 1920s western 2-story
ranch-style house w/ cedar siding and
white trim
Grounds: 3/4 acre w/ large grassy
parklike setting
Public Space: Common area w/ local
stone fireplace, 2 DRs, front porch w/
swing and Adirondack chairs
Food & Drink: Selection of 4 breakfasts: full, light, European w/ bread and
cheese, or "to go" for travelers, served
in DR, deck, or in room, depending
on room
Recreation: Badminton, croquet on
site; tennis next door; trout fishing, biking, swimming, horseback riding nearby
Amenities & Services: Barbecue,
afternoon snacks of wine, fresh fruit,
gourmet cheeses and crackers, private
parking

ACCOMMODATIONS

Units: 7 guest rooms, 3 larger than
average
All Rooms: Private bath, cable TV,
phone
Some Rooms: AC (3), four-poster,
fridge, outside entrance (2), breakfast
served in room (1), breakfast served
outside (1)
Bed & Bath: Queens, king (1)
Favorites: J. S. Caine Room, w/ private
deck and entrance, faces back garden,
pineapple mahogany four-poster,
cherry-wood inlaid dresser, matching
dark green/maroon paisley wallpaper
and Laura Ashley bedspread, large
closet, fridge
Comfort & Decor: Rooms individually decorated w/ antiques, Arts and
Crafts–style furnishings, whitewashed
pine, wicker, oak, custom window treatments, carpet, hardwood floors, area
rugs, oriental rugs

RATES, RESERVATIONS, & RESTRICTIONS

Deposit: 100% of bill on credit card;
must cancel 48 hours in advance
Discounts: None
Credit Cards: All
Check-In/Out: 3/11, late check-out by
arrangement
Smoking: No
Pets: No
Kids: OK
No-Nos: No more than 2 guests
per room
Minimum Stay: None
Open: From last weekend in April to
last weekend in Oct.
Hosts: Christopher and Marachal
Gohlich
340 Main St.
Bridgeport, CA 93517
(760) 932-7040
(800) 433-2246
Fax: (760) 932-7419
thecainhouse@msn.com

CAMINO HOTEL—SEVEN MILE HOUSE, Camino

Overall: ★★★	Room Quality: C	Value: A	Price: $50–$95

The paint is peeling a bit and the porch furniture looks a little tired, but inside this is a cute place, with a big, comfortable parlor, a great sunroom, and nine guest rooms that someone has furnished with affection and whimsy. Plus, the price is right and the location is great. Originally known as Seven Mile, Camino was a historic mill town where wagons carried miners and supplies from San Francisco to the Comstock Lode and where Pony Express riders exchanged tired horses. The Camino Hotel is a restored loggers' barrack and says right up front that it provides down-to-earth-accommodations and that "there are no Chippendale or Queen Anne chairs to strike fear in the hearts of parents."

SETTING & FACILITIES

Location: Hwy. 50 East from Placerville to Camino exit, turn right off exit and drive 1 mi.
Near: Wineries, microbreweries, apple orchards, restaurants, antiques
Building: 1888 clapboard boardinghouse
Grounds: Urban lot
Public Space: Parlor, wine-tasting room, game room, DR, sunporch
Food & Drink: Full breakfast at 9 a.m. (unless other arrangements are requested) served in the 1st-floor parlor
Recreation: Biking, horseshoes, horseback riding, whitewater rafting; 45 min. to skiing, snowboarding
Amenities & Services: Chocolate chip cookies, coffee, tea, hot cocoa in the evening; wine tasting on site, massage therapist in-house, old phone booth inside building, private parking

ACCOMMODATIONS

Units: 9 guest rooms, 2 larger than average
All Rooms: AC
Some Rooms: Four-poster, small dining area (1), extra bed (4)
Bed & Bath: Mostly queens and doubles, 6 rooms share 3 baths
Favorites: No. 1, C. D. Danaher, the largest room, w/ four-poster, handmade sampler quilt, full bath, 5 windows; No. 2, E. J. Barrett, a romantic room w/ heart-shaped headboard, fuschia pink cabbage rose decor, claw-foot tub
Comfort & Decor: Rooms individually decorated w/ local watercolors, pastels, antique sewing machine collection, theme memorabilia, handmade curtains, quilts, red fir floors throughout

RATES, RESERVATIONS, & RESTRICTIONS

Deposit: Credit card or check received w/in 48 hours; must cancel 48 hours in advance, 7 days for holidays and special events
Discounts: Long stays, weekday business groups, AAA, winter weekdays, seniors, active-duty military, corporate; extra person $10

Credit Cards: All
Check-In/Out: 2/11, late check-out by arrangement
Smoking: No
Pets: No
Kids: OK
No-Nos: No more than 2 guests per room
Minimum Stay: 2 nights on some

special events and holidays
Open: All year
Host: Paula Nobert
P.O. Box 1179
4103 Carson Rd.
Camino, CA 95709
(916) 644-7740
(800) 200-7740
Fax: (530) 647-1416

COLOMA COUNTRY INN, Coloma

Overall: ★★★★½	Room Quality: A	Value: B	Price: $95–$180

The farmhouse that became the Coloma Country Inn was built down the street from Sutter's Mill, a scant four years after James Marshall discovered traces of gold there. Now the site of the discovery is a park, generally quiet, except for summer weekends when tourists wander the town visiting the restored one-room schoolhouse and the working blacksmith, tinsmith, and gunsmith shops. But crowds don't bother guests at the pretty Coloma Country Inn, with its picket fence and wraparound veranda. It sits on five acres of land. There's a pond with a rowboat, a brick patio, and a garden full of old-fashioned roses. More cautious souls may want to rent a bicycle in Coloma and peddle through the lovely countryside in the park. There's abundant wildlife in the area, and the innkeepers provide field guides and binoculars. The decor of the inn is understated and tasteful, with an appropriately country feel. The beautiful quilts on the beds are all antiques from Cindi Ehrgott's collection.

SETTING & FACILITIES

Location: In the historic town of Coloma in Marshall Gold Discovery State Historic Park (site of Sutter's Mill), 8 mi. north of Hwy. 50 on Hwy. 49, 45 min. from Sacramento
Near: Walking distance to state park facilities, natural history programs; near 20 local wineries; Placerville, w/ antiques, shops, galleries, restaurants
Building: 1852 American farmhouse w/ clapboard siding, wraparound front porch, 1898 carriage house w/ antique weathervane
Grounds: 5 acres w/ heritage rose garden, large pond w/ rowboat, lawns, fruit

trees, perennial gardens, gazebo
Public Space: Parlor, DR, outdoor pergola
Food & Drink: Expanded cont'l breakfast served 8–9 a.m. in DR or outside overlooking the pond, breakfast in bed by request
Recreation: On-site croquet, hot air ballooning, birding, berry picking; nearby biking, gold panning, whitewater rafting, fishing, nature hikes
Amenities & Services: Barbecue, use of inn's kitchen, afternoon iced tea, lemonade and cookies, private parking, concierge service for reservations

ACCOMMODATIONS

Units: 7 guest rooms, 5 rooms in the main house, 2 suites in the carriage house, 1 of which has 2 BRs/kitchenette
All Rooms: AC, in-room sitting area
Some Rooms: Fridge, view of pond and gardens, private patio and garden, kitchenette, private entrance (5), private bath (5), shared bath (2)
Bed & Bath: Queens, doubles (2), claw-foot tubs w/ overhead showers

Favorites: Lavender Room, large, w/ lilac walls, lace curtains, windows all around, views; Rose Room, w/ double bed, sitting area, private brick courtyard, views of gazebo and gardens
Comfort & Decor: Rooms individually decorated American Country decor w/ art, both American and English antiques, wallpaper, cushions, white wicker, shutters, antique quilts

RATES, RESERVATIONS, & RESTRICTIONS

Deposit: 50% of deposit within 7 days of reservation; must cancel 2 weeks in advance
Discounts: Winter weekdays, singles; extra person $25
Credit Cards: None
Check-In/Out: 4/11, late check-out by arrangement
Smoking: No
Pets: No
Kids: OK

Minimum Stay: 2 nights on weekends April–Nov.
Open: All year
Hosts: Alan and Cindi Ehrgott
P.O. Box 502
345 High St.
Coloma, CA 95613
(530) 622-6919
Fax: (530) 622-1795
www.colomacountryinn.com

COLUMBIA CITY HOTEL AND FALLON HOTEL, Columbia

Overall: ★★★½	Room Quality: B	Value: A	Price: $50–$115

If you and your family haven't been to Columbia State Historic Park, you're missing out—it's a hoot. You can ride in a 100-year-old stagecoach, pan for gold, or tour an active gold mine. It's the best-preserved gold town in the Mother Lode, and its two beautiful, historic hotels have been authentically restored by the California State Park System. There are splendid antiques in the guest rooms, lovely parlors, and a friendly, helpful staff that often includes hotel management students from the local college. A buffet breakfast of fresh-baked breads, muffins, cereal, yogurt, and quiche is offered at both hotels. The City Hotel also boasts the What Cheer Saloon, with the original cherry-wood bar shipped around the Horn from New England. Its rowdy days are over now, and it's a pleasant spot to take a breather. The park hosts special events almost every month—art shows, a fiddle and banjo contest, a miner's Christmas, and several docent-led campfire events, to list only a few. This is a fun place, and kids are welcome.

SETTING & FACILITIES

Location: In Columbia State Historic Park, off Hwy. 49 between Angels Camp and Sonora

Near: Columbia State Historic Park, Moaning Caves, Calaveras Big Trees State Park, wine tasting and tours, shopping, theater, airport

Building: Victorian structures built in 1857 (City Hotel) and 1856 (Fallon Hotel)

Grounds: The sister hotels are centrally located in Columbia State Historic Park

Public Space: City Hotel—upstairs and downstairs parlors, restaurant DR, smaller dining room that doubles as a meeting room; Fallon Hotel—parlor

Food & Drink: Expanded cont'l breakfast served 8–9:30 a.m. in DR at the City Hotel; in the ice cream parlor adjoining the Fallon Hotel

Recreation: Tennis, golf, waterskiing, downhill skiing

Amenities & Services: Evening sherry served at the City Hotel for both hotels, children's parlor games avail. at City Hotel, private parking, disabled access at the Fallon Hotel, public restaurant and bar at City Hotel, room/dinner/theater packages

ACCOMMODATIONS

Units: City Hotel—10 guest rooms; Fallon Hotel—14 guest rooms

All Rooms: AC/heat

Some Rooms: Four-poster, extra bed (3)

Bed & Bath: City Hotel—Mostly doubles, all rooms w/ washbasins and commodes, shared shower rooms; Fallon Hotel—Mostly doubles, 1 private bath, 12 rooms w/ washbasins and commodes, shared shower rooms, 1 w/ shared bath

Favorites: City Hotel—No. 1, w/ private balcony, bed w/ ornate headboard; Fallon Hotel—No. 1, w/ large private balcony, double bed

Comfort & Decor: Rooms are individually decorated w/ Victorian antiques, Victorian wallpaper, wainscoting, velvet draperies, period lamps, oriental rugs, wicker baskets w/ all necessities for shower room, marble-topped furniture, hardwood floors, patchwork quilts, historic photos and paintings of gold rush California

RATES, RESERVATIONS, & RESTRICTIONS

Deposit: 100% of bill; must cancel 72 hours in advance

Discounts: None; extra person $10 (5 and over)

Credit Cards: AE, D, MC, V

Check-In/Out: 2/noon

Smoking: No

Pets: No

Kids: OK

Minimum Stay: None

Open: City Hotel and Fallon Hotel closed Jan. 1–10 (approximately); Fallon Hotel open weekends only Jan.–June (approximately)

Host: Tom Bender
P.O. Box 1870
Main St. in Columbia
    State Historic Park
Columbia, CA 95310
(209) 532-1479
(800) 532-1479
Fax: (209) 532-7027
www.cityhotel.com
info@cityhotel.com

TWENTY MILE HOUSE, Cromberg

| Overall: ★★★★ | Room Quality: B | Value: B | Price: $125–$135 |

This sleepy hideaway is a mile off the highway but 140 years in the past. It is quiet and relaxing—even though the Union Pacific, which used to stop here, still sends several trains up the canyon every day. A stay in this tastefully restored inn will summon up dreams of the days when stagecoaches (which in the 1860s were lucky to make 20 miles a day) stopped here three times a week as they brought gold seekers from the East via the Beckwith Trail. And when your get-up-and-go comes back, you can mosey down to the Feather and cast a fly to some of the wild trout on this little-fished section of one of America's Wild and Scenic Rivers. When your batteries get fully charged, there's a choice of six golf courses nearby (including several of world-class quality), plus several excellent restaurants. You can have your hardtack and eat it too!

SETTING & FACILITIES

Location: 1 mi. south of Hwy. 70, 7 mi. northwest of Graeagle, 3 hours northeast of Sacramento via Hwys. I-80 and I-89
Near: 6 major golf courses, X-C/ downhill skiing, trout fishing, mountain biking, gold panning, restaurants, 1 hour to Reno's casinos and shows
Building: Restored 1854 used-brick Victorian stagecoach stop w/ white porch, railings, and fretwork
Grounds: 250 acres at the junction of the Feather River and Jackson Creek,

extensive lawns and gardens
Public Space: Parlor
Food & Drink: Full gourmet breakfast served on porch, in garden, or in room at time of guest's choice
Recreation: Gold panning and fly fishing in the Feather River on site; golf, downhill/X-C skiing in nearby Plumas Eureka State Park
Amenities & Services: Barbecue, bicycles, afternoon snacks, hors d'oeuvres and wine, Adirondack chairs on lawns, porches, private parking

ACCOMMODATIONS

Units: 3 guest rooms plus 1 cabin that sleeps 4, w/ kitchen and large deck
All Rooms: Private bath, fresh flowers, coffee, tea, books
Some Rooms: Fireplace, four-poster, extra twin(s) (2)
Bed & Bath: Queens, doubles

Favorites: The downstairs room (originally the parlor for the stage stop), w/ a Victorian brass bed, marble washstand, and carved bench
Comfort & Decor: English antiques, New England pine walls, hardwood floors in a warm, period atmosphere

RATES, RESERVATIONS, & RESTRICTIONS

Deposit: 1 night's lodging; full refund if canceled 1 week ahead
Discounts: Long stays
Credit Cards: None
Check-In/Out: 2/11, late check-out

OK if room not rented next night
Smoking: No
Pets: If compatible w/ owner's 2 cats and dog
Kids: OK

Minimum Stay: None
Open: All year
Host: Barbara Gage
P.O. Box 30001
Old Cromberg Rd., 1 mi. south of

Hwy. 70
Cromberg, CA 96103
(530) 836-0375
twentymh@aol.com

RAINBOW TARNS B&B AT CROWLEY LAKE,
Crowley Lake

Overall: ★★★½	Room Quality: B	Value: A	Price: $75–$140

Crossword puzzle fans will recognize "tarns" as an often-used though obscure word for a "glacial pond." The three namesake tarns here—right outside the front door—are threaded by a small creek that rainbow trout swim up each spring to spawn, thus the name. The inn started its life in the 1920s as a log cabin and still retains its rustic charm, enhanced by contemporary creature comforts like whirlpool tubs and down beds and comforters. At 7,000 feet in the heart of the southern High Sierras, the inn is seemingly miles from civilization. In reality, it's less than 15 miles away from Mammoth Lakes, a trendy ski and vacation resort town catering to the LA crowd and offering plenty of boutiques and restaurants for the urban addict. Also close are cross-country skiing, hiking, mountain biking, and fishing. The food's pretty upscal—a recent breakfast menu included poached pears in burgundy sauce, orange-almond pound cake, baked cheese omelet soufflé, country potatoes, and sausage and bacon.

SETTING & FACILITIES

Location: Between Bishop and Mammoth west of Hwy. 395, .75 mi. north of the hamlet of Tom's Place on Crowley Lake Dr.
Near: Restaurants, dancing, hot mineral baths, Devil's Postpile, Mono Lake, Crowley Lake
Building: Log and brick inn built in the 1920s, remodeled in 1990
Grounds: 3 acres w/ huge granite boulders, pines, aspen, grassy meadows, stream and 3 ponds (tarns)
Public Space: Parlor w/ stone fireplace, game table, couches, books, dining area
Food & Drink: Full breakfast served at guests' convenience in dining area or on deck
Recreation: Fishing, boating, horseback riding, mountain biking, rock climbing, X-C/downhill skiing, birdwatching
Amenities & Services: Afternoon wine and snacks, private parking, disabled access

ACCOMMODATIONS

Units: 3 guest rooms, 2 larger than average
All Rooms: Private bath

Bed & Bath: Queens, double, whirlpool baths (2)

Favorites: Gemini Room, w/ rustic furnishings, outdoor art, garden skylight over the whirlpool tub; Rainbow Room, w/ brass bed, antiques, Tiffany lamps, whirlpool tub

Comfort & Decor: Rooms individually decorated w/ antiques, carpet, down comforters and pillows

RATES, RESERVATIONS, & RESTRICTIONS

Deposit: 50% of bill; must cancel 7 days in advance
Discounts: Long stays, seniors; children 12–18 sharing parents' room $20/child
Credit Cards: None
Check-In/Out: 3/11, late check-out by arrangement
Smoking: No
Pets: No
Kids: 12 and over
No-Nos: No more than 2 guests per room, except children
Minimum Stay: 2 nights on weekends, 3 on holiday weekends
Open: May close 2 to 3 weeks in early spring and late fall
Hosts: Brock and Diane Thoman
HC 79, Box 1053
Crowley Lake, CA 93546
(760) 935-4556
(888) 588-6269
www.rainbowtarns.com
info@rainbowtarns.com

DORRINGTON HOTEL AND RESTAURANT, Dorrington

Overall: ★★★½	Room Quality: B	Value: A	Price: $85–$125

Built in 1852, this charmingly restored hotel was originally a stagecoach stop, a depot for stockmen, and a summer resort. Pretty wallpaper and quilts, brass beds, and a judicious use of antiques characterize the five medium-sized guest rooms. The private cabin adjacent to the hotel has a wood plank floor, a large stone fireplace, a small kitchen area, and a spa tub. The hotel restaurant serves very good northern Italian cuisine, and the tiny village of Dorrington is a convenient place to stay while you're visiting the area's many attractions. A continental breakfast is delivered to your door with a morning newspaper. They may be out in the country, but they're civilized.

SETTING & FACILITIES

Location: In Dorrington on Hwy. 4, 75 mi. east of Stockton
Near: Moaning and Mercer Caverns, Calaveras Big Trees State Park, wineries, restaurants, shopping; Mt. Reba/Bear Valley ski area half-hour away
Building: 1852 Mother Lode clapboard stagecoach depot/hotel
Grounds: 38 acres of high-elevation meadow with pine and cedar forest
Public Space: Sitting room, DR
Food & Drink: Expanded cont'l breakfast served to guest's room
Recreation: Golf, horseback riding, X-C/downhill skiing, fishing
Amenities & Services: Evening sherry in sitting room, fresh fruit, newspaper; restaurant on site, private parking

ACCOMMODATIONS

Units: 5 guest rooms in main house, cabin
All Rooms: Brass bed, homemade quilt
Some Rooms: Fireplace, fridge, meadow view, sleeper sofa and private bath (cabin), shared baths (main house)
Bed & Bath: Queens
Favorites: Cabin Sweet Cabin, w/ stone fireplace, wood plank floor, spa

tub, queen bed, kitchen; No. 1 in main house, w/ brass bed, wainscoting, and a view of the meadow
Comfort & Decor: Individually decorated w/ brass beds, wingback chairs, antiques, lace curtains, wallpaper and wainscoting, hardwood floors w/ area rugs

RATES, RESERVATIONS, & RESTRICTIONS

Deposit: 1st night's lodging; must cancel 5 days in advance; $10 cancellation fee
Discounts: Midweek ski packages; extra person $20
Credit Cards: MC, V
Check-In/Out: 3–6/11
Smoking: No
Pets: No
Kids: In cabin
No-Nos: No more than 2 guests per room, except cabin

Minimum Stay: Cabin 2 nights on weekends
Minimum Stay: Cabin 2 nights on weekends
Open: All year
Hosts: Arden and Bonnie Saville
P.O. Box 4307
3431 Hwy. 4
Dorrington, CA 95223
(209) 795-5800
Fax: (209) 795-1926

FITZPATRICK WINERY AND LODGE, Fair Play

Overall: ★★★★	Room Quality: B	Value: A	Price: $79–$130

Fair Play is not a well-known tourist destination—yet. That's changing because it's one of the hottest new wine appellations in California. Its blockbuster zins, flavorsome sauvignon blancs, and unusual varieties like Rhìne and Italian reds are turning heads in Napa and Sonoma. Constructed in the late 1980s, Fitzpatrick Winery and Lodge has the ideal site and a building to match for visitors to El Dorado County. The lodge, a soaring structure made of gargantuan local white fir logs, sits on a point in the Sierra foothills and has a view that reaches all the way to the Tahoe Sierras. Wineries like Granite Springs, Single Leaf, and Charles Mitchell are all nearby, and, of course, Fitzpatrick is just out the front door. The interesting gold rush towns of Placerville and Sutter Creek are minutes away. The lodge has large rooms with good views, plus a lap pool, basketball courts, and a green for petanque, the French version of bocce ball. The spacious deck, with a backdrop of the Sierras, also has a massive outdoor wood-fired oven for baking bread and pizzas. Oh, yes, the tasting room is in the lodge building. Cheers!

SETTING & FACILITIES

Location: 18 mi. southeast of Placerville, near the hamlets of Fair Play and Somerset; call lodge or see Web site for directions
Near: Wineries, Gold Discovery Park
Building: Massive handcrafted log lodge built of peeled white fir logs
Grounds: 40 acres, vistas of Sierra foothills, working winery, organic vineyards
Public Space: Great room w/ fireplace, piano, entertainment room w/ satellite TV, movies, games and reading material, deck, DR
Food & Drink: Full made-to-order breakfast served 8–10 a.m. in DR
Recreation: Swimming, basketball, petanque, wine tasting, meditation areas on premises; whitewater rafting, wine tasting nearby, skiing 50 min. away
Amenities & Services: Complimentary beverage, coffee, and tea service; private parking, disabled access, weekend barbecue, wood-fired oven pizza nights, ploughman's lunch, catered dinners

ACCOMMODATIONS

Units: 5 guest rooms, all larger than average, including 2 suites
All Rooms: Private bath, AC, private balcony, window seat, vineyard view
Bed & Bath: Queens and kings, claw-foot tubs (3), shower and claw-foot tub (2)
Favorites: Log Suite, w/ massive log walls, king bed, Irish pine table and chairs, oversized reading chair, daybed, private deck, claw-foot tub and tile shower
Comfort & Decor: Rooms decorated w/ individual themes, artwork and photos, Irish country pine furniture, blinds and curtains, carpet, overstuffed reading chairs and hassocks, plaids, wine barrel vanities, window seats, quilted bedspreads, quilt-top mattresses

RATES, RESERVATIONS, & RESTRICTIONS

Deposit: Credit card to hold, no refund on cancellations unless room can be re-rented
Discounts: Long stays, discount on 2nd night all year round; extra person $10
Credit Cards: D, MC, V
Check-In/Out: 3/11, early check-in and late check-out by arrangement
Smoking: No
Pets: No
Kids: By prior arrangement
Minimum Stay: 2 nights on holiday weekends, special wine events
Open: Open all year
Hosts: Brian and Diana Fitzpatrick
7740 Fair Play Rd.
Fair Play, CA 95684
(530) 620-3248
(800) 245-9166
Fax: (530) 620-6838
www.fitzpatrickwinery.com
Brian@FitzpatrickWinery.com

AMERICAN RIVER INN, Georgetown

Overall: ★★★½	Room Quality: B	Value: A	Price: $85–$115

Because it's off Highway 49, the Mother Lode Highway, people touring California's Gold Country frequently overlook Georgetown, helping it to retain a lot of the rough charm and authenticity of a real mining town. The handsome, two-story American River Inn has a feel of old New Orleans, with a wraparound veranda on each floor. The owners have banished phones and TV from the Country Victorian guest rooms to ensure tranquility, but there is too much to do here to miss those distractions anyway. The inn's bicycles are a great way to explore this rich historical area, or, for those who like to push the envelope, the whitewater rafting hereabouts is legendary. Afterward—or perhaps instead of—the inn's Jacuzzi is out back.

SETTING & FACILITIES

Location: From Hwy. 49, take Hwy. 193 to Georgetown, 19 mi. southeast of Auburn, or 19 mi. north of Placerville, 1 hour from Sacramento
Near: Restaurants, shopping
Building: Victorian built originally in 1853, 2nd Queen Anne building built in 1907
Grounds: 1.75 acres w/ Victorian gardens, dove aviary
Public Space: Parlor, library, DR, outdoor game room

Food & Drink: Full breakfast served 8–10 a.m. in DR or on the porch
Recreation: Mountain bikes, croquet, horseshoes, bocce ball, badminton, and Ping-Pong on premises; fishing, whitewater rafting, golf, hot air ballooning nearby
Amenities & Services: Swimming pool, hot tub, evening wine and hors d'oeuvres, robes, off-street parking, disabled access, concierge service for reservations, free local airport pickup

ACCOMMODATIONS

Units: 18 guest rooms, 10 larger than average, including 7 suites
All Rooms: AC, ceiling fan, featherbed, down comforter
Some Rooms: Fireplace, four-poster, view of the gardens, extra twins (2), private bath (13)
Bed & Bath: Mostly queens, 4 shared baths for 5 rooms in main building

Favorites: No. 5, large room w/ special antiques; No. 14, w/ canopy bed, fireplace, and view of the garden
Comfort & Decor: Rooms individually decorated in Country Victoriana, w/ antiques, custom curtains, wallpaper, natural wood floors w/ Persian and other carpets

RATES, RESERVATIONS, & RESTRICTIONS

Deposit: Credit card; must cancel 10 days in advance; cancellation fee $10
Discounts: Weekday business groups, singles; extra person $15
Credit Cards: All
Check-In/Out: 3/11, late check-out by arrangement
Smoking: No
Pets: By special arrangement
Kids: 9 and over
Minimum Stay: 2 nights on holiday

weekends
Open: Open all year
Hosts: Will and Maria Collin
P.O. Box 43
Main and Orleans Sts.
Georgetown, CA 95634
(916) 333-4499
(800) 245-6566
Fax: (530) 333-9253
www.pcweb.net/ari
ARI@pcweb.net

MURPHY'S INN, Grass Valley

Overall: ★★★★	Room Quality: B	Value: B	Price: $105–$160

Although Grass Valley is sometimes overlooked in favor of its flashier neighbor, Nevada City, there's plenty to explore in this historic area, with its former quartz mines and mining memorabilia, plus walking, hiking, and mountain biking trails. The elegantly restored Murphy's Inn is a very pleasant place to rest after your exertions. Curl up on the spacious veranda or in a comfortable chair in front of a fireplace in one of the sitting rooms, with a decanter of sherry at hand. The guest rooms are tastefully Victorian, with mahogany, oak, and pine antiques. The inn is noted for its grand breakfast and first-rate chocolate chip cookies.

SETTING & FACILITIES

Location: At the south edge of downtown Grass Valley's historic district, 1 hour from Sacramento via Hwys. 80 and 49, 1 hour from Reno
Near: Restaurants, shopping, saloons, historical landmarks, local airport, galleries, theater, Empire Mine State Historic Park, Scotts Flat Reservoir, Rollins Reservoir, Malakoff Diggins Historic State Park
Building: Restored 1866 Gothic Revival main house, 1866 Gothic Revival Donation Day House across street w/ 2 suites
Grounds: Landscaped lot w/ giant sequoia tree, rosebushes, flower and topiary gardens, sundeck

Public Space: 2 sitting rooms w/ fireplaces, DR, veranda
Food & Drink: Full breakfast served 7:30–9 a.m. weekdays, 8:30–10 a.m. weekends, in DR
Recreation: Whitewater rafting, gold panning, mountain biking, tennis, golf, 40 min. to skiing, swimming in the South Yuba River, fishing
Amenities & Services: Afternoon snacks, port in rooms, soft drinks and chocolate chip cookies always avail., barbecue avail., private parking, assistance w/ lunch or dinner reservations, recreational information, shuttle service from airport

ACCOMMODATIONS

Units: 8 guest rooms, 4 larger than average, including 3 suites
All Rooms: Private bath, cable TV/VCR, phone, AC
Some Rooms: Private entrance (2), fireplace (4), four-poster (3), fridge (1), queen-size Hide-a-Bed (2), daybed w/ trundle (1)
Bed & Bath: Queens and kings

Favorites: Theodosia's Suite, w/ king bed, fireplace, chandeliers, tiled oversized shower w/ dual showerheads and skylight, views of veranda and gardens
Comfort & Decor: Individually decorated in Victorian style w/ artwork, antiques, lace curtains, wallpapered/ painted walls, carpet

RATES, RESERVATIONS, & RESTRICTIONS

Deposit: Credit card; must cancel 7 days in advance, 14 days for holidays
Discounts: AAA and seniors

Sun.–Thurs.; extra person $20
Credit Cards: AE, MC, V

Check-In/Out: 3–6/11, earlier/later by arrangement
Smoking: No
Pets: No
Kids: In Donation Day House suites
No-Nos: No more than 2 guests per room except suites w/ extra bed
Minimum Stay: 2 nights on weekends April–Jan.

Open: All year
Hosts: Ted and Nancy Daus
318 Neal St.
Grass Valley, CA 95945
(530) 273-6873
(800) 895-2488
Fax: (530) 273-5157
www.murphysinn.com
murphys@jps.net

GROVELAND HOTEL, Groveland

Overall: ★★★★	Room Quality: B	Value: B	Price: $115–$195

Groveland Hotel has been around since 1850 and has had more lives than a litter of cats. In 1990, innkeeper Peggy Mosley and her husband Grover rescued the rundown structure from the wrecking ball. After several million dollars in restoration, it has become a tourist destination in its own right, as well as the most entertaining way to visit nearby Yosemite. Groveland, originally known as Garrote (yes, as in hanging), is a lively gold rush town ideally situated, as the town chamber of commerce says, "above the fog and smog and below the heavy snow." A great deal of the town's liveliness is due to the acclaimed hotel and its haute cuisine dining room, winner of *Wine Spectator*'s Award of Excellence, the James Beard Foundation's 50th anniversary honors, and *Country Inns Magazine*'s Top Ten Inns. It draws people from all over the world for its comfortable lodgings and good food.

SETTING & FACILITIES

Location: On Hwy. 120 in the town of Groveland, 3 hours from San Francisco, 2.5 hours from Sacramento
Near: Half-hour from Yosemite Park; local theater, art shows, shopping, general aviation airport
Building: An 1849 adobe Monterey Colonial–style building, adjacent 1914 Queen Anne hostelry, both buildings on Nat'l Register of Historic Places
Grounds: Two urban lots w/ garden courtyard
Public Space: Parlor, conference room
Food & Drink: Extended cont'l breakfast buffet served 7:30–10 a.m. in DR

Recreation: Whitewater rafting, gold panning, tennis, golf, horseback riding, fly-fishing school, mountain climbing, boating, wind surfing, X-C skiing
Amenities & Services: Evening wine and truffles, fresh flowers, computer hookups, hairdryers, private parking, disabled access, nationally recognized restaurant, saloon, picnic baskets for Yosemite, fax and secretarial services, conference center, massage therapy, aspiring innkeeper seminars, whodunit mystery weekends, "Mark Twain" living history dinners, Elvis night (Memphis cookin'), Victorian tea

ACCOMMODATIONS

Units: 17 guest rooms, including 3 suites
All Rooms: Private bath, phone, individual heat/AC, coffeemaker w/ locally roasted coffee, computer port, ceiling fan
Some Rooms: Fireplace, spa tub, extra bed (3)
Bed & Bath: Queens, twins (2); robes
Favorites: Hetch Hetchy Suite, w/ fireplace, floral sofa, antique French bed,

private entrance to garden and courtyard, sitting room; Lyle's Room, large room decorated in shades of blues, w/ resident ghost, mirrored English armoire, French marble-topped night tables, ornate French bed, bay window, view of town
Comfort & Decor: Rooms individually decorated w/ original artwork, European antiques, down comforters, upscale linens, carpet

RATES, RESERVATIONS, & RESTRICTIONS

Deposit: Credit card guarantee; must cancel 24 hours in advance, 2 weeks for holidays and special events; $10 cancellation fee
Discounts: AAA Oct. 15–April 15, weekday business, midweek winter specials, corporate; extra adult $25, children $15
Credit Cards: All
Check-In/Out: As rooms avail., by 2/noon, late check-out by arrangement
Smoking: No
Pets: Well-behaved pets OK

Kids: OK
Minimum Stay: None
Open: All year
Hosts: Peggy A. and Grover C. Mosley
P.O. Box 481
18767 Main St.
Groveland, CA 95321
(209) 962-6674
(800) 273-3314
Fax: (209) 962-6674
www.groveland.com
peggy@groveland.com

ROCKWOOD LODGE, Homewood

Overall: ★★★★   Room Quality: B   Value: B   Price: $100–$200

Wear nice socks when you visit this lodge, because the owners preserve their fluffy white carpeting by politely requesting that you leave your shoes at the entry, as they do in Japan. The carpeting helps lighten up this woodsy mountain home with its knotty pine walls, hand-hewn beam ceilings, and huge rock fireplace in the parlor. The five guestrooms all have sitting areas, private baths, and feather beds with down comforters. Three have views of Lake Tahoe and the other two have views of the forest. Laura Ashley and other designer fabrics complement European and Early American furnishings. Breakfast features a spread including fruit, fresh pastries, and fruit crepes or Belgian waffles. After indulging, you can walk right out the back door and hike or bike on the 50 mile trail that's adjacent to the property. Don't forget to put on your shoes!

SETTING & FACILITIES

Location: On Hwy. 89 South on Lake Tahoe's west shore, 1 block south of Ski Homewood
Near: 200 ft. from Lake Tahoe, Ski Homewood, restaurants, shopping, hiking and biking trails adjacent
Building: 1930s Craftsman vacation home
Grounds: 1 acre landscaped w/ firs, cedar, and pines; fountain, flowers in summer, usually blanketed in snow from Dec. to March, large patio w/ stone fireplace
Public Space: LR w/ stone fireplace, library w/ game cabinet, formal DR
Food & Drink: Extended cont'l breakfast served in DR or on patio
Recreation: Downhill/X-C skiing, swimming, biking, tennis, golf, horseback riding, boat rentals, waterskiing
Amenities & Services: Chocolate in rooms, robes; phone avail. in LR; fax and computer hookup avail.

ACCOMMODATIONS

Units: 4 guest rooms, 2 larger than average
All Rooms: Private tiled bath w/ porcelain and brass fixtures
Some Rooms: Four-poster
Bed & Bath: Queens, double showers and Roman steeping tubs (2)
Favorites: Secret Harbor, w/ hand-painted Russian wedding bed, sitting area, built-in desk w/ power for PC and telephone jack, walk-in closet; Zephyr Cove, like a tree house, w/ private staircase
Comfort & Decor: Rooms individually decorated w/ art by Salvador Dali, Winslow Homer, and others, early American and European antiques, all-wood walls, Laura Ashley and designer fabrics, down comforters and featherbeds, carpet, lake views

RATES, RESERVATIONS, & RESTRICTIONS

Deposit: 100% of bill; no refunds, will hold credit for another visit less $10 per night cancellation fee
Discounts: Single, will upgrade when possible at no charge
Credit Cards: None
Check-In/Out: 4–6/11, late/early check-in by arrangement, late checkout by arrangement
Smoking: No
Pets: No
Kids: Not suitable
No-Nos: No more than 2 guests per room
Minimum Stay: 2 nights on weekends, 3 on holiday weekends
Open: Closed occasionally, if no prior reservations
Hosts: Constance Stevens and Lou Reinkens
P.O. Box 226
5295 W. Lake Blvd.
Homewood, CA 96141-0226
(530) 525-5273
(800) 538-2463
Fax: (530) 525-5949
info@rockwoodlodge.com
www.rockwoodlodge.com

HEIRLOOM B&B INN, Ione

| Overall: ★★★½ | Room Quality: B | Value: A | Price: $65–$98 |

Ione, a thriving town with wonderful examples of Victorian architecture, is on a road less traveled and easily overlooked. What you won't want to miss is Heirloom Bed-and-Breakfast, a rare 1863 Greek Revival house hidden in an English garden on a one-and-a-half-acre lushly landscaped lot. The guest rooms in the main house are all charmingly decorated with lace curtains and quilts, though guests with a yen for the unusual may want to try the two newer rooms in an annex made of rammed earth adobe with grass growing on the roof. In spite of the New Age construction, these rooms are quite handsome, with woodwork of hand-hewn cedar, redwood, and pine. At night you can look out the skylight and see both the stars and the lawn overhead. A typical breakfast at the Heirloom might include apple dumplings, a cornmeal soufflé with tomato sauce, and spoon rolls.

SETTING & FACILITIES

Location: In the foothill town of Ione, 45 min. southeast of Sacramento, 45 min. northeast of Stockton
Near: Gold Country sight-seeing, wineries, antiques, galleries, theater, restaurants
Building: Brick 2-story antebellum Greek Revival circa 1863 with columns, balconies, fan transom
Grounds: 1.5 acres of private grounds surrounded by century-old trees, spacious English garden
Public Space: Parlor, library, gazebo, English garden w/ tables, swings, hammocks
Food & Drink: Full breakfast served at time of choice on weekdays (9 a.m. on weekends) in DR, in bed, on balconies, or in the garden
Recreation: Biking, championship golf course, fishing, water sports
Amenities & Services: Afternoon snacks, evening wine and hors d'oeuvres, room service, croquet, private parking, disabled access

ACCOMMODATIONS

Units: 6 guest rooms
All Rooms: AC
Some Rooms: Fireplace, wood-burning stove, four-poster bed, balcony, private bath (4), shared bath (2), extra bed (2)
Bed & Bath: Mostly queens
Favorites: Spring Room, w/ antique furnishings, balcony looking out on wisteria, magnolias, and garden
Comfort & Decor: Rooms individually decorated w/ antiques, lace curtains, quilts

RATES, RESERVATIONS, & RESTRICTIONS

Deposit: 1st night's lodging; must cancel 72 hours in advance for full refund
Discounts: Long stays, state rate for weekday business, special promotions; extra person $20
Credit Cards: AE, MC, V
Check-In/Out: 2–6/11, late check-out by arrangement
Smoking: No
Pets: No
Kids: 10 and over
Minimum Stay: 2 nights on weekends, occasional availability on single Sat.
Open: Closed on Thanksgiving/Christmas Eve and Day
Hosts: Melisande Hubbs and Patricia Cross
P.O. Box 322
214 Shakeley Lane
Ione, CA 95640
(209) 274-4468
(888) 628-7896
www.theheirloominn.com

GATE HOUSE INN, Jackson

Overall: ★★★½	Room Quality: B	Value: B	Price: $100–$155

Jackson Gate Road, the old road leading to Jackson from Sutter Creek, retains its rural character, even though it's little more than a mile to bustling downtown Jackson. Nearby are the much photographed 52-foot-high tailing wheels of the famous Kennedy hard rock mine, the deepest (almost 6,000 feet) in the country, and one of the richest. Down the street the Buscaglia family has been turning out wonderful old-time Italian dinners since 1916, while just past them is a photogenic and picturesque church and cemetery that Serbian miners built in 1895. Gate House Inn was the family home for three generations of an Italian family that operated a general store next door (still standing). The house has been immaculately maintained, and it shows. It has that special patina that totally restored and rebuilt inns never seem to achieve. Breakfast is a formal affair, with candles, on the dining room table. Bread and muffins are baked daily to accompany quiches, breakfast casseroles, or the Gate House specialty, baked French toast.

SETTING & FACILITIES

Location: 1.3 mi. north of Jackson, just east of Hwy. 49 on Jackson Gate Rd.
Near: Restaurants, shopping, antiques, wineries, Historic Kennedy Wheels Park, local airport, local history museum
Building: 1903 Victorian on Nat'l Register of Historic Places
Grounds: 1 acre of landscaped lawns and gardens, swimming pool and patio, grape arbor, surrounded by rolling countryside

Public Space: Parlor w/ fireplace, DR, kitchen
Food & Drink: Full breakfast served at 9 a.m. in DR, or on porch or patio, room service avail. on request
Recreation: Table tennis on premises; tennis, golf nearby
Amenities & Services: Afternoon tea w/ fresh-baked cookies, 40-ft. swimming pool, gas barbecue, airport shuttle service, private parking, gift shop w/ local crafts

ACCOMMODATIONS

Units: 5 guest rooms, 4 larger than average, 1 separate cottage
All Rooms: Private bath, sitting area, view
Some Rooms: Fireplace, double Jacuzzi
Bed & Bath: Queens, robes
Favorites: Master Suite, w/ fireplace, Victorian queen bed, English Victorian dressing table, sitting area overlooking gardens and hillside
Comfort & Decor: Rooms individually decorated w/ original art, Victorian furniture, lace curtains, oak and mahogany parquet floor imported from Italy; beveled, leaded, and stained glass; Italian marble and tile fireplaces, oak staircase, oriental carpets, crystal chandeliers

RATES, RESERVATIONS, & RESTRICTIONS

Deposit: Credit card; must cancel 7 days in advance; $10 cancellation fee
Discounts: Weekday business, AAA; extra person $20
Credit Cards: All
Check-In/Out: 2:30/11, late check-out by arrangement
Smoking: No
Pets: No
Kids: 12 and over

Minimum Stay: 2 nights on weekends
Open: All year
Hosts: Keith and Gail Sweet
1330 Jackson Gate Rd.
Jackson, CA 95642
(209) 223-3500
(800) 841-1072
Fax: (209) 223-1299
www.gatehouseinn.com
info@gatehouseinn.com

JAMESTOWN HOTEL, Jamestown

Overall: ★★★½	Room Quality: B	Value: A	Price: $70–$135

A particularly picturesque California gold rush town, Jamestown has been the site of many Hollywood Westerns, including *Butch Cassidy and the Sundance Kid.* Fitting right into the gold rush setting, the appealing two-story brick Jamestown Hotel has moderately sized but lavishly decorated country-style guest rooms and a beautiful old-fashioned bar to wet your whistle. The rooms are named after famous women of the Old West; many have sitting rooms, and all have private baths, some with claw-foot tubs, others with whirlpool tubs. There's lots to do here year-round, including whitewater rafting, skiing, fishing, and caving. Yosemite is only an hour away.

SETTING & FACILITIES

Location: In Jamestown, just off Hwy. 49/120, 3 hours from San Francisco, 2.5 hours from Sacramento
Near: Restaurants, Columbia State Historic Park, Railtown State Park, Big Trees State Park, Stanislaus Nat'l Forest, live theater, wine tasting, antiques, shopping, art galleries, museums, rodeos
Building: Original building 1858, brick facade added later w/ brick from San Francisco earthquake
Grounds: Urban lot, patio

Public Space: Parlor, library, game room, pub, TV room
Food & Drink: Expanded cont'l breakfast served 8–10 a.m. in the pub
Recreation: Biking, all types of boating, golf, horseback riding, skiing (snow and water), snowmobiling, tennis, swimming, spelunking
Amenities & Services: Beverages and hors d'oeuvres in the pub, private parking, disabled access, fully equipped business center, pub on site

ACCOMMODATIONS

Units: 11 guest rooms, including 3 suites
All Rooms: Private bath, AC
Some Rooms: Four-poster, sleeper sofa
Bed & Bath: Mostly queens, some whirlpool tubs or claw-foot tubs
Favorites: Belle Starr, w/ queen canopy bed, private whirlpool tub, private patio; Sacajawea Suite, w/ queen bed, hand-carved wooden statue of Native American chief
Comfort & Decor: Rooms individually decorated w/ antique furniture, Laura Ashley prints, white wicker accents, some w/ sitting rooms, patios

RATES, RESERVATIONS, & RESTRICTIONS

Deposit: Credit card; must cancel 7 days in advance
Discounts: Weekday business, AAA, AARP; extra person $15
Credit Cards: All
Check-In/Out: 2/noon, late check-out by arrangement
Smoking: No
Pets: No
Kids: OK
Minimum Stay: 2 or 3 nights on holiday weekends
Open: All year
Hosts: Jerry and Lucille Weisbrot
P.O. Box 539
18153 Main St.
Jamestown, CA 95327
(209) 984-3902
(800) 205-4901
Fax: (209) 984-4149
www.jamestownhotel.com
reserve@jamestownhotel.com

JAMESTOWN NATIONAL HOTEL: A COUNTRY INN, Jamestown

Overall: ★★★½	Room Quality: B	Value: A	Price: $80–$120

Built in 1859, this Victorian country hotel is one of the oldest lodgings in California. Each of the nine nicely restored guest rooms has a brass or iron bed, a patchwork quilt, lace curtains, fresh flowers, and a teddy bear. There's a terrific saloon with a redwood bar and a popular restaurant serving brunch, lunch, and dinner in the memorabilia-filled dining room or on the vine-covered terrace. The hotel's continental breakfast includes homemade bread, fresh fruit, cereals, hard-boiled eggs, and the morning paper. The friendly staff members here go all out to please. Even pets are welcome if prior arrangement is made.

SETTING & FACILITIES

Location: On Hwy. 49 on Main St. in Jamestown; 2.5 hours from Sacramento, 3 hours from San Francisco
Near: Columbia State Historic Park, Railtown State Park, Big Trees State Park, Stanislaus Nat'l Forest, live theater, wine tasting, antiques, shopping, art galleries, museums, rodeos
Building: 1859 California gold rush building, continuously operated since 1859

Grounds: Vine arbor terrace, covered w/ 120-year-old Virginia creeper
Public Space: Parlor/saloon, DR/restaurant, soaking room w/ over-sized claw-foot bath tub for 2, balcony
Food & Drink: Expanded cont'l breakfast, served 8–10 a.m., early morning coffee at 7 a.m.
Recreation: Biking, all types of boating, horseback riding, skiing (snow and water), snowmobiling, tennis, swimming, spelunking
Amenities & Services: Wine and fruit basket in room, flowers, newspapers served w/ breakfast, hairdryers, robes, cable TV on request, room service, restaurant and saloon, fax, massage avail., picnic baskets avail.

ACCOMMODATIONS

Units: 9 guest rooms
All Rooms: Private bath, AC
Bed & Bath: Mostly queens, roll-away avail., pull-chain toilets, 3 rooms w/ large tiled showers & 2 shower heads
Favorites: No. 1 and No. 2, w/ queen bed, brass or ornate iron bed, antique dressers, table and nightstand, shared balcony w/ view of town
Comfort & Decor: Original brass beds, antique furniture, patchwork quilts, different wallpaper in each room, lace curtains, carpet

RATES, RESERVATIONS, & RESTRICTIONS

Deposit: Credit card; must cancel 72 hours in advance
Discounts: Long stays, weekday business, AAA; extra person $15
Credit Cards: All
Check-In/Out: 2/noon, late check-out by arrangement
Smoking: No
Pets: Pets welcome if housebroken and not too large, $10 and credit card
Kids: Over 8
Minimum Stay: 2 nights on major holiday weekends
Open: All year
Host: Stephen Willey
P.O. Box 502
18183 Main St.
Jamestown, CA 95327
(209) 984-3446
(800) 894-3446
Fax: (209) 984-5620
www.national-hotel.com
info@national-hotel.com

WINE AND ROSES INN, Lodi

Overall: ★★★★	Room Quality: B	Value: B	Price: $125–$165

In addition to being a well-run B&B with pretty, comfortable guest rooms, this country inn contains a regional California restaurant serving lunch, dinner, and Sunday brunch. Innkeeper Sherri Smith is a graduate of the California Culinary Academy in San Francisco, and she makes use of fresh local produce for guests' breakfasts and for the restaurant. The inn's parklike grounds feature herb and vegetable gardens, towering trees, and hundreds of roses. You will also find wild bunnies in the garden, and white barn owls that fly by at night.

SETTING & FACILITIES

Location: On the western edge of Lodi, at the corner of Turner Rd. and Lower Sacramento Rd., half-hour from Sacramento
Near: Lodi Lake, 175-acre Mokelumne River Wilderness Area
Building: 1902 Victorian home
Grounds: 5 acres of towering trees and flower gardens, 200 rosebushes, patio shaded by 100-year-old deodar cedar trees

Public Space: Parlor, sitting room w/ fireplace
Food & Drink: Extended cont'l breakfast served 6–8 a.m., full breakfast served 8–10:30 a.m. in restaurant
Recreation: Biking, golf
Amenities & Services: Evening wine, hors d'oeuvres, and homemade cookies; swimming pool, disabled access, full restaurant

ACCOMMODATIONS

Units: 10 guest rooms, 3 larger than average, including 1 suite
All Rooms: Cable TV, phone, AC, private bath,
Some Rooms: Four-poster, sleeper sofa, claw-foot tub, deck, extra twin (2)
Bed & Bath: Queens

Favorites: Honeymoon Suite, w/ 2 rooms, double French doors to private deck, tub in room, sloped ceilings, antiques
Comfort & Decor: Rooms individually decorated w/ handmade comforters, antiques, fresh flowers

RATES, RESERVATIONS, & RESTRICTIONS

Deposit: 1st night's lodging; must cancel 7 days in advance
Discounts: Long stays, weekday business, groups, AAA, corporate; extra person $15
Credit Cards: All
Check-In/Out: 3/noon, by arrangement
Smoking: No
Pets: By prior arrangement

Kids: OK
Minimum Stay: None
Open: All year
Hosts: Delwyn and Sherri Smith
2505 W. Turner Rd.
Lodi, CA 95242
(209) 334-6988
Fax: (209) 334-6570
www.winerose.com
del@winerose.come

OLD FLOWER FARM BED-AND-BREAKFAST, Loomis

| Overall: ★★★★ | Room Quality: B | Value: A | Price: $90–$125 |

This place is too cute for words. All the rooms are light and airy, the decor is a tasteful mix of contemporary and antique furnishings, and the grounds, including the swimming pool, are a treat. Family gatherings, weddings, parties, and business groups frequently rent the whole place (the innkeeper lives in a separate residence) and just have fun. The main house has a great kitchen for guests' use. Breakfast foods tend toward the healthy—fresh fruits, fresh juices, breads, yogurts, and homemade apple-sauce and jams. Popular Folsom Lake is a five-minute drive away, and there are horse stables and a bicycle path nearby.

SETTING & FACILITIES

Location: Between the towns of Folsom and Auburn on the outskirts of Loomis just south of I-80, half-hour from Sacramento
Near: Antiquing, shops, restaurants, Folsom Lake State Recreation Area
Building: Restored country farmhouse, circa 1895, 2 cottages
Grounds: 10 acres of landscaped grounds, pasture, and flowers, perennial nursery w/ 13-ft. waterwheel and pond
Public Space: Parlor, kitchen, DR, screened porch
Food & Drink: Expanded cont'l breakfast served 8–9 a.m. in DR, or by special request in room
Recreation: Biking, rafting, water sports, gold panning, horseback riding, golf
Amenities & Services: Afternoon snacks, evening wine and hors d'oeuvres, swimming pool, private parking, airport service

ACCOMMODATIONS

Units: 6 guest rooms, including 2 suites in large farmhouse, and 2 cottages
All Rooms: Private bath
Some Rooms: Fridge, robes (1); TV/VCR (1); extra bed (1)
Bed & Bath: Queens, claw-foot tubs
Favorites: Country Checker Room, w/ antiques, white wicker chaise lounge, four-poster bed, red-and-white checked curtains, claw-foot tub and shower; Honeymoon Cottage, w/ net-draped queen bed, LR w/ love seat, overstuffed chairs, in-room coffee and tea, antique wedding pictures
Comfort & Decor: Rooms individually decorated w/ artwork, antiques, wingback chairs, wicker, shutters, carpet, red Vermont stove on rock hearth

RATES, RESERVATIONS, & RESTRICTIONS

Deposit: Credit card; must cancel 14 days (30 for holidays) in advance for full refund; 1 night's lodging cancellation fee
Discounts: Long stays, weekday business, AAA; extra person $25
Credit Cards: AE, MC, V
Check-In/Out: 3/11, late check-out by arrangement
Smoking: No
Pets: No
Kids: With permission
No-Nos: No more than 2 guests per room, except in Nora's Cottage
Minimum Stay: 2 nights on weekends Dec.–Feb., 1 night March–Nov.
Open: All year
Hosts: Gary and Jenny Leonard
4150 Auburn-Folsom Rd.
Loomis, CA 95650
(916) 652-4200
Fax: (916) 652-4200
members.aol.com/rosiesmile/offi.html

SNOW GOOSE INN, Mammoth Lakes

Overall: ★★★½	Room Quality: C	Value: A	Price: $68–$168

Mammoth Lakes is a very nice resort town: not too big, but big enough to have some of the nicer urban creature comforts—good restaurants, a bookstore, a fly-fishing shop, and a decent supermarket. This is where all of LA comes to ski and remember what real snow looks like. In the summer the ski runs are turned into serious mountain bike trails (you and your bike take the ski lift to the top, and how you get down is your concern), but the pace is more relaxed. Snow Goose Inn is an ex-hostel that has been transformed into a B&B with Euro overtones. The rooms are a bit boxy, but the furnishings are nice, and the clientele is a friendly cosmopolitan mix. Just the kind of people you and your sweetie won't mind sharing the hot tub with. Breakfast time is a busy, gregarious event that anyone but a confirmed misanthrope will enjoy. Rates here are turned on their heads compared to most of the rest of the state: the rates are highest in ski season and considerably lower the rest of the year.

SETTING & FACILITIES

Location: In the resort town of Mammoth on the east side of the Sierras off Hwy. 395; 5 hours from Los Angeles, 5 hours from San Francisco in summer, 6.5 in winter; call or see Web site for directions
Near: Shopping, restaurants, local airport, hot springs, half-block from ski shuttle
Building: Former hostel, main building w/ 15 guest rooms, fourplex of 2-BR suites
Grounds: Parking lot, outside deck, sitting porch, pines and aspens

Public Space: Parlor w/ fireplace, game room
Food & Drink: Full breakfast served 7–9 a.m. in parlor
Recreation: Skiing, fishing, mountain climbing, mountain biking, horseback riding, hot air ballooning
Amenities & Services: Afternoon snacks, evening wine and hors d'oeuvres, hot tub, barbecue, athletic club privileges, magazines, games, big-screen TV/VCR, videotape library, private parking, VCRs avail.

ACCOMMODATIONS

Units: 19 guest rooms, 6 larger than average, including 4 2-BR townhouses
All Rooms: Private bath, cable TV, phone
Some Rooms: Fireplace, four-poster, sleeper sofa, fridge, Jacuzzi, kitchenette, kitchen, extra bed (6)
Bed & Bath: Queens, kings (2), Jacuzzis (4)
Favorites: No. 201, w/ shared veranda,

log four-poster, hutch w/ antique books, antique armoire and dresser decorated in blue floral prints, huge sliding glass window w/ view of trees
Comfort & Decor: Rooms individually decorated w/ country-style antiques and antique reproductions, log beds, brass beds, quilts, handmade curtains, carpets

RATES, RESERVATIONS, & RESTRICTIONS

Deposit: 50%; must cancel 30 days in advance; cancellation fee $20
Discounts: Long stays, weekday business, groups, AAA, singles, AARP; extra person $6 summer/$12 winter
Credit Cards: AE, D, MC, V
Check-In/Out: 2/10, late check-out by arrangement
Smoking: No
Pets: No
Kids: OK
Minimum Stay: 3 nights on holiday weekends
Open: All year
Hosts: Scott and Denise Robertson
P.O. Box 387
57 Forest Trail
Mammoth Lakes, CA 93546
(760) 934-2660
(800) 874-7368
Fax: (760) 934-5655
www.snowgoose-inn.com
frmvegas@aol.com

DUNBAR HOUSE, 1880, Murphys

Overall: ★★★★   Room Quality: B   Value: B   Price: $135–$190

The town of Murphys originated as a trading post for miners and retains many of the charms of its colorful past. Old stone buildings, pretty Victorians, tree-lined streets, plus a darned good beer—Murphys Red—made by the Murphys Brewery Company. What more could you want? Dunbar House, 1880, is a perfect place to pursue your trip into history. Filled with comfortable, plushy furniture, fresh flowers, lace curtains, and hand-crocheted antimacassars, it also provides lots of good food and small pleasures like appetizer trays in your room, chocolates on your turned-down bed, and a two-person hammock in the garden.

SETTING & FACILITIES

Location: In the town of Murphys, east of Hwy. 49 on Hwy. 4; 2 hours from San Francisco, 1.5 hours from Sacramento
Near: Shopping, wineries, galleries, museums, caves, Calaveras Big Trees Park, Columbia State Historic Park, local theater
Building: Italianate-style Victorian built in 1880
Grounds: 3/4 acre of gardens, including historic roses from all over the Gold Country, fountains, birdhouses, and hammock
Public Space: Parlor, DR, gazebo w/ swing for 2
Food & Drink: Full breakfast served at 8:30, 9, or 9:30 a.m. in DR, garden, or guests' room
Recreation: Downhill/X-C skiing, biking, tennis, golf, water sports
Amenities & Services: Full appetizer plate w/ fruit, cheese, and wine in room on arrival, snacks in DR anytime, turn-down w/ homemade chocolates, barbecue, hairdryers, makeup mirrors, bathrobes, English towel warmers, classic video library, private parking, concierge service for reservations

ACCOMMODATIONS

Units: 4 guest rooms, including 2 suites
All Rooms: Private bath, art, down comforter and pillows, cable TV/VCR, phone, AC, Norwegian gas-burning stove, fridge
Some Rooms: Four-poster, private entrance and garden
Bed & Bath: Queens, king, 2-person Jacuzzi spa, claw-foot tub
Favorites: Ponderosa, w/ view of gar- den and neighboring horses, claw-foot tub, four-poster king bed, gas-burning stove; Cedar, 2-room suite w/ garden motif, complimentary champagne 1st night, private entrance, private deck
Comfort & Decor: Rooms individu- ally decorated w/ antiques, overstuffed chairs and ottomans, shutters, lace cur- tains, down comforters, hardwood floors w/ oriental rugs

RATES, RESERVATIONS, & RESTRICTIONS

Deposit: 1st night's lodging; must can- cel 5 days in advance
Discounts: None
Credit Cards: AE, MC, V
Check-In/Out: 3–6/11
Smoking: No
Pets: No
Kids: Over 10
Minimum Stay: 2 nights on weekends

Open: All year
Hosts: Barbara and Bob Costa
271 Jones St.
Murphys, CA 95247
(209) 728-2897
(800) 692-6006
Fax: (209) 728-1451
www.dunbarhouse.com
innkeeper@dunbarhouse.com

REDBUD INN, Murphys

Overall: ★★★★	Room Quality: B	Value: B	Price: $90–$225

The first new inn to be built in Murphys in 136 years, the Redbud is located in the Miners' Exchange shopping and restaurant complex in the heart of town. The inn's 14 rooms and suites are all imaginatively fur- nished and decorated in styles ranging from the Anniversary Suite, done up in white eyelet, to Opi's Cabin, a re-creation of a miner's cabin, com- plete with a tin roof, wide plank floors, and the miner's nightshirt. A full breakfast is served at individual tables in the bay-windowed dining room, local wines are sampled in the evening, and you can walk to nearby restau- rants. The inn is renowned for its bread pudding.

SETTING & FACILITIES

Location: Off Hwy. 4, located on Mur- phys historic Main St.
Near: Historic buildings, shopping, caverns, wineries, galleries, restaurants, local theater and symphony productions

Building: Classic American country inn built in 1994
Grounds: Courtyard
Public Space: Parlor, DR
Food & Drink: Full breakfast served in DR 8–10 a.m.

Recreation: Fishing, gold panning, whitewater rafting, water- and snowskiing, golf

Amenities & Services: Evening sherry, wine and hors d'oeuvres, cookies, private parking, disabled access, dinners by request

ACCOMMODATIONS

Units: 14 guest rooms, 9 larger than average, including 5 suites, cottage

All Rooms: Private bath, AC/heat

Some Rooms: Fireplace, four-poster, fridge, 2-person spa, balcony, kitchen

Bed & Bath: Mostly queens, 2-person Jacuzzis (4)

Favorites: Anniversary Suite, w/ bay window, private balcony, tiled spa tub, 2-sided fireplace, wet bar, king bed w/ down comforter

Comfort & Decor: Rooms individually decorated around themes w/ coordinating fabrics, paint and wallpaper, antiques, mementos, family heirlooms, balconies, window seats

RATES, RESERVATIONS, & RESTRICTIONS

Deposit: 1 night's lodging or credit card; must cancel 7 days in advance; cancellation fee $15

Discounts: AAA, midweek for seniors; extra person $15

Credit Cards: D, MC, V

Check-In/Out: 3/11, late check-out by arrangement

Smoking: No

Pets: No

Kids: With approval

Minimum Stay: 2 nights on weekends

Open: All year

Host: Pamela Hatch
402 Main St.
Murphys, CA 95247
(209) 728-8533
(800) 827-8533
Fax: (209) 728-8132
www.redbudinn.com
innkeeper@redbudinn.com

DEER CREEK INN, Nevada City

Overall: ★★★★	Room Quality: B	Value: B	Price: $95–$150

Perched on the banks of picturesque Deer Creek, this pretty Queen Anne Victorian has wonderful tiered, landscaped grounds where you can lounge about languidly, play croquet, fish, or pan for gold in the creek. While you're swirling that gold pan, keep in mind that Deer Creek was famous in gold rush days as a "pound-a-day" creek. Four of the inn's guest rooms have four-poster or canopy beds and three have private verandas with creekside or town views. Breakfasts are a serious affair here, described by the hosts as "gourmet waddle-away-from-the-table" fare.

SETTING & FACILITIES

Location: 1 block east of Hwy. 49 on the town's main street; 1 hour from Sacramento

Near: Restaurants, shops, galleries, theater, Empire Mine State Historic Park, Scotts Flat Reservoir, Rollins Reservoir, Malakoff Diggins Historic State Park

Building: 1860 Queen Anne Victorian

Grounds: 1 landscaped acre of trees, fountain, stone benches, tiered rose gardens, paths, rose-covered arbors, creek

Public Space: 2 parlors, DR, sunroom, open kitchen, outdoor picnic area

Food & Drink: Full breakfast served at 9 a.m. in DR, or on the veranda; coffee and tea avail. for early risers

Recreation: Gold panning, fishing, croquet on premises; mountain biking, tennis, golf, swimming in the South Yuba River, river rafting, horse-drawn carriage rides nearby

Amenities & Services: Evening wine and hors d'oeuvres, afternoon snacks, cookies and brownies, brandy, complimentary beer and soft drinks, private parking, fax, computer hookups by special request

ACCOMMODATIONS

Units: 5 guest rooms, all larger than average, 2 rooms combine to make a suite, 3 w/ private balconies or patio

All Rooms: Private bath, AC

Some Rooms: Four-poster, canopy bed, claw-foot tub, Roman tub (1), extra bed (1)

Bed & Bath: Queens, king

Favorites: Elaine's Room, w/ four-poster canopy bed, private patio, sitting area overlooking creek, Roman tub for 2; Winifred's Room, done in violet w/ canopy bed, Waverly prints, private balcony

Comfort & Decor: Rooms individually decorated w/ antique photos, paintings, antiques, coordinated curtains and bedding, down comforters, carpet and hardwood floors

RATES, RESERVATIONS, & RESTRICTIONS

Deposit: Credit card; must cancel 10 days in advance

Discounts: Long stays, weekday business, AAA

Credit Cards: AE, MC, V

Check-In/Out: 3/11

Smoking: No

Pets: No

Kids: 13 and over

No-Nos: No more than 2 guests per room

Minimum Stay: 2 nights on weekends and holidays

Open: Open all year

Hosts: Chuck and Elaine Matroni
116 Nevada St.
Nevada City, CA 95959
(530) 265-0363
(800) 655-0363
www.deercreekinn.com
deercreek@gr.net

DOWNEY HOUSE B&B, Nevada City			
Overall: ★★★★	Room Quality: B	Value: B	Price: $120–$175

An 1869 Eastlake Victorian, Downey House sits on Nabob Hill, a neighborhood that's a treasure trove of restored Victorians. A block away is downtown Nevada City, with its mix of refurbished gold rush buildings, fine restaurants and shops, and, at night, as the chamber of commerce says, "the warm glow of gaslights." The inn's newly redecorated guest rooms are all color-coordinated, with extensive antiques and original artwork on the walls. The garden is particularly enticing in summer when the water lilies are in bloom. Breakfast includes fresh orange juice, fruits in season, an entrée such as garden quiche, and the inn's signature dish, Dutch Babies.

SETTING & FACILITIES

Location: In Nevada City, I block west of downtown at the corner of W. Broad and Bennett, I hour from Sacramento via Hwys. 80 and 49
Near: Restaurants, shops, galleries, theater, Empire Mine State Historic Park, Scotts Flat Reservoir, Rollins Reservoir, Malakoff Diggins Historic State Park
Building: 1869 restored Eastlake Victorian w/ curved wraparound veranda
Grounds: Landscaped gardens w/ gazebo, lily pond, and waterfall
Public Space: Parlor, veranda, gazebo, upstairs sunroom, garden room, DR

Food & Drink: Full breakfast served at 9 a.m. in DR
Recreation: Mountain biking, tennis, golf, swimming in the South Yuba River, gold panning, river rafting, horse-drawn carriage rides, fishing
Amenities & Services: Evening wine and hors d'oeuvres; coffee, tea, sodas, and homemade brownies all day; TV/VCR in upstairs sunroom or garden room, umbrellas, garage parking w/ door openers, fax and Internet service, concierge service for reservations

ACCOMMODATIONS

Units: 6 guest rooms
All Rooms: Private bath, AC, sound-proofing, ceiling fan, down comforter and pillows, radio w/ cassette player, extra blankets
Some Rooms: Sleeper sofa (1)
Bed & Bath: Queens and doubles
Favorites: Nathan's Retreat, w/ rich

red and mahogany decor, windows looking into trees, built-in faux-mahogany headboard, overstuffed reading chair
Comfort & Decor: Rooms individually decorated w/ original art, original antiques and reproductions, carpet

RATES, RESERVATIONS, & RESTRICTIONS

Deposit: 1st night's lodging; must cancel 7 days in advance Jan.–Nov., 21 days in Dec., and all major holidays
Discounts: Long stays, weekday business, midweek rates on 2 or more nights, corporate; extra person $35
Credit Cards: MC, V
Check-In/Out: 3/11, additional charge for late check-out
Smoking: No
Pets: No
Kids: Not suitable for small children

Minimum Stay: 2 nights on weekends April–Dec.
Open: All year
Hosts: Gordon Betts, owner; Jan Collins, mgr.
517 W. Broad St.
Nevada City, CA 95959
(530) 265-2815
(800) 258-2815
Fax: (530) 478-9168
www.downeyhouse.com
downeyhouse@mike-nme.com

EMMA NEVADA HOUSE, Nevada City

Overall: ★★★★½	Room Quality: A	Value: B	Price: $100–$150

Chock-full of historic buildings and good restaurants, and with charm to spare, Nevada City is Northern California's B&B heaven. Diva Emma Nevada, who spent her early childhood in Nevada City in the 1860s, is the namesake for this posh Victorian residence, a Nevada County landmark. Located on a quiet, residential street of picture-book Victorians, a street that looks like the set of a period movie, the lavishly restored, white-picket-fenced beauty contains many of the home's original antique fixtures, lovingly rescued. The six guest rooms are decorated with a blend of antiques and modern conveniences for the best of both worlds. A recent breakfast menu featured onion-caraway quiche, sticky buns, a fresh fruit plate, and mountain berry cobbler. Breakfast is served in the dining room, in the aptly designated sunroom, or on a deck overlooking the garden and the creek beyond.

SETTING & FACILITIES

Location: On the town's main street, 2 blocks west of downtown; 1 hour northeast of Sacramento via Hwys. 80 and 49
Near: Restaurants, shops, galleries, theater, Empire Mine State Historic Park, Scotts Flat Reservoir, Rollins Reservoir, Malakoff Diggins Historic State Park
Building: 2-story Victorian, restored in 1991
Grounds: 1/3 acre leading to a small creek and natural garden in back, front garden w/ roses lining the white picket fence
Public Space: Living area with fireplace, sunroom, game room, decks, wraparound veranda
Food & Drink: Coffee at 7:30 a.m., full breakfast 9 a.m. in DR, in sunroom, or on back deck
Recreation: Mountain biking, tennis, golf, swimming in the South Yuba River, gold panning, river rafting, horse-drawn carriage rides, fishing
Amenities & Services: Afternoon tea and cookies, off-street parking

ACCOMMODATIONS

Units: 6 guest rooms
All Rooms: Private bath, AC, phone jack, clock radio, down comforter, imported linens
Some Rooms: Fireplace, Jacuzzi, TV
Bed & Bath: Queens, spas (2), claw-foot tubs (2)
Favorites: Empress' Chamber, decorated in ivory and burgundy, French antique bed, wall of windows, sitting area, Jacuzzi; Nightingale's Bower, w/ bay windows, antique stove, Jacuzzi
Comfort & Decor: Professionally decorated w/ antiques, gas-lit chandeliers, custom fabrics, Italian bedding, rare water-float glass windows, pictures of Emma Nevada

RATES, RESERVATIONS, & RESTRICTIONS

Deposit: Credit card or 1 night's lodging; must cancel 7 days in advance
Discounts: Midweek Jan.–May; rooms $10 higher Thanksgiving–Dec.; extra person $20
Credit Cards: AE, MC, V
Check-In/Out: 3–6/11
Smoking: No
Pets: No
Kids: 8 and over
Minimum Stay: 2 nights on weekends

April–Dec. and on holidays
Open: All year
Hosts: Ruth Ann and Richard Riese
528 E. Broad St.
Nevada City, CA 95959
(530) 265-4415
(800) 916-3662
Fax: 530-265-4416
www.nevadacityinns.com
emmanev@oro.net

GRANDMERE'S INN—AARON SARGENT HOUSE, Nevada City

Overall: ★★★★½   Room Quality: A   Value: B   Price: $110–$165

Indisputably one of the reigning beauties in a town full of beauties, this 1856 Colonial Revival mansion is both a Nevada County Historic Landmark and on the National Register of Historic Places. Aaron Sargent was a congressman, a U.S. senator, and a foreign minister in the mid-1800s. The high-ceilinged guest rooms have tile baths, handmade quilts, and individual features such as sitting areas, a private parlor, and an enclosed sunporch overlooking the splendid half-acre formal garden. A recent breakfast included Grandmere's French toast, sausage, a tropical fruit plate, and apple-walnut crisp.

SETTING & FACILITIES

Location: 1 block west of Nevada City's historic district; 1 hour from either Sacramento or Reno via I-80 and Hwy. 49
Near: Restaurants, shops, galleries, theater, Empire Mine State Historic Park, Scotts Flat Reservoir, Rollins Reservoir, Malakoff Diggins Historic State Park
Building: 1856 Colonial Revival home, 3 stories
Grounds: Half-acre w/ formal gardens of flowering plants, shrubs, and trees, w/ year-round color

Public Space: Parlor, French Country DR
Food & Drink: Full breakfast served 9 a.m. in DR, coffee and tea avail. at 7:30 a.m.
Recreation: Mountain biking, tennis, golf, swimming in the South Yuba River, gold panning, river rafting, horse-drawn carriage rides, fishing
Amenities & Services: Afternoon snacks of homemade cookies, tea, and sodas; off-street parking, assistance w/ dinner and theater reservations

ACCOMMODATIONS

Units: 6 guest rooms, 4 larger than average, including 2 suites
All Rooms: Private bath, AC
Some Rooms: Four-poster
Bed & Bath: Queens, large tubs (3)
Favorites: Senator's Chambers, w/ antique pine four-poster, private parlor, separate porch and entrance, long claw-foot tub and separate shower
Comfort & Decor: Rooms individually decorated w/ American folk art, antique pine and oak furniture, four-poster beds, plantation shutters, carpet and parquet flooring, 10-ft. ceilings, ornate columns, original chandeliers

RATES, RESERVATIONS, & RESTRICTIONS

Deposit: Credit card; must cancel 7 days in advance, 14 days in Dec.
Discounts: Weekday business, Thanksgiving–Dec. $15 additional, extra child/adult $10/$20
Credit Cards: AE, MC, V
Check-In/Out: 3/11
Smoking: No
Pets: No
Kids: In 1 suite
Minimum Stay: 2 nights on weekends
and holidays April–Jan.
Open: All year
Hosts: Ruth Ann Riese, owner; Deborah Gutierrez, mgr.
449 Broad St.
Nevada City, CA 95959
(530) 265-4660
Fax: (530) 265-4416
www.nevadacityinns.com/grandmere.htm
grandmere@nevadacityinns.com

KENDALL HOUSE, Nevada City

Overall: ★★★★	Room Quality: B	Value: B	Price: $105–$215

Just two blocks from downtown Nevada City, Kendall House sits on two quiet acres of landscaped grounds, including a heated swimming pool surrounded by a large lounging area. The main house has four attractive guest rooms, each with a unique feature such as a reading nook or a private deck. The Barn is a separate cottage with a kitchen, a living room with a sofa bed, a bedroom and bath, and a private deck; it's suitable for two couples. Ted Kendall knows all the good hiking and jogging trails in the area, and Jan Kendall's breakfasts will give you a reason to hike them. This is a good place for folks who like the hospitality of a B&B but aren't into the fussy stuff.

SETTING & FACILITIES

Location: On Hwy. 49, 1 hour from either Sacramento or Reno
Near: Restaurants, shops, galleries, theater, Empire Mine State Historic Park, Scotts Flat Reservoir, Rollins Reservoir, Malakoff Diggins Historic State Park
Building: Pre-Victorian California farmhouse, circa 1860, w/ modern amenities
Grounds: 2 acres, heated swimming pool, pergola, redwood decks
Public Space: Large rambling LR/game room/library/common area with outside
Food & Drink: Full breakfast served 9–10:30 a.m. in DR or veranda, early coffee and tea avail.

Recreation: Mountain biking, tennis, golf, swimming in the South Yuba River, gold panning, river rafting, horse-drawn carriage rides, fishing

Amenities & Services: Evening wine and hors d'oeuvres, soft drinks, beer, brandy when appropriate, chocolate chip cookies, heated swimming pool, private parking, disabled access, concierge service for reservations

ACCOMMODATIONS

Units: 4 guest rooms in main house; I guest cottage accommodates 2 couples

All Rooms: Private bath, AC/heat, sitting area

Some Rooms: Fireplace, four-poster, sleeper sofa, fridge, private deck

Bed & Bath: Queens

Favorites: Garden Room, w/ private entrance, private porch, sitting area, antique claw-foot tub w/ handheld shower and matching pedestal sink; the Barn, separate guest house w/ private deck, LR area w/ queen sofa bed and TV, separate BR, full kitchen, picture windows looking into the trees, wood-burning stove

Comfort & Decor: Rooms individually decorated w/ original artwork, Country French furniture, wicker, custom-made armoire, reading/lounging nook w/ skylight, ceiling fans, gas fireplace/wood-burning stove

RATES, RESERVATIONS, & RESTRICTIONS

Deposit: Credit card or 50% of bill; must cancel 7 days in advance, 14 days for holidays

Discounts: Long stays

Credit Cards: AE, D, MC, V

Check-In/Out: 3/noon, early check-in by arrangement

Smoking: No

Pets: No

Kids: 12 and over, by arrangement

No-Nos: No more than 2 guests per room, except in cottage

Minimum Stay: 2 nights on weekends April–Dec. and on holidays

Open: All year

Hosts: Jan and Ted Kendall
534 Spring St.
Nevada City, CA 95959
(530) 265-0405
(888) 647-0405
Fax: (530) 265-0405
www.virtualcities.com
kenhouse@netshel.net

PIETY HILL COTTAGES B&B, Nevada City

Overall: ★★★★	Room Quality: B	Value: A	Price: $80–$150

Although this inn originated as an auto court built in 1933, owners Joan and Steve Oas have transformed Piety Hill's nine bungalows into adorable country cottages, charmingly decorated with fine wallpaper, white wicker accents, lace curtains, quilts, with added conveniences such as kitchenettes and garages. The cottages surround a grassy courtyard with picnic tables, barbecues, a gazebo-covered spa, and comfortable chairs. A breakfast basket filled with fresh fruit, quiche or French toast, and homemade breads is delivered to your cottage. Children are welcome.

SETTING & FACILITIES

Location: Southwest edge of Nevada City, 5-min. walk to downtown, 1 hour from either Sacramento or Reno via I-80 and Hwy. 49

Near: Restaurants, shops, galleries, theater, Empire Mine State Historic Park, Scotts Flat Reservoir, Rollins Reservoir, Malakoff Diggins Historic State Park

Building: 9 separate cottages built in 1933 as a tourist court, most w/ attached garages

Grounds: 1-acre open lawn, tree-shaded courtyard, and gardens w/ tables, chairs, and lounges

Public Space: Parlor, library, gazebo, covered hot tub/spa

Food & Drink: Full breakfast served 8:30–10 a.m. in cottages or outdoors in mild weather, attention to dietary needs

Recreation: Mountain biking, tennis, golf, swimming in the South Yuba River, gold panning, river rafting, horse-drawn carriage rides, fishing

Amenities & Services: Coffee, tea, cold drinks avail. in each cottage, barbecue, microwave avail., private parking

ACCOMMODATIONS

Units: 9 guest cottages in 3 sizes: room and bath; BR, kitchenette, and bath; LR, BR, kitchenette, and bath

All Rooms: Private bath, cable TV, phone, AC, coffeemaker, plug-in hot pot for tea, fridge

Some Rooms: Wood-burning stove (1), four-poster (1), VCR (1), kitchenette (8), extra bed (3)

Bed & Bath: Kings, queens (2)

Favorites: Apple Blossom sits at end of garden path, decorated in Country French yellow and blue w/ wicker, brass king bed, sitting area, private garden

Comfort & Decor: Rooms individually decorated in country styles w/ original art, numbered prints, quilt wall hangings, wicker, oak and pine furniture, lace curtains, patchwork quilts, stenciling on walls

RATES, RESERVATIONS, & RESTRICTIONS

Deposit: Credit card; must cancel 7 days in advance

Discounts: Long stays, weekday business; extra person $5/$15 night, children under 3 are free

Credit Cards: AE, MC, V

Check-In/Out: 3/11

Smoking: No

Pets: No

Kids: Welcome

Minimum Stay: 2 nights on weekends and holidays

Open: All year

Hosts: Joan and Steve Oas
523 Sacramento St.
Nevada City, CA 95959
(530) 265-2245
(800) 443-2245
Fax: (530) 265-6528
www.pietyhillcottages.com

RED CASTLE INN HISTORIC LODGINGS, Nevada City

| Overall: ★★★★½ | Room Quality: B | Value: B | Price: $85–$150 |

For those interested in period architecture, this four-story mansion built in 1859 is one of only two genuine Gothic Revival brick houses on the West

Coast. Dramatically sited on Nevada City's Prospect Hill amid giant incense cedars, the red brick structure is fringed with white icicle trim and circled with lacy white verandas. The guest rooms on the main and lower floors have high Victorian ceilings and their own verandas. On the next floor are two three-room suites with double beds. The top floor, under the eaves, is a two-bedroom suite with sloped ceilings, windows at floor level, and two double beds. A buffet breakfast includes homemade breads and muffins, fruit, cereal, and an entrée such as mushroom crepes or blueberry pancakes, plus interesting treats such as tomato-Gruyére tarts.

SETTING & FACILITIES

Location: On the east side of Hwy. 49, 2-minute walk to downtown Nevada City, 1 hour from Sacramento or Reno via I-80 and Hwys. 49 or 20
Near: Restaurants, shops, galleries, theater, Empire Mine State Historic Park, Scotts Flat Reservoir, Rollins Reservoir, Malakoff Diggins Historic State Park
Building: 1860 4-story brick Gothic Revival mansion
Grounds: 1.5 acres of terraced gardens, paths, fountain pool, views of town and foothills
Public Space: Parlor w/ 1880 pump organ, library, verandas on every level
Food & Drink: Full breakfast buffet served in foyer and parlor, or guests may take a tray to their rooms; special dietary requests accommodated
Recreation: Mountain biking, tennis, golf, swimming in the South Yuba River, gold panning, river rafting, horse-drawn carriage rides, fishing
Amenities & Services: Tea served in the afternoon (often by "Mark Twain"), ceiling fans, turn-down service, triple-sheeted beds, down comforters, hand-pieced quilts, private parking, concierge service for reservations, room delivery of ice, lavish authentic 10-course catered Victorian dinner elegantly served to guests on Christmas Day

ACCOMMODATIONS

Units: 7 guest rooms, 3 larger than average, including 3 suites
All Rooms: Private bath, private veranda or sitting area, view, oriental rugs, hardwood floor
Some Rooms: Canopy or four-poster bed, chandelier, lace curtains, parlor, AC, extra double (1)
Bed & Bath: Queens and doubles, robes, tubs (2), antique claw-foot tub (1)
Favorites: Garden Room, w/ American Empire furnishings, rich autumn colors, canopy bed, French doors to garden, ceiling fan, view of 2 sides of garden
Comfort & Decor: Rooms individually decorated w/ period antiques, including lighting, accessories, bibelots, oriental carpets over original wide plank hardwood floors, original-grain painted doors, water-float glass

RATES, RESERVATIONS, & RESTRICTIONS

Deposit: Credit card; must cancel 7 days in advance, 14 for holidays, 30 days for more than 3 rooms or 3 days
Discounts: Long stays, weekday business, AAA, seniors; extra person $20
Credit Cards: MC, V
Check-In/Out: 2 Fri. and Sat., 4 other days/11

Smoking: No
Pets: No
Kids: 10 and over
Minimum Stay: 2 nights on weekends
April–Jan.
Open: All year

Hosts: Conley and Mary Louise
Weaver
109 Prospect St.
Nevada City, CA 95959
(530) 265-5135
(800) 761-4766
www.innsofthegoldcountry.com

CHATEAU DU SUREAU, Oakhurst

Overall: ★★★★★	Room Quality: A	Value: C	Price: $315–$2,500

You don't need to go to Europe to stay in an Old World chateau—come to the town of Oakhurst, 16 miles from Yosemite National Park. Here you can experience all the pleasures of castle life, minus drafty halls and plus American plumbing. The Chateau du Sureau has carved out a niche as one of the most elegant inns in the state. From the moment the monogrammed iron gates swing shut behind you and the chambermaids in black ankle-length dresses and white aprons take you in hand, every effort is made to ensure that, for a brief period (or until you run through your inheritance), you will feel like visiting royalty. While many fine inns have lovely rooms, rare antiques, and manicured grounds, the Chateau puts them all together flawlessly, with a bit more imagination. You may never see another garden containing a chess court with three-foot-tall pieces, for instance. A separate, newly completed, individual manor house, the opulent Villa Sureau, has 14-foot ceilings, two bedrooms, steam showers, a tower library/drawing room, a small kitchen with china and crystal, a stock of guests' favorite wines, and a 24-hour personal butler. The oft-commended Erna's Elderberry House, a restaurant nationally famous for its cuisine, is also on the estate.

SETTING & FACILITIES

Location: Just west of Oakhurst, off Hwy. 41, 16 mi. from the south entrance to Yosemite Nat'l Park

Near: Yosemite Nat'l Park, Sierras, skiing, gold rush towns

Building: French-style chateau opened in 1991, w/ stone turret, terra-cotta tiled roof, Parisian wrought-iron balconies; separate villa modeled on a Parisian manor house, opened in 1999

Grounds: 9 wooded acres w/ oaks and elderberries, landscaped gardens, gazebo and reflecting pond, fountain, terraces, outdoor chess set w/ 3-ft.-tall chess pieces

Public Space: Salon, music tower and grand piano, library, breakfast room w/ fireplace

Food & Drink: European breakfast served 8–10:30 a.m. in the chateau breakfast room

Recreation: Swimming, lawn games on premises; nearby rock climbing, fly fishing, four-wheeling, skiing, horseback riding, water sports on Bass Lake, Yosemite Nat'l Park

Amenities & Services: Afternoon snacks, evening sherry and wine, gourmet treats and herbal tea in room on checking in, fresh flowers, turndown service w/ chocolate treats, swimming pool, private parking, disabled access, concierge service, award-winning restaurant on premises; therapeutic massage, hair styling, and facials avail.

ACCOMMODATIONS

Units: 10 guest rooms in chateau, 2-BR villa

All Rooms: Private bath, phone, AC, featherbed and down pillows, wood-burning fireplace

Some Rooms: Four-poster, floor-to-ceiling tapestry, black marble bath, views of the Sierras, spa tub

Bed & Bath: Mostly kings, extra beds by request

Favorites: Elderberry Room, w/ cathedral ceiling and hand-carved wooden

beams, king canopy bed, bath tiles detailed w/ hand-painted elderberries, wrought-iron Parisian balcony, views of the Sierras and gardens; Saffron Room, w/ 1834 inlaid ebony and ivory BR set, black marble fireplace and bath, floor-to-ceiling tapestry

Comfort & Decor: Individually decorated using theme of Provençal herbs and flower, w/ Italian linens, down pillows and comforters, antiques, tapestries, fine art

RATES, RESERVATIONS, & RESTRICTIONS

Deposit: 50% of bill; must cancel 7 days in advance; no charge if room subsequently rented

Discounts: None

Credit Cards: AE, MC, V

Check-In/Out: 2/noon, later by arrangement

Smoking: No

Pets: No

Kids: Over 7, by arrangement

Minimum Stay: 2 nights on week-

ends, 3 on holiday weekends

Open: Closed Jan. 3–21

Hosts: Erna Kubin-Clanin, owner; Lucy Royse, directrice

P.O. Box 577

48688 Victoria Lane

Oakhurst, CA 93644

(559) 683-6860

Fax: (559) 683-0800

www.elderberryhouse.com

chateau@sierratel.com

HOUND'S TOOTH INN, Oakhurst

Overall: ★★★½	Room Quality: B	Value: B	Price: $95–$225

This recently built, attractive inn is right off Hwy. 41, 5 miles from Bass Lake and 12 miles from the southern entrance to Yosemite National Park. It's a convenient location to everything the area has to offer, and if the rooms don't have the patina of age, they do have comfortable, pretty furnishings and choices of amenities such as spas or fireplaces. The inn's landscaping is a work in progress, and the highway is a mite close, but it beats the heck out of any motel in the area, and the hosts are pleasant and helpful.

SETTING & FACILITIES

Location: 45 mi. north of Fresno on Hwy. 41 in Oakhurst, 12 mi. south of the southern entrance to Yosemite Nat'l Park
Near: Restaurants, shopping, antiquing, Bass Lake, Yosemite Nat'l Park, gold rush towns
Building: 2-story Victorian-style house built in 1997
Grounds: 3.5 acres w/ seasonal creek, woods, spring flowers, grassy areas
Public Space: Parlor, library, sitting room, outdoor patios
Food & Drink: Full breakfast served 8–10 a.m. in the sitting room
Recreation: Biking, fishing, mountain biking, golf, horseback riding, skiing, gold panning, rock climbing, four-wheeling, water sports
Amenities & Services: Evening wine, cookies, private parking, disabled access, VCRs in rooms, Internet access, wake-up service

ACCOMMODATIONS

Units: 12 guest rooms plus cottage, 7 larger than average, including 1 suite, and 1 cottage
All Rooms: Private bath, cable TV, phone, individual AC/heat
Some Rooms: Fireplace, fridge, spa tub, VCR, private entrance, private patio and yard, kitchenette, extra daybed (1)
Bed & Bath: Queens and kings
Favorites: Hounds Tooth, w/ fireplace, king bed, couch, black and cream tai-
lored decor w/ cherry-wood, spa, view of Sierras; Tower, w/ queen bed, romantic decor in seafoam and white sheer netting, rattan chairs, corner room w/ turret seating, spa, view of Sierras
Comfort & Decor: Rooms individually decorated w/ Victorian reproductions, antiques, paint/wall coverings, lace valances, carpet and tile, vaulted upstairs ceilings, coffered ceilings, original art/prints

RATES, RESERVATIONS, & RESTRICTIONS

Deposit: Credit card; must cancel 72 hours in advance for full refund; 10% cancellation fee
Discounts: Weekday business, AAA except holidays, winter weekdays, seniors; extra person over 10 $20
Credit Cards: AE, D, MC, V
Check-In/Out: 3/noon, late check-out on approval w/ nominal charge
Smoking: No
Pets: No
Kids: OK by prior arrangement
Minimum Stay: 2 or 3 nights on holiday weekends

Open: All year
Hosts: Bill and Anna Williams and Rob
and Lisa Kiehlmeier
42071 Hwy. 41
Oakhurst, CA 93644

(559) 642-6600
(888) 642-6610
Fax: (559) 658-2946
www.sierranet.net/net/tooth
robray@sierratel.com

CHICHESTER–MCKEE HOUSE: A B&B INN, Placerville

Overall: ★★★½	Room Quality: B	Value: A	Price: $80–$125

This B&B was the subject of well-known artist Thomas Kinkade's annual Christmas print in 1993. The stately building sits on a rise in front of a sometimes busy street, but inside all is tranquil. Two of the comfortable guest rooms have half-baths and share a large shower room, while the other two have private baths. One has a fireplace. Breakfast recently featured eggs Benedict, fruit with cream, scones, and coffeecake. Doreen Thornhill is famous for her caramel brownies, which are always available, and there's a talented miniature dachshund named Heidi in residence; at breakfast she does math tricks like telling you her age and the square root of 25.

SETTING & FACILITIES

Location: In Placerville, half-block off intersection of Hwys. 49 and 50; 45 min. from Sacramento, 2 hours from San Francisco via I-80 and Hwy. 50, 2.5 hours from Reno
Near: Restaurants, wineries, galleries, antiques, museums, Apple Hill, Gold Discovery Park
Building: Queen Anne Grand Victorian built in 1892, fully restored in 1983
Grounds: 1 acre w/ gardens, rock walls, large trees

Public Space: Parlor, library, conservatory, DR, kitchen, veranda
Food & Drink: Full breakfast served 8–10 a.m. in DR
Recreation: Biking, golf, whitewater rafting, boating, horseback riding, fishing
Amenities & Services: Caramel brownies, soft drinks, fruit, robes, classical music, historical books of area, games, puzzles, off-street parking, local airport pickup, assistance w/ dining reservations

ACCOMMODATIONS

Units: 4 guest rooms, 2 larger than average
All Rooms: Individually controlled heat/AC, electric blankets
Some Rooms: Canopy bed, fireplace, private bath (2), extra twin (1)
Bed & Bath: Queens, 2 rooms w/ half-baths share large shower room
Favorites: Yellow Rose Room, w/ bay

window, oak furniture, Amish fishnet canopy bed, extra twin bed, Pullman basin, view of hillside w/ historic homes
Comfort & Decor: Rooms individually decorated w/ original watercolors, old Placerville photos; oak, Eastlake, and Amish furniture; lace curtains, wallpaper, original plank hardwood floors, carpets, fireplaces, fretwork, stained glass

RATES, RESERVATIONS, & RESTRICTIONS

Deposit: Credit card; must cancel 5 days in advance; cancellation fee $10
Discounts: None
Credit Cards: AE, D, MC, V
Check-In/Out: 4/11, late check-out by arrangement
Smoking: No
Pets: No
Kids: OK by prior arrangement
No-Nos: No more than 2 guests per room, except Yellow Rose

Minimum Stay: 2 nights during Spring Wine Passport weekend in early April
Open: Open all year
Hosts: Doreen and Bill Thornhill
800 Spring St.
Placerville, CA 95667
(530) 626-1882
(800) 831-4008
Fax: (530) 626-7801
www.innercite.com/~inn
inn@innercite.com

INDIAN CREEK B&B, Plymouth

Overall: ★★★★   Room Quality: B   Value: B   Price: $110–$140

It's hard to think of a small inn with a more dramatic living room than the one in this unusual log lodge. The cathedral beamed ceiling is 2.5 stories up there, and the 28-foot rock fireplace, suspended manzanita-rail balconies, Douglas fir floors, and Indian artifacts all combine to elicit a big "Wow." There are lots of places to hang out here—oversized couches and chairs in the living room and sunroom, rockers on the porch, recliners at the pool, and hammocks in the shade of towering oaks and pines. The lodge's four rooms range in size and decor, most with western or Native American themes. Breakfast, served at a 14-foot antique dining room table, may include tropical fruit with a peach sauce, eggs baked in puff pastry with hollandaise sauce on artichokes, Black Forest ham, and Parmesan roasted potatoes. If you can pry yourself away from all that eating and resting, you're minutes away from Fiddletown, Plymouth, Drytown, Amador City, and Sutter Creek. Git along, little dogie.

SETTING & FACILITIES

Location: 3 mi. north of Plymouth on Hwy. 49
Near: Wineries, shops, galleries, museums, state parks
Building: 1932 log lodge built by Hollywood producer, Douglas fir floors, suspended log and manzanita balcony and bridge fronting guest rooms

Grounds: 10 wooded acres w/ creek, spring-fed pond, oaks and pines, trails, mines, meadows, wildlife
Public Space: Large LR w/ 28-ft. fireplace and oversized leather couches and chairs, sunroom, DR, cowboy bar, decks, swimming pool, spa

ACCOMMODATIONS

Units: 4 guest rooms, 1 larger than average

All Rooms: Private bath, AC, ceiling fan, love seat or extra seating, view of woods, creek, or valley

Some Rooms: Four-poster, redwood deck, balcony

Bed & Bath: Queens, original deep bathtub (1)

Favorites: Margaret Breen Room, w/ redwood deck on 3 sides, panoramic view overlooking pool, spa, creek and valley below, elevated four-poster, wicker and antique pine furniture

Comfort & Decor: Rooms individually decorated w/ original art, mission oak antiques, pleated shades w/ curtains, sponged walls w/ hand-painted mural, Douglas fir floors and carpet or area rugs

RATES, RESERVATIONS, & RESTRICTIONS

Deposit: 1st night's lodging; must cancel 14 days in advance, 30 days for special events or holidays

Discounts: None

Credit Cards: D, MC, V

Check-In/Out: 3/11

Smoking: No

Pets: No

Kids: Not suitable

No-Nos: No more than 2 guests per room

Minimum Stay: 2 nights on weekends and holidays

Open: All year

Hosts: Lena Stiward and Steve Noffsinger
21950 Hwy. 49
Plymouth, CA 95669
(209) 245-4648
Fax: (209) 245-3230
www.indiancreek.com

THE FEATHER BED, Quincy

Overall: ★★★½	Room Quality: B	Value: A	Price: $80–$130

The historic area of Quincy, a sleepy town tucked in the slopes of the northern Sierra Nevada mountains, is everything you'd like a small town to be. The air is clean, the neighborhoods are quiet, and anything you need is within walking distance. The Feather Bed fits right into this friendly setting, offering attractive guest rooms, attentive hosts, and prizewinning breakfast recipes. Floral-print wallpaper and patchwork quilts complete the feeling that you're in Mayberry and Aunt Bea is going to pop her head around the corner any second.

SETTING & FACILITIES

Location: In the historic section of Quincy, 1 block north of the courthouse, 3 hours northeast of Sacramento via Hwys. 80 and 89, 2 hours east of Chico via Hwys. 70 and 89

Near: Restaurants, shopping, airport, Plumas Nat'l Forest, local history museum

Building: 2-story Queen Anne Victorian w/ Greco-Roman columns, built in 1893, 2 cottages

Grounds: 2 acres of native trees, flowers, vegetable garden; raspberry, blackberry, and strawberry patch

Public Space: Parlor w/ fireplace, sitting room w/ TV, games, covered front porch w/ chairs, DR

Food & Drink: Full breakfast w/ berry smoothies served 8:30–10 a.m. in DR, early breakfast by arrangement

Recreation: Bird-watching for bald eagles and Canada geese, fishing, biking, tennis, golf, skiing, snowmobiling

Amenities & Services: Afternoon snacks of homemade cookies, fudge, tea, cider, cocoa, lemonade; airport pickup, private parking, disabled-accessible cottage, complimentary bicycles, fax machine, concierge service for reservations

ACCOMMODATIONS

Units: 7 guest rooms, 4 larger than average, including 1 suite, 2 cottages w/ patios and fireplaces

All Rooms: Private bath, phone, AC, individually controlled heat

Some Rooms: Cable TV, fireplace, patio, extra bed (3)

Bed & Bath: Queens

Favorites: Sweetheart Cottage, w/ private deck under crabapple tree, gas fireplace, daybed, claw-foot tub/shower, cable TV; Barrett's Room, w/ Franklin stove, overlooks Victorian patio and garden, claw-foot tub/shower

Comfort & Decor: Rooms individually decorated w/ historical local photos, antiques chosen for comfort as well as style, Victorian wallpaper, lace curtains, carpet

RATES, RESERVATIONS, & RESTRICTIONS

Deposit: Credit card; must cancel 5 days in advance; no cancellation fee

Discounts: Singles, weekday business travelers, 3 nights or more; extra person $10

Credit Cards: All

Check-In/Out: 3–6/11, late check-out by arrangement

Smoking: No

Pets: No, but kennels avail. nearby

Kids: In cottages

Minimum Stay: 2 nights on summer weekend holidays

Open: All year

Hosts: Bob and Jan Janowski
P.O. Box 3200
542 Jackson St.
Quincy, CA 95971
(916) 283-0102
(800) 696-8624
www.innaccess.com/tfb

AMBER HOUSE B&B, Sacramento

Overall: ★★★★½   Room Quality: A   Value: B   Price: $109–$249

On a shady, elm-lined street in California's capital, the delightful Amber House is actually three adjacent historic homes. What they have in common is spacious guest rooms filled with fine antiques, Victorian wallpapers and draperies, and Jacuzzi tubs for two in marble-tiled bathrooms. Trés romantic. Well-fed guests have an early morning coffee tray and newspaper waiting outside their doors; sumptuous breakfasts in their rooms, the garden, or the dining room, at the time they choose; and freshly baked chocolate chip cookies and champagne in the evening. If you'd like to work off some of those calories, there are bicycles, including a tandem bike, on the premises, and the 26-mile bike trail along the American River is awesome.

SETTING & FACILITIES

Location: In midtown Sacramento 7 blocks east of Capitol Park

Near: Restaurants, the state capitol, Sutter's Fort, and the new downtown shopping mall, theaters, zoo, Towe Auto Museum State Indian Museum; Old Sacramento, w/ shops, restaurants, riverboat cruises, water taxis Military Museum State Railroad Museum

Building: Poet's Corner, a 1905 Craftsman w/ 5 rooms; Artist's Retreat, a 1913 Mediterranean w/ 4 rooms; Musician's Manor, a 1895 Colonial Revival w/ 5 rooms. The restoration of the buildings was authentically done, and they are on Sacramento's register of historically important structures

Grounds: Three 19th-century midtown city lots. Poet's Refuge and Artist's Retreat are next to each other, and Musician's Manor is diagonally across the street

Public Space: Poet's Corner and Artist's Retreat—parlors; Poet's Corner—library; Musician's Manor—private garden w/ tables, chairs, fountain for all guests

Food & Drink: Full breakfast at time and place of guests' choice

Recreation: Bicycles and a tandem bike on premises; Sacramento's extensive network of bike lanes lead to many tourist destinations and the 26-mi. American River Bike Trail; nearby river rafting, tennis, golf

Amenities & Services: Ice delivered to rooms, private phones w/ modem connection, classical background music in public spaces; evening wine, champagne, and beverages, and fresh chocolate chip cookies; off-street parking

ACCOMMODATIONS

Units: 13 guest rooms and 1 semisuite w/ sofa bed and fridge
All Rooms: Private bath, cable TV and VCR, phone w/ voice mail, table and chairs, iron and ironing board, CD or cassette player
Some Rooms: Fireplace
Bed & Bath: Queens, king, Jacuzzis (11, 3 heart-shaped), claw-foot tubs (3), bathrobes, hairdryers

Favorites: Mozart Room, w/ fireplace, armoire, private deck, bathroom w/ double heart-shaped spa
Comfort & Decor: Individually decorated w/ eclectic, comfortable mix of antiques, w/ architectural features such as boxed-beam ceilings, wingback chairs, a clinker brick fireplace, windows of beveled, leaded, and stained glass

RATES, RESERVATIONS, & RESTRICTIONS

Deposit: Credit card number (billed on arrival); must cancel 2 days in advance for weekdays or 7 days for weekends; no cancellation fee
Discounts: Weekday business travelers (single), AAA, and long-term guests
Credit Cards: All
Check-In/Out: 4/noon
Smoking: No
Pets: No
Kids: OK

Minimum Stay: None
Open: All year
Hosts: Michael and Jane Richardson
1315 22nd St.
Sacramento, CA 95816
(916) 444-8085
(800) 755-6526
Fax: 916-552-6529
www.amberhouse.com
Innkeeper@amberhouse.com

HARTLEY HOUSE B&B, Sacramento

Overall: ★★★★	Room Quality: B	Value: B	Price: $120–$170

Hartley House was built in 1906 in Sacramento's first subdivision. The house passed out of the family in 1953 but was purchased in 1987 by the original owner's great-grandson, who turned it into a B&B. Randy Hartley has impeccably restored the place, which now looks much as it did in 1906, with inlaid hardwood floors, leaded- and stained-glass windows, and original brass light fixtures converted from gas. Everywhere inside it looks much the same, with some of Grandmother Hartley's lovely furniture still in use. The urban neighborhood is still known as Boulevard Park and is one of Sacramento's friendliest, featuring many fine examples of restored Victorian and Edwardian homes. Guests can choose from a menu of items for breakfast, including entrées like apple pancakes, cheese blintzes, omelets, and quiche, plus a variety of side dishes and baked goods.

SETTING & FACILITIES

Location: In a midtown Sacramento residential area, 14 blocks northeast of the state capitol
Near: Restaurants, the state capitol, Crocker Art Museum, Sutter's Fort, the new downtown shopping mall, theaters, zoo, convention center, Towe Auto Museum State Indian Museum; Old Sacramento, w/ shops, restaurants, riverboat cruises, water taxis Military Museum State Railroad Museum
Building: Turn-of-the-century mansion, cube-type Craftsman/Colonial built in 1906
Grounds: Corner urban lot w/ gardens, secluded courtyard w/ spa
Public Space: Parlor, DR
Food & Drink: Full breakfast w/ choices of entrées and baked goods, weekdays 7:15–8:30 a.m., weekends 8:30–9:30 a.m., served in DR or courtyard
Recreation: Sacramento's extensive network of bike lanes lead to many tourist destinations and the 26-mi. American River Bike Trail; nearby river rafting, tennis, golf
Amenities & Services: Hot tub, evening sherry and wine, fresh cookies, hairdryers, irons and ironing board, robes, morning newspaper, discounts at local restaurants and health club, VCRs in room, multiline digital speaker phones, voice mail, modem ports

ACCOMMODATIONS

Units: 5 guest rooms, 1 larger than average
All Rooms: Private bath, cable TV, phone, AC, reading lamps
Some Rooms: N/A
Bed & Bath: Mostly queens
Favorites: Brighton, a light-filled corner room w/ blue walls, table and chairs, floral quilted bedcover, reading lamp; Dover, w/ king brass rail bed, desk, shutters, claw-foot tub/shower
Comfort & Decor: Rooms individually decorated w/ antique furniture, period artwork, plantation shutters, carpet, fresh flowers, original inlaid hardwood floors, oriental rugs, stained-glass windows, brass light fixtures converted from gas

RATES, RESERVATIONS, & RESTRICTIONS

Deposit: Credit card; must cancel by noon the day before reservation date
Discounts: Weekday business, single
Credit Cards: All
Check-In/Out: 3/11, late check-out $25/hr.
Smoking: No
Pets: No
Kids: 12 and over
No-Nos: No more than 2 guests per room
Minimum Stay: None
Open: All year
Host: Randy Hartley
700 22nd St.
Sacramento, CA 95816
(916) 447-7829
(800) 831-5806
Fax: (916) 447-1820
www.hartleyhouse.com
Randy@hartleyhouse.com

STERLING HOTEL, Sacramento

| Overall: ★★★★½ | Room Quality: B | Value: B | Price: $169–$360 |

The owners of the beautiful Victorian Sterling Hotel have provided Sacramento with a much-needed small European-type inn. The hotel's handsome rooms, each with a tiled bath and spa tub/shower, contain a mix of contemporary and antique furnishings with Asian touches and are quite spacious. The inn is close to Sacramento's business district, and guest rooms are equipped with voice mail and modem access. The elegant foyer has a marble floor, Art Deco chandeliers, and Chinese rugs. Many state capitol fund-raisers and political events are catered here, often taking over the hotel's parlor, so those wishing a more B&B-like setting might be more comfortable elsewhere. In the restoration of the hotel, soundproofing and double-paned windows were added, making it an island of quiet on the edge of a busy downtown.

SETTING & FACILITIES

Location: At the edge of downtown Sacramento, 5 blocks north of state capitol
Near: Restaurants, state capitol, Crocker Art Museum, Sutter's Fort, new downtown shopping mall, theaters, zoo, convention center, Towe Auto Museum State Indian Museum; Old Sacramento, w/ shops, restaurants, riverboat cruises, water taxis Military Museum State Railroad Museum
Building: 1894 Victorian, new adjoining ballroom

Grounds: Urban landscaped lot, outdoor patio restaurant
Public Space: Spacious foyer w/ marble floor, Art Deco chandeliers, Chinese rugs, lounge, grand ballroom
Food & Drink: Extended cont'l breakfast, served 6–10 a.m. in the lounge area
Recreation: Sacramento's extensive network of bike lanes lead to many tourist destinations and the 26-mi. American River Bike Trail; nearby river rafting, tennis, golf

Amenities & Services: Hot tub, delicacy from pastry chef in each room, street parking w/ public lot half-block away, special guest rates for health club 1 block away, room service from restaurant on premises

ACCOMMODATIONS

Units: 17 rooms, all larger than average, including 4 suites
All Rooms: Private bath w/ Jacuzzi, cable TV, phone, AC, voice mail and modem access
Some Rooms: Four-poster, sleeper sofa, extra queen (3), sleeper sofa (4)
Bed & Bath: Queens and kings

Favorites: Room 209, marble bath w/ Roman tub with pillars, champagne, wet bar w/ fridge, large TV; Room 202, L-shaped room w/ queen canopy bed
Comfort & Decor: Rooms individually decorated w/ designer furnishings, Italian marble-tiled bathrooms, Jacuzzis

RATES, RESERVATIONS, & RESTRICTIONS

Deposit: Must cancel 48 hours in advance
Discounts: Weekday business, groups, AAA, singles; extra person $10, no charge for children under 12
Credit Cards: AE, DC, MC, V
Check-In/Out: 3/11, late check-out noon
Smoking: No
Pets: No

Kids: OK, must be attended by parents
Minimum Stay: None
Open: All year
Host: Bill McFerson
1300 H St.
Sacramento, CA 95915
(916) 448-1300
(800) 365-7660
www.sleepingsacramento.com

VIZCAYA, Sacramento

Overall: ★★★★	Room Quality: B	Value: B	Price: $139–$239

Vizcaya sits on Poverty Ridge, a small rise just south of downtown where many of Sacramento's wealthier families built their homes as protection from the flooding that regularly inundated the town in its early, pre-levee days. Guest rooms are nicely furnished with Victorian antiques and lace curtains, and the landscaped grounds around the mansion and conference building are nothing short of spectacular, with a huge fountain and masses of flowers. The inn faces moderately busy 21st Street, but the rooms are quiet. History and architecture buffs will want to stroll through the neighborhood to view some of the other elegant Poverty Ridge mansions. A recent breakfast included vegetarian quiche, eggs, fruit, and scones.

SETTING & FACILITIES

Location: In central Sacramento
Near: State capitol, Crocker Art Museum, Sutter's Fort, theaters, zoo, convention center, Towe Auto Museum
State Indian Museum; Old Sacramento, riverboat cruises, water taxis Military Museum,
California State Railroad Museum

Building: Turn-of-the-century Victorian mansion, carriage house; connecting pavilion has a Venetian design

Grounds: Brick-lined Venetian gardens w/ fruit trees and fountains

Public Space: Parlor, DR

Food & Drink: Expanded cont'l breakfast served 7:30–9 a.m. in the mansion DR

Recreation: Sacramento's extensive network of bike lanes lead to many tourist destinations and the 26-mi. American River Bike Trail; nearby river rafting, tennis, golf

Amenities & Services: Robes, coffee, tea, soda, pastries avail.; street parking or parking lot 2 blocks away

ACCOMMODATIONS

Units: 9 guest rooms, 2 larger than average, including 1 suite

All Rooms: Private bath, cable TV, AC

Some Rooms: Extra queen (1); carriage house rooms have fireplace, four-poster, Jacuzzi

Bed & Bath: Queens, king

Favorites: Room 2 in the mansion, airy and elegant, w/ bay windows, four-poster bed, large closet, mahogany roll-top desk

Comfort & Decor: Rooms individually decorated w/ Victorian antiques, lace curtains; carriage rooms have large Italian marble whirlpool tubs

RATES, RESERVATIONS, & RESTRICTIONS

Deposit: Credit card; must cancel 24 hours in advance for Sun.–Thurs., 48 hours for Fri.–Sat.

Discounts: AAA, AARP, corporate, government; extra person $10

Credit Cards: AE, DC, MC, V

Check-In/Out: 3/11, late check-out by arrangement

Smoking: No

Pets: No

Kids: OK

Minimum Stay: None

Open: All year

Host: Sandra Wasserman
2019 21st St.
Sacramento, CA 95818
(916) 455-5243
(800) 456-2019
Fax: (916) 455-6102
www.sleepingsacramento.com

HIGH COUNTRY INN, Sierra City

Overall: ★★★½	Room Quality: B	Value: A	Price: $80–$125

The craggy peaks of the 8,586-foot-high Sierra Buttes provide the breathtaking backdrop for this choice little B&B. If that isn't enough, on one side, a mere 45 feet away, is the mighty Yuba River, a mere alpine stream at this point. On the other side is the smaller Howard Creek. Add to this scene stands of aspens and pines, a carefully kept garden, and a fishpond loaded with giant rainbow trout (pets, not food), and you have a locale that can't be beat. And that's just outside. The inn's five rooms are furnished stylishly and with an eye to comfort. All have multiple views. The new owners, Bette and Bob Latta, go all out to make a memorable breakfast. A good way to work it off is to climb the buttes, easily done in half a day.

SETTING & FACILITIES

Location: On Hwy. 49 in Tahoe Nat'l Forest, 5 mi. east of Sierra City, 2.5 hours from Sacramento, 1.5 hours from Reno

Near: Trout fishing on premises; nearby, 5 championship golf courses, Kentucky Mine museum, Plumas Eureka Ski Bowl, Lakes Basin Recreation Area, w/ 30+ lakes, X-C ski course w/ 150 mi. of groomed trails

Building: 1960 ranch-style home with addition

Grounds: 2.5 acres on North Yuba River and Howard Creek, large pond full of rainbow trout

Public Space: Common room, library, 2 hammocks on river, 2 lower patio areas on river, large deck w/ furniture

Food & Drink: Full breakfast served at guests' convenience, hot beverage tray at guest room doors 1 hour before breakfast

Recreation: Birding, wildflower walks, mountain biking, fishing, gold panning, canoeing, kayaking, river rafting, snow-shoeing, X-C/downhill skiing, sledding, snowmobiling

Amenities & Services: Afternoon wine and cheese, large-screen satellite TV/VCR, private parking

ACCOMMODATIONS

Units: 5 guest rooms, all larger than average, including 1 suite

All Rooms: View

Some Rooms: Fireplace, deck access, private bath (5)

Bed & Bath: Queens and kings

Favorites: Sierra Buttes Room, w/ king bed, tall cathedral windows across wall facing buttes, large dressing area, wood-burning stove, 6.5-ft. antique tub, shower

Comfort & Decor: Rooms individually decorated w/ combination of antique and country furnishings

RATES, RESERVATIONS, & RESTRICTIONS

Deposit: Credit card; must cancel 72 hours in advance

Discounts: None; extra person $15

Credit Cards: All

Check-In/Out: 4/11, late check-out by arrangement

Smoking: No

Pets: No

Kids: Not suitable

Minimum Stay: None

Open: All year

Hosts: Bette and Bob Latta

Hwy. 49 at Bassetts, 100 Greene Rd.

Sierra City, CA 96125

(530) 862-1530

(800) 862-1530

Fax: (530) 862-1000

www.hicountryinn.com

blatta@sccn.net

BARRETTA GARDENS B&B INN, Sonora

Overall: ★★★½	Room Quality: B	Value: B	Price: $95–$135

A rambling 5,000-square-foot restored family home built in 1903, this inn would be the perfect background for a romance novel or a period-costume movie. It's full of interesting twists and turns and lots of antique-filled rooms—living room, dining room, breakfast room, three open-air porches, a plant-filled solarium, first- and second-floor parlors, and five guest rooms.

You can easily imagine Ingrid Bergman watching the gaslights dim in one of the parlors. Sitting high on a terraced hillside overlooking downtown Sonora, the inn is located on an acre of gardens and lawns, with great views of the sunsets over the foothills. It's a short walk to Sonora restaurants and shops.

SETTING & FACILITIES

Location: In Sonora, off Washington St. (Hwys. 49/108) to Mono St., left on Barretta; 1.5 hours from Sacramento, 2 hours from San Francisco
Near: Wineries, restaurants, gold panning, live theater, shopping, antiques, airport, Calaveras Big Trees State Park, Yosemite Nat'l Park, Dodge Ridge downhill/X-C skiing, river rafting
Building: 1903 Victorian overlooking historic downtown Sonora
Grounds: 1 acre of terraced hillside gardens, lawn, gazebo
Public Space: 3 parlors, enclosed solarium, screened breakfast porch, formal DR
Food & Drink: Full breakfast served at 9 a.m. in DR or on porch
Recreation: Croquet, horseshoes on premises; biking, tennis, golf, horseback riding, skiing, fishing nearby
Amenities & Services: Stuffed animals, cookies, private parking, access to telephones and fax

ACCOMMODATIONS

Units: 5 guest rooms, 2 larger than average, including 1-BR and 2-BR suites
All Rooms: Private bath, cable TV, AC, clock radio
Some Rooms: Stained glass, crystal chandelier, view, child's roll-away (1)
Bed & Bath: Queens, king, tub/shower (3), whirlpool tub (1)
Favorites: Gennylee Suite, in shades of rose w/ Victorian mahogany BR set, parlor, private tiled bath w/ tub and shower overlooking gardens
Comfort & Decor: Rooms individually decorated w/ Victorian artwork, turn-of-the-century furniture, lace curtains, wallpaper, carpet and area rugs

RATES, RESERVATIONS, & RESTRICTIONS

Deposit: Full amount; must cancel 5 days in advance; 10% cancellation fee
Discounts: Long stays, weekday business, seniors; child $25
Credit Cards: AE, MC, V
Check-In/Out: 3/11
Smoking: No
Pets: No
Kids: 2 and over
No-Nos: No more than 2 guests per room, except child accompanying parents
Minimum Stay: 2 nights on weekends, 3 on holiday weekends
Open: All year
Host: Nancy Brandt
700 S. Barretta St.
Sonora, CA 95370
(209) 532-6039
(800) 206-3333
Fax: (209) 532-8257
www.barrettagarden.com
Barretta@mlode.com

RYAN HOUSE, 1855, Sonora

Overall: ★★★½	Room Quality: B	Value: B	Price: $90–$160

Most of the folks who come to Ryan House have been before—often. The house is cute as a button, and the hosts are delightful. The town of Sonora has moved right up to the edge of the property, but Nancy and Guy Hoffman continue to create an oasis in the midst of the busy town. Century-old handmade windowpanes, square nails, and stone walls assembled without mortar attest to Ryan House's architectural heritage. The garden is filled with old-fashioned roses, some as old as the house. Inside, the guest rooms have pretty wallpaper, antiques, and homemade quilts, and Nancy will ply you with sourdough waffles or her special scones for breakfast.

SETTING & FACILITIES

Location: In Sonora 2 blocks east of Hwy. 49; 1.5 hours from Sacramento, 2 hours from San Francisco

Near: Shopping, antiques, live theater, restaurants, golf, airport, wineries, gold panning, Calaveras Big Trees State Park, Yosemite Nat'l Park, Dodge Ridge downhill/X-C skiing, river rafting, Columbia State Historic Park, Railtown 1897

Building: Restored and modernized 1855 gold rush house

Grounds: 1/3 acre w/ 35 rosebushes

Public Space: 2 parlors w/ stoves, library, pantry room w/ TV/VCR, DR, yard w/ wicker furniture

Food & Drink: Full breakfast served at 9 a.m. in DR, early morning coffee, tea, or cocoa avail. in pantry room

Recreation: Biking, tennis, golf, horseback riding, skiing

Amenities & Services: Afternoon snacks and beverages, evening sherry and wine, homemade goodies, kitchen has fridge for guests' use, private parking, VCR for guests' use

ACCOMMODATIONS

Units: 3 guest rooms, including 1 3-room suite

All Rooms: Private bath, AC

Some Rooms: Fireplace, view of downtown Sonora and gardens, parlor, separate BR

Bed & Bath: Queens, 2-person tub (1)

Favorites: Garden View Suite, w/ private parlor, gas log stove, soaking tub

for 2, separate BR, antiques, seasonal views of the gardens

Comfort & Decor: Rooms individually decorated w/ needlework, antique Victorian furniture, Battenberg lace curtains, handmade quilts, fine china and silver, carpet, century-old handmade windowpanes

RATES, RESERVATIONS, & RESTRICTIONS

Deposit: Credit card or check to hold; must cancel 1 week in advance

Discounts: None

Credit Cards: AE, MC, V

Check-In/Out: 3/11, or when coffee runs out

Smoking: No

Pets: No

Kids: Not suitable

No-Nos: No more than 2 guests per room

Open: All year, except Christmas and New Year's Day
Hosts: Nancy and Guy Hoffman
153 S. Shepherd St.

Sonora, CA 95370
(209) 533-3445
(800) 831-4897
www.ryanhouse.com

CHRISTIANIA INN, South Lake Tahoe

Overall: ★★★½	Room Quality: B	Value: B	Price: $50–$185

This chalet, affectionately known as "Chris" by locals and the many returning guests, sits at the base of the main ski lift at Heavenly Ski Resort, a quarter mile south of Lake Tahoe. Naturally it caters to skiers, but it is also a great base for exploring the Tahoe region in the summer—the time for water skiing, landlocked salmon fishing, and sunbathing. It's also steps away from the Nevada state line where casinos are a year round sport. The inn's four suites have wet bars, wood-burning fireplaces, and two of them have their own private saunas. Your typical B&B, this isn't—Suite 4 features a sleeping loft with a mirror over its platform bed.

SETTING & FACILITIES

Location: 5 mi. from center of South Lake Tahoe, across from parking lot for Heavenly Valley Ski Resort, 1.75 hours from Sacramento, 1 hour from Reno
Near: Lake Tahoe, shopping, casinos, entertainment, restaurants, 14 major ski resorts, commercial airport, aerial tram, galleries, golf courses
Building: 1965 European-style chalet
Grounds: 2 acres of land facing Heavenly Valley Ski Resort, in a residential neighborhood
Public Space: Restaurant, DR
Food & Drink: Extended cont'l breakfast served in room at time of choice
Recreation: Biking (road and mountain), tennis, golf, skiing (snow and water), boat excursions
Amenities & Services: Brandy decanter in all rooms, private parking, bar, piano lounge w/ live jazz and blues in ski season, restaurant

ACCOMMODATIONS

Units: 6 guest rooms, 2 larger than average, including 4 suites
All Rooms: Private bath, cable TV
Some Rooms: Fireplace, fridge, private sauna (2)
Bed & Bath: Kings and queens, Jacuzzi (1)
Favorites: Suite 6, a 2-story suite w/ LR, stained-glass window, wet bar, sauna, whirlpool jet tub, king bed, wood-burning fireplace, sitting area
Comfort & Decor: Rooms individually decorated w/ antiques, European ski lodge decor

RATES, RESERVATIONS, & RESTRICTIONS

Deposit: 1st night's lodging; must cancel 7 days in advance
Discounts: Long stays
Credit Cards: MV, V
Check-In/Out: 2/11, late check-out by arrangement
Smoking: No
Pets: No

Kids: OK
Minimum Stay: 2 nights on weekends during ski season and summer, 4 on Christmas holidays
Open: All year
Hosts: Jerry and Maggie Mershon
P.O. Box 18298

3819 Saddle Rd.
South Lake Tahoe, CA 96151
(530) 544-7337
Fax: (530) 544-5342
thechris@sierra.net
www.christianiainn.com

FOXES IN SUTTER CREEK, Sutter Creek

Overall: ★★★★½	Room Quality: B	Value: B	Price: $125–$185

After 19 years of polishing and expanding their lovely B&B in picturesque downtown Sutter Creek, Min and Pete Fox have just about reached perfection. Their seven guest rooms are fulled with tasteful, comfortable furnishings, including impressive Victorian beds and armoires that look like they should be in museums. Five rooms have large, wood-burning fireplaces, and five have private entries. Breakfast is an event. Served on lovely silver trays and tea services and delivered to each room, or the gazebo if the weather is nice, guests pick their own time and menu from such choices as Swedish pancakes, Swiss eggs, or the house specialty, chile relleno.

SETTING & FACILITIES

Location: West side of Hwy. 49 (Main St.) in downtown Sutter Creek, 45 min. from Sacramento
Near: Restaurants, shopping, theater, galleries, wineries, antiques, historic gold rush buildings and sites, airport
Building: New England farmhouse built in 1857 and expanded over the years
Grounds: Landscaped city lot w/ dogwood and Japanese maples over gazebo and pond
Public Space: 2 parlors, library, gazebo

Food & Drink: Full breakfast served 8–9:30 a.m. in room or garden, dietary restrictions accommodated
Recreation: Antiquing, biking, white-water rafting, fishing, boating, golf, gold panning

Amenities & Services: Complimentary beverages, 2 fresh apples in each room, VCRs, afternoon tea or coffee to order, 5 covered parking spaces with additional parking in the rear, fax

ACCOMMODATIONS

Units: 7 guest rooms, 6 larger than average, all suites
All Rooms: Private bath, AC, armoire
Some Rooms: Cable TV/VCR (4), fireplace and private entrance (5), view of the garden
Bed & Bath: Queens, claw-foot tubs and separate showers (4)
Favorites: Victorian Suite, upstairs w/ breakfast room, library, fireplace,

spacious bath w/ old-fashioned tub and separate shower
Comfort & Decor: Rooms individually decorated w/ photography, prints, needlework, European antiques and comfortable leather chairs, lace curtains, wallpaper and faux finishes on walls, coordinated carpets and Italian tiles in baths

RATES, RESERVATIONS, & RESTRICTIONS

Deposit: 1st night's lodging within 7 days of reservation; must cancel 10 days in advance; cancellation fee $10
Discounts: AAA, seniors, Sun.–Thurs.
Credit Cards: D, MC, V
Check-In/Out: 3/11, late check-out by arrangement
Smoking: No
Pets: No
Kids: OK
No-Nos: No more than 2 guests per room

Minimum Stay: 2 nights on weekends and holidays
Open: Closed Dec. 24–26
Hosts: Min and Pete Fox
P.O. Box 159
77 Main St.
Sutter Creek, CA 95685
(209) 267-5882
(800) 987-3344
Fax: (209) 267-0712
www.foxesinn.com
foxes@cdepot.net

GREY GABLES B&B, Sutter Creek

Overall: ★★★★	Room Quality: B	Value: B	Price: $95–$150

Anglophiles will delight in this English country manor and the British tastes and customs of hosts Roger and Sue Garlick. Named after British writers and poets, each of the elegant guest rooms has fine antiques, a fireplace, and a tiled bath. Breakfast is served on English bone china in the formal DR, or in your room if you fancy, and in the afternoon, of course, there's tea with cakes or scones. Outside you'll find a manicured, terraced garden with red brick pathways, and if you look closely, that's probably Prince Charles cavorting with Camilla under the wisteria-covered archway.

SETTING & FACILITIES

Location: Hwy. 49 on the north side of Sutter Creek, 45 min. from Sacramento
Near: Restaurants, shopping, theater, galleries, wineries, antiques, historic gold rush buildings and sites, airport
Building: 108-year-old Victorian w/ recent additions
Grounds: 1/3 acre of terraced English gardens, brick pathways, and rose arbors

Public Space: Large Victorian parlor, formal DR, gazebo
Food & Drink: Full breakfast served at 9 a.m. in DR or in rooms
Recreation: Antiquing, biking, white-water rafting, fishing, boating, golf, gold panning
Amenities & Services: Afternoon tea w/ scones and cakes, evening wine and hors d'oeuvres, private parking, disabled access, touring information

ACCOMMODATIONS

Units: 8 guest rooms, 7 larger than average
All Rooms: Private tiled bath, AC, fireplace
Some Rooms: Four-poster, view of gardens, extra twin (1)
Bed & Bath: Queens and kings, claw-foot tubs/showers (3)
Favorites: Byron, w/ dark rose and forest green decor, Renaissance Revival

queen bed and side chairs, view of garden; Victorian Suite, w/ four-poster king, armoire, tea table, views of garden and churchyard
Comfort & Decor: Rooms individually decorated w/ Victorian art, pine and oak antiques, coordinated floral curtains, marble/wood fireplaces w/ gas logs, carpet

RATES, RESERVATIONS, & RESTRICTIONS

Deposit: 1st night's lodging; must cancel 7 days in advance; cancellation fee $10
Discounts: Long stays, weekday business groups; extra person $20
Credit Cards: All
Check-In/Out: 3/11
Smoking: No
Pets: No
Kids: Over 7
No-Nos: No more than 2 guests per room

Minimum Stay: 2 nights on weekends
Open: All year
Hosts: Roger and Sue Garlick
P.O. Box 1687
161 Hanford St.
Sutter Creek, CA 95685
(209) 267-1039
(800) 473-9422
Fax: (209) 267-0998
www.greygables.com
reservations@greygables.com

HANFORD HOUSE B&B INN, Sutter Creek

| Overall: ★★★★ | Room Quality: B | Value: A | Price: $69–$149 |

The large, red brick, ivy-covered Hanford House is a bit like a hotel, but a very nice hotel. It has nine spacious guest rooms, more Ralph Lauren in style than Victorian. Although it doesn't have gardens or a yard, it does have a shady patio and a sunny rooftop deck, plus a parlor, a dining room, and a large conference/reception area, imminently suitable for weddings and gatherings of all sorts. All the comforts of a good B&B are available—fresh cookies, robes, custom herbal soaps, and business amenities such as modems, a fax, and a computer. Breakfast, by the way, includes good stuff like fresh fruit smoothies, soufflés, frittatas, roasted red potatoes, granola, and interesting breads.

SETTING & FACILITIES

Location: On Hwy. 49 in Sutter Creek
Near: Restaurants, shopping, theater, galleries, wineries, antiques, historic gold rush buildings and sites, airport
Building: 2-story Gold Country brick building, Craftsman cottage annex built in 1984
Grounds: Urban lot, shaded outdoor patio, rooftop sundeck
Public Space: Hanford Room, w/ fireplace, DR
Food & Drink: Full breakfast served at 8:30, 9, and 9:30 a.m. in DR or in rooms
Recreation: Antiquing, biking, whitewater rafting, fishing, boating, golf, gold panning
Amenities & Services: Afternoon cookies and snacks, evening wine and hors d'oeuvres, robes and custom herbal soaps, home theater, cable TV/VCR, video library in parlor, private parking, disabled access, computer avail., massage therapist, facialist on call

ACCOMMODATIONS

Units: 9 guest rooms, 7 larger than average, including 3 suites
All Rooms: Private bath, AC, private entrance
Some Rooms: Fireplace, four-poster, fridge, phone, cable TV, Jacuzzi, private deck, views of hills and downtown Sutter Creek, extra bed (3)
Bed & Bath: Queens, king, Jacuzzi for 2 (1)
Favorites: Gold Country Escape, w/ 12-ft. ceilings, 10-ft. windows, pewter and brass four-poster w/ tapestry linens and bed hangings, large sitting area, private deck, CD stereo; peach and sage green walls, linens, and sitting area
Comfort & Decor: Rooms individually decorated w/ artwork from Artists on Loan program, pine furniture, carpet, designer linens

RATES, RESERVATIONS, & RESTRICTIONS

Deposit: Credit card; must cancel 7 days in advance; cancellation fee $10
Discounts: Long stays, weekday business, AAA, winter weekdays, AARP; extra person $10
Credit Cards: D, MC, V
Check-In/Out: 3/11, late check-out by arrangement
Smoking: No
Pets: No
Kids: 6 and over
Minimum Stay: 2 nights on weekends
Open: All year
Hosts: Bob and Karen Tierno
P.O. Box 1450
61 Hanford St., Hwy. 49
Sutter Creek, CA 95685
(209) 267-0747
(800) 871-5839
Fax: (209) 267-1825
www.hanfordhouse.com
bookat@hanfordhouse.com

CHANEY HOUSE, Tahoe City

Overall: ★★★★	Room Quality: B	Value: B	Price: $110–$195

If this magical stone house built by Italian masons in the 1920s were set back further into the dark forest, you might believe it was inhabited by mythical beings, or at least minor royalty. It has 18-inch stone walls, Gothic arched windows, a turret entry, a massive stone fireplace, and, inside, a high cathedral ceiling. In spite of all those rocks, Gary and Lori Chaney have fashioned a warm and comfortable B&B with three guest rooms in the house and a lavish honeymoon hideaway suite over the garage, all with private baths. Just across the street is a private beach with a pier for guests' use. Lori is a fine cook, and in nice weather breakfast is served on a lovely patio with a view of Lake Tahoe.

SETTING & FACILITIES

Location: 5.5 mi. south of Tahoe City on Hwy. 89 (W. Lake Blvd.)
Near: Lake Tahoe and Donner Lake, restaurants, shopping, commercial airport, casinos, aerial tram, galleries, museums, 10 alpine ski resorts, golf courses
Building: 70-year-old European-style building w/ 18-in. stone walls, Gothic arches
Grounds: 1 acre of native pines, gardens, private beach and pier

Public Space: Parlor w/ massive stone fireplace and cathedral ceiling, DR, 4 patios, private beach and pier
Food & Drink: Full breakfast served 8–10 a.m. in DR
Recreation: Winter sports, boating and water sports, mountain biking, golf, tennis, fishing, horseback riding
Amenities & Services: Evening wine and hors d'oeuvres, barbecue, TV/VCR in parlor, private parking

ACCOMMODATIONS

Units: 4 guest rooms, 3 larger than average, including 3 suites
All Rooms: Phone, private bath
Some Rooms: Fireplace, fridge, view of Lake Tahoe, TV/VCR, extra bed (3)
Bed & Bath: Queens, king

Favorites: Honeymoon Hideaway, w/ fireplace, TV/VCR, wet bar, fridge, featherbed, whirlpool granite tub
Comfort & Decor: Rooms individually decorated w/ antiques, mostly wood and stone walls, carpets

RATES, RESERVATIONS, & RESTRICTIONS

Deposit: 50%; must cancel 2 weeks in advance, 4 weeks for major holidays; cancellation fee $20
Discounts: Winter weekdays; extra person $20
Credit Cards: MC, V
Check-In/Out: 3/11, late check-in/out

by arrangement
Smoking: No
Pets: No
Kids: 10 and over
Minimum Stay: 2 nights on weekends, 3 on holiday weekends

Open: All year
Hosts: Gary and Lori Chaney
P.O. Box 7852
4725 Westlake Blvd.
Tahoe City, CA 96145

(530) 525-7333
Fax: (530) 525-4413
www.chaneyhouse.com
gary@chaneyhouse.com

COTTAGE INN AT LAKE TAHOE, Tahoe City

Overall: ★★★★	Room Quality: B	Value: B	Price: $145–$230

These attractive cottages were built in the "Old Tahoe" style, with knotty pine paneling and log and twig furniture. The cottages sit in a wooded area, and some have a view of Lake Tahoe through the pines. All the rooms have handsome stone fireplaces and theme decors. The Tahoe Teepee room has a—you guessed it—Native American theme, with big black-and-white cowhide on the floor and steer horns over the fireplace. It may sound a bit hokey, but the rooms are fun and nicely done. There's a sauna and access to a nearby private beach with docks, swimming, picnicking, and volleyball.

SETTING & FACILITIES

Location: West shore of Lake Tahoe, on Hwy. 89, 2 mi. south of Tahoe City
Near: Lake Tahoe and Donner Lake, restaurants, shopping, commercial airport, casinos, aerial tram, galleries, museums, 10 alpine ski resorts, golf courses
Building: Wood and stone structure built in 1938, remodeled in 1994, 7 cottages
Grounds: 1.9 acres, lawn, access to private beach w/ docks, picnic facilities

Public Space: Sitting room w/ fireplace, game table, movies, newspapers and magazines, DR
Food & Drink: Full breakfast served 8–10 a.m. in DR, on the deck, or in guest room
Recreation: Winter sports, boating and water sports, mountain biking, golf, tennis, fishing, horseback riding
Amenities & Services: Cookies and coffee bar, sauna, private parking, assistance with dining reservations

ACCOMMODATIONS

Units: 15 guest rooms, including 6 studios, 6 cottage suites, 3 deluxe suites
All Rooms: Private bath w/ spa tub, cable TV, private entrance, stone fireplace
Some Rooms: Fridge, view of Lake Tahoe, sofa bed (2)
Bed & Bath: Queens, king
Favorites: Romantic Hideaway, w/ 2-story fireplace, canopy bed, rock water-

fall Jacuzzi; Evergreen Heaven, w/ natural bark fireplace, thermal massage bath; Bit of Bavaria, w/ alpine theme, 2-room fireplace, private deck w/ hot tub, kitchen
Comfort & Decor: Rooms individually decorated w/ log, twig, and wicker furniture, knotty pine walls, wood floors w/ carpets

RATES, RESERVATIONS, & RESTRICTIONS

Deposit: 50% 2 weeks prior to check-in; must cancel 2 weeks in advance
Discounts: Winter weekdays, seniors; extra person $20
Credit Cards: MC, V
Check-In/Out: 3/11, late check-in/out by arrangement
Smoking: No
Pets: No
Kids: 12 and over
Minimum Stay: 2 nights on week-

ends, 3–4 on holiday weekends
Open: All year
Host: Susanne Muhr
P.O. Box 66
1690 W. Lake Blvd.
Tahoe City, CA 96145
(916) 581-0226
(800) 581-4073
Fax: (530) 581-0226
www.thecottageinn.com
Cottage@sierra.net

SUNNYSIDE RESTAURANT AND LODGE, Tahoe City

Overall: ★★★½	Room Quality: C	Value: B	Price: $90–$210

Although it's not the place for aficionados of intimate little B&Bs, this 23-room mountain lodge has its own appeal. Sunnyside is located at the water's edge on the west shore of Lake Tahoe. It has a marina, a restaurant, a bar, a seafood bar, and a huge redwood deck overlooking one of the most beautiful lakes in the world. For the athletes in the family, Sunnyside conducts a waterskiing school in the summer, and in the winter major ski areas like Squaw Valley and Alpine Meadows are just a few miles away.

SETTING & FACILITIES

Location: West shore of Lake Tahoe on Hwy. 89, 2 mi. south of Tahoe City
Near: Lake Tahoe and Donner Lake, restaurants, shopping, commercial airport, casinos, aerial tram, galleries, museums, 10 alpine ski resorts, golf courses
Building: Private residence built in 1908, expanded to mountain lodge in 1987
Grounds: Lakefront property w/ marina and waterski school, lakefront deck

Public Space: Upstairs nook/library, sundeck
Food & Drink: Extended cont'l breakfast buffet served 7:30–10:30 a.m. in library
Recreation: All water sports avail. on premises; winter sports, mountain biking, golf, tennis, fishing, horseback riding nearby
Amenities & Services: Afternoon snacks and tea; full restaurant, bar and grill on premises; waterski school

ACCOMMODATIONS

Units: 23 guest rooms, including 5 suites
All Rooms: Private bath, cable TV, phone, view of Lake Tahoe and Sierras,

private balcony
Some Rooms: Rock fireplace, sleeper sofa, fridge, wet bar, VCR
Bed & Bath: Queens, kings (4)

Favorites: Lakefront suites 30 and 31, w/ separate BRs, wet bars, views; Lakefront 39, w/ fireplace
Comfort & Decor: Rooms individu-ally decorated w/ artwork and wall coverings to match rooms' theme, vertical blinds, light-colored Berber carpet

RATES, RESERVATIONS, & RESTRICTIONS

Deposit: 50% for holidays; must cancel 72 hours in advance; cancellation fee 10% of 1st night
Discounts: Package discounts; extra person $15
Credit Cards: AE, MC, V
Check-In/Out: 2/11, late check-out by arrangement
Smoking: No
Pets: No
Kids: OK

Minimum Stay: 2 nights on weekends
Open: All year
Host: Janet Gregor
P.O. Box 5969
1850 W. Lake Blvd.
Tahoe City, CA 96145
(530) 583-7200
(800) 822-2754
Fax: (530) 583-2551
www.hulapie.com

TAHOMA MEADOWS B&B, Tahoma

Overall: ★★★½	Room Quality: C	Value: A	Price: $90–$105

These simple little cottages painted barn red with white trim are not only neat, attractive, and pleasingly furnished; they are also reasonably priced for the Tahoe area. Each cabin sits in a forest setting and is uniquely decorated with flower themes carried out in matching colors, fabrics, and hostess Missy Sandeman's watercolors and stencils. Some have fireplaces, and others have claw-foot soaking tubs. Host Bill Sandeman is a retired professional football player and great fun to chat with. While it is close to all the activities the Tahoe area has to offer, this little resort seems quite detached from the crowds and traffic jams that sometimes spoil this natural paradise.

SETTING & FACILITIES

Location: On Hwy. 89 in Tahoma, 8.4 mi. south of Tahoe City
Near: Lake Tahoe and Donner Lake, restaurants, shopping, commercial airport, casinos, aerial tram, galleries, museums, 10 alpine ski resorts, golf courses
Building: Old Tahoe lodge, barn red cabins w/ white trim, some duplex, some single
Grounds: 1 acre w/ cabins scattered among huge sugar pines, away from the highway
Public Space: Common area, DR, map/information room
Food & Drink: Full breakfast served 8–10 a.m. in the common area in main lodge

Recreation: Winter sports, boating and water sports, mountain biking, golf, tennis, fishing, horseback riding

Amenities & Services: Afternoon snacks, evening wine, VCRs on request, private parking; cabins w/ housekeeping services also avail.

ACCOMMODATIONS

Units: 10 guest rooms, 1 larger than average

All Rooms: Private bath and entrance, cable TV

Some Rooms: Fireplace, view of sugar pines and Lake Tahoe

Bed & Bath: Queens, kings (2), claw-foot tubs (7)

Favorites: Daffodil, in mahogany and blue w/ claw-foot tub and fireplace; Dogwood, in earth tones, w/ claw-foot tub, efficiency kitchen, private setting w/ deck

Comfort & Decor: Rooms individually decorated w/ handmade headboards, original art, stenciled walls, coordinating fabrics, carpet

RATES, RESERVATIONS, & RESTRICTIONS

Deposit: 50%; must cancel 14 days in advance; cancellation fee $20

Discounts: Winter weekdays; extra person $10

Credit Cards: All

Check-In/Out: 2/11, late check-out by arrangement

Smoking: No

Pets: 1 cottage OK for dogs, $10 cleaning fee

Kids: OK with parental supervision

Minimum Stay: 2 nights on weekends Sept.–June, 3 on summer weekends and all holiday weekends

Open: All year

Hosts: Bill and Missy Sandeman
810 Homewood
6821 W. Lake Blvd.
Tahoma, CA 96142
(530) 525-1553
(800) 355-1596
Fax: (530) 525-0335
www.tahomameadows.com
SandyTahoe@Telis.org

RICHARDSON HOUSE, Truckee

| Overall: ★★★★½ | Room Quality: B | Value: A | Price: $85–$200 |

Truckee is a charming little town surrounded on all sides by the beautiful Sierra Nevada Mountains. It is the gathering place for cross-country and downhill skiers in the winter and rock climbers, hikers, and trout fishers in the summer. When you're visiting, Richardson House is the place to stay. Sitting on a hill just a short walk from downtown Truckee, the Victorian home, built in 1886, has been luxuriously restored and redecorated. Its eight bedrooms are tastefully wallpapered and furnished with antiques, vintage light fixtures, claw-foot tubs, and featherbeds and comforters. Aunt Clara's room is fully equipped for disabled access, almost unique in Victorian B&Bs.

SETTING & FACILITIES

Location: In historic downtown Truckee off I-80, close to Reno and Lake Tahoe
Near: Lake Tahoe and Donner Lake, restaurants, shopping, commercial airport, casinos, aerial tram, galleries, museums, 10 ski resorts, golf courses
Building: 2-story Victorian circa 1886
Grounds: Urban lot, Victorian garden
Public Space: Parlor w/ player piano, TV/VCR, games, DR, gazebo
Food & Drink: Full breakfast buffet

served 8–8:30 a.m. in DR
Recreation: Winter sports, boating and water sports, mountain biking, golf, tennis, fishing, horseback riding
Amenities & Services: 24-hour complimentary snacks and beverages, morning newspaper, microwave and fridge in guests' refreshment center, fresh flowers, private parking, disabled access, pickup and delivery from/to Amtrak

ACCOMMODATIONS

Units: 8 guest rooms, 3 larger than average, 1 family suite w/ shared bath
All Rooms: Featherbed and down comforter, AC
Some Rooms: Four-poster, claw-foot tub, private bath (6), shared bath (2)
Bed & Bath: Queens (4), kings (2), twins (1), double (1)

Favorites: Bon Bon's Boudoir, w/ Truckee views, queen bed, private bath w/ slipper tub and shower
Comfort & Decor: Rooms individually decorated w/ antiques, lace and velvet curtains and drapes, original wainscoting and crown molding, carpet

RATES, RESERVATIONS, & RESTRICTIONS

Deposit: Credit card; must cancel 7 days in advance; cancellation fee $15
Discounts: Long stays, weekday business, groups, AAA; extra person $25
Credit Cards: All
Check-In/Out: 3/noon, late check-out by arrangement
Smoking: No
Pets: No
Kids: 9 and over
Minimum Stay: 2 nights on holidays and on weekends July–Sept., Dec.–April

Open: All year
Hosts: Jim and Sandi Beck, owners; Lesley King and Joel Friedman, resident mgrs.
P.O. Box 2011
10154 High St.
Truckee, CA 96160
(530) 587-5388
(888) 229-0365
Fax: (530) 587-0927
www.richardsonhouse.com
innkeeper@richardsonhouse.com

MCCAFFREY HOUSE B&B INN, Twain Harte

Overall: ★★★★½   Room Quality: B   Value: B   Price: $105–$125

Although there are many things to admire in the handsome McCaffrey House, among the most striking are the handmade Amish quilts in each guest room. They are the focal points for the coordinating colors and patterns in the seven pretty rooms. The inn is set in a woodland glade at the beginning of the Stanislaus National Forest and Emigrant Wilderness, with nearby skiing, fishing, and wineries; Yosemite is an hour away. The three-story structure was built in 1995 specifically to be an inn, incorporating such amenities as individually controlled thermostats, iron stoves in every room, and lots of private decks overlooking the forest. A recent breakfast included an egg casserole, oven-baked potatoes, sausage, muffins, and dessert.

SETTING & FACILITIES

Location: 11 mi. east of Sonora on Hwy. 108, at 4,000 ft.
Near: Stanislaus Nat'l Forest and Emigrant Wilderness, wineries, historic gold towns
Building: 3-story country inn built in 1996
Grounds: 1 acre in quiet forest setting among a grove of oaks, pines, and cedars
Public Space: LR w/ large fireplace and reading material, DR, sundeck

w/ umbrella tables and chairs, decks, gardens, spa
Food & Drink: Full breakfast served at 9 a.m. in DR or on decks, early breakfast for skiers and business travelers
Recreation: Biking, fishing, water sports, winter sports, tennis, golf
Amenities & Services: Hot tub, afternoon snacks, evening wine and hors d'oeuvres, private parking, VCRs in rooms, 500 videos, fax service avail.

ACCOMMODATIONS

Units: 7 guest rooms, 6 larger than average, 2-BR suite
All Rooms: Private bath w/ tub/shower, cable TV/VCR, phone, AC, black-iron woodstove, individual thermostat, forest view
Some Rooms: Balcony or private patio, extra queen (2)
Bed & Bath: Queens
Favorites: Wedgwood Blue Room, w/ blue-and-white Amish quilt on pencil pine bed, wallpaper and wainscoting, antique armoire, French doors w/ balcony view of front garden
Comfort & Decor: Rooms individually decorated w/ pine furniture, window treatments and wallpaper, Amish quilts, original art, fresh flowers, forest views

RATES, RESERVATIONS, & RESTRICTIONS

Deposit: 50%; must cancel 5 days in advance; processing fee $25
Discounts: Long stays, weekday business; extra person $10
Credit Cards: AE, MC, V
Check-In/Out: 2/11, late check-in/out by arrangement
Smoking: No
Pets: No
Kids: 4 and over
Minimum Stay: 2 nights on weekends
Open: All year
Hosts: Michael and Stephanie McCaffrey
P.O. Box 67
23251 Hwy. 108
Twain Harte, CA 95383
(209) 586-0757
(888) 586-0757
Fax: (209) 586-3689
www.mccaffreyhouse.com
Innkeeper@Mccaffreyhouse.com

ST. GEORGE HOTEL, Volcano

Overall: ★★★½	Room Quality: C	Value: A	Price: $65–$80

Volcano was once one of the largest towns in the Mother Lode: $90 million in gold was hauled away from the area. Built in the town's heyday in 1867, the striking three-story brick St. George Hotel has always been the town's centerpiece. After the gold rush, however, both the town and the hotel fell on hard times, becoming echoes of what they once were. Now the town is peaceful and pretty, with 85 residents, not counting dogs. New owners Mark and Tracey Beckner are breathing life into the old hotel. They've added heat and air-conditioning (a great start) and rebuilt the kitchen, and the hotel's restaurant is acquiring a growing reputation for excellence. The guest rooms in the hotel have real character in an austerely attractive way, though the single-occupancy rooms look a bit like cells. The hotel rooms all have shared baths. The parlor is very large, inviting, and impressive, with 15-foot ceilings and a massive stone fireplace. The rooms in the annex, built in 1961, are motelish in nature, but they have private baths.

SETTING & FACILITIES

Location: In Volcano, 13 mi. east of Jackson via Hwy. 88 and Pine Grove–Volcano Rd.; 1 hour from Sacramento
Near: Daffodil Hill, Indian Grinding Rocks State Park, wineries, shopping, 1 hour to Kirkwood ski resort
Building: 3-story Greek Revival built in 1862 w/ 18-in.-thick brick walls, classic gold rush hotel w/ porches and balconies
Grounds: 1.5 acres landscaped grounds, area for croquet and volleyball, horseshoes

Public Space: Parlor, DR
Food & Drink: Extended cont'l breakfast served 7:30–10 a.m. in the common area
Recreation: Croquet, volleyball, horseshoes on premises; nearby biking, golf, water sports in mountain lakes, X-C/downhill skiing
Amenities & Services: Quiet balconies on 2nd and 3rd floors, on-street parking, conference center w/ modern equipment, restaurant and bar on premises w/ brunch on weekends, Kirkwood ski-and-stay package

ACCOMMODATIONS

Units: 20 guest rooms, 2 larger than average; 14 rooms in main hotel, 6 in motel annex
All Rooms: No TV or phone
Some Rooms: Balcony, view of back garden or Sutter Creek
Bed & Bath: Queens and doubles, twin(s) (4); annex rooms have private baths, hotel rooms share 5 baths

Favorites: Twain Harte, large, sunny room overlooking gardens, w/ queen bed; Red Dog Room, opens on balcony, decorated by a Volcano couple using historic family artifacts
Comfort & Decor: Rooms individually decorated w/ old photographs, antiques, lace curtains, hardwood floors and area rugs, patchwork quilts

RATES, RESERVATIONS, & RESTRICTIONS

Deposit: Credit card or 1st night's lodging; must cancel 48 hours in advance
Discounts: Long stays, winter groups; extra person $10
Credit Cards: MC, V
Check-In/Out: 3/11, late check-out by arrangement
Smoking: No
Pets: Annex only, $20 extra
Kids: 12 and over in hotel; OK in annex

Minimum Stay: 2 nights on Thanksgiving
Open: Closed after New Year's weekend until 3rd week in Jan.
Hosts: Mark and Tracey Berkner
P.O. Box 9
16104 Main St.
Volcano, CA 95689
(209) 296-4458
Fax: (209) 296-4457
www.stgeorgehotel.com
Stgeorge@volcano.net

Zone 4
San Francisco Bay Area

Including Marin County and Point Reyes to the north; Berkeley, Oakland, and Alameda to the east; and San Jose, Silicon Valley, and the San Francisco Coast to the south and west.

Cities and Towns   San Francisco, Mill Valley, Muir Beach, Stinson Beach, Olema, Inverness, Inverness Park, San Rafael, Sausalito, Benicia, Point Richmond, Berkeley, Oakland, Pleasanton, Alameda, Fremont, San Jose, Santa Clara, Palo Alto, Half Moon Bay, Moss Beach, Princeton-by-the-Sea.

Attractions   **Golden Gate Bridge**; live theater, ballet, symphony, opera, and three major art galleries; **North Beach**; cable cars; **Fisherman's Wharf**; **Castro Street**, heart of SF's gay community; 2,000-acre **Golden Gate Park**, with a zoo, aquarium, planetarium, and natural history museum; world-famous restaurants, shopping, and nightlife; **The Exploratorium**, with 650 hands-on science exhibits; **Chinatown**; **Alcatraz**; the redwoods in **Muir Woods** and the 65,000-acre **Point Reyes National Seashore** nearby; five major league sports teams and a brand new baseball stadium; ferry rides from **San Francisco** to **Sausalito**; the **University of California at Berkeley** and the **Lawrence Hall of Science**; Oakland, with **Jack London Square**, the **Oakland Museum of California**, and bay cruises on FDR's yacht, **USS Potomac**; **Haight Street** and bittersweet memories of the Summer of Love; **Stanford University**; **San Jose Museum of Art**; **Paramount's Great America** theme park; the unforgettable elephant seal breeding grounds at **Año Nuevo State Reserve**.

Contact Information   San Francisco Visitor Information, (415) 391-2000 (www.sfvisitor.org); SF info by fax, (800) 220-5747; San Francisco International Airport, (800) 736-2008; Oakland International Airport, (510) 577-4000; Bay Area Rapid Transit, (510) 464-6000; City Box Office, (415) 392-4400; Marin County Visitors and Convention Bureau (www.visitmarin.org); Berkeley Convention and Visitors Bureau, (800) 847-4823; *USS Potomac* Visitor Center, (510) 839-8256; San Jose Visitors Information and Business Center, (408) 321-2300 (www.sanjose.org); Año Nuevo State Reserve, (800) 444-7275

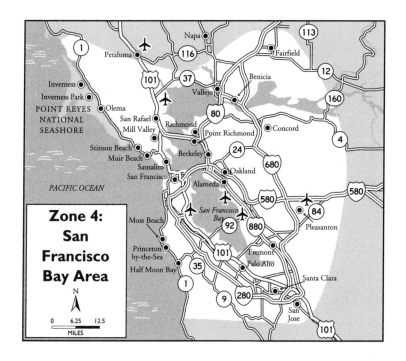

**Zone 4:
San Francisco
Bay Area**

N

0   6.25   12.5
MILES

Map labels:
113
Napa
1
Petaluma
116
Fairfield
101
37
12
Inverness
Inverness Park
Benicia
POINT REYES
NATIONAL
SEASHORE
Vallejo
160
Olema
80
San Rafael
Richmond
Concord
Mill Valley
Point Richmond
4
Stinson Beach
Muir Beach
Berkeley
24
Sausalito
San Francisco
Oakland
680
PACIFIC OCEAN
Alameda
580
580
Moss Beach
San Francisco
Bay
84
92
880
Pleasanton
Princeton
by-the-Sea
35
101
Fremont
Palo Alto
Half Moon Bay
1
Santa Clara
9
280
San
Jose
101

GARRATT MANSION, Alameda

Overall: ★★★★	Room Quality: B	Value: A	Price: $80–$145

A three-story Colonial Revival mansion in mint condition, this B&B built in 1893 has lots of architectural features to admire—hand-carved interior woodwork of oak and redwood burl, including a dramatic carved staircase leading to an orchestra balcony, large leaded- and stained-glass windows, and inlaid hardwood floors. The seven guest rooms are tucked here and there throughout the house, and two of them share a bath. Diana's Suite is light and pretty, with a bamboo canopy bed, a fireplace, and a sitting room. The Captain's Room has Bradbury & Bradbury wallpaper with gold stars on the ceiling, a particularly charming pattern. This is a very relaxed place with friendly, helpful hosts who will send you off to face the day armed with a good breakfast and a cheery disposition.

SETTING & FACILITIES

Location: On Alameda Island in San Francisco Bay, just off Oakland; from Hwy. 880, take High St. exit, go north on Central, go 1.5 mile then left on Union, corner Clinton and Union
Near: Shopping, restaurants, airport, Oakland Coliseum, rapid transit, Berkeley, San Francisco, beach
Building: Colonial Revival built in 1893, w/ redwood and oak paneling, large leaded- and stained-glass windows

Grounds: In a quiet residential neighborhood 4 blocks from bay, gardens w/ tree roses, perennials, lavender, liquidambar trees
Public Space: Parlor, library, game room, TV room w/ video library, oak-paneled DR
Food & Drink: Full breakfast served 7:30–9:30 a.m. in DR, cont'l breakfast delivered to room on request

Recreation: Tennis, golf; major league baseball, basketball, football; fishing
Amenities & Services: Hot and cold beverages avail. 24 hours, fresh chocolate chip cookies each afternoon w/ pistachios, fruit, robes; street parking, assistance w/ dining reservations and touring

ACCOMMODATIONS

Units: 7 guest rooms, 1 larger than average, includes 1 suite
All Rooms: Ceiling fan, clock radio
Some Rooms: Fireplace, four-poster, sleeper sofa, phone, private bath (5), shared bath (2), extra bed (1)
Bed & Bath: Mostly queens
Favorites: Captain's Room, w/ nautical theme, vintage blue wallpaper w/ gold stars on ceiling, four-poster queen bed, oval window, cigar box collection, antique mask from Venice, giraffes from Kenya
Comfort & Decor: Rooms individually decorated w/ personal collections, desks, comfortable reading chairs, carpet, fresh flowers, down pillows and comforters

RATES, RESERVATIONS, & RESTRICTIONS

Deposit: 1st night's lodging; must cancel 3 days in advance
Discounts: None; extra person $15
Credit Cards: AE, DC, MC, V
Check-In/Out: 3/11, late check-out by arrangement
Smoking: No
Pets: No
Kids: OK
Minimum Stay: 3 nights on holiday weekends
Open: All year
Hosts: Royce and Betty Gladden
900 Union St.
Alameda, CA 94501
(510) 521-4779
Fax: (510) 521-6796
www.garrattmansion.com
garrattm@pacbell.net

CAPTAIN WALSH HOUSE, Benicia

Overall: ★★★★½	Room Quality: A	Value: B	Price: $125–$150

Frequently selected as one of the best-decorated inns in the United States, this interesting house has no problem living up to its reputation. Designed by a prominent architect, Andrew Jackson Downing, the house was built in Boston, dismantled, and shipped to Benicia, where it was erected in 1849. These days, the five guest rooms are the stuff of fantasies, each distinctively different. Epiphania's Room is often photographed because of its massive four-poster bed swathed in fabric, sitting in glorious splendor in the middle of a room, backlighted by sun streaming through a Gothic-arched window. The romantic Harvest Room has a white brick fireplace, a towering walnut Gothic armoire and matching bed, painted plank floors, and glazed walls. The Library has vaulted ceilings, a reading loft reached by a ladder, a real zebra carpet, and a stuffed armadillo. You'll come and see the other rooms yourself.

SETTING & FACILITIES

Location: 2 blocks east of Benicia's historic 1st St., across from city hall
Near: Restaurants, shopping, historic museums, California's first state capitol, Benicia Marina, historic arsenal
Building: Gothic Revival designed by architect Andrew Jackson Downing, built in Boston and shipped around the Horn in 1849
Grounds: Double urban lot w/ gardens, statuary, fountains
Public Space: Parlor, library, DR, 2 sunporches
Food & Drink: Full breakfast served 7–9 a.m. in DR
Recreation: Tennis, golf, sailing, sculling, vintage carriage rides, swimming, wind surfing
Amenities & Services: Evening wine and hors d'oeuvres, fridge filled w/ soft drinks, silver coffee service at door in a.m., fresh flowers, evening turn-down, private parking, concierge service for reservations

ACCOMMODATIONS

Units: 5 guest rooms, 2 larger than average, including 1 suite
All Rooms: Private bath, cable TV/VCR, individually controlled AC/heat
Some Rooms: Fireplace, four-poster, fridge
Bed & Bath: Queens
Favorites: Epiphania Room, named for daughter of General Vallejo, for whom the house was once purchased, w/ massive four-poster canopy bed, Italian inlaid wood BR set, 14-ft. vaulted ceiling, Gothic windows overlooking Carquinez Strait, princess-style tub w/ 24-carat-gold-dipped claw feet and fixtures
Comfort & Decor: Rooms individually decorated w/ antiques, faux finishes and glazes on walls, China slate and hardwood floor w/ rugs, four-posters w/ draperies, vaulted ceilings, Gothic panels and windows, fireplaces, sitting areas

RATES, RESERVATIONS, & RESTRICTIONS

Deposit: 50% of bill; must cancel 7 days in advance
Discounts: None
Credit Cards: AE, MC, V
Check-In/Out: 3/noon, late check-out by arrangement
Smoking: No
Pets: No
Kids: Not suitable
No-Nos: No more than 2 guests per room
Minimum Stay: 2 nights
Open: All year
Hosts: Reed and Steve Robbins
235 E. L St.
Benicia, CA 94510
(707) 747-5653
Fax: (707) 747-6265
www.mansions-cuisine.com
aol.cwhinn.com

INN AT BENICIA BAY, Benicia

Overall: ★★★★   Room Quality: B   Value: A   Price: $89–$169

In the heart of historic downtown Benicia, this pretty yellow and white 1850s Victorian cottage has a new name and a new perspective on life. If you can tear yourself away from the large English garden in bloom in the front yard, inside you'll find a lovely library with comfortable chairs, an antique shop and art gallery to browse in, and a banquet room with cherry-wood hand-pegged plank floors. A wing added in 1985 has guest rooms with French doors opening to either a deck or a patio, both facing the garden. The upstairs rooms have cathedral ceilings, and all the rooms have a nice mix of antiques and Art Deco furnishings. This inn is a half-block off the main street, close enough to carry home just about anything from local art and antique shops.

SETTING & FACILITIES

Location: In the historic section of Benicia, 30 mi. north of San Francisco, 14 mi. south of Napa; take E. 2nd St. exit off Hwy. 780, right on Military, left on 1st St., left on D St.

Near: Restaurants, shopping, galleries, walking distance to Benicia State Park, 10 min. to Marine World Six Flags, 20 min. to Napa wine country, 35 min. to San Francisco

Building: Early Cape Cod-style Victorian, built in 1854, wing added in 1985, historic landmark

Grounds: City lot w/ English garden, brick patio w/ table, chairs, benches, gazebo, gnarled eucalyptus trees

Public Space: Parlor w/ marble fireplace, fully stocked library w/ reading chairs, DR

Food & Drink: Expanded cont'l breakfast served 7–9 a.m. on weekdays, 8–10 a.m. on weekends in DR

Recreation: Tennis, golf, sailing, sculling, wind surfing, vintage carriage rides, fishing

Amenities & Services: Afternoon snacks, evening wine and hors d'oeuvres, private parking, art and antique gallery on premises; concierge services for reservations and tours

ACCOMMODATIONS

Units: 8 guest rooms, 7 larger than average

All Rooms: Private bath, cable TV, phone

Some Rooms: Cathedral ceiling, private entrance to deck or patio, skylight, extra queen (1)

Bed & Bath: Mostly kings and queens, claw-foot tub (1), Jacuzzis (7)

Favorites: Casablanca, w/ Art Deco motif, wicker furniture, deck w/ view of garden, Ertée prints

Comfort & Decor: Rooms individually decorated w/ Deco, Victorian, and Asian antiques, original art, etchings and lithos, carpet, all rooms recently remodeled

RATES, RESERVATIONS, & RESTRICTIONS

Deposit: Credit card; must cancel 48 hours in advance

Discounts: Long stays; extra person $20

Credit Cards: All

Check-In/Out: 3/11, late check-out by arrangement

Smoking: No

Pets: No

Kids: Not suitable

Minimum Stay: None

Open: All year

Hosts: Patricia and Michael Lamb 145 E. D St. Benicia, CA 94510 (707) 746-1055 Fax: (707) 745-8361 www.theinnatbeniciabay.com theinnbb@aol.com

LORD BRADLEY'S INN, Fremont

Overall: ★★★½	Room Quality: C	Value: A	Price: $85–$135

Right next to the beautiful Mission San Jose, Lord Bradley's is as colorful as its history, with a lavishly trimmed, multicolored exterior and a papered, fringed, and lacy interior. Built in the 1870s as a stage stop, the inn has been welcoming guests for over 100 years. Each of the eight rooms is decorated in traditional Victorian style, with antiques, wallpapers, pretty quilts, and lace curtains. Mission Boulevard is a very busy street, but most guest rooms are in the rear of the property overlooking a brick courtyard.

SETTING & FACILITIES

Location: On the southeast side of Fremont, south of Hwy. 680, next to Mission San Jose
Near: Mission San Jose, restaurants, shopping, Olive Hyde Art Center, San Jose airport, BART to San Francisco
Building: Victorian, built in 1873 as a boardinghouse for miners, w/ 7 rooms, 1 suite in adjoining building
Grounds: Brick courtyard, English garden featuring variety of roses, ancient olive trees
Public Space: Parlor, tearoom, patio garden
Food & Drink: Expanded cont'l breakfast served 7–8:30 a.m. weekdays, 8:30–10:30 a.m. weekends, in the common room
Recreation: Hiking on Mission Peak, bird-watching at San Francisco Area Wildlife Refuge
Amenities & Services: Morning newspaper, private parking, disabled access, TVs avail. for nominal fee, afternoon high tea by reservation

ACCOMMODATIONS

Units: 8 guest rooms, including 2 suites
All Rooms: Private bath and entrance, phone
Some Rooms: AC, view of Mission Peak, TV avail. by request
Bed & Bath: Mostly queens and doubles
Favorites: Lady Karen bridal suite, w/ French antiques, wallpaper, sitting area w/ antique couch, bay windows, stained-glass window, whirlpool bath, private deck
Comfort & Decor: French and English furniture, lace curtains, quilts, wallpaper, wainscoting, white wicker furniture, period light fixtures, carpet

RATES, RESERVATIONS, & RESTRICTIONS

Deposit: Credit card to hold; must cancel 24 hours in advance
Discounts: Long stays; extra person $10
Credit Cards: All
Check-In/Out: 3/noon, late check-out by arrangement
Smoking: No
Pets: No
Kids: 12 and over

Minimum Stay: None
Open: All year
Hosts: Susie and Steve Wilson, owners;
Karen Wesson, innkeeper
43344 Mission Blvd.
Fremont, CA 94539

(510) 490-0520
(877) 567-3272
Fax: (510) 490-3015
www.lordbradleysinn.com
ladysusan@lordbradleysinn.com

CYPRESS INN ON MIRAMAR BEACH, Half Moon Bay

Overall: ★★★★½   Room Quality: A   Value: B   Price: $185–$295

If it weren't for the white sand beach and the blue Pacific outside, you might think you were in a New Mexico B&B when you walk in this attractive inn. Earth tones, terra-cotta tile floors, and colorful folk art are used throughout to create a luxury bungalow effect. Most of the 12 spacious, pretty guest rooms have amenities such as decks, fireplaces, and two-person whirlpool tubs. Breakfast at the inn often features its trademark peaches and cream French toast, accompanied by a granola-yogurt-berry parfait, fresh fruit, and home-baked croissants. There's also an in-house masseuse with a studio on the inn's third floor.

SETTING & FACILITIES

Location: In the community of Miramar Beach, off Hwy. I between Princeton Harbor and Half Moon Bay; take Medio to the beach, inn on left
Near: 5 mi. of sandy beach, restaurants, shopping, galleries, live theater, wineries, Pescadero Marsh Natural Preserve
Building: Contemporary inn built in 1990, additional 4 rooms in the beach house behind the inn
Grounds: Natural setting, 10 steps from the beach
Public Space: Common area w/ vaulted skylighted ceiling, fireplace, wicker furniture, radiant-heated tile

floors, deck over ocean
Food & Drink: Full breakfast served 8–10 a.m. in the common area, or brought to room
Recreation: Biking, tennis, golf, horseback riding, tide pooling, surfing, sailing, chartered deep-sea fishing, whale- and bird-watching, biplane rides
Amenities & Services: Evening wine, hors d'oeuvres, and desserts; hairdryers, robes; public rooms and El Mar Room are disabled-accessible; in-house masseuse and assistance w/ planning activities and w/ kennel reservations avail., on-site parking

ACCOMMODATIONS

Units: 12 guest rooms, 5 larger than average, including 1 suite
All Rooms: Private bath, phone, fireplace, sitting area, desk, deck, featherbed
Some Rooms: Fridge, Jacuzzi, in-room

stereo, TV/VCR, ironing system, ocean view (10), 2 rooms may be joined for suite
Bed & Bath: Queens, kings (5, 4 convert to 2 twins)

Favorites: Dunes Beach, w/ ocean views, large deck, in-room spa in front of fireplace; Las Nubes (The Clouds) penthouse, w/ ocean views, large deck, fireplace, large couch area, wicker chairs, wet bar, spa tub for 2

Comfort & Decor: Rooms individually decorated w/ folk art, rattan, pine, and wicker furniture; featherbeds, vignette shades, radiant-heated terra-cotta tile floors, ocean views

RATES, RESERVATIONS, & RESTRICTIONS

Deposit: 100% of bill 10 days in advance; must cancel 10 days in advance for full refund unless re-rented
Discounts: Weekday business, off-season midweek specials
Credit Cards: AE, D, MC, V
Check-In/Out: 3/11:30, late check-out w/ prior arrangement only
Smoking: No
Pets: No
Kids: OK
No-Nos: No more than 2 guests

per room
Minimum Stay: 2 nights on weekends
Open: All year
Hosts: Dan Floyd and Suzie Lankes
407 Mirada Rd.
Half Moon Bay, CA 94019
(650) 726-6002
(800) 832-3224
Fax: (650) 712-0380
www.cypressinn.com
lodging@cypressinn.com

OLD THYME INN, Half Moon Bay

Overall: ★★★½	Room Quality: B	Value: B	Price: $100–$255

A picket-fenced Queen Anne Victorian built in 1899, this tidy inn is named for, and built around, an English herb garden with over 50 varieties of herbs and flowers. Guest rooms are comfortably furnished with a pleasant mix of antiques and contemporary furniture and are decorated in pretty pastel fabrics. Some rooms have four-poster beds and fireplaces, and all have private baths with claw-foot tubs or double whirlpool tubs. Owner Kathy Ellis is a great cook and regularly whips out her own special dishes, such as lemon-cheese pancakes, chile rellenos, zucchini soufflé, or basil featherbed eggs. She even shares her recipes. There's lots to do around the Half Moon area—surfing, sailing, beachcombing, bird-watching, biking, golfing—and weekends there are a lot of folks in this popular resort town.

SETTING & FACILITIES

Location: Near junction of Hwy. 1 and Hwy. 92, 22 mi. south of San Francisco airport
Near: Beaches, restaurants, shopping, galleries, wine tasting, nightclubs, Pescadero Marsh Natural Preserve
Building: 1899 Queen Anne "spindle

post" Victorian, fully restored
Grounds: Herb and flower gardens w/ unusual fishpond and fountains
Public Space: Parlor, sitting areas in garden
Food & Drink: Full breakfast served 8–9:30 in the parlor

Recreation: Biking, tennis, golf, horse-back riding, tide pooling, surfing, sailing, chartered deep-sea fishing, whale- and bird-watching

Amenities & Services: Evening sherry, wine, and hors d'oeuvres, private parking

ACCOMMODATIONS

Units: 7 guest rooms, 3 larger than average
All Rooms: Private bath, double whirlpool tub, fresh flowers, stuffed animals
Some Rooms: Fireplace, four-poster, fridge, TV/VCR, extra bed (2)
Bed & Bath: Queens
Favorites: Garden Room, w/ private entrance, cathedral ceiling, carved four-

poster canopy bed, fireplace, double whirlpool tub, fridge
Comfort & Decor: Rooms individually decorated w/ original art, mixture of antiques, reproductions, and contemporary furniture, wallpaper or faux paint, featherbeds, down comforters, hardwood floors w/ area rugs, resident teddy bears

RATES, RESERVATIONS, & RESTRICTIONS

Deposit: 50% of bill; must cancel 2 weeks in advance; 10% cancellation fee
Discounts: Long stays, weekday business, groups, AAA, 2-for-1 coupons
Credit Cards: AE, D, MC, V
Check-In/Out: 3/11, late check-out by special arrangement
Smoking: No
Pets: No
Kids: 10 and over
No-Nos: 2 rooms will accommodate extra guest, otherwise no more than 2

guests per room
Minimum Stay: 2 nights on weekends
Open: Open all year
Hosts: Rick and Kathy Ellis
779 Main St.
Half Moon Bay, CA 94019
(650) 726-1616
(800) 720-4277
Fax: (650) 726-6394
www.oldthymeinn.com
innkeeper@oldthymeinn

SANDY COVE INN, Inverness

Overall: ★★★★½	Room Quality: A	Value: B	Price: $145–$250

Just beyond the village of Inverness, the road turns away from Tomales Bay and heads west to Point Reyes Lighthouse. Right there, hidden away behind a high fence, is a small Cape Cod–style inn in wonderful parklike grounds with a year-round brook and—a few steps away—a secluded cove on the bay with wildflowers, birds, and a sandy beach. And that isn't all. The three rooms in this accessible but secret hideaway all have their own entrances, fireplaces, and fridges and are smartly furnished with antique pine furniture and Turkish kilim rugs. There is certainly much to see and do here. On the premises alone you'll enjoy (in addition to the beach, brook, and gardens) some of the best bird-watching in the country, plus boating and canoeing, hiking, rafting, and bike trails. Within a mile there are antique shops, pubs, restaurants, mountains, the ocean, and tennis. The breakfasts are all prepared from organic produce grown in the inn's gardens. Don't tell anyone else about this place.

SETTING & FACILITIES

Location: Just beyond Inverness, 35 mi. north of San Francisco
Near: Point Reyes Nat'l Seashore, beaches, restaurants, shopping, oyster farm
Building: 2-story Cape Cod built in 1986, barn for 2 horses/2 sheep/1 cat
Grounds: 5 acres of landscaped gardens, organic herb and vegetable garden, year-round stream, picnic area, sandy beach and meadow facing Tomales Bay
Public Space: Solarium
Food & Drink: Full breakfast served in rooms or solarium, at time of guest's convenience, dietary restrictions

strictly respected
Recreation: Sunbathing, mountain biking, kayaking, canoeing, wind surfing, bird-watching on premises; nearby whale- and elk-watching, horseback riding, tennis, golf
Amenities & Services: Afternoon snacks; evening wine, champagne, and chocolates; beach chairs, newspaper delivered to door, binoculars, backpacks, walking sticks, terry robes and slippers in rooms, hand-milled wildflower soap, all-natural products, outdoor shower, private parking; Spanish, German, Italian spoken

ACCOMMODATIONS

Units: 3 guest rooms, all suites
All Rooms: Private bath and entrance, deck, fireplace, phone, fridge, coffeemaker w/ house blend of coffee, CD/cassette player, radio, fresh flowers, candles
Some Rooms: Window seat/bed (1)
Bed & Bath: Queens, oversized towels

Favorites: West Room, w/ wicker and pine furniture, wood-burning fireplace, books, reading lamps, sundeck, views of gardens, meadow, woods
Comfort & Decor: Original fine art, antique pine furniture, wood blinds, kilim rugs, hardwood floor, carpet

RATES, RESERVATIONS, & RESTRICTIONS

Deposit: 100% of bill in advance; must cancel 14 days in advance
Discounts: AAA, AARP, seasonal
Credit Cards: All
Check-In/Out: 4/11, late check-out by arrangement
Smoking: No
Pets: No
Kids: Not suitable
No-Nos: No more than 2 guests per room

Minimum Stay: 2 nights on weekends
Open: All year
Hosts: Kathy and Gerry Coles
P.O. Box 869
12990 Sir Francis Drake Blvd.
Inverness, CA 94937
(415) 669-2683
(800) 759-2683
Fax: (415) 669-7511
www.sandycove.com
Innkeeper@sandycove.com

TEN INVERNESS WAY, Inverness

Overall: ★★★★	Room Quality: B	Value: B	Price: $125–$180

Innkeeper Teri Mowery likes to read, hike, and cook. And there is no better place to indulge these pastimes than this three-story, shingle-covered country cottage on the edge of Inverness. A good hike is what you'll need after one of Mowery's breakfasts of pecan Belgian waffles or crepes filled with fresh local berries. As for reading, the inn is paradise. The guest rooms, except for the suite, are smallish, with room enough for one comfy reading chair, but there are good reading lights for the beds. The large living room on the second floor has a stone fireplace, three sofas, an easy chair, a wall of bookshelves and books, and soft classical music playing in the background. Out back behind the English garden, with its Adirondack (reading) chairs, is a hot tub cottage that can be reserved for private use. There's good whale- and bird-watching nearby, and several very nice restaurants are a short walk away.

SETTING & FACILITIES

Location: On the north side of Inverness, half-block off Sir Francis Drake Blvd., 45 min. north of San Francisco
Near: Point Reyes Nat'l Seashore, restaurants, shopping, beaches
Building: 3-story 1904 shingled house
Grounds: Wisteria-covered entrance, English flower garden, flagstone paths under fruit trees and shrubs lead to patio and sitting areas w/ benches and Adirondack chairs
Public Space: Redwood-paneled LR w/ stone fireplace, window seats, and books; sunroom, breakfast room
Food & Drink: Full breakfast in breakfast room 8:30–9:30 a.m., coffee and morning paper at 7:30
Recreation: Biking, kayaking, canoeing, horseback riding, bird- and whale-watching
Amenities & Services: Hot tea, coffee, cold drinks, and fresh fruit always avail. in LR; afternoon cookies, hot tub in garden cottage, robes, assistance w/ area information and reservations, picnic lunches avail. on request

ACCOMMODATIONS

Units: 5 guest rooms, including 1 suite
All Rooms: Private bath, handmade quilt, books, reading lights
Some Rooms: Private entrance, skylight, view of Tomales Bay, window seat
Bed & Bath: Queens, tubs (2)
Favorites: Garden Suite, w/ private entrance, sitting room, kitchen, private garden, breakfast served in room if requested
Comfort & Decor: Rooms are individually decorated w/ antiques, handsewn quilts, original Douglas fir floors, white wainscoting, wicker furniture, sloped ceilings, fresh flowers

RATES, RESERVATIONS, & RESTRICTIONS

Deposit: Payment in full 7 days from booking; must cancel in writing 7 days in advance; cancellation fee $10/night
Discounts: 10% for return guests all year, AAA, AARP Sun.–Thurs.; extra person $15
Credit Cards: MC, V
Check-In/Out: 4–7/11
Smoking: No
Pets: No
Kids: Welcome in suite, $15/night extra

Minimum Stay: 2 nights on weekends, 3 on holidays
Open: All year
Host: Teri Mowery
P.O. Box 63
10 Inverness Way
Inverness, CA 94937
(415) 669-1648
Fax: (415) 669-7403
www.teninvernessway.com
inn@teninvernessway.com

BLACKTHORNE INN, Inverness Park

| Overall: ★★★★ | Room Quality: B | Value: B | Price: $175–$250 |

In a heavily forested, steep-sided canyon just west of the hamlet of Inverness Park, the Blackthorne Inn climbs from the forest floor, going up and up to 70 feet, seeking the sun. The craftsmanship in the carpentry of the towering wooden structure and the stonework in the massive fireplace are awesome. The decks, the spacious public spaces, and the five rooms scattered over the inn's four levels are all invitingly stylish and comfortably furnished. They are tied together by a spiral staircase, and a fireman's pole for those who like exciting, quick descents. Guests staying in the octagonal Eagle's Nest at the top of the tower get to their bathroom by crossing a bridge to a hillside deck where the hot tub is located. But this is not, apparently, an inconvenience: though it's not the largest room, the Eagle's Nest is the most expensive and popular. It also has its own little private deck and widow's walk on the roof.

SETTING & FACILITIES

Location: In Inverness Park, left on Vallejo Ave. at Perry's Deli; 45 min. north of San Francisco
Near: Restaurants, shopping, beaches, Point Reyes Nat'l Seashore
Building: 4-story contemporary redwood, cedar, and pine lodge w/ spiral staircase, fireman's pole, and octagonal tower
Grounds: Half-acre, set in woods w/ flower beds and planters of native plants and wildflowers, creek, bordering

Point Reyes Nat'l Seashore
Public Space: A-framed LR w/ huge stone fireplace, leather couch, timbered roof beams from San Francisco piers, wet bar, library, solarium, 3,500-sq.-ft. deck
Food & Drink: Buffet breakfast served at 9:30 a.m. in the solarium; coffee, cereals, and juice are avail. from 8:30; breakfast "to go" may be arranged w/ 24-hour notice

Recreation: Bird-watching, tide pooling, swimming, horseback riding, water sports

Amenities & Services: Hot tub avail. to guests until 10 p.m., guest fridge, wineglasses and picnic ware avail.; coffee, tea, springwater, and afternoon dessert provided daily; robes, extra towels and flashlights, private parking, assistance w/ dining reservations, area information

ACCOMMODATIONS

Units: 5 guest rooms, including 2 suites that have private entrances and sitting areas and can be combined as an even larger suite for 4 persons

All Rooms: Private bath, forest view

Some Rooms: Private entrance, stained glass or arched bay window, balcony, cathedral ceiling

Bed & Bath: Queens, double, 1 bath across the deck by the hot tub

Favorites: Forest View suite, w/ private entrance, separate sitting room, glass wall opening to private redwood deck, can be combined w/ Hideaway for larger suite

Comfort & Decor: Rooms individually decorated w/ colorful contemporary furniture and linens, wicker, eyelet curtains

RATES, RESERVATIONS, & RESTRICTIONS

Deposit: Full payment due in advance; must cancel 14 days in advance

Discounts: Weekday singles

Credit Cards: MC, V

Check-In/Out: 4/11

Smoking: No

Pets: No

Kids: Not suitable for young children

No-Nos: No more than 2 guests per room

Minimum Stay: 2 nights on weekends

Open: All year

Hosts: Susan and Bill Wigert
P.O. Box 712
266 Vallejo Ave.
Inverness Park, CA 94937
(415) 663-8621
Fax: (415) 663-8635
www.blackthorneinn.com
susan@blackthorneinn.com

MOUNTAIN HOME INN, Mill Valley

Overall: ★★★½	Room Quality: B	Value: B	Price: $143–$269

This contemporary inn and restaurant, only 45 minutes from San Francisco, sits on the slopes of Mount Tamalpais with gorgeous views of San Francisco Bay, the East Bay Hills, and Mount Diablo. The restaurant's large deck is popular with hikers and mountian bikers, so the place is bustling on weekends. The clean, architectural lines of the inn's redwood exterior are continued inside with cathedral ceilings, bark-covered redwood pillars, and distinctive hickory furniture accents. Most of the 10 guest rooms have small balconies, some have fireplaces, and some have Jacuzzis that open into the main room behind folding shutters. There is no parlor, so guests who want to lounge outside their rooms can use the dining room or deck. Just outside the inn are 41 miles of hiking trails in Mount Tamalpais State Park, another 250 miles of trails in adjacent water district lands, and the giant redwoods of nearby Muir Woods Natural Monument.

SETTING & FACILITIES

Location: From Hwy. 101 between Mill Valley and Sausalito, take Stinson Beach/Hwy. 1 exit, stay on Hwy. 1 to Panoramic Hwy. (Mt. Tamalpais), at 4-way intersection take high road (Panoramic) for 1.8 mi.
Near: Restaurants, shopping, Mt. Tamalpais State Park, Muir Woods Nat'l Monument, Muir and Stinson beaches
Building: California redwood chalet, 14 years old

Grounds: On a mountainside w/ redwoods and native plants
Public Space: 2 DRs, bar, huge deck w/ views of Bay Area and Mount Tamalpais
Food & Drink: Full breakfast served 8:15–10 a.m. Mon.-Fri., 8–10 Sat.-Sun., in DR or on deck
Recreation: Mountain biking
Amenities & Services: Private parking, disabled access

ACCOMMODATIONS

Units: 10 guest rooms, 4 larger than average
All Rooms: Private bath w/ view, phone
Some Rooms: Fireplace, balcony, canopy bed
Bed & Bath: Queens and kings, roll-aways in largest rooms, Jacuzzis for 2 (4)

Favorites: Mountain View Room, w/ fireplace, king bed, spa tub, private terrace, views of bay and mountain
Comfort & Decor: Rooms individually decorated w/ wood-paneled walls, contemporary furniture, carpet, views of San Francisco Bay, Mount Diablo, East Bay

RATES, RESERVATIONS, & RESTRICTIONS

Deposit: Credit card to hold; must cancel 5 days in advance
Discounts: None; extra person $29
Credit Cards: AE, MC, V
Check-In/Out: 3/11, early check-in/late check-out by arrangement
Smoking: No
Pets: No
Kids: OK
Minimum Stay: None

Open: All year
Hosts: Ed and Susan Cunningham
810 Panoramic Hwy.
Mill Valley, CA 94941
(415) 381-9000
Fax: (415) 381-3615
www.mtnhomeinn.com
innkeeper@mtnhomeinn.com

SEAL COVE INN, Moss Beach

Overall: ★★★★½	Room Quality: A	Value: B	Price: $190–$270

A perfect blending of house and environment, this eight-year-old English-style manor house with a curving driveway, dramatic gables, soaring chimneys, and what seems like hundreds of mullioned windows is located on a dazzling site with windswept cypress trees and a wildflower garden. And it's just a short walk to a secluded beach. All is peaceful, serene, and well-run at this inn, and every effort is taken to anticipate guests' wishes. All the guest rooms are good-sized and simply but beautifully furnished, with a judicious use of antiques. They all have wood-burning fireplaces, great views, and a distinct absence of clutter and fluff; they're wonderfully calming and restorative. It's tempting to just sink into one of the comfortable chairs in front of the fireplace and never budge. On the other hand, one might miss breakfast—apple waffles or strawberry pancakes, croissants, and muffins.

SETTING & FACILITIES

Location: In Moss Beach; from Hwy. 1, go toward ocean on Cypress Ave. for .5 mile; 30-minute drive from San Francisco

Near: Restaurants, wine tasting, shopping, airport, Fitzgerald Marine Reserve, Purissima Creek Redwoods, Butano State Park, Pigeon Point Lighthouse

Building: English-style manor house, 8 years old

Grounds: 2 acres surrounded by 20 acres of parkland, secluded beaches, tree-lined paths, wildflowers, cypress trees

Public Space: LR w/ fireplace, DR, conference room

Food & Drink: Full breakfast served 8:30–10 a.m. in DR, or cont'l breakfast delivered to room, morning coffee tray and newspaper outside door at 8 a.m.

Recreation: Biking, tide pooling, salmon fishing, whale-, bird-, and elephant seal-watching

Amenities & Services: Evening sherry, wine, brandy, and hors d'oeuvres; wine and soft drinks in room, nightly turn-down service w/ chocolates, private parking, disabled access

ACCOMMODATIONS

Units: 10 guest rooms, 2 larger than average
All Rooms: Private bath, cable TV, phone, wood-burning fireplace
Some Rooms: Vaulted ceiling and private balcony, or French doors into garden
Bed & Bath: Queens, kings (2), 2 twins (2), roll-away on request, towel warmers and pedestal sinks, Jacuzzis (2)
Favorites: Cypress Room, w/ king

"tavern" bed, private Jacuzzi, views from the private deck; Fitzgerald Room, w/ canopy king bed, sofa, fireplace, French doors to balcony and views of park and ocean
Comfort & Decor: Rooms individually decorated w/ country antiques, original watercolors, floral and provincial prints, down pillows, a collection of grandfather clocks, fresh flowers

RATES, RESERVATIONS, & RESTRICTIONS

Deposit: Credit card; must cancel 7 days in advance; $20 cancellation fee
Discounts: Weekday business groups, winter weekdays; extra person $30
Credit Cards: All
Check-In/Out: 3/11, late check-out by request if possible
Smoking: No
Pets: No
Kids: Welcome in garden-level rooms
Minimum Stay: 2 nights on weekends

Open: Closed a few days prior to Christmas
Hosts: Rick and Karen Herbert
221 Cypress Ave.
Moss Beach, CA 94038
(650) 728-4114
(800) 995-9987
Fax: (650) 728-4116
www.sealcoveinn.com
sealcove@coastside.net

PELICAN INN, Muir Beach

Overall: ★★★★   Room Quality: B   Value: B   Price: $158–$198

Two of the most beautiful places in the county of Marin are Muir Woods, with its groves of virgin redwoods, and secluded, driftwood-scattered Muir Beach, with its hundreds of tide pools. Set between the two is the Pelican Inn, a re-creation of an Elizabethan inn that looks as though it were built by some deserter from Sir Francis Drake's crew in 1579. The inn, with its ground-floor pub and restaurant, is as English as you can get hereabouts. The food and drink in the pub and restaurant are all appropriately and authentically English, and a lively and friendly crowd hangs out here even on the foggiest winter nights, when the large stone fireplace is a big draw. The seven rooms are decked out in Elizabethan finery, with hanging tapestries; half-tester beds; multipaned, leaded-glass windows; and planked doors. And, yes, the breakfasts include bangers and grilled tomatoes.

SETTING & FACILITIES

Location: On Hwy. 1, 20 min. north of San Francisco at the foot of Mt. Tamalpais

Near: Restaurants, shopping, airport, 5-minute walk to Pacific beaches, 3 mi. from Muir Woods redwoods

Building: 16th-century Tudor-style inn built in 1979, whitewashed walls w/ black timbers

Grounds: Building surrounded by lawns and English gardens, covered garden patio

Public Space: DR w/ huge inglenook fireplace, daily fire, parlor ("snug") for guests only w/ fireplace, overstuffed reading chairs and books, DR w/ long refectory tables, pub w/ horseshoes on wall and dart board, English ales, full restaurant

Food & Drink: Full English breakfast served 8:15–10 a.m. in main DR or in room

Recreation: Biking, horseback riding, bird-watching, tennis, golf

Amenities & Services: Afternoon snacks, evening sherry in rooms, turndown w/ mints, private parking, massage

ACCOMMODATIONS

Units: 7 guest rooms

All Rooms: Private bath, 16th-century English antiques, oriental rugs, heavy tapestries

Some Rooms: Four-poster, sleeper sofa, balcony

Bed & Bath: Queens, king, hand-painted tiles in bath

Favorites: No. 3, w/ half-tester canopy curtained queen bed, balcony, beamed ceiling, oriental rugs, upholstered chairs, corner bedchamber w/ balcony overlooking conservatory

Comfort & Decor: Rooms individually decorated w/ English antiques and prints, heavy English tapestry drapes, oriental rugs, half-tester or canopy beds, leaded windows, fresh flowers

RATES, RESERVATIONS, & RESTRICTIONS

Deposit: 100% of bill 1 month in advance; must cancel 72 hours in advance

Discounts: None; extra person $30

Credit Cards: MC, V

Check-In/Out: 2/noon, late check-out $20/hour

Smoking: No

Pets: No

Kids: OK

Minimum Stay: None

Open: Closed Dec. 24–25

Hosts: Ed and Susan Cunningham, owners; Katrinka McKay, general mgr.

10 Pacific Way

Muir Beach, CA 94965

(415) 383-6000

Fax: (415) 383-3424

www.pelicaninn.com

innkeeper@pelicaninn.com

OLEMA INN, Olema

Overall: ★★★½	Room Quality: C	Value: B	Price: $105–$125

One hundred twenty-five years ago the Olema Inn was a wild and rowdy place where loggers and ranchers hung out and drank and fought while they waited to catch the next day's stage to San Rafael. Restored in 1988, the rooms have been redone and are decorated using a mix of antiques and contemporary furnishings, with an uncluttered, open, airy feeling. Downstairs there's a restaurant with a garden courtyard for outdoor dining, and the mild Olema climate has more than its share of al fresco days and nights. The main entrance to the 70,000-acre Point Reyes National Seashore is only minutes away, and it affords one of the widest variety of activities in a state that has them all. A hundred miles of trails lead to the beaches.

SETTING & FACILITIES

Location: In Olema, at the intersection of Hwy. 1 and Sir Francis Drake Blvd.; 1 hour north of San Francisco
Near: Point Reyes Nat'l Seashore, restaurants, shopping, beaches
Building: 120-year-old Victorian building, restored in 1988
Grounds: 1.1 acre, featuring gardens, lawns, landscaped flower beds, large patio for dining, statuary

Public Space: DR, bar area w/ piano, skylights
Food & Drink: Expanded cont'l breakfast served 8:30–10 a.m in main DR.
Recreation: Biking, bird-watching, horseback riding, water sports
Amenities & Services: Complimentary drink on arrival, private parking, full restaurant on premises

ACCOMMODATIONS

Units: 6 guest rooms, 1 larger than average
All Rooms: Private bath
Some Rooms: Can accommodate futons (2)
Bed & Bath: Queens, twin, European deep soaking tubs (4)
Favorites: No. 1, large, w/ oak and

marble dresser, tiled tub and bathroom; No. 3, quiet, w/ lace curtains, armoire, view of garden
Comfort & Decor: Rooms individually decorated w/ mix of antique and contemporary furnishings, off-white walls, wall-to-wall carpet

RATES, RESERVATIONS, & RESTRICTIONS

Deposit: Credit card; must cancel 3 days in advance
Discounts: None; extra person $10
Credit Cards: D, MC, V
Check-In/Out: 2/11:30
Smoking: No
Pets: No
Kids: In 2 rooms
No-Nos: No more than 2 guests per room except Rooms 1 and 4

Minimum Stay: None
Open: All year
Host: Roger Braun
P.O. Box 37
10000 Sir Francis Drake
Olema, CA 94950
(415) 669-9559
(800) 532-9252
Fax: (415) 663-8783
www.olemainn.com

POINT REYES SEASHORE LODGE, Olema

| Overall: ★★★★ | Room Quality: B | Value: B | Price: $95–$215 |

Though the site is on Highway 1 with a parking lot in front, don't worry. The handsome six-gabled, brick and wood exterior of the lodge is a harbinger of the comfort inside. Stylistically the building looks 19th century, but it was actually built in 1988. The rooms are spacious and light, with lots of windows and French doors leading to balconies or brick decks. Most have tiled fireplaces and Jacuzzis, and all have views of the back garden and lawn. Studded with shade trees and Adirondack chairs, the lawn abuts the 80,000-acre Point Reyes National Seashore. The inn's public spaces are all in keeping with the lodge atmosphere, featuring open-beamed ceilings in the parlor, a long reading table in the library, a wonderful antique billiard table in the game room, and a croquet green outside.

SETTING & FACILITIES

Location: At the entrance to the Point Reyes Nat'l Seashore, on the west side of Hwy. 1, just north of Olema

Near: Adjacent to Point Reyes Nat'l Seashore, near Samuel P. Taylor Redwood Park, Muir Woods Nat'l Monument, miles of beaches and park trails, restaurants, galleries, shopping

Building: 10 years old, built to replicate a turn-of-the-century country park lodge

Grounds: 2 acres of landscaped grounds bordered by natural park, rolling lawns, Olema Creek, views of meadows, Mt. Wittenberg

Public Space: Library, game room, pool room, Fireside Room w/ massive stone fireplace

Food & Drink: Expanded cont'l breakfast served 8–10 a.m. in the Fireside Room

Recreation: Road and mountain biking, horseback riding, whale- and birdwatching, golf, sea kayaking

Amenities & Services: Afternoon coffee and tea, morning papers; disabled access; assistance w/ dinner reservations, horse stabling, bike and kayak rentals

ACCOMMODATIONS

Units: 21 guest rooms, including 3 suites, 2 separate cottages used for lodging, weddings, and business conferences

All Rooms: Private bath, phone

Some Rooms: Fireplace, four-poster, sleeper sofa, fridge, deck, bay window

Bed & Bath: Queens, twins (1), doubles (1), single or double

whirlpool baths (14)

Favorites: Sir Francis Drake, Garcia, and Audubon suites, w/ Jacuzzis, fireplaces, wet bars, loft BRs, featherbeds

Comfort & Decor: Rooms individually decorated w/ featherbeds and down comforters, quilts, fireplaces, bay windows, decks, views of countryside and gardens

RATES, RESERVATIONS, & RESTRICTIONS

Deposit: Credit card to hold; must cancel 7 days in advance
Discounts: Long stays; extra adult (over 12) $25, extra child (under 12) $5
Credit Cards: AE, D, MC, V
Check-In/Out: 3–6/noon
Smoking: No
Pets: No
Kids: OK
Minimum Stay: 2 nights on weekends in fireplace rooms and suites

Open: All year
Hosts: Jeff and Nancy Harriman, owners; Greg and Susan Cockcroft, mgrs.
P.O. Box 39
10021 Hwy. 1
Olema, CA 94950
(415) 663-9000
(800) 404-5634
Fax: (415) 663-9030
www.pointreyesseashore.com
prsl@worldnet.att.net

ROUNDSTONE FARM, Olema

Overall: ★★★★½	Room Quality: B	Value: B	Price: $120–$160

On one of the most felicitous sites imaginable, a smart, talented woman built an inn and named it after a horse farm in Ireland. Roundstone Farm is part of a ten-acre horse farm specializing in Irish Connemara ponies as well as purebred Arabians. The ingenious, multilevel house has it all—views in every direction, broad decks, a living room with 16-foot-tall ceilings, and a resident telescope pointing out the sliding glass doors toward Tomales Bay in the distance. Owner/designer/decorator Inger Fischer put each of the five soundproof rooms on a different level, with a different view to contemplate; one of these views is the farm pond, with its resident flock of red-winged blackbirds. Each room has its own fireplace, lush carpets, European armoires, and headboards patterned after the ranch gates and hand-carved by a local artisan.

SETTING & FACILITIES

Location: Quarter-mile east of Olema
Near: Restaurants, shopping, galleries, Point Reyes Nat'l Seashore, Samuel P. Taylor State Park
Building: Cedar board-and-batten farmhouse built in 1988
Grounds: 10-acre horse farm, patios, deck w/ panoramic views of meadow, pond, wooded hills, and ocean; landscaped gardens, espaliered fruit trees
Public Space: Lounge w/ skylights, 16-ft. beamed ceiling, couches, fireplace, library, DR w/ horse prints, patio and decks
Food & Drink: Full breakfast served at 9:15 a.m. in DR or patio garden
Recreation: Mountain biking, horseback riding, swimming, kayaking, birdwatching (over 360 species)
Amenities & Services: Afternoon refreshments, tea and coffee avail. all day, glass-and-lath gazebo-covered hot tub, private parking, concierge services for reservations

ACCOMMODATIONS

Units: 5 guest rooms, all larger than average
All Rooms: Private bath, European armoire, down comforter, locally crafted wooden headboard, fireplace
Bed & Bath: Queens, king (or 2 twins), Danish bath fixtures
Favorites: Ridge Room, w/ wrought-iron four-poster, country-style decor, table and chairs, balloon valance, fire-place; Vision, w/ windows on three sides, sitting area, beamed ceiling, queen, 1 twin, fireplace
Comfort & Decor: Rooms individually decorated w/ contemporary artwork, some by local artists, floral curtains and spreads, fresh flowers, views of Tomales Bay, hillsides, Olema Valley; all rooms are large, light, and airy

RATES, RESERVATIONS, & RESTRICTIONS

Deposit: 1st night's lodging; must cancel 7 days in advance
Discounts: Long stays, seniors, weekdays
Credit Cards: AE, MC, V
Check-In/Out: 4/11, late check-out by arrangement
Smoking: No
Pets: No
Kids: 12 and over
No-Nos: No more than 2 guests per room, except Vision Room
Minimum Stay: 2 nights on weekends
Open: All year
Hosts: Frank Borodic and Karen Anderson
P.O. Box 217
9440 Sir Francis Drake Blvd.
Olema, CA 94950
(415) 663-1020
(800) 881-9874
Fax: (415) 663-8056
www.roundstonefarm.com
refresh@roundstonefarm.com

COWPER INN, Palo Alto

Overall: ★★★½	Room Quality: B	Value: A	Price: $65–$130

Cowper Inn is two adjacent houses and a carriage house in back with a variety of room options to meet guests' needs. It's reminiscent of big, friendly rooming house for visiting professors, but with pretty furnishings. Some small but comfortable rooms share a bath and are very reasonably priced; other rooms have partial or full kitchens and lots of space and are suitable for longer visits. The main house is a handsome brown shake Victorian featuring a wonderful parlor with redwood wainscoting, beamed ceilings, and a clinker brick fireplace. Breakfast is served here and in the equally attractive dining room. Breakfast, though not elaborate, includes top-notch items like homemade granola and fresh-squeezed orange juice. The inn is conveniently located a short walk from downtown and has off-street parking, which is very handy in this busy town, the home of Stanford University. Be forewarned: Palo Alto is one of California's greatest places to shop.

Setting & Facilities

Location: In a residential neighborhood, several blocks south of downtown Palo Alto

Near: 5-minute walk to downtown Palo Alto, restaurants, theaters, shops, galleries, Stanford University and Stanford Shopping Center less than a mile away, *Sunset Magazine*'s garden center

Building: 2 restored Victorians—main house has 5 rooms, LR, DR; Second House has 8 rooms, kitchen, parlor; carriage house has 1 room

Grounds: Landscaped urban lot, garden

Public Space: 2 parlors, 1 w/ fireplace and piano, DR, 2 porches w/ wicker furniture

Food & Drink: Expanded cont'l breakfast served 7:15–9:30 Mon.–Fri., 8–10 Sat.–Sun., in DR in the main house

Recreation: Biking, golf, tennis, wind surfing

Amenities & Services: Evening sherry, private parking, concierge services

Accommodations

Units: 14 guest rooms, 3 larger than average

All Rooms: Cable TV, phone

Some Rooms: AC, fridge, kitchen, private bath (12), shared bath (2), extra bed (5)

Bed & Bath: Queens, doubles (3), king

Favorites: No. 27, w/ king and double bed, partial kitchen w/ fridge and electric kettle; No. 30 (carriage house), full kitchen, private entrance

Comfort & Decor: Rooms individually decorated w/ antiques, floral wallpaper, quilts, wicker accents, carpets, oriental rugs

Rates, Reservations, & Restrictions

Deposit: Credit card; must cancel 48 hours in advance

Discounts: None; extra person $10

Credit Cards: AE, MC, V

Check-In/Out: 2/11, must leave by noon

Smoking: No

Pets: No

Kids: OK

Minimum Stay: None

Open: All year

Hosts: John and Peggy Woodworth
705 Cowper St.
Palo Alto, CA 94301
(650) 327-4475
Fax: (650) 329-1703

THE VICTORIAN ON LYTTON, Palo Alto

Overall: ★★★★½   Room Quality: B   Value: B   Price: $157–$240

If you're planning a trip to Palo Alto or anywhere else in the vicinity, this inn is a delightful place to stay. There are five guest rooms in the pretty restored 1895 Victorian, a historical landmark near the city's downtown area, and five more in an addition at the back of the property. All are spacious and tastefully decorated in an uncluttered way, with a mix of antiques, lace curtains, designer fabrics, and comfortable contemporary furnishings, plus all have private baths. An extended continental breakfast is served in your room. Parking is at a premium in this part of Palo Alto, so the inn's parking lot at the building's rear is a great plus. Stanford University is about a mile away, and the city's shops and restaurants are just a short stroll.

SETTING & FACILITIES

Location: In a residential neighborhood just north of downtown Palo Alto, on Lytton between Webster and Cowper

Near: Restaurants, shopping, Stanford University, Silicon Valley

Building: 1895 Queen Anne Victorian, restored in 1986, registered historical landmark, 5 rooms in main house, 5 in recent carriage house addition in back

Grounds: Surrounded by English gardens w/ more than 2,000 plants, boxwood hedges, old roses, clematis, palm trees, and a huge magnolia

Public Space: Parlor, outside benches, porch w/ willow furniture

Food & Drink: Expanded cont'l breakfast served in room

Recreation: Biking, swimming, horseback riding, golf

Amenities & Services: Cookies, coffee, tea avail.; robes, voice mail, private parking, fax

ACCOMMODATIONS

Units: 10 guest rooms, 8 larger than average

All Rooms: Private bath w/ tub/shower, cable TV, phone w/ modem hookup, down comforter, AC

Some Rooms: Fireplace, sitting area, extra twin (2)

Bed & Bath: Queens and kings, clawfoot tubs (2)

Favorites: Princess Royal, w/ fireplace, private bath w/ tub/shower and clawfoot tub, king canopy bed, view of the garden

Comfort & Decor: Individually decorated w/ English decor, rooms named after Queen Victoria and her 9 children, antique four-posters or canopy beds, down comforters, Blue Willow china, potted plants, carpet

RATES, RESERVATIONS, & RESTRICTIONS

Deposit: None

Discounts: Singles; extra person $10

Credit Cards: AE, MC, V

Check-In/Out: 3/11, late check-out by arrangement

Smoking: No

Pets: No

Kids: Not suitable

Minimum Stay: None

Open: All year

Hosts: Maxwell and Susan Hall
555 Lytton Ave.
Palo Alto, CA 94301
(650) 322-8555
Fax: (650) 322-7141

EVERGREEN, Pleasanton

Overall: ★★★★	Room Quality: B	Value: B	Price: $135–$225

Pleasanton's two B&Bs couldn't be more different, and what a nice choice to have. In contrast to the Victorian Plum Tree Inn in an urban setting, the contemporary Evergreen sits high in the hills on over an acre of oak forest surrounded by the hiking and biking trails of Augustin Bernal Park and the Pleasanton Ridgeland. All of the guest rooms are appealing, but the big favorite is the GrandView, which features a private outdoor deck, a large, white-tiled bathroom with a Jacuzzi and a view, a fireplace, and an antique king sleigh bed. The Hideaway also has an outdoor deck, a Jacuzzi, and a private entrance. There are an outdoor hot tub and an exercise room, too.

SETTING & FACILITIES

Location: On Pleasanton Ridge, just west of the city; Hwy. 680 to Bernal Ave. West, left on Foothill Rd., right on Longview

Near: Restaurants, shopping, Livermore Valley wineries, antiquing, Old Town Pleasanton, close to BART, 45 min. from San Francisco, adjacent to Augustin Bernal Park and Pleasanton Ridgeland

Building: Contemporary home, 11 years old

Grounds: 1.25 acres of oak forest

surrounded by parkland

Public Space: Parlor, breakfast room, decks, fitness room

Food & Drink: Full breakfast served 7–9:30 a.m. in DR or in rooms, or breakfast buffet in front of fireplace

Recreation: Mountain biking, golf, tennis

Amenities & Services: Hot tub, afternoon snacks, evening wine and hors d'oeuvres, robes, laundry, private parking, fax, concierge services for reservations

ACCOMMODATIONS

Units: 4 guest rooms, 2 larger than average

All Rooms: Private bath, cable TV, phone, AC, fridge w/ beverages

Some Rooms: Fireplace, four-poster, VCR

Bed & Bath: Queens and kings, Jacuzzis (2)

Favorites: GrandView, w/ antique king

sleigh bed, fireplace, private deck, huge bathroom w/ Jacuzzi and glass-block-enclosed shower

Comfort & Decor: Rooms individually decorated w/ curtains and coordinating drapes or window treatments; canopy, sleigh, or paneled beds; tasteful art, potted plants, carpet, tiled baths, views of Livermore Valley, fresh flowers

RATES, RESERVATIONS, & RESTRICTIONS

Deposit: Credit card; must cancel 48 hours in advance

Discounts: Long stays, weekday business, corporate

Credit Cards: AE, MC, V

Check-In/Out: 3/11, late check-in/out by arrangement

Smoking: No

Pets: No

Kids: Not suitable

Minimum Stay: None

Open: All year

Hosts: Jane and Clay Cameron
9104 Longview Dr.
Pleasanton, CA 94588
(925) 426-0901
Fax: (925) 426-9568
www.evergreen-inn.com
Jane@evergreen-inn.com

Credit Cards: AE, MC, V
Check-In/Out: 3/11, late check-in/out by arrangement
Smoking: No
Pets: No
Kids: Not suitable
Minimum Stay: None
Open: All year

Hosts: Jane and Clay Cameron
9104 Longview Dr.
Pleasanton, CA 94588
(925) 426-0901
Fax: (925) 426-9568
www.evergreen-inn.com
jane@evergreen-inn.com

PLUM TREE INN, Pleasanton

Overall: ★★★½　　Room Quality: B　　Value: B　　Price: $105–$135

Pleasanton has one of the most, well, pleasant central old towns you've ever seen. It's perfect for strolling, browsing, and dining. Just a hop and skip from the main street of Old Town is this charming home, put together with all the enthusiasm and talent the personable hosts, Joan and Bob Cordtz, could muster, and that's a lot. There are five suites and one guest room in a lovingly restored Victorian, filled with antiques, wicker, lace curtains and shutters, and with lots of room to loll about. A stellar breakfast is served in the dining room or on the deck of the innkeepers' home next door.

SETTING & FACILITIES

Location: In the Livermore Valley, 20 mi. southeast of Oakland; take Main St. south to Bernal Ave., north on Peters St. to W. Angela
Near: Restaurants, shopping, antiquing, Old Town Pleasanton, Livermore Valley wineries, close to BART, 45 min. from San Francisco, Augustin Bernal Park
Building: 1906 Queen Anne Victorian, 2 homes surrounded by white picket fence; 1 has inn rooms, the other is owners' home
Grounds: Two urban lots, mature trees, shrubs, large grassy areas w/ flower beds, brick parking lot, heritage redwood trees
Public Space: DR, front and back porches, patios
Food & Drink: Full breakfast served 6:30–9 a.m. in DR in innkeepers' home, or on back deck overlooking garden
Recreation: Biking, golf, horseback riding
Amenities & Services: Evening wine and hors d'oeuvres, private off-street parking

ACCOMMODATIONS

Units: 6 guest rooms, 5 larger than average, including 5 suites
All Rooms: Private bath and entrance, cable TV, phone
Some Rooms: Four-poster
Bed & Bath: Queens, twins (1)
Favorites: Cherry Room, w/ four-poster bed, antique cherry-wood furniture, large sitting room, quilt wall hanging
Comfort & Decor: Rooms individually decorated w/ antiques, pine, oak and wicker furniture, wallpaper, wall hangings, comforters, carpet, lace curtains and shutters

RATES, RESERVATIONS, & RESTRICTIONS

Deposit: Credit card; must cancel 7 days in advance; $10 cancellation fee
Discounts: Long stays
Credit Cards: AE, MC, V
Check-In/Out: 3/11, late check-out by arrangement
Smoking: No
Pets: No
Kids: 13 and over

No-Nos: No more than 2 guests per room
Minimum Stay: None
Open: All year
Hosts: Bob and Joan Cordtz
262 W. Angela
Pleasanton, CA 94566
(925) 426-9588
Fax: (925) 417-8737
www.plumtreeinn.com

EAST BROTHER LIGHT STATION, Point Richmond

Overall: ★★★★½	Room Quality: B	Value: B	Price: $290–$390

The East Brother Light Station B&B is utterly unique. It's in a 125-year-old Gothic Victorian lighthouse on a dot of an island in the middle of a whole lot of water: San Francisco Bay. Landing at the island's pier requires leaving the bobbing boat by climbing up a vertical ladder to the dock. Your reward is being welcomed with champagne and hors d'oeuvres, taken up a spiral staircase to the lighthouse tower, and, later, served an elegant dinner, accompanied by complimentary (and complementary) wines. The five guest rooms are simple and charming, and of course, the views are perfect, providing there's no fog. Two of the rooms share a bath. If you're only planning to stay one night, shower before you come, as limited water supplies permit only guests staying two nights to shower. You should also know that the U.S. Coast Guard operates an electronic foghorn 24 hours a day between October and April. Most guests find it melodious; the others are provided with earplugs.

SETTING & FACILITIES

Location: On an island just west of Richmond, in the straits that separate San Francisco and San Pablo Bays, accessible only by 10- min. boat ride from Point San Pablo Yacht Harbor
Near: Views of San Francisco skyline, Mt. Tamalpais, and surrounding small uninhabited islands
Building: Gingerbread Gothic Victorian w/ light tower, 4 rooms, Fog Signal Building w/ 1 room
Grounds: Small island inhabited only by staff and guests
Public Space: Upstairs parlor w/ books about the lighthouse restoration and journals and histories of the light keepers, wood-burning stove; downstairs parlor w/ bird, travel, and lighthouse literature
Food & Drink: Early morning popovers served in upstairs butler's pantry, full breakfast and 4-course dinner served to overnight guests in DR
Recreation: Horseshoes, fishing
Amenities & Services: Evening wine and hors d'oeuvres, earplugs; tour and history of the island

ACCOMMODATIONS

Units: 5 guest rooms
All Rooms: Nautical furnishings
Some Rooms: Fireplace (1), private bath (2), shared bath (3)
Bed & Bath: Queens, double; due to limited water, baths and showers not avail. to those staying 1 night only
Favorites: Two Sisters Room, w/ fireplace, view of Sisters Islands, brass bed, shared bath; Marin Room, w/ views of Mt. Tamalpais and Marin County, private bath; Walter's Quarters in the Fog Signal Building, a smaller room w/ a nautical motif and a view of the San Francisco skyline
Comfort & Decor: Rooms individually decorated w/ nautical motif, oriental rugs, lace curtains, antiques, and varied views—Marin, San Francisco, Two Sisters, West Brother (neighboring islands)

RATES, RESERVATIONS, & RESTRICTIONS

Deposit: 100% of bill, must be paid when reservation is made; $30 cancellation fee; cancellations made with less than 30 days' notice will be refunded at 90% of cost, less cancellation fee, if room is re-rented
Discounts: None
Credit Cards: AE, MC, V
Check-In/Out: Boat pickup at 4/check-out and return to mainland by 11 a.m.
Smoking: No
Pets: No
Kids: By arrangement
No-Nos: Candles
Minimum Stay: Only 1 room allows for stay of more than 1 night
Open: All year, Thurs.–Sun. nights, weather permitting
Hosts: Ann Selover and Gary Herdlicka
117 Park Place
Point Richmond, CA 94801
(510) 812-1207
(510) 233-2385
Fax: (510) 912-2243
www.ebls.org
ebls@ricochet.net

HOTEL MAC, Point Richmond

Overall: ★★★★	Room Quality: B	Value: A	Price: $95–$150

This hotel has the warm and charming ambience of a good B&B, plus the privacy of a small, well-run inn. Guest rooms are very attractive in a Ralph Lauren sort of way, with nicely contrasting fabrics, white plantation shutters, and tasteful room colors such as the perky yellow Country Garden Room, with a white fireplace and a big comfy floral-covered wing chair and ottoman. The Hotel Mac Restaurant, on the main floor, is all brick, mahogany, oak, and stained glass, with a great bar and lounge area. Locals of all ages seem to relish meeting and hanging out here. It serves good, if predictable, food, such as rack of lamb and chicken cordon bleu. Point Richmond, a newly restored and revitalized community on the bay, is 25 miles from San Francisco, and the rooms at Hotel Mac are far more reasonably priced than comparable rooms in the city.

SETTING & FACILITIES

Location: In the bayside community of Point Richmond, south of Hwy. 580 exit at Richmond Parkway, left at Castro, left at Tewksbury, right at Washington
Near: Restaurants, shopping, Oakland and San Francisco airports, 10 min. to Larkspur Ferry to San Francisco
Building: 3-story red brick hotel building built in 1911, listed in Nat'l Register of Historic Places
Grounds: Urban lot

Public Space: DR
Food & Drink: Expanded cont'l breakfast served downstairs in restaurant, weekdays 6–11 a.m., or at Little Louie's restaurant across the street, Sat.–Sun., 7:30–11 a.m.
Recreation: Sailing, fishing, wineries
Amenities & Services: Robes, private parking, disabled access, room service avail. from restaurant

ACCOMMODATIONS

Units: 7 guest rooms, including 2 suites
All Rooms: Private bath and entrance, cable TV, VCR, phone, fridge, AC
Some Rooms: Fireplace (4)
Bed & Bath: Queens, king, twins (1), Jacuzzi (1)
Favorites: Bellows Suite, 2-room suite w/ fireplace, sitting area w/ couch and

chairs, books, reading lamps; Country Garden Room, in English Country style w/ fireplace
Comfort & Decor: Rooms individually decorated w/ art, coordinating quilts and fabrics, fireplaces, books, comfortable reading chairs, reading lights, plantation shutters

RATES, RESERVATIONS, & RESTRICTIONS

Deposit: Credit card or check to hold; must cancel 48 hours in advance
Discounts: None; extra person $25
Credit Cards: AE, MC, V
Check-In/Out: 3/11
Smoking: No
Pets: No
Kids: Not suitable
Minimum Stay: None

Open: All year
Hosts: James S. Byers, owner; Irene Berndt, mgr.
10 Cottage Ave.
Point Richmond, CA 94801
(510) 235-0010
Fax: (510) 235-1869
www.pointrichmond.com/hotelmac

PILLAR POINT INN, Princeton-by-the-Sea

Overall: ★★★★	Room Quality: B	Value: B	Price: $150–$195

The tiny town of Princeton-by-the-Sea is the site of a busy harbor housing a fishing fleet, whale-watching charters, restaurants, and the pretty Cape Cod–style Pillar Point Inn. Although it's right in the midst of a whirlwind of activity, the inn itself is a serene environment with lots of comfortable sofas and chairs, a library, and delicious food. The 11 guest rooms contain colorful fabrics, tiled fireplaces, minifridges, window seats, and reading chairs, and all but one have views of Half Moon Bay and the harbor. There are lots of attractions in the area, such as state parks, a marine reserve, and a historic lighthouse.

SETTING & FACILITIES

Location: From Hwy. 1, take Capistrano Rd. exit west to harbor
Near: Restaurants, wineries, shopping, galleries, festivals, beaches, whale-watching tours, lighthouses, state parks, marine reserve
Building: Cape Cod-style modern 2-story building
Grounds: Landscaped urban lot w/ formal gardens and sculptured hedges, topiary garden in back, surrounded by white picket fence

Public Space: Parlor w/ 2-sided fireplace, library, breakfast room, 2nd-floor patio
Food & Drink: Full breakfast served 8–10 a.m. in the breakfast room
Recreation: Biking, horseback riding, fishing, golf
Amenities & Services: Afternoon snacks of fruit, cookies, chocolate, hot apple cider on weekends, fresh flowers, VCR library, private parking, conference center w/ fax and copier services avail.

ACCOMMODATIONS

Units: 11 guest rooms, 2 larger than average
All Rooms: Private bath, tiled fireplace, TV/VCR, minifridge
Some Rooms: Window seat (10)
Bed & Bath: Queens, kings (2), roll-away avail.
Favorites: Nos. 6 and 10, w/ harbor views, lots of light, high ceilings; No. 11, w/ mountain and garden view, partial

view of harbor
Comfort & Decor: Rooms individually decorated w/ individual local history themes, including appropriate artwork and photos, coordinated fabrics and accents, bay windows and window seats w/ pillows and afghans, featherbeds, reading chairs, tiled fireplaces

RATES, RESERVATIONS, & RESTRICTIONS

Deposit: Credit card or advance deposit; must cancel 5 days in advance
Discounts: Seniors, corporate rates; extra person $22
Credit Cards: AE, MC, V
Check-In/Out: 2/11
Smoking: No
Pets: No
Kids: OK, $22 for roll-away
No-Nos: No more than 3 guests per room, including children

Minimum Stay: 2 nights on weekends and holidays
Open: All year
Host: Marny Schuster
P.O. Box 388
380 Capistrano Rd.
Princeton-by-the-Sea, CA 94018
(650) 728-7377
(800) 400-8281
Fax: (650) 728-8345
www.pillarpointinn.com

ARCHBISHOP'S MANSION, San Francisco

Overall: ★★★★★	Room Quality: A	Value: B	Price: $139–$419

Sometimes words are just words—you have to see this place to believe it. Even if you have never before been a fan of Victorian decor, when you wander the halls of this mansion, you will understand how furniture, fabrics, fine carpets, architectural detailing, paintings, chandeliers, and fabulous fireplaces can all combine to create an opulent beauty that is the essence of the finest aspects of the Victorian era. Interestingly enough, although your guest room will look as though it belongs in a museum, it will also be inviting, comfortable, and wonderfully romantic. You will feel like a character in a Henry James novel, and you won't want the book to end.

SETTING & FACILITIES

Location: Between Civic Center and Golden Gate Park, on the northeast corner of Alamo Square
Near: Restaurants, shopping, galleries, 10 min. to downtown San Francisco or Fisherman's Wharf, .75 mile from Golden Gate Park and performing arts facilities in the civic center
Building: 1904 French chateau-style house from Belle Epoque period, restored in 1980s, former private residence and guest house of 2nd Catholic archbishop, Patrick Riordan
Grounds: Landscaped urban lot in Alamo Square, the city's largest historic district
Public Space: French parlor w/ oval stained glass skylight, grand staircase, chandelier from set of *Gone with the Wind*, Noel Coward's baby grand piano, Mary Lincoln's gold-leaf mirror, DR w/ fireplace and view of Alamo Square Park
Food & Drink: Expanded cont'l breakfast served 7:15–10 a.m. in DR or in room
Recreation: Self-guided tours of Victorian houses, tennis, golf
Amenities & Services: Coffee and tea avail. 7 a.m.–11 p.m., evening wine and hors d'oeuvres in parlor, morning newspapers, limited free parking, irons, hairdryers, robes, videocassettes; 24-hour concierge services, in-room massage therapy avail., limo and airport shuttle services

ACCOMMODATIONS

Units: 15 guest rooms, 8 larger than average, including 5 suites
All Rooms: Private bath, cable TV, 2-line phone w/ data port, VCR
Some Rooms: Fireplace, four-poster, canopy bed, downtown or park view
Bed & Bath: Queens, kings (2), roll-away beds and cribs avail., claw-foot tub (1), Jacuzzi for 2 (2)
Favorites: Large Romantic Fireplace rooms, w/ antique-filled sitting areas, dramatic fireplaces, draperies, canopies, oriental carpets, chandeliers
Comfort & Decor: Rooms individually decorated w/ paintings, antiques of historical significance, antique wallpapers, lace curtains w/ privacy shades, down comforters and pillows, tiled bathrooms, carpets, 15 fireplaces throughout the house; beamed, arched, or hand-painted ceilings

RATES, RESERVATIONS, & RESTRICTIONS

Deposit: 2 nights' room and tax at booking time; must cancel 7 days in advance
Discounts: AAA; extra person $20
Credit Cards: All
Check-In/Out: 3/1:30
Smoking: No
Pets: No
Kids: OK
Minimum Stay: 2 nights on weekends
Open: All year

Hosts: Jonathon Shannon and Jeffrey Ross, owners; Sandra Lender, mgr.
1000 Fulton St.
San Francisco, CA 94117
(415) 563-7872
(800) 543-5820
Fax: (415) 885-3193
www.sftrips.com
abm@jdvhospitality.com

BED AND BREAKFAST INN, San Francisco

Overall: ★★★★	Room Quality: B	Value: B	Price: $80–$300

Tucked away in a pretty little cul-de-sac (or mews, as the Brits would have it) right off one of San Francisco's best shopping and dining streets, San Francisco's first B&B is still thriving and still charming its patrons after 25 years. Modeled after an old English inn, the B&B is actually three adjoining Victorian houses united by ivy, window boxes, and various tasteful shades of green paint and trim. The inn offers a wide variety of accommodations, ranging from nice rooms that share two baths to six suites and two penthouses. The Garden Suite sleeps up to six people in a bedroom, on a loft, and on a pull-out sofa, and it also has a kitchen and a private deck and yard. The Mayfair Penthouse has a living room, a kitchen, a bedroom loft, a sofa bed, and a terrace. The inn's decor is a nice, eclectic mix of antiques, wicker, latticework, window shutters, delicate floral prints, and original art. The backyard garden is a particularly agreeable place to sit and have a cuppa after touring the city.

SETTING & FACILITIES

Location: In the Pacific Heights neighborhood in north central San Francisco, just off Union between Laguna and Buchanan
Near: Restaurants, shopping, boutiques, galleries, museums, outdoor cafés, Fisherman's Wharf, North Beach, Golden Gate Park
Building: A trio of 100-year-old Victorian houses
Grounds: 3 urban lots w/ garden court, container garden for suites, front porch under magnolia tree
Public Space: DR, library w/ TV, reading material, desk, garden sundeck
Food & Drink: Expanded cont'l breakfast served in DR or on tray in room
Recreation: Biking, tennis, golf
Amenities & Services: Sherry in rooms, newspaper, tea service in room on request, private parking avail., concierge services, public transportation nearby

ACCOMMODATIONS

Units: 11 guest rooms, including 5 suites, 2 penthouses
All Rooms: Down comforter, phone
Some Rooms: Garden access, foldout couch (2), private bath (6)
Bed & Bath: Mostly queens, 4 smallest rooms share 3 baths, tubs for 2 or Jacuzzi (3)
Favorites: Mayfair penthouse, BR loft w/ king bed, library w/ double sofa bed, kitchen, dining area w/ terrace overlooking garden deck; Celebration suite, w/ queen brass bed in alcove, sitting area w/ couch and coffee table, spa tub for 2
Comfort & Decor: Rooms individually decorated w/ family antiques, delicate floral and Laura Ashley wallpapers and curtains, wicker, original art, down comforters

RATES, RESERVATIONS, & RESTRICTIONS

Deposit: 1st night's lodging; must cancel 2 weeks in advance
Discounts: None, no charge for extra person
Credit Cards: MC, V
Check-In/Out: 3/noon, late check-out by arrangement
Smoking: No
Pets: No
Kids: OK, Garden Suite and Rive Gauche most suitable
Minimum Stay: None
Open: All year
Hosts: John and Bea Shields, owners; Jeanne Jensen, innkeeper
4 Charlton Court
San Francisco, CA 94123
(415) 921-9784
Fax: (415) 921-0544
www.thebandb.com
ubfi@1stb-bsf.com

CHATEAU TIVOLI, San Francisco

Overall: ★★★★½	Room Quality: B	Value: B	Price: $110–$250

Talk about painted ladies! This 22-room mansion flaunts its colorful charms on a corner in the heart of San Francisco's historic Alamo Square district, noted for spectacular Victorians. Brightly painted and dripping with woodwork, ironwork, and gold leaf, the Chateau was designed in 1892 in the rare Chateauesque style (used primarily for architect-designed landmark houses) by a renowned architect, William H. Armitage, for an Oregon lumber baron. A century later, the aging beauty enjoyed a million-dollar refurbishment, and she's the life of the party once more. The inn offers nine guest rooms and suites, all elaborately furnished, five with private baths, four with shared baths. The inn's museum-quality antiques come from the estates of the Vanderbilts, J. Paul Getty, and Madame Sally Stanford.

SETTING & FACILITIES

Location: In the geographic center of San Francisco, southwest corner of Steiner St. and Golden Gate Ave.
Near: Alamo Square, 10 min. to Golden Gate Park, 8 blocks to civic center and symphony hall, 6 blocks to Japan Center, public transportation
Building: 3-story Queen Anne French Revival Victorian, one of San Francisco's classic "painted ladies," w/ elaborate gingerbread facade, turrets and a bishop's cap, 22 colors and gold-leaf trim; received California Heritage Council's award for Best Restoration of a Victorian House
Grounds: Landscaped urban lot
Public Space: Double parlor w/ fireplace, oriental rugs, crystal chandeliers
Food & Drink: Expanded cont'l breakfast served 8–11 a.m. in DR, champagne brunch at 9, 10, and 11 a.m. on weekends

Recreation: Biking, horseback riding, walking in Golden Gate Park, tennis, golf
Amenities & Services: Afternoon tea, evening wine and cheese in the parlors; concierge services for reservations, flowers and chocolates for special occasions, luggage storage avail.

ACCOMMODATIONS

Units: 9 guest rooms, including 4 suites
All Rooms: Phone, radio
Some Rooms: Canopy bed, fireplace, stained glass, marble bath, balcony, view, tower, turret, private bath (5), shared bath (4)
Bed & Bath: Mostly doubles
Favorites: Luisa Tetrazzini, w/ queen canopy bed, private parlor w/ fireplace, balcony, frescoed ceilings, Bradbury & Bradbury wallpaper; Isadora Duncan, w/ fireplace, American Renaissance furniture, frescoed ceilings
Comfort & Decor: Rooms individually decorated w/ antiques and furniture appropriate to the theme, fireplaces, canopy beds, oriental rugs, chandeliers, French-washed walls

RATES, RESERVATIONS, & RESTRICTIONS

Deposit: Credit card; must cancel 7 days in advance
Discounts: 4 or more days; extra person $25
Credit Cards: AE, MC, V
Check-In/Out: 2/noon, late check-out by arrangement
Smoking: No
Pets: By arrangement
Kids: OK
Minimum Stay: 2 nights on weekends
Open: All year
Hosts: Shohet family, owners; Victoria Funestig, mgr.
1057 Steiner St.
San Francisco, CA 94115
(415) 776-5462
(800) 228-1647
Fax: (415) 776-0505
www.chateautivoli.com
mail@chateautivoli.com

HARPER HOUSE B&B, San Francisco

Overall: ★★★★	Room Quality: B	Value: A	Price: $80–$120

The recently opened Harper House is a great find. Conveniently located on a quiet residential street in San Francisco's famed Haight-Ashbury neighborhood, the newly restored 1905 Victorian inn has five appealing guest rooms furnished simply with antique French Provincial fabrics and furniture. Two of the rooms in the carriage house share a bath. All have queen beds. The living room and dining area have beautiful, gleaming hardwood floors, a fireplace, and comfortable seating. All the rooms are quite reasonably priced, and if you're quick there's private parking for one car for an extra $10 a night (a great deal in a town where parking spaces are an endangered species). Breakfast is on the healthy side, with home-baked breads and muffins, fresh fruit, cereals, and French roast coffee.

SETTING & FACILITIES

Location: Located in Haight-Ashbury section, 2 blocks east of Golden Gate Park and 1 block north of Haight St.
Near: Restaurants, shopping, galleries, art and history museums, Golden Gate Park, arboretum, public transportation
Building: 1905 Victorian w/ 2 rooms, carriage house w/ 3 rooms
Grounds: Urban lot w/ garden courtyard, fountain, covered walkway to

carriage house
Public Space: Parlor w/ fireplace, DR, sunroom, front reception area, garden, brick courtyard
Food & Drink: Expanded cont'l breakfast served at 8 a.m. in DR
Recreation: Tennis, golf
Amenities & Services: Afternoon wine, TV in parlor, private parking for 1 car for $10/night

ACCOMMODATIONS

Units: 5 guest rooms, 2 larger than average, including 1 suite
Some Rooms: Fridge, TV, phone, limited kitchen, dining facil., private bath (3), shared bath (2)
Bed & Bath: Queens
Favorites: Monet Suite, w/ sitting

room and breakfast area, sink and microwave, TV/VCR, country decor, BR, private bath w/ claw-foot tub
Comfort & Decor: Impressionist art in each room, iron beds, French Provincial fabrics and antique furniture, hardwood floors w/ area rugs

RATES, RESERVATIONS, & RESTRICTIONS

Deposit: 1 night's fee w/ personal check or credit card; must cancel 3 days in advance
Discounts: Long stays; extra person $20
Credit Cards: MC, V
Check-In/Out: 3/11
Smoking: No
Pets: No
Kids: 8 and over
Minimum Stay: 2 nights on weekends

Apr.–Oct.
Open: All year
Hosts: Leah Harper and Ted Loewenberg
1562 Waller St.
San Francisco, CA 94117
(415) 252-1560
Fax: (415) 252-1550
www.harperhouseb-b.com
lharper@harperhouseb-b.com

INN 1890, San Francisco

| Overall: ★★★½ | Room Quality: C | Value: A | Price: $79–$129 |

This inn is a good place to know about. In some ways, it's like a big, friendly rooming house filled with people you wish you knew. In a residential neighborhood at the edge of the upper Haight-Ashbury district and steps from Golden Gate Park, it's basically a European-style pension in a Queen Anne Victorian. The building has 12-foot ceilings, hardwood floors, and lots of bay windows. And, no surprise, it attracts a lot of European tourists. Many of the guest rooms have fireplaces, and each room has its own kitchenette or kitchen. Generously sized, the rooms contain brass or iron queen-size beds and down and feather comforters. There are a laundry room, a lending library, and even health club privileges. Some rooms sleep three to six people, for a $15 extra charge per person, making this an even greater bargain than it already is. The Castro district is nearby, as well as the University of San Francisco and UC San Francisco.

SETTING & FACILITIES

Location: In the upper Haight-Ashbury neighborhood, just east of Golden Gate Park, at Page and Shrader

Near: Restaurants, shopping, art and history museums, Haight-Ashbury and Castro districts, 1 block from Golden Gate Park, public transportation, 10 min. from downtown San Francisco

Building: 1890 Queen Anne Victorian, Landmark status, w/ 6 original working fireplaces, hardwood floors, bay windows

Grounds: Landscaped urban lot w/ patio and garden in rear

Public Space: Parlor, library, DR, kitchen

Food & Drink: Expanded cont'l breakfast served 7–10 a.m. in DR

Recreation: Biking, croquet, tennis, golf, horseshoes, horseback riding, all in Golden Gate Park

Amenities & Services: Snacks in the library, kitchen open and breakfast avail. 24 hrs., bathrobes and slippers, washer and dryer, health club privileges; limited private parking avail. at $5/night

ACCOMMODATIONS

Units: 10 guest rooms, 2 larger than average, 2 full suites/kitchens and extra beds

All Rooms: Private bath, TV, private phone line w/ voice mail, kitchenette, fridge

Some Rooms: Fireplace, room for extra bed (5)

Bed & Bath: Queens, double

Favorites: No. 1, w/ Victorian sofa, brass bed, fireplace; No. 11, w/ round turret, skylights, separate BR, full kitchen, fireplace

Comfort & Decor: Rooms individually decorated w/ artwork, Victorian furniture, comforters, drapes, hardwood floors w/ oriental rugs, 12-ft. ceilings, bay windows

RATES, RESERVATIONS, & RESTRICTIONS

Deposit: Credit card; must cancel within 1 day if the stay is 1 day or 2 days if stay is 2, etc.; no charge if room is re-rented

Discounts: Long stays; extra person $15

Credit Cards: MC, V

Check-In/Out: 3/11, late check-out by arrangement

Smoking: No

Pets: OK by prior arrangement

Kids: OK by prior arrangement

Minimum Stay: 3 nights on weekends, 2 on weekdays

Open: All year

Host: Frank Plaier
1890 Page St.
San Francisco, CA 94117
(415) 386-0486
(888) 466-1890
Fax: (415) 386-3626
www.adamsnet.com/inn1890
inn1890@worldnet.att.net

JACKSON COURT, San Francisco

Overall: ★★★★½   Room Quality: B   · Value: B   Price: $150–$205

This handsome three-story brownstone mansion in a fine San Francisco residential neighborhood has the air of an exclusive private club, with its wood-paneled parlor full of large, comfortable furniture around a striking hand-carved stone fireplace. Converted from a historic San Francisco mansion, the inn contains ten spacious guest rooms beautifully appointed with such features as Italian marble fireplaces with built-in bookcases, handcrafted wood paneling and cabinets, antique chandeliers, and window seats or sitting areas. An extended continental breakfast is served in the dining room, or you can take a tray to your room, and there are tea and cookies in the afternoon.

SETTING & FACILITIES

Location: In Pacific Heights residential neighborhood in north central San Francisco

Near: Restaurants, Union St. shopping area, Victorian mansions, public transportation, parks, museums, Golden Gate Park, Chinatown, Japantown

Building: 19th-century brownstone mansion

Grounds: Arched entrance, flower-lined courtyard

Public Space: Wood-paneled parlor

w/ hand-carved fireplace, adjoining game/reading room, upstairs sitting room

Food & Drink: Extended cont'l breakfast served 7:30–10:30 a.m. in 2nd-floor kitchen, or guests may take a tray to their room

Recreation: Tennis, golf

Amenities & Services: Afternoon tea in parlor, off-street parking for a fee, concierge service for reservations

ACCOMMODATIONS

Units: 10 guest rooms, 2 larger than average

All Rooms: Private bath, large glass shower, sitting area, TV, private phone

Some Rooms: Fireplace

Bed & Bath: Queens, king, doubles (2)

Favorites: Garden Court, originally the DR, w/ handcrafted wood paneling, antique chandelier, picture window overlooking private garden patio;

Library Room, w/ forest green accent and cream background, 3 large windows, wood-burning fireplace w/ sofa in front, oriental rug

Comfort & Decor: Rooms individually decorated w/ antique and contemporary furnishings, fireplaces, sitting areas, window seats, oriental carpet, fresh flowers

RATES, RESERVATIONS, & RESTRICTIONS

Deposit: Credit card or personal check; must cancel 7 days in advance

Discounts: None; extra adult (12 or over) $30

Credit Cards: AE, MC, V

Check-In/Out: 2/11, will hold luggage for late check-out/in

Smoking: No

Pets: No
Kids: OK (no cribs)
Minimum Stay: 2 nights on weekends
Open: All year

Host: Evelyn Jingco
2198 Jackson St.
San Francisco, CA 94115
(415) 929-7670

NOB HILL INN, San Francisco

Overall: ★★★½	Room Quality: B	Value: A	Price: $99–$249

This large 1907 Edwardian inn in a former private mansion is so . . . so San Francisco. It manages to be old, elegant, and sort of unpretentious all at once, though its four-story vertical layout makes it feel more like a small hotel than a B&B. The inn has every range of accommodation, from smallish single bedrooms (for a very reasonable price) to the spacious two-bedroom, two-bath Huntington Suite, with a kitchenette, dining room, and a master bedroom. Guest rooms are tastefully furnished with lovely antiques, some have pretty wallpaper and great fireplaces, and many have spacious sitting areas. There's a small, etched glass lift to take you to the upper floors in true European fashion. A continental breakfast is served 24 hours a day in the wine cellar, and tea and sherry are set out in the afternoon. There are even a few resident ghosts drifting about to give you something to think about in the dark.

SETTING & FACILITIES

Location: Midtown San Francisco, on Nob Hill, at the corner of Pine and Taylor Sts.
Near: Shopping, theater, restaurants, Chinatown, Union Square, cable cars, Grace Cathedral
Building: 1907 Edwardian mansion, formerly a private home, restored in 1979
Grounds: Urban lot

Public Space: Lobby, wine cellar
Food & Drink: Extended cont'l breakfast served 24 hours in the wine cellar
Recreation: Golf
Amenities & Services: Tea and sherry every afternoon in the lobby, nightly turn-down service; full 24-hour concierge services for dinner reservations, wine country trips, tours; fax and photocopy services, theater tickets

ACCOMMODATIONS

Units: 21 guest rooms, including 3 suites w/ 1 BR, 4 suites w/ 1 BR and kitchen, 2 suites w/ 2 BRs, 2 baths, and kitchen
All Rooms: Private bath, cable TV, phone
Some Rooms: Tile-faced fireplace, four-poster, love seat, kitchenette
Bed & Bath: Queens, doubles (3),

claw-foot tubs (9)
Favorites: Stanford junior suites, w/ bay windows, sitting areas, 2 TVs, fireplaces, parlors; Crocker suites, w/ fully stocked kitchenettes, private master BRs and sofa sleeper in parlor, 2 TVs
Comfort & Decor: All rooms contain restored antiques, four-poster and brass beds, armoires

RATES, RESERVATIONS, & RESTRICTIONS

Deposit: Credit card; must cancel 24 hours in advance
Discounts: AARP, AAA; no charge for extra person in nonsuite rooms
Credit Cards: AE, DC, D, MC, V
Check-In/Out: 3:30/11
Smoking: No
Pets: No

Kids: OK
Minimum Stay: None
Open: All year
Host: Sandy Miller
1000 Pine St.
San Francisco, CA 94109
(415) 673-6080
Fax: (415) 673-6098

SHERMAN HOUSE, San Francisco

Overall: ★★★★★	Room Quality: A	Value: C	Price: $360–$850

Built in 1876 by Leander Sherman, of Sherman Clay Piano Company fame, this Italianate mansion's arched, skylighted, three-story recital hall has the sounds of Caruso, Paderewski, and Lillian Russell echoing through its colorful history. Picture a full-canopy bed in gold brocade, or an immense, private, brick-floored patio with a panoramic view of the city stretching from the Golden Gate Bridge to the Bay Bridge, or walls of French-paned windows overlooking private gardens. Add to your picture China slate floors, priceless carpets, bronze Doré chandeliers, a black marble bathroom: all are components of a breathtaking hotel in a beautiful city. The Sherman House Restaurant on the premises offers inventive, seasonal dinner menus and a grand dining experience for inn guests only. •

SETTING & FACILITIES

Location: In San Francisco's wealthy Pacific Heights neighborhood, northwest of downtown and just south of the Union St. shopping district
Near: Restaurants, shopping, art and history museums, 10-minute drive to downtown San Francisco, Fisherman's Wharf, Golden Gate Park
Building: 4.5-story French Italianate Victorian built in 1878, Historic Landmark mansion; carriage house w/ 3 suites

Grounds: 1 acre w/ formal terraced English gardens, fountains, pond, gazebo, greenhouse, in urban residential neighborhood
Public Space: Parlor, DR w/ fireplace, gallery, music room, double mahogany staircase

Food & Drink: Full breakfast served 7–11 a.m. in DR or guest's room, dietary restrictions accommodated, DR serves lunch daily and dinner Tues.–Sun.
Recreation: Biking, tennis, golf, horseback riding

ACCOMMODATIONS

Units: 14 guest rooms, 6 larger than average, including 6 suites
All Rooms: Private bath, cable TV, phone
Some Rooms: Four-poster, fridge, fireplace (5), twin-sized upholstered window seat (4), view of San Francisco Bay and Golden Gate Bridge
Bed & Bath: Queens, king
Favorites: Sherman Suite, w/ huge outdoor brick terrace w/ bay views, sitting room, Roman tub; Biedermeier Suite, w/ Biedermeier antiques, upholstered walls, brocade bed hangings,

bronze Doré chandeliers, bay view, large bath w/ 2 sinks and oversized Roman tub; Paderewski Suite, w/ fireplaces in both BR and bath, dark wood wainscoting, wood-beamed ceiling, view of bay
Comfort & Decor: Rooms individually decorated w/ Old English and oriental artwork, Jacobean, French Second Empire, Biedermeier furniture, half- or full-canopy featherbeds, wood-burning fireplaces, antique tapestries, faux-wood paneling, floral carpet, inlaid wood floors

RATES, RESERVATIONS, & RESTRICTIONS

Deposit: Full payment 7 days before arrival; must cancel 7 days in advance
Discounts: Long stays, no charge for extra person
Credit Cards: AE, MC, V
Check-In/Out: 4/noon, late check-out by arrangement
Smoking: No
Pets: No
Kids: OK
Minimum Stay: 2 nights on holiday

weekends and on all weekends Aug.–Nov.
Open: All year
Host: Christine Berlin
2160 Green St.
San Francisco, CA 94123
(415) 563-3600
(800) 424-5777
Fax: (415) 563-1882
www.theshermanhouse.com
cchrisb@mhotelgroup.com

SPENCER HOUSE, San Francisco

Overall: ★★★★½	Room Quality: A	Value: B	Price: $125–$185

Occasionally you find a restored Victorian by which you judge all the others, and the Spencer House is one of these. The architecture is lovely, the furnishings are tasteful, and the objets d'art are lavishly but judiciously displayed, without causing one to fear sticking one's foot into a chamber pot or sweeping a Hummel collection to the floor with a misplaced gesture. The mansion's entry is graced by a hand-carved staircase, and Corinthian columns separate the parlor from the living room. There are green velvet sofas, an Eastlake bookcase, stained glass windows, and Persian carpets. The six guest rooms are especially beautiful, with Bradbury & Bradbury wallpaper, wonderful antique light fixtures, velvet drapes and lace net curtains, and hand-carved antique beds. The inn serves a full breakfast on silver and crystal, prepared by a chef.

SETTING & FACILITIES

Location: On the corner of Haight and Baker Sts. in a residential neighborhood, across from Buena Vista Park
Near: Golden Gate Park, restaurants, shopping, museums, public transportation to civic center, downtown, Fisherman's Wharf
Building: Restored 1887 Queen Anne Victorian w/ arched entry and corner tower
Grounds: Landscaped urban lot w/ elaborately clipped hedge in shape

of Spencer crest
Public Space: LR, parlor/w Stroud player piano, DR w/ fireplace, table for 14 set w/ crystal, china, and Grand Baroque silver
Food & Drink: Full breakfast served 8–10 a.m. in DR by candlelight
Recreation: Horseback riding in Golden Gate Park, biking, tennis, golf
Amenities & Services: Concierge service for reservations, luggage storage

ACCOMMODATIONS

Units: 6 guest rooms, 2 larger than average
All Rooms: Private bath, wallcoverings, parquet floor, original Victorian light fixtures, private phone, featherbed, down duvet, lace curtains and velvet drapes
Some Rooms: Persian rugs, Bradbury & Bradbury wallpaper, upholstered walls
Bed & Bath: Kings and queens, double
Favorites: Queen Anne Room, w/ burled-wood carved antique bed, walls upholstered w/ chintz, antique brass light fixture with hand-blown glass shade, Karastan Persian rug, sitting area

in tower window area w/ view of Buena Vista Park; Erwin's Room, w/ upholstered walls of mauve moire cotton and matching draperies, lace curtains, antique king bed w/ tester, embossed tile bathroom w/ parquet hardwood floor, Bradbury & Bradbury wallpaper, no street exposure
Comfort & Decor: Rooms individually decorated w/ carved antique furniture, featherbeds, down comforters and pillows, Persian rugs, China hooked rugs, original chandeliers, lace net curtains and drapes made in England

RATES, RESERVATIONS, & RESTRICTIONS

Deposit: 1 night's deposit; must cancel 7 days in advance, 14 days for holidays; $10 cancellation fee
Discounts: None
Credit Cards: AE, MC, V
Check-In/Out: 3/noon
Smoking: No
Pets: By previous arrangement, $10
Kids: 16 and over
Minimum Stay: 2 nights on week-

ends, 3 on holidays
Open: All year
Hosts: Barbara and Jack Chambers
1080 Haight St.
San Francisco, CA 94117
(415) 626-9205
Fax: (415) 626-9230
www.spencerhouse.com
bjc@spencerhouse.com

UNION STREET INN, San Francisco

Overall: ★★★★½	Room Quality: B	Value: B	Price: $135–$245

Union Street Inn is in the heart of one of San Francisco's most fashionable shopping and dining areas. The rooms are spacious and comfortably furnished with antique accents and fresh floral arrangements. At the back of the inn is an English garden with brick paths and lots of rosebushes, which thrive in the San Francisco's mild climate. The carriage house, a cottage with a cathedral ceiling, track lighting, a two-person in-room spa, and artful marble sculptures, is a favorite of honeymooners and has its own private garden. Individual touches such as robes, a fruit basket, and chocolates are provided by the friendly innkeeper.

SETTING & FACILITIES

Location: On Union St. between Steiner and Fillmore in the Pacific Heights/Marina district, in northern San Francisco, between Fisherman's Wharf and Golden Gate Bridge
Near: Restaurants, shopping, art and history museums, Fisherman's Wharf, Palace of Fine Arts, Exploratorium, public transportation
Building: 1903 Edwardian home w/ carriage house
Grounds: English gardens, brick paths, roses, garden ornaments; carriage house has a private garden
Public Space: Parlor, deck, gardens
Food & Drink: Full breakfast served 7:30–11 a.m. in the parlor, gardens, deck, or guest's room
Recreation: Tennis, golf
Amenities & Services: Fruit baskets in room, bottled water, chocolates, robes, fresh flowers, hairdryers; parking nearby, $12 for 24 hours, concierge services for reservations and tours

ACCOMMODATIONS

Units: 6 guest rooms, 4 larger than average
All Rooms: Private bath, cable TV, phone
Some Rooms: Four-poster, sleeper sofa, fridge, extra bed (2)
Bed & Bath: Queens, king, Jacuzzi for 2 (2), Jacuzzi (1)
Favorites: English Garden Room, w/ floral wallpaper, four-poster queen bed, private deck w/ table and chairs overlooking the garden
Comfort & Decor: Rooms individually decorated w/ eclectic English Country House furnishings, heirloom antiques, original art, collectibles, wall coverings, down comforters, carpets, antique rugs

RATES, RESERVATIONS, & RESTRICTIONS

Deposit: Credit card or 1st night's lodging; must cancel 7 days in advance
Discounts: None, singles; extra person $20
Credit Cards: AE, MC, V
Check-In/Out: 2/noon, late check-out by arrangement
Smoking: No
Pets: No
Kids: OK
Minimum Stay: 2 nights on weekends
Open: All year

Hosts: Jane Bertorelli and David Coyle
2229 Union St.
San Francisco, CA 94123
(415) 346-0424

Fax: (415) 922-8046
www.unionstreetinn.com
janeb@unionstreetinn.com

VICTORIAN INN ON THE PARK, San Francisco

Overall: ★★★★	Room Quality: B	Value: B	Price: $124–$174

Located directly across the street from the "panhandle" of Golden Gate Park, close to the downtown civic center and museums, this elegant inn was designed by William Curlett, architect of the first San Francisco City Hall (destroyed in the 1906 earthquake). On the exterior it has a distinctive octagonal-shaped belvedere open turret topped with a wooden finial, plus it contains various splendid examples of Bruce Bradbury wallpapers in its charming, antique-filled rooms. Guests can choose among room amenities including fireplaces, balconies, or Roman tubs. The innkeepers maintain an interesting collection of Victorian lampshades, which are displayed throughout the house. These friendly folks welcome kids, too.

SETTING & FACILITIES

Location: From Hwy. 101 exit at Fell St., turn right on Lyon, go to corner of Lyon and Fell
Near: Restaurants, shopping, art and history museums, adjacent to Golden Gate Park, 5 min. from civic center
Building: 1897 4-story Queen Anne Victorian, registered historic landmark known as the "Clunie House"
Grounds: Landscaped urban lot
Public Space: Parlor w/ carved maple-wood fireplace, mahogany-paneled entrance hall w/ amber and crystal stained glass windows, oak-paneled library and DR
Food & Drink: Expanded cont'l breakfast served 7:30–10:30 a.m. in DR
Recreation: Tennis, golf
Amenities & Services: Evening sherry, wine, private parking, $15/day, must be reserved in advance, honor baskets of snacks and refreshments in rooms

ACCOMMODATIONS

Units: 12 guest rooms, including 2 suites
All Rooms: Private bath, phone, fan, TV avail. on request
Some Rooms: Fireplace, four-poster, sleeping futon, extra bed (3)
Bed & Bath: Queens, twins (1), some Roman tubs
Favorites: Belvedere Room, w/ private balcony in the belvedered turret, views of the city and park, marble fireplace, Roman tub w/ shower
Comfort & Decor: Rooms individually decorated w/ Queen Anne-style antiques and reproductions, Victorian-style curtains, carpet, unique lampshades in all rooms

RATES, RESERVATIONS, & RESTRICTIONS

Deposit: 2-night deposit; must cancel 7 days in advance, 14 for holidays
Discounts: Long stays, weekday business, seniors; extra person $20
Credit Cards: All
Check-In/Out: 2/11:30, late check-out by arrangement
Smoking: No
Pets: No
Kids: Welcome
Minimum Stay: 2 nights on weekends, 3 on holidays

Open: All year
Hosts: Lisa and William Benau and Shirley and Paul Weber
301 Lyon St.
San Francisco, CA 94117
(415) 931-1830
(800) 435-1967
Fax: (415) 931-1830
www.citysearch.com/sfo/victorianinn
vicinn@aol.com

WASHINGTON SQUARE INN, San Francisco

Overall: ★★★★	Room Quality: B	Value: B	Price: $120–$210

Location is a major factor for any stay in San Francisco, and this civilized little 15-room inn is perfectly located for visitors. It faces Washington Square Park in the heart of famous North Beach, the city's fabled Italian/bohemian neighborhood—home of Joe DiMaggio, Beat poets, and great Italian restaurants. The rooms range in size and amenities, but all have been decorated by a noted SF designer with antiques and custom fabrics. In addition to breakfast in the lobby or in your room, there's an afternoon tea service, wine and hors d'oeuvres, and individual touches such as blooming orchids, newspapers, and, for an extra charge, valet parking.

SETTING & FACILITIES

Location: In the heart of North Beach, northeast corner of Washington Square Park, corner of Filbert and Stockton
Near: Restaurants, shopping, history and art museums, Fisherman's Wharf, Chinatown, Ghirardelli Square, cable cars, public transportation
Building: Small European-style hotel w/ street trees and flower boxes
Grounds: Urban corner lot facing Washington Square Park
Public Space: Parlor w/ fireplace, dining area
Food & Drink: Expanded cont'l breakfast, served 7–10 a.m. in the lobby or in room
Recreation: Tennis, golf
Amenities & Services: Afternoon tea, evening wine and hors d'oeuvres, robes, hand-milled soap, valet parking $20/day, disabled access

ACCOMMODATIONS

Units: 15 guest rooms, 5 larger than average
All Rooms: Private bath, cable TV/VCR, phone
Some Rooms: Sitting area, bay windows, sleeper sofa (2)
Bed & Bath: Kings and queens, 2 twins (1), double

Favorites: No. 11, sitting area w/ bay window, view of Coit Tower
Comfort & Decor: Rooms individu-

ally decorated w/ down pillows and comforters, flowering orchid plants

RATES, RESERVATIONS, & RESTRICTIONS

Deposit: Credit card; must cancel 48 hours in advance
Discounts: Seniors; extra person $20
Credit Cards: All
Check-In/Out: 3/noon
Smoking: No
Pets: No
Kids: OK
Minimum Stay: 2 nights on weekends

Open: All year
Host: David Norwitt
1660 Stockton St.
San Francisco, CA 94133
(415) 981-4220
(800) 388-0220
Fax: (415) 397-7242
www.wsisf.com
david@wsisf.com

GERSTLE PARK INN, San Rafael

Overall: ★★★★½	Room Quality: A	Value: B	Price: $149–$225

On the flanks of a hill in San Rafael's most historic neighborhood is an inn that deserves to be more widely known. Gerstle Park Inn sits on one and a half acres of giant oak and cedar trees and borders on the woodlands of Marin County open space. Its 12 luxury suites are decorated with an extensive selection of Asian scrolls, ceramics, and sculptures mixed with equally tasteful Western art. The rooms also contain a collection of museum-quality antiques. The inn was originally part of an estate for a San Francisco nabob—the main house was a guest house, the carriage house was, well, a carriage house, and one of the cottages was a barn. The second cottage was added in the 1950s. The terraced gardens include a stand of redwoods, a fruit orchard, and a hillside pasture. The permanent croquet field is a unique amenity for lovers of that civilized sport.

SETTING & FACILITIES

Location: On the southwest edge of downtown San Rafael; from Hwy. 101, take San Rafael/Central exit, go west on 4th St., left on D St., right on San Rafael Ave., left on Grove
Near: Restaurants, shopping, galleries, antiques, Sausalito, Tiburon, Muir Woods, airports, wine country, Point Reyes Nat'l Seashore, San Francisco
Building: 1895 guest house w/ 8 suites, 1890 carriage house w/ 2 suites

w/ kitchens, 1 cottage (former barn, age unknown), 1 cottage built in 1950s
Grounds: 1.5 acres of terraced gardens under valley oaks, croquet court, herb garden, orchard, backs onto wooded open space
Public Space: Parlor w/ massive fireplace, 16-ft. barrel-vaulted ceiling, clerestory windows, oriental art, gilt mirrors, chandelier, spacious porch w/ wicker furniture, brick terrace

Food & Drink: Full breakfast served 7:30–9:30 a.m. weekdays, 8–10 a.m. weekends, in DR, w/ separate tables for 2 to 4, 24-hour kitchen access to fridge stocked w/ drinks, yogurt, fruit, cookies, doughnuts, earlier breakfast by prior arrangement

Recreation: Tennis, golf, bird-watching, fishing
Amenities & Services: Afternoon beverages and snacks, evening sherry, wine, candy/robes in rooms, hairdryers, private parking, 1 room w/ disabled access

ACCOMMODATIONS

Units: 12 guest rooms, including 6 junior suites, 6 regular suites
All Rooms: Private bath, cable TV, phone w/ voice mail, modem port, VCR, private deck and patio
Some Rooms: Kitchen (4)
Bed & Bath: Queens and kings, twins (1), doubles (2), Jacuzzis in king suites
Favorites: Redwood Suite, w/ own staircase, windows on 3 sides, views of redwoods and grounds, French doors

open to private balcony and private deck, Jacuzzi and double marble sink in bathroom; Sunrise Suite in carriage house, w/ kitchen, LR, dining area, BR, outside patio, French doors, French decor
Comfort & Decor: Rooms individually decorated w/ antiques, fine fabrics and wallpaper, down comforters, carpet, museum-quality art

RATES, RESERVATIONS, & RESTRICTIONS

Deposit: Credit card; must cancel 5 days in advance for midweek stays, 7 days for weekend
Discounts: Long stays, weekday business; extra person $25
Credit Cards: AE, MC, V
Check-In/Out: 3/noon
Smoking: No
Pets: No
Kids: In cottages and carriage house suites
No-Nos: No more than 3 guests per room

Minimum Stay: 2 nights on weekends; inquire for exceptions
Open: All year
Hosts: Jim and Judy Dowling, owners; Barbara Hemsley, innkeeper
34 Grove St.
San Rafael, CA 94901
(415) 721-7611
(800) 726-7611
Fax: (415) 721-7600
www.gerstleparkinn.com
innkeeper@gerstleparkinn.com

PANAMA HOTEL AND RESTAURANT, San Rafael

Overall: ★★★½	Room Quality: C	Value: B	Price: $60–$145

What is it about San Rafael's Gerstle Park neighborhood that it can produce two such unusual and different B&Bs as the coolly elegant Gerstle Park Inn and, four blocks away, that oasis of funky charm, the Panama Hotel? And why is it called the Panama Hotel, you ask? Because a previous owner thought every town needed a Panama Hotel. This one lives up to its name, with a tropical feeling that reminds some of the Caribbean and others of New Orleans. The hotel is actually two 1910 homes tied together by a rambling brick patio; one of the houses contains a popular neighborhood restaurant. All of the 15 rooms are different; some have vine-covered balconies, others kitchenettes. One has a bidet. All are decorated using exuberant and eclectic items like garage sale art, travel souvenirs, and an antique bed painted baby blue.

SETTING & FACILITIES

Location: On the southwest edge of downtown San Rafael; from Hwy. 101, take San Rafael/Central exit, go west on 4th St. to B St.; inn is at B and Bayview
Near: Restaurants, shopping, galleries, antiques, SF and Oakland airports, 35 min. to wine country, 30 min. to Point Reyes Nat'l Seashore, Sausalito, Tiburon
Building: 2 1910 homes, 2-story Victorian w/ balconies decked w/ wisteria and Christmas lights and a stuccoed 2-story house with verandas that houses the restaurant

Grounds: Lushly planted gardens w/ citrus, weeping deodar, red maple trees, jasmine, succulents planted in white pointy shoes, roses and geraniums
Public Space: Patio and decks
Food & Drink: Expanded cont'l breakfast served 8–11 a.m. in the restaurant
Recreation: Tennis, golf
Amenities & Services: Shared guest kitchen for rooms w/ shared baths, on-street parking, assistance w/ dining reservations and area information, full restaurant on premises

ACCOMMODATIONS

Units: 16 guest rooms, including suites and apartments
All Rooms: Phone, ceiling fan
Some Rooms: Canopy bed, private balcony, TV, kitchenette, wet bar, microwave, skylight, private bath (10), shared bath (6), extra bed (2)
Bed & Bath: Queens and doubles
Favorites: Rosie's Room, w/ canopy

bed, private balcony, sitting room w/ wet bar, bathroom w/ claw-foot tub, shower, and bidet; Venetian Room, w/ French doors to private balcony, kitchenette
Comfort & Decor: Rooms individually decorated w/ eclectic collection of art, bright fabrics, and comfortable furniture

RATES, RESERVATIONS, & RESTRICTIONS

Deposit: Credit card, prepayment required for 2 or more rooms; must cancel 48 hours in advance
Discounts: None; extra person $10
Credit Cards: AE, MC, V
Check-In/Out: 3/noon
Smoking: No
Pets: OK in 2 rooms; must be attended at all times
Kids: OK
Minimum Stay: 2 nights on summer

weekends
Open: All year
Host: Daniel Miller
4 Bayview St.
San Rafael, CA 94901
(415) 457-3993
(800) 899-3993
Fax: (415) 457-6240
www.panamahotel.com
reservations@panamahotel.com

MADISON STREET INN, Santa Clara

Overall: ★★★½	Room Quality: C	Value: A	Price: $75–$115

A neat gray Victorian house with a rose-lined white picket fence in a residential neighborhood, this inn is just about as homey as you can get without being at home. The inn has five small-to-medium guest rooms and a family-sized suite with Victorian and country-style furnishings, plus a large pretty living room and parlor area. Two rooms share a bath. For those long, warm Santa Clara summer days, there's a swimming pool and hot tub. Breakfast is a major event, often featuring eggs Madison, an avocado dish with poached eggs and salsa. The Santa Clara and San Jose convention centers are just 15 minutes away.

SETTING & FACILITIES

Location: In the town of Santa Clara, just west of San Jose; call for directions
Near: Winchester Mystery House, Great America Park, Santa Clara University, San Jose and Santa Clara convention centers
Building: Queen Anne Victorian built in 1895
Grounds: ⅓ acre of landscaped gardens, gazebo, on an urban lot in a residential area

Public Space: Parlor, library, DR, game room
Food & Drink: Full breakfast served 7–9 a.m. in garden or DR
Recreation: Ping-Pong on premises; biking, tennis, golf close by
Amenities & Services: Hot tub, swimming pool, barbecue, evening sherry and wine, movies in parlor, fresh-baked chocolate chip cookies; concierge service for reservations

ACCOMMODATIONS

Units: 6 guest rooms, 1 larger than average
All Rooms: Phone
Some Rooms: Four-poster, sleeper sofa, TV, AC, private bath (4), shared bath (2), extra bed (2)
Units: 6 guest rooms, 1 larger
Bed & Bath: Queens, king, double
Favorites: Madison, w/ queen four-poster, Ralph Lauren diamond-etched wall and linens, exposed wood floors, private bath; Monroe, w/ queen brass bed, sitting area w/ daybed, claw-foot tub in bath
Comfort & Decor: Rooms individually decorated w/ country and Victorian furniture, hand-painted and sponged walls, wallpaper, wood floors and carpet

RATES, RESERVATIONS, & RESTRICTIONS

Deposit: Credit card or 1 night's lodging to hold; must cancel 48 hours in advance; cancellation fee 1st night's lodging
Discounts: Long stays, groups; extra person $10
Credit Cards: All

Check-In/Out: 4/noon, late check-out by arrangement
Smoking: No
Pets: No
Kids: OK
Minimum Stay: None

Open: All year
Hosts: Ralph and Theresa Wigginton
1390 Madison St.
Santa Clara, CA 95050
(408) 249-5541

(800) 491-5541
Fax: (408) 249-6676
www.santa-clara-inn.com
madstinn@aol.com

CASA DEL MAR, Stinson Beach

Overall: ★★★★	Room Quality: B	Value: B	Price: $140–$260

You enter this little piece of Eden through a bright blue gate in a stone wall. Behind the wall is the proverbial heavenly garden, overflowing with plants from around the world—jacarandas, birds of paradise, cymbidiums, bananas, palms, apple and lemon trees, cacti, passion flowers, and bougainvillea, just to mention a few. The garden originated in the 1930s and was used in the 1970s as a teaching garden for the University of California. Owner Rick Klein fell in love with the garden and then painstakingly transformed the large house into a Mediterranean-style villa of great charm. The rooms are decorated with folk art from around the world, and there are gorgeous Balinese sculptures in the garden. Rick is also a great cook.

SETTING & FACILITIES

Location: In Stinson Beach, 100 yards east of Hwy. 101 on Belvedere Ave.; 1 hour north of San Francisco
Near: Restaurants, shopping, galleries, Mount Tamalpais State Park, Muir Woods, Audubon Canyon Ranch, 3 mi. of sandy beach
Building: Mediterranean villa built in 1989
Grounds: Terraced hillside gardens overflow w/ semitropical and native plants planted in 1930, Balinese lions and other statuary, lily pond, giant boulders, cutting garden, shade garden; the gardens were used in the 1970s as a teaching garden for UC School of Landscape Architecture
Public Space: Great room w/ dramatic fireplace, books, folk art and colorful paintings by local artists, DR, woodstove in tiled eating area
Food & Drink: Full breakfast prepared by chef-innkeeper and served at 9 a.m. in DR
Recreation: Mountain and road biking, kayaking, bird- and whale-watching, horseback riding
Amenities & Services: Evening hors d'oeuvres, homemade cookies, street parking

ACCOMMODATIONS

Units: 6 guest rooms, 2 larger than average
All Rooms: Private bath, balcony, fresh flowers, view of the Pacific Ocean or Mt. Tamalpais, soothing surf sounds
Some Rooms: Fireplace, fridge
Bed & Bath: Queens, shell-shaped sinks, 2-person soaking tub (1)

Favorites: Heron Room, w/ balcony over garden, ocean view, bright wall art, colorful duvet; Penthouse, w/ 2 balconies, Balinese carvings, huge bath w/ skylights, fridge, queen and single bed, ocean views

Comfort & Decor: Original art, rattan furniture, antiques, Mexican tile and carpet, colorful bedding

RATES, RESERVATIONS, & RESTRICTIONS

Deposit: 100% of bill in advance; must cancel 7 days in advance; $10 cancellation fee

Discounts: Long stays, single; extra person $20

Credit Cards: AE, MC, V

Check-In/Out: 4/11, late check-out on request

Smoking: No

Pets: No

Kids: Welcome in Garden Room on ground floor

Minimum Stay: 2 nights on weekends, 3 on holiday weekends

Open: All year

Host: Rick Klein
P.O. Box 238
37 Belvedere Ave.
Stinson Beach, CA 94970
(415) 868-2124
(800) 552-2124
Fax: (415) 868-2305
www.stinsonbeach.com
inn@stinsonbeach.com

Zone 5
Central Coast

From Santa Cruz following Highways 1 and 101 south to Ventura, Ojai, and Santa Paula.

Cities and Towns Davenport, Santa Cruz, Soquel, Aptos, Capitola, Salinas, Monterey, Pacific Grove, Carmel, Paso Robles, San Louis Obispo, Cambria, Baywood Park, Los Alamos, Solvang, Ballard, Santa Barbara, Carpinteria, Summerland, Ojai, Santa Paula, Ventura.

Attractions Redwoods, whales, beaches, vineyards, and missions; **Santa Cruz Boardwalk**, with a 1924 wooden roller coaster, carousel, and municipal wharf; the esplanade and beach at **Capitola**; tours of **Elkhorn Slough** wildlife reserve on a pontoon boat; **Monterey** and its historic adobe buildings; **Monterey Bay Aquarium**, the world's best; **Cannery Row**, ticky-tacky souvenirs in a beautiful, historic setting; **Seventeen-Mile Drive**, with **Cypress Point** (still breathtaking after millions of photos) and four of the world's most beautiful golf courses—**Spanish Bay**, **Poppy Hills**, **Spyglass Hill**, and **Pebble Beach;** the John Steinbeck museum in **Salinas**; monarch butterflies in quiet **Pacific Grove**; cute **Carmel**, with no addresses, a fantastic beach, Doris Day, Kim Novak, and Clint Eastwood; the haunting **Big Sur** coast, with sea lions, otters, whales, millions of shore birds, and best of all, the beachfront trails along the beaches and cliffs, with a backdrop of towering redwoods; **Hearst Castle**; 11 of Father Serra's **missions,** which stretch from Santa Cruz to Ventura; the hot new wine regions of **Santa Cruz, Paso Robles**, and **Santa Barbara**; horseback riding on **Pismo Beach**; eating pastries and browsing the shops of quaint **Solvang**, home of all things Danish; the marvelous semitropical weather in **Santa Barbara**, great for shopping, outdoor dining, art gallery hopping, wharves, beaches, and ocean cruises for fishing, diving, and whale-watching; the **Channel Islands**, California as it was 400 years ago; beautiful **Ojai Valley**, home of artists, New Agers, exclusive health spas, and the endangered **California condor**, the world's largest bird.

Contact Information Santa Cruz County Conference and Visitors Council, (800) 833-3494 (www.scccvc.org); Elkhorn Slough Safari, (831) 633-5555 (www.monterey-bay.net/elkhornslough); Monterey Peninsula Visitors and Convention Bureau, (831) 649-1770; National Steinbeck Center, (831) 753-6411; Pacific Grove Chamber of Commerce, (831) 373-3304; Point Lobos State Reserve, (831) 624-4909; Hearst Castle reservations, (800) 444-4445 (www.cambria-online.com); San Louis Obispo Visitors Center, (805) 781-2777; Pismo Beach Chamber of Commerce, (805) 773-4382 (www.pismobeach.org); Paso Robles Vintners and Growers Association, (800) 549-WINE (www.pasowine.com); Santa Barbara County Vintners Association, (800) 218-0881; Solvang Conference and Visitors Bureau, (800) 688-6144 (www.solvangusa.com); Santa Barbara Municipal Airport, (805) 967-7111; Santa Barbara Amtrak, (805) 963-1015; Santa Barbara Visitor Information Center, (800) 927-4688, (www.santabarbara-ca.com); Ojai Valley Chamber of Commerce, (805) 646-2094 (www.the-ojai.org); Ventura Visitors and Convention Bureau, (800) 333-2989 (www.ventura-usa.com); Channel Islands National Park Headquarters, (805) 658-5700, or Island Packers (for transportation to islands) (805) 642-7688.

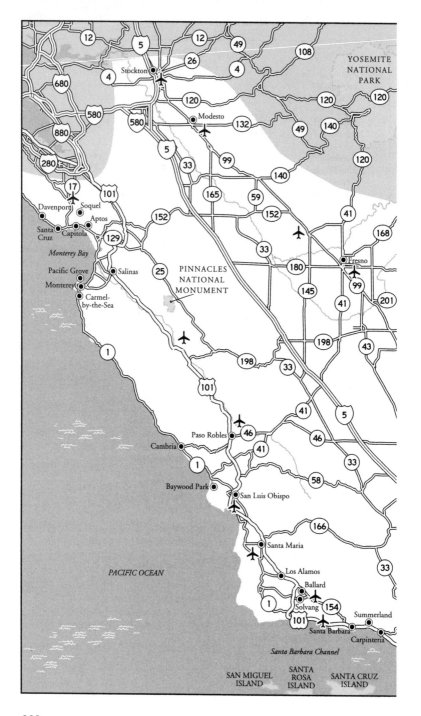

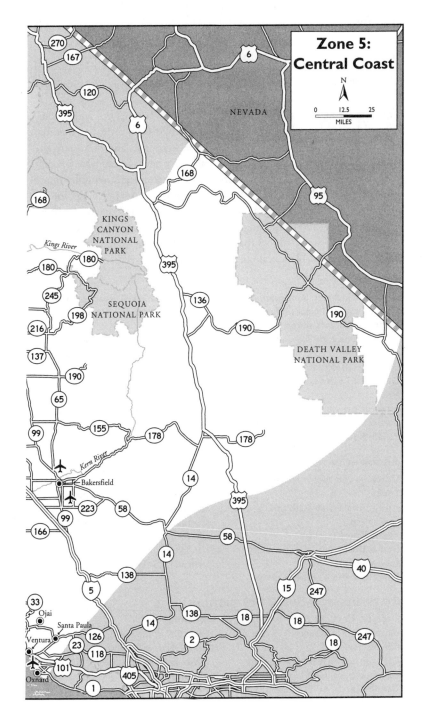

Zone 5:
Central Coast

N

0   12.5   25
MILES

NEVADA

KINGS
CANYON
NATIONAL
PARK

Kings River

SEQUOIA
NATIONAL PARK

DEATH VALLEY
NATIONAL PARK

Kern River

Bakersfield

Ojai

Santa Paula

Ventura

Oxnard

APPLE LANE INN, Aptos

Overall: ★★★★	Room Quality: B	Value: B	Price: $100–$180

This interesting four-story house is essentially a working farm with a commercial bearded iris business and all manner of farm animals clucking, quacking, mooing, and neighing in the background. The three-acre site looks like kid heaven, although there's really only one room suitable for children. Breakfast here is hearty country fare; very fresh eggs naturally figure into the main dish. The 1870s Victorian farmhouse has five guest rooms, one of which is literally the wine cellar—spacious, attractive, rather dim, deliciously cool, and containing, no surprise, neatly stored bottles of wine. This room has double doors that open onto the bright green rolling hills outside and is available for families with children or a well-behaved pet.

SETTING & FACILITIES

Location: In Aptos, 5 mi. south of Santa Cruz, just 4 blocks off Hwy. 1
Near: Restaurants, shopping, wineries, galleries, state parks, ocean beaches, spas
Building: 1870 Victorian farmhouse
Grounds: 3 acres of landscaped grounds and gardens, brick patio, apple orchards, gazebo, redwoods, commercial iris farm, barn and animal pens
Public Space: Parlor, veranda

Food & Drink: Full breakfast served at 9 a.m. in the parlor or on trays in garden
Recreation: Horseshoes, croquet on premises; nearby biking, horseback riding, golf
Amenities & Services: Homemade cookies and aperitif in parlor, private parking, concierge services for reservations, massage avail. by arrangement

ACCOMMODATIONS

Units: 5 guest rooms, including 2 suites
All Rooms: Private bath and reading area
Some Rooms: Fridge
Bed & Bath: Queens (3), double(s), roll-aways avail.
Favorites: Wine cellar, w/ private

garden entrance, old wine-making equipment, fridge, TV, coffeemaker, stained-glass window
Comfort & Decor: Rooms individually decorated w/ family antiques, Victorian fixtures, stained glass, views of the farm and meadow

RATES, RESERVATIONS, & RESTRICTIONS

Deposit: Check or credit card; must cancel 7 days in advance; $15 cancellation fee per day
Discounts: Off-season rates; extra person, crib, or dog $25
Credit Cards: AE, D, MC, V
Check-In/Out: 3/11

Smoking: No
Pets: OK in wine cellar
Kids: OK in wine cellar
No-Nos: N/A
Minimum Stay: 2 nights on weekends and holidays

Open: All year
Hosts: Diana and Doug Groom, owners; Lori Hamilton, mgr.
6265 Soquel Dr.
Aptos, CA 95003
(831) 475-6868

(800) 649-8988
Fax: (831) 464-5790
www.applelaneinn.com
ali@cruzio.com

BAYVIEW B&B INN, Aptos

Overall: ★★★★	Room Quality: B	Value: B	Price: $90–$160

A three-story Victorian built in 1878 for lodging during the Santa Cruz logging boom, this is the oldest hotel on Monterey Bay. It's located right in the heart of Aptos, an attractive little town with good restaurants, shops, and nearby beaches and redwoods. A restaurant occupies half of the inn's first floor, and the B&B's small, pretty parlor, with red velvet couches around a crackling fireplace and a dining room for guests, occupies the other half. The 11 guest rooms on the second and third floors have been completely renovated in comfortable, quietly tasteful decor that combines nice antiques, great beds, and good local art.

SETTING & FACILITIES

Location: From Hwy. 1, take Rio Del Mar exit to Soquel Dr.
Near: Restaurants, wineries, shopping, antiques, beaches
Building: 3-story 1878 Italianate Victorian w/ period furniture and 14-ft. ceilings
Grounds: Landscaped urban lot w/ edible flower and herb garden, 100-year-old rose tree

Public Space: Parlor, DR w/ fireplace
Food & Drink: Expanded cont'l breakfast served 8–9:30 in the Vintage Room by the fireplace, or on trays in room, full restaurant and bar on premise
Recreation: Biking, horseback riding trails in the redwoods
Amenities & Services: Sherry and fresh fruit always avail. in upstairs guest area, private parking

ACCOMMODATIONS

Units: 11 guest rooms, 4 larger than average, including 1 suite
All Rooms: Private bath, phone w/ modem capacity
Some Rooms: Fireplace, sleeper sofa, soaking tub, sitting area, TV/VCR, extra bed (2)
Bed & Bath: Queens, kings (2)
Favorites: Cascade Room, w/ antique

walnut bed, sitting area, garden views; Seacliff Room, w/ fireplace, TV, Roman 2-person tub and glass-enclosed shower
Comfort & Decor: Rooms individually decorated w/ local art, original antiques, featherbeds, sheers, shades and drapes, carpet, tile bathrooms

RATES, RESERVATIONS, & RESTRICTIONS

Deposit: Credit card or personal check to hold; must cancel 10 days in advance
Discounts: Weekday business; extra person $20
Credit Cards: AE, MC, V
Check-In/Out: 3/11:30
Smoking: No
Pets: No
Kids: In 2 rooms
Minimum Stay: 2 nights on weekends

Open: All year
Hosts: Dan Floyd and Suzie Lankes, owners; Gwen Burkard, mgr.
8041 Soquel Dr.
Aptos, CA 95003
(831) 688-8654
(800) 422-9843
Fax: (831) 688-5128
www.bayviewhotel.com
lodging@bayviewhotel.com

MANGELS HOUSE, Aptos

Overall: ★★★★½	Room Quality: A	Value: B	Price: $125–$165

Looking like a movie setting for an Edith Wharton tale about a wealthy Victorian family, the dramatically imposing Mangels House sits on four acres of manicured lawn and English gardens, surrounded by the thousands of acres of redwoods, creeks, and trails in the Forest of Nisene Marks State Park. The house was built in the 1880s as the country home of Claus Mangels, who, with his brother-in-law Claus Spreckels, founded the sugar beet industry in California. It is a sensational house, with large, lovely rooms, high ceilings, redwood floors, a huge stone fireplace in the attractive sitting room, a small library, and a large, formal dining room. The six guest rooms are nicely decorated and furnished with a pleasing mix of antiques and folk art that gives them a contemporary feeling. All have private baths, although two of the baths are separate from the rooms. Breakfast is a major meal, served in the dining room and featuring such good things as apple pancakes, sausage, and homemade scones and spice cake.

SETTING & FACILITIES

Location: Hwy. 1 to State Park Dr. exit, east to Soquel Dr., right on Soquel Dr. to Aptos Creek Rd., left (north) to Mangels House, half-mile along
Near: Restaurants, shopping, musical and theatrical events, Monterey Bay, redwood forests, beaches, property borders 10,000-acre Forest of Nisene Marks State Park
Building: 1886 Italianate mansion
Grounds: 4 acres of lawns, formal gardens w/ fountain, gazebo, wrap-around porches w/ canopy swing, orchard, woodlands
Public Space: Sitting room w/ massive stone fireplace, library, game room
Food & Drink: Full breakfast served at 9 or 9:15 in DR
Recreation: Ping-Pong, darts, and croquet on premises; biking, tennis, golf, surfing, whale-watching, elephant seals, monarch butterflies
Amenities & Services: Evening sherry and shortbread, cold drinks in guest refrigerator, private parking

ACCOMMODATIONS

Units: 6 guest rooms, 4 larger than average
All Rooms: Private bath
Some Rooms: Fireplace, private porch, extra twin (2)
Bed & Bath: Queens, kings (2)
Favorites: Mauve Room, w/ carved marble fireplace, stenciled walls, sheer curtains w/ balloon valances, views of lawns and trees
Comfort & Decor: Rooms individually decorated w/ eclectic furniture, local pottery and art, African artifacts, bright fabrics, down comforters, stenciled walls, wallpaper, hardwood floors, rugs and carpet, views of orchard and gardens

RATES, RESERVATIONS, & RESTRICTIONS

Deposit: Credit card; must cancel 7 days in advance
Discounts: Long stays, weekday business of 3 days or more; extra person $20
Credit Cards: AE, MC, V
Check-In/Out: 3/11
Smoking: No
Pets: No, unless they can sleep outside or in owner's car
Kids: 12 and over
Minimum Stay: 2 nights on weekends
Open: Closed Dec. 23@-26
Hosts: Jacqueline and Ron Fisher
P.O. Box 302
570 Aptos Creek Rd.
Aptos, CA 95001
(831) 688-7982
(800) 320-7401
www.innaccess.com/mangels

BAYWOOD B&B INN, Baywood Park

Overall: ★★★★	Room Quality: B	Value: A	Price: $80–$160

Baywood is a charming small town on Morro Bay that's easily overlooked. The Baywood Inn is just right for anyone who wants peace and quiet by the water. Morro Bay is more like a lagoon than a bay, so you won't get crashing breakers right outside your door, but you can walk around the bay and be tumbling in the surf in just a few minutes. The contemporary Baywood Inn is an Art Deco, rather un-innish-looking inn with 15 oversized, bay-view rooms that have been thematically but tastefully decorated.

SETTING & FACILITIES

Location: On Morro Bay, in a predominantly residential neighborhood in the small town of Baywood Park, 10 mi. west of San Louis Obispo
Near: Restaurants, shopping, wineries, Montana de Oro State Park, Morro Bay Bird Sanctuary, Mission San Luis Obispo, Hearst Castle
Building: Contemporary 2-story building across from Morro Bay
Grounds: Double urban lot w/ landscaped grounds, flower beds, and lawns
Public Space: DR, mezzanine w/ view of bay
Food & Drink: Full breakfast served 7:30–9 a.m. in DR or guest room

Recreation: Biking, kayaking, canoeing, sailing, ocean fishing, picnicking, bird-watching
Amenities & Services: Evening wine, cheese, and hors d'oeuvres, hairdryers, private parking, 1 suite is disabled-accessible

ACCOMMODATIONS

Units: 15 rooms, including 10 suites
All Rooms: Private bath w/ tub/shower, private entrance, sitting area, fireplace, microwave, fridge, TV, radio, phone
Some Rooms: Suites have separate sleeping area, dining area, bay view, VCR
Bed & Bath: Queens, hairdryers
Favorites: Tex-Mex, w/ Southwest theme, 2-BR, 2-bath suite, w/ Mexican artifacts, tile fireplace, four-poster pine bed and armoire, bay-view sitting area; Avonlea, w/ English Country-style 2-BR, 2-bath suite, brass bed, bay view, sitting area
Comfort & Decor: Each room individually decorated to fit its theme

RATES, RESERVATIONS, & RESTRICTIONS

Deposit: 1st night's lodging; must cancel 5 days prior for full refund
Discounts: None; extra person $15
Credit Cards: MC, V
Check-In/Out: 2/noon
Smoking: No
Pets: No
Kids: OK, under 6 free
Minimum Stay: 2 nights on holiday weekends
Open: All year
Host: Suzanne McCollom
1370 Second St.
Baywood Park, CA 93402
(805) 528-8888
Fax: (805) 528-8887
www.baywoodinn.com
innkeeper@baywoodinn.com

BLUE WHALE INN, Cambria

| Overall: ★★★★½ | Room Quality: A | Value: B | Price: $190–$250 |

The Cape Cod–style Blue Whale Inn sits on the bluffs of the seaside village of Cambria, minutes away from Hearst Castle. The inn has six "mini-suites," each room designed by noted interior designer Mabel Shults in an elegant country style, with light pine furniture, carefully coordinated floral fabrics and wallpaper, plantation shutters, and gas fireplaces. The contemporary inn's front room and parlor area has six large picture windows offering a panoramic view of the Pacific Ocean just across the road. All the rooms have an outdoor entrance, so you can be entirely private if you desire. It would be a shame to miss the large country breakfast served in the dining room, however, or the afternoon wine and cheese or cookies and tea. Mingle a bit, for your tummy's sake.

SETTING & FACILITIES

Location: 11 mi. south of Hearst Castle, on the ocean 1 mi. northwest of downtown; take Windsor or Moonstone exits from Hwy. 1
Near: Restaurants, shopping, galleries, antiques, wine tasting, Moonstone Beach, Hearst Castle, whale- and elephant seal-watching

Location: 11 mi. south of Hearst Castle, on the ocean 1 mi. northwest of downtown; take Windsor or Moonstone exits from Hwy. 1
Near: Restaurants, shopping, galleries, antiques, wine tasting, Moonstone Beach, Hearst Castle, whale- and elephant seal–watching
Building: Contemporary Cape Cod–style house
Grounds: Urban lot, garden area w/ benches, pond, waterfall

Public Space: Common room w/ panoramic views, DR
Food & Drink: Full breakfast served 8:30–9:30 a.m. in DR, cont'l breakfast 7–8:30 a.m.
Recreation: Biking, fishing, whale-watching
Amenities & Services: Homemade cookies and cake and tea in afternoon; evening wine, cheese, and hors d'oeuvres; private parking, disabled access in all rooms

ACCOMMODATIONS

Units: 6 minisuites w/ large dressing areas
All Rooms: Private bath and entrance, cable TV, phone, fireplace, canopy bed, fridge
Some Rooms: Four-poster
Bed & Bath: Kings, queens (2)
Favorites: Nos. 1 and 3, w/ canopy

beds, large soaking tubs
Comfort & Decor: Rooms individually decorated w/ French and English fabrics, Waverly floral wallpapers, armoires, writing desks, tiled bath rooms w/ garden windows, partial view of ocean

RATES, RESERVATIONS, & RESTRICTIONS

Deposit: 50% of bill or first night; must cancel 10 days in advance; $15 cancellation fee
Discounts: None; extra person $40
Credit Cards: MC, V
Check-In/Out: 2/11, late check-out by arrangement
Smoking: No
Pets: No
Kids: Not suitable

Minimum Stay: 2 nights on weekends, 3 on some holidays
Open: All year
Hosts: Richard Merenda and Mary Lou Lookavill
6736 Moonstone Beach Dr.
Cambria, CA 93428
(805) 927-4647
www.bluewhaleinn.com

OLALLIEBERRY INN, Cambria

Overall: ★★★★	Room Quality: B	Value: B	Price: $90–$185

Traditional B&B lovers will be very happy to make the Olallieberry Inn their home base. On the banks of Santa Rosa Creek, with three wonderful gardens, the inn originated as a home built in 1873 and is one of the oldest buildings in town. It has been fully restored, with lots of lace curtains and pretty wallpapers, and six rooms have fireplaces. Innkeepers Peter and Carol Ann Irsfeld take food seriously, offering fresh juice squeezed daily, freshly roasted coffee, and home-baked breads, muffins, and cookies.

Evening hors d'oeuvres may include baked Brie in puff pastry or goat cheese and roasted garlic with foccacia bread.

SETTING & FACILITIES

Location: 12 mi. south of Hearst Castle, 1.5 blocks outside East Village part of town
Near: Restaurants, shopping, galleries, wine tasting, Hearst Castle, beaches
Building: 1873 restored Greek Revival-style Victorian, registered historic home; main house has 6 guest rooms, newer cottage has 3 guest rooms
Grounds: 1/3 acre w/ flower and herb gardens, Santa Rosa creek, 114-year-old redwood in front
Public Space: Parlor, gathering room, deck of gathering room overlooks backyard and creek
Food & Drink: Full breakfast served at 8 or 9:15 a.m. in the gathering room
Recreation: Biking, tide pooling; bird-, elephant seal-, and whale-watching; fishing, kayaking, tennis, golf
Amenities & Services: Endless supply of home-baked cookies, 5 p.m. tasting of 3 local wines and hot hors d'oeuvres, fresh flowers, private parking, disabled access, assistance w/ dining reservations and activities

ACCOMMODATIONS

Units: 9 guest rooms, including 1 suite
All Rooms: Private bath
Some Rooms: Fireplace (6), sleeper sofa (1)
Bed & Bath: Queens and kings, some sunken or claw-foot tubs
Favorites: Creekside Suite, w/ fireplace, sitting room sofa, floral canopy king bed in its own alcove, balcony overlooking creek, dressing room; Sunrise, upstairs room w/ view of creek and pastures, fireplace
Comfort & Decor: Rooms individually decorated w/ period antiques, wall coverings, views of garden, creek, and pastures

RATES, RESERVATIONS, & RESTRICTIONS

Deposit: Credit card, prepay 7 days in advance; must cancel 7 days in advance
Discounts: Seniors (60 and over), travel agents; extra person $20
Credit Cards: AE, MC, V
Check-In/Out: 3/11
Smoking: No
Pets: No
Kids: Not suitable
No-Nos: No more than 2 guests per room except in Creekside suite
Minimum Stay: 2 nights on holiday weekends
Open: Closed approx. Jan. 1–17
Hosts: Peter and Carol Ann Irsfeld
2476 Main St.
Cambria, CA 93428
(805) 927-3222
(888) 927-3222
Fax: (805) 927-0202
www.olallieberry.com
olallieinn@thegrid.net

J. PATRICK HOUSE, Cambria

Overall: ★★★★	Room Quality: B	Value: B	Price: $125–$180

The J. Patrick House, named for a previous owner's father, is actually two houses, one of them a charming log home that contains the inn's public rooms as well as the largest of the eight guest rooms. The others are in the two-story cedar carriage house behind the garden and arbor. All are decorated in a tasteful country style, and all have wood-burning fireplaces and private baths. The interiors feature lots of knotty pine, contrasting nicely with delicately patterned wallpaper and a mix of antiques and comfortable contemporary furniture. Breakfast, which includes lots of fresh fruit and tasty vegetarian entrées, is served in the pretty Garden Room, overlooking, naturally, a garden.

SETTING & FACILITIES

Location: 6 mi. south of Hearst Castle on the southeast edge of the town of Cambria
Near: Restaurants, shopping, wine tasting, Hearst Castle, beaches, golf courses
Building: 1980 log home w/ adjacent carriage house
Grounds: Quarter-acre w/ Monterey pines and redwood trees, country garden w/ fountains and birdbaths
Public Space: Gathering room in main log home and lounge in carriage house, covered deck, gardens
Food & Drink: Full breakfast served 8–9:30 a.m. in the Garden Room
Recreation: Biking, tide pooling; bird-, elephant seal-, and whale-watching; fishing, kayaking, tennis, golf
Amenities & Services: Evening wine and hors d'oeuvres, chocolate chip cookies; fridge in lounge stocked w/ soft drinks, water, juice; private parking, assistance w/ planning activities, in-room massages avail.

ACCOMMODATIONS

Units: 8 guest rooms, all larger than average, 1 minisuite; guests who stay in the main house have the entire log home to themselves in the evening and night hours
All Rooms: Private bath, window seat
Some Rooms: Four-poster, fireplaces (7)
Bed & Bath: Queens, king, rubber duckies
Favorites: Clare, the only room in the main house, w/ views of forest and gardens, wood-burning fireplace, brass and white iron headboard on king bed; Kilkenny, w/ walnut chair rails, wood-burning fireplace w/ walnut mantel and surround, willow rocking chair, turn-of-the-century iron bed
Comfort & Decor: Rooms individually decorated w/ furniture from the 1840 rope bed to new custom-made four-posters, all custom window treatments, wallpaper, wood paneling, carpet, wood ceilings w/ crown molding, custom bedding

RATES, RESERVATIONS, & RESTRICTIONS

Deposit: 100% of bill; must cancel 7 days in advance; $20 cancellation fee
Discounts: Midweek winter specials; extra person $20
Credit Cards: AE, D, MC, V
Check-In/Out: 3/11, late check-out by request
Smoking: No
Pets: No
Kids: In Clare only
Minimum Stay: 2 nights on weekends
Open: All year
Hosts: Barbara and Melvin Schwimmer
2990 Burton Dr.
Cambria, CA 93428
(805) 927-3812
(800) 341-5258
Fax: (805) 927-6759
www.jpatrickhouse.com
jph@j patrickhouse.com

SQUIBB HOUSE, Cambria

Overall: ★★★★	Room Quality: B	Value: B	Price: $95–$155

This adorable, pale yellow Gothic Victorian house with the blooming cottage garden is as perfect as owner and renovator Bruce Black could make it. Many of the home's original fixtures were rebuilt and restored, and the house also contains handmade furniture from Amish Victorian plans. The five smallish guest rooms are simple, with pine floors, patchwork quilts, fine white curtains blowing in the breeze, and the barest touch of ornamentation in the form of dried flower wreaths—in a word, perfect. Breakfast here consists of fruit and fresh, warm bread and pastries from a nearby bakery, served in your room or the parlor. Black also established The House Next Door, a 100-year-old former carpentry shop that sells Amish furniture, antiques, and crafts by local artisans. The inn is in the heart of Cambria, close to shops and restaurants. Cambria Beach is about a mile away, and Hearst Castle about ten miles.

SETTING & FACILITIES

Location: Halfway between San Francisco and Los Angeles
Near: Restaurants, shopping, wineries, Big Sur, Hearst Castle, beaches, wineries
Building: 1877 Victorian w/ 1885 gift and antique shop, restored
Grounds: 3 urban lots, historic gardens w/ 100-year-old plants
Public Space: Sitting room, porch, gardens, gazebo
Food & Drink: Expanded cont'l breakfast served in sitting room or delivered to room 8–9:30 a.m.
Recreation: Biking, kayaking, whale-watching
Amenities & Services: Down comforters, quilts, complimentary wine tasting plus coffee, tea, beverages, and cookies across from inn at Fermentations 4–9 p.m., private off-street parking, assistance w/ restaurant reservations

ACCOMMODATIONS

Units: 5 guest rooms
All Rooms: Private bath, ornamental gas firestove, custom-built period furniture, view of gardens, hills, and village
Bed & Bath: Queens, claw-foot tub/shower (1)
Favorites: Village Room, w/ queen bed w/ patchwork quilt, wooden washstand, wicker furniture, view of Burton St.
Comfort & Decor: Rooms individually decorated w/ handbuilt furnishings, original fir floors w/ hand-rubbed finishes, quilts

RATES, RESERVATIONS, & RESTRICTIONS

Deposit: Credit card; must cancel 7 days in advance; cancellation fee $20
Discounts: Winter midweek specials
Credit Cards: MC, V
Check-In/Out: 3/11
Smoking: No
Pets: No
Kids: Not suitable

No-Nos: No more than 2 guests per room
Minimum Stay: 2 nights on weekends and holidays
Open: All year
Hosts: Bruce Black, owner; Martha and Lynn, innkeepers

4063 Burton Dr.
Cambria, CA 93428
(805) 927-9600
Fax: (805) 927-9606
www.cambria-online/thesquibbhous
    andshopnextdoor

INN AT DEPOT HILL, Capitola

Overall: ★★★★★   Room Quality: A   Value: B   Price: $190–$275

The pick of the Santa Cruz area is this stunning inn in a turn-of-the-century Capitola railroad depot. While most B&B owners claim that their rooms are individually decorated, these folks mean it. Each room is quite unique, featuring designs based on different areas of the world. Choose your vacation spot: there's the Delft Room, the Paris Room, the Côte d'Azur, the Portofino, the Stratford-on-Avon, and the Railroad Baron's Room—the latter a re-creation of a luxurious private Pullman car, with royal red fabrics of damask and silk and overstuffed red velvet chairs. All of the rooms have fireplaces, fresh flowers, and marble bathrooms, and many have private patios and outdoor whirlpool tubs. Breakfast may include entrées such as artichoke stratta or cheese soufflé with pesto sauce, plus there's wine and cheese in the afternoon and dessert in the evening.

SETTING & FACILITIES

Location: In the seaside resort town of Capitola-by-the-Sea, on a hill 2 blocks north of the beach
Near: Restaurants, shopping, wineries, antiques, beaches, redwoods
Building: 1901 railroad depot converted, enlarged, and renovated in 1990
Grounds: Urban lot w/ herringbone brick patio w/ roses, azaleas, ferns, reflecting pond, pergola
Public Space: Parlor/library, DR w/ 16-ft. ceilings, fireplace, antique piano,
private hot tub area
Food & Drink: Full breakfast served 8–10 a.m. in DR, patio, or guest room
Recreation: Biking, tennis, golf
Amenities & Services: Hot tub, afternoon snacks, evening sherry, wine and hors d'oeuvres, evening desserts, bathrobes, hairdryers, coffeemakers, clothes steamers, fresh flowers, evening turn-down service, private parking, disabled access, computer data ports in rooms, 24-hour service avail.

ACCOMMODATIONS

Units: 12 guest rooms, including 6 suites
All Rooms: Private bath, fireplace, cable TV/VCR, phone, writing desk, built-in stereo system, featherbed
Some Rooms: Bed drapes, fridge,
private entrance, private patio w/ hot tub, AC, extra twin (1)
Bed & Bath: Queens, kings (2, 1 converts to 2 twins), outdoor Jacuzzi tubs for 2 (5)

Favorites: Paris Room, w/ black-and-white toile upholstery, French lace curtains, black-and-white marble bathroom, featherbed and European linens, fireplace, Louis XVI lamps, French doors to garden; Côte d'Azur, w/ Mediterranean tiled floors, chintz-draped iron bed, semiprivate patio, private outdoor whirlpool tub

Comfort & Decor: Rooms individually decorated w/ award-winning designs, representing different parts of the world, private entrances and gardens, special wall coverings appropriate to room theme, lace curtains, drapes, fireplaces, sitting areas, fresh flowers

RATES, RESERVATIONS, & RESTRICTIONS

Deposit: 100% of bill; must cancel 10 days in advance
Discounts: Discount for volume
Credit Cards: AE, D, MC, V
Check-In/Out: 3/11:30
Smoking: No
Pets: No
Kids: By arrangement
No-Nos: No more than 2 guests per room
Minimum Stay: 2 nights on weekends

Open: All year
Hosts: Suzie Lankes and Dan Floyd
1934 Capitola-by-the-Sea
250 Monterey Ave.
Capitola, CA 95010
(831) 462-3376
(800) 572-2632
Fax: (831) 462-3697
www.innatdepothill.com
lodging@innatdepothill.com

GREEN LANTERN INN, Carmel-by-the-Sea

Overall: ★★★½	Room Quality: B	Value: A	Price: $85–$195

This inn is a real gem, particularly for families. The 18 guest rooms range in size, and some are quite "cozy" (B&B vernacular for "small"), but all are clean and neat, with fresh paint or nice wallpaper and pretty furnishings and fabrics. There are iron beds, four-posters, quilts, and all the bells and whistles you find in other Carmel B&Bs, usually for considerably higher prices. The two family units sleep five in existing beds and have wood-burning fireplaces, fridges, and TVs. An expanded continental breakfast served in the main building features fresh fruit, yogurt, cereals, bagels, and fresh pastries.

SETTING & FACILITIES

Location: In central Carmel on Casanova St. at 7th Ave.
Near: Restaurants, shopping, galleries, ocean, Carmel Mission, Monterey Bay Aquarium, Point Lobos State Park
Building: A collection of rustic cottages built in 1925, renovated in 1993
Grounds: Half-acre landscaped and terraced gardens w/ flowers, trees, and 3 patios

Public Space: Fireside Room, patios
Food & Drink: Expanded cont'l breakfast, served in Fireside Room 8–10:30 a.m.
Recreation: Biking, horseback riding, kayaking, whale- and bird-watching, tennis, golf
Amenities & Services: Afternoon cheese and wine; assistance w/ reservations

ACCOMMODATIONS

Units: 18 guest rooms, including 2 family units

All Rooms: TV, fridge, phone, private bath and entrance

Some Rooms: Fireplace, sleeper sofa, private patio, extra bed (4)

Bed & Bath: Queens (14), doubles (2), king (2)

Favorites: Cedar, w/ queen bed, wallpaper, private Carmel stone patio;

Cypress, a fireplace suite w/ a loft, 2 queen beds, soaring wood ceilings; Magnolia, a large 1930s-style suite w/ fireplace, queen sleigh bed, sitting area w/ sofa

Comfort & Decor: Individually decorated w/ wood-burning fireplaces, wallpaper, gabled and beamed ceilings, drapes, quilts, carpets, garden views

RATES, RESERVATIONS, & RESTRICTIONS

Deposit: Credit card

Discounts: None; extra person $10, prices rise during holidays and special events

Credit Cards: All

Check-In/Out: 3/11

Smoking: No

Pets: No

Kids: OK

Minimum Stay: 2 nights on weekends

Open: All year

Host: Kathy Matthews
P.O. Box 1114
7th and Casanova
Carmel-by-the-Sea, CA 93921
(831) 624-4392
(888) 414-4392
Fax: (831) 624-9591
www.greenlanterninn.com
info@greenlanterninn.com

HAPPY LANDING INN, Carmel-by-the-Sea

Overall: ★★★½	Room Quality: B	Value: B	Price: $90–$165

This is a Hugh Comstock-designed complex, or, in other words, it's cute in a distinctly Carmel-cottage way. Built in 1925 as a summer retreat for a San Francisco family, the inn shows its age in spots, but overriding the signs of wear and tear are nice touches such as cathedral ceilings, hand-painted birds and flowers on the walls, and stained glass windows. The inn's two suites are spacious, with separate bedrooms and wet bars. Other guest rooms range in size, and some are on the small side, but all open out onto the courtyard. When you're ready for breakfast in the morning, you just raise your shade and, presto, you have fruit and freshly baked sweet cake, quiche, or gingerbread with lemon sauce delivered to your door. Afternoon tea is served in the large, lovely sitting room by a great stone fireplace. Shops are a hop and a skip away, and the beach is just four blocks.

SETTING & FACILITIES

Location: In central Carmel on Monteverde between 5th and 6th Aves., 4 blocks from beach

Near: Shopping, restaurants, beach,

Carmel Mission, Point Lobos State Park, Seventeen-Mile Dr., Monterey Bay Aquarium

Building: Architect-designed 1925 summer home, restored
Grounds: Urban lot w/ garden courtyard, gazebo, frog pond and fountain, stone gnomes
Public Space: Sitting room w/ stone fireplace

Food & Drink: Extended cont'l breakfast delivered to room 8:30–10 a.m.
Recreation: Golf, biking, wine tasting
Amenities & Services: Afternoon tea in sitting room, sherry in guest room, private parking, concierge services for reservations

ACCOMMODATIONS

Units: 7 guest rooms, including 2 suites, back cottage
All Rooms: Private bath and entrance, TV, view of garden
Some Rooms: Fireplace, fridge
Bed & Bath: Queens, kings (2), double
Favorites: Suite No. 4, w/ LR, fireplace, BR w/ king bed, view of courtyard, hand-painted ceiling designs of birds,

stained-glass, tub/shower
Comfort & Decor: Rooms individually decorated w/ antiques, brass beds, curved arched doors; hand-painted ceiling designs of flowers, birds, and vines; hand-painted sinks, floral wallpaper, stained-glass windows, wicker, pine furnishings

RATES, RESERVATIONS, & RESTRICTIONS

Deposit: Credit card; must cancel 72 hours in advance
Discounts: Winter weekday specials
Credit Cards: MC, V
Check-In/Out: 2/11
Smoking: No
Pets: No
Kids: 12 and over
No-Nos: No more than 2 guests per room
Minimum Stay: 2 nights on week-

ends, 3 on holiday weekends and special occasions
Open: All year
Hosts: Dick Stewart, owner; Robert Ballard, mgr.
P.O. Box 2619
Monte Verde St. (between 5th and 6th Aves.)
Carmel-by-the-Sea, CA 93921
(831) 624-7917

SAN ANTONIO HOUSE, Carmel-by-the Sea

Overall: ★★★★	Room Quality: B	Value: B	Price: $160–$225

A few blocks from the beach, on a quiet residential street that's near the heart of Carmel shopping, the cottage-like San Antonio House sits prettily on a lawn and garden-covered site. Its five guest rooms are moderately sized, but all are attractively decorated and self-contained, with gas fireplaces, fridges, and private baths. To ensure that you never have to come out of your room if you don't want to, a breakfast of fresh fruits, hot pastries, juice, and coffee is delivered to your door in the morning. San Antonio House recently changed ownership, but the same quality of service is anticipated.

SETTING & FACILITIES

Location: In central Carmel on San Antonio between Ocean and 7th Ave., 1 block from the beach and 3 blocks from the business district
Near: Restaurants, shopping, museums, galleries, wineries, ocean beaches, Pebble Beach, Seventeen-Mile Dr., Monterey Bay Aquarium
Building: 1920s wood-shingled 2-story Victorian home, carriage house
Grounds: Double lot landscaped w/ flower gardens, trellises, lawn

Public Space: Gardens, stone patio
Food & Drink: Extended cont'l breakfast delivered to guests' rooms at 8 weekdays, at guests' convenience on weekends
Recreation: Biking, horseback riding, surfing, diving, fishing, swimming, tennis, golf
Amenities & Services: concierge services for restaurants, horseback riding, tours

ACCOMMODATIONS

Units: 5 guest rooms
All Rooms: Private bath, gas fireplace, cable TV, phone w/ modem line, coffeemaker
Some Rooms: Extra twins (1)
Bed & Bath: Queens
Favorites: Patio Suite, w/ separate

sitting area, private stone patio; Treetops, very private, over carriage house, garden view
Comfort & Decor: Rooms individually decorated w/ antiques, wood paneling, custom fabrics, lace accents, original art

RATES, RESERVATIONS, & RESTRICTIONS

Deposit: 1st night's lodging; must cancel 7 days in advance; $15 cancellation fee
Discounts: None; extra person $20
Credit Cards: AE, MC, V
Check-In/Out: 4/11, noon by arrangement
Smoking: No
Pets: Small (under 20 lbs.), $25 fee
Kids: 12 and over
Minimum Stay: 2 nights on week-

ends; special events and holidays may vary
Open: All year
Hosts: Ross Farley, owner; Melvin Mendez, mgr.
P.O. Box 6226
San Antonio between Ocean and 7th
Carmel-by-the-Sea, CA 93921
(831) 624-4334
Fax: (831) 624-4935

SANDPIPER INN BY THE SEA, Carmel-by-the-Sea

Overall: ★★★★	Room Quality: B	Value: B	Price: $95–$285

The Sandpiper looks like some lucky person's handsome California-style hacienda in a well-to-do residential area of Carmel away from the tourists, so it is surprising to learn that it was actually built as an inn in 1929. It's very close to the beach, and in a great area for walking along a scenic road that follows the curve of Carmel Bay. Most of the guest rooms are in the main house, plus there are cottage rooms behind the inn. All have comfortable beds and private baths, some have fireplaces, and some have ocean views. The inn was recently purchased by Andrew and Beth Lewis, who are gradually renovating it and sprucing it up. With a little TLC, it will easily be one of the nicest in Carmel.

SETTING & FACILITIES

Location: In a residential neighborhood at the south end of Carmel, at corner of Bay View and Martin Way, half-block from Carmel Beach
Near: Restaurants, shopping, galleries, 100 yards from Pacific Ocean, Carmel Mission, Monterey Bay Aquarium, Point Lobos State Park, Pebble Beach, Big Sur
Building: 1929 early California Ranch, stucco and plaster
Grounds: Landscaped gardens, 2 patios, terrace
Public Space: Lounge w/ fireplace and beamed ceilings, library
Food & Drink: Extended cont'l breakfast buffet, served 8–10 a.m. in the lounge, on trays in room, or on patio
Recreation: Biking, horseback riding, kayaking, whale- and bird-watching, tennis, golf
Amenities & Services: Afternoon sherry, tea, and cookies, access to kitchen refrigerator, cocoa, tea, spiced cider always avail., fresh flowers; on- and off-street parking, assistance w/ dinner reservations and activity plans

ACCOMMODATIONS

Units: 16 guest rooms, 4 larger than average, 3 cottage rooms
All Rooms: Private bath
Some Rooms: Fireplace, four-poster, sleeper sofa, ocean view, extra bed (3)
Bed & Bath: Kings, queens (6)
Favorites: Room 1, w/ king four-poster, corner fireplace, sitting area, view of garden; Room 11, w/ king four-poster, wing chairs, plantation shutters, view of beach and ocean, semiprivate entrance
Comfort & Decor: Original paintings, country antiques and contemporary furniture, shutters, drapes, carpets

RATES, RESERVATIONS, & RESTRICTIONS

Deposit: 100% of 1- or 2-night stays, 2 nights for longer visit; must cancel 7 days in advance, 14 for holidays and special events; $10 cancellation fee
Discounts: Long stays, winter specials; extra person $20
Credit Cards: AE, D, MC, V
Check-In/Out: 3/noon
Smoking: No
Pets: No
Kids: 12 and over
Minimum Stay: 2 nights on weekends, 3 on holiday weekends or for special events
Open: All year
Hosts: Andrew and Beth Lewis, owners; Audie Housman, innkeeper
2408 Bay View Ave.
Carmel-by-the-Sea, CA 93923
(831) 624-6433
(800) 633-6433
Fax: (831) 624-7148
www.sandpiper-inn.com
sandpiper-inn@redshift.com

SEA VIEW INN, Carmel-by-the-Sea

Overall: ★★★★	Room Quality: B	Value: B	Price: $90–$165

Local lore has it that world-famous architect Bernard Maybeck had a hand in the design of this three-story, 1910 Victorian-style cottage. Certainly one of the prettiest B&Bs in Carmel, the Sea View (its sea view now obscured by trees) is located in a quiet residential area of Carmel, a short walk from the village, with its shops and restaurants, and even closer to one of the best beaches in the state. The inn is beautifully maintained, and the decor throughout comprises a mix of nice antiques and comfortable contemporary furniture, great fabrics and rugs, and original art. The spacious living and dining rooms areas have beamed ceilings, wainscoting, and brick fireplaces, and the brick patio in back and the furnished porch in front are flower-filled.

SETTING & FACILITIES

Location: In a residential neighborhood on Camino Real between 11th and 12th, 3 blocks from Carmel Beach, half-mile south of downtown
Near: Restaurants, shopping, galleries, ocean beaches, Carmel Mission, Monterey Bay Aquarium, Point Lobos, Pebble Beach, Seventeen-Mile Dr.
Building: 1910 3-story Victorian, has been an inn for over 75 years
Grounds: Urban lot w/ trees and large redwood, secluded garden in rear
Public Space: Front room w/ connecting DR w/ fireplaces, flower-filled porch w/ chaise lounges
Food & Drink: Expanded cont'l breakfast served 9–10 a.m. in front room and DR, coffee and tea avail. from 8:15 a.m.
Recreation: Biking, horseback riding, kayaking, canoeing, whale- and bird-watching, tennis, golf
Amenities & Services: Afternoon tea and coffee; evening sherry, wine, and hors d'oeuvres; beach towels, street parking, phone avail. for guest use, concierge services for reservations, directions, fax

ACCOMMODATIONS

Units: 8 guest rooms, 3 larger than average
Some Rooms: Four-poster canopy bed (1), extra twin (1), private bath (6), shared bath (2)
Bed & Bath: Queens, king
Favorites: Room 7, w/ queen canopy bed, sitting area, window seat w/ garden views; Room 8, w/ brass bed, sitting area, window seat w/ view of neighboring gardens
Comfort & Decor: Newly redecorated in 1999 in an eclectic mix of antiques and comfortable furniture, shutters, oriental rugs over hardwood floors, some carpet, original art

RATES, RESERVATIONS, & RESTRICTIONS

Deposit: 1st and last night's deposit in advance; must cancel 7 days in advance
Discounts: Weekdays Nov.–March; $15 for 3rd person in only room that accommodates 3
Credit Cards: AE, MC, V

Check-In/Out: 2/11:30, late check-out by arrangement
Smoking: No
Pets: No
Kids: 12 and over
No-Nos: No more than 2 guests per room in 7 rooms
Minimum Stay: 3 nights on holiday weekends

Open: Closed Dec. 24–26 and 1 week in early Jan.
Hosts: Marshall and Diane Hydorn, owners; Margo Thomas, mgr.
P.O. Box 4138
Camino Real between 11th & 12th Sts.
Carmel-by-the-Sea, CA 93921
(831) 624-8778
Fax: (831) 625-5901

STONEHOUSE INN, Carmel-by-the-Sea

Overall: ★★★★	Room Quality: B	Value: B	Price: $110–$199

The outside of this Arts and Crafts house, with its walls of stone hand-shaped by local Native Americans, is so attractive that you will enjoy just looking at it when you arrive. Notables such as Jack London, Sinclair Lewis, and Lotta Crabtree were guests here in earlier days, when Carmel was an artist's colony. But while whispers of bohemian days and nights echo in the large, warm living room, with its great stone fireplace, the guest rooms, with their genteelly pretty antiques, quilts, and teddy bears, cater more to today's B&B fans. Five of the seven guest rooms share two baths, but returning guests don't seem to mind. Breakfast often includes cheese omelets, orange French toast, or southern-style banana rice pancakes with bacon.

SETTING & FACILITIES

Location: In central Carmel on 8th Ave. between Monte Verde and Casanova, 3.5 blocks to beach and 2 blocks to business district
Near: Restaurants, shopping, galleries, museums, ocean beaches, Pebble Beach, Seventeen-Mile Dr., Monterey Bay Aquarium, Point Lobos State Park
Building: 1906 Arts and Crafts-style home w/ stone exterior
Grounds: Triple lot w/ landscaped gardens

Public Space: LR w/ stone fireplace, sunroom, porch, DR
Food & Drink: Full breakfast served in DR 8:30–10 a.m.
Recreation: Biking, surfing, diving, fishing, swimming, horseback riding, tennis, golf
Amenities & Services: Robes in room, evening wine in front of fireplace, private parking, concierge services, aquarium tickets avail.

ACCOMMODATIONS

Units: 7 guest rooms
All Rooms: No phone or TV
Some Rooms: Ocean view, private bath (2)
Bed & Bath: Queens, kings, double, 5 rooms share 2 baths
Favorites: George Sterling Room,

w/ hand-carved king canopy bed and ocean views; Ansel Adams and Robinson Jeffers rooms, w/ private bathrooms
Comfort & Decor: Rooms individually decorated w/ antiques, down comforters, fresh flowers, teddy bears

RATES, RESERVATIONS, & RESTRICTIONS

Deposit: 1st night in advance or credit card
Discounts: Weekdays Nov. 1–May 31; extra person $20
Credit Cards: AE, MC, V
Check-In/Out: 3/noon
Smoking: No
Pets: No
Kids: 12 and over
Minimum Stay: 2 nights on weekends

Open: All year
Host: Terri Navaille
P.O. Box 2517
8th Ave. (between Monte Verde & Casanova Sts.)
Carmel-by-the-Sea, CA 93921
(831) 624-4569
(800) 748-6618
www.carmelstonehouse.com

VAGABOND'S HOUSE, Carmel-by-the-Sea

Overall: ★★★½	Room Quality: B	Value: B	Price: $95–$185

Vagabond's House—named after a poem by Don Blandings, who stayed at the inn in the 1940s—has been a popular Carmel destination for many years. Comprised of a cluster of one- and two-story attached cottages, plus a 1940s house, the guest rooms show their age a bit, but on the other hand, they're good-sized, all have fireplaces, and most have kitchens. The major attraction here, though, is the large flagstone patio, with a giant oak tree covered with twinkling lights, banked with flowers everywhere. There's a tinkling waterfall, too. The cottages have Dutch-style half-doors; you can leave them open to admire the patio and take in the ocean breezes. A continental breakfast of fruits, muffins, and boiled eggs will be brought to your room, or you can dine in the courtyard.

SETTING & FACILITIES

Location: In central Carmel on the corner of 4th and Dolores
Near: Restaurants, shopping, galleries, beaches, Seventeen-Mile Dr., Pebble Beach, Monterey Bay Aquarium, Carmel Mission, Big Sur, Point Lobos State Park
Building: 1941 brick half-timbered English Tudor buildings, restored
Grounds: Double lot, courtyard w/ outdoor furniture, ancient oak, water-falls, flowering shrubs, ferns, flowers
Public Space: Parlor
Food & Drink: Extended cont'l breakfast served in courtyard or guest's room at 8:30–10:30 a.m.
Recreation: Biking, golf, wine tasting
Amenities & Services: Afternoon teatime w/ coffee, tea, and cookies; private off-street parking, concierge services, valet, laundry

ACCOMMODATIONS

Units: 11 guest rooms, 8 larger than average, 2 rooms can combine to make a suite
All Rooms: Private bath and entrance, fridge, phone, TV, coffeemaker
Some Rooms: Kitchen, fireplace, sitting area
Bed & Bath: Kings, queens (2), 2 doubles (1)

Favorites: No. 9, w/ knotty pine, red-and-white country plaid Ralph Lauren down comforter, courtyard view, kitchen, marble bath/shower

Comfort & Decor: Rooms individually decorated w/ antiques, Ralph Lauren fabrics, floral prints, wicker furniture, wingback chairs

RATES, RESERVATIONS, & RESTRICTIONS

Deposit: Credit card; must cancel 15 days in advance
Discounts: N/A; extra person $20, rates may be higher on special-event days
Credit Cards: AE, MC, V
Check-In/Out: 3/noon
Smoking: No
Pets: $20/day for first, $10/day for second, by arrangement
Kids: 12 and over

No-Nos: No more than 4 guests per room
Minimum Stay: 2 nights on weekends
Open: All year
Host: Dawn Dull
P.O. Box 2747
4th and Dolores
Carmel-by-the-Sea, CA 93921
(831) 624-7738
(800) 262-1262
Fax: (831) 626-1243

PRUFROCK'S GARDEN INN, Carpinteria

Overall: ★★★★	Room Quality: B	Value: B	Price: $110–$230

Carpinteria, ten minutes from Santa Barbara, has "the best beach in the West," and that's not just popular opinion—it's an official designation by a beach rating group. The ocean here is calm and kid-friendly, attributes not always easy to find. Carpinteria also has Prufrock's, a quite nice B&B with lots to offer. The 1904 home was completely renovated before opening as a B&B in 1995, but the inn's ambience is still old-fashioned, with period furnishings, quilts, redwood floors and rag rugs, and a charming patio area with individual umbrella-covered tables. Judy and Jim Halvorsen, who live in a cottage at the rear of the inn, are exceptional hosts, as evidenced by the large number of repeat guests (the inn was picked as a readers' favorite by the *Los Angeles Times*).

SETTING & FACILITIES

Location: In Carpinteria, 10 min. east of Santa Barbara, 2 blocks from the beach at 6th and Linden
Near: Restaurants, shopping, wineries, galleries, boutiques, antiques, missions, state beaches, Channel Islands Boat Launch
Building: 1904 California Cottage home and 2 cottages

Grounds: 4 lots w/ landscaped gardens and extensive variety of flowers, shrubs, trees
Public Space: LR/DR, porches, garden sitting areas
Food & Drink: Early morning coffee and treats, full breakfast served in LR/DR, on porch, or in room at 9 a.m.

Recreation: Biking, swimming, horseback riding, whale-watching, sailing, golf
Amenities & Services: Bikes, beach equipment on premises; beverages, home-baked goods, fresh fruit all day, afternoon hors d'oeuvres, picnic coolers; off-street parking, one disabled-accessible room, concierge services for dinner reservations, trip maps and guides, VCR avail.

ACCOMMODATIONS

Units: 7 guest rooms, 1 suite
All Rooms: Sitting area, phone, fresh flowers
Some Rooms: Fireplace, daybed, porch w/ bistro table, swing, separate LR or reading room, antique armoire, extra bed (4), private bath (5), shared bath (2)
Bed & Bath: Queens, Jacuzzis for 2 (2), claw-foot tub (1)
Favorites: Evening Shade, w/ open-beamed ceiling, fireplace, private garden patio, quilts and matching curtains, Jacuzzi for 2; Garden Hideaway, private, w/ sitting room and daybed, French doors to garden, private porch w/ bistro table
Comfort & Decor: Rooms are individually decorated w/ period furniture, quilts and floral spreads, rag rugs and carpet on hardwood floors, sitting areas, private patios, fresh flowers

RATES, RESERVATIONS, & RESTRICTIONS

Deposit: 1st night's lodging or 50% of stay, whichever is greater; must cancel 7 days in advance; $15 cancellation fee
Discounts: Winter weekday specials; extra person $30
Credit Cards: D, MC, V
Check-In/Out: 4/11, late check-out by arrangement
Smoking: No
Pets: No
Kids: By arrangement

Minimum Stay: 2 nights on weekends, 3 on holiday weekends
Open: All year
Hosts: Judy and Jim Halvorsen
600 Linden Ave.
Carpinteria, CA 93013
(805) 566-9696
(877) 837-6257
Fax: (805) 566-9404
www.prufrocks.com

NEW DAVENPORT B&B INN, Davenport

Overall: ★★★★	Room Quality: B	Value: A	Price: $80–$130

Halfway between San Francisco and Carmel, on the Coast Highway where the Santa Cruz Mountains meet the sea, lies the tiny town of Davenport and the Davenport B&B Inn. The inn's location is handy, just across the highway from miles and miles of beaches and clifftop hiking trails. There are eight guest rooms upstairs in the main building. The guest rooms in this part of the inn open onto a wraparound deck and have great ocean views. Four more guest rooms are located in the more traditional B&B bungalow next door, without the views, but a bit more quiet and secluded. All the rooms have been decorated by the artist-owners with a pleasing mix of antiques, country touches, and ethnic furniture and art.

SETTING & FACILITIES

Location: On Hwy. 1 in Davenport, 11 mi. north of Santa Cruz, 55 mi. south of San Francisco
Near: Across highway from beach, Santa Cruz Board Walk, restaurants, shops, crafts galleries, wineries, Año Nuevo Elephant Seal Reserve, Big Basin State Park
Building: 2 buildings, 1909 bungalow w/ 4 rooms, and 2-story early California-style brick structure w/ wraparound balcony
Grounds: Double lot, small private garden on side and back of bungalow,

outside deck and veranda on main building
Public Space: Parlor/kitchen in bungalow, large enclosed deck
Food & Drink: Full breakfast served in sitting room 8:30–11:30 a.m. weekends, weekdays in restaurant, full-service restaurant and bar on site
Recreation: Biking, tide pooling, surfing, wind surfing, whale-watching
Amenities & Services: Complimentary drink in restaurant bar, kitchen in bungalow has coffeemaker, microwave, fridge; private parking

ACCOMMODATIONS

Units: 12 guest rooms, 1 larger than average
All Rooms: Private bath, phone, TV
Some Rooms: Fan, four-poster, ocean view, sleeper sofa (3)
Bed & Bath: Queens, kings (2, 1 can be converted to 2 twins)
Favorites: Captain Davenport's

Retreat, double-sized corner room w/ two walls of windows, ocean views, sitting area w/ couches, queen and double beds
Comfort & Decor: Rooms individually decorated w/ antiques, ethnic artifacts, shutters and drapes, some rooms w/ tribal rugs on floor and/or walls

RATES, RESERVATIONS, & RESTRICTIONS

Deposit: 100% of bill; individuals must cancel 4 days in advance, groups 3–6 weeks; cancellation fee $25
Discounts: Long stays, weekday business, groups, 10% Nov. 15–March 15, winter specials; extra person $15
Credit Cards: AE, D, MC, V
Check-In/Out: 3/noon, late check-out $10/hour
Smoking: No
Pets: No
Kids: 2 and over in 1 room
No-Nos: 2 guests per room except

in 4 specified rooms
Minimum Stay: 2 nights on holiday weekends
Open: All year
Hosts: Bruce and Marcia McDougal
P.O. Box J
31 Davenport Ave. and Hwy. 1
Davenport, CA 95017
(831) 425-1818
(800) 870-1817
Fax: (831) 423-1160
www.swanton.com/bnb
inn@swanton.com

UNION HOTEL AND VICTORIAN MANSION,
Los Alamos

Overall: ★★★★	Room Quality: B	Value: B	Price: $100–$242

The Victorian Mansion is the most unusual B&B in California, and maybe in the world. To describe it and its co-B&B, the Union Hotel next door, is not easy. The Victorian Mansion outwardly looks like a nice example of Queen Anne architecture, but what's inside has nothing to do with the 1890s, and a lot more to do with Pop Art and Disneyworld. In 1981, the then-owner of the Victorian Mansion had a vision, or maybe it was a hallucination. He gathered a group of over 200 artists and craftspeople, and they spent ten years transforming the interior of the building into six theme suites to end all theme suites. Each is a bizarre masterpiece. In the Cadillac Room, the windows have been covered over, and the walls are a mural depicting a drive-in movie with cars and speaker posts. The ceiling is the evening sky with stars. A 1956 Cadillac convertible with the insides removed has a bed in their place and a projection TV screen on the wall in front of the car. You lie in bed and watch movies on the big screen, listening to the sound from the drive-in post and speaker next to the car, er, bed. The Egyptian room has a life-sized sarcophagus that pulls away from the wall to reveal a secret passage to the bathroom. In the Pirate Room, ship's lanterns overhead sway in time to the swells of the sea, except the room is 20 miles from the ocean. Everything is as surreal as it sounds, but it's done with superb craftsmanship. Tiles are all handmade, TVs are hidden in the wall and pop out when you press a button, and meals appear from a hidden dumbwaiter. The Union Hotel, on the other hand, is your basic Old West hotel. The rooms are small, pretty, and authentic, some with shared baths down the hall, and the warmly colorful parlor has a billiard table in it. It's all great fun, and the proof is the people these places draw from all over the world.

SETTING & FACILITIES

Location: On the main street of Los Alamos (Hwy. 135) just west of Hwy. 101, 12 min. north of Solvang

Near: Restaurants, shopping, antiques, wineries, galleries, Solvang, Hearst Castle

Building: 1880 restored Old West adobe hotel with wooden facade, 1864 Queen Anne/Eastlake Victorian, historic landmark stagecoach stop

Grounds: 3 urban lots; the hotel and mansion share landscaped gardens, an English hedge maze, reflecting pool, gazebo

Public Space: Parlor w/ potbellied stove, game room, library, DR in Union Hotel

Food & Drink: Hotel, full breakfast served in hotel DR at 9 a.m.; mansion, full breakfast served to rooms via dumbwaiter

Recreation: Croquet, maze, antique shuffleboard, antique pool table, hotel activities such as murder mystery weekends, dinner concerts and shows, wine dinners, all on premises; nearby horseback riding, wine tastings

Amenities & Services: In hotel, hot tub, swimming pool, special guests in historic costumes; In mansion, suites, champagne, sparkling cider, or a bottle of local wine, fruit, and nuts; private off-street parking, Western bar and restaurant in hotel, room service

ACCOMMODATIONS

Units: Hotel w/ 13 rooms, including 1 suite; mansion w/ 6 themed suites
All Rooms: In mansion, private bath, cable TV, phone, AC, fireplace, themed movies and background music
Some Rooms: In hotel, private bath (5), sleigh or four-poster bed, hand-made quilt, fireplace, balcony overlooking maze
Bed & Bath: In hotel, beds vary, 8 rooms share 2 baths, most baths have claw-foot tubs and pull-chain toilets; in mansion, queens, showers and soaking tubs
Favorites: In hotel, Bridal Suite, sitting room, BR w/ carved walnut bed, lace curtains, private bath w/ claw-foot tub; in mansion, Egyptian Room, w/ stone door, swathed like a harem w/ canopy pedestal bed, desert mural, mood light-

ing, marble-faced fireplace, Near East fabrics, tapestries, Persian rugs, TV/VCR/cassette player, balcony, spa, fridge, everything remote-controlled, King Tut sarcophagus hides entry to bathroom, appropriate background music
Comfort & Decor: Hotel, 1880s antique furnishings and memorabilia, sleigh beds, handmade quilts, ceiling fans, Victorian wallpapers; mansion rooms are elaborately decorated to match their individual themes: in the Pirate Room, ships' lanterns sway to sounds of waves and seagulls, a treasure map hides the latch to the bath; Gypsy Room has a Gypsy wagon for a bed; in all rooms, murals, handmade tiles, handmade furniture, hideaway TVs, cassette players, background music and videos

RATES, RESERVATIONS, & RESTRICTIONS

Deposit: Payment in full at time of booking, no refunds, credit certificate instead; must cancel 4 days in advance
Discounts: Winter specials, group rates; extra person $25
Credit Cards: All
Check-In/Out: 2/11
Smoking: No
Pets: No
Kids: Not suitable

No-Nos: No more than 2 guests per room
Minimum Stay: None
Open: Hotel closed occasionally for special events: mansion open all year
Host: Christine Williams
362 Bell St.
Los Alamos, CA 93440
(805) 344-2744
(800) 230-2744

THE JABBERWOCK, Monterey

Overall: ★★★★	Room Quality: B	Value: B	Price: $110–$210

From the moment you squeeze through the big ivy hedge obscuring the large Craftsman-style house and the rolling manicured gardens, you are aware there is the slightest touch of eccentricity here—appropriate for a B&B with a Jabberwock theme (you do remember Lewis Carroll's nonsense poem, don't you?). The seven guest rooms are varied in size and amenities, but they all have nice antique furnishings, including large Victorian beds with down pillows and comforters, and five have private baths. This is a friendly, homey kind of place, with nice fresh flowers and warm chocolate chip cookies, and close to Cannery Row.

SETTING & FACILITIES

Location: On a hillside facing the bay, in a residential neighborhood 4 blocks south of Monterey Bay Aquarium
Near: Restaurants, shopping, galleries, Monterey Bay Aquarium, Old Adobe Walking Tour, Carmel, Seventeen-Mile Dr., Pebble Beach, Big Sur, ocean beaches, 4 blocks from Cannery Row
Building: 1911 Craftsman-style home
Grounds: Half-acre of gardens, waterfall
Public Space: LR, formal DR, sunporch

Food & Drink: Full breakfast served 8:30–9:30 a.m. in DR, on porch, or in room on request
Recreation: Biking, kayaking, whale- and bird-watching, scuba diving, boating, fishing, golf
Amenities & Services: Evening sherry and hors d'oeuvres, homemade chocolate chip cookies at bedtime, fresh flowers, unbirthday gifts in guest rooms, private parking, concierge services for reservations

ACCOMMODATIONS

Units: 7 guest rooms, 2 larger than average, including 1 suite
All Rooms: Down comforter
Some Rooms: Fireplace, bay view (5), private bath (5), shared bath (2)
Bed & Bath: Queens, kings (2), Jacuzzi (1), claw-foot tub (1)
Favorites: The Borogove, romantic king BR w/ fireplace, sitting area, spec-
tacular view of bay; The Toves, w/ private secret garden, carved queen bed, claw-foot tub
Comfort & Decor: Rooms individually decorated w/ American and Craftsman antiques, Bradbury & Bradbury wallcovers, down comforters and pillows, hardwood floors and carpet, some tile, fresh flowers

RATES, RESERVATIONS, & RESTRICTIONS

Deposit: 1 night's deposit; must cancel 7 days in advance
Discounts: Long stays, weekday business, returning guests; extra person $25
Credit Cards: MC, V
Check-In/Out: 3/noon, late check-out by arrangement
Smoking: No
Pets: No
Kids: 12 and over

Minimum Stay: 2 nights on weekends
Open: Closed Dec. 24
Hosts: Joan and John Kiliany
598 Laine St.
Monterey, CA 93940
(831) 372-4777
(888) 428-7253
Fax: (831) 655-2946
www.jabberwockinn.com

OLD MONTEREY INN, Monterey

Overall: ★★★★½	Room Quality: A	Value: B	Price: $200–$350

This is surely one of the most downright pleasant inns in California. Innkeepers Ann and Gene Swett have fashioned a gorgeous B&B from the landmark English Tudor-style home they purchased over 30 years ago to house their large family. The ten guest rooms range from a separate garden cottage, with a sitting room that contains a skylighted tub for two plus a bedroom with an antique-linen canopy bed, to rooms of varying sizes and amenities in the main house, many with wood-burning fireplaces, stained glass windows, and skylights, all lovely. A delightful gourmet breakfast is served in the dining room or in your room, and complimentary passes to the nearby Monterey Sports Center will help you work off the calories you will surely consume. A nightly turn-down, dried fruits, a fridge full of cold drinks, and a thoughtfully selected book on your nightstand are just a few of the personal touches you will enjoy here.

SETTING & FACILITIES

Location: On the side of a hill in a residential neighborhood 4 blocks south of downtown Monterey and 6 blocks from the bay
Near: Restaurants, shopping, galleries, Monterey Bay Aquarium, Cannery Row, Fisherman's Wharf, Old Adobe Walking Tour, Pebble Beach, Carmel, Point Lobos Reserve, Año Nuevo State Reserve for elephant seals
Building: 1920s English Tudor Country house covered w/ ivy and wisteria
Grounds: 1+ acres of landscaped English gardens w/ cobbled paths, fountain, tiled pond, over 100 oak, pine, and redwood trees

Public Space: LR, entry area, DR w/ beamed ceiling and fireplace
Food & Drink: Full breakfast served in DR, garden, or guest room
Recreation: Biking, new Monterey Sports Center, kayaking, bird- and whale-watching, diving, surfing, horseback riding, golf
Amenities & Services: Afternoon refreshments; evening sherry, wine, and hors d'oeuvres; robes, complimentary passes to Monterey Sports Center, picnic baskets, library, private parking, full concierge services with detailed information on area activities, fax

ACCOMMODATIONS

Units: 10 guest rooms, 4 larger than average, including 2 suites
All Rooms: Private bath, sitting area, featherbed, down comforter, CD player, phone, view of the gardens
Some Rooms: Fireplace, cable TV, VCR, stained glass window, skylight, private sundeck, extra bed (1)
Bed & Bath: Queens, kings (3),

Jacuzzis (3)
Favorites: Garden Cottage, w/ private entrance, skylights, fireplace, sitting room, in-room spa tub for 2, separate BR w/ canopy king bed, window seat overlooking the garden; the library, w/ book-lined walls, stone fireplace, private sundeck, looks out into ancient oak

Comfort & Decor: Rooms individually decorated w/ antiques, quality linens, featherbeds and down comforters, comfortable sitting areas, garden views

RATES, RESERVATIONS, & RESTRICTIONS

Deposit: Credit card to hold; must cancel 10 days in advance; some special events require longer advance cancellation
Discounts: None; extra person $50 (Ashford Suite only)
Credit Cards: MC, V
Check-In/Out: 3/noon
Smoking: No
Pets: No
Kids: 12 and over
Minimum Stay: 2 nights on weekends

Open: Closed Dec. 24 and 25
Hosts: Ann and Gene Swett
500 Martin St.
Monterey, CA 93940
(831) 375-8284
(800) 350-2344
Fax: (831) 375-6730
www.oldmontereyinn.com
omi@oldmontereyinn.com

MOON'S NEST INN, Ojai

Overall: ★★★★½   Room Quality: B   Value: A   Price: $95–$135

In 1998 new owners Rich and Joan Assenberg took an aging historic inn in Ojai and, recognizing its possibilities, transformed it into one of the most imaginative new inns in the state. They salvaged an unused side yard next door and, using its majestic old oak trees, created a private walled garden and patio area for the inn. They overhauled the building, adding heat, AC, and private baths. They used excellent design sense to create a variety of rooms in bright colors with a mix of contemporary furnishings and vintage antiques that both contrast and blend harmoniously. The color schemes are sometimes daring—for instance, the Classical Revival Room has glowing ruby walls that contrast nicely with the white-and-black patterned quilt on the bed and European antique furnishings—and sometimes traditional, as in the soft and pretty Garden Room, with an antique iron double bed, delicate floral fabrics, and French doors to a private balcony. Considering the inn's affordable prices, you should plan a trip to this delightful area before Ojai and the Moon's Nest are discovered by the rest of the world.

SETTING & FACILITIES

Location: In the heart of Ojai, 1 block north of the main street (Hwy. 150), on Matilija between N. Signal and Montgomery
Near: Restaurants, shopping, galleries, spas, antique stores
Building: 1874 American Craft style, built as Ojai's first schoolhouse, newly restored, redecorated, and landscaped
Grounds: Double urban lot, landscaped w/ private lawn, gardens, fishpond
Public Space: Parlor, library w/ TV/VCR, DR, deck
Food & Drink: Full breakfast served 8:30–9:30 a.m. in DR, or outside on deck
Recreation: Croquet on premises; biking, tennis, golf nearby
Amenities & Services: Evening sherry, wine, and hors d'oeuvres; private parking, assistance w/ reservations for dining, in-room massage, special rates at nearby athletic club, on-site salon for facials and manicures

ACCOMMODATIONS

Units: 7 guest rooms
All Rooms: AC
Some Rooms: Balcony, view of pond and mountains, private bath (5), shared bath (2)
Bed & Bath: Queens (3), doubles (3), twins (1)
Favorites: Room No. 7, the lovers' suite, w/ carved headboard and queen bed, secluded balcony; Room No. 3, black and white, in Classical Revival style, w/ brass queen bed, French doors opening onto private balcony overlooking garden and pond
Comfort & Decor: Rooms individually decorated w/ original artwork, eclectic mix of antiques and custom furniture, shutters, curtains and blinds, wood floor w/ hooked and oriental rugs

RATES, RESERVATIONS, & RESTRICTIONS

Deposit: Credit card or check for 1st night; must cancel 7 days in advance
Discounts: Long stays, weekday business groups; extra person $25
Credit Cards: AE, MC, V
Check-In/Out: 3–7/noon, late checkout by arrangement
Smoking: No
Pets: By arrangement
Kids: 6 and over
Minimum Stay: 2 nights on weekends
Open: All year
Hosts: Rich and Joan Assenberg
210 E. Matilija
Ojai, CA 93023
(805) 646-6635
Fax: (805) 646-5665
www.moonsnestinn.com

THEODORE WOOLSEY HOUSE, Ojai

Overall: ★★★½	Room Quality: B	Value: A	Price: $70–$150

One glance is all it takes to see that Theodore Woolsey House is the archetypal country inn. The 5,000-square-foot farmhouse is an imposing river stone and clapboard structure set in the middle of a grove of huge 200-year-old valley oaks. The mild weather Ojai is famous for is perfect for outdoor activities, and the spacious grounds have benches under the oaks, a pond, a waterfall, and a fountain, with space left over for croquet, horseshoes, and volleyball. The sensational 50-foot swimming pool behind the house is a magnet for tanned bodies and their paler wannabes. The decor of the rooms is predominantly country and Victorian, all of it unfussy. Some have private decks, views of the gorgeous mountains surrounding Ojai Valley, stained glass windows, fireplaces, TVs, and telephones. The fenced-in stone cottage, nestled in a grove of oaks, is very private and has a kitchen, a 2-person whirlpool tub, and a trundle bed.

SETTING & FACILITIES

Location: In the country 1 mi. east of downtown of Ojai on Hwy. 150
Near: Restaurants, shopping, antique shops, Lake Casitas, museums
Building: 1887 2-story stone and clapboard American Colonial-style farmhouse
Grounds: 7 acres of 100-year-old oaks, lawns, gardens, waterfall, fishpond, horseshoe pit, croquet course, volleyball court
Public Space: Parlor w/ beamed ceiling, antiques, stone fireplace, lobby w/ fireplace and spiral staircase, library,
DR, garden room, breakfast patio room
Food & Drink: Expanded cont'l buffet breakfast served 8:30–10:30 a.m. in DR, breakfast patio room, garden room, or pool area
Recreation: Croquet, horseshoes, and volleyball court on premises; biking, golf, tennis, horseback riding
Amenities & Services: 50-ft. swimming pool, hot tub, private parking, specials at day spa next door, massage avail.; cottage is disabled-accessible downstairs

ACCOMMODATIONS

Units: 6 guest rooms, 5 larger than average, including 1 cottage
All Rooms: Private bath, AC
Some Rooms: Cable TV, private entrance, fireplace, four-poster, down comforter, view of Topa Topa mountains, phone (5), extra twin (4)
Bed & Bath: Queens, king, Jacuzzi for 2 (1)
Favorites: Cottage, w/ knotty pine walls, loft BR w/ queen bed and brass
crib, LR w/ cast-iron fireplace, bar kitchenette w/ microwave and fridge, 2-person whirlpool tub; No. 5, w/ French motif, private entrance overlooking pool, king bed, sitting area, wraparound windows, French doors
Comfort & Decor: Rooms individually decorated w/ artwork, mirrors, antiques, wainscoting, wallpaper, hardwood floors, carpet, rugs

RATES, RESERVATIONS, & RESTRICTIONS

Deposit: 100% of bill before arrival; must cancel 5 days in advance
Discounts: Weekday singles; extra person $20
Credit Cards: None
Check-In/Out: 2–8/noon
Smoking: No
Pets: No
Kids: OK

Minimum Stay: 2 nights on weekends
Open: All year
Hosts: Ana Cross and Papi Cross
1484 E. Ojai Ave.
Ojai, CA 93023
(805) 646-9779
Fax: (805) 646-4414
www.theodorewoolseyhouse.com

THE CENTRELLA INN, Pacific Grove

Overall: ★★★★	Room Quality: B	Value: B	Price: $119–$239

The recently renovated Centrella Inn, a historic former boarding house built in 1889, has a wide range of accommodations—rooms, suites, and cottages—all of them with private baths and all charmingly furnished and decorated in an unfussy Victorian style. Many of the rooms have nice views of flower-filled gardens. Children are welcome in the five small, but private, cottages. Breakfast is a buffet with cereal, fruits, breads and pastries, and varying hot dishes.

SETTING & FACILITIES

Location: In downtown Pacific Grove on corner of Central Ave. and 17th, 1 block off Lighthouse Ave., 2 blocks from the beach
Near: Restaurants, shopping, galleries, museums, Cannery Row, Monterey Bay Aquarium, beaches, parks, Seventeen-Mile Dr., Pebble Beach
Building: 1889 Victorian hotel, a Nat'l Historic Landmark, plus 5 cottages
Grounds: Several landscaped city lots

w/ courtyards and gardens
Public Space: Parlor/lobby w/ fireplace, breakfast room, gardens
Food & Drink: Full breakfast served 8–10 a.m. in the breakfast room
Recreation: Biking, kayaking, whale- and bird-watching, tennis, golf
Amenities & Services: Evening wine and hors d'oeuvres, cookies and coffee always avail.; limited private parking, 1 room w/ disabled access

ACCOMMODATIONS

Units: 26 rooms, including 2 suites, 5 cottages
All Rooms: Private bath, phone
Some Rooms: Fireplace, TV/VCR, sleeper sofa, wet bar, potbellied stove, extra bed (7)
Bed & Bath: Queens, kings (6), twin, Jacuzzi (1)

Favorites: Garden Room, w/ private entrance, canopy bed, corner stove, TV/VCR, wet bar, white tiled bath w/ Jacuzzi for 2
Comfort & Decor: Rooms individually decorated w/ antiques, wicker, designer robes, lace curtains, down comforters, sitting areas, carpets

RATES, RESERVATIONS, & RESTRICTIONS

Deposit: 1st night's lodging; must cancel 72 hours in advance
Discounts: AAA, AARP, off-season specials
Credit Cards: AE, D, MC, V
Check-In/Out: 3/noon
Smoking: No
Pets: No
Kids: OK in cottages, other rooms suitable for 14 and over
Minimum Stay: 2 nights on weekends

Open: All year
Host: Mark Arellano
612 Central Ave.
Pacific Grove, CA 93950
(831) 372-3372
(800) 233-3372
Fax: (831) 372-2036
www.innsbythesea.com

GATE HOUSE INN, Pacific Grove

Overall: ★★★★   Room Quality: B   Value: B   Price: $110–$165

This interesting 1884 Italianate Victorian house, one of the oldest in Pacific Grove, was built as a summer home for California senator Ben Langford. The nine guest rooms in the main house and a quieter addition in back vary in size and decor, ranging from the spacious Langford Room, with a sitting area, a nice ocean view, and a claw-foot tub, to the modestly sized, modestly priced Victorian Room, with a queen bed, partial ocean view, also with a claw-foot tub. The inn has lovely silk-screened Bradbury & Bradbury wallpapers, and the charming, airy parlor, with original Victorian furniture and stained glass windows, has views of Monterey Bay. A large buffet breakfast is served in the dining room or at the kitchen table.

SETTING & FACILITIES

Location: On Central Ave., between 2nd and 3rd Sts., 1 block from Monterey Bay and .3 mi. to aquarium
Near: Restaurants, shopping, galleries, museums, Cannery Row, Monterey Bay Aquarium, beaches, parks, Seventeen-Mile Dr.
Building: 1884 Italianate Victorian
Grounds: Landscaped urban corner lot w/ gardens, lawns
Public Space: Parlor, DR, guest kitchen

Food & Drink: Full breakfast served 8–10 a.m. in DR
Recreation: Biking, in-line skating, kayaking, whale- and bird-watching, tennis, golf
Amenities & Services: Afternoon snacks, evening wine and hors d'oeuvres; cookies, coffee, tea, and hot chocolate always avail.; microwave w/ popcorn, evening turn-down w/ chocolates, private courtyard parking

ACCOMMODATIONS

Units: 9 guest rooms, 1 larger than average
All Rooms: Private bath, phone

Some Rooms: Fireplace, ocean view
Bed & Bath: Queens, king, claw-foot tubs (7)

Favorites: Langford Room, w/ sitting area, potbellied stove, ocean view, clawfoot tub in room; Steinbeck Room, w/ private large patio, fireplace, sitting area **Comfort & Decor:** Rooms individually decorated w/ Victorian antiques and bed frames, hardwood floors, oriental carpets, Bradbury & Bradbury handmade wallpapers, stained glass, exterior painted w/ original Victorian color scheme

RATES, RESERVATIONS, & RESTRICTIONS

Deposit: Credit card; must cancel 72 hours in advance
Discounts: Long stays, weekday business, AAA, singles; extra person $15
Credit Cards: AE, D, MC, V
Check-In/Out: 2/noon, late check-out by arrangement
Smoking: No
Pets: No
Kids: 8 and over
Minimum Stay: 2 nights on holiday weekends
Open: All year
Hosts: Lewis Shaefer and Susan Kuslis, owners; Lois DeFord, resident mgr.
225 Central Ave.
Pacific Grove, CA 93950
(831) 649-8436
(800) 753-1881
Fax: (831) 648-8044
www.sueandlewinns.com
lew@redshift.com

THE GOSBY HOUSE, Pacific Grove

Overall: ★★★★	Room Quality: B	Value: B	Price: $90–$170

This cheerful, gabled and turreted yellow and white Victorian mansion is in the midst of Pacific Grove's charming downtown area, steps from all sorts of shops and restaurants, and an easy walk to the beach. If quality and quantity of food is high on your list of desirable options in a B&B, this is your place. The inn's 22 rooms vary in size and amenities; some have sitting areas, private decks, fireplaces, and large baths with spas. The most private rooms are in the carriage house. The interior decor tends toward lots of busy but pretty wallpaper, lace curtains, carpet, and teddy bears. This is a lively, happy place that will take you in, take care of you, and treat you like a member of a big family. Wipe your feet before you come in, and don't be late for breakfast. You heard me!

SETTING & FACILITIES

Location: At the west end of Pacific Grove's historic downtown on Lighthouse between 18th and 19th Sts., 6 blocks from the water
Near: Restaurants, shopping, galleries, beaches, Monterey Bay Aquarium, missions, Big Sur, Seventeen-Mile Dr., Carmel
Building: 1887 Victorian mansion and carriage house, restored
Grounds: Double lot, w/ landscaped gardens and interior courtyard
Public Space: Parlor, DR
Food & Drink: Full breakfast served 8–10 a.m. in DR
Recreation: Biking, water sports, surfing, diving, fishing, golf

Amenities & Services: Bicycles, afternoon wine and hors d'oeuvres, home-baked cookies, turn-down service w/ chocolates; concierge services for reservations

ACCOMMODATIONS

Units: 22 guest rooms
Some Rooms: Fireplace, private patio or deck, window seat, private bath (20), shared bath (2)
Bed & Bath: Queens, kings (4), Jacuzzi tubs for 2 (2)
Favorites: Trimmerhill Room, w/ porch swing, fireplace, four-poster; 2 carriage house rooms w/ private entrances, spa tubs for 2, fireplaces, balconies
Comfort & Decor: Rooms individually decorated w/ antiques, wallpaper, lace curtains, carpet, teddy bears

RATES, RESERVATIONS, & RESTRICTIONS

Deposit: Credit card
Discounts: Midweek packages Nov.–March; extra person $15/day
Credit Cards: AE, DC, MC, V
Check-In/Out: 3/noon
Smoking: No
Pets: No
Kids: OK, free under 2 years
Minimum Stay: None

Open: All year
Host: Tamra Kirkland
643 Lighthouse Ave.
Pacific Grove, CA 93950
(831) 375-1287
(800) 527-8828
Fax: (831) 655-9621
www.foursisters.com
info@foursisters.com

GRAND VIEW INN, Pacific Grove

| Overall: ★★★★½ | Room Quality: A | Value: B | Price: $155–$285 |

Sitting side by side, connected by a pretty garden, the two perfectly maintained Pacific Grove inns owned and managed by the Flatley family are true dazzlers, perched grandly on the edge of Monterey Bay. The Seven Gables is the more ornate of the pair, but the Grand View is also lavishly furnished with fine antiques, statuary, oriental rugs, and chandeliers. Each guest room is an artful blending of all these elements, yet the real star is the grand view. There are wonderful ocean views every way you turn. Built in 1910 by a noted marine biologist and the first woman mayor of PG (as the locals call it), Dr. Julia Platt chose to site her mansion overlooking Lover's Point Beach. This famous beach, by the way, is named for lovers of the religious sort, as the town originated as a retreat for Methodists.

SETTING & FACILITIES

Location: On a point of land jutting out into Monterey Bay, across from Lover's Point Beach, at the corner of Ocean View Blvd. and Grand Ave., 1 mi. northwest of the aquarium

Near: Restaurants, shopping, galleries, museums, Cannery Row, Monterey Bay Aquarium, beaches, parks, Seventeen-Mile Dr., Pebble Beach, Carmel Mission, Monterey historic adobes

Building: 1910 Edwardian/post-Victorian mansion
Grounds: Landscaped grounds w/ rock walls, pond, stream; protected sitting area w/ ocean views
Public Space: Parlor/dining area w/ ocean views
Food & Drink: Full breakfast served 8–10 a.m. in the parlor area at 2 dining tables
Recreation: Biking, kayaking, whale- and bird-watching, tennis, golf
Amenities & Services: Afternoon tea 4–5 p.m., evening turn-down service, welcome baskets, robes, down comforters, private parking on- and off-street, disabled access

ACCOMMODATIONS

Units: 10 guest rooms, 9 larger than average
All Rooms: Private bath finished in marble, ocean view, crystal chandelier, sitting area
Some Rooms: Partial canopy bed
Bed & Bath: Queens
Favorites: Seal Rocks, on 2nd floor, w/ crystal chandelier, large armoire, partial canopy antique queen brass bed w/ inlaid wood, marble bath w/ shower and tub, 12-ft.-wide picture window w/ 180° view of bay and coastline, window can be left undraped with no lack of privacy; Seascape, w/ 12-ft.-high ceilings, large bay window w/ large crystal chandelier and panoramic view of coast looking toward Monterey, large armoire and matching carved bed w/ partial canopy, marble bath w/ shower
Comfort & Decor: Rooms individually decorated w/ original art, mix of antique and newer furniture, custom drapes and valences, carpet in guest rooms, hardwood floors in parlor and hall, 3-story carved oak staircase

RATES, RESERVATIONS, & RESTRICTIONS

Deposit: 100% of bill; must cancel 5 days in advance; $10 cancellation fee
Discounts: None, occasional midweek winter specials
Credit Cards: MC, V
Check-In/Out: 2:30–10/noon, late check-out by arrangement
Smoking: No
Pets: No
Kids: 12 and over
No-Nos: No more than 2 guests per room
Minimum Stay: 2 nights on weekends, 3 on holiday weekends and special events
Open: All year
Hosts: Susan Flatley and Ed Flatley
557 Ocean View Blvd.
Pacific Grove, CA 93950
(831) 372-4341
www.7gables-grandview.com

GREEN GABLES INN, Pacific Grove

| Overall: ★★★★½ | Room Quality: A | Value: B | Price: $110–$240 |

Monterey businessman William Lacy must have loved his mistress very much, because in 1888 he built her one of the most beautiful houses in California—a striking two-story Queen Anne sitting on a rise looking out across Monterey Bay with four large gables and lots of windows and a sea view from nearly every room. Bill and his nameless love are gone, but the house remains for all to admire, both inside and out. It has been meticulously maintained over the years, and carefully renovated, keeping the original moldings, the elaborate woodwork, and the maple floors. Recently the carriage house on a hill in back was also restored; five popular minisuites were added, with private entrances, baths, partial ocean views, and all the amenities for those who crave creature comforts. But true romantics will want to stay in the main house in the dormer rooms under the gables with the vaulted ceilings. Sure, four of them share two baths, but the experience is more than worth any small loss of privacy.

SETTING & FACILITIES

Location: On the corner of Central and 5th Sts. in Pacific Grove, at ocean, half-mile from aquarium
Near: Restaurants, shopping, antique shops, Monterey Bay Aquarium, Cannery Row, Fisherman's Wharf, Seventeen-Mile Dr., Carmel Mission, Monterey historic adobes, Point Lobos State Park
Building: 1888 2-story, half-timbered Queen Anne Victorian home w/ 4 gables, restored; more recent carriage house, renovated
Grounds: Double lot, landscaped w/ gardens

Public Space: 2-room parlor w/ fireplace flanked by stained glass, DR w/ crystal chandelier, view of bay
Food & Drink: Full buffet breakfast served 8–10 a.m. in DR
Recreation: Bicycles avail on premises; nearby kayaking, fishing, surfing, diving, golf, whale-, otter-, and sea lion–watching
Amenities & Services: Cookies and beverages always avail., evening wine and hors d'oeuvres, fresh flowers, teddy bears, turn-down w/ chocolates; limited parking, concierge services for reservations

ACCOMMODATIONS

Units: 11 guest rooms, including 4 minisuites (6 guest rooms in main house, 5 guest rooms in carriage house)
All Rooms: Ocean or garden view
Some Rooms: Fireplace, private entrance, sofa sitting area, window seat, TV, ocean or garden view, canopy bed, four-poster, dormer windows, private bath (7)
Bed & Bath: Queens, kings (4), double, 4 rooms share 2 baths, Jacuzzis for

2 (4), jetted tub (1)
Favorites: King bed rooms in carriage house, w/ private entrances, fireplaces, Jacuzzi tubs for 2, TV/VCR, sofa sitting area, partial ocean views
Comfort & Decor: Rooms are individually decorated w/ coordinated fabrics and wallpapers, original woodwork, maple floors, intricate molding; stained, leaded, and diamond-paned glass; beamed dormer ceilings, bay windows

RATES, RESERVATIONS, & RESTRICTIONS

Deposit: Credit card
Discounts: Midweek Dec.–Feb.; extra person $15
Credit Cards: AE, DC, MC, V
Check-In/Out: 3/noon

Smoking: No
Pets: No
Kids: OK, under 2 free
Minimum Stay: None

Open: All year
Host: Tamra Kirkland
104 5th St.
Pacific Grove, CA 93950

(831) 375-2095
(800) 722-1774
www.foursisters.com
info@foursisters.com

THE INN AT 213 SEVENTEEN MILE DRIVE, Pacific Grove

Overall: ★★★★	Room Quality: B	Value: B	Price: $135–$240

The newest B&B in Pacific Grove opened its doors in 1998 after a year of restoring the beautiful old Craftsman house back to its former glory. The original floors, beamed ceilings, and wall paneling of oak, fir, and redwood are richly attractive, and the panels of leaded-glass windows and doors between the spacious public rooms are reminiscent of a fine old college library. The inn's pleasant guest rooms, all with private baths, vary in size and amenities; they are located in the main house, in cottage units, and in redwood chalet rooms. The inn is located in the monarch butterfly tree zone, and the garden, with its native oaks, redwood, and pine trees, naturally attracts the orange-and-black lepidoptera.

SETTING & FACILITIES

Location: In a residential neighborhood at the corner of Seventeen-Mile Dr. and Lighthouse Ave., near the northern end of Seventeen-Mile Dr., 1 mi. northwest of aquarium
Near: Point Piños Lighthouse, restaurants, shopping, galleries, museums, Cannery Row, Monterey Bay Aquarium, Pebble Beach, Seventeen-Mile Dr., Carmel, beaches
Building: 1925 Craftsman-style house w/ original floors and wall paneling in oak, fir, and redwood, leaded glass windows; a 1928 redwood cottage and addition; and a 1930 cottage that won local heritage society award for best restoration
Grounds: Over half-acre of native oaks, redwoods, and pine, lawns and flower beds, fishpond
Public Space: Wood-paneled sitting, reading, and DRs, porch
Food & Drink: Full breakfast served 8–10 a.m. in DR
Recreation: Biking, kayaking, scuba diving, horseback riding, whale-watching, golf
Amenities & Services: Hot tub, evening wine and hors d'oeuvres; coffee, tea, and cookies always avail.; VCRs avail., private parking, disabled access, assistance w/ activity plans, picnics avail.

ACCOMMODATIONS

Units: 14 guest rooms, 5 larger than average
All Rooms: Private bath and entrance, cable TV, phone, down comforter
Some Rooms: Four-poster, kitchenette (1), view of bay or garden, balcony, sleeper sofa (1)
Bed & Bath: Queens, kings (2), roll-away avail.

Favorites: Blue Heron, w/ ocean views, balcony overlooking the garden, oriental rugs, king brass bed, sitting room w/ daybed; Guillemot, w/ vaulted redwood ceiling, very large and private, lots of windows, nautical decor in blues and yellows, view of garden

Comfort & Decor: Rooms individually decorated and named for local sea birds, w/ balconies, variety of 1920–30s furnishings—redwood, Mission, wicker, washed cane, leather, and brass; Laura Ashley prints, oriental rugs

RATES, RESERVATIONS, & RESTRICTIONS

Deposit: 100% at time of reservation for 2 or fewer rooms; must cancel 72 hours in advance
Discounts: Long stays, winter weekdays; extra person $20
Credit Cards: AE, MC, V
Check-In/Out: 3/noon
Smoking: No
Pets: No
Kids: In cottages
No-Nos: No more than 2 guests per room in most rooms

Minimum Stay: 2 nights on weekends, 3 on holiday weekends
Open: All year
Hosts: Tony and Glynis Greening, owners; Sally Goff, mgr.
213 Seventeen Mile Dr.
Pacific Grove, CA 93950
(831) 642-9514
(800) 526-5666
Fax: (831) 642-9546
www.innat213-17miledr.com

MARTINE INN, Pacific Grove

Overall: ★★★★½   Room Quality: A   Value: B   Price: $150–$300

Originally an 1899 Victorian, this inn has been extensively remodeled over the years and is now Mediterranean in style, with arched windows and high stucco garden walls. The 12,750-square-foot mansion's historical

grandeur is still very much in evidence, however. Guest rooms are spacious and furnished with museum-quality antiques; many have wood-burning fireplaces, and those on the ocean side have wonderful unobstructed views. Meals are served on Victorian-style china, with old Sheffield silver and crystal glassware. This inn is run like a good hotel, with extensive wine lists and wedding or conference accommodations. It's less ornate than other B&Bs on the fabled Ocean View Boulevard, but very elegant nonetheless.

SETTING & FACILITIES

Location: On Monterey Bay, across from Pacific Grove Marine Gardens Park, between 4th and 5th Sts.
Near: Restaurants, shopping, galleries, museums, 4 blocks to Cannery Row, Monterey Bay Aquarium, beaches, parks, Seventeen-Mile Dr., Pebble Beach
Building: 1890s Victorian w/ cupola, remodeled in 1920s to Mediterranean style, 4 buildings
Public Space: Parlor w/ grand piano, sitting room, library, game room, auto display of 4 MG vintage racing cars

Food & Drink: Full breakfast served 8–10 a.m. in the parlor overlooking coastline of Monterey Bay
Recreation: Biking, hiking on ocean-front trail, kayaking, whale- and bird-watching, fishing, tennis, golf
Amenities & Services: Hot tub, bathrobes and towels for spa use, afternoon snacks, evening sherry and hors d'oeuvres, fresh fruit and fresh flowers in all rooms, morning paper, disabled access, assistance w/ dining reservations, activity plans

ACCOMMODATIONS

Units: 23 guest rooms, 16 larger than average, including 4 suites
All Rooms: Private bath, museum-quality antique BR suites, phone, fridge
Some Rooms: Fireplace, four-poster
Bed & Bath: Queens, kings (5, 3 canopy), doubles w/ canopy (2), some claw-foot tubs and antique marble sinks
Favorites: Parke, w/ windows on 3 sides w/ views of surf and bay, corner Victorian fireplace, Chippendale revival BR set four-poster w/ canopy and side curtains, sitting area, claw-foot tub;

Eastlake, w/ surf views through arched windows, 1870s Eastlake furnishings, 2 settees in sitting area, canopy bed on raised platform, 7-ft. claw-foot tub w/ shower
Comfort & Decor: Rooms individually decorated w/ early California landscapes, museum-quality antiques, custom fabrics and draperies, carpets, inlaid hardwood floors, tile, each room decorated to match year and style of antiques

RATES, RESERVATIONS, & RESTRICTIONS

Deposit: 100% of bill; must cancel 72 hours in advance; $10 cancellation fee
Discounts: None
Credit Cards: AE, D, MC, V
Check-In/Out: 2/11
Smoking: No
Pets: No

Kids: OK
No-Nos: No more than 2 guests per room
Minimum Stay: 2 nights on weekends, 3 on holiday weekends and special events

Open: All year
Host: Don Martine
255 Ocean View Blvd.
Pacific Grove, CA 93950

(831) 373-3388
(800) 852-5588
Fax: (831) 373-3896
www.martineinn.com

OLD ST. ANGELA INN, Pacific Grove

Overall: ★★★★	Room Quality: B	Value: B	Price: $110–$195

This charming Cape Cod in a residential area of Pacific Grove is a former convent, perhaps the source of its air of serenity. The nine guest rooms are a warm mix of country pine furniture, beautiful hardwood floor and rugs, and colorful fabrics, and some have fireplaces and ocean views. A substantial breakfast is served in the handsome redwood and glass solarium overlooking the garden, and there's a hot tub in the garden, too. If you find High Victorian a little too intense for your taste, the Old Saint Angela is a casual, comfortable alternative to the area's "painted ladies."

SETTING & FACILITIES

Location: On Central Ave., at the corner of 7th St., 1 block from Monterey Bay, .25 mi. to aquarium
Near: Restaurants, shopping, galleries, museums, Cannery Row, Monterey Bay Aquarium, beaches, parks, Seventeen-Mile Dr.
Building: 1910 Arts and Crafts Cape Cod–style house 100 yards from the ocean
Grounds: Double lot w/ landscaped gardens, gazebo, ocean views from garden sitting area
Public Space: LR w/ cut stone fireplace, solarium
Food & Drink: Full breakfast served 8:30–10 a.m. in the solarium overlooking the garden, in the DR w/ ocean view, or outside in garden
Recreation: Biking, in-line skating, kayaking, whale- and bird-watching, tennis, golf
Amenities & Services: Hot tub, afternoon snacks; evening wine, tea, and hors d'oeuvres; cookies, popcorn, and hot and cold drinks always avail.; assistance w/ dining reservations, activity plans, tours, bike rentals, fax

ACCOMMODATIONS

Units: 9 guest rooms, 2 larger than average
All Rooms: Private bath, phone, TV avail. on request
Some Rooms: Fireplace, daybed, ocean view, extra bed (1)
Bed & Bath: Queens, king, Jacuzzis (6)
Favorites: Whale Watch, w/ blue Delft decor, private balcony w/ ocean view, canopy queen bed, fireplace w/ antique mantel; Crows Nest, w/ nautical decor, ocean view, oak antiques, cast-iron stove, sitting area
Comfort & Decor: Rooms individually decorated w/ 1880–1910 oak, walnut, and pine furniture, 7-ft. headboards, quilts, wallpaper, drapes and roman shades, hardwood floors w/ wool pile area rugs, teddy bears

RATES, RESERVATIONS, & RESTRICTIONS

Deposit: Credit card; must cancel 72 hours in advance
Discounts: Long stays, weekday business, AAA, singles; extra person $20
Credit Cards: D, MC, V
Check-In/Out: 3/noon, late check-out w/ prior arrangement
Smoking: No
Pets: No
Kids: OK when suitable rooms avail.
Minimum Stay: 2 nights on weekends

Open: All year
Hosts: Lewis Shaefer and Susan Kuslis
321 Central Ave
Pacific Grove, CA 93950
(831) 372-3246
(800) 748-6306
Fax: (831) 372-8560
www.sueandlewinns.com
lew@redshift.com

SEVEN GABLES INN, Pacific Grove

Overall: ★★★★½	Room Quality: A	Value: B	Price: $155–$475

For those who love the classical Victorian experience—a grand old manse filled with collector antiques, formal draperies, fine oriental rugs, crystal chandeliers, silver, china, and high tea—this inn is your dream come true. Each of its 14 rooms, most in the main house and the others in a guest house and cottages on the property, is ornately decorated in formal Victorian style, and most have partial canopy beds and sitting areas. Each room has an ocean view. A sit-down breakfast is served in the formal dining room, and the innkeepers also provide other nice details, such as welcome baskets and nightly turn-downs.

SETTING & FACILITIES

Location: On a point of land jutting out into Monterey Bay, across from Lover's Point Beach, at the corner of Ocean View Blvd. and Grand Ave., 1 mi. northwest of the aquarium
Near: Restaurants, shopping, galleries, museums, Cannery Row, Monterey Bay Aquarium, beaches, parks, Seventeen-Mile Dr., Pebble Beach, Carmel Mission, Monterey historic adobes
Building: 1886 3-story Victorian, 2 1886 cottages, 1884 Jewell Cottage, 1946 Victorian-style guest house
Grounds: Landscaped grounds w/ lawns, rose garden, patio areas, pathways
Public Space: Ornately decorated formal Victorian parlor w/ European antiques
Food & Drink: Full breakfast served 8–10 a.m. in the parlor area at 2 dining tables
Recreation: Biking, kayaking, whale- and bird-watching, tennis, golf
Amenities & Services: Afternoon tea 4–5 p.m., evening turn-down service, welcome baskets, robes; free on-street parking

ACCOMMODATIONS

Units: 14 guest rooms, 12 larger than average, including 1 suite, rooms located in 5 buildings on the premises

All Rooms: Private bath, oriental carpets, sitting area

Some Rooms: Partial canopy bed, fireplace

Bed & Bath: Queens

Favorites: Bellview, w/ high ceilings, antique crystal chandelier, onion-dome partial-canopy bed, 4 large windows w/ down-filled couch and excellent view down coast; Cypress Room, w/ corner bay window and window seat w/ 180° view of ocean and coastline, couch and armchairs in sitting area, oriental carpet, large armoire and sideboard, 2 large stained-glass windows

Comfort & Decor: Rooms individually decorated w/ original art, European and American antiques, custom drapes and valences, carpet and oriental rugs

RATES, RESERVATIONS, & RESTRICTIONS

Deposit: 100% of bill; must cancel 5 days in advance; cancellation fee $10

Discounts: None

Credit Cards: MC, V

Check-In/Out: 2:30/noon

Smoking: No

Pets: No

Kids: 12 and over

No-Nos: No more than 2 guests per room

Minimum Stay: 2 nights on weekends, 3 on holidays and special events

Open: All year

Hosts: Susan Flatley and Ed Flatley
555 Ocean View Blvd.
Pacific Grove, CA 93950
(831) 372-4341
Fax: (831) 372-2544
www.7gable-grandview.com

ARBOR INN B&B, Paso Robles

Overall: ★★★★½	Room Quality: B	Value: B	Price: $150–$255

Inns associated with wineries are growing increasingly popular in California, possibly because the organization and care required to grow grapes translate into the same attention to detail required to create and maintain fine accommodations. This is certainly the case with the Arbor Inn, owned by, and adjacent to, Treana Winery in Paso Robles's burgeoning wine district. The inn is surrounded by 80 acres of productive vineyards—cabernet, to be exact. The guest rooms have formal English Country furnishings with lots of delicate floral wallpaper and coordinating fabrics. French doors lead to private balconies with views of the vineyards and the countryside. All have private baths with a separate tub and tiled shower and individual climate control. For early risers, there's a continental breakfast, or, if you catch a few extra winks, an excellent, full breakfast is served in the dining room. There are also wine and chef-prepared hors d'oeuvres before dinner, and a late night snack.

SETTING & FACILITIES

Location: In a vineyard at Arbor Rd. and Hwy. 46, 2 mi. south and 1 mi. west of Paso Robles via Hwys. 101 and 46, 40 min. from Hearst Castle
Near: Restaurants, shopping, wineries, antiques, ocean beaches, Hearst Castle
Building: New 3-story English Country inn
Grounds: English gardens surrounded by vineyards
Public Space: 2-story LR w/ black marble fireplace, formal English DR, outdoor patios, gazebo

Food & Drink: Full breakfast served 8:30–10 a.m. in DR, early cont'l breakfast served at 7 a.m.
Recreation: Biking, kayaking, golf, picnicking on the Treana Winery grounds, waterskiing, elephant seal-watching
Amenities & Services: Evening Treana wine and hors d'oeuvres, late night snacks, robes, turn-down, early morning coffee service; on-site parking, concierge services, massages avail.; winery, tasting room, and deli next door

ACCOMMODATIONS

Units: 9 guest rooms, including 1 suite
All Rooms: Private bath w/ separate tub and tiled shower, fireplace, balcony, TV, vineyard view
Some Rooms: VCR, extra queen (1)
Bed & Bath: Kings, queens (3), Jacuzzi for 2 (1), 6-ft. soaking tub and 7-headed shower (1)
Favorites: Cabernet Suite penthouse, decorated in black and gold w/ 180°

view of valley from private deck, wrought-iron canopy bed, Aubusson rug, 6-ft. soaking tub, shower w/ 7 showerheads; Moscato Allegro, w/ cherry four-poster bed and Jacuzzi for 2
Comfort & Decor: Rooms individually decorated w/ classic English Country decor, down quilts

RATES, RESERVATIONS, & RESTRICTIONS

Deposit: 1st night deposit on single room, 50% deposit on multiple rooms; must cancel 48 hours in advance for single room, 14 days for multiple rooms
Discounts: AAA, seniors; extra person $65
Credit Cards: MC, V
Check-In/Out: 3/11, late check-in/out by arrangement
Smoking: No
Pets: No

Kids: Not suitable
No-Nos: No more than 2 persons per room except in room with 2 queens
Minimum Stay: None
Open: All year
Host: Denise Mertens
P.O. Box 3260
2130 Arbor Rd.
Paso Robles, CA 93447
(805) 227-4673
Fax: (805) 227-1112

JUST INN, Paso Robles

Overall: ★★★★½   Room Quality: A   Value: B   Price: $225–$275

This is probably the most remote inn in California—in feeling, if not in distance. The town of Paso Robles is booming these days, partly because of its natural unexploited charms, and increasingly because people have discovered that superb wines are being made in the rolling hills of the Santa Lucia range. If you go west 11 miles into these hills on a series of two-lane roads, you will wind your way through country dotted with virgin oaks and an occasional small winery until you reach the Justin Winery, almost at the end of the road. A small, family-owned and -operated winery, it is also a trés chic French restaurant and the namesake of the two-story, Country French-inspired Just Inn next door. The inn has three luxurious three-room suites, all with floor-to-ceiling marble baths, featherbeds, temperature-controlled air, frescoed (yes, frescoed) ceilings, wood-burning fireplaces, and tapestry-covered furnishings. Each suite is a work of art with a different theme. Outside you'll find a one-acre English garden, a swimming pool, a spa, and acres and acres of beautiful vineyards.

SETTING & FACILITIES

Location: 11 mi. northwest of Paso Robles in Santa Lucia Range, half-hour northeast of Cambria
Near: Paso Robles wine country, half-hour to ocean beaches, 45 min. to Hearst Castle
Building: California ranch style w/ French Country interiors, built in mid-1980s and early 1990s, adjacent to restaurant/DR/tasting room
Grounds: 160 acres of oak-studded hills and vineyards, 1-acre English garden, gazebo for sitting
Public Space: Lobby, DR, tasting room, gardens, pool area
Food & Drink: Full breakfast served at 9 a.m. in DR, room service avail. for $15/person, restaurant on premises

Recreation: Bicycles, wine tasting, swimming on premises; horseback riding nearby

Amenities & Services: Swimming pool, outdoor spa, complimentary wine tasting in tasting room, robes, bottled water, bottle of wine and chocolate in rooms, private hiking path, private parking, concierge services, massage avail., picnic baskets avail. w/ advance notice, fruit and cheese plates, free membership in Justin Wine Club with special offerings and discounts on limited wines

ACCOMMODATIONS

Units: 3 large 3-room suites

All Rooms: Fireplace, featherbed, private entrance from English garden

Some Rooms: Tuscany has 2 balconies w/ French doors, Provence 1 balcony w/ French doors

Bed & Bath: Queen featherbeds, floor-to-ceiling marble baths w/ hydro spas

Favorites: Sussex, the largest suite, w/ English antiques, private entrance, flower-filled window boxes, wood-burning fireplace, four-poster canopy featherbed, wall-to-wall carpet, oriental rugs, cathedral ceilings

Comfort & Decor: Suites are named and decorated in English, French, and Italian styles, w/ tapestry-covered chairs, antique pine furnishings, featherbeds, frescoed ceilings, flower-filled window boxes, swimming pool and spa just outside the door

RATES, RESERVATIONS, & RESTRICTIONS

Deposit: Credit card in advance; must cancel 10 days in advance

Discounts: 20% to Justin Wine Club members, midweek specials Jan.–March; extra person $25

Credit Cards: AE, D, MC, V

Check-In/Out: 3/noon, late check-out by arrangement

Smoking: No

Pets: No

Kids: Not suitable

Minimum Stay: 2 nights on weekends and holidays

Open: All year

Hosts: Deborah and Justin Baldwin
11680 Chimney Rock Rd.
Paso Robles, CA 93446
(805) 237-4150
(800) 726-0049
Fax: (805) 237-4109
www.justinwine.com
justinwine@aol.com

AVILA VALLEY INN, San Luis Obispo

Overall: ★★★★½	Room Quality: B	Value: B	Price: $160–$295

For over 100 years people have been coming to the Sycamore Mineral Springs to soak their parts. The Sycamore Springs resort has everything to go with its natural resources: a full-service spa, meeting rooms, an upscale restaurant, lush gardens, apartments, over 70 outdoor hot tubs, and, last but assuredly not least, a B&B, the Avila Valley Inn. The B&B consists of two side-by-side new homes. The main house has two minisuites with king beds, and a dining room where breakfast is served for both houses. The guest house has two two-bedroom suites with a king and a queen bed, and children are welcomed here. The rooms have an encyclopedic array of appointments and furnishings, including bookcases, private decks, leather and overstuffed chairs, fireplaces, and a marble solarium with an indoor spa tub and a three-head shower. Oh, yes, each building has its own seven-foot, outdoor, hot mineral water tub for some of that sybaritic Sycamore Springs soaking. The innkeepers prepare a full breakfast each day and can cater dinner with advance notice. These suites have become very popular with businesses for retreats and conferences.

SETTING & FACILITIES

Location: 8 mi. south of San Luis Obispo, 1 mi. off Hwy. 101 on Avila Beach Dr.
Near: Restaurants, shopping, ocean beaches
Building: 2 Spanish Mission Revival homes
Grounds: 116 acres w/ 5 acres of floral gardens, mature oak and sycamore trees, herb garden, gazebo
Public Space: Common room, library, DR, kitchen in main house

Food & Drink: Full breakfast served at time arranged w/ innkeeper in main house DR, vegetarian diets accommodated
Recreation: Tennis, golf, horseback riding, deep-sea fishing, kayaking, helicopter rides
Amenities & Services: Swimming pool, hot tub, afternoon snacks and freshly baked cookies; spa facilities, restaurant, motel rooms and suites, catered dinners

ACCOMMODATIONS

Units: 4 guest rooms, 2 minisuites in main house, 2 2-BR suites in guest house
All Rooms: Private bath and mineral spa, cable TV/VCR, phone, ceiling fan, individually controlled heat
Some Rooms: Fireplace, four-poster, fridge, spiral staircase, view of Avila Valley, private kitchen (2), shared kitchen (2), extra queen (1)
Bed & Bath: Kings

Favorites: Master BR in main house, w/ marble fireplace, accented w/ mahogany and cherry woods, atrium bathroom, private sundeck, private outdoor mineral spa, view of oak-studded hillsides
Comfort & Decor: Rooms individually decorated w/ leather couches in sitting rooms, artwork, lace curtains in BRs, breakfast nooks, dark green carpet, four-poster and sleigh beds, library

RATES, RESERVATIONS, & RESTRICTIONS

Deposit: Credit card; must cancel 24 hours in advance
Discounts: Weekday business groups, AAA, winter weekdays, groups; extra child $10/day
Credit Cards: All
Check-In/Out: 4/11, late check-out by arrangement

Smoking: No
Pets: No
Kids: In guest house suites
No-Nos: No more than 2 guests per room, except children
Minimum Stay: 2 nights on holiday weekends

Open: All year
Hosts: Charlie Yates, general mgr.; Judy
Begley and Isabel O'connor, innkeepers
1215 Avila Beach Dr.
San Luis Obispo, CA 93405
(805) 595-7302

(800) 234-5831
Fax: (805) 781-2598
www.sycamoresprings.com
info@smsr.com

GARDEN STREET INN, San Luis Obispo

Overall: ★★★★	Room Quality: B	Value: B	Price: $100–$170

San Louis Obispo has that increasingly endangered American species, a lively and vigorous downtown that has retained its heritage and traditions and still attracts shoppers to its stores and restaurants. Its Thursday night market is famous for throngs of crowds, stands of fresh flowers and produce, wandering musicians, and lots of finger foods like barbecued ribs and the best tacos ever. One block from main street is the Garden Street Inn, the town's finest B&B. The blue-gray and pale pink inn with a burgundy awning is the ideal base for exploring area. The guest rooms are all cleverly decorated in diverse themes. The inn's living room has a wall of well-chosen and diverse books clustered around a marble fireplace, with an oak ladder on a trolley to reach that collection of Fitzgerald short stories on the top shelf. You'll have to stay more than one day to get your reading in and still have time to do the town.

SETTING & FACILITIES

Location: In downtown San Luis Obispo, on Garden between Marsh and Osos Sts., 1.5 blocks from Higuera St., 3 blocks from the mission
Near: Restaurants, shopping, wineries, galleries, museums, theaters, California Polytechnic, Hearst Castle, Pismo Beach, Morro Bay, Mission San Luis Obispo de Tolosa
Building: 1886 restored Queen Anne/Italianate Victorian
Grounds: Landscaped gardens w/ Valencia orange and Eureka lemon trees

Public Space: Morning room, library, upper and lower decks
Food & Drink: Full breakfast served 8–9:30 a.m. in morning room or in guest room
Recreation: Biking, horseback riding, tennis, golf
Amenities & Services: Innkeepers' reception 5:30–7 p.m. w/ local wines, cider and cheeses, and hot hors d'oeuvres, robes in rooms, turn-down service w/ home-baked cookies, private parking, concierge services, some rooms equipped for physically disabled

ACCOMMODATIONS

Units: 13 guest rooms, including 4 suites
All Rooms: Private bath, AC,

12-ft. ceiling
Some Rooms: Distinctive fireplace, foothill view, sitting area (4)

Bed & Bath: Queens and kings, some Jacuzzis or claw-foot tubs
Favorites: Dollie McKeen Suite, decorated in neutral tones accented w/ black and gold, an ornate antique fireplace, original stained-glass windows; Amadeus Room, w/ rose wall coverings

and decor reminiscent of Mozart's 18th century
Comfort & Decor: Rooms individually decorated w/ antiques, armoires, wall coverings, special fabrics, spacious baths, all of which reflect the room's theme

RATES, RESERVATIONS, & RESTRICTIONS

Deposit: Check or credit card to hold
Discounts: AAA, seniors or corporate rates Sun.–Thurs.
Credit Cards: AE, MC, V
Check-In/Out: 3/11
Smoking: No
Pets: No
Kids: 16 and over
Minimum Stay: 2 nights on holiday weekends

Open: All year
Host: Elizabeth Kyle Righetti
1212 Garden St.
San Luis Obispo, CA 93401
(805) 545-9802
(800) 488-2045
Fax: (805) 545-9803
www.gardenstreetinn.com
innkeeper@gardenstreetinn.com

BATH STREET INN, Santa Barbara

Overall: ★★★★	Room Quality: B	Value: B	Price: $110–$210

In 1891 a Santa Barbara gentleman had a three-story home built for his wife as a 50th wedding anniversary present. The result was a Victorian with a hip roof containing a tiny balcony under an "eyebrow" dormer that is both charming and unusual. The house is bigger than it appears, with eight guest rooms, all but one on the second and third floors. Behind the house and its lush garden and brick patio is the summer house, a recent addition (in a compatible style) with four more guest rooms, including a suite with a kitchen. Innkeeper Susan Brown serves a substantial breakfast with things like fresh California fruit, homemade granola, cheese and egg frittata, or fresh blueberry pancakes. Guests often come down early for a cup of coffee and read the paper while breakfast is being prepared. It is served family-style in the dining room, at small tables in the living room, or outside in the garden.

SETTING & FACILITIES

Location: In a residential neighborhood between W. Islay and W. Valerio Sts., 3 blocks from State St.
Near: Restaurants, shopping, galleries, theater, wineries, ocean beaches, state parks, Mission Santa Barbara

Building: 1890s 3-story restored Queen Anne Victorian w/ newer building in rear
Grounds: Landscaped urban lot w/ flower gardens, hanging baskets, brick patio

Public Space: LR w/ fireplace, DR, library and sitting room on 3rd floor w/ views of mountains, veranda, patio
Food & Drink: Full breakfast served in DR or garden area, 8–9:30 a.m., early morning coffee avail. in kitchen from 7 a.m.

Recreation: Biking, water sports, tennis, golf
Amenities & Services: Afternoon tea, evening wine and cheese, private parking, concierge services for reservations

ACCOMMODATIONS

Units: 12 guest rooms, 8 in main house, 4 in summer house
All Rooms: Private bath, TV, phone, sitting area
Some Rooms: VCR, balcony, AC, kitchen (1), Franklin gas stove, extra bed (1)
Bed & Bath: Queens, kings (3), Jacuzzis (5)
Favorites: Balcony Room, under the eaves, w/ queen bed and sitting area,

private shower, sunset view from the historic "eyebrow" balcony; Country Suite, w/ country decor, gas Franklin stove, four-poster canopy pencil bed, kitchen, Jacuzzi spa, views of mountains
Comfort & Decor: Rooms individually decorated w/ antiques, wicker, hardwood floors, rugs, wallpapers, multipaned windows, fresh flowers, views of ocean, mountains, garden

RATES, RESERVATIONS, & RESTRICTIONS

Deposit: 50% of bill or 1st night's lodging, whichever is greater; must cancel 72 hours in advance, 14 days for 2 or more rooms
Discounts: Seniors, AAA, Mon.–Thurs. winter, no discounts on holidays; extra person $20
Credit Cards: AE, MC, V
Check-In/Out: 2/11
Smoking: No
Pets: No

Kids: OK
Minimum Stay: 2 nights on weekends
Open: All year
Host: Susan Brown
1720 Bath St.
Santa Barbara, CA 93101
(805) 682-9680
(800) 341-2284
Fax: (805) 569-1218
www.bathstinn.com
innkeeper@bathstinn.com

CHESHIRE CAT INN, Santa Barbara

Overall: ★★★★½	Room Quality: A	Value: B	Price: $140–$350

Christine Dunstan, formerly of Cheshire, England, has taken two Victorian houses, two 1920s California Craftsman cottages, and a carriage house and molded them into the city's most upscale B&B. She chose Lewis Carroll as a theme, and his characters are subtly and not annoyingly in evidence. Outside, the brick courtyard, with its wonderful displays of Santa Barbara flowers and a gazebo filled with a hot tub, ties the whole compound together. It's a glorious place to have breakfast. The staff is unobtrusive and professional, and the food is deliciously fresh California cuisine with English overtones, served on Wedgwood china.

SETTING & FACILITIES

Location: In downtown Santa Barbara at the corner of W. Valerio and Chapala, 1 block west of State St.
Near: Restaurants, shopping, theaters, wine tasting, museums, Santa Barbara Mission, beaches
Building: 2 1894 Queen Anne Victorians, 2 1920s California Craftsman cottages, recently constructed carriage house
Grounds: Double urban lot, flower-filled English gardens, fountains, deck, brick patios, gazebo
Public Space: 2 parlors w/ high ceilings and bay windows, wood-burning

fireplaces, DR w/ fireplace, sideboard, refectory table
Food & Drink: Full breakfast served 8:30–10 a.m. in the DR or on the deck
Recreation: Mountain biking, tennis, golf, wine tasting
Amenities & Services: Gazebo and spa, hot tub in cottages, afternoon snacks, evening wine and hors d'oeuvres, Bailey's liqueurs and homemade chocolates on arrival, fresh flowers, robes, private parking, disabled access, concierge service for reservations

ACCOMMODATIONS

Units: 17 guest rooms, including 1 2-room deluxe suite, 4 Jacuzzi suites, 3 junior suites
All Rooms: Private bath, phone
Some Rooms: TV/VCR, fireplace, fridge and a basket of goodies, patio, deck, private balcony, outdoor hot tub, AC
Bed & Bath: Queens, kings (4, all convertible to twins)
Favorites: Caterpillar Room, w/ window seats, split-level w/ queen bed

above, sitting area below, large private deck overlooking gardens and mountains; Tweedledee studio room, w/ wet bar, kitchen, microwave, AC, English oak table and chairs, king bed
Comfort & Decor: Rooms individually decorated w/ English antiques, Laura Ashley wallpaper and draperies, oriental rugs in public rooms, carpet and tile in guest rooms, hardwood floors; cottages have 2 BRs, private entrance, and deck

RATES, RESERVATIONS, & RESTRICTIONS

Deposit: 1st night; must cancel 7 days in advance; $15 cancellation fee
Discounts: Long stays, weekday business, AAA
Credit Cards: AE, D, MC, V
Check-In/Out: 3/noon
Smoking: No
Pets: No
Kids: In cottages
No-Nos: No more than 2 guests per room, except in cottages

Minimum Stay: 2 nights on weekends, 3 on holiday weekends
Open: All year, except Christmas Day
Hosts: Christine Dunstan, owner; Amy Taylor and Bharti Singh, mgrs.
36 W. Valerio St.
Santa Barbara, CA 93101
(805) 569-1610
Fax: (805) 682-1876
www.cheshirecat.com
cheshire@cheshirecat.com

GLENBOROUGH INN, Santa Barbara

Overall: ★★★½	Room Quality: B	Value: B	Price: $100–$360

What do you call a B&B with five different buildings? A pod? An array? Glenborough Inn, with its wonderful, um, array of Arts and Crafts buildings, has a room for every taste and just about every pocketbook. The decor is eclectic, predominantly Victorian. The rooms range from the frankly sybaritic to the fanciful. The Nouveau Luxury Suite in the Craftsman bungalow (the main building) has a sitting room, bedroom, refrigerator, and private bath, plus a private fenced yard with its own hot tub. Across the street in the Victorian cottage is the Captain's Quarters, with a great nineteenth-century sailing chart, though what sailor has ever been lucky enough to have his own Jacuzzi for two? A tasty vegetarian breakfast is delivered to your door in a picnic basket.

SETTING & FACILITIES

Location: In central Santa Barbara on Bath between W. Sola and W. Victoria, 3 blocks southwest of downtown State St.
Near: Restaurants, shopping, galleries, museums, beaches (14 blocks from the ocean), airport
Building: 5 buildings—1906 Craftsman bungalow, 1885 Victorian cottage, 1912 white farmhouse, 1890 Italianate house, and 1929 vacation rental cottage
Grounds: Private gardens and sitting areas, large yard behind Craftsman bungalow w/ chairs, tables

Public Space: Parlor in Craftsman bungalow, porches
Food & Drink: Full breakfast served in rooms at guests' convenience, no meat products served
Recreation: Biking, tennis, golf, wine tasting
Amenities & Services: Evening hors d'oeuvres, late night cookies, enclosed spa for private use on sign-up basis, robes, fresh flowers, cable TV on request, private parking, fax services, spa services

ACCOMMODATIONS

Units: 14 guest rooms, including 7 suites and 1 2-BR vacation rental cottage
All Rooms: Private bath, modem-compatible phone, coffeemaker
Some Rooms: Fireplace, four-poster, sleeper sofa, fridge, private entrance, private deck, private hot tub, garden, view, AC
Bed & Bath: Queens, kings (3),

double, Jacuzzis for 2 (3), private outdoor hot tubs (3), spa towels, robes
Favorites: The Craftsman, w/ private entrance from patio, hot tub, original wood decor, bedside fireplace, antiques, minifridge
Comfort & Decor: Rooms individually decorated w/ antiques, many w/ fireplaces, claw-foot tubs or Jacuzzis, private entrances, garden views

RATES, RESERVATIONS, & RESTRICTIONS

Deposit: 1st night's lodging or credit card; must cancel 7 days in advance; $15 cancellation fee

Discounts: Long stays, weekday business, AAA; extra person $30

Credit Cards: All

Check-In/Out: 3/11, late check-out by arrangement

Smoking: No

Pets: No

Kids: By prior arrangement

Minimum Stay: 2 nights on week-ends, 3 on holiday weekends

Open: All year

Hosts: Michael Diaz and Steve Ryan, owners; Jill Soderman, mgr.

1327 Bath St.

Santa Barbara, CA 93101

(805) 966-0589

(800) 962-0589

www.silcom.com

glenboro@silcom.com

OLD YACHT CLUB INN, Santa Barbara

Overall: ★★★★	Room Quality: B	Value: B	Price: $95–$190

No, it isn't sitting right on the water, but, yes, it was formerly a yacht club. Just a block away from Santa Barbara's East Beach, this 1912 Craftsman home was pressed into service as headquarters for the Santa Barbara Yacht Club after the organization's original clubhouse washed out to sea. The house was relocated to its current, higher and drier location in 1928 and opened as the city's first B&B in 1980. It has been so successful that the innkeepers purchased the Hitchcock House next door, so now there are a dozen nice rooms with private entrances to choose from when you stay here. The inn is furnished with European and Early American antiques, floral wallpaper, lace curtains, and oriental rugs on hardwood floors. Innkeeper Nancy Donaldson, a member of the American Wine and Food Institute, prepares memorable breakfasts and highly-sought-after five-course Saturday night dinners using only fresh local ingredients. *Bon Appetit* magazine says her meals rival the finest the city has to offer.

SETTING & FACILITIES

Location: In a quiet residential area in southeastern Santa Barbara, 1 block from East Beach, between Hwy. 101 and E. Cabrillo Blvd. near Cabrillo Park

Near: Restaurants, shopping, 1 block from beach, Santa Barbara Zoological Gardens, Santa Barbara Mission, museums

Building: 1912 2-story California Craftsman home and 1925 2-story home

Grounds: 1/3 acre w/ large patio, covered front porch on Old Yacht Club building

Public Space: Parlor, DR in main building

Food & Drink: Full breakfast served 8:30–9:30 a.m. in DR

Recreation: Biking, boating, fishing, water sports, tennis, golf
Amenities & Services: Evening sherry, wine, and hors d'oeuvres; home-made cookies always avail., fresh flow-ers and sherry in rooms, private park-ing, disabled access in 1 room, beach chairs and towels avail., Sat. dinner avail. to inn guests

ACCOMMODATIONS

Units: 12 guest rooms, 4 larger than average, including 2 suites
All Rooms: Private bath, phone
Some Rooms: Four-poster, TV, private entrance, view of Mountains of Monecito, daybed (3)
Bed & Bath: Queens, kings (5), whirlpool tubs (5)

Favorites: Channel Island Suite, large, w/ king bed, separate sitting room, whirlpool tub
Comfort & Decor: Rooms individu-ally decorated w/ Impressionist prints, European and Early American antiques, lace curtains, wallpapers, oriental rugs on hardwood floors

RATES, RESERVATIONS, & RESTRICTIONS

Deposit: Credit card to hold; must cancel 7 days in advance
Discounts: Midweek Oct.–May; extra person $30
Credit Cards: All
Check-In/Out: 1/11, late check-out negotiable
Smoking: No
Pets: No
Kids: OK, most suitable in 2 rooms w/ daybeds
No-Nos: No more than 2 guests per room unless set up for 3

Minimum Stay: 2 nights on week-ends, 3 on holiday weekends
Open: All year
Hosts: Nancy Donaldson and Sandy Hunt
431 Corona del Mar Dr.
Santa Barbara, CA 93101
(805) 962-1277
(800) 549-1676
Fax: (805) 962-3989
www.oldyachtclubinn.com
info@oldyachtclubinn.com

OLIVE HOUSE, Santa Barbara

Overall: ★★★★	Room Quality: B	Value: B	Price: $125–$185

Twenty years ago this fine example of a Craftsman home barely survived the wrecking ball, but in the nick of time it was moved to the foothills of Santa Barbara to start life over as a B&B. The typical Craftsman motif, a shingled exterior with a clean-lined, Japanese-influenced roof, is carried out inside the house as well. The redwood interior has lots of burnished redwood paneling, stained and leaded glass windows, bay windows with window seats, and coffered ceilings. The decor throughout the house is a pleasant mix of antiques and reproductions, Victorian wallpapers, and feel-good furniture such as velvet wing chairs. Several rooms have private decks, one with its own hot tub.

SETTING & FACILITIES

Location: In a residential neighborhood next to the corner of E. Arriaga and Olive, 5 blocks north of downtown
Near: Restaurants, shopping, galleries, ocean, mountains, Santa Barbara Mission
Building: 1906 California Craftsman
Grounds: Urban lot w/ terraced gardens, patio
Public Space: LR w/ wood wainscoting, window seats, fireplace, DR w/ window seats, sunporch
Food & Drink: Full breakfast served at 9 a.m. in DR, garden, or sunporch
Recreation: Biking, tennis, golf, kayaking, whale-watching, harbor tours
Amenities & Services: Afternoon snacks; evening sherry, wine, and hors d'oeuvres; morning papers, hot and iced tea and coffee, hot chocolate always avail.; off-street parking, fax

ACCOMMODATIONS

Units: 5 guest rooms
All Rooms: Private bath, phone
Some Rooms: Private patio w/ private deck, hot tub, ocean view
Bed & Bath: Queens, king (convertible to 2 twins), Jacuzzi (1)
Favorites: Bella Vista, w/ overstuffed chairs, king bed, best views, lots of windows, tub/shower; Pembroke, w/ wing chairs, cherry dresser, large private deck, views of garden, mountains, city, and ocean
Comfort & Decor: Rooms individually decorated w/ comfortable armchairs, good reading lamps, down comforters

RATES, RESERVATIONS, & RESTRICTIONS

Deposit: Credit card; must cancel 7 days in advance
Discounts: AAA, midweek business rates avail.; extra person $25
Credit Cards: AE, D, MC, V
Check-In/Out: 3–7/11, late check-out by arrangement
Smoking: No
Pets: No
Kids: 14 and over
Minimum Stay: 2 nights on weekends, 3 on major holiday weekends
Open: All year
Host: Ellen Schaub
1604 Olive St.
Santa Barbara, CA 93101
(805) 962-4902
(800) 786-6422
Fax: (805) 962-9983
www.sbinns.com/oliveinn
olivehse@aol.com

THE PARSONAGE, Santa Barbara

Overall: ★★★★½   Room Quality: B   Value: B   Price: $125–$330

For some years the Parsonage has been one of Santa Barbara's nicer B&Bs, but in 1999 it underwent a substantial redecoration that boosted it right up into the superior category. The veranda, with its dark green wicker chairs and tables, potted palms, hydrangeas, and fuchsias, is a favorite hangout for guests. The Honeymoon Suite, which runs the width of the inn, has ornately pleated canopies over the bed, with matching drapes and lace curtains that blend nicely with the period overhead light fixtures and tassled light shades. Adjoining the suite is the light-filled solarium, with three walls of arched, multipaned windows and lace café curtains that must have charmed the parson's guests in the 1890s, much as it does the Parsonage's guests today.

SETTING & FACILITIES

Location: In central Santa Barbara, 5 blocks northeast of downtown, at the corner of E. Arellaga and Olive Sts.
Near: Restaurants, shopping, theaters, walking distance to Santa Barbara Mission, museums, art galleries, wineries
Building: 1892 Queen Anne Victorian, recently renovated and redecorated
Grounds: Urban lot w/ newly landscaped grounds, veranda, outdoor dining deck
Public Space: LR w/ fireplace, period furnishings, antiques, oriental rugs, formal DR w/ fireplace, veranda w/ wicker furniture
Food & Drink: Full breakfast served 8:30–10 a.m. in the DR or on the deck
Recreation: Biking, kayaking, whale-watching, hang gliding, tennis, golf, boat excursions
Amenities & Services: Afternoon homemade cookies and cold beverages, evening wine and hors d'oeuvres, robes and fresh flowers in rooms, nightly turn-down w/ chocolates and bottled water, private parking, concierge services for reservations

Food & Drink: Full breakfast served 8:30–10 a.m. in the DR or on the deck
Recreation: Biking, kayaking, whale-watching, hang gliding, tennis, golf, boat excursions
Amenities & Services: Afternoon homemade cookies and cold beverages, evening wine and hors d'oeuvres, robes and fresh flowers in rooms, nightly turn-down w/ chocolates and bottled water, private parking, concierge services for reservations

ACCOMMODATIONS

Units: 6 guest rooms, 2 larger than average, including 1 suite
All Rooms: Private bath, phone, custom fabrics, decorator pillows
Some Rooms: Half-canopy bed, fireplace (2)
Bed & Bath: Queens, kings (2), Egyptian cotton towels, Jacuzzis (2)
Favorites: The Imperial Honeymoon Suite runs the length of the inn, w/ views of ocean, city, and mountains, king half-canopy bed, solarium, Jacuzzi for 2; the Victorian, w/ fireplace, antique furnishings, queen bed, claw-foot tub/shower
Comfort & Decor: Rooms individually decorated w/ antiques, period furniture, lace curtains, drapes, balloon valances, half-canopy and massive carved mahogany beds

RATES, RESERVATIONS, & RESTRICTIONS

Deposit: 50% of bill by credit card or check; must cancel 7 days in advance
Discounts: AAA
Credit Cards: AE, D, MC, V
Check-In/Out: 3/11, late check-out by arrangement
Smoking: No
Pets: No
Kids: Not suitable
No-Nos: No more than 2 guests per room

Minimum Stay: 2 nights on weekends, 3 on holiday weekends
Open: All year
Host: Kim Curran-Moore
1600 Olive St.
Santa Barbara, CA 93101
(805) 962-9336
(800) 775-0352
Fax: (805) 962-2285
www.parsonage.com
parsonage1@aol.com

SECRET GARDEN INN AND COTTAGES, Santa Barbara

Overall: ★★★★	Room Quality: B	Value: B	Price: $115–$225

The 1908 California Craftsman house and four tidy cottages that make up this inn have always had a homey, American Country charm about them, but under the new owners, who took over in 1994, a general sprucing up and improvement process has made a nice place even better. There are two pretty guest rooms in the main house, in addition to the comfortable living and dining rooms for guests' use. The four cottages contain nine rooms, all with private entrances. The inn's garden, bordered by high hedges, is fragrant with mock orange and jasmine and has individual tables where you can breakfast in the mild, sunny Santa Barbara weather. The inn is located in a quiet, residential neighborhood eight blocks from downtown Santa Barbara.

SETTING & FACILITIES

Location: In a residential area of Santa Barbara, on Bath St. between W. Pedregosa and W. Mission Sts., 8 blocks from downtown
Near: Restaurants, shopping, galleries, museums, wineries, Santa Barbara Mission, wharf, beach
Building: 1908 California Craftsman w/ 4 cottages also built in early 1900s, all restored
Grounds: Double lot w/ landscaped gardens, flower beds, pathways, high hedges; avocado, persimmon, and oak trees

Public Space: LR, DR, garden sitting areas
Food & Drink: Full breakfast served 8:30–10 a.m. in DR or garden, or in room by request
Recreation: Biking, swimming, fishing, kayaking, golf, tennis
Amenities & Services: Late afternoon wine and cheese in the garden, evening chocolate chip cookies or brownies w/ hot or cold cider, private off-street parking, assistance w/ dinner reservations and sight-seeing suggestions

ACCOMMODATIONS

Units: 11 guest rooms, 2 in main house, 9 in 4 cottages, including 3 suites
All Rooms: Private bath, special linens, reading area
Some Rooms: Private deck w/ hot tub (5), veranda, private garden, fireplace
Bed & Bath: Queens, king, claw-foot tubs (5)
Favorites: Nightingale Suite, w/ BR,

Chinese rug, fireplace, sitting room w/ futon, fridge, TV, private back deck w/ hot tub, dining area
Comfort & Decor: Rooms individually decorated to reflect the turn-of-the-century theme, w/ Early American and English antiques, wicker, chintz quilts and cushions, hardwood floors, rugs, carpet

RATES, RESERVATIONS, & RESTRICTIONS

Deposit: 1st night's lodging by check or credit card; must cancel 7 days in advance; cancellation fee $10
Discounts: Winter specials; extra person $20
Credit Cards: AE, D, MC, V
Check-In/Out: 3–7/noon, late check-out by arrangement
Smoking: No
Pets: No
Kids: 16 and over
Minimum Stay: 2 nights on weekends

and holidays
Open: All year
Hosts: Jack Greenwald and Christine Dunstan
1908 Bath St.
Santa Barbara, CA 93101
(805) 687-2300
(800) 676-1622
Fax: (805) 687-4576
www.secretgarden.com
garden@secretgarden.com

SIMPSON HOUSE INN, Santa Barbara

Overall: ★★★★★	Room Quality: A	Value: B	Price: $195–$500

Simpson House is on virtually every travel book's Top Ten list, and a major auto club recently judged it the best B&B in the entire United States. That's some praise for an inn in a state that has more than its share of posh B&Bs. The site contributes a lot to this—one acre in central Santa Barbara, screened off from its neighbors by a ten-foot sandstone wall in front and trees all around. Inside the big main gate, the spectacular English garden, mature trees, and a rolling lawn combine to make it into a lush oasis. But it's more than the site. The seven guest rooms in the main Eastlake Victorian mansion are the penultimate B&B rooms, with furnishings so luxe you can't imagine how they could be improved. The cottages and guest rooms in the restored barn (and "barn" doesn't seem a fitting term for lodgings this extravagant) are possibly even more lavish. The food is legendary, and the evening Mediterranean buffet can make you skip dinner. Finally, the staff is very sharp and on the job. You get to the top by doing a lot of extra things, some big and some small: handmade Victorian wallpapers, comforters of European goose down rather than ordinary down, bicycles, picnic baskets, beach chairs and towels for excursions to the ocean, free tickets on a Santa Barbara trolley tour of the town, and croquet on that gorgeous lawn.

SETTING & FACILITIES

Location: In a residential neighborhood in central Santa Barbara, 1 block northeast of State St., on E. Arrellaga between Anacapa and Santa Barbara Sts.

Near: Restaurants, shopping, wineries, theaters, museums

Grounds: 1 acre of secluded English gardens, fountains, mature trees, lawns, benches, 2 patios

Public Space: Parlor w/ fireplace, library, formal DR, verandas overlooking gardens

Food & Drink: Full breakfast served in DR, on the veranda, or in rooms

8:30–9:30 a.m., early departures can be accommodated

Recreation: Bikes, croquet, beach equipment on premises; tennis, golf nearby

Amenities & Services: Afternoon refreshments; evening sherry, wine, and Mediterranean hors d'oeuvres buffet; access to VCR library, newspaper, Santa Barbara trolley tour passes, private parking, disabled access, full concierge services, in-room European spa treatments avail., private club w/ gym and pool avail.

ACCOMMODATIONS

Units: 14 guest rooms, including 4 oversized guest rooms, 3 cottages

All Rooms: Private bath, cable TV, VCR, phone, AC, goose down comforter, flowering orchids, iron

Some Rooms: Fireplace, half-canopy bed, fridge, private patio, wet bar, extra bed (1)

Bed & Bath: Queens, kings (4), Jacuzzis (4), hairdryers

Favorites: Garden Room, w/ garden

views, patio, antique pine floor w/ oriental rug, vaulted ceiling w/ skylight, bay window w/ window seat; Sun Room, w/ white wicker furniture, cast-iron bed, views of gardens and mountains from large private deck

Comfort & Decor: Rooms individually decorated w/ original art, European antiques, hand-printed Victorian wall coverings, oriental carpets, teak and antique pine floors

RATES, RESERVATIONS, & RESTRICTIONS

Deposit: 50% of bill or 1st night's lodging if 2 nights or more; must cancel 7 days in advance

Discounts: None; extra person $35

Credit Cards: AE, D, MC, V

Check-In/Out: 3/11

Smoking: No

Pets: No

Kids: 12 and over in some rooms

No-Nos: No more than 2 guests per room

Minimum Stay: 2 nights on week-

ends, 3 on holiday weekends

Open: All year

Hosts: Linda and Glyn Davies, owners; Dixie Budke, mgr.

121 E. Arrellaga St.

Santa Barbara, CA 93101

(805) 963-7067

(800) 676-1280

Fax: (805) 364-4811

www.simpsonhouseinn.com

reservations@simpsonhouseinn.com

TIFFANY INN, Santa Barbara

Overall: ★★★★	Room Quality: B	Value: B	Price: $110–$250

There are bigger, fancier, more ornate Victorian inns, but somehow the Tiffany Inn stands out. The Stick-style architecture, with its mix of clapboard and shingles, diamond-paned bay windows, and a central gable, is handsome without ostentation. Out back there is a wonderful flower-filled patio with a specimen jacaranda tree, lots of flowers, and a old-fashioned, single-petaled ivory climbing rose that would stop traffic at a garden show. All the rooms are comfortable, but the star goes to the Penthouse Suite, with a spacious bedroom, fireplace, sitting area, terrace and balcony, and a view of the ocean.

SETTING & FACILITIES

Location: In a residential neighborhood on sometimes busy De La Vina between Victoria and Sola, 2 blocks west of State St. and the downtown area

Near: Restaurants, shopping, galleries, theater, wineries, ocean beaches, state parks, Mission Santa Barbara, art museum

Building: 1898 Stick-style Victorian

Grounds: Landscaped urban lot w/ rose gardens, deck w/ arbor and huge jacaranda tree, benches, tables

Public Space: LR w/ fireplace, formal DR, veranda overlooking rose garden

Food & Drink: Full breakfast served at 9 a.m., cont'l breakfast at 7:30 on request

Recreation: Biking, sailing, kayaking

Amenities & Services: Wine, cheese, and hors d'oeuvres at 5:30 p.m.; homemade cookies, hot chocolate, and tea at 8 p.m.; concierge services for reservations, private off-street parking

ACCOMMODATIONS

Units: 7 guest rooms, 1 2-room suite

All Rooms: Private bath, Tiffany lamps (several original)

Some Rooms: Fireplace, TV/VCR, fridge

Bed & Bath: Queens, king (can be converted to twins), spa tubs for 2 (3)

Favorites: Victoria, w/ original wood-burning fireplace, Victorian furnishings, lace curtains, overlooks gardens; Pent-house, covers entire 3rd floor, has private terrace and balcony w/ view of ocean, TV/VCR, fridge, wood-burning fireplace, spa tub for 2

Comfort & Decor: Rooms individually decorated w/ Victorian antiques, wallpapers, white lace curtains, velvet chairs; brass, walnut, and four-poster beds; garden or mountain views

RATES, RESERVATIONS, & RESTRICTIONS

Deposit: Credit card; must cancel 7 days in advance

Discounts: Midweek Oct. 1–May 31, AAA weekdays; extra person $25

Credit Cards: AE, D, MC, V

Check-In/Out: 3:30–7/11, late check-out by arrangement

Smoking: No

Pets: No

Kids: 12 and over in 2 rooms

Minimum Stay: 2 nights on weekends, 3 on holiday weekends

Open: All year
Host: Janice Hawkins
1323 De La Vina St.
Santa Barbara, CA 93101
(805) 963-2283

(800) 999-5672
Fax: (805) 962-0994
www.sbinns.com/tiffany
tiffanyinn@aol.com

VILLA ROSA, Santa Barbara

Overall: ★★★★	Room Quality: B	Value: B	Price: $100–$230

The Villa Rosa's original 1932 building was gutted and remodeled into an 18-room inn in 1981, complete with a new tile roof, archways, balconies, and an attractive, enclosed courtyard with a heated pool and Jacuzzi. Guest rooms contain contemporary southwestern furniture in terra-cotta, blue, and rose tones, Spanish and Mexican art, plantation shutters, tropical plants, and tiled baths. Some have fireplaces, sitting areas, and small kitchen facilities, and some have ocean views from private verandas. The inn provides a good continental breakfast of croissants, muffins, fruit, and freshly brewed coffee served in the lobby, in your room, or poolside. In the early evening, wine and hors d'oeuvres are out in the lounge or courtyard, and port, sherry, and coffee are offered as a nightcap in the lounge. The staff here is particularly friendly and helpful.

SETTING & FACILITIES

Location: At Chapala and Cabrillo Blvd., 1 block west of Stearn's Wharf
Near: Restaurants, shopping, galleries, beach, zoo, museums, theater
Building: 1930 renovated 2-story Spanish-style architecture
Public Space: 2 lobbies, 1 w/ fireplace, courtyard
Food & Drink: Cont'l breakfast served 8–10 a.m. in courtyard, lobby, or guest room
Recreation: Biking, in-line skating, whale-watching, parasailing, swimming, boating, fishing, horseback riding, golf
Amenities & Services: Heated swimming pool, spa, robes, hairdryers, pool towels, evening wine and hors d'oeuvres, port or sherry on request 9–11 p.m.; coffee, tea, hot chocolate, iced tea, fruit avail. in lobby; evening turn-down w/ rose and chocolate, morning paper; 24-hour concierge services, privileges at Santa Barbara Athletic Club $15/day, massage avail. on request

ACCOMMODATIONS

Units: 18 guest rooms, including one minisuite that accommodates 4
All Rooms: Private bath, phone, clock radio, sitting area
Some Rooms: Kitchen, fireplace, cable TV, French doors, private atrium; view of wharf, courtyard, and pool; balcony, sofa bed (1)
Bed & Bath: Queens, kings (3)

Favorites: No. 14, w/ view of ocean and pool, sitting area, kitchen, fireplace
Comfort & Decor: Rooms individually decorated w/ Spanish-influenced furnishings, Santa Fe decor, exposed rough wood, ivory walls, plantation shutters, tiled bathrooms

RATES, RESERVATIONS, & RESTRICTIONS

Deposit: Credit card; must cancel 5 days in advance
Discounts: Winter specials; no charge for extra persons in minisuite
Credit Cards: AE, MC, V
Check-In/Out: 3/noon
Smoking: No
Pets: No
Kids: 14 and over

Minimum Stay: 2 nights on weekends, 3 on holiday weekends
Open: All year
Host: Annie Puetz
15 Chapala St.
Santa Barbara, CA 93101
(805) 966-0851
Fax: (805) 962-7159

BABBLING BROOK B&B INN, Santa Cruz

Overall: ★★★★½	Room Quality: B	Value: B	Price: $145–$195

Although it's located along a busy road, once you enter the grounds of this pretty inn, the only sound you're aware of is that of the brook winding through the property, tumbling over waterfalls and a large picturesque waterwheel. The 14 guest rooms are light and bright and filled with Country French furniture, colorful fabrics, and French Impressionist reproductions, for which the rooms are named. There are lots of skylights, balconies, jet tubs, and decks, and all of the rooms have fireplaces and private entries. The rooms are cleverly laid out to feel very private and surrounded by greenery and water. Even the smallest rooms give the impression of being in a tree house. A large country breakfast is served in the casually attractive dining area or out on the spacious second-story deck.

SETTING & FACILITIES

Location: In a residential neighborhood in central Santa Cruz, 8 blocks west of Pacific Garden Mall
Near: Walking distance to beach, wharf, boardwalk, downtown shopping, historic homes, 200 restaurants
Building: 1909 building built on foundation of a 1790 gristmill, renovated in 1997
Grounds: 1 acre of gardens, meandering brook, waterfalls, waterwheel, gazebo

Public Space: LR/parlor w/ fireplace, deck
Food & Drink: Full breakfast buffet served 8–10 a.m. (Sun. 9–11 a.m.) in the main lobby; guests may eat there, on deck, or in room
Recreation: Tennis, golf, whale-watching, biking
Amenities & Services: Afternoon cookies, evening wine and cheese, private parking, disabled access to 2 rooms, concierge service for reservations

ACCOMMODATIONS

Units: 13 guest rooms, 3 larger than average, including 2 suites
All Rooms: Private bath and entrance, fireplace, private deck w/ view of brook and gardens, cable TV, phone
Some Rooms: VCR, hot tub (1), four-poster, coffeemaker, extra queen (1)
Bed & Bath: Queens, king, futon roll-away avail., jet tubs for 1 (3), jet tubs for 2 (2), hot tub (1), claw-foot (1)
Favorites: Artist's Retreat, w/ private deck w/ hot tub overlooking garden, corner brick fireplace, large desk; Monet, w/ jet tub for 2, wood-burning stove, view of garden
Comfort & Decor: Rooms individually decorated in styles representing artists and poets w/ French Impressionist prints appropriate to artist for which room is named, Country French furniture, wood-burning fireplaces, four-posters, floral and garden prints, carpet

RATES, RESERVATIONS, & RESTRICTIONS

Deposit: 100% prior to arrival; must cancel 10 days in advance
Discounts: Weekday business volume; extra person $20
Credit Cards: All
Check-In/Out: 3/11:30, late check-out by arrangement
Smoking: No
Pets: No
Kids: Some rooms not suitable
Minimum Stay: 2 nights on weekends

Open: All year
Hosts: Dan Floyd and Suzie Lankes
1025 Laurel St.
Santa Cruz, CA 95060
(831) 427-2437
(800) 866-1131
Fax: (831) 427-2457
www.babblingbrookinn.com
lodging@babblingbrookinn.com

DARLING HOUSE, Santa Cruz

| Overall: ★★★★ | Room Quality: B | Value: B | Price: $95–$260 |

The first thing you notice when you visit the Darling House (the owners' name, not a description of the house) is the setting—just across the street from Monterey Bay, with its dazzling blue water and wide-open sunny skies. Then you admire the house itself, a 90-year-old-Spanish Mission Revival, a work of art by noted architect William Weeks, considered his finest residential architecture. It has terra-cotta roof tiles, copper flashing, hand-tooled downspouts, and, inside, open-beamed ceilings, an Art Deco fireplace, wood inlays, and prism glass windows. Each room has a different hardwood for its interior; there are eight different woods in all. The seven guest rooms are comfortably but not lavishly outfitted in American antiques, and only one has a private bathroom. In the morning, you can have an espresso along with homemade granola, nut breads, croissants, and fresh fruits in the tiger oak dining room, and then be off to explore the pleasures of this charming beach town.

SETTING & FACILITIES

Location: In a bayside residential neighborhood, 4 blocks west of the municipal pier and boardwalk and .75 mi. south of downtown Santa Cruz
Near: Restaurants, shopping, galleries, wharf, boardwalk, beaches
Building: 90-year-old Spanish Mission Revival w/ Prairie School influence
Grounds: Half-acre of flowering gardens, palms, citrus trees, lawns, gazebo
Public Space: Parlor and DR w/ oak

paneling, beveled glass, and ocean views; large Spanish tile veranda w/ ocean view
Food & Drink: Expanded cont'l breakfast served 8–9:30 a.m. in dining area
Recreation: Croquet, biking, waterskiing
Amenities & Services: Complimentary beverage on arrival, guest fridges, private parking, disabled access

ACCOMMODATIONS

Units: 7 guest rooms, most larger than average, including 1 suite
All Rooms: Down comforter
Some Rooms: Ocean view, fireplace, private bath (1), shared bath (6)
Bed & Bath: Beds vary
Favorites: Pacific Ocean Room, w/ fireplace, telescope, private bath, ocean

view, matching tiger oak suite furnishings
Comfort & Decor: Rooms individually decorated w/ Chippendale and American antique furniture, velvet, lace curtains, hardwood floors w/ oriental rugs

RATES, RESERVATIONS, & RESTRICTIONS

Deposit: Prepayment required; must cancel 5 days in advance
Discounts: Long stays, weekday business, winter weekdays, excluding breakfast; extra person $15
Credit Cards: AE, D, MC, V
Check-In/Out: 4/11
Smoking: No
Pets: No
Kids: OK

Minimum Stay: 2 nights on weekends
Open: All year
Hosts: Darrell and Karen Darling
314 W. Cliff Dr.
Santa Cruz, CA 95060
(831) 458-1958
(800) 458-1958
Fax: (831) 458-0320
www.darling house.com

FERN OAKS INN, Santa Paula

| Overall: ★★★★ | Room Quality: B | Value: A | Price: $95–$110 |

The Fern Oaks Inn is one of those rare B&Bs that isn't in a Victorian home, but it doesn't suffer from the lack of gingerbread. The imposing two-story Spanish Revival home set on a spacious three-quarter-acre site is ideal for an inn. The owners called on the services of a well-known interior designer to pick furniture and accents that complemented the architecture, and she did just that. The living room, with its antique French settee, a 150-year-old mahogany buffet, and a baby grand piano, contrasts nicely with the casual and inviting solarium, with its Palladian windows. And the inn has four guest rooms, so you don't have to worry about the ample pool being crowded. The mountains just to the north are the site of the famous Sespe Condor Sanctuary.

SETTING & FACILITIES

Location: On Hwy. 150, 1 mi. north of downtown Santa Paula, and 15 mi. south of Ojai
Near: Restaurants, shopping, antiques, Union Oil Museum, Santa Paula Airport collection of antique planes, Filmore–Santa Paula Railroad excursions
Building: 1929 Spanish Revival w/ Arts and Crafts fireplace designed by noted California ceramist Ernest Bacheldor
Grounds: 2/3 acre, w/ native oaks, citrus and fruit trees, 75 varieties of roses
Public Space: LR w/ Chinese rug, fireplace, baby grand piano, formal DR w/ silk oriental rug, solarium w/ Palladian windows, library
Food & Drink: Full breakfast served at 9:30 a.m. in the DR or beside the pool by request
Recreation: Biking, horseback riding, boating on nearby lakes, tennis, golf
Amenities & Services: Swimming pool, afternoon snacks; evening sherry, wine, fresh fruit, and cookies; fresh flowers and chocolates in rooms, private parking, assistance w/ dining reservations, in-room massage avail. w/ 1 week's notice, cable TV in main parlor

ACCOMMODATIONS

Units: 4 guest rooms
All Rooms: Private bath, AC, separate vanity area
Some Rooms: Four-poster
Bed & Bath: Queens, roll-away bed avail.
Favorites: Casablanca has private sunporch w/ view of the Topa Topa mountains, rattan canopy four-poster, sitting area
Comfort & Decor: Rooms individually decorated w/ antiques and vintage 1930s furniture, Ralph Lauren fabrics, shutters, hardwood floors, Berber rugs, cedar closets

RATES, RESERVATIONS, & RESTRICTIONS

Deposit: 50% of bill; must cancel 7 days in advance; $15 cancellation fee
Discounts: Long stays, midweek lodging package avail.; extra person $20
Credit Cards: None
Check-In/Out: 3/noon
Smoking: No
Pets: No
Kids: OK by arrangement
Minimum Stay: 2 nights June–Sept., holidays
Open: All year
Hosts: Anthony and Marcia Landau
1025 Ojai Rd.
Santa Paula, CA 93060
(805) 525-7747
Fax: (805) 933-5001
www.fernoaksinn.com
info@fernoaksinn.com

BALLARD INN, Solvang

Overall: ★★★★½	Room Quality: A	Value: B	Price: $170–$250

At the historic crossroads of Ballard, where stagecoaches stopped on their way from Santa Barbara to San Louis Obispo, the Ballard Inn will exceed all your expectations for a country inn. Though it's only been here some 15 years, it's definitely a landmark. The gray and white two-story Cape Cod building with white wicker rockers on the veranda makes the passerby ache to go up and sit a spell. The inn's 15 oversized rooms are all decorated in different styles reflecting local lore: for instance, a historic Ballard trapper who rode with Kit Carson is remembered in the Davy Brown Room, which has walls of plank and mortar, snowshoes, a coonskin cap, and Early American antiques. The effect is tasteful, charming, and comfortable. In the evening the Ballard Inn's dining room becomes the trendy Café Chardonnay. The breakfasts at the inn are heroic stage-stop affairs, cooked to order, with bacon, smoked Idaho trout, waffles, and fruit.

SETTING & FACILITIES

Location: In the Santa Ynez Valley, 4 mi. east of Hwy. 101, 4 mi. north of Solvang, 40 min. from Santa Barbara
Near: Restaurants, shopping, galleries, museums, wineries, Solvang Scandinavian village, 3 missions within 30 min., Los Padres Nat'l Forest
Building: 1985 gray and white Cape Cod inn w/ white picket fence
Grounds: Half-acre w/ lawns and flower gardens, wraparound veranda w/ white wicker rockers
Public Space: 4 common rooms w/ hardwood floors and oriental rugs, green Italian marble fireplace, DR w/ fireplace
Food & Drink: Full breakfast served 8–10 a.m. in DR
Recreation: Mountain and road biking, horseback riding, glider rides, golf, fishing, cruises on Cachuma Lake for eagle-watching and other birding
Amenities & Services: Evening wine and hors d'oeuvres, home-baked cookies, private parking, fax, photocopying and secretarial services avail.; babysitting, beauty, barber, and massage services avail.; concierge services, restaurant on premises; 1 room fully disabled accessible, 3 partially accessible

ACCOMMODATIONS

Units: 15 guest rooms, all larger than average, including 1 suite
All Rooms: Private bath, AC, down comforter and duvet cover or handmade quilt, cable TV and phone on request
Some Rooms: Fireplace (7)
Bed & Bath: Kings (convertible to twins), queens (6), roll-away avail.
Favorites: Vineyard Room, w/ matching bent willow furniture; grape motif fabric on duvet, chairs, and drapes; sitting area in corner turret w/ bay windows, blond hardwood floors
Comfort & Decor: Rooms individually decorated w/ country, rustic, and Victorian furnishings that reflect some aspect of the area's history

RATES, RESERVATIONS, & RESTRICTIONS

Deposit: Credit card; must cancel 7 days in advance, groups 30 days; $25 cancellation fee if not rebooked
Discounts: Weekday business, groups, AAA; 10% service charge; extra person $50
Credit Cards: AE, MC, V
Check-In/Out: 3/noon, late check-out avail. on request
Smoking: No
Pets: No
Kids: OK with well-behaved parents
No-Nos: No more than 3 guests

per room
Minimum Stay: 2 nights on weekends
Open: Closed Christmas Day
Hosts: Steve Hyslop and Larry Stone, owners; Kelly Robinson, mgr.
2436 Baseline Ave.
Solvang, CA 93463
(805) 688-7770
(800) 638-2466
Fax: (805) 688-9560
www.ballardinn.com
innkeeper@ballardinn.com

STORYBOOK INN, Solvang

Overall: ★★★★	Room Quality: B	Value: B	Price: $105–$189

The Storybook Inn is just right for a storybook town. What better place to build a three-story stucco and half-timbered inn than in Solvang, that quaint little Danish town in the gorgeous Santa Ynez valley? If you've missed Solvang, it's a formerly quiet Danish colony that got discovered by LA. It's been described as "more Danish than Denmark," and "Denmark Disneyfied." *Sunset Magazine* voted it one of the ten most beautiful towns in the United States. The Storybook Inn has all of the creature comforts, such as private baths and cable, spiced up with antiques and just enough decorator touches to keep the missus happy and not ruffle the old man while he watches ESPN. Each guest room has a storybook theme and matching decor. There are lots of things to do around here—antique and knickknack shops and Danish bakeries abound, as do fine Santa Ynez Valley wineries, and four golf courses are nearby. The full Danish breakfast makes this affordable inn even better, with fresh-baked breads, eggs to order, fresh fruit, and Aebelskivvers, a Danish pancake worked over with a branding iron.

SETTING & FACILITIES

Location: In Solvang in a residential neighborhood 1 block from the main street, on Hwy. 246, 29 mi. northwest of Santa Barbara
Near: Restaurants, shopping, galleries, Hans Christian Andersen Museum, Danish Heritage and Elverhoj Fine Arts Museum, Western Wear Museum, antiques, Santa Ynez wineries, Indian casino
Building: 5-year-old 4-story European villa
Grounds: Urban lot, front patio, landscaped courtyard w/ wisteria
Public Space: Parlor, DR

Food & Drink: Full Danish breakfast served 8:30–9:30 a.m. in DR, parlor, or guest room
Recreation: Biking, golfing, live summer theater under the stars, glider rides, horseback riding, wine tours

Amenities & Services: Evening local wine and microbrewery tasting and hors d'oeuvres, fresh cookies, private parking, disabled access, restaurant on premises

ACCOMMODATIONS

Units: 9 guest rooms, 3 larger than average, including 2 suites
All Rooms: Private bath, cable TV, AC, down comforter
Some Rooms: Four-poster, patio, bay window, fireplaces (8)
Bed & Bath: Queens, Jacuzzis (2), bathrooms are tiled to match room theme
Favorites: Swan's Nest Room, w/ iron

canopy bed w/ lace netting, fireplace, patio, Jacuzzi; Princess and the Pea Room, w/ high canopy bed and stool to get in, bay window, fireplace, wall murals
Comfort & Decor: Rooms individually decorated in themes from Hans Christian Andersen, w/ artwork, antiques, down comforters, patchwork quilts; canopy, sleigh, or four-poster antique European beds

RATES, RESERVATIONS, & RESTRICTIONS

Deposit: Credit card; must cancel 7 days in advance
Discounts: AAA; extra adult $25
Credit Cards: D, MC, V
Check-In/Out: 3/11, late check-out at noon
Smoking: No
Pets: No
Kids: 12 and over
Minimum Stay: 2 nights on weekends

Open: All year
Hosts: Chip and Carol Orton
409 1st St.
Solvang, CA 93463
(805) 688-1703
(800) 786-7925
Fax: (805) 688-0953
www.solvangstorybook.com
chipcarol@solvangstorybook.com

BLUE SPRUCE INN, Soquel

Overall: ★★★★	Room Quality: B	Value: A	Price: $85–$175

Located in a nice neighborhood setting in a town that's right next door to Santa Cruz, the Blue Spruce has six rooms with featherbeds and handmade quilts; most have gas fireplaces, four have jetted tubs, and one has an outdoor tub. The inn is four miles from the Santa Cruz Civic Center and one mile from Capitola Beach, making it a great, reasonably priced headquarters from which to explore the area. A hearty breakfast features homestyle goodies such as baked apples, orange-date muffins, and quiche.

SETTING & FACILITIES

Location: In a residential neighborhood in Soquel, 3 mi. east of Santa Cruz, just north of Hwy. 1 near Bay

Ave./Porter St. exit, 1 mi. inland from Capitola Beach

Near: Restaurants, shopping, wineries, state parks, beaches, Santa Cruz casino, pier, boardwalk
Building: 1875 village farmhouse
Grounds: Half-acre w/ private gardens, fountains, grape arbor, white picket fence
Public Space: Parlor, garden, deck
Food & Drink: Full breakfast served in parlor or garden 8:30–10 a.m., or at guest's preference
Recreation: Biking, tennis, golf
Amenities & Services: Hot tub, cookies, hot and cold drinks always avail., robes, hairdryers, beach chairs and towels avail., guest fridge in common area, private parking, fax, video library

ACCOMMODATIONS

Units: 6 guest rooms, 1 (carriage house) larger than average
All Rooms: Private bath, featherbed, luxury linens, extra pillows, good reading lights, comfortable seating, wineglasses and corkscrew, phone w/ computer modem, fresh flowers
Some Rooms: Fireplace, handmade quilt, VCR, TV
Bed & Bath: Queens, king, jetted tubs (4), outdoor tub (1)
Favorites: Carriage house, w/ king bed, gas fireplace, skylights, TV, stained glass mural, private garden, in-room spa tub for 2; Seascape, w/ skylight, spa tub for 2, gas fireplace, private entrance and garden area
Comfort & Decor: Rooms are individually decorated w/ original artwork, country-style decor w/ antiques, coordinated wall coverings, carpet

RATES, RESERVATIONS, & RESTRICTIONS

Deposit: 1st night's lodging; must cancel 7 days in advance
Discounts: Corporate rates midweek
Credit Cards: AE, D, MC, V
Check-In/Out: 3/11
Smoking: No
Pets: No
Kids: Not suitable
No-Nos: No more than 2 guests per room
Minimum Stay: 2 nights on weekends, will accommodate single nights on weekend when possible
Open: All year
Hosts: Pat and Tom O'Brien
2815 S. Main St.
Soquel, CA 95073
(831) 464-1137
(800) 559-1137
Fax: (831) 475-0608
www.bluespruce.com
innkeeper@bluespruce.com

INN ON SUMMER HILL, Summerland

Overall: ★★★★½	Room Quality: B	Value: B	Price: $215–$325

Is there an award this place hasn't won since it was built in 1989? It's garnered honors from magazines, reviewers, and the public that range from "most romantic" to "most highly rated in the country." Though the architecture is Arts and Crafts, with emphasis on clean lines, materials, and workmanship, inside it's a different matter. Interior designer Mabel Shults (she and her husband, Paul, are the owners and builders) used the interior as her Sistine Chapel. The decor has been variously described as Country French, European Country, and New England Country Estate. In any case, the lavish suites are filled with canopy beds, antiques, original art, European furniture, and decorator fabrics without end. The decor would send shivers of ecstasy down the spine of a *House and Garden* editor. The building is on a snug site on the side of a hill with wonderful views of the ocean. Granted, the views are across Highway 101 (below grade here), but the soundproofed rooms and the opulent surroundings will keep you from dwelling on it.

SETTING & FACILITIES

Location: 5 mi. south of Santa Barbara in the small seaside village of Summerland
Near: Beaches, Santa Barbara museums, Mission Santa Barbara, 50 art galleries, wineries, antique shopping, restaurants
Building: Recent construction in the turn-of-the-century Arts and Crafts style, w/ heavy beams, carved woods, and built-in furniture, all of pine in California Craftsman style
Grounds: Landscaped urban hillside lot w/ brick walkways, whimsical birdhouses
Public Space: Lobby, Teapot (dining) Room w/ fireplace, pine-paneled beam ceilings, gazebo
Food & Drink: Full breakfast served buffet-style 7–10 a.m.
Recreation: Biking, horseback riding, tennis, golf, bird-watching
Amenities & Services: Hot tub, afternoon snacks, afternoon wine and hors d'oeuvres, evening desserts, fresh flowers, morning newspaper, soundproofing, private parking, concierge service for reservations

ACCOMMODATIONS

Units: 15 minisuite guest rooms, 1 deluxe suite
All Rooms: Private bath w/ 1-person Jacuzzi, private entrance, fireplace, canopy bed, books, fridge, entertainment center w/ cable TV, VCR and radio, instant hot water dispenser, phone, AC, ocean view, balcony or patio, extra queen (1)
Bed & Bath: Kings, queens (6)
Favorites: Deluxe suite has 2 rooms separated by double doors, vaulted pine ceilings, 2 baths, LR w/ 2 ocean-view balconies, wet bar, fridge, dining area, bedroom w/ king canopy bed, sitting area, fireplace, instant hot water dispenser
Comfort & Decor: Canopy beds (some so high they require steps), down comforters, floral wallpapers, hardwood floors w/ rugs, art by local artists commissioned to fit room decor; hand-crocheted doilies, runners, and afghans; wicker, wool dhurrie rugs; Payne, B. Berger, and Waverly fabrics

RATES, RESERVATIONS, & RESTRICTIONS

Deposit: 14-day advance deposit; must cancel 7 days in advance
Discounts: AAA, winter weekdays, seniors on weekdays; extra person $25
Credit Cards: All
Check-In/Out: 3/11, late check-out by request
Smoking: No
Pets: No
Kids: OK
Minimum Stay: 2 nights on weekends

Open: All year
Host: Denise LeBlanc
P.O. Box 376
2520 Lillie Ave.
Summerland, CA 93067

(805) 969-9998
(800) 845-5566
Fax: (805) 565-9946
www.innonsummerhill.com
denisel@innonsummerhill.com

LA MER, Ventura

Overall: ★★★★	Room Quality: B	Value: B	Price: $95–$185

La Mer is your real, classical European bed-and-breakfast. Owner/innkeeper Gisela Baida is from Germany and has fashioned her popular inn in the European tradition, and each antique-filled room has been decorated with the theme of a different country—France, England, Germany, Austria, and Norway. In a positive departure from B&B tradition, however, La Mer's rooms all have private baths and entrances. The handsome two-story historic Victorian is on a hillside that affords a panoramic view of downtown Ventura, the Santa Barbara Channel, and the Santa Cruz Islands on the horizon. The inn's hillside gardens are well-tended and floriferous, and the food is *wunderbar*—muesli; Black Forest ham; European cakes, breads, and cheeses; and freshly ground, house-blended coffee. Gisela's famous horse-drawn carriage outings for a picnic are legendary.

SETTING & FACILITIES

Location: At the west end of downtown Ventura, 1 block north of Main St. and 2 houses west of city hall
Near: Restaurants, shopping, beaches, antiques, Channel Islands Nat'l Park, Lake Casitas
Building: 1890 Cape Cod Victorian w/ bay windows
Grounds: Urban lot w/ landscaped hillside gardens w/ sitting areas, abuts Grant Memorial Park

Public Space: Parlor, DR
Food & Drink: Full Bavarian breakfast served 8–9:30 a.m. in DR
Recreation: Biking, ocean sports, fishing, tennis, golf
Amenities & Services: Evening wine, complimentary bottle of wine/champagne in room, private parking, antique carriage rides, German and Spanish spoken, therapeutic in-room massage, Channel Island tours arranged

ACCOMMODATIONS

Units: 5 guest rooms, 2 larger than average
All Rooms: Private bath and entrance
Some Rooms: Ocean view, fireplace (1), veranda (2)
Bed & Bath: Queens, king, claw-foot

tubs (3)
Favorites: Madame Pompadour, powder blue w/ French antique walnut carved bed, tapestries, bay window w/ ocean view, wood-burning stove, claw-foot tub

Comfort & Decor: Rooms individually decorated to capture a specific European country, w/ European antiques and paintings, comforters, tapestries, old-fashioned radios

RATES, RESERVATIONS, & RESTRICTIONS

Deposit: Credit card or 1 night's deposit; must cancel 7 days in advance

Discounts: Long stays, weekday business; extra person $20

Credit Cards: AE, MC, V

Check-In/Out: 4/noon, late check-out by arrangement

Smoking: No

Pets: No

Kids: 10 and over

Minimum Stay: 2 nights on holiday weekends and some summer weekends

Open: All year

Hosts: Gisela and Mike Baida
411 Poli St.
Ventura, CA 93001
(805) 643-3600
Fax: (805) 653-7329
www.vcol.net/lamer.com

Zone 6
Southern California

Los Angeles and Orange Counties

Cities and Towns Santa Monica, Los Angeles, South Pasadena, Rancho Cucamonga and Ontario, Playa del Rey, Venice, Seal Beach, Long Beach, Santa Catalina Island and Avalon, Newport Beach, Laguna Beach.

Attractions Movies, celebrities, stars, sun, and beaches; **Warner Brothers Studios**, the best tour; catch a flick at **Mann's Chinese Theater** and try to fit your handprint into one of the stars' on the sidewalk out front; be part of the audience at a **TV show taping**; walk along **Venice Beach** and gawk at the bikini-clad skaters, the jugglers, and the tattooed bikers; buy a movie star's castoffs at **Star Wares**; the **Getty Museum** is just one of five major art museums, with paintings ranging from Gainsborough's *Blue Boy* to enough of **Degas's** dancers to form a ballet company; other museums abound with subjects like tar pits, tolerance, lingerie, cars, TV and radio, and Gene Autry's excellent **Museum of Western Heritage**; there are innumerable beaches from **Malibu** in the north to **Laguna** in the south; the **Dodgers**, the **Lakers**, and **Santa Anita** are all here; major league shopping is everywhere, particularly on **Rodeo Drive**; live theater at the **Ahmanson Theater** and **Mark Taper Forum**; live concerts by the **Los Angeles Philharmonic** or in the **Hollywood Bowl**; live comedy at the **Comedy Store**; the *Queen Mary* is tied up at Pier J in Long Beach; try the helicopter trip to **Santa Catalina**; the reason your kids came to California, **Disneyland** (having a copy of our sister publication, *The Unofficial Guide to Disneyland*, wouldn't hurt); the Garden Grove Community Church (a.k.a. the **Crystal Cathedral**); the **Richard Nixon Library** in Yorba Linda.

Contact Information Los Angeles Visitor and Information Center, (213) 624-7300 (www.lacvb.com); Los Angeles International Airport (310) 646-5252; AMTRAK, (800) USA-RAIL; Warner Brothers Studio tours, (818) 972-TOUR; Audiences Unlimited (for tickets to TV tapings), (818) 506-0043; Star Wares, (310) 399-0224; Beverly Hills Visitors Bureau,

(800) 345-2210; Santa Monica Convention and Visitors Bureau (www.santamonica.com); Pasadena Convention and Visitors Bureau (www.pasadenavisitor.org); Ontario Convention and Visitors Authority (www.ontariocva.org); Long Beach Area Visitors and Convention Bureau (www.golongbeach.org); Richard Nixon Library, (714) 993-5075; Orange County Visitors and Convention Bureau, (714) 999-8999; Orange County/John Wayne International Airport, (714) 252-5200; Newport Beach Conference and Visitors Bureau (www.newportbeach-cvb.com); Laguna Beach Visitors Bureau (http://www.lagunabeachinfo.org).

San Bernardino Mountains

Cities and Towns   Lake Arrowhead, Big Bear Lake, Fawnskin.

Attractions   Skiing, snowboarding, and ice-skating in winter; waterskiing, horseback riding, fishing, hiking, golfing, mountain biking, and boating the rest of the year; **Lake Arrowhead** is smaller, more private than its Big Bear neighbor, with a milder climate; **Big Bear Lake** is boating heaven, with two ski resorts and big-city amenities; **Magic Mountain**, a family recreation park, with its famous snowless bobsled; get a close-up look at wolves, grizzly bears, and mountain lions at **Moonridge Animal Park**, a sanctuary for wild alpine animals.

Contact Information   Lake Arrowhead Communities Chamber of Commerce, (909) 337-3715 (www.lakearrowhead.com); Big Bear Lake Resort Association (www.bigbearinfo.com); Big Bear Tourist Bureau (www.bigbear.com/frontdesk).

Palm Springs, the desert, and the San Jacinto Mountains

Cities and Towns   In the desert—Twentynine Palms, Palm Springs, Palm Desert, La Quinta, Indio; in the San Jacinto Mountains—Idyllwild.

Attractions   Golfing, tennis, and tanning by the pool in the desert; **Joshua Trees National Park**,with 800,000 acres of mountain and lowland desert habitat filled with Joshua trees, cacti, palms, and tortoises; take the **Palm Springs Aerial Tramway** two miles up to Mount San Jacinto for a bird's-eye view of legendary **Palm Springs**, with no billboards and lots of celebrities, shopping, and palm trees; there are almost 100 golf courses here and in the nearby resort towns of **Palm Desert** and **La Quinta**; local agriculture includes figs, grapefruit, and date palms—have a date shake in **Indio** at **Shields Date Gardens; Idyllwild**, a small community in the pines, popular with hikers and rock climbers, on the western slope of the **San Jacinto Mountains.**

Contact Information   Joshua Tree National Park, (760) 367-5500 (www.desertgold.com); Palm Springs Tourism Division (www.palmsprings.org); Palm Springs Desert Resorts Convention and Visitors Bureau

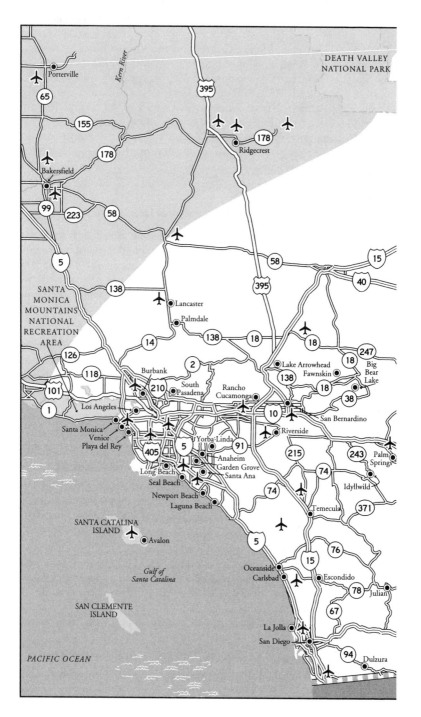

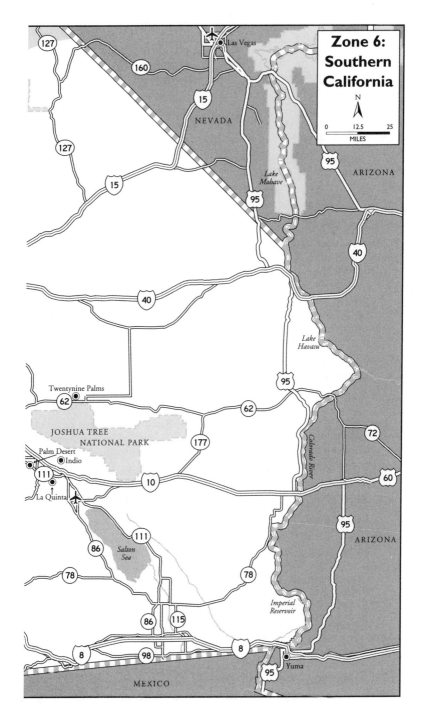

Zone 6:
Southern
California

N

0   12.5   25
MILES

127

160

Las Vegas

15

NEVADA

127

95

ARIZONA

15

Lake
Mohave

95

40

40

Lake
Havasu

95

Twentynine Palms

62

62

JOSHUA TREE
NATIONAL PARK

177

72

Palm Desert

Indio

111

60

La Quinta

10

95

111

ARIZONA

86

Salton
Sea

Colorado River

78

78

86   115

Imperial
Reservoir

78

8

8

98

95

Yuma

MEXICO

(www.desert-resorts.com/cvb.html); Shields Date Gardens, (760) 347-0996; Idyllwild Chamber of Commerce, (909) 659-3259.

San Diego County

Cities and Towns   Temecula, Oceanside, Carlsbad, Escondido, Julian, La Jolla, San Diego, Coronado, Dulzura.

Attractions   Three of the world's best wildlife attractions are in **San Diego**—the **San Diego Zoo** has over 4,000 animals, including two giant pandas living in natural surroundings; you can interact (and get wet) with dolphins at **Sea World**; or take the five-mile monorail ride through 2,200-acre **Wild Animal Park**, where white rhinos and their buddies roam unfettered; 1,200-acre **Balboa Park** has over 15 museums devoted to topics as diverse as aerospace, photography, natural history, anthropology, and model railroads; the local weather is ideal for **Padres** baseball; over 20 sunny beaches, including Coronado Beach, where *Some Like It Hot* was made; live theater at **La Jolla Playhouse** and **Old Globe Theatre; Old Town San Diego**, with California's first mission, restored Victorians, and 200-year-old adobes; in **Carlsbad**, newly opened **Legoland** amusement park has a 15-foot-tall head of Albert Einstein made with gazillions of Lego blocks; the picturesque old mining town of **Julian** in the Cuyamaca Mountains, with apple orchards and fields of wildflowers; take a jeep tour of **Anza-Borrego Desert State Park**, with 600,000 acres of canyons, dry lake beds, palm-ringed oases, and bighorn sheep; sample fine local wines in **Temecula**.

Contact Information   San Diego International Airport, (619) 231-7361; San Diego North County Convention and Visitors Bureau (www.sandiegonorth.com); Temecula Valley Chamber of Commerce, (909) 767-5090 (www.temecula.org); Oceanside Chamber of Commerce and Visitors Center (www.oceansidechamber.com); Carlsbad Visitors and Convention Bureau, (760) 434-6093 (www.carlsbadca.org); San Diego International Visitors Information Center, (619) 236-1212, (www.infosandiego.com); San Diego Zoo, (619) 234-3153, and Wild Animal Park, (760) 747-8702 (www.sandiegozoo.org); Sea World, (619) 226-3901; Coronado Visitors and Convention Bureau (www.coronado.ca.us/Visitor).

INN ON MOUNT ADA, Avalon

| Overall: ★★★★★ | Room Quality: A | Value: B | Price: $210–$595 |

As your van climbs the narrow road to the top of Mount Ada, you'll see why chewing gum magnate William Wrigley Jr. built this lovely white Georgian home atop Catalina Island's highest residential peak. The Pacific and mainland view is awesome. And it's the same view you'll gaze upon from nearly every room of the house, from the sweeping deck outside, and from the colorful gardens. Even before you check into your room, innkeepers Susie Griffin and Marlene McAdam invite you to sit down and have a bite of lunch. Afterward, you'll receive instructions on how to drive the golf cart provided for island transportation (no private autos are allowed on the island without special permit). Pretty soon you'll find yourself zipping up and down the hills and through Avalon's narrow streets and alleys. Leave yourself some time to enjoy the ambience of the inn. Sit on the expansive deck, cool drink in hand, and soak in the view of jewel-like Avalon Harbor below.

SETTING & FACILITIES

Location: On Catalina Island, 29 mi. south of Long Beach; inn provides private van transportation to and from boat or helicopter landings
Near: Restaurants, shopping
Building: 1921 restored Georgian Colonial listed in Nat'l Register of Historic Places, built by William Wrigley, who at one time owned 99% of the island

Grounds: 5.5-acre hilltop location w/ double terrace on town and harbor side, single terrace on ocean side, gardens w/ wildlife
Public Space: LR w/ fireplaces, piano, DR, den, sunporch
Food & Drink: Full breakfast served 8:30–10 a.m. in DR; ample deli-style sit-down lunch

Recreation: Biking, miniature golf, golf, horseback riding, diving, snorkeling, fishing, kayaking, ocean swimming, boating, tours, gym, golf cart w/ every room
Amenities & Services: Evening champagne, wine, and hors d'oeuvres in parlor 6–8 p.m.; fresh fruit, fresh cookies, soft drinks, beer, sherry, and port always avail.; golf carts avail. for guests' use for transportation around island; private golf cart parking, phones avail. for guests' use, fax

ACCOMMODATIONS

Units: 6 guest rooms, including 2 suites
All Rooms: Private bath, TV
Some Rooms: Fireplace, sofa bed (1), room for roll-away (2), private deck, ocean view
Bed & Bath: Queens, tub/shower (5)
Favorites: Windsor Room, a corner room w/ fireplace, full bath, harbor and ocean views; Queen's Aviary, Mrs. Wrigley's former dressing room, view of town and harbor, fireplace
Comfort & Decor: Rooms individually decorated w/ antiques, lace curtains, wallpaper (different in each room), hardwood floors and carpet; a different room is redecorated each year

RATES, RESERVATIONS, & RESTRICTIONS

Deposit: 1st night in full within 10 days of making reservation; must cancel 10 days in advance; $50 cancellation fee
Discounts: None; extra person $75
Credit Cards: MC, V
Check-In/Out: 2/11, late check-out by arrangement
Smoking: No
Pets: No
Kids: 14 and over
Minimum Stay: 2 nights on weekends and holidays
Open: Closed Dec. 24–25
Hosts: Susie Griffin and Marlene McAdam
P.O. Box 2560
398 Wrigley Rd.
Avalon, CA 90704
(310) 510-2030
(800) 608-7669
Fax: (310) 510-2237
www.catalina.com/mtada

OLD TURNER INN, Avalon

Overall: ★★★★	Room Quality: B	Value: B	Price: $120–$195

The ambience at the Old Turner Inn is casual and friendly, and staying here will give you a sense of what it's like to live in Avalon year-round. A beachy sort of place, the gray and white clapboard home with banks of windows stretching across the front of the first and second floors was built for a local family in 1927. As you might expect in a family home, the decor is a bit eclectic. The living room sports a turn-of-the-century feel, with streamlined love seats, glass-topped tables, a Steinway grand piano, and a 150-year-old hutch handmade in the Isle of Man and shipped by clipper ship around the Horn. Guest rooms are spacious, bright, and airy and contain a pleasant combination of comfortable contemporary furnishings alongside Victorian-style white wicker chairs, iron and brass beds, and mirrored armoires. All are decorated in pale, pretty colors—light green, cream, and apricot—and four have wood-burning fireplaces. Breakfast is served on the inn's cheery sunroom/porch and in the living room. The menu always features an entrée such as stratta, peach crisp, or vegetable quiche in addition to the usual fruit, juice, and baked goods.

SETTING & FACILITIES

Location: On Catalina Island in the heart of Avalon, on Catalina Ave. between Crescent Ave. and Beacon St., 1 block from Avalon Bay
Near: Restaurants, shops, within walking and biking distance of most places in town
Building: 1927 Cape Cod home
Grounds: Urban lot
Public Space: LR, enclosed front porch

Food & Drink: Extended cont'l breakfast served on the front porch 9–10 a.m., coffee from 7:30 a.m., special arrangements for early risers
Recreation: Swimming, biking, boating, fishing, golf, tennis, parasailing, kayaking, Jet Skiing, snorkeling, scuba diving
Amenities & Services: Bicycles, late afternoon hors d'oeuvres and beverages; daily maid service

ACCOMMODATIONS

Units: 5 guest rooms, including 2 suites
All Rooms: Private tiled bath, fine linens
Some Rooms: Fireplace (4), view of town and mountains, AC, daybed (2)
Bed & Bath: Kings (3), queens (2)
Favorites: The King Suite, w/ woodburning fireplace, king white iron bed, glass-enclosed sitting porch, mirrored

armoire, view of garden and mountains
Comfort & Decor: Rooms individually decorated w/ heirloom antiques, brass and white iron bedsteads, handmade afghans, large stained-glass window, Steinway grand piano, white wicker, mirrored armoires, Scandinavian love seats, rocking chairs, ceiling fans

RATES, RESERVATIONS, & RESTRICTIONS

Deposit: Credit card to hold; must cancel within 7 days
Discounts: None; extra person in suites $20–35
Credit Cards: D, MC, V
Check-In/Out: 2/11
Smoking: No
Pets: No
Kids: OK by arrangement
Minimum Stay: 2 nights most

weekends
Open: All year
Host: Jeanne Hill
P.O. Box 97
232 Catalina Ave.
Avalon, CA 90704
(310) 510-2236
(310) 510-0987
www.catalina.com/old_turner_inn
thehills@catalinas.net

APPLES B&B, Big Bear Lake

Overall: ★★★½	Room Quality: B	Value: B	Price: $130–$220

You'll be able to spot the distinctive inn created by Jim and Barbara McLean tucked among an acre of pine trees as you drive toward the ski lifts

on Moonridge Road. Look for a big, newish country Victorian-style building with a rose-pink facade, ornate decorations, and steeply gabled roof.
Since they built the inn from the ground up, the McLeans were able to put
a premium on providing creature comforts within a Victorian setting. This
is a large inn, with spacious guest rooms and expansive common areas,
including an enormous gathering room in the center of the inn. French
doors lead outside to a broad veranda out front and expansive, shady gardens out back, where there are several small decks and a hot tub. Guest
rooms, located in the main house and in a wing added later, are bright and
appealing, with colorful floral wallpapers and linens. The best rooms are the
four suites located in the turret, each with a separate sitting room and a
double Jacuzzi in the bathroom. Barbara, who ran a catering business before
opening the inn, offers a four-course sit-down breakfast each morning.
Although the menu changes seasonally, popular items include cold straw-
berry-pineapple soup, thick French toast with homemade apple cider syrup,
herb-and-cheese scrambled eggs, and honey-apple sausages.

SETTING & FACILITIES

Location: In the Moonridge section
of Big Bear Lake, 25 mi. northeast of
Redlands via Hwys. 30, 330, and 18,
2.5 hours from LA
Near: Restaurants, shopping, galleries,
Big Bear Lake, San Bernardino Nat'l
Forest
Building: New Country Victorian, built
in 1992, detached building w/ 3 garden
rooms
Grounds: 1 acre of pine forest, landscaped grounds, w/ lawns, flowerbeds,
apple trees, gazebos, tennis court
Public Space: Great room w/ wood-
burning stove, grand piano, game table,
library loft, DR, veranda
Food & Drink: Full 4-course breakfast
served at 9 a.m. in DR
Recreation: Tennis court on premises;
nearby mountain biking, horseback
riding, water sports, golf, downhill/X-C
skiing
Amenities & Services: Hot tub, all-
day snack and beverage bar in great
room, sparkling cider and herb cheese
in afternoon, evening dessert and coffee, robes, private parking, concierge
services, disabled access, massage by
arrangement

ACCOMMODATIONS

Units: 12 guest rooms, 9 in main
house, 3 garden rooms
All Rooms: Private bath, TV/VCR, fireplace, writing desk and chair, reclining
chair, down bedding
Some Rooms: Turret sitting area,
private entrance (3)
Bed & Bath: Kings, Jacuzzi tubs
for 2 (4)
Favorites: Red Delicious, w/ rose-
covered wallpaper, white iron and brass
bed, turret sitting area, glass-beaded
lamps, garden view; Royal Gala, w/ bay
window, oak four-poster w/ matching
armoire, garden view
Comfort & Decor: Rooms individually decorated w/ original art, glass
lamps, reclining chairs, down comforters, lace curtains, carpet

RATES, RESERVATIONS, & RESTRICTIONS

Deposit: 1st night's lodging; must cancel 7 days in advance; $25 cancellation fee
Discounts: AAA
Credit Cards: AE, D, MC, V
Check-In/Out: 3/noon
Smoking: No
Pets: No
Kids: OK, but only 2 people per room

Minimum Stay: 2 nights on weekends, 3 or 4 on holidays
Open: All year
Hosts: Jim and Barbara McLean
P.O. Box 7172
42430 Moonridge Rd.
Big Bear Lake, CA 92315
(909) 866-0903
www.applesbedandbreakfast.com

TRUFFLES B&B, Big Bear Lake

Overall: ★★★★	Room Quality: B	Value: B	Price: $115–$150

A 40-foot-long family room stretching across the back of this Victorian-style farmhouse affords a great winter view of the skiers schussing down the slopes at Bear Valley Mountain. There are five pleasant guest rooms at Truffles, three on the ground floor of the main house and two in attic gables. On a cold winter night, make yourself a hot drink and sit by the huge river rock fireplace, which can warm 10 guests. Or you can curl up with a good book in the privacy of the inn's upstairs library. Breakfast is usually served family-style at a large dining table placed at one end of the family room, where guests can enjoy the sweeping mountain view any time of the year.

SETTING & FACILITIES

Location: In the Moonridge area of Big Bear Lake, 25 mi. northeast of San Bernardino via Hwys. 215, 30, and 330, 1 mi. from Big Bear Mountain ski resort
Near: Restaurants, shopping, Big Bear Lake, 2 ski resorts
Building: 18-year-old English Country Manor–style farmhouse
Grounds: 3/4 landscaped acre w/ outdoor deck, sitting areas, gazebo, views of ski runs
Public Space: Parlor/gathering room w/ wood-burning stove and piano, river rock fireplace conversation pit w/ views of the ski runs, library, small exercise room, area for games, puzzles
Food & Drink: Full breakfast served at 9 a.m. in the DR or on the deck in warm weather
Recreation: Biking, skiing, snowboarding, boating, fishing, parasailing, tennis, golf
Amenities & Services: Late afternoon hors d'oeuvres, evening desserts and coffees, fresh-baked oatmeal cookies, evening turn-down w/ truffles; assistance w/ dinner reservations

ACCOMMODATIONS

Units: 5 guest rooms, 4 larger than average

All Rooms: Private bath, cable TV, featherbed, down comforter

Some Rooms: VCR, fireplace (1), four-poster, sofa bed (1)

Bed & Bath: Queens

Favorites: Queen's Legacy, w/ four-poster featherbed, armoire w/ TV/VCR, fireplace, soaking tub, private deck; Angel's Delight, w/ antique iron bed w/ cherubs, private entrance, deck, sofa bed

Comfort & Decor: Rooms individually and professionally decorated w/ traditional and antique furniture, custom coordinated bedding, carpet

RATES, RESERVATIONS, & RESTRICTIONS

Deposit: 50% of bill in advance; must cancel 7 days in advance; $10 cancellation fee

Discounts: Weekday business, groups, AAA, AARP

Credit Cards: MC, V

Check-In/Out: 3/11:30, late check-out by arrangement

Smoking: No

Pets: No

Kids: 10 and over

No-Nos: No more than 2 guests per room

Minimum Stay: 2 nights on holiday weekends

Open: All year

Hosts: Armando Sores-Alatore, owner; Lupita Alatore, innkeeper

P.O. Box 1377
43591 Bow Canyon Rd.
Big Bear Lake, CA 92315
(909) 585-2772
Fax: (909) 584-1417
www.bigbear.com/truffles

PELICAN COVE B&B, Carlsbad

Overall: ★★★★	Room Quality: B	Value: B	Price: $90–$180

If you're contemplating a visit to historic Carlsbad, as opposed to the new Carlsbad home of Legoland, Pelican Cove Inn is a good lodging choice. It's located on a quiet residential street, just a short walk from the beach. If you do visit Legoland, you'll enjoy the tranquillity at this contemporary Cape Cod-style inn, built on several levels, with rooms accessed by decks and stairways. Guests can be seen enjoying a cool ocean breeze on the decks and in the inn's colorful gardens year-round. Throughout the grounds, innkeeper Nancy Nayudu has set up tables and chairs in tiny niches, secluded corners, and sunny spots. Each of the eight rooms is nicely but simply decorated. Most rooms are spacious with big beds, small sitting areas, lots of windows, and a generally bright ambience. All have fireplaces, televisions, European-style bedding, and private entrances. There are some spa tubs. Nancy serves a full buffet breakfast featuring entrées such as cottage cheese pancakes or French toast. Guests usually take a tray outside to the garden gazebo, the sundeck, or one of the porches.

SETTING & FACILITIES

Location: On the south side of Carlsbad, 2 blocks from the ocean, 35 mi. north of San Diego

Near: Restaurants, shopping, galleries, museums, missions, theater, Mt. Palomar Observatory, Sea World, 200 yds. from ocean beaches and a short walk to Carlsbad

Building: 12-year-old Cape Cod-style building

Grounds: 2 urban lots landscaped w/ flower beds, large sundeck, gazebo, garden patio

Public Space: Parlor, decks, patio

Food & Drink: Full breakfast served 8–10 a.m. in the parlor, garden patio, or sunporch

Recreation: Biking, tennis, golf, fishing, surfing, diving, sailing, hot air ballooning

Amenities & Services: Afternoon snacks; tea, coffee, dessert avail. anytime; private parking, disabled access, beach chairs, towels and picnic baskets avail.

ACCOMMODATIONS

Units: 8 guest rooms, 4 larger than average, including 2 suites

All Rooms: Private bath, fireplace, cable TV, phone on request, down comforter, featherbed

Some Rooms: Four-poster, sleeper sofa, extra bed (2)

Bed & Bath: Queens, kings (3), twin, spa tubs for 2 (2)

Favorites: Laguna, w/ white wicker furniture, off the veranda overlooking gardens, windows on 3 sides; La Jolla, w/ round vaulted ceiling, beige and black decor, spa tub, multiple windows

Comfort & Decor: Rooms individually decorated w/ wicker and contemporary furniture, antiques, floral prints, comforters, carpet

RATES, RESERVATIONS, & RESTRICTIONS

Deposit: Credit card to hold; must cancel 7 days in advance or lose $25

Discounts: Long stays, weekday business; extra person $15

Credit Cards: AE, MC, V

Check-In/Out: 3/11, late check-out if room avail.

Smoking: No

Pets: No

Kids: In 2 rooms

Minimum Stay: 2 nights on weekends

Open: All year

Hosts: Kris and Nancy Nayudu
320 Walnut Ave.
Carlsbad, CA 92008
(760) 434-5995
(888) 735-2683
Fax: (760) 434-7649
www.pelican-cove.com
pelicancoveinn@sandcastleweb.com

BROOKSIDE FARM B&B, Dulzura

Overall: ★★★★	Room Quality: B	Value: A	Price: $85–$120

This quiet retreat, located in the mountains about 30 miles east of San Diego along the Mexican border, is about as remote as you can get in Southern California. Brookside Farm consists of a main house and several outbuildings, including an old stone dairy barn dating back to 1927. The Hunter's Cabin hangs right over the year-round brook for which the inn is named.

Originally the farm's pump house, it's decorated in an Old West theme, with a wood-burning stove standing in front of an iron bed and a screened-porch entrance. Rooms in the old barn are particularly attractive. Most have fireplaces or wood-burning stoves, screened porches, courtyards, or decks. Cooking is one of innkeeper Edd Guishard's many talents. A chef in his former life, he shares his knowledge with weekend guests by conducting informal cooking classes. Guests can learn how he uses farm-grown vegetables and fruit in the dinners served on Saturday nights. Breakfast is a bountiful buffet, particularly on Sundays, when Edd prepares Brookside eggs.

SETTING & FACILITIES

Location: 1.5 mi. east of Dulzura, 30 mi. east of San Diego via Hwy. 94
Near: In the countryside, away from everything, 10 mi. from Tecate, Mexico
Building: 1929 farmhouse w/ unique stone barn
Grounds: 5 acres of flower, herb, and vegetable gardens; fountains, koi pond, brick terraces, fruit trees, stream, California oaks, gazebo, livestock, aviaries
Public Space: Parlor, library, game room, DR w/ window wall facing

garden, pond, and dovecote
Food & Drink: Full country breakfast served at 9 a.m. in DR, complimentary dinner Sun.–Thurs.
Recreation: Croquet, horseshoes, badminton on premises
Amenities & Services: Hot tub in grape arbor, hammock on terrace, fresh flowers, private parking, disabled access, massage or aromatherapy treatments avail. on Sat., 4-course gourmet dinners on Fri. and Sat.

ACCOMMODATIONS

Units: 10 guest rooms, 6 larger than average, including 2 suites
All Rooms: Private bath
Some Rooms: Fireplace, wood-burning stove, fridge, private balcony, porch, deck, AC
Bed & Bath: Queens
Favorites: Room-with-a-View, w/ wood-burning fireplace, sitting area,

refrigerator, coffee service, private balcony; Sun Porch, w/ Monet-inspired decor, private patio overlooking gardens and koi pond
Comfort & Decor: Rooms individually decorated w/ original artwork, furniture appropriate to its theme, quilts, wallpaper, views of patios and gardens

RATES, RESERVATIONS, & RESTRICTIONS

Deposit: 1 night's fee in advance or credit card; must cancel 7 days in advance
Discounts: Long stays, weekday business, groups, AAA, singles
Credit Cards: AE, D, MC, V
Check-In/Out: 3/11
Smoking: No
Pets: No
Kids: 12 and over

No-Nos: No more than 2 guests per room
Minimum Stay: 2 nights on weekends in most rooms
Open: All year
Hosts: Edd and Sally Guishard
1373 Marron Valley Rd.
Dulzura, CA 91917
(619) 468-3043
Fax: (619) 468-9145

ZOSA GARDENS B&B, Escondido

Overall: ★★★★	Room Quality: B	Value: B	Price: $130–$250

A remote getaway in the mountains of northern San Diego County, this inn has many of the amenities of a resort, along with the comforts and personal services of a bed-and-breakfast. Zosa is the centerpiece of a 22-acre ranch where exotic fruits such as guavas, oranges, and avocados are grown. There are carefully tended flower gardens, a palm-lined entrance, sweeping green lawns, three gazebos, fountains, and a koi pond with water lilies. Resort facilities include a particularly attractive swimming pool with an outdoor Jacuzzi and inviting deck area, a tennis court, and a well-equipped indoor recreation room. Guest accommodations are located in a contemporary Spanish-style hacienda that's dripping with bougainvillea. Rooms are large but simply furnished, sporting botanical decor, with flowers everywhere. Most have garden, orchard, or mountain views and poster and canopy beds, and all have private bathrooms. Once a caterer, innkeeper Connie Vlasis specializes in stuffing her guests with her award-winning cuisine: a typical buffet breakfast includes a selection of fresh fruit (some plucked from trees on the estate), juice, muffins, and an entrée such as eggs Benedict, plus she also whips up items such as frittatas, personal pizzas, and other goodies for evening refreshments.

SETTING & FACILITIES

Location: Between Escondido and Falbrook, just east of I-15 and south of Hwy. 76

Near: 13 wineries, theater, San Diego Wild Animal Park, Palomar Observatory, Legoland

Building: 1940s Spanish-style hacienda (restored), cottage, guest house

Grounds: 22 landscaped acres w/ guavas, citrus and avocado trees, flower gardens, fountains, waterfall, koi pond, 3 gazebos

Public Space: Courtyard, recreation room, family room, DR, game room

Food & Drink: Full breakfast served in DR or outside by pool 9:30–10:30 a.m.

Recreation: Tennis court and recreation room w/ pool table on premises; biking, fishing, golf, ballooning nearby

Amenities & Services: Swimming pool, spa; afternoon wine, cheese, and appetizers; private parking, massage avail. by appointment, concierge services for reservations; horseback riding, tennis lessons avail.

ACCOMMODATIONS

Units: 9 guest rooms, plus cottage w/ 2 BRs, kitchen, LR, and guest house w/ 4 BRs, kitchen, fireplace, sunporch

Some Rooms: Four-poster, canopy, view of gardens and Moserrat Mountains, extra bed(s) in cottage and guest house

Bed & Bath: Beds vary; all private baths; Master Suite in main house has large shower w/ 2 heads and separate tub

Favorites: Protea, w/ king canopy bed, private balcony, fireplace, sitting area, dressing area, satellite TV, mountain views; Hibiscus, w/ mosquito-netting-draped four-poster, tropical plants and flowers, views of courtyard

and fountains

Comfort & Decor: Rooms individually decorated w/ garden themes, rooms named for flowers except Gardening Angel, which is filled w/ cherubs

RATES, RESERVATIONS, & RESTRICTIONS

Deposit: Credit card to hold; must cancel within 7 days; cancellation fee $25
Discounts: Seniors, midweek, AAA; extra person $25
Credit Cards: All
Check-In/Out: 2/noon, late check-out by arrangement
Smoking: No
Pets: No
Kids: Not suitable

Minimum Stay: None
Open: Closed Dec. 24–25
Host: Connie Vlasis
9381 W. Lilac Rd.
Escondido, CA 92026
(760) 723-9093
(800) 711-8361
Fax: (760) 723-3460
www.zosagardens.com
zosabnb@pacbell.net

INN AT FAWNSKIN, Fawnskin

Overall: ★★★½	Room Quality: B	Value: B	Price: $85–$175

A shaded two-story contemporary log cabin, the Inn at Fawnskin was built with wood trucked here from Wyoming. Unlike most B&Bs in the Big Bear area, this is a very homelike lodging. Of the four rooms, the best is the pine-paneled Master Suite, which has its own rock fireplace, a superlative lake view from the balcony, an open-beamed ceiling, and a private bath with his-and-hers sinks. Other rooms, all opening to an upstairs hall, offer basic accommodations with few frills. Furnishings throughout are as contemporary as the cabin. The common areas are appealing: there's a huge den furnished with a regulation-size billiards table and a burled-wood bar, and the living room has a comfortable sofa fronting a great stone fireplace. The dining room, part of the big open family room/kitchen, has its own fireplace.

SETTING & FACILITIES

Location: On the northern tip of Big Bear Lake, 32 mi. northeast of Redlands via Hwys. 30, 330, and 18, 2 hours east of LA
Near: Restaurants, shopping, community theater, across from Big Bear Lake
Building: 21-year-old contemporary log home, owners' home in back

Grounds: 1 acre of wooded pine forest across from the north shore of Big Bear Lake, w/ large lawn areas in front and back
Public Space: LR w/ large rock fireplace, game room w/ pool table, wide-screen TV and VCR, DR w/ large stone fireplace, porches, decks, patio area

Recreation: Ping-Pong, croquet, horseshoes, pool table, electronic darts, lawn bowling on premises; biking, skiing, water sports, fishing, golf nearby

Amenities & Services: Afternoon beverages and hors d'oeuvres, private parking, guest phones avail., guest fridge in game room, assistance w/ activity plans, barbecue avail.

ACCOMMODATIONS

Units: 4 guest rooms, including 1 suite
Some Rooms: Private bath (2), shared bath (1); suite has LR, fireplace, balcony, lake views, sofa bed
Bed & Bath: Queens, double
Favorites: Master Suite, w/ rock fireplace, sitting area w/ TV/VCR, private balcony overlooking lake, tub/shower

Comfort & Decor: Rooms individually decorated w/ country motif; antique, oak, and country furniture; valences, curtains, and shades; carpet, country quilts, unusual headboards

RATES, RESERVATIONS, & RESTRICTIONS

Deposit: 50% of bill; must cancel 10 days in advance; $20 cancellation fee
Discounts: Midweek, AAA, singles; extra person in suite $15
Credit Cards: AE, MC, V
Check-In/Out: 3/noon, late check-out negotiable
Smoking: No
Pets: No
Kids: OK in suite, not suitable for infants on weekends
No-Nos: No more than 2 guests per room, except suite

Minimum Stay: 2 nights on weekends and holidays
Open: Closed Dec. 23–24, Thanksgiving Day
Hosts: Todd and Kathy Murphy
P.O. Box 378
880 Canyon Rd.
Fawnskin, CA 92333
(909) 866-3200
(888) 329-6754
Fax: (909) 878-2249
www.bajalife.com/fawnskin
tmurphy@bigbear.net

WINDY POINT INN, Fawnskin

Overall: ★★★★½	Room Quality: A	Value: B	Price: $125–$245

This inn is the most romantic lodging you'll find on Big Bear Lake. Situated on a spit of land on the north shore of the lake, it's located far from the

crowds of Big Bear City, and the most noise you'll hear is the lapping of the waves against the beach. A built-from-the-ground-up creation of architect David Zimmerman and innkeepers Val and Kent Kessler, Windy Point is surrounded on three sides by water, with a private beach where you can sun and swim. The inn's living room has a sweeping 180° lake and mountain view through floor-to-ceiling windows. Whether you choose one of three guest rooms in the main house or one of the two suites in a new wing, you'll find you're sleeping in an environment that's at one with nature. Every room offers sweeping views of lake or mountains, skylights (some right over the bed) for nighttime star-gazing, and wood-burning fireplaces. Most have private decks, two-person Jacuzzis, and outside entrances. In keeping with the inn's romantic theme, breakfast is a private time, served as ordered to your room or to one couple at a time on a deck outside the kitchen.

SETTING & FACILITIES

Location: On a private peninsula on the northern tip of Big Bear Lake in the mountains of the San Bernardino Nat'l Forest, 29 mi. northeast of Redlands via Hwys. 30, 330, and 18, 2 hours from LA
Near: Restaurants, shopping, museum, Big Bear Lake, San Bernardino Nat'l Forest, 2 sandy beaches
Building: 1991 contemporary building built as B&B, recent building w/ 2 suites w/ private entrances
Grounds: Half-acre on private peninsula in Big Bear Lake w/ water on 3 sides, pine trees, 2 large decks overlooking lake
Public Space: Common area w/ sunken LR w/ fireplace, concert

grand, DR table
Food & Drink: Full breakfast served 8:30–10 a.m. in the common area or on patio, 2 suites have breakfast delivered to rooms
Recreation: Biking, fishing, boating, horseback riding, golf, snow- and waterskiing
Amenities & Services: Afternoon snacks, in-room fridges stocked w/ bottled water and soda, tea and chocolate avail. all day, private parking, concierge services for restaurant reservations and activity plans, massage avail. by appointment, robes, activity pass for San Bernardino Nat'l Forest, private dock, boats for rent nearby

ACCOMMODATIONS

Units: 5 guest rooms, including 3 suites
All Rooms: Private bath, fireplace, VCR, individually controlled heat, ceiling fan, fridge, private deck, feather comforter
Some Rooms: Cassette player (2), CD player (3), skylight (4), coffeemaker and hot water dispenser (2)
Bed & Bath: Kings, queens (2), 2-person whirlpool tubs (4), steam sauna (1)
Favorites: The Peaks, w/ views of the lake on 3 sides, skylights over both bed and bath, wraparound sofa in front of

fireplace, built-in stereo, in-room steam sauna, whirlpool tub for 2 w/ lake views; The Coves, a split-level suite w/ panoramic view of lake, sunken LR, wet bar, sofa and down-stuffed chair in front of fireplace, Jacuzzi for 2 w/ view of lake, skylights, walk-in closet, double sinks, oversized shower, built-in CD player
Comfort & Decor: Rooms individually decorated w/ internat'l artwork and accessories, minimal window treatments to take advantage of the lake views

RATES, RESERVATIONS, & RESTRICTIONS

Deposit: 1st night's lodging; must cancel 7 days in advance
Discounts: Midweek, singles
Credit Cards: AE, D, MC, V
Check-In/Out: 3/noon
Smoking: No
Pets: No
Kids: OK, but only 2 guests per room
No-Nos: No more than 2 guests per room

Minimum Stay: 2 nights on weekends, 3 on holiday weekends
Open: All year
Hosts: Val and Kent Kessler
P.O. Box 375
39015 N. Shore Dr.
Fawnskin, CA 92333
(909) 866-2746
Fax: (909) 866-1593
www.windypointinn.com

STRAWBERRY CREEK INN, Idyllwild

Overall: ★★★★½	Room Quality: B	Value: A	Price: $75–$150

Strawberry Creek is the type of inn you'd expect to find in a rustic mountain town like Idyllwild, comfortable and unpretentious. Innkeepers Diana Dugan and Jim Goff have created a country escape for harried urbanites, welcoming guests from the San Diego and Los Angeles areas for more than a decade. The inn's spacious parlor has a fireplace along one wall surrounded by inviting sofas and chairs, a coffee table you can put your feet on, and wooden floors covered with colorful rugs. There's a little alcove for one in the corner with a big chair surrounded by floor-to-ceiling stacks of books, and wall-to-wall windows on two sides. Guest rooms are located in the main house and in an adjacent annex. The rooms in the main house tend to be simply furnished and decorated with selections from Diana's antique quilt collection. Rooms in the adjacent courtyard area have more appointments: fireplaces, skylights above queen-size beds, and refrigerators. The inn has two lovely outdoor decks where guests can sit and enjoy a cool drink on a hot afternoon shaded by several large oak and pine trees.

SETTING & FACILITIES

Location: In the mountain town of Idyllwild, 25 mi. southeast of Banning on Hwy. 243, 2 hours east of LA or northeast of San Diego
Near: Restaurants, shopping, galleries, antiques, theater, concerts, Palm Springs Tramway, Living Desert Museum
Building: 1941 cedar-shake-shingled mountain home w/ dormer windows
Grounds: 1 acre of pines, oaks, cedar trees w/ summertime flower gardens

Public Space: Parlor, library, dining porch, decks w/ hammocks
Food & Drink: Full breakfast served at 9 a.m. in glassed-in dining porch
Recreation: Rock climbing, horseback riding, fishing
Amenities & Services: Coffee, teas, cookies, nuts, refreshments avail. all the time, Sat. wine hour, private parking, disabled access

ACCOMMODATIONS

Units: 9 guest rooms, 2 larger than average
All Rooms: Private bath, handcrafted quilt, rugs, baskets
Some Rooms: Fireplace, four-poster, fridge
Bed & Bath: Queens
Favorites: Autumn Room, w/ access to courtyard, skylight, wood-burning

fireplace, fridge, disabled-accessible; Evergreen Room, large, w/ direct access to house or private entrance, north woods decor, handmade quilt, river rock fireplace
Comfort & Decor: Rooms individually decorated w/ antiques, wallpapers, wood floors, carpets, handmade quilts, baskets, country decor

RATES, RESERVATIONS, & RESTRICTIONS

Deposit: 50% of bill; must cancel 2 weeks in advance, 30 days for cottage and holidays
Discounts: AAA, seniors, midweek rates avail.; extra person in cottage $20, breakfast not provided in cottage
Credit Cards: D, MC, V
Check-In/Out: 2/11, late check-out negotiable
Smoking: No
Pets: No
Kids: OK
No-Nos: No more than 2 guests per

room, except in cottage
Minimum Stay: 2 nights on weekends, 3 on holiday weekends
Open: All year
Hosts: James Goff and Diana Dugan
P.O. Box 1818
26370 SR 243
Idyllwild, Ca 92549
(909) 659-3202
(800) 262-8969
Fax: (909) 659-4707
www.strawberrycreekinn.com

JULIAN GOLD RUSH HOTEL, Julian

Overall: ★★★★	Room Quality: B	Value: A	Price: $72–$175

This hotel is one of Julian's many historic treasures. One of the oldest continuously operating hotels in Southern California, it dates back to 1897, when freed slave Albert Robinson opened it to host visitors to what was then a small boomtown. When Steve and Gig Ballinger purchased the old hotel in 1976, it hadn't changed much. In the ensuing quarter century, they've upgraded and improved, adding a few modern comforts, such as private bathrooms, but they've retained the Victorian ambience. The Victorian-style parlor displays an elegance that was scarce in historic Julian, where there was little wealth even during the only gold rush to occur in Southern California. The parlor, furnished with a settee, black leather armchairs with carved lion heads, and a Kayton tiger oak piano, always draws guests, and in winter a fire in the woodstove warms the whole room. As you might expect in a century-old hotel, rooms are small and simply furnished—pretty wallpaper, lace curtains, and polished wood floors. Guests gather each morning for breakfast served in the hotel's wicker-filled sunroom, where tables have been set up for two and four. The menu always features locally popular Dudley's bread and Queen's oats, a granola created and made at the hotel, plus an entrée.

SETTING & FACILITIES

Location: In the center of Julian, 35 mi. east of Escondido via Hwy. 78
Near: Center of historic gold mining town, restaurants, shopping, antiques, museum, gold mines
Building: 1897 Victorian w/ 2 cottages
Grounds: Urban lot, 2 stone patios, gardens; oak, pine, and pear trees
Public Space: Parlor, game room, DR

w/ wood-burning stove, rockers, antique Morris chairs
Food & Drink: Full breakfast served 8–9:30 a.m. in DR
Recreation: Hiking in 3 state parks, county park
Amenities & Services: Hosted afternoon tea in parlor 5–6 p.m.

ACCOMMODATIONS

Units: 15 guest rooms, 1 larger than average, including 1 suite, 13 rooms in original hotel, 2 cottages
All Rooms: Private bath, view of townsite, gardens, patio
Some Rooms: Fireplaces (2)
Bed & Bath: Doubles, queens (4), twin
Favorites: Patio Cottage, w/ turn-of-the-century decor, fireplace, private

veranda, views of gardens and patios; Honeymoon House, w/ LR w/ Franklin fireplace, canopy bed, separate ladies' vanity room, antique claw-foot tub
Comfort & Decor: Rooms individually decorated w/ historic photos, American antiques, Victorian wallpaper, lace curtains, drapes, floral carpets, comforters, multiple pillows

RATES, RESERVATIONS, & RESTRICTIONS

Deposit: Credit card; must cancel 48 hours in advance
Discounts: Long stays, weekday business, AAA, singles
Credit Cards: AE, MC, V
Check-In/Out: 2/noon

Smoking: No
Pets: No
Kids: OK in family suite
No-Nos: No more than 2 guests per room, except in family suite
Minimum Stay: 2 nights on weekends

Open: All year
Hosts: Steve and Gig Ballinger
P.O. Box 1856
12032 Main St.
Julian, CA 92036

(760) 765-0201
(800) 724-5854
Fax: (760) 765-0327
www.julianhotel.com
b&b@julianhotel.com

JULIAN WHITE HOUSE B&B, Julian

Overall: ★★★★½	Room Quality: B	Value: B	Price: $105–$175

The Julian White House, named by the patriot who built it in 1979, resembles a small Greek Revival southern plantation, complete with four columns marching across the front porch. Congenial innkeepers Alan and Mary Marvin fell in love with Julian on a weekend visit from San Diego, found the house, moved to the mountains, and opened their doors to guests. This is a place where guests like to spend their time sitting outside in the rose garden, making progress in a good book, strolling through the woods surrounding the inn, or stargazing while soaking in the inn's outdoor hot tub. When snow covers the ground in winter, guests can be found in front of the fire in the inn's comfortable parlor. There are four guest rooms, each with a few well-selected antiques and a bit of whimsy.

SETTING & FACILITIES

Location: 4 mi. southwest of Julian, off Pine Hills Rd., 38 mi. east of Escondido via Hwy. 78
Near: Restaurants, shopping, theater, William Hiese Park, historic gold mining town
Building: Southern Colonial built in 1979
Grounds: 1 acre of pine and oak forest, rose garden inside white lattice fence

Public Space: Parlor w/ marble fireplace, DR
Food & Drink: Full breakfast served at 9 a.m. in DR, breakfast served to Julian Suite
Recreation: Golf, biking, trout fishing
Amenities & Services: Hot tub; afternoon snacks, sweets, and tea; private parking, guest phone and fridge in common area, in-room massage avail.

ACCOMMODATIONS

Units: 5 guest rooms, including 2 suites
All Rooms: Private bath, AC
Some Rooms: Fireplace, four-poster, fridge, microwave (1)
Bed & Bath: Queens, king, Jacuzzi (1)
Favorites: East Room, w/ white iron and brass bed w/ goose down mattress, double shower, antique pedestal sink,
gas fireplace; Julian Suite, w/ black iron king bed, whirlpool tub for 2, mountain views, breakfast served to room
Comfort & Decor: Rooms individually decorated w/ antiques and Victorian reproductions, wallpaper, plantation shutters, carpet

RATES, RESERVATIONS, & RESTRICTIONS

Deposit: 1st night in advance; must cancel 7 days in advance; $25/night cancellation fee
Discounts: AAA
Credit Cards: MC, V
Check-In/Out: 4–7/noon, self check-in to 10 p.m.
Smoking: No
Pets: No
Kids: Not suitable
No-Nos: No more than 2 guests
per room
Minimum Stay: 2 nights on weekends
Open: All year
Hosts: Alan and Mary Marvin
P.O. Box 824
3014 Blue Jay Dr.
Julian, CA 92036
(760) 765-1764
(800) 948-4687
www.julian-whitehouse-bnb.com
stay@julian-whitehouse-bnb.com

LEELIN WIKIUP B&B, Julian

Overall: ★★★½	Room Quality: B	Value: B	Price: $150–$160

Wikiup is about animals—llamas, in particular. Innkeepers Linda and Lee Stanley have a string of the gentle pack animals at their inn. You'll see some of them in pens as you drive up to the house, located in a quiet residential section of Julian. Guests and children are very welcome at this rustic contemporary cedar-shingled lodge set amid oak and pine trees on three acres. Two guest rooms are separated from the house, with their own shared deck and private entrances; the third is off the living room. There is a play area with a swing and teeter-totter for the kids (human kids, that is!). In addition to the llamas, the Stanleys have goats, sheep, a donkey, and assorted dogs and cats. Guests are invited to feed and pet the animals. The main house of the inn displays a casual 1970s look, with cedar paneling, open-beamed ceilings punctuated with skylights, a common area containing a living room and dining room, Danish modern furniture, and a wood-burning stove. The two detached guest rooms share a deck furnished with a Mexican fountain and tables and chairs. "Wikiup," by the way, is Apache for "lodging," and LeeLin is short for Lee and Linda. Any more questions?

SETTING & FACILITIES

Location: Approx 1 mi. east of Julian; take Hwy. 78 to Whispering Pines Dr.
Near: Restaurants, shopping, dinner theater, carriage rides, gold mine tours, 2 parks
Building: 15-year-old contemporary cedar and brick lodge
Grounds: 3.5 acres of woods; resident animals include llamas, miniature donkey, angora goats, dogs, cats, wildlife
Public Space: Great room w/ fireplace, satellite TV, library, DR, 5 decks
Food & Drink: Full breakfast served at 9 a.m. in DR
Recreation: Biking, boating, fishing, horseback riding, glider rides, golf
Amenities & Services: Hot tub, afternoon snacks, 2 rooms w/ private cedar hot tubs in an enclosure, private parking, disabled access, day hikes w/ llamas

ACCOMMODATIONS

Units: 5 guest rooms, including 2 suites
All Rooms: Private bath and entrance, CD, radio, AC, fireplace, fridge, coffeepot, microwave, eating area
Some Rooms: Four-poster, featherbed, Franklin stove, view of woods
Bed & Bath: Queens, twin (2), king, spa tubs (2)
Favorites: Rose's Secret, w/ private deck, Victorian antiques, king canopy bed, corner fireplace, private cedar hot tub, skylights; Dreamcatcher, w/ Santa Fe decor, private entrance, rustic four-poster, sunken 2-person spa tub, Mexican terra-cotta bread oven
Comfort & Decor: Rooms individually decorated in different thematic styles: Victorian, 1890s Alaskan bordello, Santa Fe, and Stargazer, w/ contemporary furnishings and a telescope

RATES, RESERVATIONS, & RESTRICTIONS

Deposit: 100% of bill; must cancel 7 days in advance
Discounts: AAA, seniors, specials, extra person $45
Credit Cards: AE, MC, V
Check-In/Out: 4/11
Smoking: No
Pets: No
Kids: 6 and over
Minimum Stay: 2 nights on weekends, 3 on holiday weekends
Open: All year
Hosts: Lee and Linda Stanley
P.O. Box 2363
1645 Whispering Pines Dr.
Julian, CA 92036
(760) 765-1890
(800) 694-5487
Fax: (760) 765-1512
www.wikiupbnb.com
lodging@wikiupbnb.com

ORCHARD HILL COUNTRY INN, Julian

| Overall: ★★★★★ | Room Quality: A | Value: B | Price: $160–$265 |

Located in the heart of Julian's 1800s historic district, this stylish inn has every creature comfort you could want. Innkeepers Pat and Darrell Straube converted five small Craftsman cottages into 12 guest rooms and added a huge hilltop lodge with 10 more guest rooms, a two-story-high great room, a massive stone fireplace, and soaring windows to bring in the light. The cottages contain beautifully appointed rooms with private entrances, fireplaces, wet bars, window seats, whirlpool tubs in the bathrooms, and secluded gardens. Each cottage has a broad wraparound porch furnished with wicker chairs and tables. The lodge rooms are smaller and a little less luxurious, but they have the best views of the town and surrounding mountains. The guest rooms are decorated in American Country style, some painted bright, pretty colors, others with adorable wallpaper, hand-made quilts, down comforters, desks, skylights, bathtubs, and comfortable overstuffed chairs. The inn is noted for its cuisine. A full breakfast is served in the sunny muraled dining room, usually featuring quiches or blintzes in addition to fresh fruit, baked goods, and cereal. A prix fixe dinner is also available to guests on Wednesday and Saturday nights.

SETTING & FACILITIES

Location: In the center of Julian, at Washington and 2nd Sts., 35 mi. east of Escondido via Hwy. 78
Near: Restaurants, shopping, museums, dinner theater, wineries, horse-drawn carriage rides, gold mine tours
Building: 1920s Craftsman-style lodge w/ 10 guest rooms, 4 California Craftsman-style cottages w/ 3 rooms, 1 cottage w/ giftshop/conference center/massage services

Grounds: 4 acres w/ gardens of native plants, fruit trees, trails, hammocks, picnic tables, adjacent to public land w/ hiking trails
Public Space: Great room w/ massive stone fireplace, DR, lounge, game room w/ entertainment center, video library, games
Food & Drink: Full breakfast in DR 9–10 a.m. weekdays, 8:30–10 a.m. weekends

Recreation: Biking, fishing, boating, parasailing, horseback riding
Amenities & Services: Fresh-baked cookies, beverages, Belgian chocolates, split of wine in rooms; private parking, disabled access, picnic lunch, masseuse avail., dinner served Wed. and Sat. nights

ACCOMMODATIONS

Units: 22 guest rooms, 12 cottage rooms larger than average
All Rooms: Private bath and entrance, TV/VCR, down comforter, umbrella
Some Rooms: Fireplace, private garden, patio, sofa bed (2); cottage rooms have dual-sided fireplace, wet bar, private deck or veranda
Bed & Bath: Queens, kings (9), robes, whirlpool tubs for 2 (8)
Favorites: Jonathan, w/ dual-sided fireplace, sitting room w/ desk and love seat, king bed; Jonagold, w/ pillowed window seat w/ view of pasture, fireplace, tapestry-covered chair
Comfort & Decor: Rooms individually decorated w/ pine antiques, wall coverings and matching fabrics, quilts, window seats, wicker, lounge chairs, private porches and patios, wet bars, whirlpool baths, fireplaces

RATES, RESERVATIONS, & RESTRICTIONS

Deposit: 1st night in advance; must cancel 7 days in advance
Discounts: AAA Mon.–Thurs.; extra person $25
Credit Cards: AE, MC, V
Check-In/Out: 3/noon
Smoking: No
Pets: No
Kids: Only 2 rooms suitable for children, under 12 must be accompanied by adult, additional guest fee for those over 6
No-Nos: No candles

Minimum Stay: 2 nights on weekends and holidays
Open: Closed Dec. 24–25
Hosts: Pat and Darrell Straube
P.O. Box 425
2502 Washington St.
Julian, CA 92036
(760) 765-1700
(800) 716-7242
Fax: (760) 765-0290
www.orchardhill.com
information@orchard hil.cml

BED-AND-BREAKFAST INN AT LA JOLLA, La Jolla

Overall: ★★★★½   Room Quality: B   Value: B   Price: $129–$329

The Bed-and-Breakfast Inn at La Jolla is a fine example of Cubist-style architecture. It was designed by Irving Gill, who pioneered the style in the early 1900s and whose work can be seen in many San Diego–area landmark buildings, including the Museum of Contemporary Art just across the street. Gill was one of a school of architects who rejected the fussy Victorian style of the day in favor of a flat style based on straight lines and simple unadorned walls that serve as backgrounds for gardens, nature, or art. In this case the inn serves as a backdrop for brilliantly colorful subtropical gardens designed by Kate Sessions, famed for her work in Balboa Park. Inside, white walls serve a similar purpose, emphasizing the inn's tasteful furnishings: poster and canopy beds, oriental rugs, wicker and rattan tables and chairs, and nautical-themed accoutrements. There's an attractive rooftop deck and a sunny common sitting room filled with books and magazines. The innkeepers offer a full breakfast each morning in the inn's formal dining room, but many guests choose to dine in the garden.

SETTING & FACILITIES

Location: In La Jolla, in a quiet mixed residential/business area, on Draper between Silverado and Kline, 1 block from ocean
Near: Restaurants, shopping, Museum of Contemporary Art, Scripps Institute, Stephen Birch Aquarium, Sea World, zoo, Balboa Park, Deepak Chopra Center for Well-Being
Building: 1913 Irving Gill Cubist-style house, 9 rooms in main house, 6 in the annex built in 1985
Grounds: Double urban lot, landscaped gardens designed by Kate Sessions, fountain

Public Space: Library, DR, patio, decks, cloistered garden
Food & Drink: Full breakfast, served 8–9:30 a.m. in DR, patio
Recreation: Biking, ballooning, surfing, snorkeling, kayaking, wind surfing, tennis, golf
Amenities & Services: Sherry, fresh fruit, hairdryers, robes and flowers in rooms, late afternoon wine and cheese in DR; iced tea, fresh fruit, pastries, or cookies anytime; limited private parking, disabled access, VIP pass to gym, concierge services, picnic baskets avail.

ACCOMMODATIONS

Units: 15 guest rooms, 4 larger than average, including 2 suites
All Rooms: Private bath, AC, phone avail. on request
Some Rooms: Fireplace, four-poster, cable TV/VCR, fridge/minibar, ocean view
Bed & Bath: Queens, kings (3), twins (2)
Favorites: Pacific View, nautical theme

w/ antiques, sitting area, fireplace, desk, best ocean view; Holiday, w/ large fireplace, canopy four-poster, antique armoire, sitting area, double tub
Comfort & Decor: Rooms individually decorated w/ original artwork; antiques, reproductions, and designer pieces; custom-designed wallcoverings and drapes, hardwood floors w/ oriental or Aubusson rugs, some carpet

RATES, RESERVATIONS, & RESTRICTIONS

Deposit: 1 night's deposit midweek, 2 for weekends; must cancel 10 days in advance; $20 cancellation fee
Discounts: Long stays, weekday business, AAA, midweek winter
Credit Cards: AE, MC, V
Check-In/Out: 3/11, late check-out 20% of room rate
Smoking: No
Pets: No
Kids: 12 and over
No-Nos: No more than 2 guests

per room
Minimum Stay: 2 nights on weekends, 3–4 on holiday weekends
Open: All year
Host: Ron Shanks
7753 Draper Ave.
La Jolla, CA 92037
(858) 456-2066
(800) 582-2466
Fax: (858) 456-1510
www.innlajolla.com

SCRIPPS INN, La Jolla

Overall: ★★★★	Room Quality: B	Value: B	Price: $135–$355

Until recently, the view and location were the best features of this inn, which occupies some of the priciest real estate in La Jolla. Scripps Inn is perched on the edge of the Pacific overlooking La Jolla Cove, and there are blue-water views from nearly every room. Originally the facility provided accommodations for families of patients at nearby Scripps Hospital, but the hospital closed, and the facility was converted to a rather motel-like inn. It recently went through a major renovation, however: walls were moved, plumbing was redone, windows were double-paned, and new, contemporary Mediterranean furnishings were installed. Now the rooms are brighter, lighter, and airier. There is no common room in the inn, so breakfast is served in the lobby on trays for guests to take to their rooms or the outside deck. All in all, this is a comfortable, well-located place to stay, particularly for families. Breakfast is simple, featuring pastries, juice, and beverages.

SETTING & FACILITIES

Location: In La Jolla, on the ocean side of Whale Watch Point at La Jolla Cove, near Cuvier St.
Near: Restaurants, shopping, Museum of Contemporary Art, Scripps Institute, Stephen Birch Aquarium, Sea World, Zoo, Balboa Park, Legoland
Building: New England–style inn w/ Mediterranean interior, built in 1930s, renovated and redecorated in 1999
Grounds: U-shaped 3-level lot w/ lanai deck overlooking ocean, bougainvilleas, potted plants
Public Space: 2nd-floor deck w/ outdoor furniture
Food & Drink: Cont'l breakfast from local French bakery served 7:30–10 a.m. in lobby
Recreation: Biking, ballooning, surfing, snorkeling, kayaking, wind surfing, tennis, golf
Amenities & Services: Complimentary newspaper, cable TV, private parking

ACCOMMODATIONS

Units: 13 guest rooms, all larger than average, including 4 suites
All Rooms: Private bath, cable TV, phone, sleeper sofa, small fridge, ceiling fan
Some Rooms: Fireplace, extra queen (3)
Bed & Bath: Kings, queens (3)
Favorites: No. 14, Honeymoon Suite, w/ a 20-ft. expanse of double-paned windows overlooking ocean, full kitchen, dining area w/ ocean view, 2 sinks, tub/shower, separate toilet room
Comfort & Decor: Contemporary Mediterranean whitewashed furniture w/ tan-and-white fabrics, white walls, beige wall-to-wall carpet, white taffeta bedspreads w/ tan-striped bedskirts, ocean views, tiled bathrooms w/ double granite sinks

RATES, RESERVATIONS, & RESTRICTIONS

Deposit: 1st night's lodging; must cancel 7 days in advance
Discounts: Long stays, AAA; extra adult (over 6) $10
Credit Cards: AE, D, MC, V
Check-In/Out: 3/noon
Smoking: No
Pets: No
Kids: OK on ground-floor rooms
Minimum Stay: 2 nights on weekends, 3 on weekends June 1–Sept.

15, 3 or 4 on holiday weekends
Open: All year
Host: Pamela Millan
555 Coast Blvd. South
La Jolla, CA 92037
(619) 454-3391
(800) 439-7529
Fax: (619) 456-0389
www.jcresorts.com
plmlajolla@aol.com

TWO ANGELS INN, La Quinta

Overall: ★★★★½   Room Quality: A   Value: B   Price: $140–$350

No, it isn't a mirage, there really is a great gray stone French chateau looming over the typical red-tile-roofed, adobe-style buildings in the desert. The idea of a chateau here came to innkeepers Hap and Holly Harris in a vision, and they created the Two Angels Inn alongside Lake La Quinta in the shadow of the Santa Rosa Mountains. An antique tapestry adorns the salon walls, cool tiles cover the floors, and French doors provide access to the lakeside lawn. Guest rooms decorated in a variety of styles display antiques collected by family members over a lifetime. The guest rooms also have fireplaces, double sinks and whirlpool tubs, and balconies or patios. In addition to the salon, common areas include a dark, cool library (where Holly sometimes holds meditation and yoga classes), a swimming pool, and lots of lawn and patio between the inn and the lake.

SETTING & FACILITIES

Location: In the desert resort and golfing town of La Quinta, southeast of Palm Springs, Rancho Mirage, and Palm Desert, via Hwy. 111; go south on Washington St., left on Ave. 47, and right on Caleo Bay

Near: Restaurants, shopping, galleries, Living Desert Wildlife Refuge, 100 golf courses within 10-minute drive, 5 min. from new Indian Wells Tennis Garden and complex

Building: French Chateau–style inn, plus suites building, both built in 1997
Grounds: 1 acre overlooking Lake La Quinta, w/ gardens, trees, landscaped meditation garden
Public Space: Salon w/ 28-ft. ceiling, DR, meditation library, terrace
Food & Drink: Full 3-course breakfast, including breakfast dessert, served 8:30–9:30 a.m. in the DR or on the terrace, early coffee outside rooms at 7:30 a.m.
Recreation: Biking, tennis, golf, horseback riding, jeep tours
Amenities & Services: Swimming pool, hot tub, late afternoon wine and hors d'oeuvres, robes, evening turndown services w/ treat, private parking, disabled access; concierge services for reservations, etc.; in-room massage

ACCOMMODATIONS

Units: 11 guest rooms, 9 in chateau and 2 minisuites in boathouse
All Rooms: Private bath, patio or balcony, fireplace, cable TV, phone, AC, view of Lake La Quinta
Some Rooms: Four-poster, private entrance
Bed & Bath: Kings (8, 2 convertible to twins), queens (3), double sinks and oversized showers, Jacuzzis for 2 (6)
Favorites: Papillon, w/ antique headboard, king (or 2 twins), European open shower, accommodates special needs; Marrakesh, w/ Moroccan arched entry, Empire campaign chairs, slate tile fireplace, musk-scented teak cabinets, whirlpool tub for 2, custom iron four-poster bed
Comfort & Decor: Rooms individually decorated w/ beds and bedding suited to room theme, Roman shades, French doors to patio or balcony, carpet, tiled baths, art objects including Masai carved work

RATES, RESERVATIONS, & RESTRICTIONS

Deposit: 50% of stay on credit card or by check in advance; must cancel 14 days in advance
Discounts: AAA, seniors, singles
Credit Cards: AE, D, MC, V
Check-In/Out: 3/11, late check-in/out by arrangement
Smoking: No smoking on property
Pets: No
Kids: 16 and over
No-Nos: No more than 2 guests per room
Minimum Stay: 2 nights on weekends and holidays
Open: All year
Hosts: Hap and Holly Harris
78120 Caleo Bay
La Quinta, CA 92253
(760) 564-7332
(888) 226-4546
Fax: (760) 564-6356
deuxanges@aol.com

CARRIAGE HOUSE, Laguna Beach

Overall: ★★★★	Room Quality: B	Value: B	Price: $140–$165

Some of the first B&Bs in Southern California were opened in Laguna Beach. The Carriage House, located on a quiet side street a few blocks from the beach and the hectic heart of Laguna, is one of these. Since the early 1980s, it's been a popular hideaway for quiet-seeking visitors to the beach city. Prior to that it was an apartment building, which it still resembles in layout. It's a U-shaped 2-story building surrounding a central courtyard that contains a verdant tropical garden, one of the inn's most appealing aspects. Because of the apartment origin of the building, accommodations are actually unusually spacious suites that can hold families or two couples, complete with kitchens, dining, and sitting areas. Innkeepers Andy and Lesley Kettley, longtime residents of the area, are particularly knowledgeable about restaurants and other attractions in Laguna Beach. An ample continental breakfast features homemade granola, muesli, and bread baked on the premises.

SETTING & FACILITIES

Location: In Laguna Beach, in the village area 1 mi. south of downtown, on corner of Catalina and Cress, 2.5 blocks from beach
Near: Restaurants, shopping, galleries, specialty shops, beaches
Building: 1920s colonial home, former beach house of Louis B. Mayer, renovated 1998–99, designated historic building
Grounds: Double lot w/ U-shaped building surrounding a brick courtyard, 3-tiered fountain, flowering gardens
Public Space: Breakfast room, courtyard
Food & Drink: Expanded cont'l breakfast served 8:30–10 a.m. in the breakfast room or courtyard
Recreation: Deep-sea fishing, sailing, kayaking
Amenities & Services: Cheese, fruit, and snack avail. in each suite; evening sherry, wine in fridge, private parking

ACCOMMODATIONS

Units: 6 guest rooms, all suites
All Rooms: Private bath, cable TV/VCR, DR, 1 or 2 BRs
Some Rooms: Fireplace, fridge (4), full kitchen (5)
Bed & Bath: Queens, kings (2)
Favorites: Green Palms, w/ white wicker furniture against tropical green, bay window overlooking courtyard fountain, queen bed w/ tropical net canopy; Lilac Time, w/ cranberry and lilac tones, antiques, queen brass bed, French doors to courtyard
Comfort & Decor: Suites individually decorated, antiques, wicker, memorabilia, carpets

RATES, RESERVATIONS, & RESTRICTIONS

Deposit: Credit card to hold; must cancel 72 hours in advance
Discounts: Long stays, AAA; extra person $20, children (under 10) $10
Credit Cards: AE, MC, V
Check-In/Out: 2/11, late check-out by arrangement
Smoking: No
Pets: OK, $10/pet, must not be left unattended
Kids: OK
Minimum Stay: 2 nights on weekends
Open: All year
Hosts: Andy and Lesley Kettley
1322 Catalina St.
Laguna Beach, CA 92651
(949) 494-8945
(888) 335-8945
Fax: (949) 494-6829
www.carriagehouse.com
crgehsebb@aol.com

CASA LAGUNA INN, Laguna Beach

Overall: ★★★★	Room Quality: B	Value: B	Price: $79–$225

This striking inn, located right on a quiet stretch of the Pacific Coast Highway, has much to recommend it. The hilltop location is high enough to afford blue-water ocean views from a number of rooms. Portions of the inn, including the signature Spanish Revival bell tower, mission house, and hilltop cottage, were built by Frank Miller, who was responsible for similar architectural touches in Riverside's famed Mission Inn. Many rooms have been set around a central courtyard to take advantage of the blooms and the soothing sounds of a fountain. There's a wide choice of guest rooms, ranging from small courtyard rooms to one-bedroom suites. Furnishings are simple, in keeping with the Mediterranean architecture. There are ceiling fans, louvered windows, sea breezes, and other touches of the languid life, which may lead to a hibiscus behind your ear and an urge for a mai-tai. The innkeepers serve an expanded continental breakfast in the library. Evening wine, tea, lemonade, teatime dessert, and hors d'oeuvres are also served in the library.

SETTING & FACILITIES

Location: In a residential neighborhood, 1 mi. south of downtown Laguna Beach, 5 min. to 2 secluded beaches
Near: Restaurants, shopping, galleries, Laguna Art Museum, ocean beaches
Building: 1930s whitewashed Spanish-style architecture w/ red-tiled roof, bell tower
Grounds: 1 acre of terraced hillside overlooking the ocean, w/ queen palms, 5 patios, tropical gardens w/ views of the ocean, fountains, greenhouses, aviary w/ doves

Public Space: Library, 4 patios scattered throughout grounds, bell tower w/ observation deck
Food & Drink: Expanded cont'l breakfast served 8–10 a.m. in the library
Recreation: Swimming, biking, fishing, tennis, golf
Amenities & Services: 1930s heated swimming pool; afternoon tea, wine, and cookies; evening sherry, wine, and hors d'oeuvres; private parking

ACCOMMODATIONS

Units: 19 guest rooms, 6 larger than average, including 3 suites; Cape Cod–style cottage w/ BR, fireplace; and Mission House, w/ 2 BRs, 2 fireplaces, large DR, sleeps 6
All Rooms: Private bath, TV, phone, fridge
Some Rooms: Fireplace, LR, kitchen, ocean view (14), extra bed (6)
Bed & Bath: Queens, kings (5, convertible to twins)

Favorites: Suites (Rooms 1–4), w/ LR, dining area, full kitchen, 1 BR, sofa sleepers in LR, private balconies, ocean or garden views; cottage, w/ stained glass, private ocean-view deck, sitting room w/ fireplace, full kitchen
Comfort & Decor: Rooms individually decorated w/ antiques and contemporary furnishings, stained glass, bas reliefs, 1930s Catalina Island tiles

RATES, RESERVATIONS, & RESTRICTIONS

Deposit: Credit card; must cancel 72 hours in advance; cancellation fee full rate
Discounts: Weekday business, groups, AAA; extra adult (13 and over) $20
Credit Cards: All
Check-In/Out: 2/11, late check-out by arrangement
Smoking: No
Pets: Small pets by arrangement, $5

Kids: OK
Minimum Stay: 2 nights on weekends July–Aug. and holidays
Open: All year
Host: Kathleen Flint
2510 S. Coast Hwy.
Laguna Beach, CA 92651
(949) 494-2996
(800) 233-0449
Fax: (949) 494-5009

EILER'S INN, Laguna Beach

Overall: ★★★★	Room Quality: B	Value: B	Price: $120–$195

This engagingly European-influenced bed-and-breakfast is the creation of German-born Henk Wirtz, who was a bit ahead of his time when he opened it more than 25 years ago. Henk's son Nico now operates the B&B with the same style that has lured returning fans for all these years. Smallish, simply furnished rooms on first and second floors surround a central courtyard that holds a burbling fountain and overflows with plants and flowers. There's also a sundeck with an ocean exposure on the second floor. The guest rooms have been refurbished and redecorated with new art and antiques in recent years. Expect to dine on European-style breads, cereals, fresh fruit, boiled eggs, and apple strudel at breakfast. In the evening the innkeepers put out a selection of cheeses and other hors d'oeuvres. From time to time a musician is on hand to entertain. All in all, this is a very relaxed and pleasant inn.

SETTING & FACILITIES

Location: On the ocean side of Hwy. 1 just past the intersection with Cleo St., half-mile from center of town, 2 blocks from beach
Near: Restaurants, shopping, small boutiques, galleries, state parks, ocean beaches, museums
Building: 1940 2-story New Orleans–style apartment building
Grounds: 4 urban lots w/ inside courtyard w/ flower gardens, fountain, steps away from the beach
Public Space: LR w/ fireplace, library/TV room, sundeck, courtyard
Food & Drink: European-style breakfast served 8:30–10:30 in courtyard
Recreation: Biking, swimming, surfing, tennis, sailing, sunset ocean cruises, golf
Amenities & Services: Evening wine and cheese, classical guitar in courtyard on Sat., fresh fruit in rooms, homemade apple strudel on Sun.; limited parking in back, assistance w/ dinner reservations, public phone in lobby, in-room massage avail.

ACCOMMODATIONS

Units: 12 guest rooms, including 1 suite
All Rooms: Private bath
Some Rooms: Courtyard view (10), sundeck access (2), ocean view (3), sofa bed (1)
Bed & Bath: Queens, kings (2), 2 doubles (2)
Favorites: Room 209, w/ sundeck

view, Art Nouveau inlaid dresser; Room 207, a suite w/ original artwork, fireplace, ocean views, sitting room w/ sofa bed
Comfort & Decor: Rooms individually decorated w/ antiques, white wicker, original artwork, special linens, lace curtains, carpets

RATES, RESERVATIONS, & RESTRICTIONS

Deposit: Credit card; must cancel 5 days in advance; cancellation fee 1 night's lodging
Discounts: Off-season specials; extra person $20
Credit Cards: AE, D, MC, V
Check-In/Out: 2/noon
Smoking: No
Pets: No
Kids: OK, but not suitable

Minimum Stay: 2 nights on weekends, 3 on holidays
Open: All year
Hosts: Nico Wirtz, owner;
Maria Mestas, mgr.
741 S. Coast Hwy.
Laguna Beach, CA 92651
(949) 494-3004
Fax: (949) 497-2215

BRACKEN FERN MANOR, Lake Arrowhead

| Overall: ★★★★ | Room Quality: B | Value: A | Price: $80–$350 |

Bracken Fern Manor, a very nice B&B in the San Bernardino Mountains, has a colorful and torrid history. It was built in the late 1920s as a private club catering to movie stars and mobsters like Bugsy Segal and Mickey Cohen. Upstairs they had a brothel and lured aspiring actresses to staff it. Here was a chance to make money and meet important people. No one knows whether any of the women made it to the screen, but their letters and keepsakes were found in the attic when the inn was restored. The inn's ten rooms have been named for them, and their names are memorialized as flowers in the stained glass transoms. The rooms are modestly sized and simply but attractively furnished with brass, wrought-iron, or sleigh beds; European antiques; and cat mascots, a reminder of the inn's "cathouse" history. The exception is the Bridal Suite, with Mombassa veiling and a canopy over a four-poster oak bed, and a bathroom with a two-person Jacuzzi. Innkeeper Cheryl Weaver has added many touches: an art gallery, a library, a wine-tasting cellar, and a gently swaying hammock.

Setting & Facilities

Location: 5 min. from Lake Arrowhead and Arrowhead Villas, 29 mi. northeast of LA via Hwy. 18
Near: Restaurants, shopping, antiques, Lake Arrowhead
Building: 1929 restored English Tudor country manor, historic landmark
Grounds: 3 urban lots, w/ 3 patios, gardens, gazebo
Public Space: Parlor w/ fireplace, library, art gallery w/ changing exhibits, game parlor w/ antique snooker table, wine-tasting cellar, patios
Food & Drink: Full breakfast served in DR at reserved time
Recreation: Biking, fishing, water sports, horseback riding, skiing, ice-skating, bowling, theaters, boating
Amenities & Services: Garden hot tub, indoor sauna, afternoon wine and refreshments, artesian well water, candies, 7 a.m. beverage service, private parking, concierge services, picnic baskets

Accommodations

Units: 10 guest rooms, including 4 suites; cottage has kitchen and sleeps 4 for families w/ children, breakfast not included
All Rooms: Stained glass, occasional chairs, armoire
Some Rooms: Family unit has shared bath
Bed & Bath: Beds vary
Favorites: Bridal Suite, w/ hand-carved queen four-poster bed w/ canopy of Mombassa veiling, Jacuzzi tub, wet bar, fridge, coffeemaker; Rosey, a minisuite w/ roses and lace, antique shower/tub
Comfort & Decor: Rooms individually decorated w/ eclectic decor—antiques from around the world, stained glass transoms; four-poster, brass, sleigh, and wrought-iron beds; wicker, lace accents, floral fabrics, skylights

Rates, Reservations, & Restrictions

Deposit: 1 night's lodging in advance; must cancel 3 days in advance, 7 days on holidays and summer
Discounts: Seniors, AAA, Sun.–Thurs.
Credit Cards: MC, V
Check-In/Out: 3:30–10/11:30, late check-out 2 p.m. $50
Smoking: No
Pets: No, except assistance dogs
Kids: Angelic children considered
Minimum Stay: 2 nights on holidays and during summer
Open: All year
Host: Cheryl Weaver
P.O. Box 1006
815 Arrowhead Villas Rd.
Lake Arrowhead, CA 92352
(909) 337-8557
Fax: (909) 337-3323
www.brackenfernmanor.com

CARRIAGE HOUSE B&B, Lake Arrowhead

Overall: ★★★★   Room Quality: B   Value: A   Price: $95–$135

This gray New England–style clapboard house is located in a quiet residential section of Lake Arrowhead. The innkeepers will make you comfortable and offer advice on what to see and do, and if you opt to lounge on the tree-shaded back deck in the two-person hammock with a good book, that's OK, too. The inn was designed to take advantage of lake views framed by pine trees. The Surrey Room has French doors onto a private balcony with a lake view. The Brougham has a fireplace, a claw-foot tub with a skylight over it, and, of course, a lake view. The Victoria Room has a high antique bed and a large window seat from which you can get a glimpse of Papoose Lake. Furnishings at the Carriage House are pleasantly eclectic, including items from the innkeepers' antique collection.

SETTING & FACILITIES

Location: In community of Lake Arrowhead on the east shore of Lake Arrowhead, 18 mi. north of San Bernardino via Hwys. 30, 18, and 173, 2 hours east of LA
Near: Restaurants, shopping, antiques, boat tours
Building: 40-year-old New England-style clapboard house
Grounds: Urban lot w/ lawns and gardens, flagstone patio, deck
Public Space: Parlor w/ fireplace, DR, English sunroom w/ TV/VCR, large decks, flagstone patio, all w/ lake views
Food & Drink: Full breakfast served 8–9:30 a.m. in DR
Recreation: Biking, horseback riding, ice-skating, lake swimming, fishing, tennis, downhill/X-C skiing
Amenities & Services: Afternoon appetizers and beverages, passes for Lake Arrowhead access; off-street parking, concierge service for reservations

ACCOMMODATIONS

Units: 3 guest rooms, 1 suite
All Rooms: Private bath, cable TV, featherbed, down comforter, view of lake and pines
Some Rooms: Extra bed (1); suite has fireplace, skylight above tub, VCR
Bed & Bath: Queens, king, claw-foot tub (1)
Favorites: Brougham Room, w/ king bed, window seat, fireplace, lake view, antique tub; Surrey Room, w/ French doors to balcony, lake view
Comfort & Decor: Rooms individually decorated w/ American Country furnishings, antique whitewashed pine and brass, and white iron beds, wallpaper, Belgian lace curtains, hooked rugs, paned and leaded windows, oak woodwork and floors

RATES, RESERVATIONS, & RESTRICTIONS

Deposit: 1st night's lodging; must cancel 7 days in advance, 14 for holidays
Discounts: Long stays, midweek 2-night stays, singles; extra person in suite $15
Credit Cards: All
Check-In/Out: 3/noon
Smoking: No
Pets: No
Kids: 12 and over
No-Nos: No more than 2 guests per room except in suite
Minimum Stay: 2 nights on weekends, 3 on some holidays
Open: All year
Hosts: Lee and Johan Karstens
P.O. Box 982
472 Emerald Dr.
Lake Arrowhead, CA 92352
(909) 336-1400
(800) 526-5070
Fax: (909) 336-6092
www.lakearrowhead.com/
    carriagehouse
joleekar@js-net.com

CHATEAU DU LAC, Lake Arrowhead

Overall: ★★★★	Room Quality: B	Value: B	Price: $125–$250

If you won the lottery and wanted to build a waterfront house with a view to knock folks' socks off, it might look a lot like Château du Lac. Set on a hillside above the blue water of Lake Arrowhead's north shore, this inn built in 1986 boasts more than 100 windows on all sides, some three stories high. There are spacious outdoor decks, some cool and tree-shaded, others affording a lake view. You can even climb upstairs into a third-floor tower nook and try out your binoculars. Best of the five rooms is the Lakeview Suite, with open beams and trusses, a brick fireplace, inspirational views everywhere you turn, and a Jacuzzi in the bathroom. Other rooms are tucked into dormers and hidden down halls. Innkeepers Oscar and Jody Wilson are gracious hosts who offer a breakfast buffet that might include home-baked croissants along with stratta, quiche, or stuffed French toast. Jody, once a caterer, serves tea in the afternoon.

SETTING & FACILITIES

Location: On the east side of Lake Arrowhead, 2 blocks from the lake, 20 mi. north of San Bernardino via Hwys. 18 and 173, 2.5 hours east of Los Angeles
Near: Restaurants, shopping, antiques, boat tours, Lake Arrowhead
Building: 1986 Victorian w/ Country French interior
Grounds: Double lot w/ forest setting, gazebo

Public Space: Parlor w/ fireplace and game table, library, DR w/ fireplace, tower room w/ view of north woods
Food & Drink: Full breakfast served at 9 a.m. in DR
Recreation: Swimming, horseback riding, fishing, ice-skating, X-C/downhill skiing
Amenities & Services: Afternoon tea, evening wine, videotape library, private parking, guest fridge in DR

ACCOMMODATIONS

Units: 5 guest rooms, 4 larger than average
All Rooms: Private bath, cable TV/VCR, phone
Some Rooms: Fireplace, sleeper sofa (1), balcony
Bed & Bath: Queens, Jacuzzis (3)
Favorites: Lakeview, w/ open beams, wallpaper, antique armoire, white lace

eyelet comforter, fireplace, private balcony overlooking the lake, Jacuzzi for 2 set in bay window w/ lakeview
Comfort & Decor: Rooms individually decorated w/ wallpaper, featherbeds, teddy bears, Country French furnishings, sitting areas, comforters, lake and forest views

RATES, RESERVATIONS, & RESTRICTIONS

Deposit: Credit card; must cancel 3–4 days in advance; $15 cancellation fee
Discounts: Long stays, weekday business

Credit Cards: All
Check-In/Out: 1/11, late check-out by arrangement

Smoking: No
Pets: No
Kids: 14 and over
Minimum Stay: 2 nights on weekends
and holidays
Open: All year
Hosts: Oscar and Jody Wilson
P.O. Box 1098

911 Hospital Rd.
Lake Arrowhead, CA 92352
(909) 337-6488
(800) 601-8722
Fax: (909) 337-6746
www.lakearrowhead.com
chateau@js-net.com

EAGLE'S LANDING, Lake Arrowhead

Overall: ★★★★	Room Quality: B	Value: B	Price: $95–$185

The eagles that once fished in the North Bay section of Lake Arrowhead before it was developed inspired Dorothy and Jack Stone to call their lodge Eagle's Landing. Indeed, if the eagles ever come back, they will find many perches waiting for them at the Stones' dramatic trilevel "mountain Gothic" home. There are two wraparound redwood decks with sweeping lake views, plus a tower in the back of the house that soars up into the pines. Inside, there's a 24-foot wall of glass overlooking the lake in the common room. In spite of its contemporary origin, this is an old-fashioned sort of B&B in which the grace of the hosts is essential to its charm. These are accomplished, well-traveled people who delight in sharing the experiences of their lives with guests. Ask about an Indian basket mounted on the wall, and Dorothy will tell you about interesting, out-of-the-way places in Arizona and Utah. She'll tell you where she found the green and white Amish quilt on the bed, and the story of the huge trestle dining table that dominates the family room. You won't starve here, either. A full breakfast consisting of French toast or Irish oatmeal is served in the tower breakfast room, and on Sundays Jack takes over and barbecues sausages for brunch.

SETTING & FACILITIES

Location: On the west shore of Lake Arrowhead, 27 mi. north of San Bernardino via Hwys. 18 and 189, 2 hours east of LA
Near: Across the road from Lake Arrowhead, near restaurants, shopping, boutiques, galleries, lake tours
Building: 15-year-old "mountain Gothic" retreat
Grounds: Half-acre surrounded by national forest, massive pines and cedars, naturally landscaped
Public Space: Common room w/ 24-ft. wall of windows, huge fireplace, 10-ft. trencher table, library, breakfast room, 1,000 feet of redwood decks, picnic area w/ double hammocks
Food & Drink: Full breakfast served 8–10 a.m in the breakfast room, Sun. brunch served in the common room at 9:30 a.m

Recreation: Skiing, ice-skating, tennis, lake fishing, and swimming
Amenities & Services: Afternoon snacks; evening wine, hot spiced cider, and hors d'oeuvres; private beach club membership extended to guests, private off-street parking, concierge services for reservations

ACCOMMODATIONS

Units: 4 guest rooms, including 1 suite
All Rooms: Private bath, down comforter
Some Rooms: TV, private deck w/ lake view, VCR/TV/stereo, fireplace, fridge, dishes, full bar, leather sofa bed (1)
Bed & Bath: Queens, kings
Favorites: Lake View Suite, w/ wood-burning fireplace, sitting room, full bar, TV/VCR, fridge, private deck; Woods Room, w/ private deck overlooking woods and lake
Comfort & Decor: Rooms individually decorated w/ artwork, antiques and reproductions, carpets, collections from owners' travels in Europe

RATES, RESERVATIONS, & RESTRICTIONS

Deposit: Credit card; must cancel 7 days in advance, 2 weeks for major holidays
Discounts: Weekday business Mon.–Thurs., 2-night stay required
Credit Cards: AE, D, MC, V
Check-In/Out: 3/noon
Smoking: No
Pets: No
Kids: 14 and over
No-Nos: No more than 2 guests per room

Minimum Stay: 2 nights on weekends
Open: All year
Hosts: Dorothy and Jack Stone
P.O. Box 1510
Blue Jay, CA 92317
27406 Cedarwood Dr.
Lake Arrowhead, CA 92352
(909) 336-2642
(800) 835-5085
Fax: (909) 336-2642
www.southerncalonline.com/
    eagles_landing.html

LORD MAYOR'S INN, Long Beach

Overall: ★★★★	Room Quality: B	Value: A	Price: $85–$185

A lovely blue and white Edwardian home built by the first mayor of Long Beach, this house has been painstakingly restored and decorated. It's filled with antiques: genuine Eastlake pieces, pineapple and mahogany beds, and heirlooms passed down through the family of retired educators Reuben and Laura Brasser. The elegant inn has five spacious bedrooms, gleaming oak floors, handmade quilts, generous amounts of woodwork, and brass fittings. The Brassers operate two cottages in addition to their classic inn. Just around the corner are Apple House and Cinnamon House, designed to serve families and business groups traveling together. They offer fairly small, simply furnished bedrooms, a few antiques, living and dining rooms, and small gardens. Laura serves an ample breakfast to her guests in the formal dining room in the main house, which may include eggs Benedict, popovers with lemon curd, or scrambled eggs. As this book goes to press, the Brassers are at it again, restoring a nearby six-unit 1906 apartment house.

SETTING & FACILITIES

Location: In downtown Long Beach, on Cedar near 5th St., 2 blocks north of civic center, half-hour south of LA Internat'l Airport
Near: Queen Mary, Aquarium of the Pacific, beaches, LA entertainment, Disneyland, shopping, restaurants, water sports, ocean fishing, Catalina Island tours, deep-sea fishing
Building: 1904 2-story Edwardian home, studio in converted horse barn in back, restored historic landmarks, 2 1906 city cottages, restored, around corner on 5th St.
Grounds: 3 separate urban lots w/ large garden in rear of main building

Public Space: Main House LR, 3 sunporches on upper and lower decks, DR, cottages each have a LR, DR
Food & Drink: Full breakfast in Main House DR, or on decks; served 7–9:30 a.m.; popovers w/ warm fresh lemon curd on Sun.
Recreation: Water sports, biking, golf, theater, symphony, professional and collegiate sports, museums
Amenities & Services: Hand-ironed decorator sheets, antiques, down comforters, evening beverage and dessert, private parking, local restaurant menus avail.

ACCOMMODATIONS

Units: 12 guest rooms, 5 in main house, 1 in garden cottage, 3 each in each city cottage
All Rooms: Down comforter, fine linens, quilt, hand-crocheted rugs
Some Rooms: Fridge, kitchen, featherbed, high ceiling, afghan, private bath (8), data port (5)
Bed & Bath: Queens, doubles (3), twins (2), 4 rooms share 2 baths, clawfoot soaking tubs (5)
Favorites: Fireplace Room, spacious,

original BR of Long Beach's 1st mayor, 10-ft. ceiling, fireplace, four-poster bed, antique light fixtures, 11-ft.-wide bow windows, private bath w/ claw-foot soaking tub and shower, wood and marble sink, wainscoting, access to sundeck
Comfort & Decor: Rooms are individually decorated w/ antiques appropriate to the age of the house; original eastern golden oak woodwork, original granite stone fireplace, hand-tied Persian rugs

RATES, RESERVATIONS, & RESTRICTIONS

Deposit: Credit card to hold; must cancel 7 days in advance; $15 cancellation fee
Discounts: Singles
Credit Cards: AE, D, MC, V
Check-In/Out: Before 10:30/11:30
Smoking: No
Pets: No
Kids: OK, most suitable in Apple or Cinnamon Houses; 12 and over in Main House

No-Nos: No more than 2 guests per room
Minimum Stay: None
Open: All year
Hosts: Laura and Reuben Brasser
435 Cedar Ave.
Long Beach, CA 90802
(562) 436-0324
Fax: (562) 436-0324
www.lordmayors.com
innkeepers@lordmayors.com

TURRET HOUSE, Long Beach

Overall: ★★★★   Room Quality: B   Value: B   Price: $100–$140

The newest B&B in Long Beach's emerging tourist-oriented downtown, the Turret House is a pretty Queen Anne Victorian graced with its namesake turret, gables, and a "painted lady" facade featuring 11 colors. It was built in 1906 by a local master carpenter whose fine craftsmanship can be found in the original built-in china closets, custom butler's pantry, beveled and leaded glass windows, and ornate scrollwork around the front porch. Rooms range in size, and the littlest one, the Turret, is a charmer in many ways. It has a 12-foot ceiling and a view from the king-sized trundle bed of five leaded-glass windows set in the turret, and a bath just outside the door. The largest of the rooms, the Balcony Suite, contains a romantic poster bed with a white tulle canopy. Breakfast is served in the inn's High Victorian dining room, and a typical breakfast may include stuffed French toast along with home-baked breads and fresh fruit.

SETTING & FACILITIES

Location: At corner of 6th St. and Chestnut Ave., in a residential area of Long Beach's historic district
Near: Historic district, Queen Mary, aquarium, bike/walking paths on beach, Shoreline Village and marina, Catalina Island, restaurants, shopping, antiques, beaches, farmers' market, maritime museum, galleries, convention center
Building: 1906 turreted Queen Anne Victorian, restored w/ authentic paint job using 11 colors
Grounds: Urban lot, w/ flower beds, fountain, resting bench, lawn
Public Space: Parlor w/ player piano, DR, sitting room w/ fireplace, games, books, TV/VCR, front porch w/ wicker furniture
Food & Drink: Full breakfast served at guests' arranged time in DR or room
Recreation: Biking, surfing, parasailing, kayaking, swimming, Jet Skiing, waterskiing, deep-sea fishing, tennis, golf, vintage airplane rides
Amenities & Services: Afternoon snacks, robes, fresh flowers, down comforters, signature soaps/toiletries, breakfast and snacks on historic Civil War china, crystal, and silver; hatbox lunches, on-site parking, special dinner packages w/ local restaurants, special aquarium rates

ACCOMMODATIONS

Units: 5 guest rooms, all on 2nd floor
All Rooms: Private bath w/ claw-foot tubs/showers, AC, armoire, overhead fan
Some Rooms: Four-poster, trundle bed (1)
Bed & Bath: Queens, kings (2), sinks in antique dressers
Favorites: Balcony Suite, in whites and blues, ceiling angles from 20 ft. to 9 ft., antique four-poster w/ white tulle canopy, matching wood dresser, in-room bath, French doors to private balcony w/ white iron ice cream table and chairs

Comfort & Decor: Rooms individually decorated, leaded glass windows, antiques, armoires, floral wallpapers, overstuffed chairs, lace curtains, Chinese wool floral rugs, original hardwood floors

RATES, RESERVATIONS, & RESTRICTIONS

Deposit: Credit card; must cancel 7 days in advance; cancellation fee $20
Discounts: None; extra person $20
Credit Cards: AE, D, MC, V
Check-In/Out: 3–9/11, late check-out by arrangement
Smoking: No
Pets: No
Kids: Not suitable for small children
Minimum Stay: 2 nights on Long

Beach Grand Prix weekend and holiday weekends
Open: All year
Hosts: Nina and Lee Agee
556 Chestnut Ave.
Long Beach, CA 90802
(562) 983-9812
Fax: (562) 437-4082
www.turrethouse.com
innkeepers@turrethouse.com

INN AT 657, Los Angeles

| Overall: ★★★★ | Room Quality: B | Value: B | Price: All Suites $125 |

Innkeeper Patsy Carter, a former trial lawyer, just loves Los Angeles and the people who are drawn to it. Her guests include professors, speakers, museum directors, and researchers who are spending some time at nearby University of Southern California or Marymount University, so the conversation around the breakfast table can be quite stimulating. The inn, the closest B&B to downtown L.A., consists of an apartment building with one- and two-bedroom apartments that have been converted to guest accommodations. Each has a private entrance from a gated patio or balcony. Rooms are spacious and furnished with a comfortable blend of sofas, easy chairs, and tables. Patsy can usually be found presiding over the inn's kitchen, where she cooks up legendary breakfasts for her guests. Menus are cooked to order and might include ham and French toast, pork chops and cheese omelets, or pancakes with bacon.

SETTING & FACILITIES

Location: In downtown LA, 1 block west of Figueroa St. between the Los Angeles Convention Center and the University of Southern California
Near: Restaurants, shopping, museums, theater, Convention Center, Exposition Park, both state and federal courthouses, financial district, music center, garment district, Staples Center sports complex
Building: 1940s apartment building
Grounds: Urban lot w/ gardens, patios, fountains
Public Space: DR
Food & Drink: Full breakfast served in DR cooked to order, approx. 7–10 a.m.

Recreation: Shopping, professional and collegiate sports, museums
Amenities & Services: Hot tub, gardens, private off-street parking, laundry, catered dinner, intracity shuttle 1 block away

ACCOMMODATIONS

Units: 5 apartment-sized 1- and 2-BR suites w/ dining area, kitchen, private entrance, 4 w/ LR
All Rooms: Private bath, cable TV/VCR, phone, AC, fridge, microwave, coffeemaker, goose down comforter, private line phone for fax and computer, private entrance from patio or balcony

Bed & Bath: Queens
Favorites: Oriental Blue Suite, w/ large LR, fully equipped kitchen, Japanese silk hangings, Turkish rug
Comfort & Decor: Rooms individually decorated w/ comfortable furniture, rugs and carpet, LRs, dining areas, kitchens, goose down comforters, sitting areas

RATES, RESERVATIONS, & RESTRICTIONS

Deposit: 1st night's lodging; must cancel 5 days in advance
Discounts: Singles; extra person $25
Credit Cards: None; checks are accepted
Check-In/Out: 2/11, late check-out by arrangement
Smoking: No
Pets: No
Kids: OK

No-Nos: No more than 2 guests per room
Minimum Stay: None
Open: All year
Host: Patsy Carter
657 W. 23rd St.
Los Angeles, CA 90007
(213) 741-2200
(800) 347-7512
www.patsysinn657.com

DORYMAN'S OCEANFRONT INN, Newport Beach

Overall: ★★★★½	Room Quality: B	Value: B	Price: $175–$325

For over a century, a flotilla of dory fisherman have made the beach next to the pier in trendy Newport Beach their home. Each morning the men land their fish-filled dories here and sell the catch to local housewives and chefs. The Doryman's Inn, located on the second floor of a structure that also houses a restaurant, is named for the morning fishing boat ritual. Indeed, you can watch the activity from most rooms. The Doryman is elegantly decorated with draped Victorian canopy beds, French and American antiques, handcrafted woodwork, and deep pile carpet. All have fireplaces and sunken marble tubs. The innkeepers serve an expanded continental breakfast in a somewhat formal dining room, or guests can take their meal to their rooms or the sundeck on the roof. Over the years, Doryman's has drawn its share of celebrities who come to hide out a few days.

SETTING & FACILITIES

Location: In Newport Beach, on the beach across from the municipal pier, at intersection of W. Ocean Front, W. Balboa, and 21st Sts., 15 min. west of Orange Country Airport

Near: Restaurants, shopping, beaches, Newport Harbor Art Museum, UC Irvine, Disneyland, Anaheim Stadium

Building: 1891 historic 2-story brick hotel, 5-year, multi-million-dollar restoration

Grounds: Urban lot, parking lot

Public Space: 2nd-floor breakfast parlor, sundeck/terrace, 2nd-floor patio

Food & Drink: Expanded cont'l breakfast served in breakfast room or guest room 7:30–10:30 a.m.

Recreation: Swimming, biking, deep-sea fishing, boating

Amenities & Services: Morning newspaper, coffee and tea always avail., evening cookies and hot chocolate, elevator, soundproofed rooms, 1-way glass windows, redwood sundeck/terrace on roof, private parking lot, full 24-hour concierge service, restaurant on ground floor

ACCOMMODATIONS

Units: 10 rooms, including 3 suites

All Rooms: Private bath w/ sunken marble spa tub for 2, remote-controlled gas marble fireplace, down comforter, potted plants, individual climate control

Some Rooms: Canopy bed, four-poster, brass bed, ocean view, door to patio, extra bed (3)

Bed & Bath: Kings, queens (3)

Favorites: Master Suite, w/ draped canopy bed, 3-window ocean view, dining table for 2, sunken spa tub for 2

Comfort & Decor: Rooms individually decorated w/ American and French antiques, window seats, potted tropical plants and ferns, fireplaces, Italian marble sunken spas, solid oak doors; carved, canopy, and brass beds; matching floral draperies and down comforters, ruffled pillow shams, lace curtains, beveled mirrors, brass fittings, oak woodwork, etched glass light globes, hand-stenciled ceiling trim

RATES, RESERVATIONS, & RESTRICTIONS

Deposit: Credit card; must cancel 7 days in advance

Discounts: AAA, senior, corporate, government

Credit Cards: AE, MC, V

Check-In/Out: 3/noon

Smoking: No

Pets: No

Kids: OK

Minimum Stay: None

Open: All year

Host: Jeannie Lawrence
2102 W. Ocean Front
Newport Beach, CA 92663
(949) 675-7300
Fax: (949) 675-7300

PORTOFINO BEACH HOTEL, Newport Beach

Overall: ★★★★	Room Quality: B	Value: B	Price: $129–$339

The Portofino Beach Hotel is definitely the elegant alternative to the strand's casual side. This richly appointed Italian-style hotel would fit right into the scene on the Italian Riviera. It's filled with bouffant balloon curtains framing ocean-view windows, faux-marble columns, brocade wing chairs and curved-back settees, and oriental rugs. The guest rooms are decorated in lavish style with antique furnishings such as brass beds, carved headboards, and French side chairs. Many have appealing bathrooms with skylights or step-down marble whirlpool tubs; the two rooms across the front have views from the Jacuzzis. Several have full or partial ocean views, and there's also a rooftop sundeck with an ocean view. The innkeepers serve an extended continental breakfast with freshly baked muffins, fruit, yogurt, and cereal in the lobby or the hotel's La Gritta bar.

SETTING & FACILITIES

Location: In Newport Beach, at corner of W. Ocean Front and 23th Sts., on the beach, 2 blocks north of municipal pier, 15 min. west of Orange County Airport
Near: Restaurants, shopping, beaches, Newport Harbor Art Museum, UC Irvine, Disneyland, Anaheim Stadium
Building: 1890 Victorian train station, restored
Grounds: Urban lot, beach in front

Public Space: Parlor, European-style lobby, antique bar w/ fireplace
Food & Drink: Expanded cont'l breakfast served 7–10 a.m. in the lobby or bar
Recreation: Swimming, biking, deep-sea fishing, boating, golf
Amenities & Services: Coffee, tea avail., towels, private parking, room service 5:30–10 p.m. from adjoining Renato Ristorante Italian restaurant

ACCOMMODATIONS

Units: 15 guest rooms, including 3 suites
All Rooms: Private bath, cable TV, phone, AC
Some Rooms: Fireplace, four-poster, sleeper sofa, fridge, panoramic views of ocean, extra bed (10)
Bed & Bath: Queens

Favorites: Portofino Room, w/ Italian antique furnishings, Roman drapes, wall of windows w/ panoramic view of ocean, Jacuzzi for 2 w/ view of ocean
Comfort & Decor: Rooms individually decorated w/ Victorian Italian antiques, elegant fabrics, plush carpet

RATES, RESERVATIONS, & RESTRICTIONS

Deposit: Credit card; must cancel 72 hours in advance
Discounts: AAA, corporate, government, seniors; no charge for extra person
Credit Cards: AE, DC, D, MC, V, Transmedia
Check-In/Out: 3/noon, late check-out $50 if after 3 p.m.
Smoking: No
Pets: No
Kids: In 2 rooms

Minimum Stay: None
Open: All year
Hosts: Ken and Betty Ricamore, owners; Nick Atakan, mgr.
2306 W. Ocean Front
Newport Beach, CA 92663
(949) 673-7030
(800) 571-8749
Fax: (949) 723-4370
www.portofinobchhotel.com
portofino@newportbeach.com

TRES PALMAS B&B, Palm Desert

Overall: ★★★★	Room Quality: B	Value: B	Price: $80–$185

Everything is up-to-date in trendy Palm Desert, including Tres Palmas Bed-and-Breakfast. It's a built-for-the-purpose inn located in a quiet residential area, just steps from the shops, galleries, and restaurants of chic El Paseo, the "Rodeo Drive of the desert." The inn is the creation of Terry and Karen Bennett, who designed and built this Mediterranean-style, sand-colored stucco desert home in 1993. Inside it has open-beamed ceilings, tile floors, floor-to-ceiling windows, and southwestern-style decor throughout. The guest rooms also have a southwestern theme. Coyote has lodgepole pine furnishings, a king bed, and a couch. Kokopelli, the largest of the rooms, has a contemporary pencil point bed, a love seat, a private patio, and direct access to the pool area. In typical desert fashion, much of life here centers around the sparkling backyard pool and spa. There's a small desert garden, and for real relaxation, you can contemplate the Bennetts' desert tortoises. Each morning Karen makes a buffet-style continental breakfast that features her famous homemade muffins.

SETTING & FACILITIES

Location: In the desert resort town of Palm Desert, between Palm Springs and La Quinta, 2 blocks southwest of the intersection of Hwys. 11 and 74 via El Paseo and Ocotillo
Near: Restaurants, shopping, galleries, boutiques, Living Desert and Palm Springs, 10 public golf courses nearby
Building: Mediterranean/Spanish-style inn built in 1993
Grounds: Half-acre w/ citrus trees, desert boulders, lawn and palm trees, blooming flowers all year
Public Space: Living/dining area
Food & Drink: Expanded cont'l breakfast served 8–10 a.m. in DR or on trays for room or pool
Recreation: Tennis, golf
Amenities & Services: Swimming pool, hot tub, afternoon snacks, lemonade and iced tea always avail., private parking, guest phone avail. in wet bar area

ACCOMMODATIONS

Units: 4 guest rooms, all larger than average
All Rooms: Private bath, cable TV, AC, ceiling fan
Some Rooms: Four-poster, room for extra twin (1)
Bed & Bath: Queens and kings, double sinks (1)
Favorites: Kokopelli, w/ direct access to pool, private patio, king four-poster, love seat; Gecko, w/ queen bed, sitting/eating area, whitewashed and green iron furnishings
Comfort & Decor: Rooms individually decorated w/ cross-stitchery, plantation shutters, southwestern decor and linens in all rooms, high ceilings, wall-to-wall carpet

RATES, RESERVATIONS, & RESTRICTIONS

Discounts: Long stays; extra person $20

Credit Cards: AE, MC, V

Check-In/Out: 3/11

Smoking: No

Pets: No

Kids: 10 and over

Minimum Stay: 2 nights on weekends mid-Oct.–mid-June

Open: All year

Hosts: Karen and Terry Bennett

73–135 Tumbleweed Lane

Palm Desert, CA 92260

(760) 773-9858

(800) 770-9858

Fax: (760) 776-9159

www.innformation.com/ca/trespalmas

CASA CODY B&B COUNTRY INN, Palm Springs

Overall: ★★★★	Room Quality: B	Value: A	Price: $49–$349

This is an appealing, attractively priced inn located in the heart of Palm Springs, just steps from Palm Canyon Drive and the area's nightlife. Casa Cody, founded by Hollywood pioneer Harriet Cody (a cousin of Buffalo Bill) in the 1920s, consists of five interconnected one-story buildings with guest accommodations around central courtyards, two of which contain swimming pools. Guest rooms, attractively decorated in a southwestern style, come in a variety of configurations: standard motel-style rooms, studios, one- and two-bedroom suites, a one-bedroom cottage, and a two-bedroom historic adobe. Most have kitchens, making this a good choice if you plan to spend more than a couple of days in Palm Springs. There are cool Saltillo tiles on the floors, dhurrie rugs, handmade Santa Fe-style furniture, original art, Mexican tin mirrors, and woven baskets. The larger units have private patios, fireplaces, fully equipped kitchens, and cable television. Longtime innkeeper Elissa Goforth knows which Palm Springs restaurants are the best, where to see wildflowers in spring, and where to find the best bargains at the in the area's many resale shops. A casual continental breakfast is served poolside each morning.

SETTING & FACILITIES

Location: On the west side of Palm Springs, in heart of the Palm Springs Village area, half-block south of E. Tahquitz Canyon Way

Near: Restaurants, shopping, boutiques, galleries

Building: 4 1-story buildings built over 5 decades from 1910, early California adobe hacienda style, oldest operating hotel in Palm Springs

Grounds: 1.5 acres of rolling lawns, 3 bougainvillea- and citrus-filled courtyards, many private patios

Public Space: Patios and courtyards

Food & Drink: Expanded cont'l breakfast served poolside at 1 of 2 pools, 8–10 a.m.

Recreation: Biking, tennis, horseback riding, golf, swimming

Amenities & Services: 2 heated swimming pools, tree-shaded hot tub, private parking, disabled access

ACCOMMODATIONS

Units: 23 guest rooms, 21 larger than average, including 9 suites; total comprises 2 hotel rooms, 2 small studios, 10 large studios, 6 1-BR suites, 1 2-BR suite, 1 1-BR cottage, 1 2-BR adobe
All Rooms: Private bath, cable TV, phone, AC, VCR on request
Some Rooms: Fireplace, sleeper sofa (7), fridge (21); studios and suites have full kitchens
Bed & Bath: Kings (some convertible to twins), roll-aways avail.

Favorites: Nos. 16 and 24, located at the end of the buildings, w/ mountain views over spacious lawns, private; 1-BR cottage, w/ kitchen, LR, BR, separate yard
Comfort & Decor: Rooms individually decorated w/ paintings, prints, ethnic wall hangings, handmade pine furnishings, southwestern-design quilts, curtains and blinds, Saltillo tile floors, dhurrie rugs

RATES, RESERVATIONS, & RESTRICTIONS

Deposit: Credit card; must cancel 72 hours in advance
Discounts: Long stays, weekday business
Credit Cards: All
Check-In/Out: 2/11, late check-out by arrangement
Smoking: Allowed, but not encouraged
Pets: $10/night per pet plus $100 refundable deposit, $10 extra for holiday weekends
Kids: OK

No-Nos: Some rooms accommodate 4 guests, otherwise no more than 2 guests per room
Minimum Stay: 2 nights on weekends
Open: All year
Hosts: Therese Hayes and Frank Tysen, owners; Elissa Goforth, mgr.
175 S. Cahuilla Rd.
Palm Springs, CA 92262
(760) 320-9346
(800) 231-2639
Fax: (760) 325-8610
www.palmsprings.com/hotels/casacody

KORAKIA PENSIONE, Palm Springs

Overall: ★★★★½	Room Quality: B	Value: B	Price: $109–$365

When he acquired the walled Moroccan-style villa in the chic Las Palmas section of Palm Springs, innkeeper Doug Smith set out to create a salon of sorts where he would entertain artists, writers, and performers. The villa had previously been a temporary or full-time home to many artists, including Scottish painter Gordon Coutts, who built the house to replicate a villa in Tangiers, and Winston Churchill, who came to the desert to paint in the late 1920s. Smith, a retired architect, then acquired some additional buildings, including a small but stylish Mediterranean house across the street that belonged to 1930s and 1940s character actor J. Carrol Naish. Currently Smith is living in and working on a recently acquired adobe next to the Mediterranean Villa, which will house a spa for the inn. The result of this one-man show is that the inn has achieved a reputation as a place where artists, actors, and journalists like to come and hang out.

SETTING & FACILITIES

Location: In the southwest section of downtown Palm Springs, on Patencio between W. Baristo and W. Arena Rds.
Near: Restaurants, shopping, galleries, 3 blocks from Palm Canyon Dr.
Building: 1924 Moroccan and Mediterranean villas, surrounding bungalows and guest houses
Grounds: 1.5 acres w/ fruit trees, rock gardens, mosaic pools, stone waterfalls, at foot of San Jacinto Mountains
Public Space: Community kitchen

Food & Drink: Full breakfast served 8–11 a.m. in the courtyards or poolside, or in rooms on weekends, cont'l breakfast weekdays
Recreation: Biking, swimming, tennis, golf
Amenities & Services: Swimming pool, afternoon snacks, traditional Moroccan mint tea, pistachios, orange wedges, ginger cookies; European turndowns, in-room massage

ACCOMMODATIONS

Units: 20 guest rooms, 16 larger than average, including 9 suites
All Rooms: Private bath, phone, AC, featherbed, fridge
Some Rooms: Fireplace, four-poster, kitchen
Bed & Bath: Queens, kings (6), twins (5), double
Favorites: The Library, w/ high wood-beamed ceilings, fireplace, French doors to shaded patio, bookshelves w/ rare and first-edition books, separate dressing area, handmade queen four-poster, oriental rugs
Comfort & Decor: Rooms individually decorated w/ artwork from Italy, Greece, Morocco, Afghan, Thailand; all white walls or chocolate-washed walls, canvas curtains; tile, stone, and hardwood floors w/ kilims, sisal, and antique rugs

RATES, RESERVATIONS, & RESTRICTIONS

Deposit: 2 nights' lodging in advance; must cancel 2 weeks in advance, 45 days on holidays
Discounts: None
Credit Cards: None
Check-In/Out: 3/noon, half-day rate past 1 p.m.
Smoking: No
Pets: No
Kids: 15 and over
Minimum Stay: 2 nights on weekends, 3 on holiday weekends
Open: Closed from mid-July to mid-Sept.
Hosts: Doug Smith, owner; Melissa McDaniel, general mgr.
257 S. Patencio Rd.
Palm Springs, CA 92262
(760) 864-6411
Fax: (760) 864-4147
www.palmsprings.com/hotels/korakia

L'HORIZON, Palm Springs

Overall: ★★★½	Room Quality: B	Value: B	Price: $115–$225

Several generations of Lassies romped the expansive lawns and gardens surrounding the seven buildings that comprise this inn. It was created in the 1950s by Jack and Bonita Granville Wrather, movie producer and actress, respectively, who owned the original Lassie. The Wrathers entertained their Hollywood friends extensively in the desert using this property as guest houses and a hotel. The 1950s-style flat-roofed ranch-style pods have been nicely updated and restored, each with three guest rooms that can be arranged in different configurations (as a single unit with two bedrooms, three individual units, or two units, with or without kitchens) depending on the needs of guests. The decor is contemporary, done mostly in soft desert colors of blues and pinks, with handsome floor-to-ceiling plantation shutters. Large windows reveal expansive views of sometimes snowcapped Mount San Jacinto. Each room has its own private patio, where one can enjoy a morning cup of coffee while reading the paper. The innkeepers provide guests with a simple breakfast featuring beverages, pastries, and juice.

SETTING & FACILITIES

Location: In a mixed residential neighborhood at E. Palm Canyon and Deepwell Rd., 1 mi. east of downtown Palm Springs

Near: Restaurants, shopping, galleries, museums, concerts, 5 public golf courses within 1.5 mi.

Building: 7 buildings designed by architect William Cody in 1954, restored

Grounds: 2 acres of lawns, flower beds, palm trees, private patios off each room

Public Space: Library, patios, pavilion w/ barbecue

Food & Drink: Expanded cont'l breakfast served 8–9:30 a.m., guests choose what is served, and when and where—room, patio, or poolside

Recreation: Classic lawn and table games and bicycles on premises; biking, swimming, ballooning, horseback riding, ice-skating, tennis, golf nearby

Amenities & Services: Swimming pool, hot tub, barbecue, water and juice always avail., complimentary newspaper, private parking, assistance w/ activity plans and reservations, in-room massages

ACCOMMODATIONS

Units: 22 guest rooms, including 6 suites

All Rooms: Private bath, cable TV, phone, AC, patio

Some Rooms: Fireplace (1), fridge (6), private patio for sunbathing

Bed & Bath: Kings

Favorites: No. 3A, larger room w/ fireplace, kitchen, private enclosed patio; No. 6B, panoramic view of mountains and swimming area

Comfort & Decor: Simple, well-lit rooms in desert tones w/ plantation shutters, carpet, kitchenettes, showers w/ sliding glass doors opening onto private enclosed patios

RATES, RESERVATIONS, & RESTRICTIONS

Deposit: Credit card; must cancel 48 hours in advance, 72 for holidays
Discounts: Long stays, AAA
Credit Cards: All
Check-In/Out: 3/noon
Smoking: No
Pets: No
Kids: 16 and over
No-Nos: No more than 2 guests per room

Minimum Stay: 2 nights on weekends
Open: Closed June 1–Sept. 30
Host: Nickie McLaughlin, general mgr.
1050 E. Palm Canyon Dr.
Palm Springs, CA 92264
(760) 323-1858
(800) 377-7855
Fax: (760) 327-2933
www.lhorizonhotel.com
innkeeper@lhorizonhotel.com

WILLOWS HISTORIC PALM SPRINGS INN, Palm Springs

Overall: ★★★★★   Room Quality: A   Value: B   Price: $195–$550

"Einstein not only slept here, he dreamt here." That's the reason Tracy Conrad and Paul Marut rescued this historic Palm Springs estate and brought it back to life as one of the most elegant bed-and-breakfast inns in California. Originally the home of Samuel Untermyer, Secretary of the U.S. Treasury in the 1920s, it was a winter hideout for many of his wealthy and celebrated friends. Elegantly decorated to reflect the 1920s and 1930s, the Mediterranean-style inn features mahogany-beamed frescoed ceilings, stone and marble fireplaces, slate and hardwood floors, private garden patios, and original, handmade tiles. There's even a waterfall that cascades down a mountain slope into a pool just outside the dining room. Rooms are simply but elegantly furnished with period pieces, including antique bird's-eye maple dressers and hand-carved and sleigh beds. Bathrooms are luxurious, with two-person showers, two-person claw-foot tubs, pedestal sinks, pewter and crystal chandeliers, and a shower that splashes onto a rock protruding from the floor. Public spaces are just as posh: a pair of sofas fronting the fireplace in the expansive living room; curtained verandas overlooking the pool; and a fireplace framed with hand-painted tiles in the dining room. The inn's gardens date back nearly 70 years, when Einstein used to take the trail to Inspiration Point at the top of the hill behind the mansion and watch the desert sun rise.

SETTING & FACILITIES

Location: In the old Palm Springs Village section of Palm Springs, on W. Tahquitz, 3 blocks west of Palm Canyon Dr.
Near: Downtown shopping, restaurants, Desert Museum, antique shops, Mount San Jacinto
Building: 1927 Mediterranean villa, restored
Grounds: 1 acre w/ landscaped gardens
Public Space: LR, DR, veranda

Food & Drink: Full breakfast served in DR 8:30–11 a.m.
Recreation: Biking, golf, tennis, swimming, Palm Canyons oasis
Amenities & Services: Egyptian cotton towels, fine linens, swimming pool, complimentary beverages and wine, afternoon hors d'oeuvres and occasional live music, evening turn-down; off-street, gated parking, disabled access, full concierge service

ACCOMMODATIONS

Units: 8 guest rooms, 4 larger than average
All Rooms: Private bath, individual climate control, phone, 2nd modem line, voice mail, cable TV/VCR, fridge, iron/board, full toiletries including sunscreen
Some Rooms: Fireplace, separate entrance, private balcony, view of waterfall
Bed & Bath: Queens, kings (3), hairdryers, robes
Favorites: Marion Davies Room, w/ original antique furnishings, elaborately carved bed, 2-person claw-foot tub, silver chandelier, chaise lounge, separate

marble shower w/ pillowed stone floor, garden view; The Library, where Gable and Lombard honeymooned, w/ mahogany furniture, cherry hand-carved fireplace and coffered ceiling, private entrances open under a frescoed ceiling of the veranda and onto a private garden patio, king bed, antique pedestal sink, extra-long Art Deco bathtub and separate shower
Comfort & Decor: Rooms individually decorated w/ antiques, upholstered furniture, fine linens, handmade tiles, fireplaces, hardwood floors, private garden patios, mountain and garden views

RATES, RESERVATIONS, & RESTRICTIONS

Deposit: Credit card; must cancel 7 days in advance; cancellation fee 50%
Discounts: None; extra person $100, infants free
Credit Cards: All

Check-In/Out: 4/noon
Smoking: None on premises
Pets: No
Kids: 16 and over
Minimum Stay: 2 nights on weekends

Open: Sept. 1–July 15
Hosts: Tracy Conrad, owner;
Connie Stevens, mgr.
412 W. Tahquitz Canyon Way
Palm Springs, CA 92262

(760) 320-0771
(800) 966-9597
Fax: (760) 320-0780
www.thewillowspalmsprings.com
innkeeper@thewillowspalmsprings.com

INN AT PLAYA DEL REY, Playa del Rey

Overall: ★★★★½	Room Quality: A	Value: B	Price: $150–$295

This brand-new, built-from-the-ground-up Cape Cod-style inn has two appeals: as a very convenient location for business travelers arriving and departing from Los Angeles International Airport, just minutes away, and as a seaside hideaway (well, almost seaside) for romantic couples. Innkeeper Susan Zolla designed it that way, with rooms to match guests' needs. Business travelers will find economical, no-nonsense rooms equipped with desks, data ports, phones, and other items they may need. Romantic travelers will find other rooms featuring great views of sailboats moving silently down the Main Channel of Marina del Rey, and sweeping ocean vistas beyond. They'll find romance in bathrooms featuring over-sized Jacuzzi tubs, see-through fireplaces, and other luxury appointments. Decor is contemporary, with handcrafted beds and armoires, quilts, and fresh flowers. Not only are the rooms lovely, but the spacious living and dining rooms are inviting, with fresh sea breezes wafting through French doors that open to the ocean. The inn overlooks both the blue waters of Marina del Rey and the Ballona wetlands, a 350-acre bird sanctuary. Susan puts out an expansive buffet breakfast featuring home-baked breads, entrées such as cheese soufflé or egg puffs, bagels, fresh fruit, and yogurt.

SETTING & FACILITIES

Location: In the small community of Playa del Rey, at Culver and Pershing, 5 mi. north of LA Internat'l Airport and 3 blocks from the beach
Near: Restaurants, shopping, 3 blocks to beach, Ballona wetlands bird sanctuary, coastal bike path; a bit farther are Disneyland, Getty Art Center, Century City, Beverly Hills, Universal Studios
Building: 3-year-old Cape Cod inn
Grounds: On 350 acres of nature preserve, rose garden
Public Space: Parlor, library w/ books, movies, and games, breakfast room
Food & Drink: Full breakfast served 7:30–10 a.m. in breakfast room or on tray in guest room
Recreation: Biking (bikes on premises), bird-watching, golf
Amenities & Services: Garden Jacuzzi, afternoon wine and cheese, tea all day, robes, extra-large towels, private parking, disabled access, massages and facials avail., guest business center w/ fax, e-mail, and computer

ACCOMMODATIONS

Units: 21 guest rooms, 4 larger than average, including 2 suites
All Rooms: Private bath, cable TV, VCR, phone, AC, data port
Some Rooms: Fireplace, four-poster, sleeper sofa, fridge, porch (17)
Bed & Bath: Queens, kings (9), twins (4), Jacuzzis (11)
Favorites: Romance Suite, w/ over-sized tub in front of fireplace, surrounded by windows overlooking the bird sanctuary and the sailboats in the marina

Comfort & Decor: Rooms individually decorated w/ books and reading chairs; canopy, sleigh, and antique iron and brass beds; fireplaces, decks, robes, extra-large towels, views

RATES, RESERVATIONS, & RESTRICTIONS

Deposit: 1 night's stay; must cancel 48 hours in advance
Discounts: None; extra person $15
Credit Cards: AE, MC, V
Check-In/Out: 3/noon, late check-ins and check-outs by arrangement
Smoking: No
Pets: No
Kids: OK
Minimum Stay: None

Open: All year
Hosts: Susan Zolla and Donna Donnelly
435 Culver Blvd.
Playa del Rey, CA 90293
(310) 574-1920
Fax: (310) 574-9920
www.innatplayadelrey.com
playainn@aol.com

CHRISTMAS HOUSE B&B INN, Rancho Cucamonga

Overall: ★★★★½   Room Quality: B   Value: A   Price: $80–$180

Once home to a family of wealthy ranchers who entertained lavishly, this three-story 1904 Queen Anne mansion has always been known locally as the Christmas House because of the abundant red and green stained glass windows throughout. When Janice Ilsley opened the inn in the mid-1980s, she continued the tradition of entertaining her guests and visitors but also set out to make a name for the inn among the increasing numbers of businesspeople traveling to the Ontario area. Indeed, the charming inn makes a spacious and comfortable headquarters for any reason you can think of, with pretty rooms, large parlors, shady verandas, and nearly an acre of landscaped grounds. Guest rooms are located on the first and second floors of the main house and in a carriage house out back. Janice serves breakfast in the inn's sunny dining room. A typical menu might feature sausage/apple/cheddar quiche or blueberry custard crepes with red wine sauce or German apple pancakes.

SETTING & FACILITIES

Location: In a mixed residential neighborhood in Rancho Cucamonga, 1.3 mi. north of I-10, 1.5 mi. north of Ontario Internat'l Airport, 1 hour east of LA Internat'l Airport
Near: Shopping, restaurants, 1 hour or less to most LA attractions
Building: 1904 3-story Queen Anne Victorian w/ red and green stained glass, intricate wood carving, 7 fireplaces
Grounds: 1 acre of landscaped gardens w/ gazebo, carriage house, English gardens
Public Space: 2 parlors, library, formal DR, veranda w/ wicker furniture and hammock
Food & Drink: Full breakfast served in DR or rooms 7–9:30 weekdays, 8–9:30 weekends
Recreation: Mountain biking, downhill skiing, golf
Amenities & Services: Afternoon tea in the parlor, homemade cookies in rooms, private off-street parking, TV avail. on request

ACCOMMODATIONS

Units: 6 guest rooms, 2 larger than average, including 1 suite
All Rooms: AC
Some Rooms: Fireplace(s), four-poster, VCR, popcorn popper, private bath (4), shared bath (2)
Bed & Bath: Doubles, queens (2), outdoor Jacuzzis for 2 in private courtyard (2)
Favorites: Celebration Suite, w/ fireplace in both parlor and BR, antique mahogany canopy bed draped in lace, in-room breakfast, bay window; Garden Suite, w/ floral prints, white wooden shutters, white iron bed, ceiling fan, brick courtyard garden, private gazebo w/ spa
Comfort & Decor: Rooms individually decorated w/ antique furniture, satin drapes, shutters, carpet, 1915 grand piano, stained glass windows

RATES, RESERVATIONS, & RESTRICTIONS

Deposit: 1st night's lodging; must cancel 7 days in advance
Discounts: Weekday corporate rates, weekdays
Credit Cards: AE, D, MC, V
Check-In/Out: 4/11, late check-out negotiable
Smoking: No
Pets: No
Kids: OK
No-Nos: No more than 2 guests per room
Minimum Stay: None
Open: All year
Host: Janice Ilsley
9240 Archibald Ave.
Rancho Cucamonga, CA 91730
(909) 980-6450

HERITAGE PARK B&B INN, San Diego

Overall: ★★★★½	Room Quality: B	Value: B	Price: $100–$235

Heritage Park Inn, tucked into an eight-acre historic Victorian park on the edge of San Diego's Old Town, is part of the city's historic preserve, where many fine old buildings were relocated to save them from the wrecker's ball. The inn consists of two adjacent Victorians, both charming, moved to the park about 15 years ago. The 1889 Queen Anne has a turret, a wraparound porch, stained-glass windows, ornate millwork on banisters, and wainscoting. It's wonderfully furnished with antiques, including a double Eastlake panel bed with carved sunflowers, poster and canopy beds, fainting couches, and antique quilts. The cheerful guest rooms in the Queen Anne range in size, and some have Mission Bay views. All have private bathrooms, although some are detached. The three very spacious rooms in the adjacent manor house are also furnished with antiques, featherbeds, and whirlpool tubs. The innkeepers make an occasion of serving breakfast in the formal dining room of the main house by candlelight. Entrées may include eggs Florentine with broiled Parmesan potatoes or baked Victorian French toast with apple cider syrup and country sausages.

SETTING & FACILITIES

Location: In a neighborhood of historic homes next to Old Town San Diego just southeast of the junction of I-5 and I-8

Near: Restaurants, shopping, museums, galleries, Balboa Park, San Diego Zoo, Sea World, beaches

Building: 1889 Queen Anne Victorian mansion and 1889 Italianate manor house w/ turreted tower, fish-scale shingles, wraparound veranda, restored

Grounds: In an 8-acre Victorian village w/ cobblestone street, rose garden

Public Space: Main house parlor, formal DR, library, veranda w/ rockers, rose garden

Food & Drink: Full breakfast served at 8:30 a.m. in DR

Recreation: Biking, ballooning, swimming, diving, deep-sea fishing, sailing

Amenities & Services: Afternoon tea on veranda, robes, evening turndown, 24-hour beverages and homemade cookies, evening classic films shown in parlor, communal jigsaw puzzle, private parking, disabled access, concierge services for reservations

ACCOMMODATIONS

Units: 12 guest rooms, 3 larger than average, including 1 suite

All Rooms: Private bath, phone, fresh flowers, featherbed

Some Rooms: Ornamental fireplace, four-poster, sleeper sofa, fridge, private entrance, trundle bed (3)

Bed & Bath: Queens, doubles (2), king, hairdryers, Jacuzzi for 2 (3)

Favorites: Drawing Room, w/ window seat overlooking Victorian park, large Jacuzzi for 2, 13-ft. ceilings, antique ceiling wallpaper; Forget-Me-Not, w/ antique sleigh bed, fireplace, winner of Waverly fabric national contest for best B&B room, stenciled ceiling, claw-foot tub

Comfort & Decor: Rooms individually decorated w/ period antiques, featherbeds, Victorian lace curtains, period historic wallcoverings, oriental carpets, hardwood floors

RATES, RESERVATIONS, & RESTRICTIONS

Deposit: Credit card; must cancel 7 days in advance
Discounts: Weekday business, AAA; extra person $20
Credit Cards: All
Check-In/Out: 3/11, late check-out by arrangement
Smoking: No
Pets: No
Kids: OK

Minimum Stay: 2 nights on weekends
Open: All year
Hosts: Charles and Nancy Helsper
2470 Heritage Park Row
San Diego, CA 92110
(619) 299-6832
(800) 995-2470
Fax: (619) 299-9465
www.heritageparkinn.com
innkeeper@heritageparkinn.com

CHANNEL ROAD INN, Santa Monica

Overall: ★★★★½	Room Quality: A	Value: B	Price: $145–$295

The closest to the beach of all Los Angeles-area B&Bs, Channel Road Inn is also one of the most gracious. Innkeeper Susan Zolla, who saved the century-old home from certain demolition and turned it into an inn, deserves the credit for making every room comfortable and for treating guests as though they were personal friends on a visit. Pure Craftsman architectural details of the building define many of its best features: large windows facing the ocean bring in late afternoon breezes; there are balconies or decks where one can sit with a cool drink in hand; common areas include a large living room, small sitting room/library, and colorful outdoor gardens. Rooms range from small to ample, and some have a glimpse of the ocean. Each guest room is unique and beautiful, with subtle colors, elegant antiques, and tasteful draperies and bedcovers. Beds are highlights of the rooms: four-posters, canopies, and sleigh beds are represented, with lace coverings, Amish quilts, or more tailored effects. The inn is a block from the wide, white sand beach, albeit along the busy Pacific Coast Highway. Susan and her staff serve a generous breakfast in a sunny dining room, where the atmosphere is convivial. The menu might feature apple French toast (featured in the book *Chicken Soup for the Soul*), fresh fruit, yogurt, and other healthy items.

SETTING & FACILITIES

Location: In a residential neighborhood just north of Pacific Coast Hwy. and San Vicente Blvd., 2 mi. north of downtown Santa Monica
Near: Restaurants, shopping, galleries, museums, Getty Center, Santa Monica Pier, Universal Studios, Disneyland, 1 block from beach
Building: 1910 shingle-clad 3-story Colonial Revival house
Grounds: 4 urban lots, w/ hillside gardens
Public Space: LR w/ tiled fireplace, library, breakfast room overlooking hillside gardens, patios
Food & Drink: Full breakfast served 7:30–10 a.m. in the breakfast room or guest room
Recreation: Biking (bikes on premises), ocean and pool swimming, health clubs, tennis, golf nearby
Amenities & Services: Hot tub, afternoon cookies and tea, evening wine and hors d'oeuvres, robes, fresh flowers, private parking, disabled access, concierge services for reservations

ACCOMMODATIONS

Units: 14 guest rooms, 7 larger than average, including 2 suites
All Rooms: Private bath, cable TV, phones w/ data port
Some Rooms: VCR, fireplace, four-poster, sleeper sofa, fridge, AC, deck, partial ocean or garden view, extra bed (5)
Bed & Bath: Queens, kings (2, convertible to twins), hairdryers, Jacuzzis (2)
Favorites: Room No. 9, a sunny room w/ queen antique wicker bed, fireplace, private deck, view of ocean, double-sink bathroom
Comfort & Decor: Rooms individually decorated w/ bleached pine, antique wicker, Amish quilts, appliquéd lace bedcovers, wingback chairs and armchairs, wrought iron, wallpaper, hardwood floors and carpet, balconies and decks

RATES, RESERVATIONS, & RESTRICTIONS

Deposit: 1st night's lodging; must cancel 72 hours in advance
Discounts: Weekday business, corporate; extra person $15
Credit Cards: AE, MC, V
Check-In/Out: 3/noon, late check-out by arrangement
Smoking: No
Pets: No
Kids: OK
Minimum Stay: None
Open: All year
Hosts: Susan Zolla, owner; Heather Suskin, innkeeper
219 W. Channel Rd.
Santa Monica, CA 90402
(310) 459-1920
Fax: (310) 454-9920
www.channelroadinn.com
channelinn@aol.com

SEAL BEACH INN AND GARDENS, Seal Beach

Overall: ★★★★½	Room Quality: B	Value: B	Price: $155–$375

Like many inns, Seal Beach has a colorful past. This now quiet, beautiful inn was once a rumrunners' hideout. Marjorie Bettenhausen-Schmaehl gradually transformed the neglected 1920s resort into a luxury inn after she purchased it in 1972. It has French-Mediterranean charm to spare. Interconnected one- and two-story buildings surround a central flower-decked, plant-filled courtyard with a brick patio, a fern grotto, trellises, fountains, hanging baskets of flowers, and Old World statuary. The buildings have white iron balustrades, geranium-filled window boxes set off by classic blue awnings, and little flower-decked corners everywhere. Guest rooms range from small and simple to large and lavish. Some are suites with kitchens, separate sitting rooms, two-person Jacuzzis, poster beds, stained glass windows, and colorful floral wallpapers. The place abounds with antiques Marjorie has picked up over the years in her European travels. These components are adroitly assembled into lovely rooms. Good food is a serious matter here; the chef regularly cooks up Belgian waffles and salmon or vegetarian quiches, always accompanied by seasonal fruit and home-baked pastries. Guests dine in the small breakfast room or, in fine weather, take breakfast outdoors beside the pool. The inn is one block from the beach.

SETTING & FACILITIES

Location: In Seal Beach at 5th St. and Central Ave., 5 blocks from municipal pier, 25 mi. southeast of LA Internat'l Airport
Near: Restaurants, shopping, galleries, theaters, museums, Disneyland, Long Beach Aquarium, Queen Mary, Long Beach Marina, pier, Old Town Main St.
Building: 1920s French Mediterranean inn consisting of interconnected 1- and 2-story buildings, renovated w/ antique streetlights, awnings, and shutters
Grounds: 1/3 acre w/ brick courtyards, gardens, antique fountains, 100 varieties of trees, vines, and shrubs
Public Space: Parlor, library, formal DR, tearoom, 3 patios, and nooks and crannies
Food & Drink: Full breakfast served 7–9 a.m. weekdays and 7–10 a.m. weekends in the tearoom
Recreation: Biking, tennis, golf, surfing, bird-watching at Bolsa Chica bird and wildlife preserve
Amenities & Services: Swimming pool, evening tea w/ appetizers, turndown service on request, robes, newspaper, private off-street parking, concierge service; German, Swedish, Spanish, and other foreign language assistance; shuttle service to surrounding areas avail.

ACCOMMODATIONS

Units: 24 guest rooms, including 7 suites
All Rooms: Private bath and entrance, TV, phone, AC
Some Rooms: Fireplace, four-poster, sleeper sofa, fridge, canopy bed
Bed & Bath: Beds vary, Jacuzzi for 2 (5), tiled Roman tubs for 2 (6)
Favorites: Honeysuckle Room, w/ 3-sided fireplace, 2 skylights, lighting on dimmers, ceiling fans, kitchenette, canopy bed, bay windows, whirlpool tub for 2 w/ waterfall and stenciled ceiling, sitting area, armoire w/ entertainment center; Wisteria Room, w/ French doors to patio, antique Persian tile wall hanging, lace curtains, marble-topped tea table, Roman tiled tub for 2; Vienna Woods, w/ California redwood walls, pre-Civil War bed, German lace draperies, leather lounging chairs, Roman tiled tub for 2

Comfort & Decor: Rooms individually decorated w/ artwork, European furniture, Victorian headboards, down comforters, hand-painted wall murals in some rooms, carpet or antique rugs

RATES, RESERVATIONS, & RESTRICTIONS

Deposit: 1st night's lodging; must cancel 72 hours in advance
Discounts: Weekday business, AAA; extra person $20
Credit Cards: AE, D, DC, JCB, MC, V
Check-In/Out: 4/11
Smoking: No
Pets: No
Kids: Not suitable
Minimum Stay: None
Open: All year

Hosts: Marjorie Bettenhausen-Schmaehl and Harty Schmaehl
212 5th St.
Seal Beach, CA 90740
(562) 493-2416
(800) 443-3292
Fax: (562) 799-0483
www.sealbeachinn.com
hideaway@sealbeachinn.com

ARTISTS' INN, South Pasadena

| Overall: ★★★★½ | Room Quality: B | Value: B | Price: $110–$205 |

The Artists' Inn is about art and the art of hospitality. Inspired by the paintings of Van Gogh, Gauguin, Degas, and the English masters that hang in nearby museums, owner Janet Marangi, an interior designer, composed rooms evocative of the works. The blue Van Gogh room, with sunflowers on a bathroom wall, resembles the bedroom in one of his early paintings. The eighteenth-century English room is filled with reproductions of Gainsborough, Reynolds, and Constable paintings and has a rose-patterned wall covering and a canopy bed. The inn is actually two adjacent buildings, one a century-old Victorian farmhouse and the other a former 1909 duplex made over into cottage-style accommodations. The cottage contains five spacious rooms with canopy and poster beds, sitting areas, fireplaces, and decks. The farmhouse has an inviting shaded front porch where guests can sit and sip tea and read the paper, surrounded by a prizewinning rose garden with more than 100 plants. Breakfast, served in the dining room or on the front porch, features entrées such as apple puff pancakes, oatmeal pancakes with orange sauce, or quiche.

SETTING & FACILITIES

Location: In South Pasadena, on Magnolia between Meridian and Fairview, 1 block south of 110 Fwy., 3 blocks from city hall, 45 min. from LA Internat'l Airport
Near: Restaurants, shopping, galleries, theater, Mission West district, Old Town Pasadena, Wrigley Mansion, Rose Bowl, Norton Simon Museum, Asian Museum, Huntington Library
Building: 1895 Victorian farmhouse, 1909 cottage, historical landmark

Grounds: Double lot w/ gardens, 100 rosebushes, fruit trees, herb garden
Public Space: LR w/ fireplace, oriental rug, TV library, DR, large front porch
Food & Drink: Full breakfast served in DR, on front porch, or in room at 7:30–9:30 a.m., weekdays 8–10 a.m.

Recreation: Biking, tennis, golf
Amenities & Services: English afternoon tea on porch or in LR, port in rooms, hairdryers, candies, fresh flowers, private off-street parking, assistance w/ reservations and activity planning

ACCOMMODATIONS

Units: 9 guest rooms, 3 larger than average, including 3 suites, 5 rooms in cottage
All Rooms: Private bath, phone, AC
Some Rooms: TV, fireplace, four-poster, sleeper sofa, fridge, private entrance, extra twins (1)
Bed & Bath: Queens, kings (2), double, Jacuzzis (3)
Favorites: Expressionist, w/ fireplace,

queen bed, sitting area, TV, deck, large red Jacuzzi and shower; Gauguin, w/ bamboo queen bed, fireplace, TV, view of garden, Jacuzzi, and shower
Comfort & Decor: Rooms individually decorated in style of an artist or art period w/ antiques, bamboo, and brass canopy beds, custom curtains and wall coverings, rugs on hardwood floors, original art

RATES, RESERVATIONS, & RESTRICTIONS

Deposit: Credit card; must cancel 7 days in advance; cancellation fee $20
Discounts: Long stays, weekday business; extra person $20
Credit Cards: AE, MC, V
Check-In/Out: 3/11, late check-out by arrangement
Smoking: No
Pets: No
Kids: Not suitable except in Italian Suite

Minimum Stay: 2 nights on weekends
Open: All year
Host: Janet Marangi
1038 Magnolia St.
South Pasadena, CA 91030
(626) 799-5668
(888) 799-5668
Fax: (626) 799-3678
www.artistsinns.com
artistsinn@artistsinns.com

BISSELL HOUSE B&B, South Pasadena

Overall: ★★★★½	Room Quality: B	Value: B	Price: $115–$160

This three-story mansion was once the home of Anna Bissell McCay, daughter of the carpet sweeper tycoon. Albert Einstein was once a guest at dinner here; he created something of a stir when he preferred chatting with McCay's seven-year-old niece to conversing with the family's adults. You enter through a porte cochere covered by a trellised canopy, through a foyer into the living room with gleaming oak floors and large windows framed by elegant drapes. The dining room, with its bay window and pink and green botanical stencilwork on the walls, could accommodate a ball. Bedrooms have been carefully renovated and decorated to reflect life in this household in the 1920s. Indeed, shortly after the inn opened, a Bissell descendant dropped by to inspect "her" room, Morning Glory (all done in china blue and white), and proclaimed it just as she remembered. The Garden Room, tucked into a gable, has a sunny bathroom with backyard treetop view and double whirlpool tub. The innkeepers serve a continental breakfast during the week but go all out with a full breakfast on weekends.

SETTING & FACILITIES

Location: In South Pasadena on "Millionaire's Row" at the corner of Orange Grove and Columbia, just south of Ventura Fwy., and north of 110 Fwy., half-hour from LA Internat'l Airport
Near: Restaurants, shopping, antiques, theater, Old Town Pasadena, Wrigley Mansion, Rose Bowl, Norton Simon Museum, Asian Museum, Gamble House, Huntington Library
Building: 1887 3-story Victorian, historic landmark
Grounds: Half-acre lot enclosed by 50-ft. hedge, rose gardens
Public Space: LR, library, DR, veranda
Food & Drink: Full breakfast on weekends served at 9 a.m. in DR, expanded cont'l breakfast 7:30–9 a.m. during week
Recreation: Swimming, golf, tennis
Amenities & Services: Swimming pool, hot tub, wine, fresh fruit, fresh flowers, robes and slippers in rooms; afternoon aperitifs, tea, and pastries; private off-street parking, elevator to 2nd floor

ACCOMMODATIONS

Units: 5 guest rooms, 4 larger than average
All Rooms: Private bath, down quilt and pillows, sitting and reading area, individual heat/AC
Bed & Bath: Queens, tub/shower (3), Jacuzzi for 2 (1)
Favorites: Garden Room, w/ antique carved bed, floral chintz decor, sitting area, Jacuzzi tub for 2; Rose Room, w/ gable ceilings, 2 oversized chairs, tall windows w/ view of neighborhood, gold-framed mirrors, brass shower
Comfort & Decor: Rooms individually decorated w/ antiques, art, chintz fabrics, lace curtains, wallpaper, leaded glass windows, pedestal sinks, claw-foot tubs, hardwood floors, grand piano

RATES, RESERVATIONS, & RESTRICTIONS

Deposit: Credit card; must cancel 7 days in advance
Discounts: None; extra person in Prince Albert Room $35
Credit Cards: AE, MC, V
Check-In/Out: 3/noon, late check-out by arrangement
Smoking: No
Pets: No
Kids: Not suitable for small children
Minimum Stay: 2 nights on weekends
Open: All year
Hosts: Russell and Leonore Butcher, owners; Ivis and Annette, mgrs.
201 Orange Grove Ave.
South Pasadena, CA 91030
(626) 441-3535
(800) 441-3530
Fax: (626) 441-3671
www.bissellhouse.com
info@bissellhouse.com

LOMA VISTA B&B, Temecula

| Overall: ★★★★½ | Room Quality: B | Value: B | Price: $100–$150 |

If you're visiting the Temecula wine country in northern San Diego County, this hilltop Spanish-style hacienda with the red-tiled roof surrounded by vineyards and wineries is a great place to stay. The view from the second floor stretches forever, and you can see the dome of Palomar Mountain Observatory in the distance. Built as an inn in 1988, Loma Vista has every modern convenience in a quiet, romantic setting. The inn is surrounded by colorful gardens, including a small grapefruit orchard on the hillside below. Inside, guests tend to gather in the inn's great room, which has large picture windows, open-beamed ceilings, and comfortable sofas. The guest rooms upstairs are attractively but not ornately appointed. Breakfast here is festive, starting with champagne. Innkeepers Walt and Sheila Kurczynski serve it family-style in the big dining room, and menus often include Canadian bacon and eggs or ham-and-chicken crepes. At press time the inn was in the process of adding four new rooms to be opened in 2000.

SETTING & FACILITIES

Location: In wine and grapefruit region, 5 mi. north and east of Temecula via I-5 and Rancho California Rd., 41 mi. south of Riverside, 61 mi. north of San Diego
Near: Restaurants, shopping, wineries, museums, antiques
Building: 10-year-old Spanish Mission-style inn
Grounds: 5 acres of landscaped grounds, gardens, and grapefruit groves

Public Space: Common area, DR, large patio
Food & Drink: Full breakfast w/ champagne served at 9 a.m. in DR
Recreation: Biking, tennis, golf, ballooning, fishing
Amenities & Services: Hot tub; evening sherry, wine, and hors d'oeuvres; complimentary sherry in rooms, private parking, disabled access

ACCOMMODATIONS

Units: 6 guest rooms, 2 larger than average
All Rooms: Private bath, AC, fresh flowers

Some Rooms: Four-poster, balcony
Bed & Bath: Queens and kings, roll-away avail.

Favorites: Fumé Blanc, light and airy, w/ white wicker, king bed, plants, private balcony overlooking the vineyards; Sauvignon Blanc, w/ southwestern motif, white pine furniture, four-poster, private balcony overlooking entire

Temecula Valley
Comfort & Decor: Rooms individually decorated w/ Art Deco, Queen Anne, Southwestern, and wicker furniture, full-length drapes, carpet

RATES, RESERVATIONS, & RESTRICTIONS

Deposit: Credit card; must cancel 7 days in advance; cancellation fee $25
Discounts: None; extra person $25
Credit Cards: MC, V
Check-In/Out: 3/11
Smoking: No
Pets: No
Kids: OK, but not suitable
No-Nos: No more than 3 guests

per room
Minimum Stay: 2 nights on weekends for balcony rooms
Open: Closed Dec. 24–25
Hosts: Sheila and Walt Kurczynski
33350 La Serena Way
Temecula, CA 92591
(909) 676-7047
Fax: (909) 676-0077

HOMESTEAD INN, Twentynine Palms

Overall: ★★★½	Room Quality: B	Value: B	Price: $95–$175

If you're going to visit Joshua Tree National Park and you'd like to stay someplace that reflects the eccentric nature of life in the desert, this is the place. The Homestead was one of the original buildings in this area. The unpretentious house, built in 1928, is located on 15 not-quite-arid acres with cactus gardens and all manner of desert wildlife. Innkeeper Jerri Hagman, who inherited the property in 1978, has maintained it so that it reflects the style of life of early desert homesteaders. The decor is eclectic, with fine examples of botanical art and original Erté prints from the 1920s. There are overstuffed sofas in the living room, along with stocked bookcases with abundant information about the desert. Guest rooms have comfortable furnishings, private baths, private patios, and views of the desert. Jerri is warm and friendly and will do anything to accommodate her guests. She makes a mean frittata or blueberry pancakes for breakfast, served in the dining room or on the patio.

SETTING & FACILITIES

Location: In Twentynine Palms, on Two Mile Rd. between Desert Knoll and Marine Ave., approx. 1 mi. north of Hwy. 62
Near: Joshua Tree Nat'l Park, 1 hour to Palm Springs
Building: 1928 homestead house,

restored sheriff's stable w/ 3 rooms, office building w/ 1 guest room
Grounds: 15 acres, 5 acres fenced w/ cactus gardens, tortoise habitat, wildlife including roadrunners, quail, many other birds

Public Space: LR w/ local history library, fireplace, DR, patios in front and back
Food & Drink: Full breakfast served in DR or on patios, at guests' convenience
Recreation: Biking, rock climbing, horseback riding, golf
Amenities & Services: Robes, well water, afternoon tea, house label bottled water, open cookie jar, telescopes for stargazing, binoculars for bird-watching, private parking, disabled access, assistance w/ horseback riding, bike reservations, picnic baskets avail. on request, dinner avail. by prior arrangement

ACCOMMODATIONS

Units: 7 guest rooms, 3 in main house, 3 minisuites in former stable, 1 large guest room in office building
All Rooms: Private bath, contemporary furniture
Some Rooms: Private entrance and patio, coffeemaker, microwave, fridge, TV/VCR, wet bar
Bed & Bath: Queens, whirlpool baths (3), 2-person whirlpool/soaking tub (1)
Favorites: Gypsy Queen, w/ Victorian settee, tables, and chairs, decorated w/ antique perfume bottles and antique purses, private patio and entrance, whirlpool for 2, his-and-hers dressing rooms; White Star, w/ queen and twin beds, fireplace, private patio, writing desk, and whirlpool tub
Comfort & Decor: Rooms individually decorated w/ antiques, original art by well-known desert artists John and Kathy Hilton, desert views

RATES, RESERVATIONS, & RESTRICTIONS

Deposit: Credit card; must cancel 7 days in advance
Discounts: Seniors, AAA; extra person $15
Credit Cards: AE, MC, V
Check-In/Out: 3/11, late check-out by arrangement
Smoking: No
Pets: No
Kids: OK

Minimum Stay: 2 nights on weekends, 3 on holiday weekends
Open: Closed July 6–Oct. 1
Host: Jerri Hagman
74153 Two Mile Rd.
Twentynine Palms, CA 92277
(760) 367-0030
Fax: (760) 367-1108
www.joshuatreelodging.com
homstdin@cci-29palms.com

ROUGHLEY MANOR, Twentynine Palms

Overall: ★★★★	Room Quality: B	Value: A	Price: $75–$125

In 1928, this was one of the original homesteads in Twentynine Palms. It was settled by the young Campbell family, who loved the desert setting and the cloudless blue skies. Like most homesteads in the area, it had humble beginnings, portions of which you can see in the attached shed-roofed house. Shortly after settling on the land, however, the Campbells inherited a fortune, allowing them to construct this attractive manor. It is made of native stone with Vermont maple flooring, a large stone fireplace in the formal great room, leaded and stained glass windows, and fine architectural detailing throughout. Guest rooms upstairs in the manor and in the four cottages on the property are furnished with antiques collected by owners Jan and Gary Peters. There are fireplaces, poster and canopy beds, and original tile in the bathrooms. The inn is set on 25 beautifully landscaped acres with a rose garden, a hot tub set in a gazebo, a fine stand of native Washingtonia palms, and an expansive stone patio. Breakfast includes fresh fruit followed by entrées such as potato quiche or stuffed twice-baked potato topped with scrambled eggs and bacon, served in the garden, the gazebo, or the formal dining room.

SETTING & FACILITIES

Location: East end of Twentynine Palms, 1 mi. north of Hwy. 62 (Twentynine Palms Hwy.), 2 mi. north of Joshua Tree Nat'l Park Visitors Center
Near: Restaurants, shopping, Joshua Tree Nat'l Park, Twentynine Palms Murals, Big Morongo Canyon Preserve bird sanctuary
Building: 1924 3-story Victorian-style stone house w/ 4 cottages, historic landmark, restored
Grounds: 25 acres, 6 landscaped w/ gardens, lawn, 2 gazebos, palm and cedar trees

Public Space: Great room w/ fireplace and dining area, family room w/ fireplace and sitting area, patio w/ fountain
Food & Drink: Full breakfast served 8–9 a.m. in DR or on patio
Recreation: Horseshoes, croquet on premises; rock climbing, glider rides, golf nearby
Amenities & Services: Hot tub; dessert, coffee, tea in evening; robes, private parking, concierge services, massage avail.

ACCOMMODATIONS

Units: 9 guest rooms, 4 cottage rooms larger than average
All Rooms: Comforter, view of desert
Some Rooms: Kitchenette w/ fridge, microwave, coffeemaker, TV, fireplace (4), private patio (3), private bath (4)
Bed & Bath: Mostly queens, 5 rooms share 2 baths
Favorites: Magnolia Room, w/ lace canopy bed, fireplace, wallpapers, orien-

tal rug, views of fountain courtyard; Campbell Room, w/ four-poster, fireplace, wallpaper, swag drapes, views of fountain courtyard
Comfort & Decor: Rooms individually decorated w/ antiques, coordinating drapes, wallpapers, comforters; in main house, floors of original Vermont maple, area rugs, 22-by-35-ft. rug hand-braided by movie actress Fanny Brice

RATES, RESERVATIONS, & RESTRICTIONS

Deposit: Credit card; must cancel 72 hours in advance
Discounts: None; extra person $15
Credit Cards: AE, MC, V
Check-In/Out: 2/11, late check-out by arrangement
Smoking: No
Pets: No
Kids: By prior arrangement

Minimum Stay: None
Open: All year
Hosts: Gary and Jan Peters
74744 Joe Davis Dr.
Twentynine Palms, CA 92277
(760) 367-3238
Fax: (760) 367-4483
www.virtual29.com/themanor
themanor@cci-29palms.com

VENICE BEACH HOUSE, Venice

Overall: ★★★½	Room Quality: B	Value: B	Price: $95–$165

Venice Beach is one of California's most famous landmarks and a magnet for the fun-in-the-sun crowd. Scantily clad Rollerbladers, street performers, bodybuilders, and latter-day hippies create a carnival atmosphere that's wildly popular with out-of-towners seeking the "real" Southern California beach scene. The Venice Beach House, a block from the beach, is a nice place to stay because you can retreat into its pretty gardens and tranquil rooms when you've had enough of the beachside promenade. The 1911 Craftsman-style inn has a comfortable lived-in quality about it. There's a pretty parlor with a curved bay window, oak floors, and oriental carpets, and the guest rooms are bright and airy. Breakfast, served in the parlor, varies, but it generally includes items such as coffeecake, cereal, fruit, granola, and a hot entrée.

SETTING & FACILITIES

Location: On Venice Beach at Speedway and 30th Ave., 1 block north of Venice Pier, 6 mi. north of LA Internat'l Airport
Near: Restaurants, shopping, boutiques, Venice Pier, beaches
Building: 1906 Craftsman-style home, former home of Venice's founder
Grounds: Double lot w/ large garden surrounded by tall hedge

Public Space: Parlor w/ fireplace, veranda
Food & Drink: Expanded cont'l breakfast served 7:30–9:30 a.m. weekdays, 7:30–10:30 weekends, on the veranda
Recreation: Biking, ocean swimming, paddle tennis and volleyball on beach
Amenities & Services: Hot tea and fresh cookies, evening refreshments, private parking

ACCOMMODATIONS

Units: 9 guest rooms, 5 larger than average
All Rooms: Cable TV, phone
Some Rooms: Fireplace (1), private entrance (1), balcony (2), private bath (5), extra bed (1)
Bed & Bath: Kings, queens (3), double, 4 rooms share 2 baths, Jacuzzi for 2 (1)
Favorites: James Peasgood's Room, w/ king bed, balcony, double Jacuzzi, bath-

tub, cathedral wood ceilings; Pier Suite, bright, w/ view of ocean, sitting room, fireplace, private bath, antiques
Comfort & Decor: Rooms individually decorated w/ contemporary furniture and accents in some rooms, white wicker and pink accents in Cara's Corner, Scottish plaid wool w/ green carpet in Abbott Kinney's Room

RATES, RESERVATIONS, & RESTRICTIONS

Deposit: Credit card; must cancel 5 days in advance

Discounts: AAA on rooms w/ private bath; extra person $20

Credit Cards: AE, MC, V

Check-In/Out: 2/11

Smoking: No

Pets: No

Kids: OK

Minimum Stay: None

Open: All year

Host: Karen Stern
15 30th Ave.
Venice, CA 90291
(310) 823-1966
Fax: (310) 823-1842

Appendix

Additional Bed-and-Breakfasts and Small Inns

While our 300 profiles give you a fine range of bed-and-breakfasts and small inns, some may be fully booked when you want to visit, or you may want to stay in areas where we have not included a property. So we have included this listing of over 200 additional bed-and-breakfasts and small inns, spread geographically throughout California. All properties meet our basic criteria for this guide: They usually have about 3–25 guest rooms, a distinct personality and individually decorated guest rooms, are open regularly, and include breakfast in the price (with a few exceptions). Prices are a range from low to high season. Unlike the previous 300 profiles, we have not visited all of these properties so we cannot recommend them across the board. We suggest you get a brochure, look on the Internet, or call and ask about some of the categories that are on the profile format to find out more. While many of these supplementals are famed and excellent, some may not be up to the level of the profiled properties.

Zone 1: Northern California

Arcata
Lady Ann
$90–$105
(707) 822-2797

Cassel
Clearwater House
$330 (3 meals)
(530) 335-5500 or
    (415) 381-1173

Cazadero
Timberhill Ranch Resort
$395–$415
(707) 784-7325 or
    (800) 847-3470

Cedarville
J. K. Metzker House B&B
$65–$75
(530) 279-2650

Chester
Cinnamon Teal
$65–$95
(530) 258-3993

Drakesbad Guest Ranch
$210–$238 (3 meals)
(530) 529-9820

Chico
Music Express Inn
$75–$85
(530) 891-9833

Esplanade B&B
$75–$95
(530) 345-8084

Clio
White Sulphur Springs
    Ranch B&B
$85–$140
(530) 836-2387 or
    (800) 854-1797

Etna
Bradley's Alderbrook
    Mansion
$50–$70
(530) 467-3917

Eureka
Old Town B&B Inn
$95–$185
(707) 445-3951 or
    (800) 331-5098

Fall River Mills
Lava Creek Lodge
$75–$130
(530) 336-6288

Ferndale
Shaw House B&B
$85–$185
(707) 786-9958

Fort Bragg
Glass Beach B&B Inn
$50–$160
(707) 964-6774

Old Stewart House Inn
$75–$165
(707) 961-0775

Pudding Creek Inn B&B
$75–$135
(707) 964-9529 or
    (800) 227-9529

Loyalton
Clover Valley Mill House
$85–$105
(530) 993-4819

McCloud
Hogin House
$70
(530) 964-2882 or
    (530) 964-3125

McCloud Guest House
    and Spa
$85–$95
(530) 964-3160

McCloud River Inn
$69–$145
(530) 964-2130

Mendocino
Blue Heron Inn
$85–$105
(707) 937-3611

Brewery Gulch Inn
$85–$135
(707) 937-4752

Captain's Cove Inn
$173–$197
(707) 937-5159 or
    (800) 780-7905

Headlands Inn
$90–$195
(707) 937-0421 or
    (800) 354-4431

MacCallum House
$100–$190
(707) 937-0289 or
    (800) 609-0492

Reed Manor
$175–$450
(707) 937-5446

Seagull Inn B&B
$45–$145
(707) 937-5204 or
    (800) 937-5204

Victorian Farm House
$98–$165
(707) 937-0697 or
    (800) 264-4723

Mill Valley
Mill Valley Inn
$155–$240
(415) 389-6608 or
    (800) 595-2100

Monte Rio
Huckleberry Springs
    Country Inn and Spa
$155–$165
(707) 865-2683

Mount Shasta
Strawberry Valley Inn
$58–$94
(530) 926-2052

Myers Flat
Myers Inn
$100–$135
(707) 943-3259

O'Brien
O'Brien Mountain Inn
$97–$147
(530) 238-8026 or
    (888) 799-8026

Oroville
Jean Pratt's Riverside B&B
$65–$125
(530) 533-1413

Petrolia
Lost Inn B&B
$95
(707) 629-3394

Portola
Pullman House Inn
$58–$95
(530) 832-0107 or
    (800) 996-0107

Red Bluff
Jefferson House
$75
(530) 527-4133

Jeter Victorian Inn
$65–$140
(530) 527-7574

Shelter Cove
Shelter Cove Inn
$65–$105
(707) 986-7161

Shingletown
Weston House
$85–$145
(530) 474-3738

Susanville
Roseberry House
$60–$85
(530) 257-5675

Trinidad
Trinidad Bay B&B
$125–$170
(707) 677-0840

Turtle Rocks Inn
$110–$170
(707) 677-3707

Valley Ford
Inn at Valley Ford
$65–$90
(707) 876-3182

Westport
Bowen's Pelican Lodge
and Inn
$50–$85
(707) 964-5584

Willits
Emandal Farm
$250
(707) 459-5439 or
(800) 262-9597

Zone 2:
Wine Country

Calistoga
Calistoga Country Lodge
$105–$160
(707) 942-5555

Calistoga Inn
$55–$70
(707) 942-4101

Calistoga's Wine Way Inn
$90–$165
(707) 942-0680 or
(800) 572-0679

Christopher's Inn
$135–$295
(707) 942-5755

Meadowlark Country
House and Inn
$150–$205
(707) 942-5651

Pink Mansion
$135–$235
(707) 942-0558 or
(800) 238-7465

Quail Mountain B&B Inn
$130–$185
(707) 942-0316

Scarlett's Country Inn
$115–$175
(707) 942-6669

Silver Rose Inn
$155–$270
(707) 942-9581 or
(800) 995-9381

Trailside Inn
$165–$185
(707) 942-4106

Wine Way Inn
$95–$165
(707) 942-0680

Zinfandel House
$100–$125
(707) 942-0733

Cloverdale
Shelford House
$105–$250
(707) 894-5956 or
(800) 833-6479

Forestville
Farmhouse Inn
$105–$195
(707) 887-3300 or
(880) 464-6642

Freestone
Green Apple Inn
$85–$90
(707) 874-2526

Glen Ellen
Above the Clouds
$175
(707) 996-7371 or
(800) 600-7371

Guerneville
Ridenhour Ranch
House Inn
$95–$140
(707) 887-1033

Santa Nella House
$100–$110
(707) 869-9488

Healdsburg
Grape Leaf Inn
$115–$185
(707) 433-8140

Haydon Street Inn
$95–$165
(707) 433-5228 or
(800) 528-3703

Raford House B&B Inn
$130–$250
(707) 887-9573 or
(800) 887-9503

George Alexander House
$145–$255
(707) 433-1358 or
(800) 310-1358

Hopland
Thatcher Inn
$115–$175
(707) 744-1890 or
(800) 266-1891

Napa
Blue Violet Mansion
$169–$339
(707) 253-2583

Crossroads Inn
$250
(707) 944-0646

Tall Timbers Chalets
$105–$150
(707) 252-7810

Trubody Ranch B&B
$110–$205
(707) 255-5907

Nice
Featherbed Railroad Co.
$96–$145
(707) 274-8378 or
(800) 966-6322

Petaluma
Chileno Valley Ranch
B&B
$120–$145
(707) 765-6664 or
(877) 280-6664

Philo
Philo Pottery Inn
$95–$115
(707) 895-3069

Rutherford
Rancho Caymus Inn
$175–$305
(707) 963-1777 or
    (800) 845-1777

Santa Rosa
Melitta Station Inn
$95–$120
(707) 538-7712 or
    (800) 504-3099

Sonoma
El Dorado Hotel
$120–$195
(707) 996-3030

Trojan Horse Inn
(on freeway)
$135–$165
(707) 996-2430 or
    (800) 899-1925

St. Helena
Ambrose Bierce House
$159–$195
(707) 963-3003

Bartels Ranch and
    Country Inn
$165–$425
(707) 963-4001 or
    (800) 265-5328

Chestelson House
$120–$245
(707) 963-2238 or
    (800) 959-4545

Hotel St. Helena
$145–$275
(707) 963-4388 or
    (888) 478-4355

Sutter Home Inn
$190
(707) 963-3104

Windsor Country
Meadow Inn
$100–$195
(707) 431-1276 or
    (800) 238-1728

Yountville
Bordeaux House
$138–$171
(707) 944-2855

Zone 3: Sacramento, Gold Rush Country, Lake Tahoe, and the Sierras

Ahwahnee
Silver Spur B&B
$60
(559) 683-2896 or
    (888) 359-9178

Amador City
Mine House Inn
$85–$185
(209) 267-5900 or
    (800) 646-3473

Angels Camp
Cooper House B&B
$105
(209) 736-2145

Bishop
Matlick House
$75–$85
(760) 873-3133 or
    (800) 898-3133

Brownsville
Mountain Seasons Inn
$60
(530) 675-2180

Columbia
Harlan House
$85–$130
(209) 533-4862

Dorrington
Dorrington Inn
$100–$140
(209) 795-2164 or
    (888) 874-2165

Fiddletown
Casa de la Pradera
$80
(209) 245-6681

Grass Valley
Elam Biggs B&B
$75–$110
(530) 477-0906

Peacock Inn
$70–$100
(530) 477-2179

Swan-Levine House
$75–$95
(530) 272-1873

Groveland
Berkshire Inn
$79–$89
(209) 962-6744 or
    (800) 679-6904

Hope Valley
Sorensen's
$80–$130
(916) 694-2203 or
    (800) 423-9949

Independence
Winnedumah Hotel,
    A B&B Inn
$40–$70
(760) 878-2040

Jackson
Court Street Inn
$95–$150
(209) 223-0416 or
    (800) 200-0416

Wedgewood Inn
$100–$175
(209) 296-4300 or
    (800) 933-4393

Jamestown
Palm Hotel B&B
$85–$145
(209) 984-3429

Royal Hotel
$45–$85
(209) 984-5271

Loomis
Emma's B&B
$100–$145
(916) 652-1392

Mammoth Lakes
Cinnamon Bear Inn B&B
$79–$119
(760) 934-2873 or
    (800) 845-2873

White Horse Inn
$85–$180
(760) 924-3656 or
    (800) 982-5657

Mariposa
Mariposa Hotel Inn
$90–$105
(209) 966-4676

Meadow Creek Ranch
$95
(209) 966-3843

Poppy Hill B&B
$110
(209) 742-6273 or
    (800) 587-6779

Mokelumne Hill
Mokelumne River
    Lodge B&B
$110–$160
(209) 286-1000

Nevada City
Flume's End B&B
$85–$145
(530) 265-9665 or
    (800) 991-8118

M. L. Marsh House
$135–$230
(530) 265-5709 or
    (800) 874-7458

Parsonage B&B Inn
$80–$135
(530) 265-9478

Placerville
Combellack-Blair House
$110
(530) 622-3764

Plymouth
Amador Harvest Inn
$95–$120
(209) 245-5512 or
    (800) 217-2304

Sacramento
Capitol Park
    Bed-and-Breakfast
$99–$175
(916) 414-1300 or
    (877) 753-9982

San Andreas
Robin's Nest
$65–$125
(209) 754-1076 or
    (888) 214-9202

Sonora
Lavender Hill B&B Inn
$75–$95
(209) 532-9024

Serenity
$100–$125
(209) 533-1441

Soulsbyville
Benjamin Soulsby
    B&B Inn
$85–$125
(209) 533-2030 or
    (800) 643-8731

South Lake Tahoe
Christiania Inn
$50–$175
(530) 544-7337

Sutter Creek
Picture Rock Inn
$90–$100
(209) 267-5500 or
    (800) 399-2389

Sutter Creek Inn
$65–$175
(209) 267-5606

Tahoe City
Mayfield House
$95–$225
(530) 583-1001

Tahoe Vista
Shore House at
    Lake Tahoe
$135–$255
(530) 546-7270 or
    (800) 207-5160

Tahoma
Norfolk Woods Inn
$90–$160
(530) 525-5000

Truckee
Donner Country Inn
$120
(530) 587-5574 or
    (925) 938-0695

Truckee Hotel
$45–$125
(530) 587-4444 or
    (800) 659-6921

Yosemite
Yosemite Peregrine
$130–$180
(209) 372-8517 or
    (800) 396-3639

Yuba City
Harkey House B&B Inn
$83–$126
(530) 674-1942

Zone 4: San Francisco Bay Area

Benicia
Union Hotel
$119–$159
(707) 746-0100 or
    (800) 544-2278

Berkeley
Hillegass House
$95–$110
(510) 548-5517 or
    (800) 400-5517

Bolinas
Thomas' White House Inn
$100–$110
(415) 868-0279

Half Moon Bay
Mill Rose Inn
$165–$285
(650) 726-9794

San Benito House
$60–$126
(415) 726-3425

Zaballa House
$75–$250
(650) 726-9123

Inverness
Hotel Inverness
$125–$190
(415) 669-7393

Patterson House
$98–$167
(415) 669-1383

Marshall
Inn on Tomales Bay
$130–$145
(415) 663-9002

Mill Valley
Mill Valley Inn
$155–$240
(415) 389-6608 or
    (800) 595-2100

Miramar
Pacific Victorian B&B
$175–$185
(415) 712-3900

Montara
Goose and Turrets
$100–$135
(650) 728-5451

Olema
Bear Valley Inn B&B
$85–$135
(415) 663-1777

Pescadero
Old Saw Mill Lodge
$90–$160
(650) 879-0111

Point Reyes Station
Carriage House
$110–$160
(415) 663-8627 or
    (800) 613-8351

Holly Tree Inn
$125–$250
(415) 663-1554

Jasmine Cottage
$185
(415) 663-1166

Knob Hill
$55–$110
(415) 663-1784

San Francisco
Alamo Square Inn
$85–$195
(415) 922-2055 or
    (800) 345-9888

Albion House
$125–$195
(415) 621-0896 or
    (800) 625-2466

Bock's B&B
$45–$80
(415) 664-6842

Casa Arguello
$89–$124
(415) 752-9482

Edward II Inn
$77–$235
(415) 922-3000

Golden Gate Hotel
$72–$109
(415) 392-3702 or
    (800) 835-1118

Hotel Boheme
$139
(415) 433-9111

Inn at Union Square
$175–$350
(415) 397-3510 or
    (800) 288-4346

Inn San Francisco
$85–$235
(415) 641-0188 or
    (800) 359-0913

The Mansions
$149–$350
(415) 929-9444 or
    (800) 826-9398

Petite Auberge
$120–$165
(415) 928-6000 or
    (800) 365-3004

San Gregario
Rancho San Gregario
$90–$150
(415) 747-0810

San Jose
Hensley House
$135–$255
(408) 298-3537 or
    (800) 498-3537

Sausalito
Hotel Sausalito
$135–$250
(415) 332-0700 or
    (888) 442-0700

Zone 5: Central Coast

Arroyo Grande
Arroyo Village Inn
$125–$375
(805) 543-9075 or
    (800) 563-7762

Crystal Rose Inn
$95–$185
(805) 481-1854 or
    (800) 767-3466

Ben Lomond
Château des Fleurs
$100–$130
(831) 336-8943 or
    (800) 291-9966

Fairview Manor
$119
(831) 336-3355 or
    (800) 553-8840

Carmel-by-the-Sea
Carmel Country Inn
$115–$205
(831) 625-3263 or
    (800) 215-6343

Carmel Garden Court
$125–$295
(831) 624-6926

Carmel Wayfarer Inn
$93–$158
(831) 624-0831 or
(800) 533-2711

Carriage House Inn
$209–$279
(831) 625-2585 or
(800) 433-4732

Cobblestone Inn
$95–$175
(831) 625-5222 or
(800) 833-8836

Crystal Terrace Inn
$140–$230
(831) 624-6400 or
(800) 600-4488

Sunset House
$160–$190
(831) 624-4884

Carmel Valley
Acacia Lodge Country
Garden
$110–$162
(408) 659-2297

Carmel Valley Lodge
$119–$299
(831) 659-2261 or
(800) 641-4646

Stonepine
$295–$900
(831) 659-2245

Dinuba
Reedley Country Inn
$66–$90
(209) 638-2585

Felton
Inn at Felton Crest
$275–$345
(408) 335-4011 or
(800) 474-4011

Hanford
Irwin Street Inn
$70–$125
(209) 583-8000

Kernville
Kern River Inn B&B
$79–$99
(760) 376-6750 or
(800) 986-4382

Lemon Cove
Mesa Verde
Plantation B&B
$69–$159
(209) 597-2555 or
(800) 240-1466

Monterey
Del Monte Beach Inn
$77–$110
(831) 649-4410

Morro Bay
Marina Street Inn
$89–$109
(805) 772-4016

Nipomo
Kaleidoscope Inn
$95
(805) 929-5444

Pacific Grove
Centralia B&B Inn
$149–$239
(831) 372-3372 or
(800) 233-3372

Pacific Grove Inn
$125–$225
(831) 375-2825 or
(800) 732-2825

Paso Robles
Gillie Archer Inn
$90–$165
(805) 238-0879

Randsburg
Cottage Hotel B&B
$60–$65
(760) 374-2285 or
(800) 268-4622

San Luis Obispo
Heritage Inn
$85–$130
(805) 544-7440

San Martin
Country Rose Inn B&B
$129–$199
(831) 842-0441

Santa Barbara
Blue Dolphin Inn
$125–$225
(805) 965-2333

Eagle Inn
$85–$169
(805) 965-3586 or
(800) 767-0030

Mary May Inn
$165–$180
(805) 569-3398

Santa Cruz
Château Victorian,
a B&B Inn
$110–$140
(831) 458-9458

Cliff Crest B&B Inn
$95–$150
(831) 427-2609

Santa Paula
White Gables Inn
$85–$115
(805) 933-3041

Springville
Annie's B&B
$95
(559) 539-3827

Mountain Top B&B
$70–$85
(559) 542-2639

Ventura
Bella Maggiore Inn
$75–$150
(805) 652-0277 or
(800) 523-8479

Visalia
Ben Maddox House
$85
(209) 739-0721

Zone 6: Southern California

Avalon
Zane Grey Pueblo Hotel
$59–$150
(310) 510-0966 or
    (800) 378-3256

Big Bear City
Gold Mountain Manor
Historic B&B
$125–$190
(909) 585-6997

Big Bear Lake
Switzerland Haus B&B
$70–$200
(909) 866-3729

Wainwright Inn B&B
$95–$$175
(909) 585-6914

Coronado
Coronado Victorian
    House
$250–$500
(619) 435-2200

Dana Point
Blue Lantern Inn
$150–$500
(949) 661-1304 or
    (800) 950-1236

Desert Hot Springs
Travellers Repose B&B
$65–$85
(760) 329-9584

Duarte
White Horse Estate B&B
$125
(818) 568-8172 or
    (800) 653-8886

Encinitas
Sea Breeze B&B
$75–$150
(760) 944-0318

Homeland
Pierson's Country Place
$85–$125
(909) 926-4546

Idyllwild
Fern Valley Inn
$80–$130
(909) 659-2205

Wilkum Inn
$65–$95
(909) 659-4087 or
    (800) 659-4086

Julian
Butterfield B&B
$115–$155
(760) 765-2179 or
    (800) 379-4262

Shadow Mountain Ranch
$100–$130
(760) 765-0323

La Jolla
Prospect Park Inn
$80–$325
(619) 454-0133 or
    (800) 433-1609

Lake Arrowhead
Romantique Lakeview
    Lodge
$65–$225
(909) 337-6633 or
    (800) 358-5253

Nipton
Hotel Nipton
$55
(619) 856-2335

Ramona
Lake Sutherland Lodge
    B&B
$110–$205
(760) 789-6483 or
    (800) 789-6483

San Clemente
Casa Tropicana B&B Inn
$85–$350
(714) 492-1234 or
    (800) 492-1245

San Diego
Balboa Park Inn
$80–$200
(619) 298-0823 or
    (800) 938-8181

The Cottage
$65–$109
(619) 299-1564

Index